Life in the UK Test
Handbook

Everything you need to study for the British citizenship test

Published by Red Squirrel Publishing

Red Squirrel Publishing

Suite 235, 15 Ingestre Place,

London W1F 0DU, United Kingdom

www.redsquirrelbooks.com

First edition published in 2006

Eleventh Edition – First Impression

Handbook: 978-1-907389-85-6

Edited by Henry Dillon & Alastair Smith

Proofreading by Robert Clark

Picture research by Isaac Strang

Typeset by Antony Gray

Printed and bound in the UK by Micropress

Table of contents

Foreword – Mario López-Goicoechea

Dear Reader:

Forget Brexit and its toxic legacy. For as long as I've lived in the UK (almost twenty-five years), the long-standing, unresolvable, contentious issue has been: milk in first or last?

Welcome to Great Britain, a country where people take their tea-drinking seriously. Few topics generate as much controversy as this one, so taking the Life in the UK Test should be a doddle.

Joking aside (only slightly, mind), becoming a citizen of another country points at a commitment that few dare to make. Relocating to another nation, and learning another language in many cases, takes courage.

By now you've probably become part of the fabric of British life. You might have taken up walking in the Peak District, or eating sand-covered, cold sandwiches on the beach in Cornwall in the summer while getting rained on, or downing a pint at your local boozer on a Friday evening after work. Congratulations! You've passed your test.

The truth is that your years of living in this country have by now hopefully helped you to prepare for your test. Admittedly, you will still need to learn that many West Indians from the Windrush generation were recruited to drive buses in the 1950s. But you might have already met some of these veterans and got to know them well. In a sense, the Life in the UK Test marries your lived experience with new knowledge.

In my book, *Cuban, Immigrant, and Londoner*, I describe the feeling of being an immigrant and juggling a multitude of identities. Some of these identities, we choose. Others are chosen for you. Either way, the minute you land in Heathrow or Gatwick airport, a whole new universe opens up. A universe of identity markers. In this new universe questions like what a quango is (answer: a non-departmental public body) might throw you off at first. Yet, give it time and the fog will clear. You might even end up working for a quango yourself. And there, right there, there's the beauty of a Life in the UK test. The theory and practice have come together. Joined at the hip, if you like.

I'm pretty sure that you've found that there are other issues more relevant to your life in the UK than the ones in the test. Like, for instance, which side of the road do we drive and cycle on? How do you pronounce 'scone' And do people ever get cold in Yorkshire?

I mentioned identity before. With identity comes also a sense of belonging. Of being accepted for who I am, funny accent included. For me belonging has never been about one moment in particular but the total, ever-growing sum of tiny snapshots. One sticks in the mind and brings a tear to the eye. Super Saturday, 4th August 2012, when Jessica Ennis-Hill, Mo Farah and Greg Rutherford all won gold medals in less than three quarters of an hour at the London Olympics.

This is what living in the UK is about. Being part of a multicultural family and celebrating that family. The Life in the UK Test is yet another step towards that goal. And it doesn't matter if you are a Miffy (milk in first) or a Tiffy (tea in first). You'll still have your cuppa.

Mario López-Goicoechea is a London-based, Cuban-born writer. He's the author of *Cuban, Immigrant, and Londoner*. He has written for various publications, including *The Guardian* and *Prospect*. His hobbies include writing, reading, cycling, running, walking and dancing.

Introduction

Thousands of people choose to make the UK their home every year. Your decision to join them in becoming a British citizen or permanent resident is only the start of what can be a long and challenging journey. The application process is complex, time-consuming and expensive.

An essential part of the process is the Life in the UK Test. This book includes the complete text of the official study materials, *Life in the United Kingdom: A Guide for New Residents*. The test requires you to learn about British history, culture and law, based on information set by the Home Office. This book will make learning this information a lot easier.

Home Office statistics show that around two in ten people fail the test. At £50 for every test taken this is an expensive mistake, and an unnecessary one. We actively seek feedback from readers after their test so we can track how effective our guides are – last year 97% passed. If you closely follow the advice in this book, a pass is very achievable.

Get in touch

We are always delighted when we hear from our readers. If you have any comments or questions about your studies and test, the book or website, or would like to share a particular experience, please get in touch with us.

To send us feedback please visit:
www.lifeintheuk.net/feedback

Find us on Facebook
www.facebook.com/lifeintheuk.net

Follow us on Twitter
@lifeintheuk

WHAT'S IN THIS BOOK?

This guide gives you everything you need to prepare for the Life in the UK Test:

- The complete official testable materials, which are chapters 2–6. **The material here is exactly the same as given by the Home Office in *Life in the United Kingdom: A Guide for New Residents***
- Free access to online tests at www.lifeintheuk.net
- Diagrams, illustrations and appendices.

The current version of the Life in the UK Test contains a lot of dates, events and numbers. We have picked out the most complicated parts and provided illustrations to help you learn them, as well as providing extra appendices to help you study, something which you won't find in the official guide.

How to use this study guide

This guide has many parts and features, but the sections that you must focus on are the official study materials (see chapters 2–6). These chapters are reproduced in full from the Home Office publication *Life in the United Kingdom: A Guide for New Residents*. You must make sure you read and understand these chapters as the questions that you will be asked in your test are based on all of the information provided there.

The testable study materials are divided into five sections:

- The values and principles of the UK
- What is the UK?
- A long and illustrious history
- A modern, thriving society
- The UK government, the law and your role.

Chapter 1 is not testable but includes information on the questions as well as advice from people who passed the test and answers to frequently asked questions.

The other parts of this book will help you understand and learn the study materials. There are also practice tests that will help you prepare for your test by checking your knowledge.

APPENDICES

Chapter 7 contains timelines that summarise some of the study materials. There is also an extensive glossary of words that you need to know. These are words or phrases that you will need to understand for your test. Each word or phrase is explained fully, in easy-to-understand language. As you work your way through the materials, you can use the glossary to check any terms or expressions that are not familiar to you.

PRACTICE QUESTIONS

Once you have finished revising the study materials, try taking practice tests. This will help you test your knowledge and identify any topics you need to study further.

Further practice tests, along with news and up-to-date information about the material in this guide, can also be found online at www.lifeintheuk.net.

REGISTER YOUR BOOK

When you are ready to start taking practice tests, you can use this book to claim a free subscription to the online tests at www.lifeintheuk.net/test.

Once you have created your account, follow the instructions to get a free subscription.

Before you begin

The study materials for the Life in the UK Test contain several references to the British monarchy and, specifically, to Queen Elizabeth II. When the Queen died on 8 September 2022 this meant these and other references became out of date.

For example, there is a reference to Prince Charles as the heir to the throne. Prince Charles has now acceded to the throne and is now known as King Charles III.

These outdated references are marked in the materials with blue asterisks like this *. You can view explanations of these references at lifeintheuk.net/clarify.

The government has advised that people taking the Life in the UK Test will not be asked questions about the Queen and the British monarchy. We have updated this edition with the most current official materials at the time of going to print, however, the government is yet to publish updates regarding the monarchy. We expect these changes to be released later in 2023. You can check if an updated version has been published by visiting the link below.

Scan this QR code to check for updates at lifeintheuk.net/2023update

CHAPTER 1
About the test

→ THE LIFE IN THE UK TEST is designed to test your knowledge of British life and ability to use the English language.

The 3rd edition of the citizenship test was launched on 25 March 2013. This guide is for this 3rd version of the citizenship test only.

- You have 45 minutes to complete the test
- The test is made up of 24 multiple-choice questions
- Questions are chosen at random
- The pass mark is 75% (18 questions correct out of 24)
- Each attempt to pass the test costs £50 (as of January 2023)
- The test is conducted at Life in the UK Test centres across the UK
- You take the test using a computer, which is provided by the test centre

1

Why do I need to take the test?

If you are applying for Indefinite Leave to Remain in the UK (also known as settlement) or British citizenship then you must demonstrate that you have sufficient 'knowledge of life and language in the UK'. This is also called the KOL requirement.

You must do two things to meet this requirement:

- pass the Life in the UK Test **AND**
- have a speaking and listening qualification in English at B1 CEFR or higher, or its equivalent.

Some exemptions to the language requirements apply. For instance, if you are from a majority English speaking country, such as the USA or Australia, you are exempt. You are also exempt if you have a degree-level qualification, or higher, taught in English.

What do I need to study?

The Home Office has given some official advice as to what to study. However, the test itself is still very much shrouded in secrecy. The following advice is based on feedback from our readers – people like you who have taken the test – and our personal experience of taking the test. It is intended to help you plan your studies, and not to provide shortcuts!

DO I REALLY NEED TO LEARN EVERYTHING?

The questions in your test 'will be based on the whole book, including [Chapter 2], so make sure you study the entire book thoroughly' (see pages 4–5).

The questions in your test could be drawn from any part of chapters 2–6. For example, they may be on the values and principles of the UK explained in Chapter 2 alongside the information about the test itself. You may get questions on the Second World War or Parliament today, both of which are covered at length. But you may also be asked about the Statute of Rhuddlan (see page 17) or British Crown dependencies (see page 8), both of which are only mentioned briefly.

What are the questions like?

The following offers specific advice on the kind of knowledge you must have to pass the test. There are detailed notes on question formats at the start of Chapter 8.

DATES

The study materials say 'Questions are based on ALL parts of the handbook, but you will not need to remember dates of birth or death' (see page 4). You must understand, however, when key events happened, or when certain people lived. For example, you will not be asked a question such as 'What year was Emmeline Pankhurst born in?', but you could be asked 'In which year were equal voting rights for men and women introduced in the UK?'

ANNUAL EVENTS

One exception with dates is annual events and festivals. Where something happens on the same date each year, such as Christmas or St George's Day, you must know the specific date. These dates are summarised on page 157. For moveable festivals such as Easter or Hannukah, you need to know in which months of the year they normally fall.

FAMOUS PEOPLE, PLACES AND WORKS

You need to be able to correctly identify the famous people described in the text. This means you should know who they are, their nationality and what they are famous for, and be able to name their works. This applies to people described in the text and also people summarised in boxes or lists, including: writers (see page 86), artists (see page 83), films and directors (see page 91), sportspeople (see pages 74–5) and architects (see pages 84–5).

The same is true of famous works or places such as British inventions (see pages 56–7), cities of the UK (see pages 62–3) or the Commonwealth (see pages 123–4). You may be required to correctly identify inventions or inventors, identify British cities or answer a question on who wrote a particular novel, for example.

FAMOUS BATTLES AND EVENTS

There are many different battles mentioned throughout Chapter 4. You should be familiar with the key figures involved and where and why these things happened. Example questions could be 'Which of the following is a famous battle fought with the French during the Hundred Years War?', 'Where was the Battle of Britain fought?' or 'Which king united the Anglo-Saxon kingdoms to defeat the Vikings?'

Take some time to understand the differences between criminal and civil law.

Key pieces of legislation are just as important. You need to know when they happened and what the outcomes were. You should also be able to spot an incorrect combination, for true or false questions. For example, 'Is the statement below TRUE or FALSE?: The Bill of Rights provided the basis for the modern welfare state'. The correct answer is False, as it was the Beveridge Report that formed the basis for the modern welfare state. You should also think about who was monarch or Prime Minister at the time of key events. The timelines in the appendices at the back of this book help by summarising the different historical periods.

THE UK COURTS

Take some time to understand the differences between criminal and civil law (see pages 126–7). You also need to understand which courts deal with certain offences, and how they vary in their processes, in particular the differences between countries in the UK. You should know about Scottish courts even if you are taking the test in London.

You should also take the time to learn some of the more specific details of the criminal and civil courts. For example, the number of members in a jury or the maximum amount that can be claimed in the small claims procedure.

QUESTION STYLES

You should expect facts in the test to be presented in a different way to the study materials.

For example, you might be asked 'Is the statement below TRUE or FALSE?' about statements such as 'The hovercraft was invented in the 1950s' or 'The Chancellor of the Exchequer is responsible for crime, police and immigration.' To answer these questions, you need to know that the hovercraft was invented in the 1950s (see page 56) and that the Chancellor of the Exchequer is responsible for the economy (see page 113).

If you learn the materials like a script, you may find certain questions difficult. For example, as well as being asked 'What is Roger Bannister famous for?', you may be asked 'Who ran the first four-minute mile in 1954?' Or, instead of 'When were women first given the right to vote?', you may be asked 'Why is 1918 an important date in the history of women's rights?'

You are being tested on your understanding of the subjects covered in the materials rather than your ability to memorise facts.

A question might include dates alongside other facts and ask you which are correct. For example, you might be asked:

Which famous female novelist, born in 1775, wrote novels concerned with marriage and family relationships?

- A J K Rowling
- B Hilary Mantel
- C Jane Austen
- D Agatha Christie

This question requires you to know that Jane Austen wrote novels that are concerned with marriage and family relationships, but also to be aware of when she was born.

The key is that you should expect to be tested on a whole topic, and not single facts. You can't just learn that Jane Austen wrote *Pride and Prejudice*. You must learn when she lived and what her novels are concerned with.

> "You must not ignore anything because it seems too obvious or too general."

UNDERSTANDING IS CRUCIAL

The most important thing is to make sure you read and understand all of the materials completely. Ideally you should be able to explain the contents of the materials in your own words. You should also try and learn how each fact relates to when it happened.

You can test your understanding on different topics by asking yourself questions such as:

- Who was monarch at the time?
- What was the period known as and why?
- What were the causes or outcomes of key events?

For example, you should know about Florence Nightingale and Isambard Kingdom Brunel (see pages 42–3) but also need to think of them as famous Victorians, and people who were alive during the British Empire. You should know that the Tower of London was built on the orders of William the Conqueror after the Norman Conquest, and that its White Tower is an example of a Norman castle keep. As well as that, it is home to Beefeaters and the Crown Jewels, and is also the place where Anne Boleyn was executed.

Our appendices are designed to help you develop this kind of understanding. By providing a summary of key information, they demonstrate the associations you should be making between facts. You should use the appendices to supplement your studies. If you only study the appendices you will not pass your test.

Do not assume that the test questions will be phrased in the same way as this book, or that you will be asked any of the same questions. You cannot simply learn the practice questions and expect to pass. You must understand the complete study materials.

Clarifications

While reading this book you may notice blue asterisks * beside some of the text. This means that the official text from the Home Office is either out of date, inaccurate or a simplification. For the purposes of your test, you should learn the text as it's written but if you want to understand more we have published clarifications online.

We receive regular feedback from readers when they come across information in the study materials that they don't think is correct. For some people it creates confusion as they are not sure whether they should rely on their personal knowledge, other sources of information or trust what they have read in the study materials. This is an unwelcome distraction from their preparations for the test.

Whatever the reason for the issue in the text, when a piece of information in the materials is incorrect, outdated or obsolete the official advice from the government is consistent: 'learn the material as reproduced in the book for your test'.

We keep an online record of these issues and inaccuracies at lifeintheuk.net/clarify to help our readers when something in the materials is not correct. This online record is regularly updated and revised. However, if you come across anything that you have concerns about that isn't already marked with an asterisk you can email us at help@redsquirrelbooks.com to let us know.

Scan this QR code to read the clarifications at lifeintheuk.net/clarify

How to pass your test

STEP 1: STUDY THE MATERIALS

All the questions that can be asked in the Life in the UK Test are based on the official study materials provided by the Home Office. The relevant material has been fully reproduced in this guide.

Your official test will only ask questions based on chapters 2, 3, 4, 5 and 6 of this publication. The questions in this book are also drawn only from those chapters.

Make sure you read the advice from our readers below – this comes from people, just like you, who have already taken the test. Included are specific tips on the kind of thing the test covers, and problems previous customers have faced.

Also remember, **there is no substitute for studying chapters 2–6 thoroughly!**

STEP 2: TAKE PRACTICE TESTS

Once you've finished reviewing the study materials you should check if you are ready to take the official test by completing practice tests from this book. It is important to make sure that you fully understand the content and haven't just memorised the information as written, or worse just memorised the questions and answers.

Each of the practice tests contains 24 questions covering all parts of the study materials. These questions will not necessarily be phrased in the same way as the text in the chapters.

If you do not pass the practice tests consistently, or do not feel confident enough to sit your official test, then you should continue your study.

Once you've finished with the questions in this book, additional questions can be found in our book *Life in the UK Test: Practice Questions*. You can also access further tests with our free subscription offer at www.lifeintheuk.net/test.

Although they are not the same questions that you will receive in your official test, they are in a similar format, use the same approach and test you on the same official material. The practice tests are not a substitute for reading and understanding chapters 2–6.

STEP 3: BOOK YOUR TEST

You must book your test online through the Life in the UK Test booking website. You will need valid photo ID, a debit or credit card and an email address to book. You must pay the test fee when you book.

When you create an account to book your test you must provide information such as your place and date of birth, address and nationality. You must also provide your Home Office reference number if you have one. You will have been issued with this if you have had previous contact with the Home Office (for example, when applying for an extension of stay).

The following are acceptable forms of photographic ID:

- a Biometric Residence Permit or Biometric Residence Card – this document must be in date
- a passport from your country of origin – this document must be in date
- a European Union Identity Card – this document must be in date, or
- a Travel Document – this document must be in date.

It is very important to make sure that the details you register when booking **exactly** match the ID and supporting documents you take with you on the day.

If they do not match – for instance, you registered your full middle name but your ID only shows an initial – you will not be allowed to take the test and your test fee will not be refunded. **We have had lots of reports from candidates who have been turned away at the test centre because of this**.

If you have registered for the test with your married name and your ID is in your maiden name, then you must bring an original UK marriage certificate, or a UK Spouse Visa (this must be in date). Without one of these your test will be refused and you will not receive a refund.

You will be directed to the five test centres closest to you when you book. You must take your test at one of these five centres. If you book your test elsewhere you will not be allowed to take the test and your fee will not be refunded.

You may have to wait a few weeks for your test appointment. The earliest you can take your test is three days after booking. You can cancel your test without charge up to three days before your test. If you cancel within three days your test fee will not be refunded. You can change your test appointment using your online account.

You can call the Life in the UK Test Helpline on 0800 015 4245 with any queries about the booking process.

STEP 4: TAKE AND PASS YOUR TEST

Make sure that you have a good night's sleep before the test and that you have eaten beforehand. Being tired or hungry severely affects your concentration and will make the test harder.

Be sure to arrive earlier than your appointed test time. If you arrive when your test is due to start you may not be allowed to take your test. If this happens you will have to rebook and pay again.

When you arrive at the test centre the staff will register your details. The registration process before the test itself can take some time, as there may be many candidates to register.

You will be given a locker to put your belongings in. You are not allowed to take anything into the test, including study notes, mobile phones and wristwatches, so everything will have to go in the locker. Try not to bring too much with you!

You will take the test using a computer provided by the test centre. You will be allowed to run through a few practice questions so that you are familiar with the test software. Do not worry if you don't know the answers for the practice questions: these questions do not count towards your result.

Each applicant's test is begun individually by the test supervisor, so your test will not begin until you say that you are ready. There have been several cases over the years of people trying to cheat in the test using methods ranging from the simple to the high tech. The test centres are wary of this. Do not be surprised if you are asked to put your collar down, or roll your sleeves up, to show you are not hiding any equipment or trying to cheat.

Once your test begins you will have 45 minutes. There will be equipment allowing you to hear the questions and answers read to you. You can review and change your answers to questions at any stage during the test.

If you pass then you will be given a 'unique reference number'. This is very important as you will need this number to complete your citizenship or settlement application. The Home Office will use it to check that you have passed the test.

If you don't pass you can take the test again. However, you will need to rebook and pay again, and wait at least seven days before retaking your test. You should not make an application for naturalisation as a British citizen or for Indefinite Leave to Remain if you fail. You may need to apply for further leave to remain if your existing leave to remain has expired, or is close to expiring.

Share your experiences

We are able to give you advice like this because of the hugely helpful feedback we have had from our readers. We read everything people write to us and use it all when we make new editions of this book every year.

The more feedback we get the better we can make this advice. So we want to hear about your experiences of the test. In particular, we want to hear what you think we did well or what we didn't do so well. Was there a particular type of question you weren't expecting? Did one of our study aids really help you?

Everything from a single thought to a detailed critique of every question in your test is useful. To send us feedback just visit www.lifeintheuk.net/feedback.

Test preparation checklist

There are a lot of things that you need to remember to do for the Life in the UK Test. Avoid problems and get organised by completing this checklist.

○ **Test appointment booked**

Book your test through the Life in the UK Test booking website

Test Date ....

Time ....

Test Centre Address ....

....

....

Phone ....

○ **Finished reading study materials (see chapters 2–6)**

○ **Completed all practice tests in study guide**

○ **Completed free online practice tests at www.lifeintheuk.net**

○ **Checked latest tips and advice at www.lifeintheuk.net**

○ **Checked your registered details exactly match your photo ID**

○ **Confirmed test centre location and travel route**

CHAPTER 2
The values and principles of the UK

IN THIS CHAPTER you will learn about the fundamental rights and responsibilities which apply to everyone who lives in the UK, citizen or not. There is also some information about the format of the Life in the UK Test and the requirements for becoming a permanent resident.

The questions you get in the real test will be based on the whole book, including this introductory chapter, so make sure that you are familiar with the details of the application process for permanent residence as well as the rights and responsibilities of UK residents.

IN THIS CHAPTER THERE IS INFORMATION ABOUT:

- The fundamental principles of British life
- Responsibilities and freedoms of all UK residents
- Becoming a permanent resident
- Taking the Life in the UK Test
- The testable sections of this book

2

Britain is a fantastic place to live: a modern, thriving society with a long and illustrious history. Our people have been at the heart of the world's political, scientific, industrial and cultural development. We are proud of our record of welcoming new migrants who will add to the diversity and dynamism of our national life.

Applying to become a permanent resident or citizen of the UK is an important decision and commitment. You will be agreeing to accept the responsibilities which go with permanent residence and to respect the laws, values and traditions of the UK. Good citizens are an asset to the UK. We welcome those seeking to make a positive contribution to our society.

Passing the Life in the UK Test is part of demonstrating that you are ready to become a permanent migrant to the UK. This handbook is designed to support you in your preparation. It will help you to integrate into society and play a full role in your local community. It will also help ensure that you have a broad general knowledge of the culture, laws and history of the UK.

British society is founded on fundamental values and principles which all those living in the UK should respect and support.

The values and principles of the UK

British society is founded on fundamental values and principles which all those living in the UK should respect and support. These values are reflected in the responsibilities, rights and privileges of being a British citizen or permanent resident of the UK. They are based on history and traditions and are protected by law, customs and expectations. There is no place in British society for extremism or intolerance.

The fundamental principles of British life include:

- democracy
- the rule of law
- individual liberty
- tolerance of those with different faiths and beliefs
- participation in community life.

As part of the citizenship ceremony, new citizens pledge to uphold these values. The pledge is:

'I will give my loyalty to the United Kingdom and respect its rights and freedoms. I will uphold its democratic values. I will observe its laws faithfully and fulfil my duties and obligations as a British citizen.'

Flowing from the fundamental principles are **responsibilities and freedoms** which are shared by all those living in the UK and which we expect all residents to respect.

If you wish to be a permanent resident or citizen of the UK, you should:

- respect and obey the law
- respect the rights of others, including their right to their own opinions
- treat others with fairness
- look after yourself and your family
- look after the area in which you live and the environment.

In return, the UK offers:

- freedom of belief and religion
- freedom of speech
- freedom from unfair discrimination
- a right to a fair trial
- a right to join in the election of a government.

Becoming a permanent resident

To apply to become a permanent resident or a naturalised citizen of the UK, you will need to:

- speak and read English
- have a good understanding of life in the UK.

This means you will need to:

- Pass the Life in the UK Test

AND

- Produce acceptable evidence of speaking and listening skills in English at B1 of the Common European Framework of Reference. This is equivalent to ESOL Entry Level 3. You can demonstrate your knowledge of English by having a recognised English test qualification from an approved test centre. For further details on how to demonstrate evidence of the required level of speaking and listening skills in English, please visit the Home Office website.

> “Questions are based on ALL parts of the handbook.”

It is possible that the requirements may change in the future. You should check the information on the Home Office website for current requirements before applying for settlement or citizenship.

Taking the Life in the UK Test

This handbook will help prepare you for taking the Life in the UK Test. The test consists of 24 questions about important aspects of life in the UK. Questions are based on ALL parts of the handbook, but you will not need to remember dates of birth or death. The 24 questions will be different for each person taking the test at that test session.

The Life in the UK Test is usually taken in English, although special arrangements can be made if you wish to take it in Welsh or Scottish Gaelic.

You can only take the test at a registered and approved Life in the UK test centre. There are over 30 test centres in the UK. You can only book your test online, at www.gov.uk/life-in-the-uk-test. You should not take your test at any other establishment as the Home Office will only accept certificates from registered test centres. If you live on the Isle of Man or in the Channel Islands, there are different arrangements for taking the Life in the UK test.

When booking your test, read the instructions carefully. Make sure you enter your details correctly. You will need to take some identification and proof of your address with you to the test. If you don't take these, you will not be able to take the test.

HOW TO USE THIS HANDBOOK

Everything that you will need to know to pass the Life in the UK Test is included in this handbook. The questions will be based on the whole book, including this introduction, so make sure you study the entire book thoroughly. The handbook has been written to ensure that anyone who can read English at ESOL Entry Level 3 or above should have no difficulty with the language.

The glossary at the back of the handbook contains some key words and phrases, which you might find helpful.

The 'Check that you understand' boxes are for guidance. They will help you to identify particular things that you should understand. Just knowing the things highlighted in these boxes will not be enough to pass the test. You need to make sure that you understand everything in the book, so please read the information carefully.

The glossary at the back of the handbook contains some key words and phrases, which you might find helpful.

WHERE TO FIND MORE INFORMATION

You can find out more information from the following places:

- the Home Office website (www.gov.uk/browse/visas-immigration/settle-in-the-uk) for information about the application process and the forms you will need to complete
- the Life in the UK test website (www.gov.uk/life-in-the-uk-test) for information about the test and how to book a place to take one
- gov.uk (www.gov.uk) for information about ESOL courses and how to find one in your area.

Check that you understand:

- The origin of the values underlying British society
- The fundamental principles of British life
- The responsibilities and freedoms which come with permanent residence
- The process of becoming a permanent resident or citizen

CHAPTER 3
What is the UK?

→ **IN THIS CHAPTER** you will learn about the countries that make up the Union as well as the various phrases used to describe them. Although this chapter is very short you should make sure that you read and understand all the facts presented. For instance it is very likely there will be questions about the differences between Great Britain, the British Isles and Britain, or what the Crown dependencies are.

IN THIS CHAPTER THERE IS INFORMATION ABOUT:

- The different countries that make up the UK

3

What is the UK?

The UK is made up of England, Scotland, Wales and Northern Ireland. The rest of Ireland is an independent country.

'Great Britain' refers only to England, Scotland and Wales, not to Northern Ireland.

The official name of the country is the United Kingdom of Great Britain and Northern Ireland. 'Great Britain' refers only to England, Scotland and Wales, not to Northern Ireland. The words 'Britain', 'British Isles' or 'British', however, are used in this book to refer to everyone in the UK.

There are also several islands which are closely linked with the UK but are not part of it: the Channel Islands and the Isle of Man. These have their own governments and are called 'Crown dependencies'. There are also several British overseas territories in other parts of the world, such as St Helena and the Falkland Islands. They are also linked to the UK but are not a part of it.

The UK is governed by the Parliament sitting in Westminster. Scotland, Wales and Northern Ireland also have parliaments or assemblies of their own, with devolved powers in defined areas.

Check that you understand:

- The different countries that make up the UK

SCOTLAND
NORTHERN IRELAND
ENGLAND
WALES

CHAPTER 4
A long and illustrious history

→ IN THIS CHAPTER you will learn about British history starting from the Stone Age. The beginning focuses on arriving populations which affected the language and religions of Britain. After that the focus is on the development of the monarchy, church and Parliament. Major battles and significant periods are covered, including the civil war, the industrial revolution and the Empire. There is a lot of information about the First and Second World Wars and after the Second World War the chapter focuses on the governments of the UK and devolution in Northern Ireland, Wales and Scotland.

Make sure that you understand the relationship between the monarchy and Parliament, Protestants and Catholics and Britain and the colonies of the Empire. Think about how the right to vote developed. You should also make sure you know about each of the people described. You will need to know about Acts of Parliament and other major events.

IN THIS CHAPTER THERE IS INFORMATION ABOUT:

- The history of early Britain
- The Middle Ages
- The Tudor and Stuart monarchs
- The establishment of Parliament
- The unification of the United Kingdom
- The Enlightenment and Industrial Revolution
- The Victorian Age and the British Empire
- The First World War
- The Great Depression
- The Second World War
- Britain since 1945 and the welfare state
- Great British inventions and sporting figures
- Government since the Second World War

Early Britain

The first people to live in Britain were hunter-gatherers, in what we call the Stone Age. For much of the Stone Age, Britain was connected to the continent by a land bridge. People came and went, following the herds of deer and horses which they hunted. Britain only became permanently separated from the continent by the Channel about 10,000 years ago.

The first farmers arrived in Britain 6,000 years ago. The ancestors of these first farmers probably came from south-east Europe. These people built houses, tombs and monuments on the land. One of these monuments, Stonehenge, still stands in what is now the English county of Wiltshire. Stonehenge was probably a special gathering place for seasonal ceremonies. Other Stone Age sites have also survived. Skara Brae on Orkney, off the north coast of Scotland, is the best preserved prehistoric village in northern Europe, and has helped archaeologists to understand more about how people lived near the end of the Stone Age.

The World Heritage Site of Stonehenge

Around 4,000 years ago, people learned to make bronze. We call this period the Bronze Age. People lived in roundhouses and buried their dead in tombs called round barrows. The people of the Bronze Age were accomplished metalworkers who made many beautiful objects in bronze and gold, including tools, ornaments and weapons. The Bronze Age was followed by the Iron Age, when people learned how to make weapons and tools out of iron. People still lived in roundhouses, grouped together into larger settlements, and sometimes defended sites called hill forts. A very impressive hill fort can still be seen today at Maiden Castle, in the English county of Dorset. Most people were farmers, craft workers or warriors. The language they spoke was part of the Celtic language family. Similar languages were spoken across Europe in the Iron Age, and related languages are still spoken today in some parts of Wales, Scotland and Ireland. The people of the Iron Age had a sophisticated culture and economy. They made the first coins to be minted in Britain, some inscribed with the names of Iron Age kings. This marks the beginnings of British history.

THE ROMANS

Julius Caesar led a Roman invasion of Britain in 55 BC. This was unsuccessful and for nearly 100 years Britain remained separate from the Roman Empire. In AD 43 the Emperor Claudius led the Roman army in a new invasion. This time, there was resistance from some of the British tribes but the Romans were successful in occupying almost all of Britain. One of the tribal leaders who fought against the Romans was Boudicca, the queen of the Iceni in what is now eastern England. She is still remembered today and there is a statue of her on Westminster Bridge in London, near the Houses of Parliament.

Areas of what is now Scotland were never conquered by the Romans, and the Emperor Hadrian built a wall in the north of England to keep out the Picts (ancestors of the Scottish people). Included in the wall were a number of forts. Parts of Hadrian's Wall, including the forts of Housesteads and Vindolanda, can still be seen. It is a popular area for walkers and is a UNESCO (United Nations Educational, Scientific and Cultural Organization) World Heritage Site.

The Romans remained in Britain for 400 years. They built roads and public buildings, created a structure of law, and introduced new plants and animals. It was during the 3rd and 4th centuries AD that the first Christian communities began to appear in Britain.

“The Romans remained in Britain for 400 years. They built roads and public buildings, created a structure of law, and introduced new plants and animals.”

THE ANGLO-SAXONS

The Roman army left Britain in AD 410 to defend other parts of the Roman Empire and never returned. Britain was again invaded by tribes from northern Europe: the Jutes, the Angles and the Saxons. The languages they spoke are the basis of modern-day

English. Battles were fought against these invaders but, by about AD 600, Anglo-Saxon kingdoms were established in Britain. These kingdoms were mainly in what is now England. The burial place of one of the kings was at Sutton Hoo in modern Suffolk. This king was buried with treasure and armour, all placed in a ship which was then covered by a mound of earth. Parts of the west of Britain, including much of what is now Wales, and Scotland, remained free of Anglo-Saxon rule.

A helmet from the time of the Anglo-Saxons and Vikings

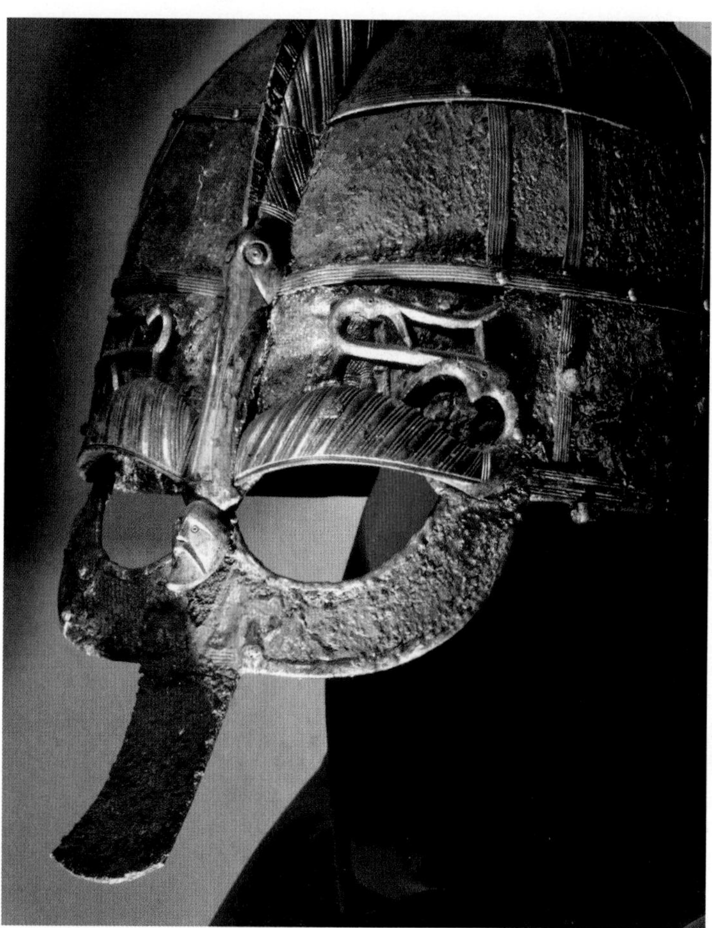

The Anglo-Saxons were not Christians when they first came to Britain but, during this period, missionaries came to Britain to preach about Christianity. Missionaries from Ireland spread the religion in the north. The most famous of these were St Patrick, who would become the patron saint of Ireland (see page 68 for more about patron saints), and St Columba, who founded a monastery on the island of Iona, off the coast of what is now Scotland. St Augustine led missionaries from Rome, who spread Christianity in the south. St Augustine became the first Archbishop of Canterbury (see page 67 for more about the Archbishop of Canterbury and the Church in Britain today).

THE VIKINGS

The Vikings came from Denmark, Norway and Sweden. They first visited Britain in AD 789 to raid coastal towns and take away goods and slaves. Then, they began to stay and form their own communities in the east of England and Scotland. The Anglo-Saxon kingdoms in England united under King Alfred the Great, who defeated the Vikings. Many of the Viking invaders stayed in Britain – especially in the east and north of England, in an area known as the Danelaw (many place names there, such as Grimsby and Scunthorpe, come from the Viking languages). The Viking settlers mixed with local communities and some converted to Christianity.

“

The Anglo-Saxon kingdoms in England united under King Alfred the Great, who defeated the Vikings.

Anglo-Saxon kings continued to rule what is now England, except for a short period when there were Danish kings. The first of these was Cnut, also called Canute.

In the north, the threat of attack by Vikings had encouraged the people to unite under one king, Kenneth MacAlpin. The term Scotland began to be used to describe that country.

THE NORMAN CONQUEST

In 1066, an invasion led by William, the Duke of Normandy (in what is now northern France), defeated Harold, the Saxon king of England, at the Battle of Hastings. Harold was killed in the battle. William became king of England and is known as William the Conqueror. The battle is commemorated in a great piece of embroidery, known as the Bayeux Tapestry, which can still be seen in France today.

Marcel Douwe Dekker

Part of the Bayeux Tapestry – the linen cloth is nearly 70 metres (230 feet) long and is embroidered with coloured wool

The Norman Conquest was the last successful foreign invasion of England and led to many changes in government and social structures in England. Norman French, the language of the new ruling class, influenced the development of the English language as we know it today. Initially the Normans also conquered Wales, but the Welsh gradually won territory back. The Scots and the Normans fought on the border between England and Scotland; the Normans took over some land on the border but did not invade Scotland.

William sent people all over England to draw up lists of all the towns and villages. The people who lived there, who owned the land and what animals they owned were also listed. This was called the Domesday Book. It still exists today and gives a picture of society in England just after the Norman Conquest.

Check that you understand:

- The history of the UK before the Romans
- The impact of the Romans on British society
- The different groups that invaded after the Romans
- The importance of the Norman invasion in 1066

The Middle Ages

WAR AT HOME AND ABROAD

Broadly speaking, the Middle Ages (or medieval period) spans a thousand years, from the end of the Roman Empire in AD 476 up until 1485. However, the focus here is on the period after the Norman Conquest. It was a time of almost constant war.

The English kings fought with the Welsh, Scottish and Irish noblemen for control of their lands. In Wales, the English were able to establish their rule. In 1284 King Edward I of England introduced the Statute of Rhuddlan, which annexed Wales to the Crown of England. Huge castles, including Conwy and Caernarvon, were built to maintain this power. By the middle of the 15th century the last Welsh rebellions had been defeated. English laws and the English language were introduced.

In Scotland, the English kings were less successful. In 1314 the Scottish, led by Robert the Bruce, defeated the English at the Battle of Bannockburn, and Scotland remained unconquered by the English.

“In 1314 the Scottish, led by Robert the Bruce, defeated the English at the Battle of Bannockburn.”

At the beginning of the Middle Ages, Ireland was an independent country. The English first went to Ireland as troops to help the Irish king and remained to build their own settlements. By 1200, the English ruled an area of Ireland known as the Pale, around Dublin. Some of the important lords in other parts of Ireland accepted the authority of the English king.

During the Middle Ages, the English kings also fought a number of wars abroad. Many knights took part in the Crusades, in which European Christians fought for control of the Holy Land. English kings also fought a long war with France, called the Hundred Years War (even though it actually lasted 116 years). One of the most famous battles of the Hundred Years War was the Battle of Agincourt in 1415, where King Henry V's vastly outnumbered English army defeated the French. The English largely left France in the 1450s.

THE BLACK DEATH

The Normans used a system of land ownership known as feudalism. The king gave land to his lords in return for help in war. Landowners had to send certain numbers of men to serve in the army. Some peasants had their own land but most were serfs.

They had a small area of their lord's land where they could grow food. In return, they had to work for their lord and could not move away. The same system developed in southern Scotland. In the north of Scotland and Ireland, land was owned by members of the 'clans' (prominent families).

In 1348, a disease, probably a form of plague, came to Britain. This was known as the Black Death. One third of the population of England died and a similar proportion in Scotland and Wales. This was one of the worst disasters ever to strike Britain. Following the Black Death, the smaller population meant there was less need to grow cereal crops. There were labour shortages and peasants began to demand higher wages. New social classes appeared, including owners of large areas of land (later called the gentry), and people left the countryside to live in the towns. In the towns, growing wealth led to the development of a strong middle class.

In Ireland, the Black Death killed many in the Pale and, for a time, the area controlled by the English became smaller.

LEGAL AND POLITICAL CHANGES

In the Middle Ages, Parliament began to develop into the institution it is today. Its origins can be traced to the king's council of advisers, which included important noblemen and the leaders of the Church.

> **"The Magna Carta established the idea that even the king was subject to the law. It protected the rights of the nobility and restricted the king's power to collect taxes or to make or change laws."**

There were few formal limits to the king's power until 1215. In that year, King John was forced by his noblemen to agree to a number of demands. The result was a charter of rights called the Magna Carta (which means the Great Charter). The Magna Carta established the idea that even the king was subject to the law. It protected the rights of the nobility and restricted the king's power to collect taxes or to make or change laws. In future, the king would need to involve his noblemen in decisions.

In England, parliaments were called for the king to consult his nobles, particularly when the king needed to raise money. The numbers attending Parliament increased and two separate parts, known as Houses, were established. The nobility, great landowners and bishops sat in the House of Lords. Knights, who were usually smaller landowners, and wealthy people from towns and cities were elected to sit in the House of Commons. Only a small part of the population was able to join in electing the members of the Commons.

A similar Parliament developed in Scotland. It had three Houses, called Estates: the lords, the commons and the clergy.

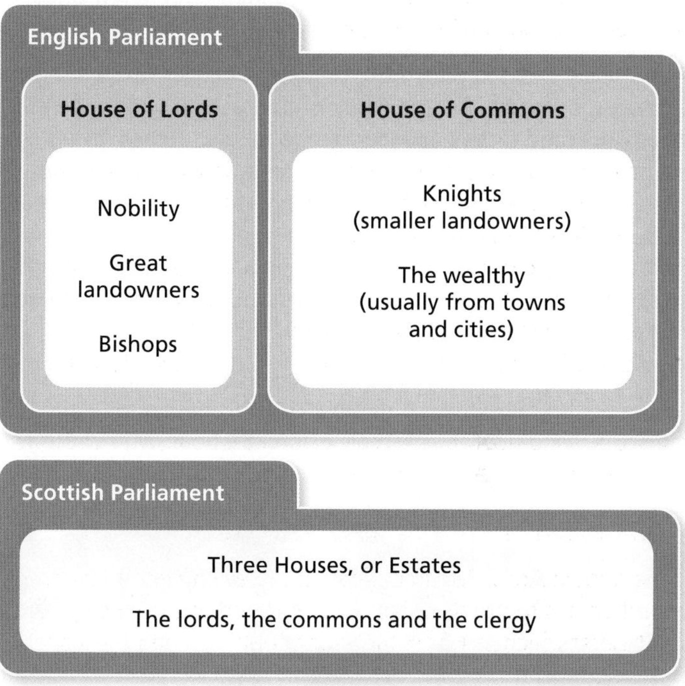

This was also a time of development in the legal system. The principle that judges are independent of the government began to be established. In England, judges developed 'common law' by a process of precedence (that is, following previous decisions) and tradition. In Scotland, the legal system developed slightly differently and laws were 'codified' (that is, written down).

A DISTINCT IDENTITY

The Middle Ages saw the development of a national culture and identity. After the Norman Conquest, the king and his noblemen had spoken Norman French and the peasants had continued to speak Anglo-Saxon. Gradually these two languages combined to become one English language. Some words in modern English – for example, 'park' and 'beauty' – are based on Norman French words. Others – for example, 'apple', 'cow' and 'summer' – are based on Anglo-Saxon words. In modern English there are often two words with very similar meanings, one from French and one

> By 1400, in England, official documents were being written in English, and English had become the preferred language of the royal court and Parliament.

from Anglo-Saxon. 'Demand' (French) and 'ask' (Anglo-Saxon) are examples. By 1400, in England, official documents were being written in English, and English had become the preferred language of the royal court and Parliament.

In the years leading up to 1400, Geoffrey Chaucer wrote a series of poems in English about a group of people going to Canterbury on a pilgrimage. The people decided to tell each other stories on the journey, and the poems describe the travellers and some of the stories they told. This collection of poems is called *The Canterbury Tales*. It was one of the first books to be printed by William Caxton, the first person in England to print books using a printing press. Many of the stories are still popular. Some have been made into plays and television programmes.

In Scotland, many people continued to speak Gaelic and the Scots language also developed. A number of poets began to write in the Scots language. One example is John Barbour, who wrote *The Bruce* about the Battle of Bannockburn.

York Minster stained glass

The Middle Ages also saw a change in the type of buildings in Britain. Castles were built in many places in Britain and Ireland, partly for defence. Today many are in ruins, although some, such as Windsor and Edinburgh, are still in use. Great cathedrals – for example, Lincoln Cathedral – were also built, and many of these are still used for worship. Several of the cathedrals had windows of stained glass, telling stories about the Bible and Christian saints. The glass in York Minster is a famous example.

During this period, England was an important trading nation. English wool became a very important export. People came to England from abroad to trade and also to work. Many had special skills, such as weavers from France, engineers from Germany, glass manufacturers from Italy and canal builders from Holland.

THE WARS OF THE ROSES

In 1455, a civil war was begun to decide who should be king of England. It was fought between the supporters of two families: the House of Lancaster and the House of York. This war was called the Wars of the Roses, because the symbol of Lancaster was a red rose and the symbol of York was a white rose. The war ended with the Battle of Bosworth Field in 1485. King Richard III of the House of York was killed in the battle and Henry Tudor, the leader of the House of Lancaster, became King Henry VII. Henry then married King Richard's niece, Elizabeth of York, and united the two families. Henry was the first king of the House of Tudor. The symbol of the House of Tudor was a red rose with a white rose inside it as a sign that the Houses of York and Lancaster were now allies.

The red rose of Lancaster | The white rose of York | The red and white rose of the House of Tudor

Check that you understand:

- The wars that took place in the Middle Ages
- How Parliament began to develop
- The way that land ownership worked
- The effects of the Black Death
- The development of English language and culture
- The Wars of the Roses and the founding of the House of Tudor

The Tudors and Stuarts

RELIGIOUS CONFLICTS

After his victory in the Wars of the Roses, Henry VII wanted to make sure that England remained peaceful and that his position as king was secure. He deliberately strengthened the central administration of England and reduced the power of the nobles. He was thrifty and built up the monarchy's financial reserves. When he died, his son Henry VIII continued the policy of centralising power.

Henry VIII was most famous for breaking away from the Church of Rome and marrying six times.

Henry VIII was king of England from 21 April 1509 until his death on 28 January 1547

THE SIX WIVES OF HENRY VIII

Catherine of Aragon – Catherine was a Spanish princess. She and Henry had a number of children but only one, Mary, survived. When Catherine was too old to give him another child, Henry decided to divorce her, hoping that another wife would give him a son to be his heir.

Anne Boleyn – Anne Boleyn was English. She and Henry had one daughter, Elizabeth. Anne Boleyn was unpopular in the country and was accused of taking lovers. She was executed at the Tower of London.

Jane Seymour – Henry married Jane Seymour after Anne Boleyn's execution. She gave Henry the son he wanted, Edward, but she died shortly after the birth.

Anne of Cleves – Anne was a German princess. Henry married her for political reasons but divorced her soon after.

Catherine Howard – Catherine Howard was a cousin of Anne Boleyn. She was also accused of taking lovers and executed.

Catherine Parr – Catherine Parr was a widow who married Henry late in his life. She survived him and married again but died soon after.

You may be asked specific questions about Henry VIII's wives. As well as the facts given here, you should learn the order he married them in.

To divorce his first wife, Henry needed the approval of the Pope. When the Pope refused, Henry established the Church of England. In this new Church, the king, not the Pope, would have the power to appoint bishops and order how people should worship.

To divorce his first wife, Henry needed the approval of the Pope. When the Pope refused, Henry established the Church of England.

At the same time the Reformation was happening across Europe. This was a movement against the authority of the Pope and the ideas and practices of the Roman Catholic Church. The Protestants formed their own churches. They read the Bible in their own languages instead of in Latin; they did not pray to saints or at shrines; and they believed that a person's own relationship with God was more important than submitting to the authority of the Church. Protestant ideas gradually gained strength in England, Wales and Scotland during the 16th century.

In Ireland, however, attempts by the English to impose Protestantism (alongside efforts to introduce the English system of laws about the inheritance of land) led to rebellion from the Irish chieftains, and much brutal fighting followed.

During the reign of Henry VIII, Wales became formally united with England by the Act for the Government of Wales. The Welsh sent representatives to the House of Commons and the Welsh legal system was reformed.

Henry VIII was succeeded by his son Edward VI, who was strongly Protestant. During his reign, the Book of Common Prayer was written to be used in the Church of England. A version of this book is still used in some churches today. Edward died at the age of 15 after ruling for just over six years, and his half-sister Mary became queen. Mary was a devout Catholic and persecuted Protestants (for this reason, she became known as 'Bloody Mary'). Mary also died after a short reign and the next monarch was her half-sister, Elizabeth, the daughter of Henry VIII and Anne Boleyn.

QUEEN ELIZABETH I

Elizabeth I was the younger daughter of Henry VIII

Queen Elizabeth I was a Protestant. She re-established the Church of England as the official Church in England. Everyone had to attend their local church and there were laws about the type of religious services and the prayers which could be said, but Elizabeth did not ask about people's real beliefs. She succeeded in finding a balance between the views of Catholics and the more extreme Protestants. In this way, she avoided any serious religious conflict within England. Elizabeth became one of the most popular monarchs in English history, particularly after 1588, when the English defeated the Spanish Armada (a large fleet of ships), which had been sent by Spain to conquer England and restore Catholicism.

THE REFORMATION IN SCOTLAND AND MARY, QUEEN OF SCOTS

“Elizabeth became one of the most popular monarchs in English history, particularly after 1588, when the English defeated the Spanish Armada.”

Scotland had also been strongly influenced by Protestant ideas. In 1560, the predominantly Protestant Scottish Parliament abolished the authority of the Pope in Scotland and Roman Catholic religious services became illegal. A Protestant Church of Scotland with an elected leadership was established but, unlike in England, this was not a state Church.

The queen of Scotland, Mary Stuart (often now called 'Mary, Queen of Scots') was a Catholic. She was only a week old when her father died and she became queen. Much of her childhood was spent in France. When she returned to Scotland, she was the centre of a power struggle between different groups. When her husband was murdered, Mary was suspected of involvement and fled to England. She gave her throne to her Protestant son, James VI of Scotland. Mary was Elizabeth I's cousin and hoped that Elizabeth might help her, but Elizabeth suspected Mary of wanting to take over the English throne, and kept her a prisoner for 20 years. Mary was eventually executed, accused of plotting against Elizabeth I.

EXPLORATION, POETRY AND DRAMA

The Elizabethan period in England was a time of growing patriotism: a feeling of pride in being English. English explorers sought new trade routes and tried to expand British trade into the Spanish colonies in the Americas. Sir Francis Drake, one of the commanders in the defeat of the Spanish Armada, was one of the founders of England's naval tradition. His ship, the *Golden Hind*, was one of the first to sail right around ('circumnavigate') the world. In Elizabeth I's time, English settlers first began to colonise the eastern coast of America. This colonisation, particularly by people who disagreed with the religious views of the next two kings, greatly increased in the next century.

The Elizabethan period is also remembered for the richness of its poetry and drama, especially the plays and poems of William Shakespeare.

Shakespeare is widely regarded as the greatest writer in the English language

WILLIAM SHAKESPEARE (1564–1616)

Shakespeare was born in Stratford-upon-Avon, England. He was a playwright and actor and wrote many poems and plays. His most famous plays include *A Midsummer Night's Dream, Hamlet, Macbeth* and *Romeo and Juliet.* He also dramatised significant events from the past, but he did not focus solely on kings and queens. He was one of the first to portray ordinary Englishmen and women. Shakespeare had a great influence on the English language and invented many words that are still common today. Lines from his plays and poems which are often still quoted include:

- Once more unto the breach (*Henry V*)
- To be or not to be (*Hamlet*)
- A rose by any other name (*Romeo and Juliet*)
- All the world's a stage (*As You Like It*)
- The darling buds of May (*Sonnet 18 – Shall I Compare Thee To A Summer's Day*).

Many people regard Shakespeare as the greatest playwright of all time. His plays and poems are still performed and studied in Britain and other countries today. The Globe Theatre in London is a modern copy of the theatres in which his plays were first performed.

JAMES VI AND I

Elizabeth I never married and so had no children of her own to inherit her throne. When she died in 1603 her heir was James VI of Scotland. He became King James I of England, Wales and Ireland but Scotland remained a separate country.

THE KING JAMES BIBLE

One achievement of King James' reign was a new translation of the Bible into English. This translation is known as the 'King James Version' or the 'Authorised Version'. It was not the first English Bible but is a version which continues to be used in many Protestant churches today.

"One achievement of King James' reign was a new translation of the Bible into English. This translation is known as the 'King James Version' or the 'Authorised Version'."

IRELAND

During this period, Ireland was an almost completely Catholic country. Henry VII and Henry VIII had extended English control outside the Pale (see page 17) and had established English authority over the whole country. Henry VIII took the title 'King of Ireland'. English laws were introduced and local leaders were expected to follow the instructions of the Lord Lieutenants in Dublin.

During the reigns of Elizabeth I and James I, many people in Ireland opposed rule by the Protestant government in England. There were a number of rebellions. The English government encouraged Scottish and English Protestants to settle in Ulster, the northern province of Ireland, taking over the land from Catholic landholders. These settlements were known as plantations. Many of the new settlers came from south-west Scotland and other land was given to companies based in London. James later organised similar plantations in several other parts of Ireland. This had serious long-term consequences for the history of England, Scotland and Ireland.

THE RISE OF PARLIAMENT

Elizabeth I was very skilled at managing Parliament. During her reign, she was successful in balancing her wishes and views against those of the House of Lords and those of the House of Commons, which was increasingly Protestant in its views.

James I and his son Charles I were less skilled politically. Both believed in the 'Divine Right of Kings': the idea that the king was directly appointed by God to rule. They thought that the king should be able to act without having to seek approval from Parliament. When Charles I inherited the thrones of England, Wales, Ireland and Scotland, he tried to rule in line with this principle. When he could not get Parliament to agree with his religious and foreign policies, he tried to rule without Parliament at all. For 11 years, he found ways in which to raise money without Parliament's approval but eventually trouble in Scotland meant that he had to recall Parliament.

THE BEGINNING OF THE ENGLISH CIVIL WAR

Charles I wanted the worship of the Church of England to include more ceremony and introduced a revised Prayer Book. He tried to impose this Prayer Book on the Presbyterian Church in Scotland and this led to serious unrest. A Scottish army was formed and Charles could not find the money he needed for his own army without the help of Parliament. In 1640, he recalled Parliament to ask it for funds. Many in Parliament were Puritans, a group of Protestants who advocated strict and simple religious doctrine and worship. They did not agree with the king's religious views and disliked his reforms of the Church of England. Parliament refused to give the king the money he asked for, even after the Scottish army invaded England.

Charles was held prisoner by the parliamentary army. He was still unwilling to reach any agreement with Parliament and in 1649 he was executed.

Another rebellion began in Ireland because the Roman Catholics in Ireland were afraid of the growing power of the Puritans. Parliament took this opportunity to demand control of the English army – a change that would have transferred substantial power from the king to Parliament. In response, Charles I entered the House of Commons and tried to arrest five parliamentary leaders, but they had been warned and were not there. (No monarch has set foot in the Commons since.) Civil war between the king and Parliament could not now be avoided and began in 1642. The country split into those who supported the king (the Cavaliers) and those who supported Parliament (the Roundheads).

OLIVER CROMWELL AND THE ENGLISH REPUBLIC

The king's army was defeated at the Battles of Marston Moor and Naseby. By 1646, it was clear that Parliament had won the war. Charles was held prisoner by the parliamentary army. He was still unwilling to reach any agreement with Parliament and in 1649 he was executed.

England declared itself a republic, called the Commonwealth. It no longer had a monarch. For a time, it was not totally clear how the country would be governed. For now, the army was in control. One of its generals, Oliver Cromwell, was sent to Ireland, where the revolt which had begun in 1641 still continued and where there was still a Royalist army. Cromwell was successful in establishing the authority of the English Parliament but did this with such violence that even today Cromwell remains a controversial figure in Ireland.

Oliver Cromwell was the leader of the English republic

The Scots had not agreed to the execution of Charles I and declared his son Charles II to be king. He was crowned king of Scotland and led a Scottish army into England. Cromwell defeated this army in the Battles of Dunbar and Worcester. Charles II escaped from Worcester, famously hiding in an oak tree on one occasion, and eventually fled to Europe. Parliament now controlled Scotland as well as England and Wales.

After his campaign in Ireland and victory over Charles II at Worcester, Cromwell was recognised as the leader of the new republic. He was given the title of Lord Protector and ruled until his death in 1658. When Cromwell died, his son, Richard, became Lord Protector in his place but was not able to control the army or the government. Although Britain had been a republic for 11 years, without Oliver Cromwell there was no clear leader or system of government. Many people in the country wanted stability. People began to talk about the need for a king.

THE RESTORATION

In May 1660, Parliament invited Charles II to come back from exile in the Netherlands. He was crowned King Charles II of England, Wales, Scotland and Ireland. Charles II made it clear that he had 'no wish to go on his travels again'. He understood that he could not always do as he wished but would sometimes need to reach agreement with Parliament. Generally, Parliament supported his policies. The Church of England again became the established official Church. Both Roman Catholics and Puritans were kept out of power.

“ **Habeas corpus is Latin for 'you must present the person in court'. The Act guaranteed that no one could be held prisoner unlawfully.**

During Charles II's reign, in 1665, there was a major outbreak of plague in London. Thousands of people died, especially in poorer areas. The following year, a great fire destroyed much of the city, including many churches and St Paul's Cathedral. London was rebuilt with a new St Paul's, which was designed by a famous architect, Sir Christopher Wren. Samuel Pepys wrote about these events in a diary which was later published and is still read today.

The Habeas Corpus Act became law in 1679. This was a very important piece of legislation which remains relevant today. Habeas corpus is Latin for 'you must present the person in court'. The Act guaranteed that no one could be held prisoner unlawfully. Every prisoner has a right to a court hearing.

Charles II was interested in science. During his reign, the Royal Society was formed to promote 'natural knowledge'. This is the oldest surviving scientific society in the world. Among its early members were Sir Edmund Halley, who successfully predicted the return of the comet now called Halley's Comet, and Sir Isaac Newton.

ISAAC NEWTON (1643–1727)

Born in Lincolnshire, eastern England, Isaac Newton first became interested in science when he studied at Cambridge University. He became an important figure in the field. His most famous published work was *Philosophiae Naturalis Principia Mathematica* ('Mathematical Principles of Natural Philosophy'), which showed how gravity applied to the whole universe. Newton also discovered that white light is made up of the colours of the rainbow. Many of his discoveries are still important for modern science.

A CATHOLIC KING

Charles II had no legitimate children. He died in 1685 and his brother, James, who was a Roman Catholic, became King James II in England, Wales and Ireland and King James VII of Scotland. James favoured Roman Catholics and allowed them to be army officers, which an Act of Parliament had forbidden. He did not seek to reach agreements with Parliament and arrested some of the bishops of the Church of England. People in England worried that James wanted to make England a Catholic country once more. However, his heirs were his two daughters, who were both firmly Protestant, and people thought that this meant there would soon be a Protestant monarch again. Then, James' wife had a son. Suddenly, it seemed likely that the next monarch would not be a Protestant after all.

THE GLORIOUS REVOLUTION

James II's elder daughter, Mary, was married to her cousin William of Orange, the Protestant ruler of the Netherlands. In 1688, important Protestants in England asked William to invade England and proclaim himself king. When William reached England, there was no resistance. James fled to France and William took over the throne, becoming William III in England, Wales and Ireland, and William II of Scotland. William ruled jointly with Mary. This event was later called the 'Glorious Revolution' because there was no fighting in England and because it guaranteed the power of Parliament, ending the threat of a monarch ruling on his or her own as he or she wished. James II wanted to regain the throne and invaded Ireland with the help of a French army. William defeated James II at the Battle of the Boyne in Ireland in 1690, an event which is still celebrated by some in Northern Ireland today.

“ William defeated James II at the Battle of the Boyne in Ireland in 1690, an event which is still celebrated by some in Northern Ireland today.

William re-conquered Ireland and James fled back to France. Many restrictions were placed on the Roman Catholic Church in Ireland and Irish Catholics were unable to take part in the government.

*For more information see **Clarifications** in Chapter 1 and lifeintheuk.net/clarify

There was also support for James in Scotland. An attempt at an armed rebellion in support of James was quickly defeated at Killiecrankie*. All Scottish clans were required formally to accept William as king by taking an oath. The MacDonalds of Glencoe were late in taking the oath and were all killed. The memory of this massacre meant some Scots distrusted the new government.

These kings were known by different titles in Scotland compared to the rest of the Union

Kings of England and Scotland

England, Wales and Ireland	Scotland
James I	James VI
James II	James VII
William III	William II

Some continued to believe that James was the rightful king, particularly in Scotland. Some joined him in exile in France; others were secret supporters. James' supporters became known as Jacobites.

Check that you understand:

- How and why religion changed during this period
- The importance of poetry and drama in the Elizabethan period
- About the involvement of Britain in Ireland
- The development of Parliament and the only period in history when England was a republic
- Why there was a restoration of the monarchy
- How the Glorious Revolution happened

A global power

CONSTITUTIONAL MONARCHY – THE BILL OF RIGHTS

At the coronation of William and Mary, a Declaration of Rights was read. This confirmed that the king would no longer be able to raise taxes or administer justice without agreement from Parliament. The balance of power between monarch and Parliament had now permanently changed. The Bill of Rights, 1689, confirmed the rights of Parliament and the limits of the king's power. Parliament took control of who could be monarch and declared that the king or queen must be a Protestant. A new Parliament had to be elected at least every three years (later this became seven years and now it is five years). Every year the monarch had to ask Parliament to renew funding for the army and the navy.

> **"The Bill of Rights, 1689, confirmed the rights of Parliament and the limits of the king's power."**

These changes meant that, to be able to govern effectively, the monarch needed to have advisers, or ministers, who would be able to ensure a majority of votes in the House of Commons and the House of Lords. There were two main groups in Parliament, known as the Whigs and the Tories. (The modern Conservative Party is still sometimes referred to as the Tories.) This was the beginning of party politics.

This was also an important time for the development of a free press (newspapers and other publications which are not controlled by the government). From 1695, newspapers were allowed to operate without a government licence. Increasing numbers of newspapers began to be published.

The laws passed after the Glorious Revolution are the beginning of what is called 'constitutional monarchy'. The monarch remained very important but was no longer able to insist on particular policies or actions if Parliament did not agree. After William III, the ministers gradually became more important than the monarch but this was not a democracy in the modern sense. The number of people who had the right to vote for members of Parliament was still very small. Only men who owned property of a certain value were able to vote. No women at all had the vote. Some constituencies were controlled by a single wealthy family. These were called 'pocket boroughs'. Other constituencies had hardly any voters and were called 'rotten boroughs'.

A GROWING POPULATION

This was a time when many people left Britain and Ireland to settle in new colonies in America and elsewhere, but others came to live in Britain. The first Jews to come to Britain since the Middle Ages settled in London in 1656. Between 1680 and 1720 many refugees called Huguenots came from France. They were Protestants and had been persecuted for their religion. Many were educated and skilled and worked as scientists, in banking, or in weaving or other crafts.

THE ACT OR TREATY OF UNION IN SCOTLAND

William and Mary's successor, Queen Anne, had no surviving children. This created uncertainty over the succession in England, Wales and Ireland and in Scotland. The Act of Union, known as the Treaty of Union in Scotland, was therefore agreed in 1707, creating the Kingdom of Great Britain. Although Scotland was no longer an independent country, it kept its own legal and education systems and Presbyterian Church.

The Act of Union, known as the Treaty of Union in Scotland, was agreed in 1707, creating the Kingdom of Great Britain.

THE PRIME MINISTER

When Queen Anne died in 1714, Parliament chose a German, George I, to be the next king, because he was Anne's nearest Protestant relative. An attempt by Scottish Jacobites to put James II's son on the throne instead was quickly defeated. George I did not speak very good English and this increased his need to rely on his ministers. The most important minister in Parliament became known as the Prime Minister. The first man to be called this was Sir Robert Walpole, who was Prime Minister from 1721 to 1742.

THE REBELLION OF THE CLANS

In 1745 there was another attempt to put a Stuart king back on the throne in place of George I's son, George II. Charles Edward Stuart (Bonnie Prince Charlie), the grandson of James II, landed in Scotland. He was supported by clansmen from the Scottish highlands and raised an army. Charles initially had some successes but was defeated by George II's army at the Battle of Culloden in 1746. Charles escaped back to Europe.

The clans lost a lot of their power and influence after Culloden. Chieftains became landlords if they had the favour of the English king, and clansmen became tenants who had to pay for the land they used.

A process began which became known as the 'Highland Clearances'. Many Scottish landlords destroyed individual small farms (known as 'crofts') to make space for large flocks of sheep and cattle. Evictions became very common in the early 19th century. Many Scottish people left for North America at this time.

ROBERT BURNS (1759–96)

Known in Scotland as 'The Bard', Robert Burns was a Scottish poet. He wrote in the Scots language, English with some Scottish words, and standard English. He also revised a lot of traditional folk songs by changing or adding lyrics. Burns' best-known work is probably the song *Auld Lang Syne*, which is sung by people in the UK and other countries when they are celebrating the New Year (or Hogmanay as it is called in Scotland).

THE ENLIGHTENMENT

During the 18th century, new ideas about politics, philosophy and science were developed. This is often called 'the Enlightenment'. Many of the great thinkers of the Enlightenment were Scottish. Adam Smith developed ideas about economics which are still referred to today. David Hume's ideas about human nature continue to influence philosophers. Scientific discoveries, such as James Watt's work on steam power, helped the progress of the Industrial Revolution. One of the most important principles of the Enlightenment was that everyone should have the right to their own political and religious beliefs and that the state should not try to dictate to them. This continues to be an important principle in the UK today.

THE INDUSTRIAL REVOLUTION

Before the 18th century, agriculture was the biggest source of employment in Britain. There were many cottage industries, where people worked from home to produce goods such as cloth and lace.

“Before the 18th century, agriculture was the biggest source of employment in Britain.”

The Industrial Revolution was the rapid development of industry in Britain in the 18th and 19th centuries. Britain was the first country to industrialise on a large scale. It happened because of the development of machinery and the use of steam power. Agriculture and the manufacturing of goods became mechanised. This made things more efficient and increased production. Coal and other raw materials were needed to power the new factories. Many people moved from the countryside and started working in the mining and manufacturing industries.

The development of the Bessemer process for the mass production of steel led to the development of the shipbuilding industry and the railways. Manufacturing jobs became the main source of employment in Britain.

You may be asked about key historical figures and their work. Focus on what their achievements meant for Britain, for example how Arkwright made the textile industry more efficient.

RICHARD ARKWRIGHT (1732–92)

Born in 1732, Arkwright originally trained and worked as a barber. He was able to dye hair and make wigs. When wigs became less popular, he started to work in textiles. He improved the original carding machine. Carding is the process of preparing fibres for spinning into yarn and fabric. He also developed horse-driven spinning mills that used only one machine. This increased the efficiency of production. Later, he used the steam engine to power machinery. Arkwright is particularly remembered for the efficient and profitable way that he ran his factories.

Richard Arkwright's carding machine

Better transport links were needed to transport raw materials and manufactured goods. Canals were built to link the factories to towns and cities and to the ports, particularly in the new industrial areas in the middle and north of England.

Working conditions during the Industrial Revolution were very poor. There were no laws to protect employees, who were often forced to work long hours in dangerous situations. Children also worked and were treated in the same way as adults. Sometimes they were treated even more harshly.

This was also a time of increased colonisation overseas. Captain James Cook mapped the coast of Australia and a few colonies were established there. Britain gained control over Canada, and the East India Company, originally set up to trade, gained control of large parts of India. Colonies began to be established in southern Africa.

Britain traded all over the world and began to import more goods. Sugar and tobacco came from North America and the West Indies; textiles, tea and spices came from India and the area that is today called Indonesia. Trading and settlements overseas sometimes brought Britain into conflict with other countries, particularly France, which was expanding and trading in a similar way in many of the same areas of the world.

SAKE DEAN MAHOMET (1759–1851)

Mahomet was born in 1759 and grew up in the Bengal region of India. He served in the Bengal army and came to Britain in 1782. He then moved to Ireland and eloped with an Irish girl called Jane Daly in 1786, returning to England at the turn of the century. In 1810 he opened the Hindoostane Coffee House in George Street, London*. It was the first curry house to open in Britain. Mahomet and his wife also introduced 'shampooing', the Indian art of head massage, to Britain.

*For more information see **Clarifications** in Chapter 1 and lifeintheuk.net/clarify

THE SLAVE TRADE

This commercial expansion and prosperity was sustained in part by the booming slave trade. While slavery was illegal within Britain itself, by the 18th century it was a fully established overseas industry, dominated by Britain and the American colonies.

Slaves came primarily from West Africa. Travelling on British ships in horrible conditions, they were taken to America and the

Caribbean, where they were made to work on tobacco and sugar plantations. The living and working conditions for slaves were very bad. Many slaves tried to escape and others revolted against their owners in protest at their terrible treatment.

There were, however, people in Britain who opposed the slave trade. The first formal anti-slavery groups were set up by the Quakers in the late 1700s, and they petitioned Parliament to ban the practice. William Wilberforce, an evangelical Christian and a member of Parliament, also played an important part in changing the law. Along with other abolitionists (people who supported the abolition of slavery), he succeeded in turning public opinion against the slave trade. In 1807, it became illegal to trade slaves in British ships or from British ports, and in 1833 the Emancipation Act abolished slavery throughout the British Empire. The Royal Navy stopped slave ships from other countries, freed the slaves and punished the slave traders. After 1833, 2 million Indian and Chinese workers were employed to replace the freed slaves. They worked on sugar plantations in the Caribbean, in mines in South Africa, on railways in East Africa and in the army in Kenya.

“In 1807, it became illegal to trade slaves in British ships or from British ports, and in 1833 the Emancipation Act abolished slavery throughout the British Empire.”

THE AMERICAN WAR OF INDEPENDENCE

By the 1760s, there were substantial British colonies in North America. The colonies were wealthy and largely in control of their own affairs. Many of the colonist families had originally gone to North America in order to have religious freedom. They were well educated and interested in ideas of liberty. The British government wanted to tax the colonies. The colonists saw this as an attack on their freedom and said there should be 'no taxation without representation' in the British Parliament. Parliament tried to compromise by repealing some of the taxes, but relationships between the British government and the colonies continued to worsen. Fighting broke out between the colonists and the British forces. In 1776, 13 American colonies declared their independence, stating that people had a right to establish their own governments. The colonists eventually defeated the British army and Britain recognised the colonies' independence in 1783.

WAR WITH FRANCE

During the 18th century, Britain fought a number of wars with France. In 1789, there was a revolution in France and the new French government soon declared war on Britain. Napoleon, who became Emperor of France, continued the war. Britain's navy fought against combined French and Spanish fleets, winning the Battle of Trafalgar in 1805. Admiral Nelson was in charge of the British fleet at Trafalgar and was killed in the battle. Nelson's Column in Trafalgar Square, London, is a monument to him. His ship, *HMS Victory*, can be visited in Portsmouth. The British army also fought against the French. In 1815, the French Wars ended with the defeat of the Emperor Napoleon by the Duke of Wellington at the Battle of Waterloo. Wellington was known as the Iron Duke and later became Prime Minister.

The Battle of Trafalgar (21 October 1805) was a naval engagement fought by the British Royal Navy against the combined fleets of the French Navy and Spanish Navy

THE UNION FLAG

Although Ireland had had the same monarch as England and Wales since Henry VIII, it had remained a separate country. In 1801, Ireland became unified with England, Scotland and Wales after the Act of Union of 1800. This created the United Kingdom of Great Britain and Ireland. One symbol of this union between England, Scotland, Wales and Ireland was a new version of the official flag, the Union Flag. This is often called the Union Jack. The flag combined crosses associated with England, Scotland and Ireland. It is still used today as the official flag of the UK.

The Union Flag consists of three crosses:

- The cross of St George, patron saint of England, is a red cross on a white ground.
- The cross of St Andrew, patron saint of Scotland, is a diagonal white cross on a blue ground.
- The cross of St Patrick, patron saint of Ireland, is a diagonal red cross on a white ground.

The Union Flag, also known as the Union Jack

The crosses of the three countries which combined to form the Union Flag

The cross of St George

The cross of St Andrew

The cross of St Patrick

There is also an official Welsh flag, which shows a Welsh dragon. The Welsh dragon does not appear on the Union Flag because, when the first Union Flag was created in 1606 from the flags of Scotland and England, the Principality of Wales was already united with England.

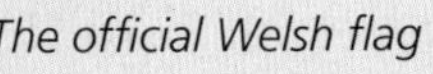

The official Welsh flag

THE VICTORIAN AGE

In 1837, Queen Victoria became queen of the UK at the age of 18. She reigned until 1901, almost 64 years. Her reign is known as the Victorian Age. It was a time when Britain increased in power and influence abroad. Within the UK, the middle classes became increasingly significant and a number of reformers led moves to improve conditions of life for the poor.

THE BRITISH EMPIRE

During the Victorian period, the British Empire grew to cover all of India, Australia and large parts of Africa. It became the largest empire the world has ever seen, with an estimated population of more than 400 million people.

Many people were encouraged to leave the UK to settle overseas. Between 1853 and 1913, as many as 13 million British citizens left the country. People continued to come to Britain from other parts of the world. For example, between 1870 and 1914, around 120,000 Russian and Polish Jews came to Britain to escape persecution. Many settled in London's East End and in Manchester and Leeds. People from the Empire, including India and Africa, also came to Britain to live, work and study.

TRADE AND INDUSTRY

Britain continued to be a great trading nation. The government began to promote policies of free trade, abolishing a number of taxes on imported goods. One example of this was the repealing of the Corn Laws in 1846. These had prevented the import of cheap grain. The reforms helped the development of British industry, because raw materials could now be imported more cheaply.

Working conditions in factories gradually became better. In 1847, the number of hours that women and children could work was limited by law to 10 hours per day. Better housing began to be built for workers.

Transport links also improved, enabling goods and people to move more easily around the country. Just before Victoria came to the throne, the father and son George and Robert Stephenson pioneered the railway engine and a major expansion of the railways took place in the Victorian period. Railways were built throughout the Empire. There were also great advances in other

> **“During the Victorian period, the British Empire grew to cover all of India, Australia and large parts of Africa.”**

areas, such as the building of bridges by engineers such as Isambard Kingdom Brunel.

ISAMBARD KINGDOM BRUNEL (1806–59)

Brunel was originally from Portsmouth, England. He was an engineer who built tunnels, bridges, railway lines and ships. He was responsible for constructing the Great Western Railway, which was the first major railway built in Britain. It runs from Paddington Station in London to the south west of England, the West Midlands and Wales. Many of Brunel's bridges are still in use today.

The Clifton Suspension Bridge, designed by Isambard Kingdom Brunel, spanning the Avon Gorge

British industry led the world in the 19th century. The UK produced more than half of the world's iron, coal and cotton cloth. The UK also became a centre for financial services, including insurance and banking. In 1851, the Great Exhibition opened in Hyde Park in the Crystal Palace, a huge building made of iron and glass. Exhibits ranged from huge machines to handmade goods. Countries from all over the world showed their goods but most of the objects were made in Britain.

THE CRIMEAN WAR

From 1853 to 1856, Britain fought with Turkey and France against Russia in the Crimean War. It was the first war to be extensively covered by the media through news stories and photographs. The conditions were very poor and many soldiers died from illnesses they caught in the hospitals, rather than from war wounds. Queen Victoria introduced the Victoria Cross medal during this war. It honours acts of valour by soldiers.

FLORENCE NIGHTINGALE (1820–1910)

Florence Nightingale was born in Italy to English parents. At the age of 31, she trained as a nurse in Germany. In 1854, she went to Turkey and worked in military hospitals, treating soldiers who were fighting in the Crimean War. She and her fellow nurses improved the conditions in the hospital and reduced the mortality rate. In 1860 she established the Nightingale Training School for nurses at St Thomas' Hospital in London. The school was the first of its kind and still exists today, as do many of the practices that Nightingale used. She is often regarded as the founder of modern nursing.

IRELAND IN THE 19TH CENTURY

Conditions in Ireland were not as good as in the rest of the UK. Two-thirds of the population still depended on farming to make their living, often on very small plots of land. Many depended on potatoes as a large part of their diet. In the middle of the century the potato crop failed, and Ireland suffered a famine. A million people died from disease and starvation. Another million and a half left Ireland. Some emigrated to the United States and others came to England. By 1861 there were large populations of Irish people in cities such as Liverpool, London, Manchester and Glasgow.

“In the middle of the century the potato crop failed, and Ireland suffered a famine.

The Irish Nationalist movement had grown strongly through the 19th century. Some, such as the Fenians, favoured complete independence. Others, such as Charles Stuart* Parnell, advocated 'Home Rule', in which Ireland would remain in the UK but have its own parliament.

THE RIGHT TO VOTE

As the middle classes in the wealthy industrial towns and cities grew in influence, they began to demand more political power. The Reform Act of 1832 had greatly increased the number of people with the right to vote. The Act also abolished the old pocket and rotten boroughs (see page 33) and more parliamentary seats were given to the towns and cities. There was a permanent shift of political power from the countryside to the towns but voting was still based on ownership of property. This meant that members of the working class were still unable to vote.

A movement began to demand the vote for the working classes and other people without property. Campaigners, called the Chartists, presented petitions to Parliament. At first they seemed to be unsuccessful, but in 1867 there was another Reform Act. This created many more urban seats in Parliament and reduced the amount of property that people needed to have before they could vote. However, the majority of men still did not have the right to vote and no women could vote.

Politicians realised that the increased number of voters meant that they needed to persuade people to vote for them if they were to be sure of being elected to Parliament. The political parties began to create organisations to reach out to ordinary voters. Universal suffrage (the right of every adult, male or female, to vote) followed in the next century.

In common with the rest of Europe, women in 19th-century Britain had fewer rights than men. Until 1870, when a woman got married, her earnings, property and money automatically belonged to her husband. Acts of Parliament in 1870 and 1882 gave wives the right to keep their own earnings and property. In the late 19th and early 20th centuries, an increasing number of women campaigned and demonstrated for greater rights and, in particular, the right to vote. They formed the women's suffrage movement and became known as 'suffragettes'.

"In the late 19th and early 20th centuries, an increasing number of women campaigned and demonstrated for greater rights and, in particular, the right to vote. They formed the women's suffrage movement and became known as 'suffragettes'.

EMMELINE PANKHURST (1858–1928)

Emmeline Pankhurst was born in Manchester in 1858. She set up the Women's Franchise League in 1889, which fought to get the vote in local elections for married women. In 1903 she helped found the Women's Social and Political Union (WSPU). This was the first group whose members were called 'suffragettes'. The group used civil disobedience as part of their protest to gain the vote for women. They chained themselves to railings, smashed windows and committed arson. Many of the women, including Pankhurst, went on hunger strike. In 1918, women over the age of 30 were given voting rights and the right to stand for Parliament, partly in recognition of the contribution women made to the war effort during the First World War. Shortly before Pankhurst's death in 1928, women were given the right to vote at the age of 21, the same as men.

THE FUTURE OF THE EMPIRE

Although the British Empire continued to grow until the 1920s, there was already discussion in the late 19th century about its future direction. Supporters of expansion believed that the Empire benefited Britain through increased trade and commerce. Others thought the Empire had become over-expanded and that the frequent conflicts in many parts of the Empire, such as India's north-west frontier or southern Africa, were a drain on resources. Yet the great majority of British people believed in the Empire as a force for good in the world.

The Boer War of 1899 to 1902 made the discussions about the future of the Empire more urgent. The British went to war in South Africa with settlers from the Netherlands called the Boers. The Boers fought fiercely and the war went on for over three years. Many died in the fighting and many more from disease. There was some public sympathy for the Boers and people began to question whether the Empire could continue. As different parts of the Empire developed, they won greater freedom and autonomy from Britain. Eventually, by the second half of the 20th century, there was, for the most part, an orderly transition from Empire to Commonwealth, with countries being granted their independence.

“The Boer War of 1899 to 1902 made the discussions about the future of the Empire more urgent.”

RUDYARD KIPLING (1865–1936)

Rudyard Kipling was born in India in 1865 and later lived in India, the UK and the USA. He wrote books and poems set in both India and the UK. His poems and novels reflected the idea that the British Empire was a force for good. Kipling was awarded the Nobel Prize in Literature in 1907. His books include the *Just So Stories* and *The Jungle Book*, which continue to be popular today. His poem *If* has often been voted among the UK's favourite poems. It begins with these words:

> 'If you can keep your head when all about you
> Are losing theirs and blaming it on you;
> If you can trust yourself when all men doubt you,
> But make allowance for their doubting too;
> If you can wait and not be tired by waiting,
> Or being lied about, don't deal in lies,
> Or being hated, don't give way to hating,
> And yet don't look too good, nor talk too wise'
> (*If*, Rudyard Kipling)

Check that you understand:

- The change in the balance of power between Parliament and the monarchy
- When and why Scotland joined England and Wales to become Great Britain
- The reasons for a rebellion in Scotland led by Bonnie Prince Charlie
- The ideas of the Enlightenment
- The importance of the Industrial Revolution and development of industry
- The slave trade and when it was abolished
- The growth of the British Empire
- How democracy developed during this period

The 20th century

THE FIRST WORLD WAR

On 28 June 1914, Archduke Franz Ferdinand of Austria was assassinated. This set off a chain of events leading to the First World War (1914–18).

The early 20th century was a time of optimism in Britain. The nation, with its expansive Empire, well-admired navy, thriving industry and strong political institutions, was what is now known as a global 'superpower'. It was also a time of social progress. Financial help for the unemployed, old-age pensions and free school meals were just a few of the important measures introduced. Various laws were passed to improve safety in the workplace; town planning rules were tightened to prevent the further development of slums; and better support was given to mothers and their children after divorce or separation. Local government became more democratic and a salary for members of Parliament (MPs) was introduced for the first time, making it easier for more people to take part in public life.

This era of optimism and progress was cut short when war broke out between several European nations. On 28 June 1914, Archduke Franz Ferdinand of Austria was assassinated. This set off a chain of events leading to the First World War (1914–18). But while the assassination provided the trigger for war, other factors – such as a growing sense of nationalism in many European states; increasing militarism; imperialism; and the division of the major European powers into two camps – all set the conditions for war.

The conflict was centred in Europe, but it was a global war involving nations from around the world. Britain was part of the Allied Powers, which included (amongst others) France, Russia, Japan, Belgium, Serbia – and later, Greece, Italy, Romania and the United States. The whole of the British Empire was involved in the conflict – for example, more than a million Indians fought on behalf of Britain in lots of different countries, and around 40,000 were killed. Men from the West Indies, Africa, Australia, New Zealand and Canada also fought with the British. The Allies fought against the Central Powers – mainly Germany, the Austro-Hungarian Empire, the Ottoman Empire and later Bulgaria. Millions of people were killed or wounded, with more than 2 million British casualties. One battle, the British attack on the Somme in July 1916, resulted in about 60,000 British casualties on the first day alone.

"The British attack on the Somme in July 1916 resulted in about 60,000 British casualties on the first day alone."

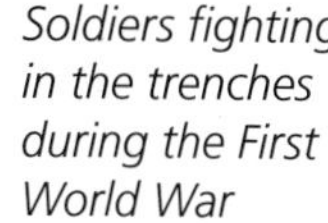

Soldiers fighting in the trenches during the First World War

The First World War ended at 11.00 am on 11 November 1918 with victory for Britain and its allies.

THE PARTITION OF IRELAND

In 1913, the British government promised 'Home Rule' for Ireland. The proposal was to have a self-governing Ireland with its own parliament but still part of the UK. A Home Rule Bill was introduced in Parliament. It was opposed by the Protestants in the north of Ireland, who threatened to resist Home Rule by force.

The outbreak of the First World War led the British government to postpone any changes in Ireland. Irish Nationalists were not willing to wait and in 1916 there was an uprising (the Easter Rising) against the British in Dublin. The leaders of the uprising were executed under military law. A guerrilla war against the British army and the police in Ireland followed. In 1921 a peace treaty was signed and in 1922 Ireland became two countries. The six counties in the north which were mainly Protestant remained part of the UK under the name Northern Ireland. The rest of Ireland became the Irish Free State. It had its own government and became a republic in 1949.

There were people in both parts of Ireland who disagreed with the split between the North and the South. They still wanted Ireland to be one independent country. Years of disagreement led to a terror campaign in Northern Ireland and elsewhere. The conflict between those wishing for full Irish independence and those wishing to remain loyal to the British government is often referred to as 'the Troubles'.

In 1929, the world entered the 'Great Depression' and some parts of the UK suffered mass unemployment.

THE INTER-WAR PERIOD

In the 1920s, many people's living conditions got better. There were improvements in public housing and new homes were built in many towns and cities. However, in 1929, the world entered the 'Great Depression' and some parts of the UK suffered mass unemployment. The effects of the depression of the 1930s were felt differently in different parts of the UK. The traditional heavy industries such as shipbuilding were badly affected but new industries – including the automobile and aviation industries – developed. As prices generally fell, those in work had more money to spend. Car ownership doubled from 1 million to 2 million between 1930 and 1939. In addition, many new houses were built. It was also a time of cultural blossoming, with writers such as Graham Greene and Evelyn Waugh prominent. The economist John Maynard Keynes published influential new theories of economics. The BBC started radio broadcasts in 1922 and began the world's first regular television service in 1936.

THE SECOND WORLD WAR

Adolf Hitler came to power in Germany in 1933. He believed that the conditions imposed on Germany by the Allies after the First World War were unfair; he also wanted to conquer more land for the German people. He set about renegotiating treaties, building up arms, and testing Germany's military strength in nearby countries. The British government tried to avoid another war. However, when Hitler invaded Poland in 1939, Britain and France declared war in order to stop his aggression.

The war was initially fought between the Axis powers (fascist Germany and Italy and the Empire of Japan) and the Allies. The main countries on the allied side were the UK, France, Poland, Australia, New Zealand, Canada, and the Union of South Africa.

Having occupied Austria and invaded Czechoslovakia, Hitler followed his invasion of Poland by taking control of Belgium and the Netherlands. Then, in 1940, German forces defeated allied troops and advanced through France. At this time of national crisis, Winston Churchill became Prime Minister and Britain's war leader.

As France fell, the British decided to evacuate British and French soldiers from France in a huge naval operation. Many civilian volunteers in small pleasure and fishing boats from Britain helped the Navy to rescue more than 300,000 men from the beaches around Dunkirk. Although many lives and a lot of equipment were lost, the evacuation was a success and meant that Britain was better able to continue the fight against the Germans. The evacuation gave rise to the phrase 'the Dunkirk spirit'.

Many civilian volunteers in small pleasure and fishing boats from Britain helped the Navy to rescue more than 300,000 men from the beaches around Dunkirk.

From the end of June 1940 until the German invasion of the Soviet Union in June 1941, Britain and the Empire stood almost alone against Nazi Germany.

Hitler wanted to invade Britain, but before sending in troops, Germany needed to control the air. The Germans waged an air campaign against Britain, but the British resisted with their fighter planes and eventually won the crucial aerial battle against the Germans, called 'the Battle of Britain', in the summer of 1940. The most important planes used by the Royal Air Force in the Battle of Britain were the Spitfire and the Hurricane – which were designed and built in Britain. Despite this crucial victory, the German air force was able to continue bombing London and other British cities at night-time. This was called the Blitz. Coventry was almost totally destroyed and a great deal of damage was done in other cities, especially in the East End of London. Despite the destruction, there was a strong national spirit of resistance in the UK. The phrase 'the Blitz spirit' is still used today to describe Britons pulling together in the face of adversity.

Make sure you know the planes used in the Battle of Britain, and which parts of the UK were most affected by the Blitz.

Winston Churchill, best known for his leadership of the UK during the Second World War

WINSTON CHURCHILL (1874–1965)

Churchill was the son of a politician and, before becoming a Conservative MP in 1900, was a soldier and journalist. In May 1940 he became Prime Minister. He refused to surrender to the Nazis and was an inspirational leader to the British people in a time of great hardship. He lost the General Election in 1945 but returned as Prime Minister in 1951.

He was an MP until he stood down at the 1964 General Election. Following his death in 1965, he was given a state funeral. He remains a much-admired figure to this day, and in 2002 was voted the greatest Briton of all time by the public. During the War, he made many famous speeches including lines which you may still hear:

'I have nothing to offer but blood, toil, tears and sweat'

Churchill's first speech to the House of Commons after he became Prime Minister, 1940

'We shall fight on the beaches,
we shall fight on the landing grounds,
we shall fight in the fields and in the streets,
we shall fight in the hills;
we shall never surrender'

Speech to the House of Commons after Dunkirk (see above), 1940

'Never in the field of human conflict was so much owed by so many to so few'

Speech to the House of Commons during the Battle of Britain (see above), 1940

?

You may be asked to identify famous quotes from speeches by people such as Churchill. Make sure you know who said what.

At the same time as defending Britain, the British military was fighting the Axis on many other fronts. In Singapore, the Japanese defeated the British and then occupied Burma, threatening India. The United States entered the war when the Japanese bombed its naval base at Pearl Harbor in December 1941.

That same year, Hitler attempted the largest invasion in history by attacking the Soviet Union. It was a fierce conflict, with huge losses on both sides. German forces were ultimately repelled by the Soviets, and the damage they sustained proved to be a pivotal point in the war.

The Royal Air Force helped to defend Britain in the Second World War

The allied forces gradually gained the upper hand, winning significant victories in North Africa and Italy. German losses in the Soviet Union, combined with the support of the Americans, meant that the Allies were eventually strong enough to attack Hitler's forces in Western Europe. On 6 June 1944, allied forces landed in Normandy (this event is often referred to as 'D-Day'). Following victory on the beaches of Normandy, the allied forces pressed on through France and eventually into Germany. The Allies comprehensively defeated Germany in May 1945.

The war against Japan ended in August 1945 when the United States dropped its newly developed atom bombs on the Japanese cities of Hiroshima and Nagasaki. Scientists led by New-Zealand-born Ernest Rutherford, working at Manchester and then Cambridge University, were the first to 'split the atom'. Some British scientists went on to take part in the Manhattan Project in the United States, which developed the atomic bomb. The war was finally over.

ALEXANDER FLEMING (1881–1955)

Born in Scotland, Fleming moved to London as a teenager and later qualified as a doctor. He was researching influenza (the 'flu') in 1928 when he discovered penicillin. This was then further developed into a usable drug by the scientists Howard Florey and Ernst Chain. By the 1940s it was in mass production. Fleming won the Nobel Prize in Medicine in 1945. Penicillin is still used to treat bacterial infections today.

Check that you understand:

- What happened during the First World War
- The partition of Ireland and the establishment of the UK as it is today
- The events of the Second World War

Britain since 1945

> In 1948, Aneurin (Nye) Bevan, the Minister for Health, led the establishment of the National Health Service (NHS), which guaranteed a minimum standard of health care for all, free at the point of use.

THE WELFARE STATE

Although the UK had won the war, the country was exhausted economically and the people wanted change. During the war, there had been significant reforms to the education system and people now looked for wider social reforms.

In 1945 the British people elected a Labour government. The new Prime Minister was Clement Atlee, who promised to introduce the welfare state outlined in the Beveridge Report. In 1948, Aneurin (Nye) Bevan, the Minister for Health, led the establishment of the National Health Service (NHS), which guaranteed a minimum standard of health care for all, free at the point of use. A national system of benefits was also introduced to provide 'social security', so that the population would be protected from the 'cradle to the grave'. The government took into public ownership (nationalised) the railways, coal mines and gas, water and electricity supplies.

Another aspect of change was self-government for former colonies. In 1947, independence was granted to nine countries, including India, Pakistan and Ceylon (now Sri Lanka). Other colonies in Africa, the Caribbean and the Pacific achieved independence over the next 20 years.

The UK developed its own atomic bomb and joined the new North Atlantic Treaty Organization (NATO), an alliance of nations set up to resist the perceived threat of invasion by the Soviet Union and its allies.

Britain had a Conservative government from 1951 to 1964. The 1950s was a period of economic recovery after the war and increasing prosperity for working people. The Prime Minister of the day, Harold Macmillan, was famous for his 'wind of change' speech about decolonisation and independence for the countries of the Empire.

CLEMENT ATTLEE (1883–1967)

Clement Attlee was born in London in 1883. His father was a solicitor and, after studying at Oxford University, Attlee became a barrister. He gave this up to do social work in East London and eventually became a Labour MP. He was Winston Churchill's Deputy Prime Minister in the wartime coalition government and became Prime Minister after the Labour Party won the 1945 election. He was Prime Minister from 1945 to 1951 and led the Labour Party for 20 years. Attlee's government undertook the nationalisation of major industries (like coal and steel), created the National Health Service and implemented many of Beveridge's plans for a stronger welfare state. Attlee also introduced measures to improve the conditions of workers.

You may be asked questions about the formation of the welfare state. Take some time to study the key figures and how they contributed to it, as well as key reports and legislation.

WILLIAM BEVERIDGE (1879–1963)

William Beveridge (later Lord Beveridge) was a British economist and social reformer. He served briefly as a Liberal MP and was subsequently the leader of the Liberals in the House of Lords but is best known for the 1942 report *Social Insurance and Allied Services* (known as the Beveridge Report). The report was commissioned by the wartime government in 1941. It recommended that the government should find ways of fighting the five 'Giant Evils' of Want, Disease, Ignorance, Squalor and Idleness and provided the basis of the modern welfare state.

R A BUTLER (1902–82)

Richard Austen Butler (later Lord Butler) was born in 1902. He became a Conservative MP in 1923* and held several positions before becoming responsible for education in 1941. In this role, he oversaw the introduction of the Education Act 1944 (often called 'The Butler Act'), which introduced free secondary education in England and Wales. The education system has changed significantly since the Act was introduced, but the division between primary and secondary schools that it enforced still remains in most areas of Britain.

*For more information see **Clarifications** in Chapter 1 and lifeintheuk.net/clarify

DYLAN THOMAS (1914–53)

Dylan Thomas was a Welsh poet and writer. He often read and performed his work in public, including for the BBC. His most well-known works include the radio play *Under Milk Wood*, first performed after his death in 1954, and the poem *Do Not Go Gentle into That Good Night*, which he wrote for his dying father in 1952. He died at the age of 39 in New York. There are several memorials to him in his birthplace, Swansea, including a statue and the Dylan Thomas Centre.

MIGRATION IN POST-WAR BRITAIN

Rebuilding Britain after the Second World War was a huge task. There were labour shortages and the British government encouraged workers from Ireland and other parts of Europe to come to the UK and help with the reconstruction. In 1948, people from the West Indies were also invited to come and work.

During the 1950s, there was still a shortage of labour in the UK. Further immigration was therefore encouraged for economic reasons, and many industries advertised for workers from overseas. For example, centres were set up in the West Indies to recruit people to drive buses. Textile and engineering firms from the north of England and the Midlands sent agents to India and Pakistan to find workers. For about 25 years, people from the West Indies, India, Pakistan and (later) Bangladesh travelled to work and settle in Britain.

SOCIAL CHANGE IN THE 1960s

The decade of the 1960s was a period of significant social change. It was known as 'the Swinging Sixties'. There was growth in British fashion, cinema and popular music. Two well-known pop music groups at the time were The Beatles and The Rolling Stones. People started to become better off and many bought cars and other consumer goods.

It was also a time when social laws were liberalised, for example in relation to divorce and to abortion in England, Wales and Scotland. The position of women in the workplace also improved. It was quite common at the time for employers to ask women to leave their jobs when they got married, but Parliament passed new laws giving women the right to equal pay and made it illegal for employers to discriminate against women because of their gender.

The 1960s was also a time of technological progress. Britain and France developed the supersonic commercial airliner, Concorde. New styles of architecture, including high-rise buildings and the use of concrete and steel, became common.

The number of people migrating from the West Indies, India, Pakistan and what is now Bangladesh fell in the late 1960s because the government passed new laws to restrict immigration to Britain. Immigrants were required to have a strong connection to Britain through birth or ancestry. Even so, during the early 1970s, Britain admitted 28,000 people of Indian origin who had been forced to leave Uganda.

SOME GREAT BRITISH INVENTIONS OF THE 20TH CENTURY

Britain has given the world some wonderful inventions. Examples from the 20th century include:

The **television** was developed by Scotsman John Logie Baird (1888–1946) in the 1920s. In 1932 he made the first television broadcast between London and Glasgow.

Radar was developed by Scotsman Sir Robert Watson-Watt (1892–1973), who proposed that enemy aircraft could be detected by radio waves. The first successful radar test took place in 1935.

Working with radar led Sir Bernard Lovell (1913–2012) to make new discoveries in astronomy. The radio telescope he built at **Jodrell Bank** in Cheshire was for many years the biggest in the world and continues to operate today.

A **Turing machine** is a theoretical mathematical device invented by Alan Turing (1912–54), a British mathematician, in the 1930s. The theory was influential in the development of computer science and the modern-day computer.

The Scottish physician and researcher John MacLeod (1876–1935) was the co-discoverer of **insulin**, used to treat diabetes.

The **structure of the DNA molecule** was discovered in 1953 through work at British universities in London and Cambridge. This discovery contributed to many scientific advances, particularly in medicine and fighting crime. Francis Crick (1916–2004), one of those awarded the Nobel Prize for this discovery, was British.

The **jet engine** was developed in Britain in the 1930s by Sir Frank Whittle (1907–96), a British Royal Air Force engineer officer.

Sir Christopher Cockerell (1910–99), a British inventor, invented the **hovercraft** in the 1950s.

Britain and France developed **Concorde**, the supersonic passenger aircraft. It first flew in 1969 and began carrying passengers in 1976. Concorde was retired from service in 2003.

The **Harrier jump jet**, an aircraft capable of taking off vertically, was also designed and developed in the UK.

In the 1960s, James Goodfellow (1937–) invented the **cash-dispensing ATM** (automatic teller machine) or 'cashpoint'. The first of these was put into use by Barclays Bank in Enfield, north London in 1967.

IVF (in-vitro fertilisation) therapy for the treatment of infertility was pioneered in Britain by physiologist Sir Robert Edwards (1925–2013) and gynaecologist Patrick Steptoe (1913–88). The world's first 'test-tube baby' was born in Oldham, Lancashire in 1978.

In 1996, two British scientists, Sir Ian Wilmut (1944–) and Keith Campbell (1954–2012), led a team which was the first to succeed in cloning a mammal, Dolly the sheep. This has led to further research into the possible use of **cloning** to preserve endangered species and for medical purposes.

Sir Peter Mansfield (1933–2017), a British scientist, is the co-inventor of the **MRI (magnetic resonance imaging)** scanner. This enables doctors and researchers to obtain exact and non-invasive images of human internal organs and has revolutionised diagnostic medicine.

The inventor of the **World Wide Web**, Sir Tim Berners-Lee (1955–), is British. Information was successfully transferred via the web for the first time on 25 December 1990.

PROBLEMS IN THE ECONOMY IN THE 1970s

In the late 1970s, the post-war economic boom came to an end. Prices of goods and raw materials began to rise sharply and the exchange rate between the pound and other currencies was unstable. This caused problems with the 'balance of payments': imports of goods were valued at more than the price paid for exports.

You should be able to identify all 15 British inventions (on this and the previous page) and when they were invented. You also need to be able to identify the inventors.

Many industries and services were affected by strikes and this caused problems between the trade unions and the government. People began to argue that the unions were too powerful and that their activities were harming the UK.

The 1970s was also a time of serious unrest in Northern Ireland. In 1972, the Northern Ireland Parliament was suspended and Northern Ireland was directly ruled by the UK government. Some 3,000 people lost their lives in the decades after 1969 in the violence in Northern Ireland.

MARY PETERS (1939–)

Born in Manchester, Mary Peters moved to Northern Ireland as a child. She was a talented athlete who won an Olympic gold medal in the pentathlon in 1972. After this, she raised money for local athletics and became the team manager for the women's British Olympic team. She continues to promote sport and tourism in Northern Ireland and was made a Dame of the British Empire in 2000 in recognition of her work.

EUROPE AND THE COMMON MARKET

West Germany, France, Belgium, Italy, Luxembourg and the Netherlands formed the European Economic Community (EEC) in 1957. The EEC became a part of the European Union when it was formed in 1993. The UK was a full member of the European Union but did not use the Euro currency. The UK formally left the European Union on 31 January 2020.

CONSERVATIVE GOVERNMENT FROM 1979 TO 1997

MARGARET THATCHER (1925–2013)

© Getty Images

Margaret Thatcher was the daughter of a grocer from Grantham in Lincolnshire. She trained as a chemist and lawyer. She was elected as a Conservative MP in 1959 and became a cabinet minister in 1970 as the Secretary of State for Education and Science. In 1975 she was elected as Leader of the Conservative Party and so became Leader of the Opposition.

Following the Conservative victory in the General Election in 1979, Margaret Thatcher became the first woman Prime Minister of the UK. She was the longest-serving Prime Minister of the 20th century, remaining in office until 1990.

During her premiership, there were a number of important economic reforms within the UK. She worked closely with the United States President, Ronald Reagan, and was one of the first Western leaders to recognise and welcome the changes in the leadership of the Soviet Union which eventually led to the end of the Cold War.

Margaret Thatcher, Britain's first woman Prime Minister, led the Conservative government from 1979 to 1990. The government made structural changes to the economy through the privatisation of nationalised industries and imposed legal controls on trade union powers. Deregulation saw a great increase in the role of the City of London as an international centre for investments, insurance and other financial services. Traditional industries, such as shipbuilding and coal mining, declined. In 1982, Argentina invaded the Falkland Islands, a British overseas territory in the South Atlantic. A naval taskforce was sent from the UK and military action led to the recovery of the islands.

John Major was Prime Minister after Mrs Thatcher, and helped establish the Northern Ireland peace process.

ROALD DAHL (1916–90)

Roald Dahl was born in Wales to Norwegian parents. He served in the Royal Air Force during the Second World War. It was during the 1940s that he began to publish books and short stories. He is most well known for his children's books, although he also wrote for adults. His best-known works include *Charlie and the Chocolate Factory* and *George's Marvellous Medicine*. Several of his books have been made into films.

“In Northern Ireland, the Blair government was able to build on the peace process, resulting in the Good Friday Agreement signed in 1998.”

LABOUR GOVERNMENT FROM 1997 TO 2010

In 1997 the Labour Party led by Tony Blair was elected. The Blair government introduced a Scottish Parliament and a Welsh Assembly (now called the Senedd – see page 115). The Scottish Parliament has substantial powers to legislate. The Welsh Assembly was given fewer legislative powers but considerable control over public services. In Northern Ireland, the Blair government was able to build on the peace process, resulting in the Good Friday Agreement signed in 1998. The Northern Ireland Assembly was elected in 1999 but suspended in 2002. It was not reinstated until 2007. Most paramilitary groups in Northern Ireland have decommissioned their arms and are inactive. Gordon Brown took over as Prime Minister in 2007.

CONFLICTS IN AFGHANISTAN AND IRAQ

Throughout the 1990s, Britain played a leading role in coalition forces involved in the liberation of Kuwait, following the Iraqi invasion in 1990, and the conflict in the Former Republic of Yugoslavia. Since 2000, British armed forces have been engaged in the global fight against international terrorism and against the proliferation of weapons of mass destruction, including operations in Afghanistan and Iraq. British combat troops left Iraq in 2009. The UK now operates in Afghanistan as part of the United Nations

(UN) mandated 50-nation International Security Assistance Force (ISAF) coalition and at the invitation of the Afghan government. ISAF is working to ensure that Afghan territory can never again be used as a safe haven for international terrorism, where groups such as Al Qa'ida could plan attacks on the international community. As part of this, ISAF is building up the Afghan National Security Forces and is helping to create a secure environment in which governance and development can be extended. International forces are gradually handing over responsibility for security to the Afghans, who will have full security responsibility in all provinces by the end of 2014.

“The UK voted by a margin of 51.9% to 48.1% to leave the European Union.

2010 ONWARDS AND BREXIT

In May 2010, and for the first time in the UK since February 1974, no political party won an overall majority in the General Election. The Conservative and Liberal Democrat parties formed a coalition and the leader of the Conservative Party, David Cameron, became Prime Minister.

The Conservative Party won a majority at the general election of 7 May 2015 and David Cameron remained Prime Minister. The Conservative government called a referendum on the UK's membership of the European Union. This was held on 23 June 2016. The UK voted by a margin of 51.9% to 48.1% to leave the European Union. David Cameron was succeeded as Prime Minister after the referendum by Theresa May on 13 July 2016. She in turn was succeeded by Boris Johnson* on 24 July 2019. The UK formally left the European Union on 31 January 2020.

Check that you understand:

- The establishment of the welfare state
- How life in Britain changed in the 1960s and 1970s
- British inventions of the 20th century (you do not need to remember dates of births and deaths)
- Events since 1979

CHAPTER 5
A modern, thriving society

→ IN THIS CHAPTER you will learn about the population and culture of the UK. The start of the chapter shows you where the major cities of the UK are. You should be sure you can identify the various cities, such as Leeds and Bradford, confidently. Because the UK is a multicultural country you will also have to know the sizes of the different ethnic and religious groups in the UK, as well as their main festivals.

The chapter focuses on British culture after that and you should make sure you know who each of the people described are and what they have achieved. Britain's recent sporting success at the Olympics features heavily so focus on who won medals and for what as well as the general information about sport in the UK. Make sure you familiarise yourself with the poems, films, books and other works listed too, as well as the artists, composers, architects, authors, poets and other famous people. You should also familiarise yourself with the extracts of poems provided and be able to recognise the famous landmarks at the end of the chapter.

IN THIS CHAPTER THERE IS INFORMATION ABOUT:

- The cities and population of the UK
- Religious festivals of the UK
- Popular sports and famous sportsmen and women
- The development of music, including famous composers
- British theatre and cinema through the ages
- British artists and architects
- Famous British poets and authors
- Sections of famous British poems
- British comedy and leisure activities
- Famous British landmarks

5

The UK today

Post-war immigration means that nearly 10% of the population has a parent or grandparent born outside the UK.

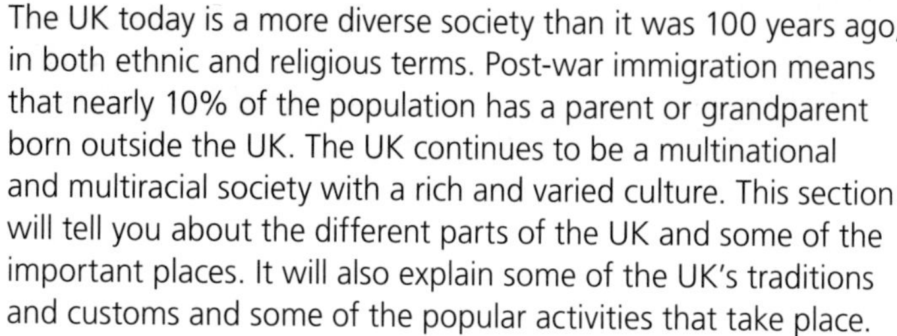

The UK today is a more diverse society than it was 100 years ago, in both ethnic and religious terms. Post-war immigration means that nearly 10% of the population has a parent or grandparent born outside the UK. The UK continues to be a multinational and multiracial society with a rich and varied culture. This section will tell you about the different parts of the UK and some of the important places. It will also explain some of the UK's traditions and customs and some of the popular activities that take place.

THE NATIONS OF THE UK

The UK is located in the north west of Europe. The longest distance on the mainland is from John O'Groats on the north coast of Scotland to Land's End in the south-west corner of England. It is about 870 miles (approximately 1,400 kilometres).

Most people live in towns and cities but much of Britain is still countryside. Many people continue to visit the countryside for holidays and for leisure activities such as walking, camping and fishing.

CITIES OF THE UK

ENGLAND

1 London
2 Birmingham
3 Liverpool
4 Leeds
5 Sheffield
6 Bristol
7 Manchester
8 Bradford
9 Newcastle Upon Tyne
10 Plymouth
11 Southampton
12 Norwich

WALES

13 Cardiff
14 Swansea
15 Newport

NORTHERN IRELAND

16 Belfast

SCOTLAND

17 Edinburgh
18 Glasgow
19 Dundee
20 Aberdeen

CAPITAL CITIES

The capital city of the UK is London

Scotland
The capital city of Scotland is Edinburgh

Wales
The capital city of Wales is Cardiff

Northern Ireland
The capital city of Northern Ireland is Belfast

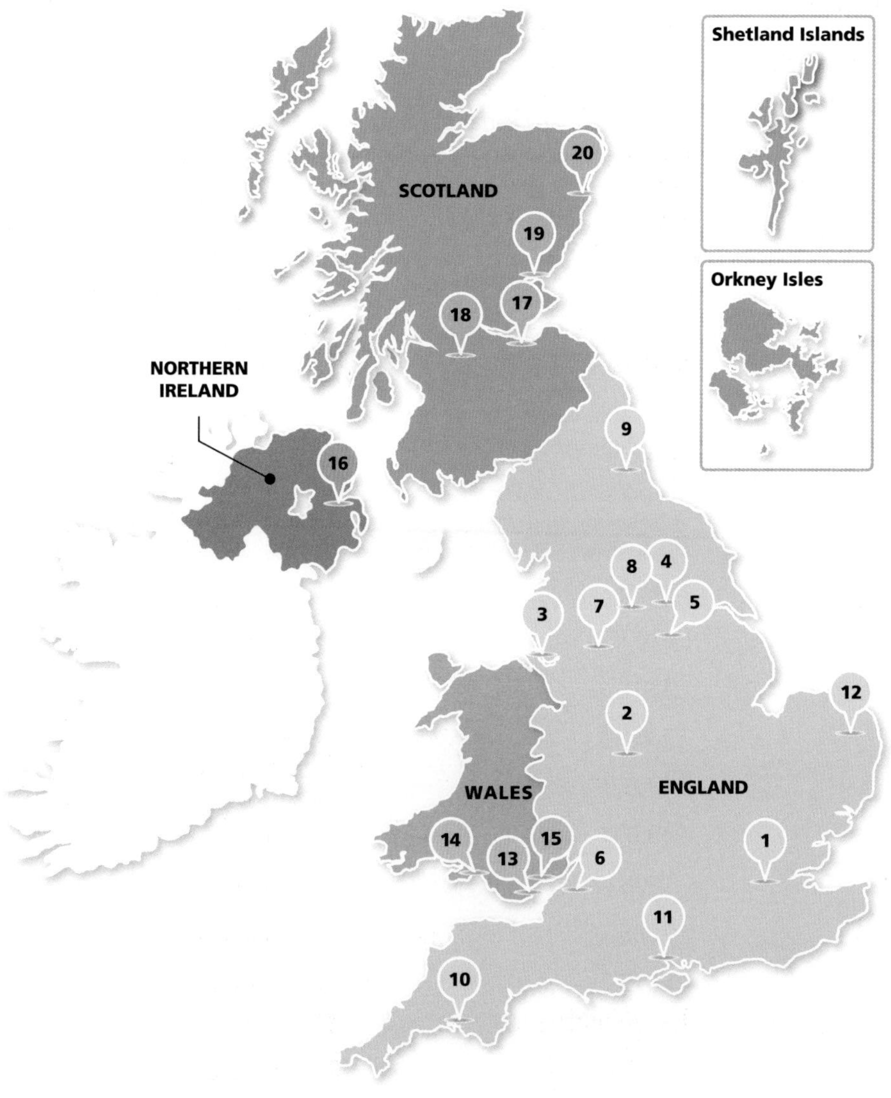

UK CURRENCY

The currency in the UK is the pound sterling (symbol £). There are 100 pence in a pound. The denominations (values) of currency are:

coins: 1p, 2p, 5p, 10p, 20p, 50p, £1 and £2

notes: £5, £10, £20, £50.

Northern Ireland and Scotland have their own banknotes, which are valid everywhere in the UK. However, shops and businesses do not have to accept them.

LANGUAGES AND DIALECTS

In Scotland, Gaelic is spoken in some parts of the Highlands and Islands, and in Northern Ireland some people speak Irish Gaelic.

There are many variations in language in the different parts of the UK. The English language has many accents and dialects. In Wales, many people speak Welsh – a completely different language from English – and it is taught in schools and universities. In Scotland, Gaelic (again, a different language) is spoken in some parts of the Highlands and Islands, and in Northern Ireland some people speak Irish Gaelic.

POPULATION

The table below shows how the population of the UK has changed over time.

Population growth in the UK

Year	Population
1600	Just over 4 million
1700	5 million
1801	8 million
1851	20 million
1901	40 million
1951	50 million
1998	57 million
2005	Just under 60 million
2010	Just over 62 million
2017	Just over 66 million

Source: National Statistics

Population growth has been faster in more recent years. Migration into the UK and longer life expectancy have played a part in population growth.

The population is very unequally distributed over the four parts of the UK. England more or less consistently makes up 84% of the total population, Wales around 5%, Scotland just over 8% and Northern Ireland less than 3%.

Population distribution across the UK

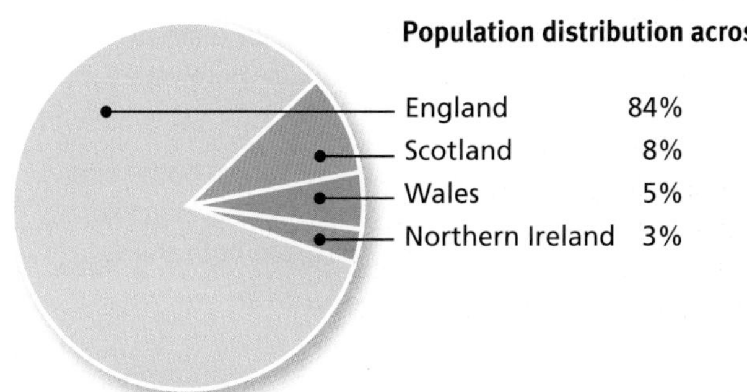

AN AGEING POPULATION

People in the UK are living longer than ever before. This is due to improved living standards and better health care. There are now a record number of people aged 85 and over. This has an impact on the cost of pensions and health care.

ETHNIC DIVERSITY

The UK population is ethnically diverse and changing rapidly, especially in large cities such as London. It is not always easy to get an exact picture of the ethnic origin of all the population.

There are people in the UK with ethnic origins from all over the world. In surveys, the most common ethnic description chosen is white, which includes people of European, Australian, Canadian, New Zealand and American descent. Other significant groups are those of Asian, black and mixed descent.

AN EQUAL SOCIETY

Within the UK, it is a legal requirement that men and women should not be discriminated against because of their gender or because they are, or are not, married. They have equal rights to

“Within the UK, it is a legal requirement that men and women should not be discriminated against because of their gender or because they are, or are not, married.”

work, own property, marry and divorce. If they are married, both parents are equally responsible for their children.

Women in Britain today make up about half of the workforce. On average, girls leave school with better qualifications than boys. More women than men study at university.

Employment opportunities for women are much greater than they were in the past. Women work in all sectors of the economy, and there are now more women in high-level positions than ever before, including senior managers in traditionally male-dominated occupations. Alongside this, men now work in more varied jobs than they did in the past.

It is no longer expected that women should stay at home and not work. Women often continue to work after having children. In many families today, both partners work and both share responsibility for childcare and household chores.

Check that you understand:

- The capital cities of the UK
- What languages other than English are spoken in particular parts of the UK
- How the population of the UK has changed
- That the UK is an equal society and ethnically diverse
- The currency of the UK

Religion

The UK is historically a Christian country. In the 2011 Census, 59% of people identified themselves as Christian. Much smaller proportions identified themselves as Muslim (4.8%), Hindu (1.5%), Sikh (0.8%) and Jewish or Buddhist (both less than 0.5%). There are religious buildings for other religions all over the UK. This includes Islamic mosques, Hindu temples, Jewish synagogues, Sikh gurdwaras and Buddhist temples. However, everyone has the legal right to choose their religion, or to choose not to practise a religion. In the 2011 Census, 25% of people said they had no religion*.

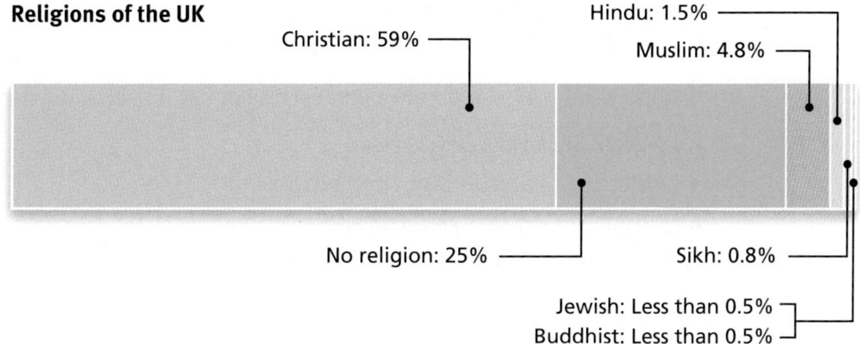

CHRISTIAN CHURCHES

In England, there is a constitutional link between Church and state. The official Church of the state is the Church of England (called the Anglican Church in other countries and the Episcopal Church in Scotland and the United States). It is a Protestant Church and has existed since the Reformation in the 1530s (see pages 23 for an explanation).

The monarch is the head of the Church of England. The spiritual leader of the Church of England is the Archbishop of Canterbury.

The monarch is the head of the Church of England. The spiritual leader of the Church of England is the Archbishop of Canterbury. The monarch has the right to select the Archbishop and other senior church officials, but usually the choice is made by the Prime Minister and a committee appointed by the Church. Several Church of England bishops sit in the House of Lords (see page 111).

In Scotland, the national Church is the Church of Scotland, which is a Presbyterian Church. It is governed by ministers and elders. The chairperson of the General Assembly of the Church of Scotland is the Moderator, who is appointed for one year only and often speaks on behalf of that Church.

There is no established Church in Wales or Northern Ireland.

Other Protestant Christian groups in the UK are Baptists, Methodists, Presbyterians and Quakers. There are also other denominations of Christianity, the biggest of which is Roman Catholic.

PATRON SAINTS' DAYS

England, Scotland, Wales and Northern Ireland each have a national saint, called a patron saint. Each saint has a special day:

- 1 March: St David's Day, Wales
- 17 March: St Patrick's Day, Northern Ireland
- 23 April: St George's Day, England
- 30 November: St Andrew's Day, Scotland.

Only Scotland and Northern Ireland have their patron saint's day as an official holiday (although in Scotland not all businesses and offices will close). Events are held across Scotland, Northern Ireland and the rest of the country, especially where there are a lot of people of Scottish, Northern Irish and Irish heritage.

While the patron saints' days are no longer public holidays in England and Wales, they are still celebrated. Parades and small festivals are held all over the two countries.

Westminster Abbey has been the coronation church since 1066 and is the final resting place of many monarchs

Check that you understand:

- The different religions that are practised in the UK
- That the Anglican Church, also known as the Church of England, is the Church of the state in England (the 'established Church')
- That other branches of the Christian Church also practise their faith in the UK without being linked to the state
- That other religions are practised in the UK
- About the patron saints

Customs and traditions

THE MAIN CHRISTIAN FESTIVALS

Christmas Day, 25 December, celebrates the birth of Jesus Christ. It is a public holiday. Many Christians go to church on Christmas Eve (24 December) or on Christmas Day itself.

Christmas is celebrated in a traditional way. People usually spend the day at home and eat a special meal, which often includes roast turkey, Christmas pudding and mince pies. They give gifts, send cards and decorate their houses. Christmas is a special time for children. Very young children believe that Father Christmas (also known as Santa Claus) brings them presents during the night before Christmas Day. Many people decorate a tree in their home.

A typical Christmas Day meal

The 40 days before Easter are known as Lent. It is a time when Christians take time to reflect and prepare for Easter.

Boxing Day is the day after Christmas Day and is a public holiday.

Easter takes place in March or April. It marks the death of Jesus Christ on Good Friday and his rising from the dead on Easter Sunday. Both Good Friday and the following Monday, called Easter Monday, are public holidays.

The 40 days before Easter are known as Lent. It is a time when Christians take time to reflect and prepare for Easter. Traditionally, people would fast during this period and today many people will give something up, like a favourite food. The day before Lent starts is called Shrove Tuesday, or Pancake Day. People eat pancakes, which were traditionally made to use up foods such as eggs, fat and milk before fasting. Lent begins on Ash Wednesday. There are church services where Christians are marked with an ash cross on their forehead as a symbol of death and sorrow for sin.

Easter is also celebrated by people who are not religious. 'Easter eggs' are chocolate eggs often given as presents at Easter as a symbol of new life.

OTHER RELIGIOUS FESTIVALS

Diwali normally falls in October or November and lasts for five days. It is often called the Festival of Lights. It is celebrated by Hindus and Sikhs. It celebrates the victory of good over evil and the gaining of knowledge. There are different stories about how the festival came about. There is a famous celebration of Diwali in Leicester.

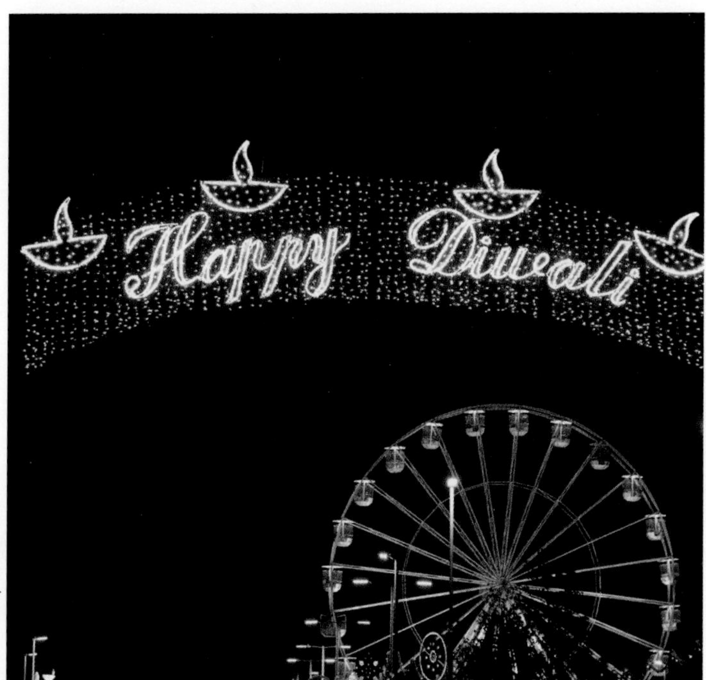

Diwali is popularly known as the Festival of Lights

Hannukah is in November or December and is celebrated for eight days. It is to remember the Jews' struggle for religious freedom. On each day of the festival a candle is lit on a stand of eight candles (called a menorah) to remember the story of the festival, where oil that should have lasted only a day did so for eight*.

*For more information see **Clarifications** in Chapter 1 and lifeintheuk.net/clarify

Eid al-Fitr celebrates the end of Ramadan, when Muslims have fasted for a month. They thank Allah for giving them the strength to complete the fast. The date when it takes place changes every year. Muslims attend special services and meals.

Eid ul Adha remembers that the prophet Ibrahim was willing to sacrifice his son when God ordered him to. It reminds Muslims of their own commitment to God. Many Muslims sacrifice an animal to eat during this festival. In Britain this has to be done in a slaughterhouse.

Vaisakhi (also spelled Baisakhi) is a Sikh festival which celebrates the founding of the Sikh community known as the Khalsa. It is celebrated on 14 April each year with parades, dancing and singing.

OTHER FESTIVALS AND TRADITIONS

New Year, 1 January, is a public holiday. People usually celebrate on the night of 31 December (called New Year's Eve). In Scotland, 31 December is called Hogmanay and 2 January is also a public holiday. For some Scottish people, Hogmanay is a bigger holiday than Christmas.

Valentine's Day, 14 February, is when lovers exchange cards and gifts. Sometimes people send anonymous cards to someone they secretly admire.

April Fool's Day, 1 April, is a day when people play jokes on each other until midday. The television and newspapers often have stories that are April Fool jokes.

Mothering Sunday (or Mother's Day) is the Sunday three weeks before Easter. Children send cards or buy gifts for their mothers.

You need to know the dates of key festivals and traditions. Take some time to learn what is associated with each event as well, such as special foods or traditions.

Father's Day is the third Sunday in June. Children send cards or buy gifts for their fathers.

Halloween, 31 October, is an ancient festival and has roots in the pagan festival to mark the beginning of winter. Young people will often dress up in frightening costumes to play 'trick or treat'. People give them treats to stop them playing tricks on them. A lot of people carve lanterns out of pumpkins and put a candle inside.

Bonfire Night, 5 November, is an occasion when people in Great Britain set off fireworks at home or in special displays. The origin of this celebration was an event in 1605, when a group of Catholics led by Guy Fawkes failed in their plan to kill the Protestant king with a bomb in the Houses of Parliament.

Remembrance Day, 11 November, commemorates those who died fighting for the UK and its allies. Originally it commemorated the dead of the First World War, which ended on 11 November 1918. People wear poppies (the red flower found on the battlefields of the First World War). At 11.00 am there is a two-minute silence and wreaths are laid at the Cenotaph in Whitehall, London.

Unveiled in 1920, the Cenotaph is the centrepiece to the Remembrance Day service

BANK HOLIDAYS

As well as those mentioned previously, there are other public holidays each year called bank holidays, when banks and many other businesses are closed for the day. These are of no religious significance. They are at the beginning of May, in late May or early June, and in August. In Northern Ireland, the anniversary of the Battle of the Boyne in July is also a public holiday.

Check that you understand:

- The main Christian festivals that are celebrated in the UK
- Other religious festivals that are important in the UK
- Some of the other events that are celebrated in the UK
- What a bank holiday is

Sport

Sports of all kinds play an important part in many people's lives. There are several sports that are particularly popular in the UK. Many sporting events take place at major stadiums such as Wembley Stadium in London and the Principality Stadium in Cardiff.

Local governments and private companies provide sports facilities such as swimming pools, tennis courts, football pitches, dry ski slopes and gymnasiums. Many famous sports, including cricket, football, lawn tennis, golf and rugby, began in Britain.

The UK has hosted the Olympic Games on three occasions: 1908, 1948 and 2012. The main Olympic site for the 2012 Games was in Stratford, East London. The British team was very successful, across a wide range of Olympic sports, finishing third in the medal table.

“ The UK has hosted the Olympic Games on three occasions: 1908, 1948 and 2012.

The Paralympic Games for 2012 were also hosted in London. The Paralympics have their origin in the work of Dr Sir Ludwig Guttman*, a German refugee, at the Stoke Mandeville hospital in Buckinghamshire. Dr Guttman developed new methods of treatment for people with spinal injuries and encouraged patients to take part in exercise and sport.

NOTABLE BRITISH SPORTSMEN AND WOMEN

Sir Roger Bannister (1929–2018) was the first man in the world to run a mile in under four minutes, in 1954.

Sir Jackie Stewart (1939–) is a Scottish former racing driver who won the Formula 1 world championship three times.

Bobby Moore (1941–93) captained the English football team that won the World Cup in 1966.

Sir Ian Botham (1955–) captained the English cricket team and held a number of English Test cricket records, both for batting and for bowling.

Jayne Torvill (1957–) and **Christopher Dean (1958–)** won gold medals for ice dancing at the Olympic Games in 1984 and in four consecutive world championships.

Sir Steve Redgrave (1962–) won gold medals in rowing in five consecutive Olympic Games and is one of Britain's greatest Olympians.

Baroness Tanni Grey-Thompson (1969–) is an athlete who uses a wheelchair and won 16 Paralympic medals, including 11 gold medals, in races over five Paralympic Games. She won the London Marathon six times and broke a total of 30 world records.

Dame Kelly Holmes (1970–) won two gold medals for running in the 2004 Olympic Games. She has held a number of British and European records.

Dame Ellen MacArthur (1976–) is a yachtswoman and in 2004 became the fastest person to sail around the world single-handed.

Sir Chris Hoy (1976–) is a Scottish cyclist who has won six gold and one silver Olympic medals. He has also won 11 world championship titles.

David Weir (1979–) is a Paralympian who uses a wheelchair and has won six gold medals over two Paralympic Games. He has also won the London Marathon six times*.

*For more information see **Clarifications** in Chapter 1 and lifeintheuk.net/clarify

Sir Bradley Wiggins (1980–) is a cyclist. In 2012, he became the first Briton to win the Tour de France. He has won eight Olympic medals, including Gold in the 2004, 2008, 2012 and 2016 Olympic Games.

Sir Mo Farah (1983–) is a British distance runner, born in Somalia. He won gold medals in the 2012 and 2016 Olympics for the 5,000 and 10,000 metres and is the first Briton to win the Olympic gold medal in the 10,000 metres.

Dame Jessica Ennis-Hill (1986–) is an athlete. She won the 2012 Olympic gold medal in the heptathlon and silver medal in the 2016 Olympic Games, which includes seven different track and field events. She also holds a number of British athletics records.

Make sure you are familiar with this list of sportsmen and women, including which sports they are famous for and any medals won or records achieved.

Sir Andy Murray (1987–) is a Scottish tennis player who in 2012 won the men's singles in the US Open. He is the first British man to win a singles title in a Grand Slam tournament since 1936. In the same year, he won Olympic gold and silver medals. In 2013 and 2016 he won the men's singles at Wimbledon (see page 78). He also went on to win Gold at the 2016 Olympics.

Ellie Simmonds (1994–) is a Paralympian who won gold medals for swimming at the 2008, 2012 and 2016 Paralympic Games and holds a number of world records. She was the youngest member of the British team at the 2008 Games.

CRICKET

Cricket originated in England and is now played in many countries. Games can last up to five days but still result in a draw! The idiosyncratic nature of the game and its complex laws are said to reflect the best of the British character and sense of fair play. You may come across expressions such as 'rain stopped play', 'batting on a sticky wicket', 'playing a straight bat', 'bowled a googly' or 'it's just not cricket', which have passed into everyday usage. The most famous competition is the Ashes, which is a series of Test matches played between England and Australia.

Cricket is one of the many famous sports originating in Britain

FOOTBALL

Football is the UK's most popular sport. It has a long history in the UK and the first professional football clubs were formed in the late 19th century.

England, Scotland, Wales and Northern Ireland each have separate leagues in which clubs representing different towns and cities compete. The English Premier League attracts a huge international audience. Many of the best players in the world play in the Premier League. Many UK teams also compete in competitions such as the UEFA (Union of European Football Associations) Champions League, against other teams from Europe. Many towns and cities have a professional club and people take great pride in supporting their home team. There can be great rivalry between different football clubs and among fans.

Each country in the UK also has its own national team that competes with other national teams across the world in tournaments such as the FIFA (Fédération Internationale de Football Association) World Cup and the UEFA European Football Championships. England's only international tournament victory was at the World Cup of 1966, hosted in the UK.

Football is also a popular sport to play in many local communities, with people playing amateur games every week in parks all over the UK.

RUGBY

Rugby originated in England in the early 19th century and is very popular in the UK today. There are two different types of rugby, which have different rules: union and league. Both have separate leagues and national teams in England, Wales, Scotland and Northern Ireland (who play with the Irish Republic). Teams from all countries compete in a range of competitions. The most famous rugby union competition is the Six Nations Championship between England, Ireland, Scotland, Wales, France and Italy. The Super League is the most well-known rugby league (club) competition.

> **"The modern game of golf can be traced back to 15th-century Scotland."**

HORSE RACING

There is a very long history of horse racing in Britain, with evidence of events taking place as far back as Roman times. The sport has a long association with royalty. There are racecourses all over the UK. Famous horse-racing events include: Royal Ascot, a five-day race meeting in Berkshire attended by members of the Royal Family; the Grand National at Aintree near Liverpool; and the Scottish Grand National at Ayr. There is a National Horseracing Museum in Newmarket, Suffolk.

GOLF

The modern game of golf can be traced back to 15th-century Scotland. It is a popular sport played socially as well as professionally. There are public and private golf courses all over the UK. St Andrews in Scotland is known as the home of golf. The Open Championship is the only 'Major' tournament held outside the United States. It is hosted by a different golf course every year.

TENNIS

Modern tennis evolved in England in the late 19th century. The first tennis club was founded in Leamington Spa in 1872. The most famous tournament hosted in Britain is The Wimbledon Championships, which takes place each year at the All England Lawn Tennis and Croquet Club. It is the oldest tennis tournament in the world and the only 'Grand Slam' event played on grass.

WATER SPORTS

Sailing continues to be popular in the UK, reflecting our maritime heritage. A British sailor, Sir Francis Chichester, was the first person to sail single-handed around the world passing the Cape of Good Hope (Africa) and Cape Horn (South America), in 1966/67. Two years later, Sir Robin Knox-Johnston became the first person to do this without stopping. Many sailing events are held throughout the UK, the most famous of which is at Cowes on the Isle of Wight.

“

A British sailor, Sir Francis Chichester, was the first person to sail single-handed around the world, in 1966/67. Two years later, Sir Robin Knox-Johnston became the first person to do this without stopping.

Rowing is also popular, both as a leisure activity and as a competitive sport. There is a popular yearly race on the Thames between Oxford and Cambridge Universities.

MOTOR SPORTS

There is a long history of motor sport in the UK, for both cars and motor cycles. Motor-car racing in the UK started in 1902. The UK continues to be a world leader in the development and manufacture of motor-sport technology. A Formula 1 Grand Prix event is held in the UK each year and a number of British Grand Prix drivers have won the Formula 1 World Championship. Recent British winners include Damon Hill, Lewis Hamilton and Jenson Button.

SKIING

Skiing is increasingly popular in the UK. Many people go abroad to ski and there are also dry ski slopes throughout the UK. Skiing on snow may also be possible during the winter. There are five ski centres in Scotland, as well as Europe's longest dry ski slope near Edinburgh.

Arts and culture

MUSIC

Music is an important part of British culture, with a rich and varied heritage. It ranges from classical music to modern pop. There are many different venues and musical events that take place across the UK.

The Proms is an eight-week summer season of orchestral classical music that takes place in various venues, including the Royal Albert Hall in London. It has been organised by the British Broadcasting Corporation (BBC) since 1927. The Last Night of the Proms is the most well-known concert and (along with others in the series) is broadcast on television.

Classical music has been popular in the UK for many centuries. **Henry Purcell (1659–95)** was the organist at Westminster Abbey. He wrote church music, operas and other pieces, and developed a British style distinct from that elsewhere in Europe. He continues to be influential on British composers.

The German-born composer **George Frederick Handel (1685–1759)** spent many years in the UK and became a British citizen in 1727. He wrote the *Water Music* for King George I and *Music for the Royal Fireworks* for his son, George II. Both these pieces continue to be very popular. Handel also wrote an oratorio, *Messiah*, which is sung regularly by choirs, often at Easter time.

“The German-born composer George Frederick Handel (1685–1759) spent many years in the UK and became a British citizen in 1727.

More recently, important composers include **Gustav Holst (1874–1934)**, whose work includes *The Planets*, a suite of pieces themed around the planets of the solar system. He adapted *Jupiter*, part of the *Planets* suite, as the tune for *I vow to thee my country*, a popular hymn in British churches.

Sir Edward Elgar (1857–1934) was born in Worcester, England. His best-known work is probably the *Pomp and Circumstance Marches. March No 1 (Land of Hope and Glory)* is usually played at the Last Night of the Proms at the Royal Albert Hall.

Ralph Vaughan Williams (1872–1958) wrote music for orchestras and choirs. He was strongly influenced by traditional English folk music.

The Royal Albert Hall is the venue for the Last Night of the Proms

© Adam Woolfitt/Robert Harding

You should be familiar with the lives and works of these famous composers (here and on the previous page).

Sir William Walton (1902–83) wrote a wide range of music, from film scores to opera. He wrote marches for the coronations of King George VI and Queen Elizabeth II but his best-known works are probably *Façade*, which became a ballet, and *Belshazzar's Feast*, which is intended to be sung by a large choir.

Benjamin Britten (1913–76) is best known for his operas, which include *Peter Grimes* and *Billy Budd*. He also wrote *A Young Person's Guide to the Orchestra*, which is based on a piece of music by Purcell and introduces the listener to the various different sections of an orchestra. He founded the Aldeburgh festival in Suffolk, which continues to be a popular music event of international importance.

Other types of popular music, including folk music, jazz, pop and rock music, have flourished in Britain since the 20th century. Britain has had an impact on popular music around the world, due to the wide use of the English language, the UK's cultural links with many countries, and British capacity for invention and innovation.

Since the 1960s, British pop music has made one of the most important cultural contributions to life in the UK. Bands including The Beatles and The Rolling Stones continue to have an influence on music both here and abroad. British pop music has continued to innovate – for example, the Punk movement of the late 1970s, and the trend towards boy and girl bands in the 1990s.

There are many large venues that host music events throughout the year, such as: Wembley Stadium; The O2 in Greenwich, south-east London; and The SEC Centre in Glasgow.

Festival season takes place across the UK every summer, with major events in various locations. Famous festivals include Glastonbury, the Isle of Wight Festival and Creamfields. Many bands and solo artists, both well-known and up-and-coming, perform at these events.

The National Eisteddfod of Wales is an annual cultural festival which includes music, dance, art and original performances largely in Welsh. It includes a number of important competitions for Welsh poetry.

The Mercury Prize is awarded each September for the best album from the UK and Ireland. The Brit Awards is an annual event that gives awards in a range of categories, such as best British group and best British solo artist.

THEATRE

There are theatres in most towns and cities throughout the UK, ranging from the large to the small. They are an important part of local communities and often show both professional and amateur productions. London's West End, also known as 'Theatreland', is particularly well known. *The Mousetrap*, a murder-mystery play by Dame Agatha Christie, has been running in the West End since 1952 and has had the longest initial run of any show in history.

"The National Eisteddfod of Wales is an annual cultural festival which includes music, dance, art and original performances largely in Welsh."

There is also a strong tradition of musical theatre in the UK. In the 19th century, Gilbert and Sullivan wrote comic operas, often making fun of popular culture and politics. These operas include *HMS Pinafore*, *The Pirates of Penzance* and *The Mikado*. Gilbert and Sullivan's work is still often staged by professional and amateur groups. More recently, Andrew Lloyd Webber has written the music for shows which have been popular throughout the world, including, in collaboration with Tim Rice, *Jesus Christ Superstar* and *Evita*, and also *Cats* and *The Phantom of the Opera*.

One British tradition is the pantomime. Many theatres produce a pantomime at Christmas time. They are based on fairy stories and are light-hearted plays with music and comedy, enjoyed by family audiences. One of the traditional characters is the Dame, a woman played by a man. There is often also a pantomime horse or cow played by two actors in the same costume.

The Edinburgh Festival takes place in Edinburgh, Scotland, every summer. It is a series of different arts and cultural festivals, with the biggest and most well-known being the Edinburgh Festival Fringe ('the Fringe'). The Fringe is a showcase of mainly theatre and comedy performances. It often shows experimental work.

The Laurence Olivier Awards take place annually at different venues in London. There are a variety of categories, including best director, best actor and best actress. The awards are named after the British actor Sir Laurence Olivier, later Lord Olivier, who was best known for his roles in various Shakespeare plays.

ART

During the Middle Ages, most art had a religious theme, particularly wall paintings in churches and illustrations in religious books. Much of this was lost after the Protestant Reformation but wealthy families began to collect other paintings and sculptures. Many of the painters working in Britain in the 16th and 17th centuries were from abroad – for example, Hans Holbein and Sir Anthony Van Dyck. British artists, particularly those painting portraits and landscapes, became well known from the 18th century onwards.

Works by British and international artists are displayed in galleries across the UK. Some of the most well-known galleries are The National Gallery, Tate Britain and Tate Modern in London, the National Museum in Cardiff, and the Scottish National Gallery in Edinburgh.

Tate Modern is based in the former Bankside Power Station in central London

The Turner Prize was established in 1984 and celebrates contemporary art. It was named after Joseph Turner. Four works are shortlisted every year and shown at Tate Britain before the winner is announced. The Turner Prize is recognised as one of the most prestigious visual art awards. Previous winners include Damien Hirst and Richard Wright.

NOTABLE BRITISH ARTISTS

Thomas Gainsborough (1727–88) was a portrait painter who often painted people in country or garden scenery.

David Allan (1744–96) was a Scottish painter who was best known for painting portraits. One of his most famous works is called *The Origin of Painting*.

Joseph Turner (1775–1851) was an influential landscape painter in a modern style. He is considered the artist who raised the profile of landscape painting.

John Constable (1776–1837) was a landscape painter most famous for his works of Dedham Vale on the Suffolk–Essex border in the east of England.

The Pre-Raphaelites were an important group of artists in the second half of the 19th century. They painted detailed pictures on religious or literary themes in bright colours. The group included Holman Hunt, Dante Gabriel Rossetti and Sir John Millais.

Sir John Lavery (1856–1941) was a very successful Northern Irish portrait painter. His work included painting the Royal Family.

Henry Moore (1898–1986) was an English sculptor and artist. He is best known for his large bronze abstract sculptures.

John Petts (1914–91) was a Welsh artist, best known for his engravings and stained glass.

Lucian Freud (1922–2011) was a German-born British artist. He is best known for his portraits.

David Hockney (1937–) was an important contributor to the 'pop art' movement of the 1960s and continues to be influential today.

?

You may be asked questions about these artists and their work. Make sure you know about trends in British art as well, such as the development of landscape painting.

ARCHITECTURE

The architectural heritage of the UK is rich and varied. In the Middle Ages, great cathedrals and churches were built, many of which still stand today. Examples are the cathedrals in Durham, Lincoln, Canterbury and Salisbury. The White Tower in the Tower of London is an example of a Norman castle keep, built on the orders of William the Conqueror (see pages 15 and 102).

Gradually, as the countryside became more peaceful and landowners became richer, the houses of the wealthy became more elaborate and great country houses such as Hardwick Hall in Derbyshire were built. British styles of architecture began to evolve.

In the 17th century, Inigo Jones took inspiration from classical architecture to design the Queen's House at Greenwich and the Banqueting House in Whitehall in London. Later in the century, Sir Christopher Wren helped develop a British version of the ornate styles popular in Europe in buildings such as the new St Paul's Cathedral.

"In the 17th century, Inigo Jones took inspiration from classical architecture to design the Queen's House at Greenwich and the Banqueting House in Whitehall in London.

In the 18th century, simpler designs became popular. The Scottish architect Robert Adam influenced the development of architecture in the UK, Europe and America. He designed the inside decoration as well as the building itself in great houses such as Dumfries House in Scotland. His ideas influenced architects in cities such as Bath, where the Royal Crescent was built.

In the 19th century, the medieval 'gothic' style became popular again. As cities expanded, many great public buildings were built in this style. The Houses of Parliament and St Pancras Station were built at this time, as were the town halls in cities such as Manchester and Sheffield.

In the 20th century, Sir Edwin Lutyens had an influence throughout the British Empire. He designed New Delhi to be the seat of government in India. After the First World War, he was responsible for many war memorials throughout the world, including the Cenotaph in Whitehall. The Cenotaph is the site of the annual Remembrance Day service attended by the Queen, politicians and foreign ambassadors (see pages 72–3).

The firms of modern British architects continue to work on major projects throughout the world as well as within the UK. These include those of Sir Norman Foster (1935–), Lord (Richard) Rogers (1933–)* and Dame Zaha Hadid (1950–2016).

Alongside the development of architecture, garden design and landscaping have played an important role in the UK. In the 18th century, Lancelot 'Capability' Brown designed the grounds around country houses so that the landscape appeared to be natural, with grass, trees and lakes. He often said that a place had 'capabilities'. Later, Gertrude Jekyll often worked with Edwin Lutyens to design colourful gardens around the houses he designed. Gardens continue to be an important part of homes in the UK. The annual Chelsea Flower Show showcases garden design from Britain and around the world.

FASHION AND DESIGN

Britain has produced many great designers, from Thomas Chippendale (who designed furniture in the 18th century) to Clarice Cliff (who designed Art Deco ceramics) to Sir Terence Conran (a 20th-century interior designer). Leading fashion designers of recent years include Mary Quant, Alexander McQueen and Vivienne Westwood.

LITERATURE

The UK has a prestigious literary history and tradition. Several British writers, including the novelist Sir William Golding, the poet Seamus Heaney, and the playwright Harold Pinter, have won the Nobel Prize in Literature. Other authors have become well known in popular fiction. Agatha Christie's detective stories are read all over the world and Ian Fleming's books introduced James Bond. In 2003, *The Lord of the Rings* by JRR Tolkien was voted the country's best-loved novel.

The Man Booker Prize for Fiction is awarded annually for the best fiction novel written by an author from the Commonwealth, Ireland or Zimbabwe*. It has been awarded since 1968. Past winners include Ian McEwan, Hilary Mantel and Julian Barnes.

*For more information see **Clarifications** in Chapter 1 and lifeintheuk.net/clarify

NOTABLE AUTHORS AND WRITERS

Jane Austen (1775–1817) was an English novelist. Her books include *Pride and Prejudice* and *Sense and Sensibility*. Her novels are concerned with marriage and family relationships. Many have been made into television programmes or films.

Charles Dickens (1812–70) wrote a number of very famous novels, including *Oliver Twist* and *Great Expectations*. You will hear references in everyday talk to some of the characters in his books, such as Scrooge (a mean person) or Mr Micawber (always hopeful).

Robert Louis Stevenson (1850–94) wrote books which are still read by adults and children today. His most famous books include *Treasure Island*, *Kidnapped* and *Dr Jekyll and Mr Hyde*.

You may be asked to identify famous British authors and poets, as well as famous books and poems. Make sure you know British winners of the Nobel Prize in Literature as well.

Thomas Hardy (1840–1928) was an author and poet. His best-known novels focus on rural society and include *Far from the Madding Crowd* and *Jude the Obscure*.

Sir Arthur Conan Doyle (1859–1930) was a Scottish doctor and writer. He was best known for his stories about Sherlock Holmes, who was one of the first fictional detectives.

Evelyn Waugh (1903–66) wrote satirical novels, including *Decline and Fall* and *Scoop*. He is perhaps best known for *Brideshead Revisited*.

Sir Kingsley Amis (1922–95) was an English novelist and poet. He wrote more than 20 novels. The most well known is *Lucky Jim*.

Graham Greene (1904–91) wrote novels often influenced by his religious beliefs, including *The Heart of the Matter*, *The Honorary Consul*, *Brighton Rock* and *Our Man in Havana*.

J K Rowling (1965–) wrote the Harry Potter series of children's books, which have enjoyed huge international success. She now writes fiction for adults as well.

BRITISH POETS

British poetry is among the richest in the world. The Anglo-Saxon poem *Beowulf* tells of its hero's battles against monsters and is still translated into modern English. Poems which survive from the

Middle Ages include Chaucer's *Canterbury Tales* and a poem called *Sir Gawain and the Green Knight*, about one of the knights at the court of King Arthur.

As well as plays, Shakespeare wrote many sonnets (poems which must be 14 lines long) and some longer poems. As Protestant ideas spread, a number of poets wrote poems inspired by their religious views. One of these was John Milton, who wrote *Paradise Lost*.

Other poets, including William Wordsworth, were inspired by nature. Sir Walter Scott wrote poems inspired by Scotland and the traditional stories and songs from the area on the borders of Scotland and England. He also wrote novels, many of which were set in Scotland.

Poetry was very popular in the 19th century, with poets such as William Blake, John Keats, Lord Byron, Percy Shelley, Alfred Lord Tennyson, and Robert and Elizabeth Browning. Later, many poets – for example, Wilfred Owen and Siegfried Sassoon – were inspired to write about their experiences in the First World War. More recently, popular poets have included Sir Walter de la Mare, John Masefield, Sir John Betjeman and Ted Hughes.

Some of the best-known poets are buried or commemorated in Poet's Corner in Westminster Abbey.

“Some of the best-known poets are buried or commemorated in Poet's Corner in Westminster Abbey.”

Some famous lines include:

> 'Oh to be in England now that April's there
> And whoever wakes in England sees, some morning, unaware,
> That the lowest boughs and the brushwood sheaf
> Round the elm-tree bole are in tiny leaf
> While the Chaffinch sings on the orchard bough
> In England – Now!'
> (Robert Browning, 1812–89 – *Home Thoughts from Abroad*)

> 'She walks in beauty, like the night
> Of cloudless climes and starry skies;
> And all that's best of dark and bright
> Meet in her aspect and her eyes'
> (Lord Byron, 1788–1824 – *She Walks in Beauty*)

'I wander'd lonely as a cloud
That floats on high o'er vales and hills
When all at once I saw a crowd,
A host of golden daffodils'
(William Wordsworth, 1770–1850 – *The Daffodils*)

'Tyger! Tyger! Burning bright
In the forests of the night,
What immortal hand or eye
Could frame thy fearful symmetry?'
(William Blake, 1757–1827 – *The Tyger*)

'What passing-bells for these who die as cattle?
Only the monstrous anger of the guns.
Only the stuttering rifles' rapid rattle
Can patter out their hasty orisons.'
(Wilfred Owen, 1893–1918 – *Anthem for Doomed Youth*)

Check that you understand:

- Which sports are particularly popular in the UK
- Some of the major sporting events that take place each year
- Some of the major arts and culture events that happen in the UK
- How achievements in arts and culture are formally recognised
- Important figures in British literature

Leisure

People in the UK spend their leisure time in many different ways.

GARDENING

A lot of people have gardens at home and will spend their free time looking after them. Some people rent additional land called 'an allotment', where they grow fruit and vegetables. Gardening and flower shows range from major national exhibitions to small local events. Many towns have garden centres selling plants and gardening equipment. There are famous gardens to visit throughout the UK, including Kew Gardens, Sissinghurst and Hidcote in England, Crathes Castle and Inveraray Castle in Scotland, Bodnant Garden in Wales, and Mount Stewart in Northern Ireland.

The countries that make up the UK all have flowers which are particularly associated with them and which are sometimes worn on national saints' days:

England – the rose

Scotland – the thistle

Wales – the daffodil

Northern Ireland – the shamrock

SHOPPING

There are many different places to go shopping in the UK. Most towns and cities have a central shopping area, which is called the town centre. Undercover shopping centres are also common – these might be in town centres or on the outskirts of a town or city. Most shops in the UK are open seven days a week, although trading hours on Sundays and public holidays are generally reduced. Many towns also have markets on one or more days a week, where stallholders sell a variety of goods.

COOKING AND FOOD

Many people in the UK enjoy cooking. They often invite each other to their homes for dinner. A wide variety of food is eaten in the UK because of the country's rich cultural heritage and diverse population.

TRADITIONAL FOODS

There are a variety of foods that are traditionally associated with different parts of the UK:

England: Roast beef, which is served with potatoes, vegetables, Yorkshire puddings (batter that is baked in the oven) and other accompaniments. Fish and chips are also popular.

Wales: Welsh cakes – a traditional Welsh snack made from flour, dried fruits and spices, and served either hot or cold.

Scotland: Haggis – a sheep's stomach stuffed with offal, suet, onions and oatmeal.

Northern Ireland: Ulster fry – a fried meal with bacon, eggs, sausage, black pudding, white pudding, tomatoes, mushrooms, soda bread and potato bread.

Eminent directors included Sir Alexander Korda and Sir Alfred Hitchcock, who later left for Hollywood and remained an important film director until his death in 1980.

FILMS

British film industry

The UK has had a major influence on modern cinema.

Films were first shown publicly in the UK in 1896 and film screenings very quickly became popular. From the beginning, British film makers became famous for clever special effects and this continues to be an area of British expertise. From the early days of the cinema, British actors have worked in both the UK and USA. Sir Charles (Charlie) Chaplin became famous in silent movies for his tramp character and was one of many British actors to make a career in Hollywood.

British studios flourished in the 1930s. Eminent directors included Sir Alexander Korda and Sir Alfred Hitchcock, who later left for Hollywood and remained an important film director until his death in 1980. During the Second World War, British movies (for example, *In Which We Serve*) played an important part in boosting morale. Later, British directors including Sir David Lean and Sir Ridley Scott found great success both in the UK and internationally.

The 1950s and 1960s were a high point for British comedies, including *Passport to Pimlico*, *The Ladykillers* and, later, the *Carry On* films.

Many of the films now produced in the UK are made by foreign companies, using British expertise. Some of the most commercially successful films of all time, including two of the highest-grossing film franchises (Harry Potter and James Bond), have been produced in the UK. Ealing Studios has a claim to being the oldest continuously working film studio facility in the world. Britain continues to be particularly strong in special effects and animation. One example is the work of Nick Park, who has won four Oscars for his animated films, including three for films featuring Wallace and Gromit.

Actors such as Sir Laurence Olivier, David Niven, Sir Rex Harrison and Richard Burton starred in a wide variety of popular films. British actors continue to be popular and continue to win awards throughout the world. Recent British actors to have won Oscars include Colin Firth, Sir Anthony Hopkins, Dame Judi Dench, Kate Winslet and Tilda Swinton.

The annual British Academy Film Awards, hosted by the British Academy of Film and Television Arts (BAFTA), are the British equivalent of the Oscars.

“The annual British Academy Film Awards, hosted by the British Academy of Film and Television Arts (BAFTA), are the British equivalent of the Oscars.”

SOME FAMOUS BRITISH FILMS

The 39 Steps (1935), directed by Sir Alfred Hitchcock

Brief Encounter (1945), directed by Sir David Lean

The Third Man (1949), directed by Carol Reed

The Belles of St Trinian's (1954), directed by Frank Launder

Lawrence of Arabia (1962), directed by Sir David Lean

Women in Love (1969), directed by Ken Russell

Don't Look Now (1973), directed by Nicolas Roeg

Chariots of Fire (1981), directed by Hugh Hudson

The Killing Fields (1984), directed by Roland Joffé

Four Weddings and a Funeral (1994), directed by Mike Newell

Touching the Void (2003), directed by Kevin MacDonald.

You may be asked questions about these films and their directors, as well as the history of British cinema and famous actors.

BRITISH COMEDY

The traditions of comedy and satire, and the ability to laugh at ourselves, are an important part of the UK character.

Medieval kings and rich nobles had jesters who told jokes and made fun of people in the Court. Later, Shakespeare included comic characters in his plays. In the 18th century, political cartoons attacking prominent politicians – and, sometimes, the monarch or other members of the Royal Family – became increasingly popular. In the 19th century, satirical magazines began to be published. The most famous was *Punch*, which was published for the first time in the 1840s. Today, political cartoons continue to be published in newspapers, and magazines such as *Private Eye* continue the tradition of satire.

Comedians were a popular feature of British music hall, a form of variety theatre which was very common until television became the leading form of entertainment in the UK. Some of the people who had performed in the music halls in the 1940s and 1950s, such as Morecambe and Wise, became stars of television.

Everyone in the UK with a TV, computer or other medium which can be used for watching TV must have a television licence.

Television comedy developed its own style. Situation comedies, or sitcoms, which often look at family life and relationships in the workplace, remain popular. Satire has also continued to be important, with shows like *That Was The Week That Was* in the 1960s and *Spitting Image* in the 1980s and 1990s. In 1969, *Monty Python's Flying Circus* introduced a new type of progressive comedy. Stand-up comedy, where a solo comedian talks to a live audience, has become popular again in recent years.

TELEVISION AND RADIO

Many different television (TV) channels are available in the UK. Some are free to watch and others require a paid subscription. British television shows a wide variety of programmes. Popular programmes include regular soap operas such as *Coronation Street* and *EastEnders*. In Scotland, some Scotland-specific programmes are shown and there is also a channel with programmes in the Gaelic language. There is a Welsh-language channel in Wales. There are also programmes specific to Northern Ireland and some programmes broadcast in Irish Gaelic.

Everyone in the UK with a TV, computer or other medium which can be used for watching TV must have a television licence. One licence covers all of the equipment in one home, except when people rent different rooms in a shared house and each has a separate tenancy agreement – those people must each buy a separate licence. Some people over 75 can apply for a free TV licence and blind people can get a 50% discount. You will receive a fine of up to £1,000 if you watch TV but do not have a TV licence.

The money from TV licences is used to pay for the British Broadcasting Corporation (BBC). This is a British public service broadcaster providing television and radio programmes. The BBC is the largest broadcaster in the world. Although it receives some state funding, it is independent of the government. Other UK channels are primarily funded through advertisements and subscriptions.

There are also many different radio stations in the UK. Some broadcast nationally and others in certain cities or regions. There are radio stations that play certain types of music and some broadcast in regional languages such as Welsh or Gaelic. Like television, BBC radio stations are funded by TV licences and other radio stations are funded through advertisements.

"The money from TV licences is used to pay for the British Broadcasting Corporation (BBC). This is a British public service broadcaster providing television and radio programmes."

SOCIAL NETWORKING

Social networking websites such as Facebook and Twitter are a popular way for people to stay in touch with friends, organise social events, and share photos, videos and opinions. Many people use social networking on their mobile phones when out and about.

PUBS AND NIGHT CLUBS

Public houses (pubs) are an important part of the UK social culture. Many people enjoy meeting friends in the pub. Most communities will have a 'local' pub that is a natural focal point for social activities. Pub quizzes are popular. Pool and darts are traditional pub games. To buy alcohol in a pub or night club you must be 18 or over, but people under that age may be allowed in some pubs with an adult. When they are 16, people can drink wine or beer with a meal in a hotel or restaurant (including eating areas in pubs) as long as they are with someone over 18.

Pubs are usually open during the day from 11.00 am (12 noon on Sundays). Night clubs with dancing and music usually open and close later than pubs. The licensee decides the hours that the pub or night club is open.

BETTING AND GAMBLING

In the UK, people often enjoy a gamble on sports or other events. There are also casinos in many places. You have to be 18 to go into betting shops or gambling clubs. There is a National Lottery for which draws are made every week. You can enter by buying a ticket or a scratch card. People under 18 are not allowed to participate in the National Lottery.

PETS

A lot of people in the UK have pets such as cats or dogs. They might have them for company or because they enjoy looking after them. It is against the law to treat a pet cruelly or to neglect it. All dogs in public places must wear a collar showing the name and address of the owner. The owner is responsible for keeping the dog under control and for cleaning up after the animal in a public place.

Vaccinations and medical treatment for animals are available from veterinary surgeons (vets). There are charities which may help people who cannot afford to pay a vet.

“ The National Trust was founded in 1895 by three volunteers. There are now more than 61,000 volunteers helping to keep the organisation running.

Places of interest

The UK has a large network of public footpaths in the countryside. There are also many opportunities for mountain biking, mountaineering and hill walking. There are 15 national parks in England, Wales and Scotland. They are areas of protected countryside that everyone can visit, and where people live, work and look after the landscape.

There are many museums in the UK, which range from small community museums to large national and civic collections. Famous landmarks exist in towns, cities and the countryside throughout the UK. Most of them are open to the public to view (generally for a charge).

Many parts of the countryside and places of interest are kept open by the National Trust in England, Wales and Northern Ireland and the National Trust for Scotland. Both are charities that work to preserve important buildings, coastline and countryside in the UK. The National Trust was founded in 1895 by three volunteers. There are now more than 61,000 volunteers helping to keep the organisation running.

UK LANDMARKS

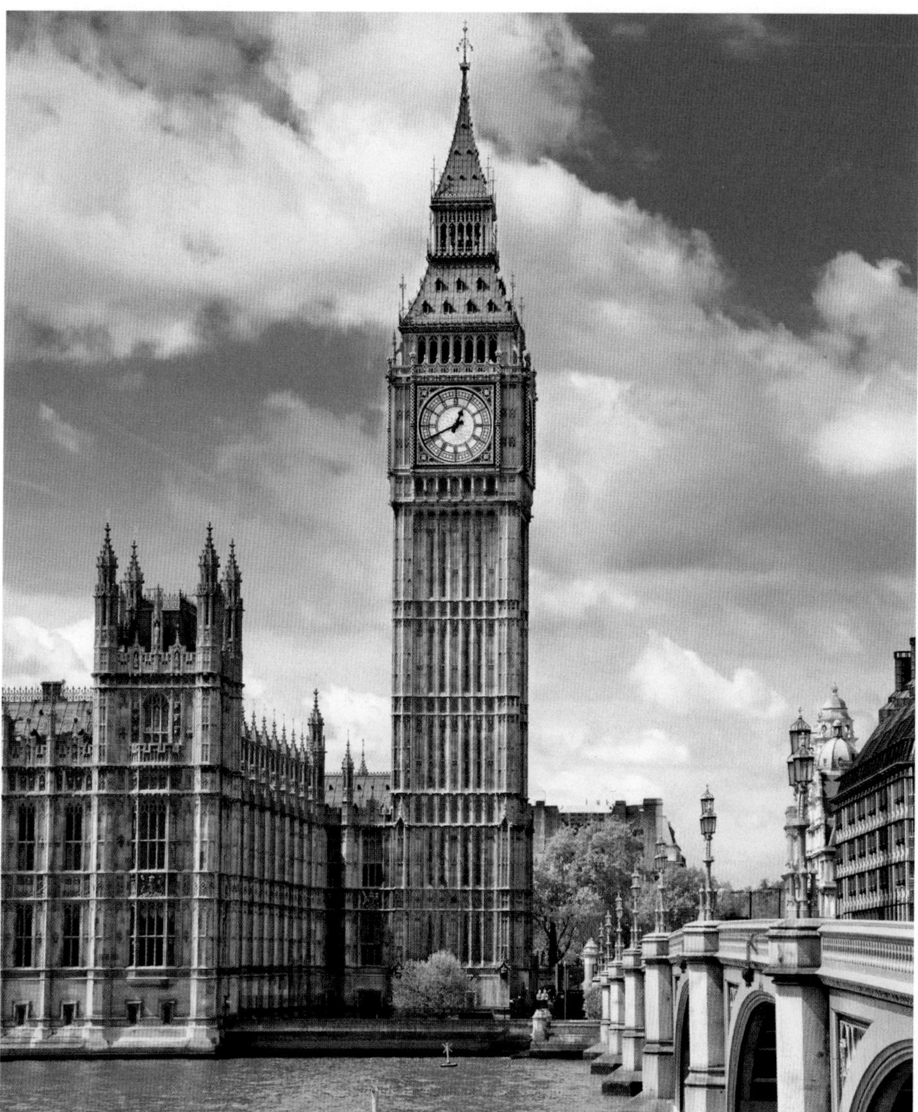

Big Ben

Big Ben is the nickname for the great bell of the clock at the Houses of Parliament in London. Many people call the clock Big Ben as well. The clock is over 150 years old and is a popular tourist attraction. The clock tower is named 'Elizabeth Tower' in honour of Queen Elizabeth II's Diamond Jubilee in 2012.

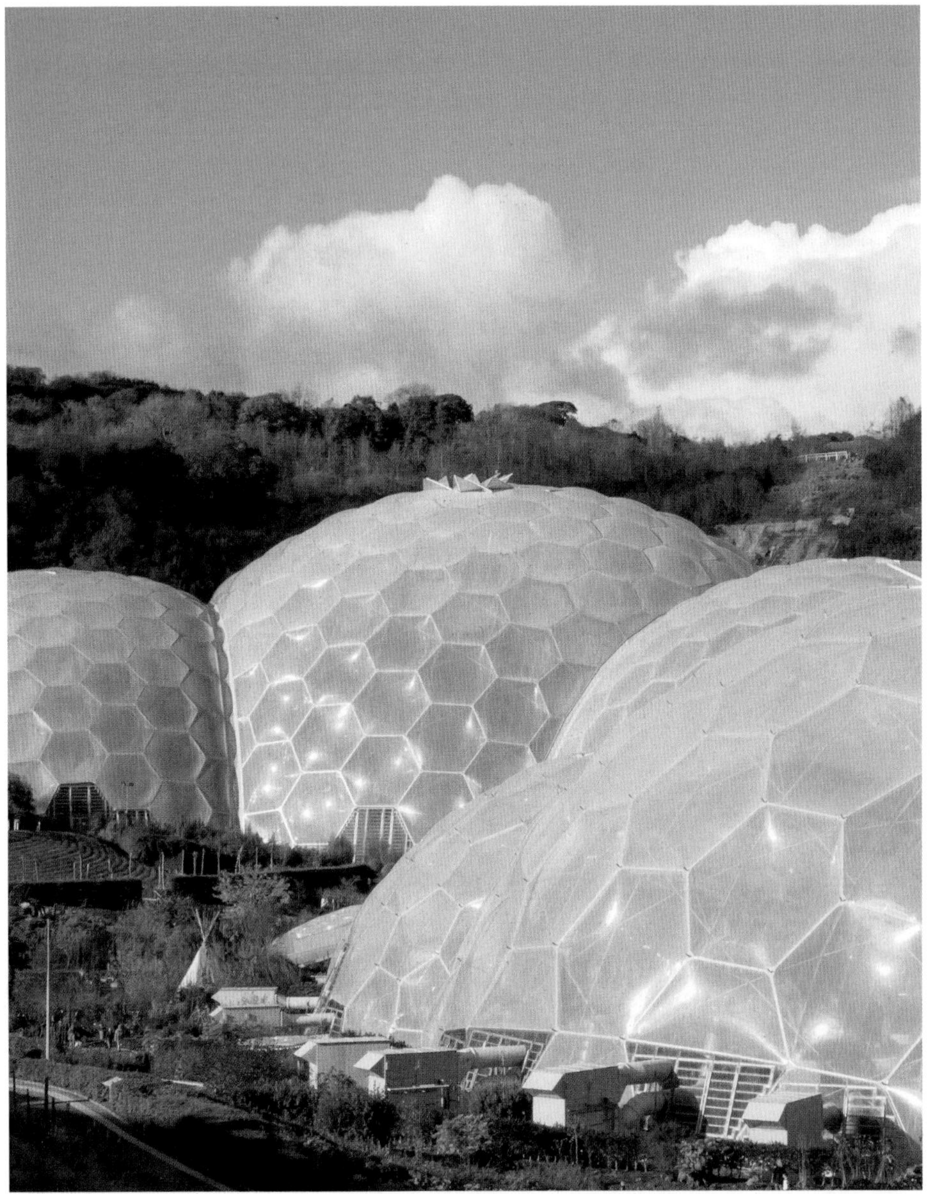

The Eden Project

The Eden Project is located in Cornwall, in the south west of England. Its biomes, which are like giant greenhouses, house plants from all over the world. The Eden Project is also a charity which runs environmental and social projects internationally.

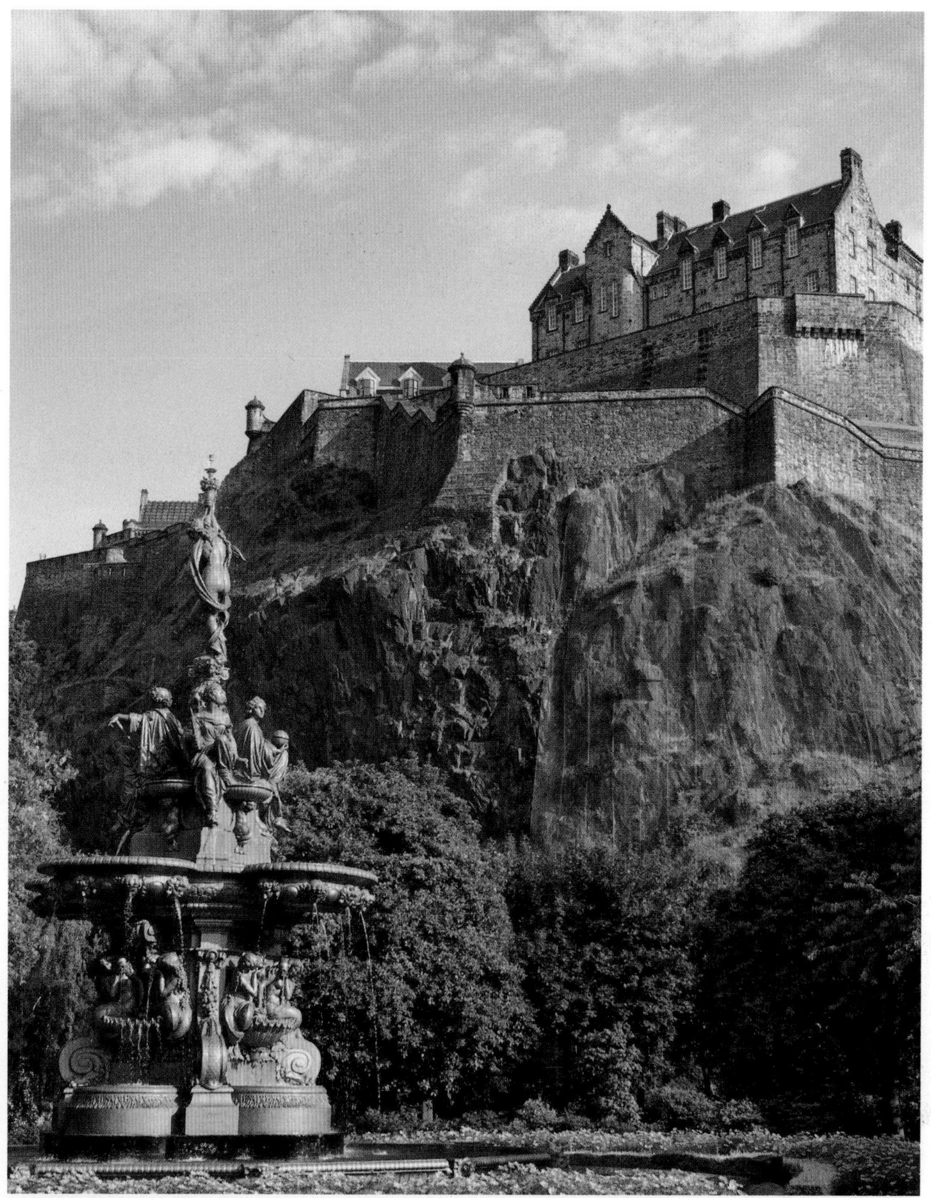

Edinburgh Castle

The Castle is a dominant feature of the skyline in Edinburgh, Scotland. It has a long history, dating back to the early Middle Ages. It is looked after by Historic Environment Scotland.

The Giant's Causeway

Located on the north-east coast of Northern Ireland, the Giant's Causeway is a land formation of columns made from volcanic lava. It was formed about 50 million years ago. There are many legends about the Causeway and how it was formed.

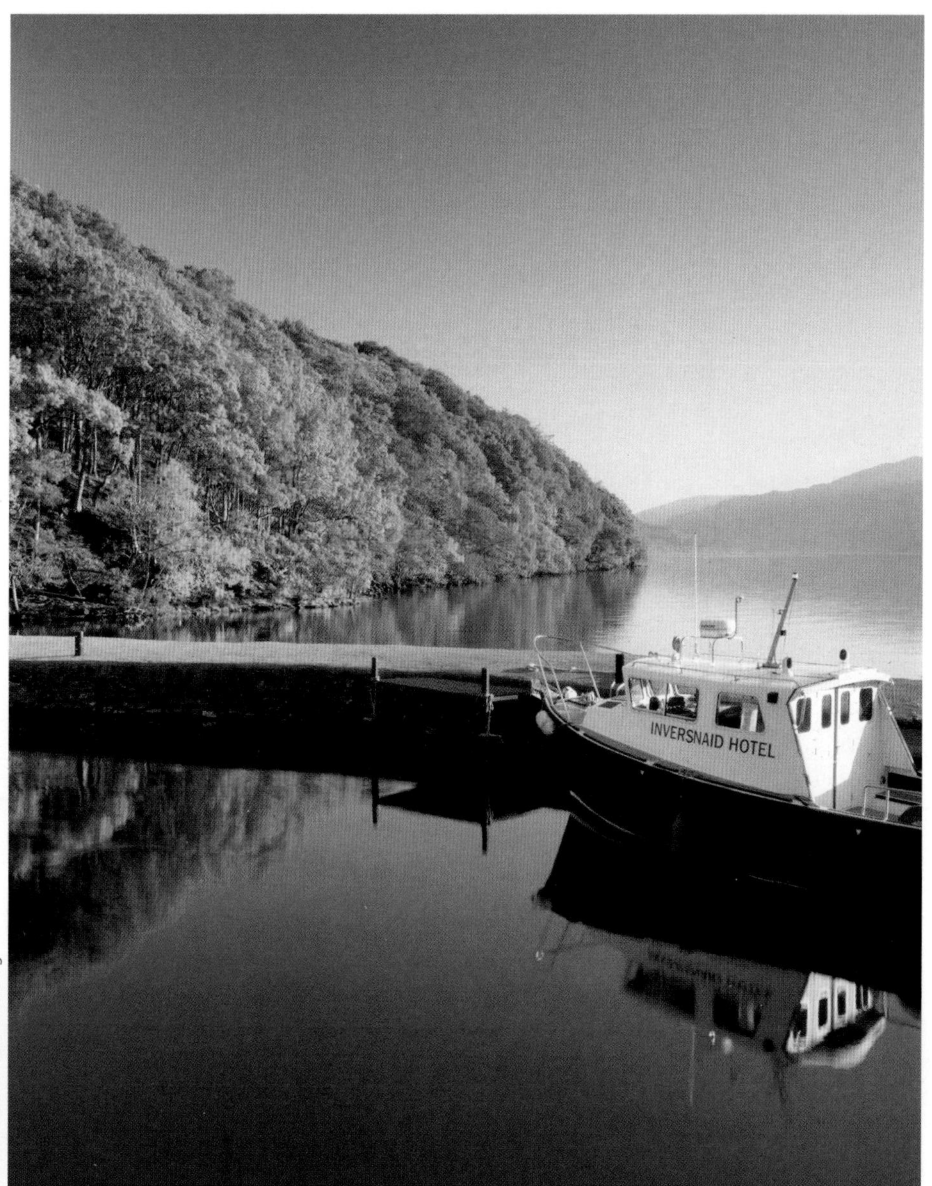

Loch Lomond and the Trossachs National Park

This national park covers 720 square miles (1,865 square kilometres) in the west of Scotland. Loch Lomond is the largest expanse of fresh water in mainland Britain and probably the best-known part of the park.

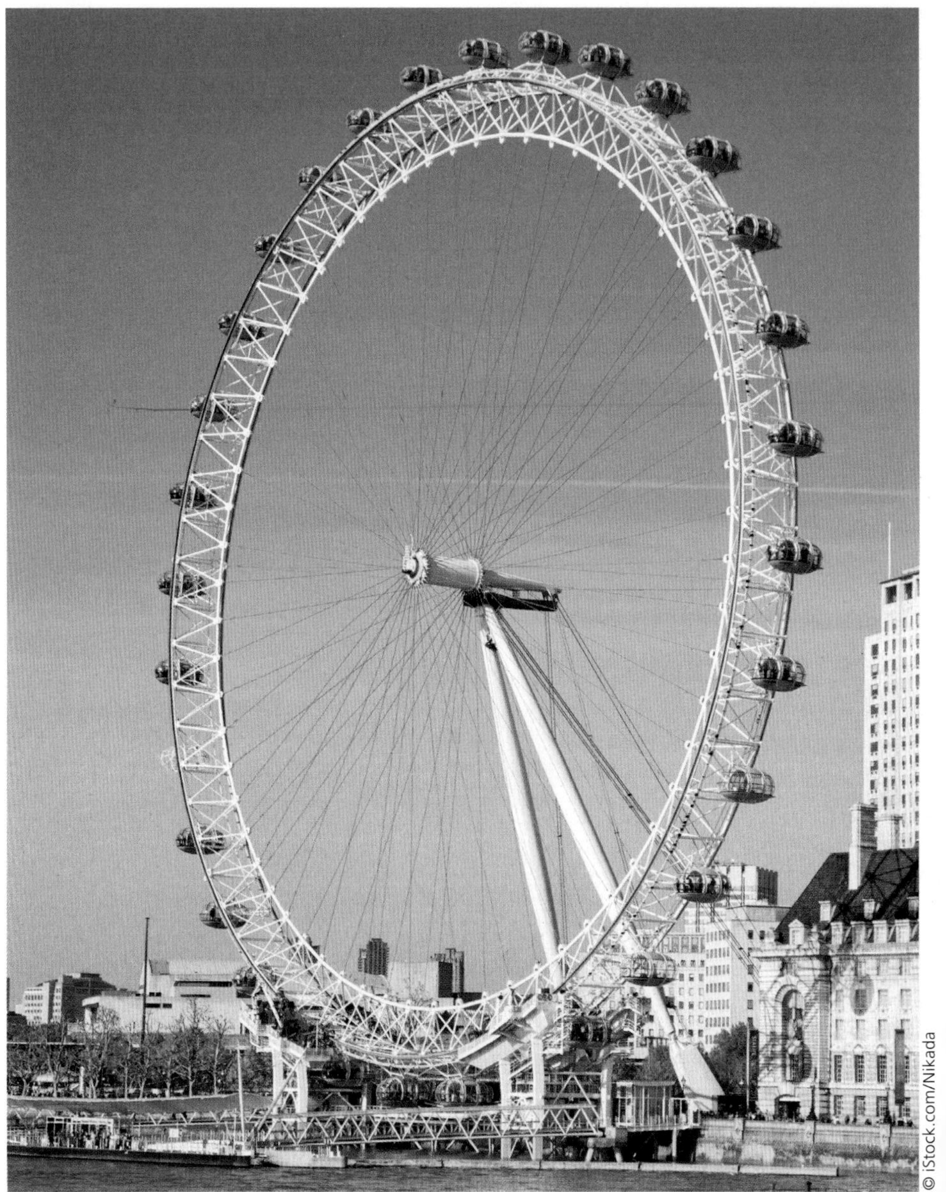

London Eye

The London Eye is situated on the southern bank of the River Thames and is a Ferris wheel that is 443 feet (135 metres) tall. It was originally built as part of the UK's celebration of the new millennium and continues to be an important part of New Year celebrations.

Snowdonia

Snowdonia is a national park in North Wales. It covers an area of 823 square miles (2,132 square kilometres). Its most well-known landmark is Snowdon, which is the highest mountain in Wales.

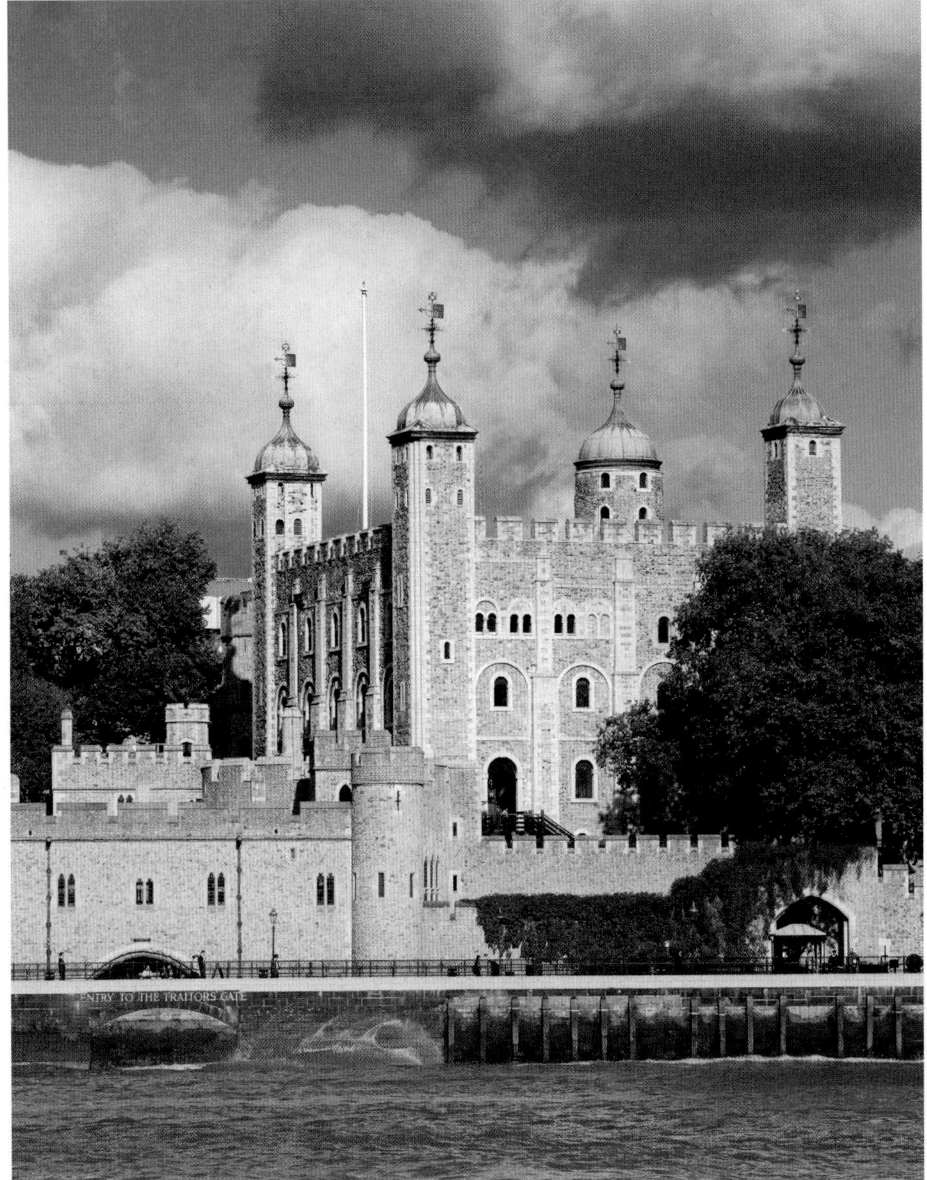

The Tower of London

The Tower of London was first built by William the Conqueror after he became king in 1066. Tours are given by the Yeoman Warders, also known as Beefeaters, who tell visitors about the building's history. People can also see the Crown Jewels there.

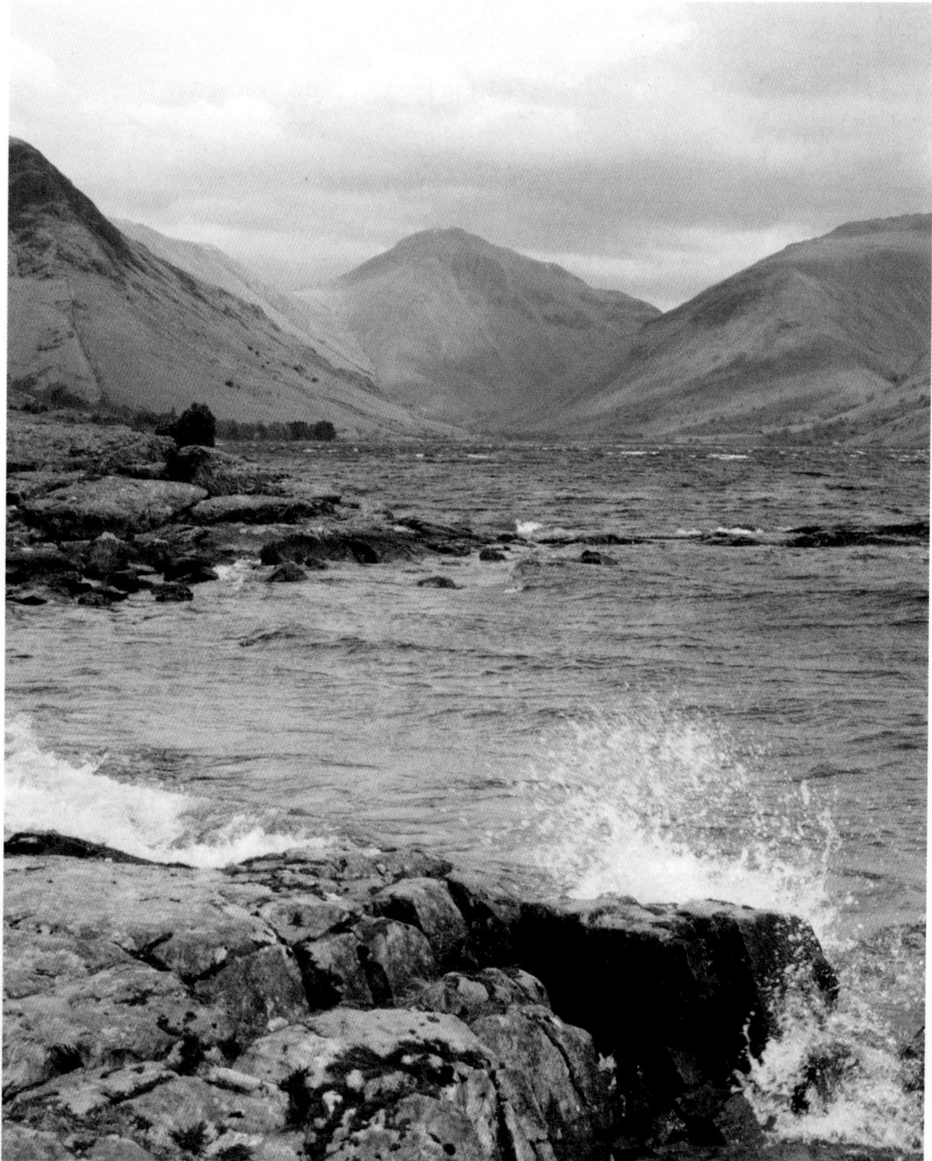

The Lake District

The Lake District is England's largest national park. It covers 912 square miles (2,362 square kilometres). It is famous for its lakes and mountains and is very popular with climbers, walkers and sailors. The biggest stretch of water is Windermere. In 2007, television viewers voted Wastwater as Britain's favourite view.

Check that you understand:

- Some of the ways in which people in the UK spend their leisure time
- The development of British cinema
- What the television licence is and how it funds the BBC
- Some of the places of interest to visit in the UK

CHAPTER 6
The UK government, the law and your role

→ IN THIS CHAPTER you will learn how the UK is governed. You need to understand the Queen's* role in government and her powers. Make sure you understand how people are appointed to the two Houses of Parliament and the specific roles detailed, such as the Speaker and cabinet, and your rights to vote and stand for election. Everyone should understand the workings of the devolved administrations but pay particular attention if you are taking the test in Scotland, Wales or Northern Ireland.

The UK's international role is explained through the Commonwealth, UN and other institutions so focus on the differences between these bodies and their member countries. The chapter then explains common laws, fundamental rights, policing and the courts of the UK. Pay particular attention to this so you know the differences between the various courts and offences they deal with. Finally the chapter deals with taxation, driving and community activity.

IN THIS CHAPTER THERE IS INFORMATION ABOUT:

- Britain as a constitutional monarchy
- How Parliament works
- Elections, the government and the opposition
- Devolved administrations of the UK
- The Commonwealth, UN and NATO
- British law and justice
- The courts
- Fundamental principles and rights
- Tax
- Driving
- Community work and getting involved

6

The UK is a parliamentary democracy with the monarch as head of state. This section will tell you about the different institutions which make up this democratic system and explain how you can play a part in the democratic process.

The development of British democracy

Democracy is a system of government where the whole adult population gets a say. This might be by direct voting or by choosing representatives to make decisions on their behalf.

At the turn of the 19th century, Britain was not a democracy as we know it today. Although there were elections to select members of Parliament (MPs), only a small group of people could vote. They were men who were over 21 years of age and who owned a certain amount of property.

The franchise (that is, the number of people who had the right to vote) grew over the course of the 19th century and political parties began to involve ordinary men and women as members.

In the 1830s and 1840s, a group called the Chartists campaigned for reform. They wanted six changes:

- for every man to have the vote
- elections every year
- for all regions to be equal in the electoral system
- secret ballots
- for any man to be able to stand as an MP
- for MPs to be paid.

At the time, the campaign was generally seen as a failure. However, by 1918 most of these reforms had been adopted. The voting franchise was also extended to women over 30, and then in 1928 to men and women over 21. In 1969, the voting age was reduced to 18 for men and women.

“The voting franchise was also extended to women over 30, and then in 1928 to men and women over 21. In 1969, the voting age was reduced to 18 for men and women.

The British constitution

A constitution is a set of principles by which a country is governed. It includes all of the institutions that are responsible for running the country and how their power is kept in check. The constitution also includes laws and conventions. The British constitution is not written down in any single document, and therefore it is described as 'unwritten'. This is mainly because the UK, unlike America or France, has never had a revolution which led permanently to a totally new system of government. Our most important institutions have developed over hundreds of years. Some people believe that there should be a single document, but others believe an unwritten constitution allows for more flexibility and better government.

CONSTITUTIONAL INSTITUTIONS

In the UK, there are several different parts of government. The main ones are:

- the monarchy
- Parliament (the House of Commons and the House of Lords)
- the Prime Minister
- the cabinet
- the judiciary (courts)
- the police
- the civil service
- local government.

> **The British constitution is not written down in any single document, and therefore it is described as 'unwritten'.**

In addition, there are devolved governments in Scotland, Wales and Northern Ireland that have the power to legislate on certain issues.

THE MONARCHY

Queen Elizabeth II is the head of state of the UK*. She is also the monarch or head of state for many countries in the Commonwealth. The UK has a constitutional monarchy. This means that the king or queen does not rule the country but appoints the government, which the people have chosen in a democratic election. The monarch invites the leader of the party with the largest number of MPs, or the leader of a coalition between more than one party, to become the Prime Minister. The monarch has regular meetings with the Prime Minister and can advise, warn and encourage, but the decisions on government policies are made by the Prime Minister and cabinet (see the section on 'The government').

Queen Elizabeth II, head of state of the UK

The Queen has reigned since her father's death in 1952, and in 2012 she celebrated her Diamond Jubilee (60 years as queen). She was married to Prince Philip, the Duke of Edinburgh, until his death in 2021. Her eldest son, Prince Charles (the Prince of Wales), is the heir to the throne*.

The Queen has important ceremonial roles, such as the opening of the new parliamentary session each year. On this occasion the Queen makes a speech which summarises the government's policies for the year ahead. All Acts of Parliament are made in her name.

The Queen represents the UK to the rest of the world. She receives foreign ambassadors and high commissioners, entertains visiting heads of state, and makes state visits overseas in support of diplomatic and economic relationships with other countries.

The Queen has an important role in providing stability and continuity. While governments and Prime Ministers change regularly, the Queen continues as head of state. She provides a focus for national identity and pride, which was demonstrated through the celebrations of her Jubilee.

“The Queen has important ceremonial roles, such as the opening of the new parliamentary session each year. On this occasion the Queen makes a speech which summarises the government's policies for the year ahead.”

THE NATIONAL ANTHEM

The National Anthem of the UK is 'God Save the Queen'*. It is played at important national occasions and at events attended by the Queen or the Royal Family. The first verse is:

> 'God save our gracious Queen!
> Long live our noble Queen!
> God save the Queen!
> Send her victorious,
> Happy and glorious,
> Long to reign over us,
> God save the Queen!'

New citizens swear or affirm loyalty to the Queen as part of the citizenship ceremony*.

Oath of allegiance

'I (name) swear by Almighty God that on becoming a British citizen, I will be faithful and bear true allegiance to Her Majesty Queen Elizabeth the Second, her Heirs and Successors, according to law.'

Affirmation of allegiance

'I (name) do solemnly, sincerely and truly declare and affirm that on becoming a British citizen, I will be faithful and bear true allegiance to Her Majesty Queen Elizabeth the Second, her Heirs and Successors, according to law.'

SYSTEM OF GOVERNMENT

The system of government in the UK is a parliamentary democracy. The UK is divided into parliamentary constituencies. Voters in each constituency elect their member of Parliament (MP) in a General Election. All of the elected MPs form the House of Commons. Most MPs belong to a political party, and the party with the majority of MPs forms the government. If one party does not get a majority, two parties can join together to form a coalition.

The Houses of Parliament, one of the centres of political life in the UK and a World Heritage Site

THE HOUSE OF COMMONS

The House of Commons is regarded as the more important of the two chambers in Parliament because its members are democratically elected. The Prime Minister and almost all the members of the cabinet are members of the House of Commons (MPs). Each MP represents a parliamentary constituency, which is a small area of the country. MPs have a number of different responsibilities. They:

- represent everyone in their constituency
- help to create new laws
- scrutinise and comment on what the government is doing
- debate important national issues.

THE HOUSE OF LORDS

Members of the House of Lords, known as peers, are not elected by the people and do not represent a constituency. The role and membership of the House of Lords has changed over the last 50 years.

Until 1958, all peers were:

- 'hereditary', which means they inherited their title, or
- senior judges, or
- bishops of the Church of England.

Since 1958, the Prime Minister has had the power to nominate peers just for their own lifetime. These are called life peers. They have usually had an important career in politics, business, law or another profession. Life peers are appointed by the monarch on the advice of the Prime Minister. They also include people nominated by the leaders of the other main political parties or by an independent Appointments Commission for non-party peers.

Since 1999, hereditary peers have lost the automatic right to attend the House of Lords. They now elect a few of their number to represent them in the House of Lords.

Since 1999, hereditary peers have lost the automatic right to attend the House of Lords. They now elect a few of their number to represent them in the House of Lords.

The House of Lords is normally more independent of the government than the House of Commons. It can suggest amendments or propose new laws, which are then discussed by MPs. The House of Lords checks laws that have been passed by the House of Commons to ensure they are fit for purpose. It also holds the government to account to make sure that it is working in the best interests of the people. There are peers who are specialists in particular areas, and their knowledge is useful in making and checking laws. The House of Commons has powers to overrule the House of Lords, but these are not used often.

THE SPEAKER

Debates in the House of Commons are chaired by the Speaker. This person is the chief officer of the House of Commons. The Speaker is neutral and does not represent a political party, even though he or she is an MP, represents a constituency and deals with constituents' problems like any other MP. The Speaker is chosen by other MPs in a secret ballot.

The Speaker keeps order during political debates to make sure the rules are followed. This includes making sure the opposition (see the section on 'The government') has a guaranteed amount of time to debate issues which it chooses. The Speaker also represents Parliament on ceremonial occasions.

ELECTIONS

UK elections

MPs are elected at a General Election, which is held at least every five years.

If an MP dies or resigns, there will be a fresh election, called a by-election, in his or her constituency.

MPs are elected through a system called 'first past the post'. In each constituency, the candidate who gets the most votes is elected. The government is usually formed by the party that wins the majority of constituencies. If no party wins a majority, two parties may join together to form a coalition.

MPs are elected through a system called 'first past the post'. In each constituency, the candidate who gets the most votes is elected.

CONTACTING ELECTED MEMBERS

All elected members have a duty to serve and represent their constituents. You can get contact details for all your representatives and their parties from your local library and from www.parliament.uk. MPs, Senedd members (SMs) and members of the Scottish Parliament (MSPs) are also listed in *The Phone Book*, published by BT.

You can contact MPs by letter or telephone at their constituency office, or at their office in the House of Commons: The House of Commons, Westminster, London SW1A 0AA, telephone 020 7219 3000. In addition, many MPs, SMs and MSPs hold regular local 'surgeries', where constituents can go in person to talk about issues that are of concern to them. These surgeries are often advertised in the local newspaper.

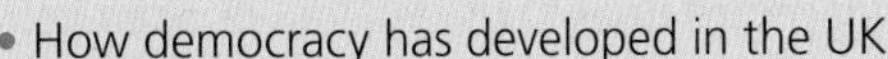

Check that you understand:

- How democracy has developed in the UK
- What a constitution is and how the UK's constitution is different from those of most other countries
- The role of the monarch
- The role of the House of Commons and House of Lords
- What the Speaker does
- How the UK elects MPs

The government

THE PRIME MINISTER

The Prime Minister (PM) is the leader of the political party in power. He or she appoints the members of the cabinet (see below) and has control over many important public appointments. The official home of the Prime Minister is 10 Downing Street, in central London, near the Houses of Parliament. He or she also has a country house outside London called Chequers.

The Prime Minister can be changed if the MPs in the governing party decide to do so, or if he or she wishes to resign. The Prime Minister usually resigns if his or her party loses a General Election.

THE CABINET

The Prime Minister appoints about 20 senior MPs to become ministers in charge of departments. These include:

- Chancellor of the Exchequer – responsible for the economy
- Home Secretary – responsible for crime, policing and immigration
- Foreign Secretary – responsible for managing relationships with foreign countries
- other ministers (called 'Secretaries of State') responsible for subjects such as education, health and defence.

These ministers form the cabinet, a committee which usually meets weekly and makes important decisions about government policy. Many of these decisions have to be debated or approved by Parliament.

Each department also has a number of other ministers, called Ministers of State and Parliamentary Under-Secretaries of State, who take charge of particular areas of the department's work.

THE OPPOSITION

The second-largest party in the House of Commons is called the opposition. The leader of the opposition usually becomes Prime Minister if his or her party wins the next General Election.

The leader of the opposition leads his or her party in pointing out what they see as the government's failures and weaknesses. One important opportunity to do this is at Prime Minister's Questions, which takes place every week while Parliament is sitting. The leader of the opposition also appoints senior opposition MPs to be 'shadow ministers'. They form the shadow cabinet and their role is to challenge the government and put forward alternative policies.

THE PARTY SYSTEM

Anyone aged 18 or over can stand for election as an MP* but they are unlikely to win unless they have been nominated to represent one of the major political parties. These are the Conservative Party, the Labour Party, the Liberal Democrats, or one of the parties representing Scottish, Welsh or Northern Irish interests.

*For more information see **Clarifications** in Chapter 1 and lifeintheuk.net/clarify

There are a few MPs who do not represent any of the main political parties. They are called 'independents' and usually represent an issue important to their constituency.

"There are a few MPs who do not represent any of the main political parties. They are called 'independents' and usually represent an issue important to their constituency.

The main political parties actively look for members of the public to join their debates, contribute to their costs, and help at elections for Parliament or for local government. They have branches in most constituencies and hold policy-making conferences every year.

Pressure and lobby groups are organisations which try to influence government policy. They play an important role in politics. Some are representative organisations such as the CBI (Confederation of British Industry), which represents the views of British business. Others campaign on particular topics, such as the environment (for example, Greenpeace) or human rights (for example, Liberty).

THE CIVIL SERVICE

Civil servants support the government in developing and implementing its policies. They also deliver public services. Civil servants are accountable to ministers. They are chosen on merit and are politically neutral – they are not political appointees. People can apply to join the civil service through an application process, like other jobs in the UK. Civil servants are expected to carry out their role with dedication and a commitment to the civil service and its core values. These are: integrity, honesty, objectivity and impartiality (including being politically neutral).

LOCAL GOVERNMENT

Towns, cities and rural areas in the UK are governed by democratically elected councils, often called 'local authorities'. Some areas have both district and county councils, which have different functions. Most large towns and cities have a single local authority.

Local authorities provide a range of services in their areas. They are funded by money from central government and by local taxes.

Many local authorities appoint a mayor, who is the ceremonial leader of the council. In some towns, a mayor is elected to be the effective leader of the administration. London has 33 local authorities, with the Greater London Authority and the Mayor of London coordinating policies across the capital. For most local authorities, local elections for councillors are held in May every year. Many candidates stand for council election as members of a political party.

“**Civil servants are accountable to ministers. They are chosen on merit and are politically neutral – they are not political appointees.**”

DEVOLVED ADMINISTRATIONS

Since 1997, some powers have been devolved from the central government to give people in Wales, Scotland and Northern Ireland more control over matters that directly affect them. There has been a Welsh Assembly (now called the Senedd) and a Scottish Parliament since 1999. There is also a Northern Ireland Assembly, although this has been suspended on a few occasions.

Policy and laws governing defence, foreign affairs, social security and most taxation all remain under central UK government control. However, many other public services, such as education, are controlled by the devolved administrations.

The devolved administrations each have their own civil servants.

Devolved administrations of the UK

The Senedd

Formed in 1999 in Cardiff, capital of Wales

Members: 60 MSs

Elections: Every four years

Powers: Since 2011 can make law without UK Parliament in 21 areas including:

- education and training
- health and social services
- economic development
- housing

The Scottish Parliament

Formed in 1999 in Edinburgh

Members: 129 MSPs

Elections: Use a form of proportional representation

Powers: In all areas not specifically reserved by UK Parliament (see above), including:

- civil and criminal law
- health
- education
- planning
- additional tax-raising powers

The Northern Ireland Parliament

First established in 1922

Abolished in 1972, after The Troubles started in 1969

The Northern Ireland Assembly

Established after the Belfast Agreement in 1998

Members: 90 MLAs

Elections: Use a form of proportional representation. Ministerial offices shared between main parties

Powers: In areas including:

- education
- agriculture
- the environment
- health
- social services

Has been suspended several times

The Welsh government

The Welsh government and the Senedd are based in Cardiff, the capital city of Wales. There are 60 members of the Senedd (MSs) and elections are held every four years using a form of proportional representation.* Members can speak in either

Welsh or English, and all of the Senedd's publications are in both languages.

The Senedd has the power to make laws for Wales in 21 areas, including:

- education and training
- health and social services
- economic development
- housing.

Since 2011, the Senedd has been able to pass laws on these topics without the agreement of the UK Parliament.

© Allan Baxter/Getty Images

The Senedd building, opened in March 2006

© Kim Traynor

The Scottish Parliament building, opened in October 2004

The Scottish Parliament

The Scottish Parliament was formed in 1999. It sits in Edinburgh, the capital city of Scotland.

There are 129 members of the Scottish Parliament (MSPs), elected by a form of proportional representation. The Scottish Parliament can pass laws for Scotland on all matters which are not specifically reserved to the UK Parliament. The matters on which the Scottish Parliament can legislate include:

You should know about all of the devolved administrations, wherever you live in the UK. Make sure you know how they were formed and the powers they have.

- civil and criminal law
- health
- education
- planning
- additional tax-raising powers.

The Northern Ireland Assembly

A Northern Ireland Parliament was established in 1922, when Ireland was divided, but it was abolished in 1972, shortly after the Troubles broke out in 1969 (see pages 47–8).

The Northern Ireland Assembly was established soon after the Belfast Agreement (or Good Friday Agreement) in 1998. There is a power-sharing agreement which distributes ministerial offices amongst the main parties. The Assembly has 90 elected members, known as MLAs (members of the Legislative Assembly). They are elected with a form of proportional representation.

The Northern Ireland Assembly building, known as Stormont

The Northern Ireland Assembly can make decisions on issues such as:

- education
- agriculture
- the environment
- health
- social services.

The UK government has the power to suspend all devolved assemblies. It has used this power several times in Northern Ireland when local political leaders found it difficult to work together.

THE MEDIA AND GOVERNMENT

Proceedings in Parliament are broadcast on television and published in official reports called *Hansard*. Written reports can be found in large libraries and at www.parliament.uk. Most people get information about political issues and events from newspapers (often called 'the press'), television, radio and the internet.

“Proceedings in Parliament are broadcast on television and published in official reports called *Hansard*.”

The UK has a free press. This means that what is written in newspapers is free from government control. Some newspaper owners and editors hold strong political opinions and run campaigns to try to influence government policy and public opinion.

By law, radio and television coverage of the political parties must be balanced and so equal time has to be given to rival viewpoints.

Check that you understand:

- The role of the Prime Minister, cabinet, opposition and shadow cabinet
- The role of political parties in the UK system of government
- Who the main political parties are
- What pressure and lobby groups do
- The role of the civil service
- The role of local government
- The powers of the devolved governments in Wales, Scotland and Northern Ireland
- How proceedings in Parliament are recorded
- The role of the media in keeping people informed about political issues

Who can vote?

The UK has had a fully democratic voting system since 1928 (see page 106). The present voting age of 18 was set in 1969 and (with a few exceptions) all UK-born and naturalised adult citizens have the right to vote.

Adult citizens of the UK, and citizens of the Commonwealth and Ireland who are resident in the UK, can vote in all public elections.

THE ELECTORAL REGISTER

To be able to vote in a parliamentary or local election, you must have your name on the electoral register.

If you are eligible to vote, you can register by contacting your local council electoral registration office. This is usually based at your local council (in Scotland it may be based elsewhere). If you don't know which local authority you come under, you can find out by visiting www.aboutmyvote.co.uk and entering your postcode. You can also download voter registration forms in English, Welsh and some other languages.

The electoral register is updated every year in September or October. An electoral registration form is sent to every household and this has to be completed and returned with the names of everyone who is resident in the household and eligible to vote*.

*For more information see **Clarifications** in Chapter 1 and lifeintheuk.net/clarify

In Northern Ireland a different system operates. This is called 'individual registration' and all those entitled to vote must complete their own registration form. Once registered, people stay on the register provided their personal details do not change. For more information see the Electoral Office for Northern Ireland website at www.eoni.org.uk.

By law, each local authority has to make its electoral register available for anyone to look at, although this has to be supervised. The register is kept at each local electoral registration office (or council office in England and Wales). It is also possible to see the register at some public buildings such as libraries.

WHERE TO VOTE

People vote in elections at places called polling stations, or polling places in Scotland. Before the election you will be sent a poll card. This tells you where your polling station or polling place is and when the election will take place. On election day, the polling station or place will be open from 7.00 am until 10.00 pm.

"People vote in elections at places called polling stations, or polling places in Scotland."

When you arrive at the polling station, the staff will ask for your name and address. In Northern Ireland you will also have to show photographic identification. You will then get your ballot paper, which you take to a polling booth to fill in privately. You should make up your own mind who to vote for. No one has the right to make you vote for a particular candidate. You should follow the instructions on the ballot paper. Once you have completed it, put it in the ballot box.

If it is difficult for you to get to a polling station or polling place, you can register for a postal ballot. Your ballot paper will be sent to your home before the election. You then fill it in and post it back. You can choose to do this when you register to vote.

STANDING FOR OFFICE

Most citizens of the UK, Ireland or the Commonwealth aged 18 or over can stand for public office. There are some exceptions, including:

- members of the armed forces
- civil servants
- people found guilty of certain criminal offences.

Members of the House of Lords may not stand for election to the House of Commons but are eligible for all other public offices.

VISITING PARLIAMENT AND THE DEVOLVED ADMINISTRATIONS

The UK Parliament

The public can listen to debates in the Palace of Westminster from public galleries in both the House of Commons and the House of Lords.

You can write to your local MP in advance to ask for tickets or you can queue on the day at the public entrance. Entrance is free. Sometimes there are long queues for the House of Commons and people have to wait for at least one or two hours. It is usually easier to get in to the House of Lords.

You can find further information on the UK Parliament website at www.parliament.uk.

Northern Ireland Assembly

In Northern Ireland elected members, known as MLAs, meet in the Northern Ireland Assembly at Stormont, in Belfast.

If you wish to visit Stormont, you can either contact the Northern Ireland Assembly Education Service (http://education.niassembly.gov.uk/visit), go to the Northern Ireland Assembly website (http://www.niassembly.gov.uk/visit-and-learning/) or contact an MLA.

Scottish Parliament

In Scotland the elected members, called MSPs, meet in the Scottish Parliament building at Holyrood in Edinburgh (for more information, see www.parliament.scot).

You can get information, book tickets or arrange tours through visitor services. You can write to them at the Scottish Parliament, Edinburgh, EH99 1SP, telephone 0131 348 5200, freephone 0800 092 7600 or email visit@parliament.scot

The Senedd

In Wales the elected members, known as SMs*, meet in the Senedd building in Cardiff Bay (for more information, see www.senedd.wales).

*For more information see **Clarifications** in Chapter 1 and lifeintheuk.net/clarify

You can book guided tours or seats in the public galleries for the Senedd. To make a booking, contact the Senedd Booking Service on 0300 200 6565, email contact@senedd.wales or visit www.senedd.wales for an online booking form.

Check that you understand:

- Who is eligible to vote
- How you register to vote
- How to vote
- Who can stand for public office
- How you can visit Parliament, the Northern Ireland Assembly, the Scottish Parliament and the Senedd

The UK and international institutions

THE COMMONWEALTH

The Commonwealth is an association of countries that support each other and work together towards shared goals in democracy and development. Most member states were once part of the British Empire, although a few countries which were not have also joined.

The Queen is the ceremonial head of the Commonwealth*, which currently has 54* member states (see table below). Membership is voluntary. The Commonwealth has no power over its members, although it can suspend membership. The Commonwealth is based on the core values of democracy, good government and the rule of law.

Commonwealth members

Antigua and Barbuda	Australia	The Bahamas
Bangladesh	Barbados	Belize
Botswana	Brunei Darussalam	Cameroon
Canada	Cyprus	Dominica
Fiji	The Gambia	Ghana
Grenada	Guyana	India
Jamaica	Kenya	Kiribati
Lesotho	Malawi	Malaysia
Maldives	Malta	Mauritius
Mozambique	Namibia	Nauru
New Zealand	Nigeria	Pakistan
Papua New Guinea	Rwanda	Samoa
Seychelles	Sierra Leone	Singapore
Solomon Islands	South Africa	Sri Lanka
St Kitts and Nevis	St Lucia	St Vincent and the Grenadines
Swaziland*	Tanzania	Tonga
Trinidad and Tobago	Tuvalu	Uganda
UK	Vanuatu	Zambia

THE COUNCIL OF EUROPE

The Council of Europe has 47 member countries, including the UK, and is responsible for the protection and promotion of human rights in those countries. It has no power to make laws but draws up conventions and charters, the most well-known of which is the European Convention on Human Rights and Fundamental Freedoms, usually called the European Convention on Human Rights.

THE UNITED NATIONS

The UK is part of the United Nations (UN), an international organisation with more than 190 countries as members.

The UN was set up after the Second World War and aims to prevent war and promote international peace and security. There are 15 members on the UN Security Council, which recommends action when there are international crises and threats to peace. The UK is one of five permanent members of the Security Council.

THE NORTH ATLANTIC TREATY ORGANIZATION (NATO)

The UK is also a member of NATO. NATO is a group of European and North American countries that have agreed to help each other if they come under attack. It also aims to maintain peace between all of its members.

Check that you understand:

- What the Commonwealth is and its role
- Other international organisations of which the UK is a member

Respecting the law

One of the most important responsibilities of all residents in the UK is to know and obey the law. This section will tell you about the legal system in the UK and some of the laws that may affect you. Britain is proud of being a welcoming country, but all residents, regardless of their background, are expected to comply with the law and to understand that some things which may be allowed in other legal systems are not acceptable in the UK. Those who do not respect the law should not expect to be allowed to become permanent residents in the UK.

The law is relevant to all areas of life in the UK. You should make sure that you are aware of the laws which affect your everyday life, including both your personal and business affairs.

THE LAW IN THE UK

Every person in the UK receives equal treatment under the law. This means that the law applies in the same way to everyone, no matter who they are or where they are from.

“Every person in the UK receives equal treatment under the law. This means that the law applies in the same way to everyone, no matter who they are or where they are from.

Laws can be divided into criminal law and civil law:

- Criminal law relates to crimes, which are usually investigated by the police or another authority such as a council, and which are punished by the courts.
- Civil law is used to settle disputes between individuals or groups.

Examples of criminal laws are:

- Carrying a weapon: it is a criminal offence to carry a weapon of any kind, even if it is for self-defence. This includes a gun, a knife or anything that is made or adapted to cause injury.
- Drugs: selling or buying drugs such as heroin, cocaine, ecstasy and cannabis is illegal in the UK.
- Racial crime: it is a criminal offence to cause harassment, alarm or distress to someone because of their religion or ethnic origin.
- Selling tobacco: it is illegal to sell tobacco products (for example, cigarettes, cigars, roll-up tobacco) to anyone under the age of 18.
- Smoking in public places: it is against the law to smoke tobacco products in nearly every enclosed public place in the UK. There are signs displayed to tell you where you cannot smoke.

- Buying alcohol: it is a criminal offence to sell alcohol to anyone who is under 18 or to buy alcohol for people who are under the age of 18. (There is one exception: people aged 16 or over can drink alcohol with a meal in a hotel or restaurant – see page 93.)
- Drinking in public: some places have alcohol-free zones where you cannot drink in public. The police can also confiscate alcohol or move young people on from public places. You can be fined or arrested.

This list does not include all crimes. There are many that apply in most countries, such as murder, theft and assault. You can find out more about types of crime in the UK at www.gov.uk.

Examples of civil laws are:

- Housing law: this includes disputes between landlords and tenants over issues such as repairs and eviction.
- Consumer rights: an example of this is a dispute about faulty goods or services.
- Employment law: these cases include disputes over wages and cases of unfair dismissal or discrimination in the workplace.
- Debt: people might be taken to court if they owe money to someone.

"The police are organised into a number of separate police forces headed by Chief Constables. They are independent of the government.

THE POLICE AND THEIR DUTIES

The job of the police in the UK is to:

- protect life and property
- prevent disturbances (also known as keeping the peace)
- prevent and detect crime.

The police are organised into a number of separate police forces headed by Chief Constables. They are independent of the government.

In November 2012, the public first elected Police and Crime Commissioners (PCCs) in England and Wales. These are directly elected individuals who are responsible for the delivery of an efficient and effective police force that reflects the needs of their local communities. PCCs set local police priorities and the local policing budget. They also appoint the local Chief Constable.

The police in the UK protect life and property, prevent disturbances, and prevent and detect crime

© Peter Dazeley/Getty Images

The police force is a public service that helps and protects everyone, no matter what their background or where they live. Police officers must themselves obey the law. They must not misuse their authority, make a false statement, be rude or abusive, or commit racial discrimination. If police officers are corrupt or misuse their authority they are severely punished.

Police officers are supported by police community support officers (PCSOs). PCSOs have different roles according to the area but usually patrol the streets, work with the public, and support police officers at crime scenes and major events.

All people in the UK are expected to help the police prevent and detect crimes whenever they can. If you are arrested and taken to a police station, a police officer will tell you the reason for your arrest and you will be able to seek legal advice.

If something goes wrong, the police complaints system tries to put it right. Anyone can make a complaint about the police by going to a police station or writing to the Chief Constable of the police force involved. Complaints can also be made to an independent body in England and Wales (www.policeconduct.gov.uk). In Scotland, if you are unhappy with the way your complaint has been handled, you can contact the Police Investigations and Review Commissioner at https://pirc.scot/. In Northern Ireland, you should contact the Police Ombudsman's Office (www.policeombudsman.org).

TERRORISM AND EXTREMISM

The UK faces a range of terrorist threats. The most serious of these is from Al Qa'ida, its affiliates and like-minded organisations. The UK also faces threats from other kinds of terrorism, such as Northern Ireland-related terrorism.

All terrorist groups try to radicalise and recruit people to their cause. How, where and to what extent they try to do so will vary. Evidence shows that these groups attract very low levels of public support, but people who want to make their home in the UK should be aware of this threat. It is important that all citizens feel safe. This includes feeling safe from all kinds of extremism (vocal or active opposition to fundamental British values), including religious extremism and far-right extremism.

If you think someone is trying to persuade you to join an extremist or terrorist cause, you should notify your local police force.

Check that you understand:

- The difference between civil and criminal law and some examples of each
- The duties of the police
- The possible terrorist threats facing the UK

The role of the courts

THE JUDICIARY

Judges (who are together called 'the judiciary') are responsible for interpreting the law and ensuring that trials are conducted fairly. The government cannot interfere with this.

Sometimes the actions of the government are claimed to be illegal. If the judges agree, then the government must either change its policies or ask Parliament to change the law. If judges find that a public body is not respecting someone's legal rights, they can order that body to change its practices and/or pay compensation.

Judges also make decisions in disputes between members of the public or organisations. These might be about contracts, property or employment rights or after an accident.

CRIMINAL COURTS

There are some differences between the court systems in England and Wales, Scotland and Northern Ireland.

Magistrates' and Justice of the Peace Courts

In England, Wales and Northern Ireland, most minor criminal cases are dealt with in a Magistrates' Court. In Scotland, minor criminal offences go to a Justice of the Peace Court.

Magistrates and Justices of the Peace (JPs) are members of the local community. In England, Wales and Scotland they usually work unpaid and do not need legal qualifications. They receive training to do the job and are supported by a legal adviser. Magistrates decide the verdict in each case that comes before them and, if the person is found guilty, the sentence that they are given. In Northern Ireland, cases are heard by a District Judge or Deputy District Judge, who is legally qualified and paid.

In England, Wales and Northern Ireland, serious offences are tried in front of a judge and a jury in a Crown Court.

Crown Courts and Sheriff Courts

In England, Wales and Northern Ireland, serious offences are tried in front of a judge and a jury in a Crown Court. In Scotland, serious cases are heard in a Sheriff Court with either a sheriff or a sheriff with a jury. The most serious cases in Scotland, such as murder, are heard at a High Court with a judge and jury. A jury is made up of members of the public chosen at random from the local electoral register (see pages 120–1). In England, Wales and Northern Ireland a jury has 12 members, and in Scotland a jury has 15 members. Everyone who is summoned to do jury service must do it unless they are not eligible (for example, because they have a criminal conviction) or they provide a good reason to be excused, such as ill health.

The jury has to listen to the evidence presented at the trial and then decide a verdict of 'guilty' or 'not guilty' based on what they have heard. In Scotland, a third verdict of 'not proven' is also possible. If the jury finds a defendant guilty, the judge decides on the penalty.

The Old Bailey is probably the most famous criminal court in the world

Youth Courts

In England, Wales and Northern Ireland, if an accused person is aged 10 to 17, the case is normally heard in a Youth Court in front of up to three specially trained magistrates or a District Judge. The most serious cases will go to the Crown Court. The parents or carers of the young person are expected to attend the hearing. Members of the public are not allowed in Youth Courts, and the name or photographs of the accused young person cannot be published in newspapers or used by the media.

In Scotland a system called the Children's Hearings System is used to deal with children and young people who have committed an offence.

Northern Ireland has a system of youth conferencing to consider how a child should be dealt with when they have committed an offence.

?

Make sure you understand the differences between criminal and civil law. This includes the types of case each court handles and the differences across the UK.

Criminal Courts

(Scotland only) Most serious offences, such as murder

Scotland: High Court
Cases are heard by judge and jury

Serious offences

England, Wales and Northern Ireland: Crown Court
Trials are before a judge and jury

Scotland: Sheriff Court
Trials are before a sheriff, or a sheriff and jury

Most minor criminal cases

England and Wales: Magistrates' Court
Magistrates are unpaid and do not need legal qualifications

Scotland: Justice of the Peace Court
Justices (JPs) are unpaid and do not need legal qualifications

Northern Ireland: Magistrates' Court
District Judges or Deputy District Judges are legally qualified and paid

Youth Courts

England, Wales and Northern Ireland: Youth Court

- Where accused is aged 10–17
- Cases heard by up to three specially trained magistrates or a District Judge
- Most serious cases go to Crown Court
- Parents/Carers are expected to attend
- Closed courts – public cannot attend and names/photos of accused cannot be used by the media

Scotland: Children's Hearings System is used

Northern Ireland only: Youth conferencing system used to consider punishment/treatment of children

Juries of the UK

England, Wales and Northern Ireland – 12 members
Verdicts 'guilty' or 'not guilty'

Scotland – 15 members
Verdicts 'guilty', 'not guilty' or 'not proven'

CIVIL COURTS

County Courts

County Courts deal with a wide range of civil disputes. These include people trying to get back money that is owed to them, cases involving personal injury, family matters, breaches of contract, and divorce. In Scotland, most of these matters are dealt with in the Sheriff Court. More serious civil cases – for example, when a large amount of compensation is being claimed – are dealt with in the High Court in England, Wales and Northern Ireland. In Scotland, they are dealt with in the Court of Session in Edinburgh.

The small claims procedure is an informal way of helping people to settle minor disputes without spending a lot of time and money using a lawyer.

The small claims procedure

The small claims procedure is an informal way of helping people to settle minor disputes without spending a lot of time and money using a lawyer. This procedure is used for claims of less than £10,000 in England and Wales and £3,000 in Scotland and Northern Ireland*. The hearing is held in front of a judge in an ordinary room, and people from both sides of the dispute sit around a table. Small claims can also be issued online through Money Claims Online (www.moneyclaim.gov.uk).

*For more information see **Clarifications** in Chapter 1 and lifeintheuk.net/clarify

You can get details about the small claims procedure from your local County Court or Sheriff Court. Details of your local court can be found as follows:

- England and Wales: at www.gov.uk
- Scotland: at www.scotcourts.gov.uk
- Northern Ireland: at www.courtsni.gov.uk.

Civil Courts

Serious civil cases, e.g. large compensation claims

England, Wales and Northern Ireland: High Court

Scotland: Court of Session, in Edinburgh

Civil disputes, e.g. personal injury claims, family matters, breaches of contract and divorce

England, Wales and Northern Ireland: County Courts

Scotland: Sheriff Court

Small civil claims

England and Wales: Small claims procedure for anything under £10,000

Scotland and Northern Ireland: Small claims procedure for anything under £3,000

Hearings are with judge and both parties around a table

All UK: Money Claims Online
Online alternative to the small claims procedure

LEGAL ADVICE

Solicitors

Solicitors are trained lawyers who give advice on legal matters, take action for their clients and represent their clients in court.

There are solicitors' offices throughout the UK. It is important to find out which aspects of law a solicitor specialises in and to check that they have the right experience to help you with your case. Many advertise in local newspapers. Citizens Advice (www.citizensadvice.org.uk) can give you names of local solicitors and which areas of law they specialise in. You can also get this information from the Law Society (www.lawsociety.org.uk) in England and Wales, the Law Society of Scotland (www.lawscot.org.uk) or the Law Society of Northern Ireland (www.lawsoc-ni.org). Solicitors' charges are usually based on how much time they spend on a case. It is very important to find out at the start how much a case is likely to cost.

Check that you understand:

- The role of the judiciary
- About the different criminal courts in the UK
- About the different civil courts in the UK
- How you can settle a small claim

Fundamental principles

Britain has a long history of respecting an individual's rights and ensuring essential freedoms. These rights have their roots in the Magna Carta, the Habeas Corpus Act and the Bill of Rights of 1689 (see pages 18, 30 and 33), and they have developed over a period of time. British diplomats and lawyers had an important role in drafting the European Convention on Human Rights and Fundamental Freedoms. The UK was one of the first countries to sign the Convention in 1950.

Some of the principles included in the European Convention on Human Rights are:

- right to life
- prohibition of torture
- prohibition of slavery and forced labour
- right to liberty and security
- right to a fair trial
- freedom of thought, conscience and religion
- freedom of expression (speech).

The Human Rights Act 1998 incorporated the European Convention on Human Rights into UK law. The government, public bodies and the courts must follow the principles of the Convention.

EQUAL OPPORTUNITIES

UK laws ensure that people are not treated unfairly in any area of life or work because of their age, disability, sex, pregnancy and maternity, race, religion or belief, sexuality or marital status. If you face problems with discrimination, you can get more information from Citizens Advice or from one of the following organisations:

- England and Wales: Equality and Human Rights Commission (www.equalityhumanrights.com)
- Scotland: Equality and Human Rights Commission in Scotland (www.equalityhumanrights.com/en/commission-scotland) and Scottish Human Rights Commission (www.scottishhumanrights.com)
- Northern Ireland: Equality Commission for Northern Ireland (www.equalityni.org)
- Northern Ireland Human Rights Commission (www.nihrc.org).

Any man who forces a woman to have sex, including a woman's husband, can be charged with rape.

DOMESTIC VIOLENCE

In the UK, brutality and violence in the home is a serious crime. Anyone who is violent towards their partner – whether they are a man or a woman, married or living together – can be prosecuted. Any man who forces a woman to have sex, including a woman's husband, can be charged with rape.

It is important for anyone facing domestic violence to get help as soon as possible. A solicitor or Citizens Advice can explain the available options. In some areas there are safe places to go and stay in, called refuges or shelters. The 24-hour National Domestic Violence Freephone Helpline is available on 0808 2000 247 at any time, and its voicemail service allows callers to leave a message to be called back. You can find out more by visiting its website on https://www.nationaldahelpline.org.uk/. Alternatively, you can try the Women's Aid website on https://www.womensaid.org.uk. In an emergency, you should always call the police, who can also help you to find a safe place to stay.

FEMALE GENITAL MUTILATION

Female genital mutilation (FGM), also known as cutting or female circumcision, is illegal in the UK. Practising FGM or taking a girl or woman abroad for FGM is a criminal offence.

FORCED MARRIAGE

A marriage should be entered into with the full and free consent of both people involved. Arranged marriages, where both parties agree to the marriage, are acceptable in the UK.

Forced marriage is where one or both parties do not or cannot give their consent to enter into the partnership. Forcing another person to marry is a criminal offence.

Forced Marriage Protection Orders were introduced in 2008 for England, Wales and Northern Ireland under the Forced Marriage (Civil Protection) Act 2007. Court orders can be obtained to protect a person from being forced into a marriage, or to protect a person in a forced marriage. Similar Protection Orders were introduced in Scotland in November 2011.

A potential victim, or someone acting for them, can apply for an order. Anyone found to have breached an order can be jailed for up to two years for contempt of court.

“A marriage should be entered into with the full and free consent of both people involved. Arranged marriages, where both parties agree to the marriage, are acceptable in the UK.”

Taxation

INCOME TAX

People in the UK have to pay tax on their income, which includes:

- wages from paid employment
- profits from self-employment
- taxable benefits
- pensions
- income from property, savings and dividends.

Money raised from income tax pays for government services such as roads, education, police and the armed forces.

For most people, the right amount of income tax is automatically taken from their income from employment by their employer and paid directly to HM Revenue & Customs (HMRC), the government department that collects taxes. This system is called 'Pay As You Earn' (PAYE). If you are self-employed, you need to pay your own tax through a system called 'self-assessment', which includes completing a tax return. Other people may also need to complete a tax return. If HMRC sends you a tax return, it is important to complete and return the form as soon as you have all the necessary information.

You can find out more about income tax at www.gov.uk/income-tax. You can get help and advice about taxes and completing tax forms from the HMRC self-assessment helpline on 0300 200 3310, and by visiting https://www.gov.uk/government/organisations/hm-revenue-customs.

NATIONAL INSURANCE

Almost everybody in the UK who is in paid work, including self-employed people, must pay National Insurance Contributions. The money raised from National Insurance Contributions is used to pay for state benefits and services such as the state retirement pension and the National Health Service (NHS).

“The money raised from National Insurance Contributions is used to pay for state benefits and services such as the state retirement pension and the National Health Service (NHS).”

Employees have their National Insurance Contributions deducted from their pay by their employer. People who are self-employed need to pay National Insurance Contributions themselves.

Anyone who does not pay enough National Insurance Contributions will not be able to receive certain contributory benefits such as Jobseeker's Allowance or a full state retirement pension. Some workers, such as part-time workers, may not qualify for statutory payments such as maternity pay if they do not earn enough.

Further guidance about National Insurance Contributions is available on https://www.gov.uk/national-insurance.

Getting a National Insurance number

A National Insurance number is a unique personal account number. It makes sure that the National Insurance Contributions and tax you pay are properly recorded against your name. All young people in the UK are sent a National Insurance number just before their 16th birthday.

A non-UK national living in the UK and looking for work, starting work or setting up as self-employed will need a National Insurance number. However, you can start work without one. If you have permission to work in the UK, you will need to telephone the National Insurance number application line. After you've applied, you'll get a letter from the Department for Work and Pensions (DWP) asking you to come to a National Insurance number interview at Jobcentre Plus. The letter will also tell you which documents to bring to prove your identity.

You can find out more information about how to apply for a National Insurance number at https://www.gov.uk/apply-national-insurance-number.

Driving

In the UK, you must be at least 17 years old to drive a car or motor cycle and you must have a driving licence to drive on public roads. To get a UK driving licence you must pass a driving test, which tests both your knowledge and your practical skills. You need to be at least 16 years old to ride a moped, and there are other age requirements and special tests for driving large vehicles.

Drivers can use their driving licence until they are 70 years old. After that, the licence is valid for three years at a time.

In Northern Ireland, a newly qualified driver must display an 'R' plate (for restricted driver) for one year after passing the test.

If you have a licence from another country, you may use it in the UK for up to 12 months. To continue driving after that, you must get a UK full driving licence*. To check that you can drive in the UK with a non-GB licence, visit www.gov.uk/driving-nongb-licence.

*For more information see **Clarifications** in Chapter 1 and lifeintheuk.net/clarify

If you are resident in the UK, your car or motor cycle must be registered at the Driver and Vehicle Licensing Agency (DVLA). You must pay an annual vehicle tax, which cannot be passed on when a vehicle changes hands. If the vehicle is parked off the road and not being used, you must tell DVLA by making a Statutory Off Road Notification (SORN). SORN cannot be transferred if the vehicle is sold or given to a new owner. You must also have valid motor insurance. It is a serious criminal offence to drive without insurance. If your vehicle is over three years old, you must take it for a Ministry of Transport (MOT) test every year. It is an offence not to have an MOT certificate if your vehicle is more than three years old. You can find out more about vehicle tax and MOT requirements from www.gov.uk.

Check that you understand:

- The fundamental principles of UK law
- That domestic violence, FGM and forced marriage are illegal in the UK
- The system of income tax and National Insurance
- The requirements for driving a car

Your role in the community

Becoming a British citizen or settling in the UK brings responsibilities but also opportunities. Everyone has the opportunity to participate in their community. This section looks at some of the responsibilities of being a citizen and gives information about how you can help to make your community a better place to live and work.

VALUES AND RESPONSIBILITIES

Although Britain is one of the world's most diverse societies, there is a set of shared values and responsibilities that everyone can agree with. These values and responsibilities include:

- to obey and respect the law
- to be aware of the rights of others and respect those rights
- to treat others with fairness
- to behave responsibly
- to help and protect your family
- to respect and preserve the environment
- to treat everyone equally, regardless of sex, race, religion, age, disability, class or sexual orientation
- to work to provide for yourself and your family
- to help others
- to vote in local and national government elections.

Taking on these values and responsibilities will make it easier for you to become a full and active citizen.

BEING A GOOD NEIGHBOUR

When you move into a new house or apartment, introduce yourself to the people who live near you. Getting to know your neighbours can help you to become part of the community and make friends. Your neighbours are also a good source of help – for example, they may be willing to feed your pets if you are away, or offer advice on local shops and services.

You can help prevent any problems and conflicts with your neighbours by respecting their privacy and limiting how much noise you make. Also try to keep your garden tidy, and only put your refuse bags and bins on the street or in communal areas if they are due to be collected.

GETTING INVOLVED IN LOCAL ACTIVITIES

Volunteering and helping your community are an important part of being a good citizen. They enable you to integrate and get to know other people. It helps to make your community a better place if residents support each other. It also helps you to fulfil your duties as a citizen, such as behaving responsibly and helping others.

“As well as getting the right to vote, people on the electoral register are randomly selected to serve on a jury.”

How you can support your community

There are a number of positive ways in which you can support your community and be a good citizen.

JURY SERVICE

As well as getting the right to vote, people on the electoral register are randomly selected to serve on a jury. Anyone who is on the electoral register and is aged 18 to 70 (18–75 in England and Wales) can be asked to do this.

HELPING IN SCHOOLS

If you have children, there are many ways in which you can help at their schools. Parents can often help in classrooms, by supporting activities or listening to children read.

Many schools organise events to raise money for extra equipment or out-of-school activities. Activities might include book sales, toy sales or bringing food to sell. You might have good ideas of your own for raising money. Sometimes events are organised by parent–teacher associations (PTAs). Volunteering to help with their events or joining the association is a way of doing something good for the school and also making new friends in your local community. You can find out about these opportunities from notices in the school or notes your children bring home.

Parents often help in classrooms, by supporting activities or listening to children read

School governors

School governors are people from the local community who wish to make a positive contribution to children's education. They must be aged 18 or over at the date of their election or appointment. There is no upper age limit.

Governors have an important part to play in raising school standards. They have three key roles:

- setting the strategic direction of the school
- ensuring accountability
- monitoring and evaluating school performance.

You can contact your local school to ask if they need a new governor. In England, you can also apply online at the Governors for Schools website at www.governorsforschools.org.uk.

In England, parents and other community groups can apply to open a free school in their local area. More information about this can be found at https://www.gov.uk/set-up-free-school.

SUPPORTING POLITICAL PARTIES

Political parties welcome new members. Joining one is a way to demonstrate your support for certain views and to get involved in the democratic process.

Political parties are particularly busy at election times. Members work hard to persuade people to vote for their candidates – for instance, by handing out leaflets in the street or by knocking on people's doors and asking for their support. This is called 'canvassing'. You don't have to tell a canvasser how you intend to vote if you don't want to.

> **"Political parties are particularly busy at election times. Members work hard to persuade people to vote for their candidates. This is called 'canvassing'."**

British citizens can stand for office as a local councillor or a member of Parliament (or the devolved equivalents). This is an opportunity to become even more involved in the political life of the UK. You may also be able to stand for office if you are an Irish citizen or an eligible Commonwealth citizen.

You can find out more about joining a political party from the individual party websites.

HELPING WITH LOCAL SERVICES

There are opportunities to volunteer with a wide range of local service providers, including local hospitals and youth projects. Services often want to involve local people in decisions about the way in which they work. Universities, housing associations, museums and arts councils may advertise for people to serve as volunteers in their governing bodies.

You can volunteer with the police, and become a special constable or a lay (non-police) representative. You can also apply to become a magistrate. You will often find advertisements for vacancies in your local newspaper or on local radio. You can also find out more about these sorts of roles at www.gov.uk.

BLOOD AND ORGAN DONATION

Donated blood is used by hospitals to help people with a wide range of injuries and illnesses. Giving blood only takes about an hour to do. You can register to give blood at:

- England and North Wales: www.blood.co.uk
- Rest of Wales: www.welsh-blood.org.uk
- Scotland: www.scotblood.co.uk
- Northern Ireland: https://nibts.hscni.net

Many people in the UK are waiting for organ transplants. If you register to be an organ donor, it can make it easier for your family to decide whether to donate your organs when you die. You can register to be an organ donor at www.organdonation.nhs.uk.* Living people can also donate a kidney.

Some volunteer activities will give you a chance to practise your English or develop work skills that will help you find a job or improve your curriculum vitae (CV).

OTHER WAYS TO VOLUNTEER

Volunteering is working for good causes without payment. There are many benefits to volunteering, such as meeting new people and helping make your community a better place. Some volunteer activities will give you a chance to practise your English or develop work skills that will help you find a job or improve your curriculum vitae (CV). Many people volunteer simply because they want to help other people.

Activities you can do as a volunteer include:

- working with animals – for example, caring for animals at a local rescue shelter
- youth work – for example, volunteering at a youth group
- helping improve the environment – for example, participating in a litter pick-up in the local area
- working with the homeless in, for example, a homelessness shelter
- mentoring – for example, supporting someone who has just come out of prison
- work in health and hospitals – for example, working on an information desk in a hospital
- helping older people at, for example, a residential care home.

Voluntary organisations work to improve the lives of people, animals and the environment in many different ways

There are thousands of active charities and voluntary organisations in the UK. They work to improve the lives of people, animals and the environment in many different ways. They range from the British branches of international organisations, such as the British Red Cross, to small local charities working in particular areas. They include charities working with older people (such as Age UK), with children (for example, the National Society for the Prevention of Cruelty to Children (NSPCC)), and with the homeless (for example, Crisis and Shelter). There are also medical research charities (for example, Cancer Research UK), environmental charities (including the National Trust and Friends of the Earth) and charities working with animals (such as the People's Dispensary for Sick Animals (PDSA)).

Volunteers are needed to help with their activities and to raise money. The charities often advertise in local newspapers, and most have websites that include information about their opportunities. You can also get information about volunteering for different organisations from https://do-it.org

There are many opportunities for younger people to volunteer and receive accreditation which will help them to develop their skills. These include the National Citizen Service programme, which gives 16- and 17-year-olds the opportunity to enjoy outdoor activities, develop their skills and take part in a community project. You can find out more about these opportunities as follows:

It is important to recycle as much of your waste as you can. Using recycled materials to make new products uses less energy and means that we do not need to extract more raw materials from the earth.

- National Citizen Service: at https://wearencs.com
- England: at www.vinspired.com
- Wales: at https://volunteering-wales.net/vk/volunteers/index.htm
- Scotland: at www.volunteerscotland.net
- Northern Ireland: at www.volunteernow.co.uk.

Looking after the environment

It is important to recycle as much of your waste as you can. Using recycled materials to make new products uses less energy and means that we do not need to extract more raw materials from the earth. It also means that less rubbish is created, so the amount being put into landfill is reduced.

You can learn more about recycling and its benefits at www.recyclenow.com. At this website you can also find out what you can recycle at home and in the local area if you live in England. This information is available for Wales at www.wasteawarenesswales.org.uk*, for Scotland at wasteless.zerowastescotland.org.uk and for Northern Ireland from your local authority.

*For more information see **Clarifications** in Chapter 1 and lifeintheuk.net/clarify

A good way to support your local community is to shop for products locally where you can. This will help businesses and farmers in your area and in Britain. It will also reduce your carbon footprint, because the products you buy will not have had to travel as far.

Walking and using public transport to get around when you can is also a good way to protect the environment. It means that you create less pollution than when you use a car.

Check that you understand:

- The different ways you can help at your child's school
- The role of school governors and how you can become one
- The role of members of political parties
- The different local services people can volunteer to support
- How to donate blood and organs
- The benefits of volunteering for you, other people and the community
- The types of activities that volunteers can do
- How you can look after the environment

CHAPTER 7
Appendices

→ IN THIS CHAPTER you will find a glossary of words and terms used throughout the earlier chapters. You need to read through all of the listed terms and be sure that you understand all of them. Each word or phrase is fully explained in easy-to-understand language.

You will also find some useful summaries of the dates and events listed in the main chapters. These lists summarise sections of the key information but they do not give you every date or event featured in the chapters. They should be used to aid your studies and not as an alternative for studying the chapters.

IN THIS CHAPTER THERE IS:

- A glossary of key terms
- Key dates in the calendar
- A timeline of key legislation
- A timeline of key dates in how the UK is governed
- A timeline of key battles and wars

7

Glossary

This glossary will help you understand the meaning of key terms which appear in the study materials. Where words may be difficult to understand, an example of their use may follow the definition.

The word that is bracketed after an entry relates to the particular context in which the word is being defined – for example, arrested (police). A slash (/) separates different definitions.

AD	Anno Domini – referring to the number of years after the birth of Jesus Christ – used as a time reference
allegiance	Loyalty to something – for example, to a leader, a faith or a country
annexed	Joined
architect	Someone who designs buildings
armed forces	The army, navy and air force which defend a country in times of peace and war
arrested (police)	Taken by the police to a police station and made to stay there to answer questions about illegal actions or activity
arson	The criminal act of deliberately setting fire to a building
assault	The criminal act of using physical force against someone or of attacking someone – for example, hitting someone
bank holiday	A day when most people have an official day off work and many businesses are closed. A bank holiday can also be called a public holiday
baron	A man who has one of the ranks of the British **nobility**. The title was particularly common during the **Middle Ages**
BC	Before Christ – referring to the number of years before Jesus Christ was born – used as a time reference
bishop	A senior member of the clergy in the Christian religion, often in charge of the churches in a particular area
boom	A sharp rise in something – very often in business activity or the economy
brutality	Behaviour towards another which is cruel and violent and causes harm

by-election	An election held in a parliamentary **constituency** or local authority area to fill a vacancy (see also **General Election**)
cabinet (government)	A group of senior ministers who are responsible for controlling government policy
casualties (medical)	People who are wounded or killed (for example, in a war)
cathedral	The most important church in an area
charter (government)	An official written statement which describes the rights and responsibilities of a state and its citizens
chieftain	The leader of a **clan** in Scotland or Ireland
civil disobedience	The refusal of members of the public to obey laws, often because they want to protest about political issues
civil law	The legal system that deals with disputes between people or groups of people
civil service	The departments within the government which manage the business of running the country – people who work for the government can be called civil servants
civil war	A war between groups who live in the same country
clan	A group of people or families who live under the rule of a **chieftain** and may be descendants of the same person – a term used traditionally in Scotland
clergy	Religious leaders, used here to describe religious leaders in Christian churches
coalition	A partnership between different political parties
colonise	Inhabit and take control of another country. People who colonise are called colonists
commemorate	Show that something or someone is remembered
composer	Someone who writes music
conquered	Beaten in battle
constituency	A specific area where the voters who live in that place (its constituents) can elect an MP to represent them in Parliament
constitution (law)	The legal structure of established laws and principles which is used to govern a country
convention (government)	An agreement, often between countries, about particular rules or codes of behaviour
criminal law	The legal system that deals with illegal activities

decree (law)	Official order, law or decision
democratic country	A country which is governed by people who are elected by the population to represent them in Parliament
devolution	The passing of power from a central government to another group at a regional or local level, which can then be called a devolved administration
dialect	A form of a language spoken by a particular group or people living in a particular area
domestic policies	Political decisions that relate to what is happening within a country (as opposed to in another country)
electoral register	The official list of all the people in a country who are allowed to vote in an election
electorate	All the people who are allowed to vote in an election
eligible	Allowed by law
ethnic origin	The country of birth, someone's race or the nationality of someone when they were born/the customs and place from which a person and their family originated (or came from)
executed	Killed as a punishment
first past the post	A system of election in which the candidate with the largest number of votes in a particular **constituency** wins a seat in Parliament
franchise	The right to vote
General Election	An event in which all the citizens of a country who are allowed to vote choose the people they wish to represent them in their government
gothic	A style of art or architecture that developed in the Middle Ages
government policies	Official ideas and beliefs that are agreed by a political party about how to govern the country
guilty	Found by a court to have done something which is illegal
heir	Someone who will legally receive a person's money or possessions after their death. The heir to the throne is the person who will become the next king or queen
House (history)	A family (for example, House of York)
household	A home and the people who live in it/something that relates to a home. (For example, household chores are tasks that are done around the house, such as cleaning and cooking)

House of Commons	That part of the **Houses of Parliament** where MPs who are elected by the voting public debate political issues
House of Lords	That part of the **Houses of Parliament** where people who have inherited their place or been chosen by the government debate political issues
Houses of Parliament	The building in London where the **House of Commons** and **House of Lords** meet
illegal	Something which the law does not allow
infrastructure	Structured network that is necessary for successful operation of a business or transport system – for example, roads or railways
innocent (law)	Found by a court not to have done something illegal
judge	The most important official in court. The judge makes sure what happens in court is fair and legal
judiciary	All the **judges** in a country. Together, they are responsible for using the law of the land in the correct way
jury (legal)	People who are chosen to sit in court, listen to information about a crime, and decide if someone is guilty or innocent
legal	Allowed by law
legislative power	The power to make laws
liberty	Freedom
magistrate	A person who acts as a **judge** in a court case where the alleged crime is not a serious one
marital status	Information about whether a person is single, married, separated or divorced. This is often asked for on official forms
media, the	All the organisations which give information to the public, i.e. newspapers, magazines, television, radio and the internet
Middle Ages (medieval period)	In history, the period between 1066 and about 1500
missionary	Someone who travels to teach about a religion
monarch	The king or queen of a country
national issues	Political problems that can affect everyone who lives in a country
nationalised	Bought and then controlled by central government – relating to an industry or service that was previously owned privately
nobility	The people in a country who belong to the highest social class, some of whom may have titles – for example, Lord, Duke, Baron

office, to be in	To be in power in government
Olympics	International sporting event held every four years
opposition	In the **House of Commons**, the largest political party which is not part of the government is officially known as the opposition
oratorio	A piece of music for an orchestra (musicians) and singers, often about a religious idea
Pale (history)	Part of Ireland once governed by England
party politics	The shared ideas and beliefs of an organised group of politicians
patron saint	A Christian saint who is believed to protect a particular area or group of people
penalty (law)	Punishment for breaking the law
plague	A very serious, infectious disease
Pope, the	The head of the Roman Catholic Church
portrait	A picture of a person
practise a religion	Live according to the rules and beliefs of a religion
Presbyterian	The main Protestant Church in Scotland
Prime Minister	The politician who leads the government
prohibit/ prohibition	Make something illegal
proportional representation	A system of election in which political parties are allowed a number of seats in Parliament that represents their share of the total number of votes cast
Protestants	Christians who are not members of the Roman Catholic Church
public body	A governmental department or a group of people who represent or work for the government and who work for the good of the general public
public house/ pub	A place where adults can buy and drink alcohol
Quakers	A Protestant religious group
rebellion	Organised fighting against a government
Reformation, the	The religious movement in the 16th century that challenged the authority of the **Pope** and established **Protestant** churches in Europe

refugee	A person who must leave the country where they live, often because of a war or for political reasons
residence	The place where someone lives
rival viewpoints	Opinions held by different groups of people
rural	Countryside
scrutinise	Examine all the details
seat (Parliament)	A **constituency**
sentence	A punishment imposed by a court
shadow cabinet	Senior opposition (see above) MPs who challenge the government and put forward alternative policies
sheriff (law)	A **judge** in Scotland
slavery	A system in which people bought and sold other people (slaves) who were forced to work without pay
sonnet	A poem which is 14 lines long and rhymes in a particular way
Speaker, the	The member of the **House of Commons** who controls the way issues are debated in Parliament
stand for office	Apply to be elected – for example, as an MP or councillor
strike, to go on	Refuse to work in order to protest against something
successor (government)	A person who comes after another and takes over an office or receives some kind of power – for example, a son who becomes king when his father dies is his successor
suspend	To stop something from happening or operating, usually for a short time
terrorism	Violence used by people who want to force a government to do something. The violence is usually random and unexpected, so that no one can feel really safe from it
The Phone Book	A book which contains names, addresses and phone numbers of organisations, businesses and individuals
theft	The criminal act of stealing something from a person, building or place
trade union	An association of workers formed to protect its members
treaty	An official written agreement between countries or governments
uprising	A violent revolt or rebellion against an authority
voluntary work	Work which someone does because they want to and which they do for free, i.e. they do not receive any payment

volunteer	Someone who works for free or who offers to do something without payment (see **voluntary work**)
war effort	The work people did in order to help the country in any way they could during wartime

Dates in the calendar

This page lists all the key dates of the British calendar that are mentioned in the official study materials.

1 January	New Year's Day	page 72
14 February	Valentine's Day	page 72
1 March	St David's Day	page 68
17 March	St Patrick's Day	page 68
1 April	April Fool's Day	page 72
14 April	Vaisakhi (also Baisakhi)	page 71
23 April	St George's Day	page 68
31 October	Halloween	page 72
5 November	Bonfire Night	page 72
11 November	Remembrance Day	page 72
30 November	St Andrew's Day	page 68
24 December	Christmas Eve	page 69
25 December	Christmas Day	page 69
26 December	Boxing Day	page 72
31 December	New Year's Eve / Hogmanay	page 72

Up to the Norman Conquest

Pages 12–16

This table lists the key events that happened up to and including the Norman Conquest.

Period	Monarch	Year	What?
Stone Age		6,000 years ago	First farmers arrive in Britain
Roman Empire		55 BC	Julius Caesar unsuccessfully invades Britain
		AD 43	Emperor Claudius successfully invades Britain
		3rd–4th centuries	Christian communities appear in Britain
		410	The Roman army leaves Britain
Anglo-Saxon		600	Anglo-Saxon kingdoms are established in Britain
		789	The Vikings first visit Britain
Norman Conquest	William I	1066	William the Conqueror, Duke of Normandy, becomes King William I of England after defeating Harold, the Saxon King of England, at the Battle of Hastings
			Westminster Abbey first used as coronation church

The Middle Ages (1066–1485)

Pages 17–21

The Middle Ages cover the time after the Norman Conquest until the Wars of the Roses.

Century	Monarch	Year	What?
13th	John	1215	Magna Carta introduced during King John's rule
	Edward I	1284	Edward I of England introduces Statute of Rhuddlan, annexing Wales to the Crown of England
14th		1314	The Scottish, led by Robert the Bruce, defeat the English at the Battle of Bannockburn
15th		By 1400	In England, official documents are written in English and English becomes the preferred language of the royal court and Parliament
	Henry V	1415	The Battle of Agincourt, the most famous battle of the Hundred Years War, sees King Henry V's vastly outnumbered army beat the French
		Mid-15th century	Last Welsh rebellions are defeated. English law and language are introduced in Wales
		1450	English leave France
		1455	The Wars of the Roses start between the Houses of Lancaster and York over who should be king of England
		1485	The Wars of the Roses end with the Battle of Bosworth Field. King Richard III of the House of York is killed and Henry Tudor of the House of Lancaster becomes Henry VII

The Reformation to the Glorious Revolution

Pages 22–33

This period was marked by series of major changes to British society. The Reformation changed religious practices in the country. Tensions between Parliament and the king resulted in the English Civil War. This ultimately led to the Restoration and a new balance of power between royalty and Parliament.

Period	Monarch	Year	What?
The Reformation	Henry VIII	21 Apr 1509	Henry VIII becomes king
		1530s	The Reformation in England and Wales leads to the formation of the Protestant Church
		28 Jan 1547	Henry VIII dies and Edward VI, a Protestant, becomes king
	Edward VI / Bloody Mary	1553	Edward VI dies at the age of 15, having ruled for six years. 'Bloody' Mary, a Catholic, becomes Queen
	Elizabeth I	1560	The Reformation in Scotland. The predominantly Protestant Scottish Parliament abolishes the authority of the Pope and Roman Catholic services become illegal
Elizabethan		1588	Elizabeth I defeats the Spanish Armada, which had been sent to restore Catholicism to England
		1603	Elizabeth I dies. James I of England, Wales and Ireland and VI of Scotland, Elizabeth's cousin, becomes king
English Civil War	Charles I	1640	Charles I tries to introduce a revised Prayer Book in Scotland, causing rebellion. He recalls Parliament to try and raise money for an army to repel the Scots. The Protestant and Puritan Parliament refuse to give Charles the money, even after the Scottish invade
		1641	Revolt begins in Ireland, where there is a Royalist army. Cromwell eventually subdues the revolt with great violence, still remembered today

Period	Monarch	Year	What?
English Civil War	Charles I	1642	Civil war begins between Royalist Cavaliers loyal to Charles I and Parliamentarian Roundheads
		1646	The Roundheads defeat Charles I's army at the Battles of Marston Moor and Naseby and take him prisoner
		1649	Charles I, who is unwilling to reach agreement with Parliament, is executed
	Cromwell	1658	Lord Protector Oliver Cromwell dies
			His son, Richard Cromwell, becomes Lord Protector
The Restoration	Charles II	1 May 1660	Charles II is invited back from exile in the Netherlands
		1679	The Habeas Corpus Act becomes law
		1685	Charles II dies with no legitimate heir. His Catholic brother, James II of England, Wales and Ireland and James VII of Scotland, becomes king
The Glorious Revolution	William III	1688	William of Orange is asked to invade by important Protestants. This is the Glorious Revolution because it is non-violent. He becomes William III of England, Wales and Ireland and William II of Scotland and rules jointly with Mary, James II's elder daughter
		1689	The Bill of Rights becomes law, meaning that the monarch must now be Protestant and ask Parliament for funding for the army and navy every year. Parliament now has to be elected every three years
		1690	William II/III defeats James II, brother of Charles II, at Battle of the Boyne in Ireland. James flees back to France

The 18th and 19th centuries

Pages 34–46

This period is marked by major economic change in Britain. The growth of industry changed how people worked and also how and where they lived. This is also a period that saw the growth of the British Empire around the world.

Period	Monarch	Year	What?
The Enlightenment	Anne	1707	The Act of Union 1707, known as the Treaty of Union in Scotland, creates Great Britain, the union of England, Wales and Scotland
		1714	Queen Anne dies
	George I	1714	George I (a German Protestant) becomes king
	George II	1745	Charles Edward Stuart (Bonnie Prince Charlie), grandson of James II, lands in Scotland to try and usurp George II
		1746	Bonnie Prince Charlie is defeated by George II at the Battle of Culloden. Charles escapes back to Europe
The Industrial Revolution		1776	13 American colonies declare independence, leading to the American War of Independence between the colonial and British forces
		1783	The American colonial forces defeat the British army and the independence of the colonies is recognised
		1789	Following a revolution in France, the new government declares war on Britain. Napoleon later becomes Emperor of France and continues the war
		1801	The Act of Union 1800 unifies Ireland with England, Scotland and Wales
		21 Oct 1805	The British navy, lead by Admiral Nelson, defeats the combined Spanish and French fleets at the Battle of Trafalgar. Nelson is killed in battle

Period	Monarch	Year	What?
The Industrial Revolution		1807	It becomes illegal to trade slaves in British ships or from British ports
		1815	The French Wars end with the defeat of Emperor Napoleon by the Duke of Wellington at Waterloo
		1832	The first Reform Act grants many more people the right to vote and abolishes both rotten and pocket boroughs
		1833	The Emancipation Act abolishes slavery throughout the Empire. Two million Indian and Chinese workers are employed to replace the freed slaves
The Victorian Age and the Industrial Revolution	Victoria	1837	Victoria becomes Queen at the age of 18
		1846	The Corn Laws are repealed, allowing the import of cheap grain
		1847	Working limits for women and children are introduced at 10 hours a day
		1853–1856	The Crimean War is fought with Turkey and France against Russia
		1867	The second Reform Act creates more urban seats in Parliament and reduces the amount of property people must own in order to vote
		1870	An Act of Parliament allows women to keep their earnings, property and money when they get married

Period	Monarch	Year	What?
The Victorian Age and the Industrial Revolution	Victoria	1882	An Act of Parliament gives women the right to keep their own earnings and property
		1899–1902	The Boer War is fought against Dutch settlers in South Africa. The war raises public sympathy for the Boers and leads to questioning of the Empire's role
		1901	Victoria dies after almost 64 years on the throne

The 20th century to the present day

Pages 46–60

The study materials break the 20th century down into several sections. These are the First World War, the inter-war period, the Second World War, and then the decades that make up post-war Britain, such as the 'Swinging Sixties'.

Period	Prime Minister	Year	What?
		1913	The Home Rule Bill is introduced in Parliament proposing a self-governing Ireland with its own parliament
First World War		1914–1918	World War One (WW1)
		28 Jun 1914	Archduke Franz Ferdinand of Austria is assassinated, setting off a chain of events which leads to WWI
		1 Jul 1916	A British attack, known as the Battle of the Somme, results in 60,000 British casualties on the first day alone
		1916	Irish nationalists revolt against delays in the implementation of Home Rule for Ireland. Leaders of the failed revolt, which was known as the Easter Rising, are executed under martial law
		1918	Women over the age of 30 are given the right to vote and stand for Parliament
		11 Nov 1918	WW1 ends at 11.00 am
Inter-war period		1921	Following a guerrilla war against the police and British army in Ireland, a peace treaty is signed with Irish nationalists
		1922	Ireland is separated into two countries. The six mainly Protestant counties in the north remain part of the UK as Northern Ireland. The rest of Ireland becomes the Irish Free State. A Northern Ireland Parliament is established
		1928	Women are given the right to vote at 21, the same age as men

Period	Prime Minister	Year	What?
Inter-war period		1933	Adolf Hitler comes to power in Germany
Second World War		1939	Hitler invades Poland. Britain and France declare war on Germany in response to this aggression
	Winston Churchill	1 May 1940	Winston Churchill becomes Prime Minister
		1940	German forces defeat allied troops and advance through France
		Summer 1940	The Royal Air Force wins the crucial air battle, the Battle of Britain, against the German air force
		June 1940–June 1941	Until German invasion of Soviet Union in June 1941, Britain and the Empire stand alone against Nazi Germany
		1941	The Social Insurance and Allied Services report (the Beveridge Report) is commissioned
		Dec 1941	Japan bombs US naval harbour, Pearl Harbor, and the US enters World War Two
		1942	The Social Insurance and Allied Services report (the Beveridge Report) is published by William Beveridge
		1944	R A Butler oversees introduction of the Education Act 1944 (often called 'The Butler Act') introducing free secondary education in England and Wales and creating primary and secondary stages of education
		6 Jun 1944	Allied forces land in Normandy. This is known as D-Day
		May 1945	The Allies comprehensively defeat Germany
		Aug 1945	The US drops atomic bombs on Hiroshima and Nagasaki. Japan surrenders

Period	Prime Minister	Year	What?
Post-war Britain	Clement Attlee	1945	Clement Attlee becomes Prime Minister of a Labour government after Winston Churchill loses the General Election
		1947	Independence is granted to nine colonies of the Empire including India, Pakistan and Ceylon (now Sri Lanka)
		1947–1967	Other colonies of the Empire in the Caribbean and Pacific achieve independence
		1948	Aneurin (Nye) Bevan, then Minister for Health, leads establishment of the NHS
		1949	Irish Free State becomes a republic
		1950	UK is one of the first countries to sign the European Convention on Human Rights and Fundamental Freedoms
		1951	Winston Churchill returns as Prime Minister after defeating Clement Attlee
		1951–1964	There is a Conservative government in the UK
		1952	Elizabeth II becomes queen
		25 Mar 1957	Belgium, France, Germany, Italy, Luxembourg and the Netherlands sign the Treaty of Rome, forming the EEC
		1958	The Prime Minister is given the power to nominate life peers
'Swinging Sixties'		1960s	Strict new immigration rules require immigrants to have a connection to the UK through birth or ancestry. This leads to a fall in the numbers of immigrants coming from West Indies, India, Pakistan and what is now Bangladesh
		1964	Winston Churchill stands down as an MP at the General Election
		1969	The voting age is reduced to 18 for men and women

Period	Prime Minister	Year	What?
1970s and The Troubles		1969	The Troubles, a conflict between those wishing for full Irish independence and those wishing to remain part of the UK, begin in Northern Ireland
		1970s	There is serious unrest in Northern Ireland, including terror campaigns
		1972	The Northern Ireland Parliament is abolished
		1973	The UK joins the EEC
Conservative government	Margaret Thatcher	1979	Margaret Thatcher, a Conservative MP, becomes Prime Minister
		1979–1990	Thatcher's Conservative government leads the UK
		1982	Argentina invades the Falkland Islands, a British overseas territory in the South Atlantic. A naval task force is sent from the UK, which recovers the islands
	John Major	1990s	The UK plays a leading role in coalition forces during liberation of Kuwait following the Iraqi invasion in 1990 and the conflict in the Former Republic of Yugoslavia
Labour government	Tony Blair	1997	Tony Blair, a Labour MP, is elected as Prime Minister
		1997	Some powers are devolved from central government to give people in Wales, Scotland and Northern Ireland more control over domestic matters
		1998	The Belfast (or Good Friday) Agreement is signed in Northern Ireland, leading to the establishment of the Northern Ireland Assembly
		1998	The Human Rights Act incorporates the European Convention on Human Rights and Fundamental Freedoms into UK law
		1999	The first Northern Ireland Assembly is elected

Period	Prime Minister	Year	What?
Labour government	Tony Blair	1999	The Welsh Assembly (Senedd) and Scottish Government are formed
		1999	Hereditary peers lose the automatic right to attend the House of Lords. They now elect a few of their number to represent them in the Lords
		Since 2000	British forces are engaged in a global fight against terrorism and the proliferation of weapons of mass destruction, including operations in Afghanistan and Iraq
		2002–2007	The Northern Ireland Assembly is suspended
	Gordon Brown	2007	Gordon Brown, a Labour MP, becomes Prime Minister
		2008	Forced Marriage Protection Orders are introduced in England, Wales and Northern Ireland, allowing the courts to issue orders to protect a person from being forced into a marriage, or a person in a forced marriage
		2009	British combat troops leave Iraq
Coalition government	David Cameron	1 May 2010	The first coalition government since Feb 1974 is elected. David Cameron, a Conservative MP, becomes Prime Minister
		2011	Forced Marriage Protection Orders are introduced in Scotland
		2011	The Senedd gets powers to pass laws on education & training, health & social services, economic development and housing
		Nov 2012	The first Police and Crime Commissioners (PCCs) are elected in England and Wales
		2012	Elizabeth II celebrates her Diamond Jubilee (60 years on the throne)
		2014	Afghanistan has full security responsibility in all of its provinces

Period	Prime Minister	Year	What?
Conservative government	David Cameron	7 May 2015	The Conservative party wins a majority at the General Election. David Cameron remains Prime Minister
		23 June 2016	The UK votes to leave the European Union in a referendum
	Theresa May	13 July 2016	Theresa May succeeds David Cameron as Prime Minister
	Boris Johnson	24 July 2019	Boris Johnson succeeds Theresa May as Prime Minister
		31 January 2020	The UK formally leaves the European Union

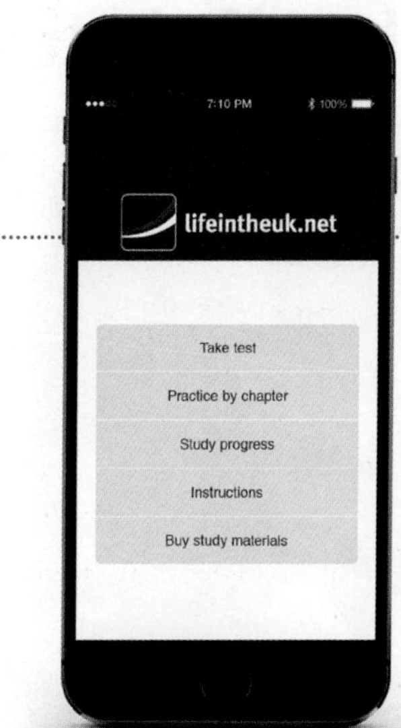

Get the BritTest app

Take practice tests wherever you go with hundreds of questions and randomised practice tests in your hand.

The essential revision aid for anyone on the move. Find out more at **www.lifeintheuk.net/app.**

Power and Society in the GDR, 1961–1979

The 'Normalisation of Rule'?

edited by
Mary Fulbrook

Berghahn Books
New York • Oxford

First edition published in 2009 by

Berghahn Books
www.berghahnbooks.com

Library of Congress Cataloging-in-Publication Data

Power and society in the GDR, 1961-1979 : The "normalisation of rule"? / edited by Mary Fulbrook.
p. cm.
Includes bibliographical references and index.
ISBN 978-1-84545-435-7 (hbk. : alk. paper)
1. Germany (East)–Social life and customs. 2. Germany (East)–Social conditions. 3. Social norms. 4. Social stability–Germany (East) 5. Power (Social sciences)–Germany (East) 6. Popular culture–Germany (East) 7. Political culture–Germany (East) 8. Germany (East)–Politics and government. 9. Germany (East)–Social policy. 10. Socialism–Germany (East) I. Fulbrook, Mary, 1951– II. Title: Power and society in the German Democratic Republic, 1961–1979.
DD288.P69 2009
943'.10875–dc22 2008053751

British Library Cataloguing in Publication Data

A catalogue record for this book is available from the British Library

Printed in the United States on acid-free paper

ISBN-13: 978-1-84545-435-7 hardback

Contents

Abbreviations

BGW	Berlin electric light bulb factory *(Berliner Glühlampenwerk)*
CFW	Synthetic materials production factory, Premnitz *(Chemiefaserwerk Premnitz)*
DFD	Democratic Women's League of Germany *(Demokratischer Frauenbund Deutschlands)*
DTSB	German League of Sport and Gymnastics *(Deutscher Turn- und Sportbund)*
ESP	Introduction to socialist production *(Einführung in die sozialistische Produktion)*
EVW	Oil refinery, Schwedt *(Erdölverarbeitungswerk Schwedt)*
FDGB	Free German Trade Unions League *(Freier Deutscher Gerwerkschaftsbund)*
FDJ	Free German Youth organisation *(Freie Deutsche Jugend)*
FES	Recreational and leisure sports *(Freizeit- und Erholungssport)*
GDR	German Democratic Republic (*DDR- Deutsche Demokratische Republik)*
GST	Society for Sport and Technology *(Gesellschaft für Sport und Technik)*
HFO	Semi-conductor plant (*Halbleiterwerk)* in Frankfurt/Oder
HSSG	Sports community of an educational institution (*Hochschulsportgemeinschaft)*
IM	Unofficial collaborator or informer for the Stasi (*inoffizielle Mitarbeiter)*
KLR	District economic council (*Kreislandwirtschaftsrat)*
KOG	Cooperative community (*Kooperationsgemeinschaft)*
KOR	Cooperative council (*Kooperationsrat)*
LDPD	Liberal Democratic Party of Germany *(Liberal-Demokratische Partei Deutschlands)*
LPG	Collective farm (*Landwirtschaftliche Produktionsgenossenschaft)*
MfS	Ministry for State Security (*Ministerium für Staatssicherheit,* or *Stasi*)

MfV	Ministry for People's Education *(Ministerium für Volksbildung)*
MTS	Machine and tractor lending station (*Maschinen-Traktoren-Station)*
NES	New Economic System (of Planning and Management) (*NÖS(PL), Neues ökonomisches System (der Planung und Leitung))*
NVA	National People's Army *(Nationale Volksarmee)*
OdF	Victims of fascism *(Opfer des Faschismus*)
PA	Productive work (*Produktive Arbeit)*
SBZ	Soviet Occupation Zone *(Sowjetische Besatzungszone*)
SPK	State Planning Commission (*Staatliche Plankommission)*
ThHStAW	Thuringian Principal State Archive, Weimar (*Thüringisches Hauptstaatsarchiv Weimar)*
TRO	Transformer production factory, Berlin (*Transformatorenwerk)*
TZ	Technical drawing (*Technisches Zeichnen)*
UTP	Educational 'Day in Production', or regular school-linked work experience *(Unterrichtstag in der Produktion)*
VdgB	Farmers' Mutual Assistance Association *(Verein der gegenseitigen Bauernhilfe)*
VEB	People's Own Factory *(Volkseigener Betrieb*)
VVB	Combine of People's Own Factories (*Vereinigung Volkseigener Betriebe)*
VWR	Peoples' Economic Council *(Volkswirtschaftsrat)*
WKU	Military education in schools (*Wehrkundeunterricht)*
WPA	Applied scientific work *(Wissenschaftlich-praktische Arbeit*)
ZIJ	Central Institute for Youth Research *(Zentralinstitut für Jugendforschung*)

Chapter 1

The Concept of 'Normalisation' and the GDR in Comparative Perspective

Mary Fulbrook

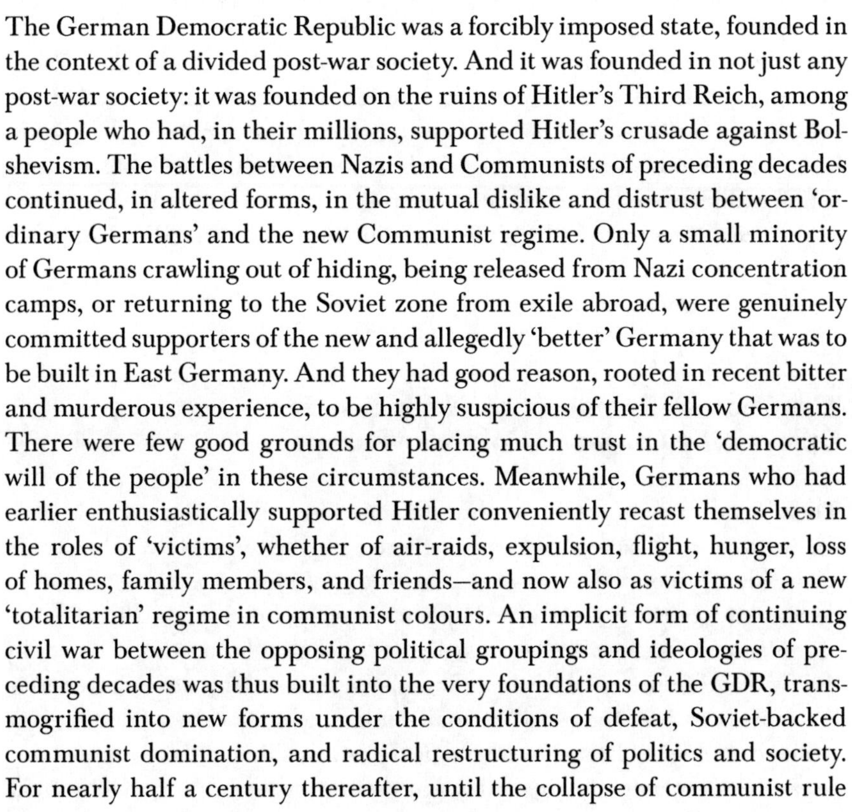

The German Democratic Republic was a forcibly imposed state, founded in the context of a divided post-war society. And it was founded in not just any post-war society: it was founded on the ruins of Hitler's Third Reich, among a people who had, in their millions, supported Hitler's crusade against Bolshevism. The battles between Nazis and Communists of preceding decades continued, in altered forms, in the mutual dislike and distrust between 'ordinary Germans' and the new Communist regime. Only a small minority of Germans crawling out of hiding, being released from Nazi concentration camps, or returning to the Soviet zone from exile abroad, were genuinely committed supporters of the new and allegedly 'better' Germany that was to be built in East Germany. And they had good reason, rooted in recent bitter and murderous experience, to be highly suspicious of their fellow Germans. There were few good grounds for placing much trust in the 'democratic will of the people' in these circumstances. Meanwhile, Germans who had earlier enthusiastically supported Hitler conveniently recast themselves in the roles of 'victims', whether of air-raids, expulsion, flight, hunger, loss of homes, family members, and friends–and now also as victims of a new 'totalitarian' regime in communist colours. An implicit form of continuing civil war between the opposing political groupings and ideologies of preceding decades was thus built into the very foundations of the GDR, transmogrified into new forms under the conditions of defeat, Soviet-backed communist domination, and radical restructuring of politics and society. For nearly half a century thereafter, until the collapse of communist rule in the GDR and the more general implosion of the Soviet bloc in 1989–90, force was an ever-present factor in East German politics; visibly manifest in the highly fortified inner-German border holding East Germans effectively prisoners within their state, less visibly but no less inhumanely in the ubiquitous surveillance measures and malign interventions on the part of the State Security Service or *Staatssicherheitsdienst*, widely known as the *Stasi*. Until the building of the Berlin Wall in August 1961, around three million citizens took the opportunity to flee to what they hoped would be a better life in the west; and once the Iron Curtain began to crumble in the summer of 1989, mass exodus precipitated the final challenge to communist rule in the GDR.

How then, in this context, could one possibly want to apply any concept of 'normalisation' to the history of the GDR?

In this chapter, I shall first outline the way in which this highly contested concept has in fact been widely deployed to analyse periods variously designated by ruling elites and/or by members of the population as a 'return to normal' after periods of crisis, with respect both to post-war western European democratic states (notably West Germany in the 1950s) and eastern European communist states following the forcible suppression of challenges to Soviet domination (notably Poland, Hungary, and Czechoslovakia). I shall then go on to propose a more abstract notion of normalisation as a theoretical concept or 'ideal type', which can in principle be applied widely across historical periods and places, and which serves to link the levels of structure, action, subjective experience, and perceptions framed within the discourses of the time. Finally, I shall seek to place the history of the GDR within the broader comparative framework of both eastern and western Europe in the light of this conceptual approach.

The Contested Concept of 'Normalisation': Contrasting Usages in Cold War Europe

There is in many quarters an almost immediate reaction of outrage when the word 'normalisation' comes anywhere near the term 'GDR'. How could an artificially created rump state, lacking any kind of either national or democratic legitimacy, sustained by Soviet occupation and the threat or use of indigenous force, with a supposedly terrified population watched over by the *Stasi* and imprisoned by the infamous Wall, be in any way referred to in the same breath as the word 'normal'—unless, of course, by some unreconstructed apologist blinded by ideological brainwashing and communist propaganda? Conveniently forgetting that there is no such thing as a 'normal' state—the notion of the modern democratic nation state which implicitly underlies this reaction of outrage is itself, we have to remember, a fragile and recent invention and in a tiny minority in any kind of world-historical comparison—such gut reactions allow personal political preferences to preclude the possibility of scholarly analysis of historical experiences. 'Normal' is, on this view, essentially 'A Good Thing'; and the GDR, clearly 'abnormal' by the standards of a democratic nation state, should not be considered in relation to any such concept.[1] Such reactions fail, however, to appreciate the anthropological, historical, and political scope of the term as an analytic concept, caught as they are in their own implicit assumptions and normative prejudices about what constitutes 'normality'. It is necessary, therefore, to look more explicitly at the varied meanings and usages of the term.

'Normalisation' is an intrinsically relational, comparative term, with an element of movement or time frame involved: returning to, or making conform to, or aspiring to, some conception of 'normality'. Within the very word itself are built in notions of what would constitute 'deviance from' or challenges to some state of presumed 'normality', conceived as a 'healthy' state; or, put differently, notions of 'normalisation' inevitably entail also assumptions about what would constitute 'abnormality'. This close entanglement with potentially invidious comparisons, intrinsic to the term itself, renders the notion of normalisation problematic as a theoretical concept to be applied in historical research. This is particularly the case when the concept is lifted, un-problematised, from everyday usages of the term—and even more so if those everyday usages are those only of particular political actors, with their own, contested, views of what would be a desirable or 'normal' state of affairs.

Scholarly approaches, in consequence, differ quite remarkably on the usages of the term 'normalisation', on occasion using it relatively unthinkingly as though what is meant is self-evident, at other times more explicitly as a concept perhaps derived from the usages of contemporaries, but raised to attention as in some sense problematic. There is an additional twist relating to its application to the GDR. The history of the GDR is located in—or, frequently, is lost between—the 'double' comparative context of the histories of both its western twin, the increasingly affluent democratic Federal Republic of Germany, and of the other Eastern European states with which the GDR shared the fate of being under Soviet domination and influence. Curiously, the concept of 'normalisation' has been applied to both these spheres, yet with widely different meanings in each case. While analysts of

---

1. This is an extremely common reaction among lay members of audiences during discussions following the delivery of any lecture referring to normalisation in the GDR.

West German history have picked up on the notion of normalisation as a 'bottom up' concept widely deployed by ordinary people to refer to continual improvements in their private lives in the 1950s, Eastern European specialists have focussed rather on the use of the term to refer to top-down Soviet policies of repression following challenges to communist rule from the 1950s to the 1980s. On both sides, there have been varying degrees of awareness of the intrinsically loaded and normative character of any usage by contemporaries, whether from 'above' or 'below'; the loaded character tends to be somewhat more evident to scholars discussing Eastern Europe, given the evident dissonance between official claims to 'normalisation' and what should be seen as an entirely 'abnormal' deployment of force. The contrast between the two usages appears at first glance to be significant: bottom-up versus top-down, experienced reality of improvements in everyday life versus the claimed restoration of repressive rule against the express will of the people. On closer inspection, however, wide variations in substantive usage may be rooted in similar underlying theoretical issues, as will be explored further in a moment. First, a brief survey of the current range of usage will be helpful.

'Normalisation' is, for historians of Western Europe, particularly associated with the relative peace and growing prosperity of the 1950s, after decades of instability and violence in the preceding 'Thirty Years War' from 1914 to 1945, and most particularly after the horrors of the Second World War and genocide. Across Western Europe, as Richard Bessel and Dirk Schumann comment:

> One of the most striking characteristics of the period that followed the 'decade of violence' was its relative peacefulness, stability and conservatism—not only in terms of politics but also in terms of social and cultural life. If the 1940s may described as the 'decade of violence', the 1950s arguably may be described as the 'decade of normality'—a decade in which one saw an apparent 'normalization' and stabilisation of political, social, and cultural relationships . . . However, the normality of the 1950s—coming as it did after the greatest outpouring of violence in human history—was anything but normal. It was, both collectively and individually, life after death.[2]

The 'return to normality', in terms of the (re-)building of shattered private lives, the reunions of families, and the reconstructions of the physical

---

2. Richard Bessel and Dirk Schumann, 'Introduction: Violence, Normality and the Construction of Post-war Europe', in R. Bessel and D. Schumann, eds., *Life after Death: Approaches to a Cultural and Social History of Europe during the 1940s and 1950s* (Cambridge: Cambridge University Press, 2003), p. 12.

infrastructure under peace-time conditions, had common elements across post-war Western Europe.

West Germany, shattered as it was in some areas by massive bombing raids, and subjected to the further constraints of defeat and occupation, shared these wider elements of physical rebuilding, economic recovery, and the associated construction of what was perceived as 'normal life' in the 'private sphere'. It was massively helped in this by the influx of both political and economic aid under the auspices of the Marshall Plan, from which it was the greatest beneficiary. But in Germany, the term had an extra, if largely suppressed (and hence all the more sinister) twist. Among contemporaries, conceptions of a supposed 'return to normality' in the Federal Republic of the 1950s referred to improvements in their private lives, with increasing affluence, job security, stable family lives, better living conditions, and enhanced leisure activities in the course of the 'economic miracle'–accompanied in many quarters by a degree of silence about the recent past. The term should thus not be taken entirely at face value, or lifted un-problematically from the usage of contemporaries, as Hanna Schissler points out:

> 'Normality' and 'normalization' were code words of the 1950s. They were part of the collective symbolism of the time. . . . Germans had lived through the rigors of war, including Allied bombardments. Millions had been displaced from their homes; hunger had become a common experience. The revelations of Germany's genocidal policies had shocked them. Now people were longing for a return to 'normality' . . . The frequent and matter-of-fact use of the terms 'normality' and 'normalization" in everyday life during the 1950s renders the project of 'normalization' highly suspicious and demands explanation. 'Normality' and 'normalization' are loaded ideological terms . . . Because 'normality' supposedly does not need explanation or justification, the normativity that was attached to the normalization project was (at least partly) veiled . . . [This] is precisely what made it such a powerful tool in the social and ideological reality of the 1950s.[3]

Lutz Niethammer similarly points out that normalisation is a term that has to be treated with care in a longer-term historical perspective:

> The need for liberating experience beyond certain ideological guiding concepts is easily recognizable in the catchword of the 1950s: 'normalization'. It is one of the most important code words used in both self-understandings

3. Hanna Schissler, '"Normalization" as project: Some thoughts on gender relations in West Germany during the 1950s', in Hanna Schissler, ed., *The Miracle Years. A Cultural History of West Germany, 1949–1968* (Princeton: Princeton U. P., 2001), pp. 359–75; here, pp. 359–60.

> and contemporary historical characterizations of that decade. It is even recognized in economic-historical debates on the reconstruction period as a major subconscious category. But what does it actually express? Does its definition of 'normal' extend only to the fact that at this time people were crawling out the cellars and no longer ate out of tin dishes? Doesn't it label in fact as 'normal' the entire dramatic change in German society—at least in the West—after World War II? . . . According to which operative norms did the 1950s 'return to normal'?[4]

For the working class Germans in the Ruhr area on whose experiences Niethammer's observations were based, such conceptions actually have as an implicit reference point the 'silent years' or 'good years' of a return to full employment under Hitler in the peace-time years of the 1930s, and not the 'normality' of poverty, or of political and economic chaos that formed the widespread experience of the 1920s in this area.

From another perspective, such conceptions among large numbers of Germans in the 1950s display an extraordinary (and indeed by their indifference arguably callous) self-centredness and disregard for the millions of victims of the Nazi regime. The physical rebuilding from the ruins could never make life 'normal' again for those who would never return to their former homes and homeland, whether because they had been murdered in the Holocaust or had managed to flee abroad to try to make new lives in foreign places; nor could life within post-Holocaust Germany ever be the same again, or develop in patterns expected before the Nazi takeover, for the often deeply traumatised survivors and friends. Post-war relationships with fellow (but non-Jewish) Germans could 'never again be normalised', as one close friend of a woman murdered in Auschwitz later explicitly reflected; 'it was not made good again' was her acerbic comment on the supposed restitution or 'Wiedergutmachung' trumpeted by Adenauer's Germany.[5] 'Normalisation' for many post-war West Germans, as essentially a good experience, was thus predicated not merely on the earlier exploitation, exclusion, and murder of millions of those considered to be 'racially inferior', but also on varying degrees of post-war silence or repression of any prior knowledge of or complicity in these crimes and their long-lasting consequences. The desire to be 'normal' was hence not merely a desire to pick up again on strands of family life that had been disrupted by war, flight, and hunger, but

4. Lutz Niethammer, '"Normalization" in the West: Traces of memory leading back into the 1950s', in Hanna Schissler, ed., *The Miracle Years. A Cultural History of West Germany, 1949–1968* (Princeton: Princeton U. P., 2001), pp. 237–65; here, p. 238.

5. Martin Doerry, *'Mein verwundetes Herz'. Das Leben der Lilli Jahn 1900–1944* (Stuttgart and Munich; Deutsche Verlags-Anstalt, and Bundeszentrale für politische Bildung, 2004), p. 338.

also, if less consciously expressed at the time, the desire not to have been associated with the horrendous experiences and actions of the Nazi era; to pick up the pieces as if nothing had happened. It was thus predicated on a silent non-recognition of the fact that Germans were now inhabiting a society which had been successfully 'purged' of distinctive groups among its prewar population (and very significant percentages of the population in cities such as Frankfurt and Berlin), representing also a dramatic shift in Germany's social, intellectual, and cultural profile. At intervals, nevertheless, tensions erupted as challenges rooted in the realities of the past disturbed the comfortable materialism and affluent superficiality of the present.

Aspirations for some form of 'normality' with respect to the Nazi past were never completely submerged in public discourse over the years, as any even cursory glance at West Germany's 'policies with respect to the past' (*Vergangenheitspolitik*) will readily reveal. From Adenauer's gestures towards 'restitution' and proclamations of public shame without personal responsibility in the 1950s, through the debates on the war crimes trials and the issue of limitations on liability to prosecution for murder in the 1960s, to the widespread discussion of recapitulations of the Nazi past in films, documentaries, and historical analyses from the later 1960s onward, the notion of being a 'normal' nation persistently dogged West German discourses over 'German identity' both past and present.[6] This was, in Ernst Nolte's infamous phrase, the 'past that would not pass away' (*die Vergangenheit, die nicht vergehen will*). Thus, the concept of 'normalisation' returned explicitly as a term of public debate in the Helmut Kohl era of mid 1980s West Germany. Conservative historians and philosophers—Andreas Hillgruber, Michael Stürmer, Ernst Nolte—called for a 'normalisation' of the treatment of the Third Reich, arguing that it was time for Germany to be a 'normal nation' again, understood as a nation with a past in which Germans could take some pride, just as other nations allegedly could take pride in the deeds and achievements of their own respective forefathers. This proposed relativisation of the crimes of the Holocaust provoked widespread outrage on the part of Jürgen Habermas and many others, reaching its peak in the notorious 'historians' dispute' or *Historikerstreit* of 1986–87.[7]

6. There is a huge literature in this area. See for example Norbert Frei, *Vergangenheitspolitik* (Munich: C. H. Beck, 1996); Ralph Giordano, *Die zweite Schuld, oder, Von der Last Deutscher zu sein* (Hamburg: Rasch and Röhrig, 1987); for my own brief summary of relevant developments in both East and West Germany, see Mary Fulbrook, *German National Identity after the Holocaust* (Cambridge: Polity, 1999).

7. The original literature is well-known and does not need to be rehearsed again here; for a recent discussion from a later perspective, see the discussion contributions in 'The *Historikerstreit* Twenty Years On', *German History*, vol. 24 (Oct. 2006): 587–607. For the use of the term 'normalisation' in this context, see for example Heide Gerstenberger and Dorothea Schmidt, eds., *Normalität oder Normalisierung?* (Münster: Westfälisches Dampfboot Verlag, 1987).

While the focus in this debate was on whether German history itself could in any way be treated as a 'normal' past rather than as a subject for constant shame and outrage, a somewhat different focus was to be found in the debate between Saul Friedländer and Martin Broszat over the proposed 'historicisation' of approaches to the Third Reich. The key issue in that debate was over whether historians could or should adopt 'normal' historical methods and approaches to a period that was, on both sides of this debate, recognised as 'abnormal' on any measure of the scale of the crimes committed.

So, for West Germany, issues of 'normalisation' revolved around the early development of the materialistic, affluent society, with appeals regarding the alleged 'return to normality' of everyday life—at least for 'Aryan' survivors, including not only those who had personally remained at a distance (both politically and geographically) from complicity in Nazi crimes, but also many former perpetrators and accomplices in Nazi policies of genocide—and also around later appeals for there to be, finally, a 'line drawn' (*Schlußstrich*) under this unsavoury 'episode' of an otherwise entirely 'normal' national history. A trivial footnote, perhaps, to the tale of 'normalisation' in the West lies in the extraordinarily late revelation, in an autobiography published in the summer of 2006, on the part of the renowned writer and generally acclaimed 'moral voice of the nation', Günter Grass, that he had himself not merely been a member of the Waffen-SS as a teenager at the end of the war, but that he only now, half a century later, felt able to reveal this fact—despite having made a career of castigating others for their repression and denial of complicity in the Nazi system.

On the other hand, scholars of Eastern Europe have used the concept of 'normalisation' in an entirely different sense: to analyse the top-down politics and policies employed by the Communist Party of the Soviet Union (CPSU) and its local representatives in its 'satellite states', in order to suppress attempts at liberalisation and reform and restore Soviet control following the political upheavals in Hungary in 1956, Poland in 1956 and 1980–81, and Czechoslovakia following Dubček's 'Prague Spring' of 1968. Usage of this concept with respect to Eastern European states derives very directly from the Soviet Union's own official terminology and distinctive conceptions of 'normality'. As Kieran Williams points out, earlier uses of the term (with reference to 'orthographical and metallurgical standardization' from the 1860s, or to the standardisation of relations between two states from the 1930s onward), were, for scholars of communist states, displaced by the Soviet use of the term:

> In Russian *normalizatsiia* has two meanings: the process of 'making normal'; and the adaptation of an object to conform to a norm. After the 1956 crises it entered Soviet parlance as a euphemism for the restoration of communist control, the return to a 'normal' Soviet-type system, or, to use its second Russian

> gloss, the re-calibration of the local system to match the norm represented by the Soviet model.[8]

And as Zdenek Mlynar comments,

> [T]he term 'normalization of the situation' is in fact designed to obscure the reality of the forced restoration of a Soviet-type socio-political system in a situation where the individual national communities have clearly rejected such a system (in Hungary in 1956, in Czechoslovakia in 1968, and in Poland in 1980–81) and have made an attempt to bring about its qualitative change. 'Normalization of the situation' means the restoration of a system rejected by a majority of society, at a point when it can be saved solely by the use of large-scale military and police repression.[9]

Moreover, 'the Soviet leadership considers "normal" only a very specific internal political situation. Such a normal situation means there must be a centre of absolute power (in the form of the Politburo of the given Communist Party), willing and able to enforce Soviet interests in the event of a contradiction between Soviet interests and the will of a national society.'[10] Similarly, Kusin argues that:

> 'Normalisation' in Czechoslovakia can be defined as restoration of authoritarianism in conditions of a post-interventionist lack of indigenous legitimacy, carried out under the close supervision of a dominant foreign power which retains the prerogative of supreme arbitration and interpretation but which prefers to work through its domestic agents. It had two principal aims: to remove reformism as a political force, and to legitimate a new regime resting on old pre-reformist principles . . . Towards its attainment, two simultaneous processes were pursued with determination. The population at large was intimidated into acceptance of imposed rules, and both real and potential opposition was pushed out from positions of influence, authority and control.[11]

As indicated, both coercion and a degree of cooption of the subjugated population were key elements in such processes. Thus, in academic usage,

---

8. Kieran Williams, *The Prague Spring and its Aftermath: Czechoslovak Politics, 1968–1970* (Cambridge: Cambridge University Press, 1997), pp. 39–40.

9. Zdenek Mylnar, 'Introduction', in W. Brus, P. Kende, and Z. Mlynar, *'Normalization' Processes in Soviet-dominated Central Europe: Hungary Czechoslovakia Poland* (N.P: Research Project: Crises in Soviet-type systems, Study No. 1 © Z. Mlynar, 1982), p. 3.

10. Zdenek Mlynar, 'Normalization in Czechoslovakia after 1968' in W. Brus, P. Kende, Z. Mlynar, *'Normalization' Processes* (pp. 15–36), p. 16.

11. Vladimir Kusin, *From Dubček to Charter 77: A study of 'normalisation' in Czechoslovakia 1968–1978* (Edinburgh: Q Press, 1978), p. 145.

the term has become rather more complex and multi-facetted than in the original Soviet version.

The concept of normalisation is used in slightly varying ways by specialists in this area: sometimes to refer to Soviet intentions and repressive responses to political challenge; sometimes to refer to domestic policies introduced or imposed by local Communists under Soviet hegemony in the medium term; and sometimes to the whole bundle of features including the changing roles of functionaries and the adaptations of behaviour and attitude among intellectuals, workers, and peasants over a longer period of time.[12] In an attempted systematic comparison among selected Eastern European states, Peter Hübner has sought to apply the concept rather narrowly to a particular time period, focussing on policy changes in the Soviet block in the early 1970s, and restricting the concept to what he calls '*Normalisierungspolitik*', or 'policies of normalisation', with specific reference to post–1970 East European economics reversals in the GDR, CSSR, and Poland after the reform attempts of the 1960s.[13] This approach is of course doubly limited by seeking to restrict the term not only to the substantive usage by a dominant political actor, but also to a particular set of policies at a specific point in time. Other scholars apply the term in a broader sense, ranging fairly widely across the three principal cases and exploring relations between rulers, functionary classes, and the ruled, over extended periods of time.[14] While commentators have differed slightly in the way in which the term is applied, and the extent to which the original Soviet use of it is treated with a degree of distance, the term has gained widespread currency as a substantive appellation for processes of 'social pacification' through a combination of the stick of forcible repression and the carrot of consumerism in these three states.

The injuries and deaths involved in forcible suppression of mass demonstrations, the subsequent prison sentences, executions, exclusions from office and professional life, and other longer-term consequences of radical political upheavals and reinstatement of communist control, were frequently accompanied by attempts at social pacification through improved working conditions, enhanced supplies of consumer goods, and higher living

12. See for example the wide-ranging analysis by Milan Simecka, *The Restoration of Order: The Normalization of Czechoslovakia*, trans. A.G. Brain (London: Verso, 1984).

13. Peter Hübner, 'Norm, Normalität, Normalisierung: Quellen und Ziele eines gesellschaftlichen Paradigmenweschsels im sowjetischen Block um 1970', *Potsdamer Bulletin* Nr 28/29, Jan. 2003: 24–40.

14. On the 'paradigm case' of Czechoslovakia see also, for example, H. Gordon Skilling, *Czechoslovakia's Interrupted Revolution* (Princeton: Princeton University Press, 1976); Fred Eidlin, *The Logic of 'Normalization': The Soviet Intervention in Czechoslovakia of 21 August 1968 and the Czechoslovak Response* (New York: Columbia University Press and Boulder, 1980).

standards for a now resigned and politically passive population. Social peace was, in short, bought at a high price, particularly for the victims of the initial wave of repression and restructuring. On this view, 'normalisation' has generally been considered, both by most contemporaries (with of course the exception of the political forces imposing such policies) and by subsequent scholarly observers, in contrast to the use of the term when applied to western post-war developments, to be utterly abhorrent. Almost without exception, from the point of view of historians of Eastern Europe the term has been treated as a loaded concept, an unacceptable euphemism, posing for some scholars a serious obstacle in wanting to adopt a term derived from the political discourse of repressive rulers as an analytical term in academic discourse.

Academic analyses of normalisation as a top-down policy of social pacification in Eastern European states have, with a few exceptions, largely tended to leave the GDR out of the comparison. Perhaps the 1953 June Uprising in the GDR came just too early for scholars of Communist states to explore it under a conceptual heading that became common currency in the Soviet bloc only after 1956; perhaps the degree of Soviet intervention and control in the GDR was different in ways which did not lend themselves to a similar use of the term; perhaps any 'normalisation' after 1953 had a delayed inception only after the renewed trauma and use of force with the building of the Berlin Wall in 1961. Perhaps, too, there has subconsciously reigned among Eastern European specialists an implicit assumption that GDR history does not 'really' belong to the history of the repeatedly subjugated states of Eastern Europe, rooted as the GDR was in the very different war-time history of the German aggressor state. Similarly, few scholars have thought to apply to the GDR the concept of normalisation in the western sense of 'bottom-up experiences', of a 'return to normality' after the war and post-war periods of violence and deprivation, given the continuation of uncertainties, radical social restructuring, political repression, economic miseries, and extended rationing in the GDR through the 1950s. Observers of the affluent, materialistic, capitalist democratic West Germany have generally felt that any notion of normalisation would be in principle inapplicable to the condition of East Germans eking out what was, by western standards, a miserable existence behind the 'Iron Curtain'.

Altogether the GDR has tended to escape embedding itself in the wider historical narratives of post-war Europe. While before German unification in 1990 many western scholars tended to write the history of Germany as moving seamlessly from the Third Reich to the Federal Republic, with the GDR as a mere appendage to be mentioned in passing, primarily in the context of initial division and subsequent West German *Ostpolitik*, specialists in Eastern Europe also did not really consider it as central to their scholarly stamping ground. Only after the opening of the East German archives in the 1990s did the GDR become an object of extensive analysis on its own right, with an explosion of research projects on its domestic political and social history; but even by the early twenty-first century, cries were still being heard, calling for it to be treated as part of a broader European history, rather than merely a 'footnote' of interest only to a select band of academic specialists, and to a variegated mixture of romantic 'Ostalgics' harbouring rose-tinted views of the world they had lost, or former political victims trying to come to terms with their wounds. Such calls for the broader contextualisation of GDR history fit in with the wider recognition that, to adapt a phrase, 'no state is an island complete of itself', which was accompanied more generally by pleas for the 'trans-nationalisation' of historical approaches.

Moreover, the history of the GDR itself has been written with an eye largely to its beginnings and endings, with a widespread tendency to skim rapidly over the middle decades. Particularly in the first decade after the opening of the archives, historians tended to concentrate primarily on the early years of the establishment and development of the new structures of the dictatorship, up to the building of the Wall in 1961, and on the closing years of economic decline, political destabilisation, and the growth of oppositional movements leading up to the collapse of communist rule and the end of the GDR in 1989–90. With the exception of certain areas–church/state relations, the *Stasi*, relations between the two German states in the era of *Ostpolitik*–relatively little attention was initially paid to underlying developments in political structure and related patterns of social and behavioural change during the more stable years of the 1960s and 1970s. These were years of détente characterised by some limited optimism for a degree of apparent liberalisation, improvements in social and economic conditions, and hopes for a better future in this world rather than the next; despite the constraints of the Wall, utopia appeared to be giving way to pragmatism, and meeting the needs of the people appeared to be taking priority over ideological zeal. This was a period characterised many years ago by Peter Christian Ludz as one of 'consultative authoritarianism'; and a period which even those theorists clinging to the 'totalitarian' model had difficulty in conceptualising, with variants on 'post-totalitarian' and 'late totalitarian' being devised in an attempt to accommodate recognition of difference within a conceptual framework which did not quite fit. While this situation has been changing in the scholarship of the twenty-first century, with the proliferation of specialist studies and monographs on a range of particular topics, the question of the parameters and character of relative stabilisation in the middle period of the GDR is one that has remained relatively under-theorised. Here, we believe an investigation in the light of the concept of normalisation may be fruitful; first, however, it is important to clarify the ways in which this term is being applied as a theoretical rather than a descriptive or normative concept.

Normalisation as an Ideal Type

Given the wide range of usage by both contemporaries within and analysts of Eastern and Western Europe, how may the contested concept of normalisation be of more general use? It is important to make it very clear from the outset that this concept is used here not as a descriptive label for a particular period, nor as a term borrowed from the usage of contemporaries, but rather as a heuristic tool for further analysis of a range of processes in different areas. The outcomes of such an investigation are by no means predetermined.

The notion of normalisation is best deployed as an ideal type, in the Weberian sense, against which particular processes and developments can be measured and set in broader comparative context. The concept is thus deployed here *not* as a descriptive phrase (let alone a political evaluation), but rather as an analytic tool of potentially wider significance and applicability. The claim is *not*, then, that the GDR in the 1960s and 1970s can be substantively characterised in this way; but rather, that for comparative and interpretive purposes, it is fruitful for this period of the GDR's history to explore questions concerning the relative stabilisation of domestic political structures and processes, the degrees of routinisation and predictability of everyday practices, and to examine, with an anthropological sensitivity, patterns and variations in widespread conceptions of what is held to be 'normal'.

In deploying the concept of normalisation in this way, it is not a matter of simply inventing a new term from thin air, but (as with other historical concepts such as 'dictatorship' or 'democracy') necessarily at the same time picking up from and relating to the usage of both contemporaries and other scholars. Historians can, after all, not talk purely in terms of entities comparable to the Table of the Elements prevalent in the natural sciences, and the complex overlay of meanings (or 'double hermeneutic') in historical analysis is accordingly often highly problematic.[15] The meaning of 'normal' in some contexts is simple: for physiological organisms, there is a 'normal range' of body temperatures or blood sugar levels, for example, beyond which–at

15. For fuller discussion of my approach to the theoretical issues involved in concept formation and value neutrality in history, see my book on *Historical Theory* (London: Routledge, 2002).

either extreme–life is fatally threatened. For collective social and political entities, such as states, societies, and communities (at whatever level), the situation is very different, with widely varying cultural constructions of what might be meant by a 'return to normality'. Yet the concept of normalisation has seemed, in practice, to be of considerable relevance in different quarters. It may also, if we consider the prospect of developing it more explicitly as an analytic construct for heuristic purposes, prove to be of far wider applicability than the particular cases considered in this context. We need then to return to the construction of the term as a more abstract ideal type, a usable concept in the social and historical field.

The varied applications sketched in above–whether referring to West Germany in the 1950s, or to Eastern European states from the 1950s through the 1980s–at first glance appear very different in their definitions. Interestingly, however, for all their obvious differences they nevertheless share certain intrinsic features. They pick up on the usage of contemporaries to point to the ways in which key collective actors sought to define a particular set of changes as being a 'return' to the 'way things were', understood not necessarily as how they 'actually' were, but certainly conforming to some conception of how they 'ought to be': a curious mixture of reference both to a construction of the past, and to aspirations for the future. In the West, the relevant collective actors consisted, at different times, of significant numbers of 'ordinary Germans', as well as sections of the political and cultural elites; and it is precisely because of the relatively broad area of consensus between post-war elites and the population that the term appeared unproblematic to all but a few. In the Eastern European cases, by contrast, the politically loaded character of the term lies precisely in the fact that the claims and aspirations of a repressive Soviet power and its local post-reformist leaderships were not shared by significant sections of the population, including ousted intellectuals and vocal oppositionalists. The Soviet conception was a definition of 'normality' that many explicitly felt to be utterly unacceptable, and an active minority were even prepared to risk (or actively sacrifice, as in the case of the self-immolation of Jan Pallach) their lives to demonstrate against it. Yet the widespread tendency to find the western notion intrinsically less problematic should not disguise the fact that both versions of what constitutes 'normality' are–as the etymology of the word itself proclaims–intrinsically normative and loaded.

The issue of shared norms, and of associated social constructions of 'normality', is important, alongside the implicit or explicit claim on the part of one or another group (whether dominant or subordinate) that this is the way things 'should' be. Built into any notion of 'normalisation' also is explicit reference to a process of change over time, to the ways in which an 'abnormal' situation is–or should be–turning into a 'normal' one, as defined by key collective actors. Over the course of this period of time, which may be quite extended and strongly contested, processes of political, economic, and social change take place in which people's changing experiences affect their attitudes and patterns of behaviour; they adapt to new circumstances and seek to realise their interests in changing socio-political environments, in the process also changing their own conceptions of 'normality'. Conflicting norms are negotiated as new definitions of the situation are worked through, and new dominant patterns of behaviour and interaction emerge, or people learn to adapt to uncomfortable conditions in an effort to make tolerable lives within (or despite) less than ideal circumstances.

Important too, therefore, is the question of significant periods of stabilisation (however impermanent in any longer-term historical perspective), and the associated possible routinisation of institutional structures and regular patterns of behaviour. As the 'new' eventually becomes experienced as 'routine', expectations settle down: people begin to assume that tomorrow will be pretty much like today (no longer existentially threatened), and that the rules themselves will not change very much, so that it is worth learning to play by the rules in order to achieve personal ends. 'Private lives' are no longer radically disrupted by the course of 'collective history'; ruptures are rooted rather in what are perceived as individual life crises (work problems, illness, divorce, death) and not in the collective impact of major external events, the chaos of the economic system or the demands of politics or warfare. 'Life plans' become possible in the light of now familiar parameters, in the context of which it is possible to act today in ways which will produce predictable results in the medium and longer-term future–including the choice of taking risks in not conforming, with the knowledge of the likely penalties weighed up against personal moral and political considerations. It is important to note explicitly that predictability of consequences does not necessarily entail or imply belief in or conformity to the rules. Normalisation is not the same thing as legitimisation. After a longer or shorter period of time, following a period of upheaval and rapid change, new norms may be successfully internalised, inculcated into the minds of rising generations–or may not, as the case may be. One can, then, begin to explore empirically the extent to which people are aware of and take into account the new 'rules', both explicit and implicit, of the circumstances in which they make their lives; the extent to which they choose to challenge, to ignore, to confront, or to play by these rules while retaining a sense of inner distance; or the extent to which they have, perhaps entirely unconsciously, internalised certain aspects of the new norms and rules, assuming that their lives are in some unexamined sense 'perfectly normal'.

It is in this way possible to reconsider processes of 'normalisation' in a rather more abstract, multi-facetted and comprehensive manner, rather than simply taking over, with a greater or lesser degree of scholarly distancing and disapproval, a substantive concept derived from the usage of contemporaries. The concept, when used in this more abstract fashion, is an 'ideal type' (in Max Weber's theoretical sense rather than the normative meaning of the term!), which could in principle be applied to any historical case and period: it is an empirical question to explore the extent to which any of these aspects might obtain at any particular time among selected social groups. The concept can, then, be applied just as fruitfully to the German states in the later seventeenth century, after decades of turmoil and warfare in the Thirty Years War, to Londoners after the Blitz in the Second World War, to New Yorkers and Londoners after the terrorist attacks of '9/11' and '7/7', or to the people of Iraq after the removal of Saddam Hussein and the occupation of armed forces under American hegemony, as it can to the experiences of people in the GDR; in all of these cases, a moment's thought will readily reveal both the extent to which such a notion is problematic, and the ways in which it can be a useful tool for investigating the links between wider historical changes and people's experiences and perceptions on the ground, as they believe that a situation is 'returning to normal'. The concept of normalisation thus in itself presupposes nothing about how any situation following a period of existential crisis is 'actually' experienced and theorised by different groups among contemporaries living through periods of upheaval and change; rather, it poses the question of the relations between rapid change and the emergence of possible perceptions, in different quarters, of a 'return to normal'—with all the attendant issues of constructions of 'normality' as a reference point in a mythologised past, as an ideal and as a future aspiration, referred to above. Thus, if treated in this way, the concept of normalisation as a theoretical tool or ideal type can provide a very useful means of exploring the links between 'structural' changes (in political, economic, and social structure), on the one hand, and changes in mentalities, patterns of behaviour, and discourse, on the other; and it serves to raise questions about the 'degrees of fit' between the demands of the external world and the perceptions and experiences of the inner life among people in different social and generational groups, in those longer, slower, 'less memorable' times following periods of major upheaval and historical turmoil that have visible implications for people's experiences and perceptions of their 'private lives'.

Normalisation in the GDR in Comparative Perspective

When the history of the GDR is revisited in this broader theoretical and comparative context, some interesting patterns begin to emerge. Economic, international, political, and social factors all combine in different ways to suggest the conditions under which any aspect of the bundle of processes of 'normalisation' might be observed.

The material basis for a tolerable physical existence is certainly a crucial precondition for any sense of normalisation. The American election campaign headquarters reminder slogan, 'the economy, stupid', seems to hold good across systems of whatever political colour. In the West, widespread popular claims to 'normalisation' were clearly predicated on the long period of post-war economic growth. In West Germany, a sense of 'normalisation' set in with the Marshall Plan and currency reform in 1948; in the course of the 1950s, support for democracy in principle rose alongside per capita income, in a context of sustained economic growth and moves towards western European economic integration. The 'post-war period' in the GDR in terms of economic shortages, political uncertainties, and continued upheavals lasted far longer than in West Germany: there was no Marshall Aid to speed up recovery, and war-time damage was compounded by reparations to the Soviet Union and the consequences of radical socioeconomic restructuring in both industry and agriculture as early as 1945–46, as well as by the separation from western economic links and later integration into the system of the less well-developed economies of eastern Europe in Comecon. Yet by the early 1960s, with the end of rationing and the emergence of improvements in living and working conditions, life began at least to appear more 'normal' with respect to many everyday needs, in contrast, for those old enough to remember, with the dire conditions of the very early post-war years.

What becomes clear in the Eastern European cases more generally is that, despite the very different economic system and conditions obtaining under communism, a modicum of material well-being plays an important role in the longer-term question of whether a politically unstable situation can be successfully 'normalised' after the shock waves of a revolt. In Hungary following the upheavals of 1956, in the context of general post-war economic recovery and growth, a policy of 'mixed capitalism' fostered a fairly productive economy. 'Kadarism'—the politics of pragmatic materialism pursued by Hungary's new leader Janos Kadar—thus played an important role in stabilising the system in the years following the brutal and bloody suppression of the 1956 Hungarian uprising. In different ways, there was sufficient leeway in the system for consumerist measures in Czechoslovakia in the post-Dubček era of the early 1970s. The same strategies could, however, not be repeated by General Jaruzelski in Poland after taking over in face of the challenges from the Solidarity movement in 1980–81, in the new context of oil crises, world economic recession, and renewed Cold War pressures for rising military expenditure in the 1980s. This general economic and political context formed the backdrop too, to the change in policies under Mikhail Gorbachev in the USSR in the later 1980s, and ultimately to the revolutionary challenges that swept away communist rule in the Soviet bloc in 1989–90.

The GDR's early political shock, the June Uprising of 1953, was followed by (somewhat short-lived) consumer concessions; but the still somewhat open border with the West, while the loophole of escape remained through Berlin, meant that a constant haemorrhage of skilled labour continually drained the economy, leaving any successful policy of 'Kadarism' less available in the SED's arsenal of potential responses at this time. East Germans realised very early on the disadvantages of their system in comparison to the rapidly improving conditions in the West, and material dissatisfaction was expressed in the high rates of flight to the Federal Republic during the 1950s. It was only after the building of the Wall in 1961 that the East German labour supply was at last stabilised, with some degree of certainty that the work force in any given enterprise or institution would be the same from one day to the next. In 1963, the New Economic System introduced a range of reforms in the organisation of industrial production, with a limited degree of decentralisation of economic decision-making, while the waves of enforced collectivisation of agriculture in 1959–60 inaugurated a more predictable, stabilised agrarian sector. While the East German economy was never able to keep pace with (let alone overtake, as Ulbricht had optimistically proclaimed) the productivity of the West, for close on two decades, East Germans in the 1960s and 1970s were able to enjoy an increasingly comfortable if always modest standard of living, with a shorter working week, growing leisure time, and ownership of concomitant consumer goods such as television sets. Such modest improvements were of course marred both by constant shortages in particular goods, replacement parts, and 'exotic' fresh fruit, as well as continued comparisons with the more affluent West, and the construction of domestic idylls filled with the material products of modern design was continually hampered by problems with adequate provision of housing; but, particularly in the context of Honecker's proclaimed 'unity of economic and social policy' in the early 1970s, there were widespread expectations for continued improvements in the foreseeable future. It was not until the later 1970s and particularly from the early 1980s, in the context of oil crises and world recession, that the adverse consequences in the GDR of Honecker's generous social subsidies began to be evident in a visibly deteriorating environmental and economic system. Thus, for nearly two decades in the GDR, the basic economic preconditions for a degree of 'normalisation' were present, even if constantly under the situation of adverse comparisons with the West, in ways which will be analysed in greater detail in a number of chapters below.

Normalisation is of course intrinsically related to questions of political stabilisation and domestic challenges to any given regime in a broader international context. Germany's first experiment at democracy in the Weimar Republic was repeatedly challenged from both the Left and the Right; in conditions of rising unemployment and the economic depression of the early 1930s, the right-wing elites' resort to the demagogic NSDAP in the hope of harnessing popular unrest in support of conservative autocracy was a wild gamble that eventuated in the Hitler state. Experiences of a 'return to normality' among those Germans untouched by the political terror and racism of the 1930s, and glad to gain employment and a degree of security, was a chimera, with the 'Hitler myth' blinding many Germans to the spiral of radical state-sponsored violence and further fatal destabilisation of an already unstable interwar political situation in central Europe. The effect of Hitler's war of aggression—a World War, and not 'merely' the revisionist war that might in any event have been fought—was to bring the two new superpowers into Europe, with the USA and the Soviet Union dominating European history for the better part of the following half century. It is only in the context of the fragile stability and changing flashpoints of the Cold War context that the histories of the post-war European states—most obviously in the East, in less visible ways in the West—can be understood. And domestic challenges to Communist rule within the Soviet bloc states—1953, 1956, 1968, 1980–81—came at different times within the broader context of the Cold War as it affected Europe, and within their own histories as 'satellite states'.

The ruling communist Socialist Unity Party in the GDR, the SED, experienced only one major challenge to its domination that was comparable to the events of 1956, 1968, and 1980–81 in its Eastern European neighbours: the uprising of June 1953, the first serious shudder to run through the new area of Soviet domination in eastern Europe. But this was not an event comparable to the later upheavals in terms of immediate processes of 'normalisation'—perhaps another reason why this term has rarely if ever been applied to the GDR—for a number of reasons. The June 1953 Uprising was not merely a 'workers' uprising', as sometimes portrayed, in part because the general strike of 17 June was initially sparked by a protest against raised work norms on the part of building workers in East Berlin's Stalinallee, which subsequently snowballed into a more general demonstration and general strike on 17 June; by the time political demands for the downfall of the Ulbricht regime and reunification with the West had been raised, the demonstrations involved a much wider cross-section of the population. Yet, despite a degree of factionalism and difference within the SED at this time, the 1953 Uprising neither arose out of nor significantly involved ideas of reform from within on the part of factions within the ruling communist party along the lines of debates in Hungary, Czechoslovakia or Poland. Nor did the demonstrations on the streets on 17 June involve significant numbers of the East German intelligentsia—a term that is, in any event, perhaps somewhat anachronistic when applied to this early stage of GDR history. Although there were notable exceptions, members of those professional and social groups who would eventually be termed the socialist 'intelligentsia' tended to remain in the wings in 1953, on the whole '*abwartend*' or 'waiting to see how things would develop', to use the standard language of contemporary reports. In the course of the 1950s, disproportionate numbers of these groups would take the opportunity to flee to the West, where there were far better career prospects as well as opportunities for the education of the children of the previously privileged classes. And, unlike the change of leadership that took place in Hungary, Czechoslovakia, and Poland, the 1953 challenge to communist rule in the GDR was followed by the consolidation of Ulbricht in power, rather than his replacement. Although there was a significant purge of party membership, there was at this very early stage in GDR history no serious transformation of the landscape of functional and intellectual elites, as took place after 1968 in Czechoslovakia.

In many respects, in the early 1950s the transformation of East German social and political structure was still at such a formative stage that the violent repression of the 1953 uprising was essentially an early 'foundational' shock, rather than a rude reminder that subordinate communist states could not, at least not before the changes in the Soviet Union at the very end of the 1980s, contemplate trying to do things 'their way' (to use Soviet spokesman Gennady Gerasimov's adoption of the 'Sinatra doctrine'). And although the events of 1953 were, as in the other later Eastern European cases, followed by very widespread resignation on the part of a significant percentage of the population, there was for several years thereafter still the escape hatch of an alternative version of living one's life in a German state after Hitler, namely the option of flight to the West. We have perhaps to remind ourselves that, with the benefit of hindsight, we know there were no real prospects for reunification after, at the very latest, the first Stalin note of 1952; but this was not the perception of many contemporaries, who in the 1950s lived between constant fear of a Third World War and the hope for reunification. There can be little talk about predictability, routinisation, and stabilisation, when the very state in which the 'rules' are supposed to apply might cease to exist from one day to the next. The future, in the 1950s, appeared far more uncertain in the GDR than it did in West Germany at the same time, or in the other Eastern European states which did not share the curious situation of having a western alternative sharing a common language and in which one had automatic citizenship rights. Issues of national legitimacy were, therefore, in the other cases rather different. In the case of Poland in 1980–81, for example, national identity was focussed in very different ways around an opposition between atheist Communist domination and the Catholic Church as an enduring symbol of the Polish people, rooted in experiences of invasion and occupation over the centuries, and particularly powerful at a time when there was a Polish Pope in Rome. Arguably, then, for reasons of the GDR's uncertain status and future as a state at all, until the building of the Berlin Wall in 1961, there could be no real talk of 'normalisation' in the tenuous, continually uncertain conditions of what was still widely referred to as 'the Zone'.

'Lessons' were certainly learned on the part of participants in all of the cases of repressed uprisings. Pierre Kende has indeed argued, for the case of Hungary, that Hungary's normalisation 'began with the nation's complete defeat' in 1956. The experience of suppression of hopes for reform was, according to Kende, worse in Hungary than in Czechoslovakia in 1968 because:

> [I]n Hungary awareness of defeat had been immediate and total while in Czechoslovakia it was attenuated by the hopes temporarily entertained by the routed team. Nor did Poland—even after 13 December 1981—ever know this feeling of complete and irremediable defeat which stole over the Hungarians in late autumn 1956 . . . Hungarian public opinion firmly thought they were finished as a nation.
>
> Paradoxically, this despair was to be one of the assets in the hands of the normalizers. Since Hungary had reached the fathoms of despair, anything that it could be offered that was less horrible than the worst . . . was likely to be considered as an unhoped-for gift.[16]

Awareness not merely of defeat, but also abandonment by the West, was certainly a key feature in the experiences of those involved in the 1953 Uprising in the GDR. The echoes of '17.6.53' reverberated right through the subsequent history of the GDR, affecting both ordinary workers who felt another challenge would be pointless in the absence of any practical support from the West, as well as Party apparatchiks seeking to retain their hold on power, demonstrated even in *Stasi* chief Erich Mielke's

16. Pierre Kende, 'The post–1956 Hungarian normalization', in W. Brus, P. Kende, and Z. Mlynar, *'Normalization' Processes* (pp. 5–13), here, p. 6.

remarks–'is this another 17.6'?–more than a third of a century later, in the autumn of 1989.

There were major developments over the longer term in terms of both strategies of the use of power and responses on the ground. These can perhaps best be summarised in terms of an almost paradoxical concomitant growth of both the apparatus of coercion, and its simultaneous displacement by relationships embodying practices of authority. This development too is characteristic of processes of normalisation.

The use of physical force and visible violence was at its most brutal in the period of the Soviet occupation and the very early years of the newly founded GDR. Whether in terms of the hundreds of thousands of deaths from starvation, maltreatment, and disease in post-war internment centres, or in terms of the political abuse of the system of legal 'justice' in show trials, or in terms of the constraints on political activities, any real or imagined opposition to the new system was brutally crushed, including among the victims not only of former Nazis and contemporary political competitors and opponents across the whole spectrum, but also entirely innocent youngsters caught up in the chaotic post-war system of brutality. Yet over time the deployment of visible, naked force gradually gave way to the growth of a less visible apparatus of repression through the *Stasi*. Caught relatively unawares in 1953, the State Security Service grew steadily larger through the later 1950s and 1960s. Ironically, it was in the period of greater openness and apparent semi-liberalisation following Ostpolitik that the *Stasi* experienced its greatest expansion, however, mushrooming in the Honecker period to become proportionately (per head of population) probably the largest security service in the twentieth-century world.[17]

The apparatus of power, defined in Max Weber's terms as 'the capacity to exert one's will against the will of others', and the growth of the state in terms of its 'monopoly of the legitimate use of force within given territorial boundaries' is thus beyond question. But this should not blind us to a concomitant and as yet less well-explored aspect of the ways in which the East German state changed during this period: the simultaneous, and perhaps paradoxical growth of 'legitimate authority', in the Weberian sense of the willingness of the ruler's staffs or functionary classes to act as though they believed in the legitimacy of the ruler's claims to power, and 'the likelihood that orders will be obeyed', for whatever combination of reasons. '*Macht*' was accompanied by a growth of '*Herrschaft*', in a more complex manner than has generally been represented.

17. See particularly Jens Gieseke, *Mielke-Konzern. Die Geschichte der Stasi 1945–1990* (Munich: Deutsche Verlags-Anstalt, 2001).

One key element in this situation is that of the roles of functionaries, whose role certainly requires more detailed investigation. In the context of normalisation processes in other Eastern European states, functionaries in a phase of normalisation are generally regarded as apparatchiks of the Moscow-dominated ruling elite, often displacing previous functionary groups who had supported indigenous attempts at reform or the development of 'socialism with a human face'. On this view, functionaries are essentially top-down policy transmitters, alienated from the grassroots. Thus in the Czechoslovakian case, according to Kieran Williams:

> Ultimately, of course, normalization took place because Moscow demanded it. . . . The Soviets, however, communicated only a general set of expectations and left the actual detail of normalization to local cadres . . . [A]ny factionalism within ruling communist parties had to be concealed and decision-making restricted to the innermost circle of party functionaries. The duty of any functionary or institution outside the inner circle, especially the media, was to relay and execute, not debate, official policy. The army and security police had to be operational, either for war or surveillance and riot control.[18]

While the general gist of this also holds true, of course, for the case of the GDR, particularly with respect to the roles of the army and security police, there are significant differences in the East German case. During the 1950s, the SED experienced great difficulty in building up a stable system of functionaries in the GDR, a situation perhaps exacerbated by the uncertainty over the future of the state. But in the course of the 1960s and 1970s, with the stabilisation of the economy and the international political situation and the coming to maturity of new generations, we can see the growth of what I have elsewhere termed the 'societal state', or 'honeycomb state'.[19] Despite and alongside the growth in the apparatus of power, there was a simultaneous growth in the less malign aspects of the East German state. Increasing numbers of GDR citizens came to take on positions as paid or honorary functionaries in a very wide range of positions: in the 'people's own' economic enterprises, in the trade union organisation (FDGB), as cultural functionaries, volunteers in youth work, and so on. Increasingly, the 'state' was carried by its citizens: large numbers of people became simply part of the way the regime functioned. Many of the chapters that follow explore the changing patterns of interrelationships between low-level and medium-ranking functionaries and their immediate local 'constituents', as

18. Williams, *Prague Spring and its Aftermath*, p. 59.

19. Mary Fulbrook, *The People's State: East German Society from Hitler to Honecker* (Yale: Yale University Press, 2005).

well as the relations between the latter and higher levels of the state apparatus. This contributes, too, to the realisation that traditional dichotomous approaches with their sharp separation of 'state' and 'society' are very difficult to apply in practice with respect to the way in which the 'societalised state' operated in the GDR.

Only a minority, of course—even if a fairly substantial minority—became actively involved in the state apparatus as functionaries. What about changing patterns of behaviour and opinion among the wider population? Different domestic institutional structures, inherited and reinterpreted patterns of political culture and 'repertoire', and the constraints and opportunities of the wider international situation affected the extent to which, and the ways in which, people adapted to the changing demands of their environment. Again, we can see differences across the Eastern European cases, although in all cases 'normalisation' presupposes some measure of adaptation, even if only grudging and grumbling, to conditions which people feel they can no longer challenge or seek to change. In Williams' discussion of 'patterns of conformity and resistance in society' in the Czechoslovak case, he suggests that:

> The broader normalization of society, like many forms of authoritarian control, required not an unrelenting terror but the retransformation of autonomous interest groups into monopolistic structures of mobilization which ... help to thwart opposition to dictatorship by channelling most citizens' energies into activities (often ritualized or diversionary) staged by official associations for youth, workers, professionals, women, national minorities, and intellectuals. Through these [organizations], time is consumed, ideology is transmitted, rewards are bestowed, an illusion of participation is created, and material dependency on the state is imposed.[20]

The assumption built into this assertion is that there is a sharp differentiation between the 'regime' and 'people'—even if there is some exploration of how people resign themselves and 'adapt'—and that the latter participate in a way that is acknowledged to be merely a matter of lip service or ritual obedience, in some sense essentially inauthentic.

Yet with respect both to the roles of functionaries and the involvement of the people, the situation in the GDR was arguably different from that in Poland or Czechoslovakia. In the GDR, as many of the chapters in this collection make clear, functionaries appeared in the course of the 1970s to have developed somewhat more leeway and room for a limited degree of partially

---

20. Williams, *Prague Spring and its Aftermath,* p. 249.

autonomous action within the local sphere; and, by the later 1970s and early 1980s, local and lower level functionaries frequently appeared as representatives not only of those above, but also of those whose interests they professed to serve, occupying an increasingly difficult position characterised by rising frustration, as spokespeople on behalf of those 'below' as well as at the behest of those 'above'. This appears to have been particularly the case by the later 1970s and early 1980s, when functionaries voiced increasing frustration with the shortcomings of the system. And it was precisely these relatively loyal servants of the regime who became increasingly critical of the failures of the Honecker government in the 1980s even to acknowledge, let alone deal adequately with, the mounting crises and failures to deliver the goods in a situation of economic decline heading towards ultimate collapse.

The consequences of this phenomenon for attitudes and behaviour patterns of the majority of East Germans are also subjected to closer examination in many of the chapters which follow. One interesting feature to emerge is the way in which many East Germans felt able to articulate their grievances and interests with at least some limited hope of redress or input into future policy. Thus, they were, if only to a limited degree and within certain boundaries (not least the physical boundaries of the East German state itself as a geographical entity), able to 'work the system' for their own ends. Many felt simultaneously committed to and critical of the system within which they lived and worked. This highlights the fact that it is not sufficient simply to talk about '*Eigen-Sinn*' in terms of a defence of a person's 'own interests' and the bestowal of his or her 'own meanings', important though such a stance also is in some contexts. The notion of '*Eigen-Sinn*' presupposes still some distance between an individual's 'own' and 'society's' interests and norms. What is interesting—in addition—in the GDR is the as yet insufficiently explored question of the extent of overlap and merging of these two areas. The notion of normalisation allows us to explore the extent to which certain norms were shared, or internalised, to such a degree that the sense of '*Eigen-Sinn*' becomes almost irrelevant.

This approach also has implications for wider debates about the roles of 'conformity and consent', or 'repression and opposition' in dictatorships (a debate frequently re-run with respect to the Third Reich). No serious historian would suggest that there was anything like the degree of popular enthusiasm for the GDR as there was for the preceding Hitler regime. But there were probably more areas of consent and consensus than historians have generally been prepared to acknowledge (commitment to greater social equality, or to a comprehensive health system in principle, while critiquing shortcomings in the GDR in practice, are probably good examples). To resolve such questions empirically, we need to look at lived experiences and degrees of internalisation of new norms; popular attitudes in the GDR cannot be described or summed up purely in terms of an assumed long-term general mood of gloomy resignation. Widespread popular opposition had clearly been present in the 1950s, and grew again in new ways (particularly under the protective umbrella of the Protestant Churches) in the 1980s. But the GDR population did not consist, after 1953, of repressed and muted oppositionalists; members of any kind of intellectual opposition were in only a tiny minority in the 1960s and 1970s, and there was no evidence, before 1989, of the kinds of alliance between workers and intellectuals evident in Poland.

Thus arguably normalisation in the GDR was rather more successful than in the neighbouring Eastern European states, even if the fact of being a divided nation, with a far more affluent western twin, meant that the East German status quo was never as unthinkingly accepted as a 'return to normal' as experienced in post-war West Germany. Yet East Germans did come to terms with and develop new ways of living in their changing state. In comparison to Poland, Hungary, and Czechoslovakia, the greater apparent stability of the GDR over two decades or so was predicated on a combination of having a stronger economy, perhaps an increasingly widespread willingness to act as functionaries, greater ease of isolation (or export to the West) of articulate opposition among the intelligentsia over a long period of time, and the relatively late emergence of the Protestant Churches as a focus for opposition in the late 1970s and 1980s. The character of the intellectual opposition, the words and works of the East German intelligentsia in the literary and creative arena, the roles of pastors, environmentalists, human rights activists, and others in the environs of the Protestant Churches, have long been the focus of discussion and debate, not least in the immediate aftermath of the fall of the Wall and the reunification with—or takeover by—the West, which many prominent voices from within the GDR had argued against. Similarly, the character and development of the ruling communist party, and the structures of power and repression in the *Stasi*, have been the subject of intensive analysis. But the ways in which the system was carried and sustained from within, by lower-level functionaries and ordinary people, has to date received less attention than they arguably deserve. These, too, were key elements in the 'normalisation of rule' in the middle decades of the GDR's history; and the erosion of this system was a significant factor in the de-legitimisation that preceded the more dramatic events of 1989.

Overview and Preview

A journalist, researching for an article on the complex political situation in Northern Ireland, was in a pub in a war-torn area of Belfast. One of his potential informants leaned over his pint of Guinness and suspiciously cross-examined the journalist: 'Are you a Catholic or a Protestant?' the Irishman asked. 'Neither,' replied the journalist, 'I'm an atheist'. The Irishman, not content with this answer, put a further question: 'Ah, but are you a Catholic atheist or a Protestant atheist?'

There is a similar complexity and ambiguity about commitment to the GDR, if focussed around a rather more secular political religion. Large numbers of East Germans may have refused to believe in the official gods of the SED regime, yet they were irrevocably involved in the institutions, activities, and organisations that sustained this state. Over time, these activities, and the values and attitudes that underpinned them, became 'second nature' to increasing numbers of GDR citizens, particularly those of younger generations who had never consciously experienced life under any other political or geographical boundaries. Arguably, a process of 'normalisation' set in, in which people both learnt the written and unwritten rules of the game, and operated according to the relevant norms. Those who transgressed were subjected to a wide range of penalties, from the most severe (incarceration and brutal maltreatment in a *Stasi* prison, even at times death) through to the quite informal (a friendly warning by an avuncular head teacher or police officer, ostracism by a work brigade, critical support from a neighbour or colleague). People learned to live within and generally abided by the visible and invisible boundaries of the regime; or they knew what consequences were likely to follow from any decision to transgress the boundaries. And within these boundaries, many developed ways of seeking to lead fulfilled and satisfying lives, in which they could pursue self-defined projects and personal goals. Patterns of conflict resolution became predictable, routinised.

To point to processes of normalisation in this sense is not to suggest that the GDR was a legitimate or a stable state: its very existence as a separate state was predicated on forcibly restraining the population behind a fortified border; and its economic foundations were far too fragile, the equation of mounting debt and generous social policy subsidies was entirely unrealistic, particularly in the altered international situation of the oil crises and arms race of the 1980s. People increasingly challenged and pushed the boundaries, particularly in the later 1980s once the signal had been given by the new Soviet leader Mikhail Gorbachev. For, as the official slogans in the GDR had always proclaimed, 'to learn from the Soviet Union is to learn to be victorious' (*von der Sowjetunion lernen heißt siegen lernen*). A lengthy period in which it is possible to discern processes of normalisation, if constantly contested, gave way to a period of economic decline and associated political destabilisation, opening the way for revolutionary change once the outer conditions were altered.

All of this is not to suggest that the GDR was a state that was at any time carried on a wave of popular enthusiasm, or that active commitment and popular support played a similar role in the GDR as did faith in the Führer in the Third Reich. But while the latter was at times carried on a tidal wave of popular support among significant numbers of the 'Volksgemeinschaft', levels of popular support which the GDR could never hope to achieve, the Third Reich was in essence intensely dynamic, inherently unstable, in ways in which the successor state built on its ruins in the Soviet zone was not. And the stabilisation of the GDR was built on more than merely force. We need, then, to develop more complex and nuanced ways of interpreting the relatively stable middle decades of the GDR, of understanding the changing character of East German society, and of representing the people who were formed by and lived through the distinctive socio-political structures of the 'societal state'. They did not, as some historians would have it, live constantly in a state of real or latent civil war. Nor was 1989 a simple continuation of 1953. In very large measure, 1989 was born out of a growing frustration with a system that had gone into visible economic decline in a period of heightened international instability; and 1989 was carried by those who were largely products of this system, had participated in its structures, and played a significant role in making it work. For a couple of decades, the GDR had—even while the *Stasi* was invisibly mushrooming—essentially (also) operated in large measure on a quite extended basis of 'legitimate authority' in Weber's sense: that is, authority in the sense of the willingness of functionaries to uphold the system, and the willingness of large numbers of people to obey (from whatever combination of motives), to play by the rules, whether or not they were in private agreement with these rules. What is extraordinary about the later months of 1989 is the fact that, even as the system was challenged and then crumbled, the loss of legitimacy in this purely functional sense also rendered the use of naked power impossible.

The fact that the GDR was born out of violence, was imposed by violence, yet collapsed with what has been termed the 'gentle revolution', should give us some pause for thought. So too should the high post-unification levels of 'Ostalgia' for an East Germany that had passed away: without mourning in any way the end of the SED regime, East Germans still appeared to feel some nostalgia for distinctive styles of life and patterns of social relationships. We need of course to focus on the key moments of crisis, of repression, dissent, and opposition: but this should not make us lose from sight the wide swathes of time, and the significant numbers of people who at the same time participated in and sustained the structures and processes that also made up the history of the GDR. It is to this end that the concept of normalisation may be of some use. The extent to which this concept proves fruitful in practice, in detailed and specific areas of inquiry, can only be judged in its application.

The chapters that follow are roughly divided into two major sections. In Part One, the focus is particularly on the conditions for stabilisation and routinisation of domestic political processes, understood broadly to range from exploration of the external conditions of détente at the international level (Merrilyn Thomas), through the transformation and routinisation of economic structures and processes in industry (Jeannette Madarász) and agriculture (George Last), to contestations over popular music and sport (Daniel Wilton), culture for the masses (Esther von Richthofen), and *Heimat* activitivists (Jan Palmowski). In many of these chapters, there is a strong focus on the intermediary roles of mid-level functionaries, who may have begun by seeking to represent 'the state' to 'the people', but who often ended by speaking on behalf of their own 'constituencies'. Although contributors differ quite markedly in their willingness to deploy or critique the notion of normalisation, all of these essays serve in effect to underline the significance of the roles of functionaries in the socio-political system of the GDR in the middle decades. Whatever their separate individual motives, and varying degrees of frustration or willingness to cooperate with central authorities, intermediate functionaries played a key role in negotiating what it was or was not possible to achieve in the pursuit of meaningful lives, and in social, economic, and cultural practices, for ordinary citizens in the GDR. And there is a history to be told, which varied according to area in rhythm, pace, and trajectory, of the degrees of stabilisation of structures and routinisation of practices, which had been more or less rapidly introduced in the post-war decade and a half or so of radical transformation and '*Aufbau*'.

Part Two turns to the question of subjective perceptions and norms—whether these are evidenced by way of internalisation, outward behavioural conformity, sporadic or continual contestation. While Alf Lüdtke emphasises the need to adopt an approach which starts from the acting individual and is sensitive to the complexity of inner perceptions, the simultaneity of apparently contradictory behaviours, and the active construction of individual life projects, Ina Merkel reminds us of the transnational, pan-European character of both the challenges of different phases of 'modernisation' and of cultural transfers across the Wall. The different experiences, patterns of behaviour, and inter-relations of succeeding generations are explored by Dorothee Wierling, while Angela Brock explores the character and impact of an education system determined to produce the 'socialist personality'. Mark Allinson identifies key tensions and common themes in 1977: a year in which, at first glance, ' nothing out of the ordinary' happened; and yet in which the 'abnormalities' or less than desirable features of life in the

GDR–division, frustrations, shortages, constraints–had become entirely expected, indeed, paradoxically, a more or less 'normal' state of affairs. Finally, Mary Fulbrook discusses the results of a survey carried out in 2005, fifteen years after unification, in which East Germans reflect on their lives and experiences during, after, and in the case of older respondents, also before the existence of the GDR. These subjective perceptions serve to highlight very different patterns of experience and memory, and underline the significance of notions of regularity, predictability, and ways of coping.

Overall, the volume seeks to engage with a range of aspects of life in the middle decades of the GDR's history, using the notion of normalisation as a heuristic device in the light of which systematic comparisons can be made. It does not seek to provide any kind of comprehensive characterisation, or to impose any artificial uniformity of interpretation, but rather to raise key issues for discussion and set out lines for further inquiry, proposing a more complex approach to the parameters and processes of 'rule' within a post-crisis period.

Part I

Normalisation as Stabilisation and Routinisation?

Systemic Parameters and the Roles of Functionaries

Chapter 2

'Aggression in Felt Slippers': Normalisation and the Ideological Struggle in the Context of Détente and *Ostpolitik*

Merrilyn Thomas

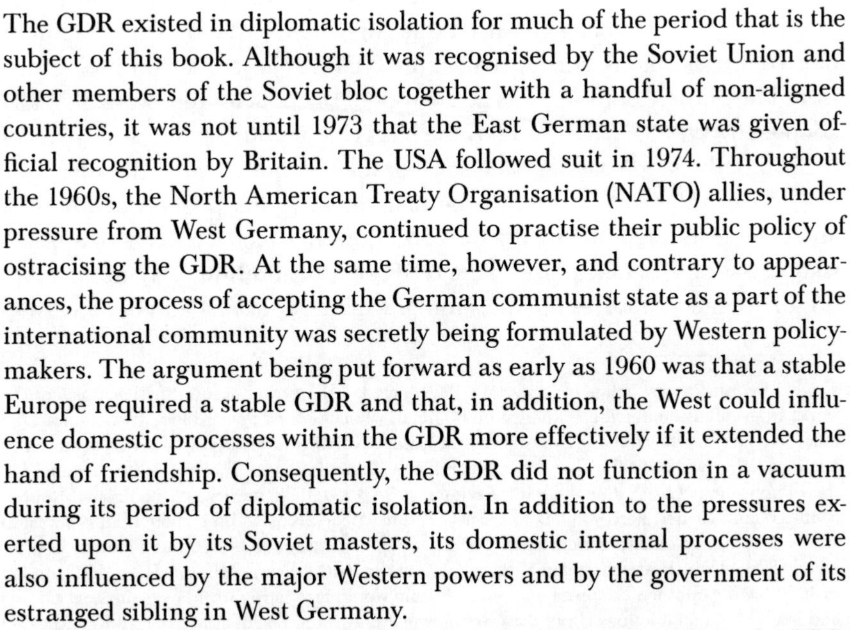

The GDR existed in diplomatic isolation for much of the period that is the subject of this book. Although it was recognised by the Soviet Union and other members of the Soviet bloc together with a handful of non-aligned countries, it was not until 1973 that the East German state was given official recognition by Britain. The USA followed suit in 1974. Throughout the 1960s, the North American Treaty Organisation (NATO) allies, under pressure from West Germany, continued to practise their public policy of ostracising the GDR. At the same time, however, and contrary to appearances, the process of accepting the German communist state as a part of the international community was secretly being formulated by Western policy-makers. The argument being put forward as early as 1960 was that a stable Europe required a stable GDR and that, in addition, the West could influence domestic processes within the GDR more effectively if it extended the hand of friendship. Consequently, the GDR did not function in a vacuum during its period of diplomatic isolation. In addition to the pressures exerted upon it by its Soviet masters, its domestic internal processes were also influenced by the major Western powers and by the government of its estranged sibling in West Germany.

The object of this chapter is to examine the 1960s and 1970s in the GDR within the context of Cold War international relations. The period of normalisation was a period during which the NATO allies and West Germany adopted a policy of co-operation rather than confrontation towards the Soviet Union and its satellite states, including the GDR. In other words, at the same time as a process of internal normalisation was taking place within the GDR, a similar process was taking place in relation to external affairs. This chapter will argue that these policies were instrumental in enabling the GDR leaders, Walter Ulbricht, and later Erich Honecker, to pursue their goal of creating a strong and permanent socialist German state.

In the context of the Western powers and the Soviet bloc in general, the policy of co-operation became known as détente. In the context of relations between the two German states it was known as *Ostpolitik*. The adoption of these policies by the West in its dealings with the Soviet bloc was driven by two major judgements. Firstly, failed revolts in East Berlin, Poland and Hungary in the 1950s had persuaded the West that other ways needed to be found with which to defeat communism. In addition, the Cuban Missile Crisis in 1962 had concentrated minds on the dangers of brinkmanship and on the threat of nuclear annihilation. Secondly, the West believed that the future threat from the Soviet Union lay in the non-aligned world where Western influence was being undermined. It needed to be able to concentrate its political and military resources in Asia and Africa rather than Europe.[1] A reduction of tension in Europe, therefore, appeared to be in the West's interests. The idea of co-existence rather than confrontation with the Soviet bloc countries, and particularly with the GDR because of its position at the front line of the Cold War, was at the root of the policies that were officially adopted by West Germany and by the NATO allies during the latter years of the 1960s, the seeds having been sown at the beginning of the decade.

The chapter first examines the manner in which policies of *Ostpolitik* and détente assisted in creating the conditions in which a process of normalisation was able to take place in the GDR and, in addition, were designed to do so. Secondly, it raises the question of whether *Ostpolitik* and détente were

1. British foreign policy objectives in 1960 included the prevention of 'further areas of the world from falling under the influence or domination of the Sino-Soviet bloc'. It was envisaged that 'détente will allow a reduction of forces in Europe which is necessary if we are to achieve our "politico-military" policy elsewhere'. See Macmillan Cabinet Papers 1957–1963 Online, Adam Matthew Publications Ltd, National Archives reference CAB 134/1929, meeting of the Prime Minister, Ministers and Armed Forces chiefs to discuss Future Policy Study, 7 June 1959, final report and subsequent discussion and memoranda. The Future Policy Study 1960–1970 was a lengthy Top Secret document which was compiled at the request of the British Prime Minister Harold Macmillan in 1959/60. It examined the problems which Britain would face in the world over the next decade and made recommendations about the ways in which they should be handled; questions addressed included should the British try to reach a *modus vivendi* with the Russians in Europe; would détente be to British advantage and what sort of geo-political price would be paid for this policy. The document provides a useful insight not only into the mindset of British foreign policy makers during this period, but also of their allies and their opponents, chiefly the USA and the Soviet Union.

not so much a bridge between East and West as a boarding plank which the West used in order to undermine the ideological convictions on which communism was based. This, in turn, raises the question of the extent to which, in the context of international relations, the normalisation of the GDR was not an end in itself but a stage along the road to the end of the GDR. To what extent was normalisation an illusion, outside the control of Honecker and his regime?

The suggestion that the West secretly influenced events inside the GDR–and other Soviet bloc countries–is one that is, by definition, difficult to prove. These matters were largely secret at the time and remain so now. In this context, though, it is necessary to remember that during the Second World War, both Britain and the USA created impressive psychological warfare departments and acquired the expertise with which to undermine hostile states–in this instance chiefly the Third Reich.[2] They were able to draw on this legacy of experience during the Cold War. Probably the two most important skills acquired during the Second World War were the ability to use psychological techniques in order to undermine the enemy, and to maintain and control resistance groups in occupied countries. Both these skills were secretly put to use during the Cold War, against a different enemy.

Some of these secret Cold War activities have begun to emerge into the public arena in various ways. A few years ago, the father of *Ostpolitik*, Egon Bahr, told a meeting of former Cold War players in Washington that GDR Foreign Minister Otto Winzer had been right to refer to *Ostpolitik* as 'aggression in felt slippers'.[3] Indeed, Bahr himself had made this claim at the time in the 1960s when he referred to the fact that his and Brandt's goal was 'to liberate Eastern Europe from a disease called communism'. Subsequently, both men had agreed to keep silent about that aim. Likewise, in a discussion on the Future Policy Study, the British Foreign Secretary told his Cabinet colleagues that détente 'was not a policy of appeasement but a means of carrying the offensive into the Communist camp'.[4] This comment was made

---

2. See, for example, Michael Stenton, *Radio London and Resistance in Occupied Europe: British Political Warfare 1939–1943* (Oxford: Oxford University Press, 2000); Ellic Howe, *The Black Game: British subversive operations against the Germans during the Second World War* (London: Michael Joseph, 1982); Paul Lashmar and James Oliver, *Britain's Secret Propaganda War* (Stroud: Sutton, 1998).

3. Egon Bahr, *Bulletin of the German Historical Institute*, American Détente and German *Ostpolitik*, 1969–1972, Supplement 1 2004: 138. Bahr was the right-hand man of West German Chancellor Willy Brandt for many years and has been credited with being the architect of *Ostpolitik*. He was Secretary and later Minister of State in the Brandt government. 'Under the title of state secretary, Bahr essentially functioned as Brandt's personal emissary to the Soviet Union and the GDR from 1969 onwards.' M.E. Sarotte, *Dealing with the Devil: East Germany, Détente and Ostpolitik* (Chapel Hill and London: University of North Carolina Press, 2001), p. 28.

4. Macmillan Cabinet Papers, meeting of the Prime Minister and Ministers to discuss the Future Policy Study, 23 March 1960.

in 1960–ten years before East and West German leaders met for the first time in the East German city of Erfurt. These hidden agendas were a reflection of the manner in which international relations were conducted during the Cold War. Western foreign policy frequently consisted of two distinct strands–official policy and unofficial policy. Official policy was that which was aired publicly; unofficial policy was spoken of behind closed doors.[5]

Cold War International Relations Before 1965

An examination of Western policy towards the Soviet bloc before 1965 demonstrates the way in which strategy changed in later years. During the earlier period, particularly during the 1950s, Western policy towards the Soviet bloc, including the GDR, focused initially on the idea of the containment of communism and subsequently on what was known optimistically as rollback. Rollback meant liberating the Soviet bloc countries from communism by encouraging, organising, and financing resistance groups along the lines of the resistance operations to the Nazis that had been supported covertly during the Second World War. The aim, in the words of the British, was to liberate Soviet bloc countries short of war. US and British backed operations of this type were carried out, for example, in Albania, Ukraine, Poland, and the Baltic states.[6]

A detailed account of US policy in relation to the GDR during this period has been published by the German historian, Anjana Buckow. Her research in US archives has provided a mass of evidence to demonstrate that the USA actively supported opposition, and was prepared to use psy-

---

5. See Merrilyn Thomas, *Communing with the Enemy: Covert Operations, Christianity and Cold War Politics in Britain and the GDR* (Oxford and Bern: Peter Lang, 2005), chap. 6 for more on unofficial Cold War policy. The secrecy and duplicity of the Cold War creates problems for historians, but a failure to address these issues because of the difficulties of 'proving' them results in an incomplete interpretation of events. To skirt around unofficial policy or intelligence activity places an artificial restriction upon the sum of knowledge. This chapter addresses some of the problems faced by historians examining the murky world of Cold War international relations. It is worth noting that during the last couple of decades many historians have found it necessary to revise their interpretations of this period with the passing of time. What may have appeared to have been 'proved' at one time, can cease to be 'proved' at another, whether one is basing one's interpretation on official records, or not. It is ever thus.

6. W Scott Lucas and C.J. Morris, 'A Very British Crusade: The Information Research Department and the Beginning of the Cold War' in Richard Aldrich, *British Intelligence*. Quoted in Peter Grose, *Operation Rollback: America's Secret War Behind the Iron Curtain*, (Boston, New York: Houghton Mifflin, 2000), p. 155. An example of the rollback policy can be seen in Albania where, in the late 1940s, unsuccessful attempts were made by the British and the Americans to instigate a revolt, these plans being betrayed by Kim Philby. Also see Mike Sewell, *The Cold War* (Cambridge: Cambridge University Press, 2002), p. 41.

chological warfare techniques in order to encourage anti-Soviet resistance.[7] This was true of the West in general. While not desiring an opposition that caused an explosion, it did want one which caused turmoil; one which threatened, weakened, and possibly overturned the communist regime. As with Hungary and Poland though, the West looked to the people of the GDR to accomplish this and was not prepared to become militarily involved in support of a revolt. In the words of an instruction from the US Department of State to Bonn and Berlin, dated 1953, on US policy towards the GDR:

> We wish to emphasize that overt measures should be used only to nourish the spirit of resistance, not to advocate openly specific acts of resistance. The reasons for these limitations . . . are: 1) that we do not want to risk precipitating prematurely a mass, open rebellion or, if one does take place prematurely, to incur blame for the consequences; and 2) that we do not want to throw doubt on the spontaneous nature of the resistance.[8]

The GDR during this period was an abnormal state by virtue of its international isolation. This lack of normality was a state of affairs that the West fostered as part of its Cold War strategy. It was experienced by GDR citizens in a number of ways. One of these was their inability to travel to countries outside the Soviet bloc. This inability arose, not only because of restrictions imposed by their own government, but, more importantly, because the NATO countries frequently put obstacles in the way or refused to allow them to travel to the West. A closer examination of this NATO policy is useful to an understanding of Western foreign policy in that it provides an illustration of the sometimes devious ways in which the West used apparently overt methods with which to achieve covert aims. In this particular instance, the use of travel restrictions against GDR citizens was, on one level, a reinforcement of and an essential part of the policy of non-recognition. But, in addition, its rigid implementation had a demoralising effect upon GDR citizens, a fact of which there is evidence that the British Foreign Office was well aware. Later, it can be seen how policy changed in line with the shift towards recognition and stability.

Allied Travel Office

One of the results of the policy of non-recognition was that the GDR passport was also not recognised by NATO countries. The psychological game

---

7. Anjana Buckow, *Zwischen Propaganda und Realpolitik: die USA und der sowjetisch besetzte Teil Deutschland 1945–1955* (Stuttgart: Franz Steiner, 2003), p. 9.

8. Quoted in Buckow, *Zwischen Propaganda und Realpolitik*, p. 578.

adopted by the West of creating a sense of abnormality went so far that, until 1962, the British entered the nationality of GDR citizens on travel documents as 'Presumed German'.[9] The process of granting permission for GDR citizens to travel to the West was conducted through an organisation known as the Allied Travel Office (ATO), based in West Berlin and run by NATO, which had been established at the end of the Second World War. Initially, the ATO was seen as a relief organisation since, in the post-war chaos, there was a need to facilitate travel by Germans from both East and West despite a lack of documents. As the years went by, and West Germany became a sovereign state with its own passport, the ATO dealt purely with GDR citizens. The British government was at pains to disguise the restrictive role of the ATO publicly, its aim being to create the impression that it was solely GDR-imposed restrictions that prevented its citizens from travelling to the West. For example, in 1965, in response to correspondence relating to a woman living in Britain who wanted her East German parents to visit her, a Foreign Office official advised in a handwritten note that Members of Parliament should blame the East German government for the inability to travel, especially when it concerned elderly people wishing to visit relatives, and to give no hint that it was any fault of NATO.[10] When a Labour MP made the claim in Parliament that 'people in the Eastern Zone were prevented from visiting the West, not by the East German Government, but by these . . . regulations', the response was that the 'main obstacle to pensioners or anyone else leaving East Germany consists in the nature of the East German regime and not in any regulations relating to visas'.[11]

The reality was, however, that East Germans who wished to travel to the West were obliged to obtain a document known as a Temporary Travel Document (TTD) issued by the ATO. The rules governing who was eligible for a TTD and the manner in which those rules were interpreted varied from time to time depending on political tensions. One

9. Bell, *Britain and East Germany: The Politics of Non-Recognition* (MPhil thesis, University of Nottingham, 1977), p. 133. Although the practice ceased in 1962, this designation was still in use on Temporary Travel Documents used by GDR citizens until 1967 since the documents were valid for five years. See National Archives, FCO 33/515, TTD Policy, 1969.

10. National Archives, FO 371/183140 RG1621/78, correspondence relating to a visit by the East German parents of a woman living in Britain, November 1965. 'Mr Thomson [George Thomson, Minister of State at the Foreign Office] has asked me firstly to make a general point that any letter to Members of Parliament should put the blame for the lack of travel facilities, especially for old folk, from East Germany squarely on the East German authorities and not give any hint that the NATO allies are at fault'.

11. Hansard, Oral Answers, Columns 897–898, question from Stan Newens to the Secretary of State for Foreign Affairs, 13 December 1965.

British official described the TTD weapon 'as a bludgeon, not a rapier'.[12] Fundamentally, the principle was to refuse a TTD to anyone who could be said to hold a political position or who claimed to be a member of an official delegation. However, innocent individuals were often caught up in these restrictions and found themselves unable to obtain the documents needed to be allowed into Britain. For example: during the three years between October 1961 and September 1964, 195 East Germans were refused permission by the ATO to travel to Britain. Of these, 135 were sportsmen and women, 19 musicians and actors, and 13 scientists.[13] There were two main reasons for this state of affairs. One was because the definition of 'political' could be stretched to include anyone who claimed to be a citizen of the GDR because, in Western eyes, the GDR did not exist and, therefore, claiming citizenship was a political statement. Indeed, when an MP asked the government what criteria governed the issue of TTDs, the response was that the criteria were 'confidential', being agreed to by NATO.[14] Since the criteria were unknown, it was therefore impossible to comply with them. When an MP asked what 'non-political' meant, suggesting that it meant East Germans had to divest themselves of all political ideas, the government responded that it was a 'general description', but applied to people who purported to represent the Soviet zone as a sovereign or national entity. This catchall could include football teams or children's choirs.[15]

The second reason why ordinary people were unable to visit the West was because the ATO required the GDR applicant to make two visits to its West Berlin office, the first to make the application and the second in order to pick up the documents. This was obviously impossible for most people to do from 1961 onwards after the building of the Berlin Wall and difficult even before that date. However, the situation was such that, when in 1966 a parliamentary question was put in Britain asking the government to lift this requirement, the government responded that it had 'no evidence' that the ATO requirements impeded travel by East Germans to Britain.[16] This assertion was made despite the fact that a Foreign Office document dated 1964 includes extracts from letters from around a dozen East German citizens, wishing to be reunited with relatives in Britain, who wrote personally

12. National Archives, FO 371/177988, RG 1622/27, handwritten note, 25 March 1964.

13. Hansard, Written Answers, Columns 202–203, 7 November 1966.

14. Hansard, Written Answers, Columns 7–8, question from Mrs Renée Short to the Secretary of State for Foreign Affairs, 26 July 1965.

15. Hansard, Oral Answers, Columns 11–13, 13 April 1964.

16. Hansard, Written Answers, Column 13, question from Mr Brooks to the Secretary of State for Foreign Affairs, 12 December 1966.

to the British government pleading with it to post their TTDs to them as they were unable to comply with the requirement to personally attend at the ATO.[17] It is interesting to note that the restrictions also affected leading East German clergy—people who were seen by the GDR itself as opponents of the regime. Foreign Office documents show that the leading GDR bishop, Frederich-Wilhelm Krummacher, found it difficult to visit Britain and succeeded in doing so only by obtaining documents 'surreptitiously' from an unknown American. When Paul Oestreicher, a British priest and long-standing GDR intermediary, contacted the Foreign Office in 1965 to ask if this method could be used again, the answer was no.[18] The issue of travel restrictions became increasingly live in Britain during the 1960s, with a number of parliamentary questions being asked about the role of the ATO. In 1963, the subject became a matter for Cabinet discussion in the wake of British refusal to allow the Berliner Ensemble to take part in the Edinburgh Festival, this decision resulting in strong protests from many British people.[19] One MP described the restrictions as treating GDR citizens like 'Stateless persons'.[20]

Nevertheless, British government statistics do show that a number of East Germans were given permission to travel to Britain. Between October 1963 and May 1964, 399 East Germans applied to visit Britain, 298 travel documents were issued and seven were refused.[21] The government explained that the totals did not tally because many East Germans did not collect their documents after they were issued which, as we have seen, would have been impossible for many because they were required to collect them from West Berlin. If, usually for commercial reasons, both the British and the East German authorities were anxious for the visit to go ahead, a courier service was arranged, but this was not an option for ordinary travellers. The British gave two reasons for their insistence on applications being made in person. One was that they did not trust TTDs to the GDR postal service. The other was that the British intelligence service often used the opportunity to question applicants. As one Foreign

17. National Archives, FO 371/177988, RG 1622/12, TTDs policy 1964. In one instance, it is recorded that special arrangements were made for a Frau Missbach to receive her TTD when she arrived at the airport in London on 12 April 1964, but most applicants were not so fortunate.

18. National Archives, FO 371/183140 RG 1621/52, Krummacher travel arrangements, April 1965.

19. National Archives, FO 371/172194, papers relating to the refusal to allow the Berliner Ensemble to visit Britain, 1963.

20. Hansard, Written Answers, Column 78, question from Will Owen to George Thomson, Minister of State for Foreign Affairs, 15 November 1966.

21. Hansard, Oral Answers, Columns 134–135, question from Will Griffiths to Walter Padley, Minister of State for Foreign Affairs, 21 June 1965.

Office official explained: 'in addition our friends [a term used to describe the intelligence services] wish to vet the East Germans and try to squeeze some information out of them on the first visit.'[22]

NATO policy was amended in 1965, in keeping with the growing policy of NATO countries towards preserving the status quo in Central Europe and particularly in relation to the GDR. The office issued a statement in December 1965 which said that it had been decided to introduce a 'simplified procedure' to facilitate the entry of pensioners into NATO countries.[23] This in itself is an admittance of the fact that previously pensioners had fallen foul of ATO regulations.

Cold War International Relations After 1965

The concept that was the main plank of Western policy towards the GDR during the latter part of the 1960s and first half of the 1970s was stability.[24] The West no longer wanted to promote revolt in Soviet bloc countries.[25] To quote the Future Policy Study: 'We do not wish to stimulate unrest which Russia would be certain to suppress.'[26] The British government, while publicly maintaining a belligerent stance, secretly talked in terms of maintaining the status quo. The strategy was to bring about a normalisation of conditions in relation to bilateral and multilateral relations with the communist state, and also within the state itself. This included support for Brandt's *Ostpolitik* ideas behind the scenes, even during the very early years.[27]

There were various ways in which this strategy was put into practice, one of the main steps being the recognition of the GDR in the early 1970s, which brought the state into the international community of nations. This was a lengthy and tortuous process with Western policymakers keeping a

---

22. National Archives, FO 371/177988, RG 1622/11, memo from D Beevor about the need for two personal visits to West Berlin, 14 February 1964.

23. Hansard, Oral Answers, Columns 897–898, question from Stan Newens to the Secretary of State for Foreign Affairs, 13 December 1965.

24. 'The revitalisation of Cold War tensions from 1979 ended a period of détente and heralded a return to rhetoric and actions reminiscent of the late 1940s and early 1950s.' Sewell, *The Cold War*, p. 112. The voices of opponents of détente in both the USA and the Soviet Union began to be heard more loudly from around 1975 onward.

25. Egon Bahr, *GHI Washington Bulletin*, Détente and *Ostpolitik*, p. 137. It had become clear that communist regimes could not be overthrown by internal revolt.

26. Macmillan Papers, Future Policy Study, February 1960.

27. National Archives, FO 953/2347, a briefing note for 'information talks' between British and West German diplomats notes with reference to a plan for Brandt to visit Karl Marx Stadt that 'we warmly approve of the SPD initiative but we must avoid giving the impression that we are more enthusiastic than the Federal Government', May 1966.

watchful eye on every small step taken by the GDR towards international recognition. For example, one British Foreign Office file for 1971 deals with GDR attempts to be represented in a variety of international organisations and the possible repercussions. The file ends with the Prime Minister writing to his Foreign Secretary to ask if a 'fresh look' at GDR policy is not now due because 'our policy now–with the Federal Republic in the van–is to recognise them as a state, and to accept their entry into the United Nations, when certain conditions are fulfilled'.[28]

The acceptance of the GDR as a member of various international organisations and the taking of steps to improve communications was an important part of the process leading to recognition and normalisation. For example:

- in 1971, the allies discussed (without reaching agreement) the possibility of commercial flights into Schönefeld airport in East Berlin;
- in 1971, the GDR applied for membership of the World Health Organisation. A decision was deferred until the following year;
- in the same year, the British discussed allowing the use of the GDR's flag and national anthem in NATO countries (by way of contrast, two years' earlier, the GDR hockey team had cancelled a visit to Britain because of a ban on the use of the flag and anthem);[29]
- in 1972, the GDR was given observer status at the UN and became a member of UNESCO.

All these developments and many more were significant in bringing about normalisation within the GDR. Another most important factor was trade. Moves were made to increase trade between the GDR and capitalist countries and credit arrangements were agreed upon which were to become a necessary part of the GDR economy.

Superficially, these developments appeared to be beneficial to the GDR and, in the short term, this was no doubt the case. GDR citizens experienced an improvement in economic conditions and were no longer made to feel like outcasts. They had become members of the international community and were increasingly able to travel to other countries in the interests of economic, cultural, and sporting activities. However, the long-term purpose behind the new strategy adopted by the Western allies and West Germany can be seen in views expressed in the Future Policy Study. Here, the argument was put forward that the best way of defeating communism was to expose it to

---

28. National Archives, FCO 33/1334, minute from Edward Heath to Sir Alec Douglas-Home, 29 October 1971.

29. Hansard, Written Answers, Columns 101–102, 26 April 1968.

Western capitalist influences. The best and probably only hope for a peaceful end to the East-West conflict, it stated, was that the East would 'mellow into a bourgeois prosperity' and thereby 'lose its urge to win the world for Communism. . . . we must do anything we can to assist the process.' Communist ideology, it went on, 'can best be eroded away by exposure to another system which is shown to be equally successful and more attractive'.[30] The report recommended that steps which could be taken in this direction included visits, meetings, and cultural and commercial exchanges.

A major plank of the *Ostpolitik*/détente strategy was to encourage the GDR to become more economically dependent on the West. The aim was 'to limit the further consolidation of Soviet domination by encouraging the development of economic independence in the Satellites.'[31] Economic independence of the Soviet Union, though, meant *dependence* on the West. The US Secretary of State Dean Rusk told Prime Minister Harold Macmillan as early as 1962 that the West Germans 'recognised the importance of making East Germany dependent economically on the West'.[32] Over the next 20 years or so, West Germany made unconditional loans amounting to billions of Deutsch Marks to the GDR. A senior Soviet diplomat, Juli Kvitzinsky, observed post-reunification that the West Germans only invested in the GDR in order to bring about the *Wandel durch Annäherung* (change through rapprochement) which Brandt and Bahr had conceived in 1963.[33] Honecker also recognised the threat as time went by, but was, according to Kvitzinsky, 'unable to escape the noose once he was in it'. The historian Manfred Görtemaker has observed that 'the GDR faced the dilemma of weighing up its desire for international recognition and co-operation against the danger of allowing the West to undermine its internal cohesion via the so-called "exchange of people, information and ideas"'.[34]

Ideological infiltration

Ideological infiltration of the GDR was the political goal behind *Ostpolitik* and détente. The aim was to undermine the ideological beliefs on which the communist world was based so that eventually the countries concerned

30. Macmillan Papers, Future Policy Study, February 1960.

31. Ibid.

32. Macmillan Papers, meeting between Rusk, Macmillan and others, London, 24 June 1962.

33. Juli Kvitzinsky, *Vor dem Sturm: Erinnerungen eines Diplomaten* (Berlin: Siedler, 1993), p. 261.

34. Manfred Görtemaker, 'The Collapse of the German Democratic Republic and the Role of the Federal Republic', in the *Bulletin of the German Historical Institute London*, Vol; XXV, No. 2, November 2003: 49–70.

would collapse—or implode—as they eventually did in 1989. In this sense, ideological infiltration does not refer to paid up members of the intelligence services secretly penetrating the Iron Curtain in order to undertake subversive activities; rather, it refers to the ways in which Western ideas and values were spread to the Eastern bloc through the activities of non-state organisations and private individuals. As Egon Bahr told the Cold War seminar in Washington in 2002, the communist world was held together by a belief in a shared ideology—remove that belief and there would be nothing left to fight for. It was for this reason that the 'ideological struggle was a central intellectual component of *Ostpolitik*'.[35]

Personal networks played a major part in the ideological infiltration of the East. One of the networks having the greatest impact on the outcome of the Cold War was the Christian network. Christianity was extraordinarily significant in the struggle between capitalism and communism. It was a faith that had the power to rival communism in the manner in which it gripped its believers. The Christian network was, and is, an international network. It did not have to be created in order to combat the atheist ideology of communism because it already existed. Its power and influence ranged from that exerted by the late Pope John Paul II, who some historians argue 'instigated the public process leading to the end of the Cold War and the break-up of the Soviet Union',[36] to the work of organisations such as the World Council of Churches, and individual Christians such as the British priest Paul Oestreicher and the American Quaker Robert Reuman.[37] The Church, as the Soviet diplomat Kvitzinsky noted, was an important secret channel used in order to find a way, firstly, to normalise relations with the East and, secondly, in order to infiltrate those countries.[38]

---

35. Egon Bahr, *GHI Washington Bulletin*, Détente and *Ostpolitik*, p. 140.

36. Peter C Kent, 'The Lonely Cold War of Pope Pius XII', in *Religion and the Cold War*, Dianne Kirby, ed. (Basingstoke: Palgrave, 2003), p. 67.

37. For an account of Paul Oestreicher's activities in the GDR, see Thomas, *Communing with the Enemy*. A 10-page report by Robert Reuman on attitudes in the GDR is contained in the British Foreign Office archive. See National Archives, FO 371/183002 RG 1016/42A, report by Reuman dated 30 June 1965.

38. Juli Kvitzinsky, *Vor dem Sturm*, 'They [representatives of the West German Protestant Church] were more prepared to talk to us than the worldly authorities and rejected possible doubts with the argument that clergymen should proclaim God's word to everyone. Therefore they could foster contact with Soviet diplomats . . . Without doubt, the Church was not simply interested in bringing the word of God to the Soviet people. As preparers of the way for contact with the Soviet Union, the Church drew the attention of all those who themselves wanted this possibility. There were quite a few, for, among the Germans, efforts were growing to find a way to normalise relations with the people of the USSR. The Church was a channel for this.' p. 207.

The words 'ideological infiltration' do not spring out from Western archives which are available to researchers (in contrast to the *Stasi* archives where such references proliferate). There are, however, other ways of expressing such things. One British Foreign Office document, for example, refers to 'ideological contamination' in relation to détente and the GDR.[39] The Future Policy Study refers to the 'ideological struggle' and the need to construct 'an infrastructure of political and spiritual sympathies without which our economic and military effort cannot be fully effective'.[40] Here, the use of the word 'spiritual' is interesting in the context of the use of Christianity in this ideological struggle. A study of British Foreign Office archives shows that the British were extremely interested in what they referred to as 'the attitudes' of East German people. For example, in 1965, the Foreign Office circulated with approval a document written by Robert Reuman, a frequent visitor to the GDR, entitled *Attitudes in the DDR (East Germany)*. This was passed on to the department responsible for anti-communist propaganda and support of opposition groups, the Information Research Department.[41] The same year the British representative in West Berlin submitted a lengthy report on the 'mood of the East German people'. Attitudes are the raw material of ideological infiltration. What the infiltrators need to know is what they are and how they are changing. In this context, Foreign Office files also reveal that the British went to the lengths of intercepting letters written by East Germans to friends and relatives abroad to find out what they were thinking.[42]

Ideological infiltration was both overt and covert—sometimes both at the same time. Activity could be overt in that it was not disguised, but the true purpose might be covert in that it was hidden. Overt ideological infiltration was achieved through increased contact between the East and West, between East Germany and West Germany. The movement of people and the opening up of communications chipped away at communist ideology in a manner that could not be suppressed. The material well-being of the capi-

---

39. National Archives, FCO 33/2068, annual review of the GDR, 1973. 'It will be interesting to see whether, through fear of ideological contamination, the East German authorities will feel constrained to back track in 1973 . . . we all know that when the chips are down, internal repression and restrictions are likely to have the upper hand.'

40. Macmillan Papers, Future Policy Study, 1960.

41. National Archives, FO 371/183002, RG 1016/42A, Attitudes in the DDR (East Germany), 30 June, 1965. The IRD drew up reports in 1960, for example, on the East German lie factory, the East German incitement campaign, and East German subversive organisations (FO 975/139, 140, 141).

42. National Archives, FO 371/183002 RG 1016/35, private letters from the GDR intercepted by British Secret Service revealed that people had no great pride in the GDR but they wanted reunification so that families could be united, not because the FRG was better, 1965. Also FO 371/183002 RG 1016/41, intercepts mentioned in a report on GDR youth rock culture, 8 November 1965.

talist world was held out to the people of the East with the aim of achieving the conditions described by the British Future Policy report; the replacement of socialist hardship by the aspirations of bourgeois prosperity. At the same time, covert activity took place designed to build up structures within Soviet bloc countries on which the movement towards a more relaxed reformed form of socialism could be built. The goal was long-term. The aim was to create the conditions within which a reform movement could become effective in a peaceful and stable manner. The process demanded extreme caution, as was demonstrated by the debacle in Czechoslovakia in 1968.

Covert Activities

The nature of covert operations means that it is difficult to provide hard evidence of their existence. The archives of Western intelligence services are not open for inspection by researchers. An insight into Western activity, however, is provided by the *Stasi* archive. Although there is considerable, and sometimes, heated debate about the weight that should be attached to the contents of the *Stasi* archive, it can be argued that they are a useful source because they provide researchers with glimpses not only of the activities of GDR intelligence operations, but also those of other countries. While allegations of spying or subversive operations must always be treated with caution, from whichever side the allegation comes, these allegations are pointers to the complexity and duplicity of Cold War international relations.

During the Cold War, both sides tried to subvert the other. The West feared infiltration by Communist agents, not only seeking to obtain information, but, more importantly, seeking to influence events. The same was true for the Eastern bloc. It was constantly on guard against the subversive activities of the capitalist countries. Nowhere was this more the case than in the GDR. The extent to which the GDR feared ideological infiltration as a result of *Ostpolitik* can be seen in the huge growth of the *Stasi* as an organisation during this period.[43] Between 1969 and 1975, the number of IMs (unofficial informers) almost doubled from about 100,000 to 180,000. This type of action was something the West foresaw and hoped to be able to avert. As noted above, the question of whether the 'ideological contamination' created by détente and *Ostpolitik* would increase repression within the GDR was a matter of interest to the British Foreign Office.[44] The situation in the GDR

43. Manfred Görtemaker, 'The Collapse of the German Democratic Republic and the Role of the Federal Republic' in the *Bulletin of the German Historical Institute London*, Vol. XXV, No. 2, November 2003: 52. The *Stasi* grew to become an 'instrument of state-wide control'.

44. National Archives, FCO 33/2068, annual review of East Germany for 1972, note from James of FO to Major General Earl Cathcart in Berlin, 15 February 1973.

reflected that in the Soviet Union. Bryan Cartledge, Head of Chancery at the British Embassy in Moscow, drew up a report entitled *Détente and the 'Ideological Struggle'* in 1974 in which he described the ideological struggle from the Soviet perspective as being a 'struggle against' rather than a 'struggle for', prophylactic rather than missionary.[45] That is to say, the main aim was not the propagation of communist ideology in the West, but the prevention of the incursion of capitalist ideology into the Soviet bloc. In Soviet eyes, it was the period of détente rather than the period of conflict that presented the greatest ideological threat. Cartledge's paper on the ideological struggle was widely circulated within the Foreign Office, winning plaudits for its analysis, and thereby demonstrating the weight that the British attached to the concept of the ideological struggle. One diplomat, commenting on the report, wrote: 'I keep it next to my heart as a Bible!'[46] In reality, the West and the GDR were actually facing the same problem, namely keeping control of the destabilising effects of *Ostpolitik* and détente. Neither side wanted the boat to be rocked—or at least not until the boarding plank had been placed firmly in position.

Aktion Sühnezeichen

If it is accepted that efforts made by the West to subvert the Soviet bloc were comparable with communist attempts to undermine the West, the major question which presents itself is in what manner and by what means did the West subvert the Soviet Union, the GDR, and the other members of the Soviet bloc, and how did it undertake this task while at the same time preserving the stability of these countries. A partial answer to this question is provided by the use that countries such as Britain and West Germany made of private individuals and non-state institutions behind the Iron Curtain in helping to build up hidden networks within the Soviet bloc countries linking those who had, or in the future would have, influence. These were not people who were going to take to the streets and confront Soviet tanks, but people who, it was hoped, could steer the Soviet bloc countries in a

45. National Archives, FCO 28/2564, Détente and the Ideological Struggle by Bryan Cartledge, 29 January 1974. 'Just as those responsible for the direction of the ideological offensive see in détente a period of special opportunity, so those entrusted with the more crucial defensive campaign profess to see in it a period of special danger. . . . it is precisely during the period of détente [according to Soviet counter-intelligence] that the hostile forces of imperialism and counter-revolution can be expected to be at their most dangerous . . . in the employment of subversive and underhand techniques for the dissemination of lies and slander.' The report was sent to the Foreign Secretary, Sir Alec Douglas-Home. Cartledge went on to become British Ambassador to the Soviet Union during the Gorbachev period, retiring to become an Oxford academic in 1988.

46. National Archives, FCO 28/2564, comment on Cartledge paper, 8 April 1974.

direction that was amenable to the West. It is in this area that the Church and Christian groups played a major role.[47]

One such all-German Christian organisation was called *Aktion Sühnezeichen* (action as a sign of atonement). It was founded in 1958 with the stated aim of making atonement for Nazi atrocities in those countries which had suffered most and carried out this work by arranging for groups of young volunteers from both East and West Germany to take part in construction projects. The countries which were particularly targeted by *Aktion Sühnezeichen* were Poland, Czechoslovakia, and the Soviet Union.[48] The organisation was inter-denominational with both Protestants and Catholics taking part. The activities of *Aktion Sühnezeichen* were closely monitored by the *Stasi*. Many reports on the organisation and its leaders are contained within the *Stasi* archive.[49] Particular attention was paid to its founder, Lothar Kreyssig, a leading Church figure in the GDR, and his friend and colleague in West Berlin, Erich Müller-Gangloff, a member of the West Berlin *Aktion Sühnezeichen* leadership circle and the head of the West Berlin *Evangelische Akademie*. Both men were politically well-connected. Müller-Gangloff's contacts included Egon Bahr and the West German Foreign Minister, Gerhard Schröder. The *Stasi* suspected that he worked for the CIA, though, of course, this cannot be proved. Müller-Gangloff confided in a senior *Stasi* agent, Hans-Joachim Seidowsky, who worked behind the scenes in the international field and in particular with operations related to the Churches, up until the demise of the GDR.[50] This relationship began at the end of the 1950s, at which time Seidowsky was posing as a disaffected young Marxist and Müller-Gangloff was attempting to recruit him into the network of reform-minded socialists that he had established in the GDR. Seidowsky's true identity became known to Müller-Gangloff in the mid 1960s. *Aktion Sühnezeichen* also had close British links, in particular with Coventry Cathedral.[51]

The *Stasi* saw *Aktion Sühnezeichen* as a subversive and ideologically hostile organisation. It placed its activities within the global strategy of the West, in particular *Ostpolitik*. It linked the founding of the organisation in 1958 to the start of a 'reorientation' by the West towards the use of what

---

47. For information about the activities of Church organisations and Church leaders in the GDR see Thomas, *Communing with the Enemy*.

48. With the lifting of travel restrictions in 1963, young East Germans were able to take part in work camps in these countries and did so in great numbers.

49. See, for example, MfS AP 20985/92, 20983/92, 7632/79 and 279/57 on Lothar Kreyssig; and MfS HA XX/4 1477, 2278 and 2303 on *Aktion Sühnezeichen* in the Bundesbeauftragte für die Unterlagen des Staatssicherheitsdienstes der ehemaligen Deutschen Demokratischen Republik.

50. See Thomas, *Communing with the Enemy*, chap. 2.

51. See Thomas, *Communing with the Enemy*, chaps. 8 and 9.

the *Stasi* described as 'more flexible methods' in the fight against the Soviet bloc.[52] The *Stasi* perception was that *Aktion Sühnezeichen*'s 'ultimate goal [was] to penetrate the GDR and other socialist states in order to create a hostile ideology there through the creation and exploitation of contacts and connections with the Church and other people'.[53] The two other countries most threatened, in the eyes of the *Stasi*, were Czechoslovakia and Poland. *Aktion Sühnezeichen* did indeed run work camps manned by idealistic young volunteers. By doing so, it also assisted in lifting the Soviet bloc countries out of the isolation in which they had existed hitherto. In addition, using the work camps as its raison d'être, it was able to build up networks, not just among young people, but among Church leaders, intellectuals, and others of influence—people who were dissatisfied with the rigid communist system. The *Stasi*'s view was that, in this way, *Aktion Sühnezeichen* operated as a systematic part of the West's psychological warfare and ideological infiltration programme.

There are those who argue that the *Stasi* as an organisation was paranoid and saw conspiracy where none existed. However, it cannot be disputed that *Aktion Sühnezeichen* was a politically important organisation of far greater significance than its low profile would suggest. Probably the greatest evidence of this is the meeting which two *Aktion Sühnezeichen* leaders, one of them Müller-Gangloff, had in East Berlin with Khrushchev in 1963 during the very early days of *Ostpolitik*. This had been planned as a secret meeting between Brandt and the Soviet leader, but Brandt was forced to cancel at the last minute because of political pressure. The two *Aktion Sühnezeichen* leaders took his place. The message that Müller-Gangloff gave to Khrushchev was that people such as Brandt were moving towards a less confrontational attitude towards the Soviet Union and the other socialist countries. Egon Bahr's 'Wandel durch Annäherung speech' was made a few months later at a West German *Evangelische Akademie.*

In Czechoslovakia, Müller-Gangloff founded an organisation called the Comenius Club (named after the medieval Czech philosopher), which operated in concert with *Aktion Sühnezeichen* and which was aimed specifically at promoting the idea of co-existence through private networks rather than official channels. In Müller-Gangloff's own words, the reason for founding this organisation was to reach out to Germans in East and West as well as the CSSR, Poland, Hungary, and the USSR. 'We want to use our freedom, our private initiative, to open up in the public area that which cannot be

52. BStU, MfS HA XX/4 1477, report on *Aktion Sühnezeichen*, circa 1969, p. 18.
53. BStU, MfS HA XX/4 1477, report on *Aktion Sühnezeichen*, circa 1969.

done officially,' he said, and close the 'abyss' between East and West.[54] The abyss must be actively overcome with a new policy with concrete objectives. 'Governments which are entrenched in Cold War positions cannot solve this problem', he said. The GDR was included in the plans from the start, although, according to Müller-Gangloff, it was 'clear to us that the abyss between the two Germanies is the hardest to bridge and will remain so for the foreseeable future'.[55] In the event, the Club was most active in Czechoslovakia, but lost its importance after the events of 1968.

Following the suppression of the Czech reform movement in 1968, Poland became the main target of *Aktion Sühnezeichen*. In Poland, for example, the *Stasi* recorded that *Aktion Sühnezeichen* worked closely with the Clubs of the Catholic Intelligentsia (KIK) and publications such as Tygodnik Powszechny, dissident organisations which were also associated with the late Pope John Paul II.[56] One of the aims was to counteract the feelings of resignation that had resulted following the crushing of the reform movement in Czechoslovakia. Activities were stepped up post–1968 with the *Stasi* reporting that *Aktion Sühnezeichen* had opened a bank account in Warsaw in 1969 and allocated the sum of 43,000 Deutsch Marks for activities in Poland that year, more than double the previous year.

Conclusion

The greatest period of domestic stability in the GDR, as discussed in other chapters in this book, was also a period during which the Western world adopted a policy of co-operation rather than confrontation with the Soviet bloc. The aim was to achieve stability in Europe. As the GDR emerged from the turbulence of the post-war years and the systems of the socialist regime began to bed in, the governments of the NATO allies and West Germany gradually edged away from their hard-line rejection of the GDR as a legitimate state. Western post-war policy, which had envisaged the rollback of communism with the GDR being the most vulnerable of the socialist states, was transformed into a policy that not only accepted the GDR as a sovereign state, but positively encouraged it to achieve a sense of identity. Thus, the GDR was accepted into the international community, provided with economic assistance, and allowed to participate in the cultural, academic,

54. Evangelische Zentralarchiv, 97/639, Müller-Gangloff's description of the Comenius Club, 13 August 1967.

55. Ibid.

56. See George Weigel, *Witness to Hope: the Biography of Pope John Paul II* (New York: HarperCollins, 1999), pp. 110 and 231.

and sporting world. In terms of international relations, the GDR during this period could almost be described as a normal state, although the presence of West Berlin within GDR territory and the existence of the Berlin Wall were constant reminders of the ease with which normality could turn to crisis.

During this period of 'normalisation', the West rejected the idea of isolating the GDR and moved instead towards a policy of changing it. Through increased contact, it was anticipated that slowly, over a period of many years, the GDR together with other Soviet bloc countries could be transformed. One of the main reasons why Brandt and Bahr committed themselves to *Ostpolitik* and therefore to the acceptance of the GDR was because they believed that this slow incursion into the GDR and other Soviet bloc countries would lead to their ultimate defeat. The archives of both the East and the West refer to similar strategies during this period of normalisation, although the terminology may differ. The *Stasi* feared Western subversion. The West talked in terms of undermining communism through closer contact. Importantly, neither side appeared to be referring to violent revolutions, as had been the case in the early days of the Cold War. Détente and *Ostpolitik* allowed and encouraged the GDR to function as a relatively normal state, but also enabled Western influences to permeate GDR society much more effectively than had been the case when the communist state existed in isolation. These policies were thus a contributory cause both of the period of stability that the GDR enjoyed during the 1960s and 1970s and of the country's eventual downfall.

Chapter 3

Economic Politics and Company Culture: The Problem of Routinisation[1]

Jeannette Madarász

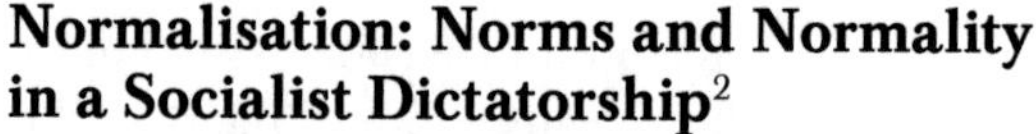

Normalisation: Norms and Normality in a Socialist Dictatorship[2]

After the building of the Berlin Wall in August 1961, the situation in the German Democratic Republic (GDR) changed. East Germans of all political and social opinions were confronted with circumstances beyond their control, circumstances that had a massive impact on their personal and working lives. People had to adjust to these changed circumstances; they realised this quickly and adapted without much ado. Processes of adaptation could last a lifetime and led to ever-finer nuances of behaviour. Social norms emerged based both on traditional expectations and the socialist values propagated by the East German communist party, the SED. They affected most East Germans in one way or another. Political acquiescence does not describe the situation adequately: much more was going on in all sections of society. Particular patterns of behaviour developed: the avoidance of open confrontation by assessing accurately the political implications of any situation; distrust to-

1. This chapter summarises some of the arguments developed in the author's recent publication: Jeannette Madarász, *Working life in East Germany, 1961 to 1979. Arriving in the Everyday* (Basingstoke: Palgrave, 2006).

2. The author was part of a research project entitled *The 'Normalisation of Rule'? State and Society in the GDR, 1961–1979,* based at the German Department of UCL. Many thanks are due to the AHRC for its continuous and generous financial support of this project.

wards anybody who was not a close friend or relative, although even this was no guarantee against surveillance by the Ministry of State Security (MfS or *Stasi*); careful positioning within political, professional, and social structures, depending on the individual's career aims; the use of a specific language to communicate effectively with governmental and party institutions; and so on. These methods allowed people to feel that they were shaping their own lives and those of their families despite an intrusive political system. They also learned to live with and exploit given circumstances because socialist values and the promises made by the SED became a part of the East German value system.[3] In fact, attitudes began to prevail criticising those who felt unable or refused to comply with this value system for political reasons.

East German society was shaped by compromise. It included notions of collective life, basic ideals, and practical values, such as social fairness and guaranteed jobs, but largely excluded many of the SED's ideological tenets, such as socialist internationalism or hostility towards Western imperialism.[4] In response to given circumstances, expectations, and popular reluctance to accept whole-scale re-socialisation, new norms and behaviour patterns formed slowly. The 1960s also marked the beginning of a process of standardisation and institutionalisation, which affected not only the education system, professional qualifications, and the economic sector, but also cultural activity, communication practices, and language. With time, norms became set in stagnating institutions, which distorted their original meaning. Both their rigidity and the notable difference between propaganda and everyday life motivated, at least in some parts of East German society, a backlash against both standardised biographies and unsatisfying realities. By the late 1970s, societal expectations of 'normality' that had been introduced at least partly by the SED were not fulfilled anymore, leading to widespread resignation, frustration, and a stronger focus on personal interests. Ensuing tendencies towards individualisation undermined East German society in the longer term.

Normalisation

Normalisation is a concept referring to various processes that contextualise societal evolution not just in a socialist dictatorship such as the GDR, but

3. Cf. also the patterns of opinion expressed in 2005, summarised in Chapter 13, below.

4. Harry Müller, *Jugend im Wandel ihrer Werte* (Leipzig: ZIJ, 1985), pp. 13–14. See also Dieter Geulen, *Politische Sozialisation in der DDR. Autobiographische Gruppengespräche mit Angehörigen der Intelligenz* (Opladen: Leske+Budrich, 1998), p. 103. Ina Merkel, *Utopie und Bedürfnis. Die Geschichte der Konsumkultur in der DDR* (Cologne et al.: Böhlau, 1999), p. 160. Felix Mühlberg, *Bürger, Bitten und Eingaben. Geschichte der Eingabe in der DDR* (Berlin: Dietz Verlag, 2004), p. 27.

almost any socio-political system.[5] Stabilisation after political or social upheaval will be followed by routinisation that, if given enough time, will lead to the internalisation of at least some of the repeatedly propagated and experienced norms. In turn, these norms will define the popular perception of 'normality', especially when comparisons with other socio-political systems are restricted. It is particularly relevant that the normalisation concept refers to a variety of processes. It is not intended to announce the 'arrival of normal life', however this difficult concept may be defined, but rather to refer to the steps that lead towards a 'perceived normality', which always also includes a variety of difficulties and crises.

Furthermore, the normalisation concept does not assume the totality of these processes. Within any society, there will always be niches, subcultures, and behaviour that run counter to the mainstream. No state or party will ever be able to control entirely a country and its population. Rather, just as in parenthood, some latitude may go a long way towards acquiescence. Even this, however, will depend on issues such as social and cultural opportunities and an imperative economic success.

This chapter applies the normalisation concept to company politics and company culture in East German state-owned concerns during the 1960s and 1970s. It will be argued that stabilisation during the 1960s relied to a large extent on finding common interests and the establishment of a limited interaction between central decision makers and the working population.

When talking of state-owned concerns or factories as acting entities, it is to be understood that a number of persons and groups with different interests and intentions influenced and prepared the actions that issued from any specific state-owned concern. To explain this further: the works director was the person directly responsible to superior institutions such as the *Vereinigung Volkseigener Betriebe* (VVB) and the appropriate ministry. However, the party secretary of the SED also had an impact on decisions, and in many cases this was not restricted to political issues. Furthermore, the works director was in a position in which one of his main tasks was to negotiate between his employees and central institutions. Administrative staff, economic functionaries, trade union functionaries, and functionaries representing other mass organisations such as the Free German Youth (FDJ)—all of these people and groups contributed to an internal exchange and shaped the dialogue with central institutions. Production workers and technical staff also had their own individual agendas, which they tried to defend within the context of ongoing interaction, often relying on seemingly suitable functionaries for the representation of their interests.

5. See also the discussion of this concept in Chapter One, above.

This complex constellation of interests furthered the mutual exchange of expectations, demands, and offers, which led to fine adjustments and shifts within original interest patterns at all levels. It is the interaction between different interest groups and individual personalities in state-owned concerns and also with central institutions, i.e., vertical relations within the East German economic system, which lies at the heart of this analysis. Horizontal relations, for example cooperation between state-owned concerns or with the local community, enriched this complex pattern further.

Interaction is delineated by the context in which it takes places, even more so in dictatorial societies.[6] Therefore, the following three themes will be discussed: economic changes over time; differences between factories; and interaction between central authorities and the working population. Here, the influence of both central policy on individual factories and that of the workforce on central policy will be traced.

The East German Economy: Changes Over Time

The economy in the GDR was based on a planned system, which encountered crises repeatedly. It stood in constant competition with the West German economy and was dependent on supplies of raw materials, specifically oil, from the Soviet Union. Also, the East German economic system was hampered by its political context.[7] In the GDR, workers were the most sought after social group, but also, after the upheaval on 17 June 1953, the most feared (potential) opponents of both state and party. Much was done to avoid open confrontation—a major problem in terms of economic effectiveness. Work in the GDR was a highly political issue.

The economic crisis of the late 1950s had manifestly contributed to the decision to build the Berlin Wall in 1961. In spite of Cold War polemics, one of the main motives at the central level had been to stabilise the workforce to allow for more substantiated economic planning. However, although the Berlin Wall effectively prevented the bleeding out of a skilled workforce, the economic difficulties were not resolved. Accordingly, Ulbricht introduced economic reforms in 1963. The New Economic System of Planning and Management (NES) was intended to improve the economic system structurally. However, its introduction was piecemeal and caused problems for many

6. Sandrine Kott, 'Pour une histoire sociale du pouvoir en Europe communiste', in Kott, ed., *Pour une histoire sociale du pouvoir en Europe communiste, Revue d'histoire moderne et contemporaire 49* (2002), pp. 5–23.

7. Jeffrey Kopstein, *The Politics of Economic Decline in East Germany, 1945–1989* (Chapel Hill, London: University of North Carolina Press, 1997), p. 2.

state-owned concerns as it undermined their often already precarious position further by, for example, introducing new and more realistic methods of bookkeeping.[8] Although the NES did not offer immediate remedy to the crisis-shaken East German economy, it comprised some necessary reforms. For example, the influence of the SED's organisational units in factories changed clearly during the 1960s and 1970s. With the introduction of the NES, the party organisations within state-owned concerns were reduced in importance, especially regarding actual management decisions. The rise of technocratic thinking during this period, which was much encouraged by Ulbricht, and the economic reforms with their focus on providing management with more decision making power, together helped to strengthen the position of works directors and economic functionaries at an intermediate level.[9] This forced party functionaries into retreat, at least in the short-term, although they never stopped trying to get involved.[10] Already in 1967, this process was reversed and party influence started to grow again, arguably reflecting Honecker's increasing influence on domestic politics.[11]

Towards the end of the 1960s, the GDR underwent another economic crisis, which was a crucial accessory to Ulbricht's replacement by Honecker. Honecker's concept of the 'unity of economic and social policy' (*Einheit der Wirtschafts- und Sozialpolitik*) defined the political priorities of the new leader. The unity of economic and social policy was based on debt-funded investment policy. In the long-term, it led to an immense increase in indebtedness as oil prices soared and finances were used to increase standards of living, particularly accommodating higher levels of consumption. Economic reproduction was not ensured by the new leadership. From the middle of the 1970s, the negative results of this policy became apparent in many state-owned concerns heralding the advent of another economic crisis in the late 1970s. Neither the introduction of massive savings measures, nor drastic rationalisation, nor the creation of *Kombinate* provided the necessary structural solutions required by a centrally planned economy that promised the right to work.

---

8. See for example LAB, C Rep. 409–01 Nr. 54, Parteileitungssitzung 18.1.1965, p. 13.

9. André Steiner, *Die DDR-Wirtschaftsreform der sechziger Jahre–Konflikt zwischen Effizienz- und Machtkalkül* (Berlin: Akademie Verlag, 1999), p. 65. See also Steiner, 'Betriebe im DDR-Wirtschaftssystem', pp. 55 and 59, in Renate Hürtgen, Thomas Reichel, eds., *Der Schein der Stabilität–DDR-Betriebsalltag in der Ära Honecker* (Berlin: Metropol Verlag, 2001), pp. 53–67.

10. Wolfgang Biermann, *Demokratisierung in der DDR? Ökonomische Notwendigkeiten, Herrschaftsstrukturen, Rolle der Gewerkschaften 1961–1977* (Cologne: Verlag Wissenschaft und Politik, 1978), p. 56.

11. For a more detailed account, see also Madarász, 'Normalisation in East German enterprises, 1961–79', in *Debatte* 1/2005, pp. 45–63. See also Peter C. Caldwell, *Dictatorship, State Planning, and Social Theory in the GDR* (Cambridge, New York: Cambridge University Press, 2003), p. 185.

Changes at the central level had an impact on company culture in terms of management style, socio-political relations, and behaviour patterns. For example, the status of a factory could change dramatically in the context of changing central policy, which then affected many other aspects such as working and living conditions, recruitment, the supply of materials, and hence, economic performance. However, beyond large-scale changes there could be many other reasons for such internal developments.

The general trend was divided into many different instances, events, and processes that were influenced by both central policy and developments at the grassroots level. Neither ever progressed in a straight line or was applicable to every social group or section of society across-the-board. For example, central policy favoured specific industrial sectors, but these priorities changed over time. Also, company culture differed widely according to the history of an individual factory, its location, size, the gender ratio of its workforce, and its status. Accordingly, within different factories different problems occurred, were prioritised or ignored. Furthermore, central policy in some cases took years to reach a specific factory and its workforce. As a result, the situation within one economic unit may have differed greatly from the experience of another in the same area, of similar size or part of the same industrial sector. Therefore, the differences between state-owned concerns must be considered meticulously when trying to describe company culture in the wider context of central policy.

Differentiation Between Enterprises

The differences between state-owned concerns is an issue worth studying in detail, particularly in response to totalitarian approaches to GDR history that assume general applicability of central intention to the everyday life of most people. Even some of those historians who recognise the 'limits' of control with which central authorities were continuously confronted tend to neglect specific experience in favour of general trends. This approach, however, bears the danger of writing local history whilst claiming to describe a country's experience, discussing policy-making at the highest level whilst ignoring influences from below, or the other way round. Even in the centrally planned economic system, problems differed and various methods were applied to deal with difficulties.

Of course, all state-owned concerns were confronted more or less by the same basic problems. Working conditions were dire and social relations could be tense. André Steiner has stressed the economy's dependence on political decisions that undermined efficiency throughout the GDR's existence.[12] One aspect of this political context was the right to work, which limited the economy's flexibility.[13] Also, almost every workforce had to deal with unreliable supplies of materials and prefabricated parts, a lack of qualified staff, and insufficient investment and capacities. However, even with regard to these very basic issues, the real situation in different factories could vary dramatically. A comparative approach seems needed to paint a nuanced picture of life and work in the GDR that allows for both general trends and distinct experiences.

Sources are a problem in this context, as it seems that, at least generally, archives for large, state-owned, and centrally administered concerns that were part of the capital goods industry are the most easily accessible. However, the least a historian can do is to select factories that existed prior to the war to compare their position to those that were founded during GDR times; to choose enterprises in diverse locations, with workforces of varying gender ratios and, crucially, of dissimilar status within the economic system; and, to pay attention to the impact of individual personalities.[14]

Many excellent studies have already given some indication of the relevance of specific themes within the East German economic system. Sandrine Kott, for example, has traced general structures and the experiences of the workforce in five Berlin factories.[15] Petra Clemens has written on a traditional factory employing primarily women, and Leonore Ansorg has written on a state-owned concern that also employed mostly women, but was built from scratch in a previously agricultural area.[16] Francesca Weil compared two Leipzig factories and came to the conclusion that both size and composition were central to their individual company culture. Weil also noted the importance of the works director's networks for the economic performance of a state-owned concern.[17] Furthermore, within the East German economic

12. Steiner, *DDR-Wirtschaftsreform*, p. 556.

13. Heike Knortz, *Innovationsmanagement in der DDR 1973/79–1989. Der sozialistische Manager zwischen ökonomischen Herausforderungen und Systemblockaden* (Berlin: Duncker & Humblot, 2004), p. 186.

14. See Thomas Reichel, Die 'durchherrschte Arbeitsgesellschaft'–Zu den Herrschaftsstrukturen und Machtverhältnissen in DDR-Betrieben, p. 91, in Hürtgen, Reichel, *Der Schein der Stabilität*, pp. 85–110.

15. Sandrine Kott, *Le communisme au quotidien. Les Enterprises d'Etat dans la société est-allemande. Edition Belin* (Paris, 2001).

16. Leonore Ansorg, '"Ick hab immer von unten Druck gekriegt und von oben". Weibliche Leitungskader und Arbeiterinnen in einem DDR-Textilbetrieb. Eine Studie zum Innenleben der DDR-Industrie', in *Archiv für Sozialgeschichte* 39 (Berlin: Dietz Verlag, 1999), pp. 123–65. Petra Clemens, *Die aus der Tuchbude–Alltag und Lebensgeschichten Forster Textilarbeiterinnen* (Münster: Waxmann Verlag, 1998).

17. Francesca Weil, *Herrschaftsanspruch und Wirklichkeit. Zwei Sächsiche Betriebe in der DDR während der Honecker-Ära* (Cologne et al.: Böhlau Verlag, 2000).

system, the status of a factory requires consideration, as has been pointed out by Ingrid Deich specifically with regard to a company's social efforts.[18] However, despite many insightful individual analyses, a comparative approach is still missing. The individuality of state-owned concerns needs to be stressed with reference to a variety of themes in the context of the centrally planned economic system. An older factory employing mostly women, with a long tradition, faced a different situation to one that employed mostly men; and both were in an entirely different position from a factory newly built in the countryside.

Significantly, such differences need to be discussed as essential characteristics rather than picking and choosing from the various state-owned concerns to put together a general picture, discerning major trends rather than exploring what in my opinion is the most definitive aspect of economic units in the GDR: their distinctiveness. To highlight this point, in the following the experiences of five selected factories will be compared.

Both the *Berliner Glühlampenwerk* (BGW) and the *Transformatorenwerk* in Berlin (TRO) were factories that had existed prior to the Second World War. Both were principal suppliers for their products within the GDR and both exported worldwide. They both employed large workforces of about four to five thousand people in the 1960s and 1970s. However, whilst the TRO employed mostly men, the bulk of the BGW's employees—about 65 percent—was female. Accordingly, they were confronted with different problems.

In the 1960s, the need to employ women wherever possible to compensate for labour shortages was growing within the East German economy. Part of this effort was the provision of suitable places of work and childcare facilities to get mothers into employment. It is no surprise, then, that the BGW was at the forefront of the new drive to improve working and living conditions, discussed in more detail below. Already in 1965, a suitable programme had been devised for the BGW; TRO, which employed mostly men, had to wait until 1967 for a similarly extensive package. A major contributory factor to the BGW's early success at expanding its social efforts, however, had been the activities of its works director Rudi Rubbel.[19]

The influence of the works director was crucial. In the GDR, the principle of individual responsibility (*Einzelleitung*) applied. It meant that works directors were held responsible for the economic performance of a factory

18. See Ingrid Deich, Wolfhard Kohte, *Betriebliche Sozialeinrichtungen* (Opladen: Leske+Budrich, 1997).

19. Rudi Rubbel (1920–71) had been active in the *Neuerer* (innovator)-movement during the 1950s, member of the *Bundesvorstand* of the FDGB (East Germany's trade union), and of the SED's Berlin district organisation before becoming works director at the BGW in 1964.

by both central authorities and the workforce. Success was measured by the plan, working and living conditions, wages and bonuses. It has been rightly argued that the works director and his management team were in a difficult position between the plan and the workforce as a result of this constellation.[20] It is crucial to show how this constellation worked on the ground and how it was dealt with by central authorities, the works director, and the various layers of the workforce.

In many cases, a power struggle ensued between the works director and the party secretary as a result of an opposition of economic and political interests. Often enough, it was decided by personality traits or an individual's length of service and, thereby, social standing. In the *Chemiefaserwerk Premnitz* (CFW), for example, relations between the party secretary and the works director Hermann Danz, who came to Premnitz in 1967, were tense right from the outset. The party secretary had been in his position for many years before the arrival of Danz, and former employees of the CFW remember him as an authoritarian personality with little by way of interpersonal skills. To say the least, he made it difficult for the new works director to establish his authority.[21] In other cases, however, such a power struggle never came to fruition. The works director of the *Erdölverarbeitungswerk Schwedt* (EVW), for example, automatically became a member of the SED's central committee and therefore had a direct link to the centre of the communist party, which no party secretary would have been able to rival.

The authority of any works director, and his success, also depended on his or her connections. Top functionaries such as Rudi Rubbel at the BGW, Helmut Wunderlich at TRO, or Werner Frohn at the EVW could rely on strong and continuous backing from central authorities. Rubbel maintained good relations with Paul Verner, who was a member of the Politburo, and with the executive board of the FDGB. Wunderlich, as a former Minister for General Mechanical Engineering, and vice chairman in both the State Planning Commission (SPK) and the Peoples' Economic Council (VWR), was well connected to central state authorities; and Frohn was a member of the SED's central committee and had close connections to the Minister of the Chemical Industry, Günther Wyschofsky. Although there were limits to their powers, these people, more than less elevated functionaries, could move things; they were motivated, hard-working and insisted on good relations with the workforce. Their arrival at a state-owned concern almost guaranteed success.

---

20. Kott, *Le communisme au quotidien*, p. 177.

21. See the oral history interviews with the works director Hermann Danz, the technical director, and other former employees of the CFW (transcripts in possession of the author).

Quite apart from such crucial aspects having to do with internal power structures, factories outside of Berlin and any of the other larger cities were in an entirely different situation again from both the BGW and TRO. The CFW had also had a long company tradition, but it was not only removed from the capital of the GDR, it also had a lower status within East German industry than, for example, the EVW, which was also located in the countryside. Chemical fibres and textiles were less important to the East German economy than aggregates, bulbs, and products of raw oil that could be sold on the world market for hard currency. However, the CFW was of immense importance for the surrounding territory for which it was the main employer. People came not only from Premnitz, but from surrounding villages and small towns such as Rathenow to work at the CFW. To enable sufficient provision of childcare facilities, schools, accommodation, and other services necessary for everyday life, the CFW supported local authorities by offering financial assistance, technical expertise, and labour.[22]

This type of cooperation was vital to the establishment of a reliable work force, especially in small towns or in agricultural areas, still more so for new economic units such as the EVW in Schwedt and the *Halbleiterwerk* in Frankfurt/Oder (HFO). Both were founded in the early 1960s and had to put much effort into recruiting their workforce. Almost every East German factory had difficulties recruiting suitably qualified employees. Here, it was even more important to work with local authorities to build up a suitable environment where young families might see a future for themselves and their children. When trying to encourage people to move into an area or seek employment at a specific factory removed from the usual amenities offered by larger towns, management and local authorities had to work together to improve surroundings. In this context, cooperation was based on a mutual interest and benefited both sides. Local patriotism (*Ortspatriotismus*), in contrast to a state-owned concern's egoism (*Betriebsegoismus*), which carried much more negative connotations as similar efforts were concentrated solely on the factory and its workforce, was welcomed and encouraged by central authorities.

It has been argued that central authorities forced state-owned concerns to share their resources with the local community.[23] It is certainly correct that, in the late 1960s and early 1970s, laws and decrees centralised coopera-

22. BLHA Rep. 503 CFW 5236, 15.3.1970, *Grundkonzeption des VEB Chemiefaserkombinat Schwarza 'W.Pieck'–Chemiefaserwerk 'Friedrich Engels' Premnitz zur Verbesserung der Arbeits- und Lebensbedingungen für den Zeitraum 1970–75*, p. 13. See also BLHA Rep. 503 CFW 5654, *Bericht über den Stand der Erfüllung der Massnahmen aus den abgeschlossenen Kommunalverträgen des CFW*, 15.10.1971.

23. See Kott, *Le communisme au quotidien*, p. 88.

tion efforts, thereby in effect ordering all factories to support their localities. The motivation behind these efforts was the state's growing difficulty in financing and realising the necessary investments. State-owned concerns were supposed to help out a desperate economy that was encountering problems in the late 1960s, and they simply had more resources than local communities. In September 1964, Honecker had stated in the Politburo that it would be much better to leave responsibility for childcare facilities and accommodation with the individual factories. Honecker expected them to have greater financial clout than regional bodies, and also feared constant fights with local authorities.[24]

However, to some extent at least, this sharing of resources was also in the interest of the factory, which could expect valuable concessions concerning social and cultural provisions in return for resources such as material, workers, and specialists.[25] There was a notable difference between factories that were located in large towns and cities, where they were not the only employers, and those in small towns or out in the countryside, where a single firm provided all of the jobs and resources: in the latter, *Ortspatriotismus* was essential to the area, and managers recognised local influence as significant to their economic success.

In turn, members of the workforce, from production workers to technologists, administrative staff, and economic functionaries, were very much interested in working at a successful plant. Employment at a factory that fulfilled its plans and had a high status within the East German economic system would ensure high wages, bonuses, and good working and living conditions.[26] Naturally, many fundamental problems were rooted in the deficiency of the centrally planned economic system, and could not easily be solved; but they were dealt with sufficiently to ensure, at least outwardly, a more efficient organisation of work and a smoother production process. Success could contribute to an improvement in social relations. To a greater extent at least than in unsuccessful economic units, production workers were given a chance to be productive, technologists had the opportunity to be innovative, and administrative staff and economic functionaries avoided some of the possible confrontations with exasperated subordinates and superiors. Social peace was kept more easily in state-owned concerns with a high status than in failing ones. This was in the interest of almost everybody: central authorities, management, and, increasingly in the 1960s and 1970s, also the workforce.

24. BAB DE 1 / VA 48523, Report on discussion in Politburo, 30.9.1964, p. 12.

25. See for example BLHA Rep. 703 EVW 374, Kommunalvertrag 1969/70 EVW–Rat der Stadt Schwedt, 13.9.1969.

26. Deich, Kohte, *Betriebliche Sozialeinrichtungen*, pp. 155ff.

These are just a few examples to highlight issues that had an impact on the development and positions of state-owned concerns within an economic system that worked on the basis of selection. One other relevant issue was the influence of the SED, which not only depended on the personalities of both the works director and the party secretary, but also on changes in central policy. Furthermore, the interest of central authorities in a state-owned concern could vary widely and have diverse consequences, both negative and positive. Various aspects contributed to a factory's placement and those that were deemed deserving of promotion met with different responses than those of lesser status. Status, however, depended on various aspects and could change with time; changes in central economic policy, a new works director or technological advancements could either hinder or help a particular factory in the constant struggle for a privileged position.

Dynamics of Power: Interaction Between the Centre and the Grassroots

Even slight shifts and fine differences had an impact on company culture, specifically within the centrally planned economic system. There have been excellent studies on economic policy,[27] on the evolution of consumerism, and, linked to it, social policy at the central level[28] and developments at the grassroots.[29] However, the interaction or mutual permeation between central policy and the grassroots has not yet been analysed with reference to the individuality of state-owned concerns. Here, it is crucial to consider the experience of individual factories within the context of wider economic policy and socio-political developments over two decades.

Any factory depended on decisions that were made at the central level. However, short-lived upheavals were paralleled and, seen in retrospect, overlain by processes that affected people in the longer term. Specifically when considering the attitudes and opinions of people, whether the production worker, an economic functionary or the works director, behaviour patterns in the early years of a decade differed greatly from those in the later part of the same decade. In the 1960s, this was partly in response to a changing political climate caused by the power struggle accompanying the advent of a new head of state.

---

27. See in particular works by André Steiner and Jeffrey Kopstein.

28. See particularly Philipp Heldmann, *Herrschaft, Wirtschaft, Anoraks. Konsumpolitik in der DDR der Sechzigerjahre* (Göttingen: Vandenhoeck & Ruprecht, 2004).

29. See, for example, works by Peter Hübner, Sandrine Kott, and Jörg Roessler.

Workplaces were the primary intersection between the working population and the state. It was here that the ideological theory of the working class as the leading force in communism, which was after all one of the founding myths of the GDR, needed to be substantiated.

Social relations at the grassroots were influenced by central policy. Throughout the 1960s and 1970s, the SED reserved its right to send intellectuals, specifically artists, students, and failing party members into production to learn to appreciate working class life. In many cases, the newcomers were shocked by the situation in the factory halls, the behaviour, and the attitude of their new colleagues.[30] Sometimes, good working relations and mutual respect developed.[31] Sometimes, a sense of distance and lack of understanding prevailed. Production workers mostly blamed economic functionaries for inadequate work organisation and the higher levels of management for their inability to provide required materials or better working conditions. Technologists were unhappy and became cynical regarding their own work, which was seldom applied to production processes. Administrative staff were in a particularly difficult situation, positioned between complaining workers and management, but themselves mostly unable to out possible solutions into practice. Here also relations were not necessarily contented, but rather influenced by 'office politics'. It would be inadequate to describe this complex situation as simply divided into blue- and white-collar workers.

Policy over wages, for example, changed various times in the 1960s and 1970s, thereby influencing the hierarchical position of workers and technologists.[32] In the early 1960s, it was not unusual for production workers to earn more than an engineer, thus upsetting the traditional hierarchy, partly because real wages were generally negotiated internally and here the production worker, mostly skilled and male, had a strong position.[33] With the rise of new elites during the NES period, more emphasis was put on supporting and encouraging technologists, thereby improving their position within the factory hierarchy again. This changed towards the end of the 1960s and in the Honecker period, when Ulbricht's focus on technological progress and its carriers was deemed politically incorrect.[34] In the

30. LAB, C Rep. 409–01 Nr. 215, 'Lunik III', 31.1.1961, 6.2.1961.

31. LAB, C Rep. 409–01 Nr. 214, 'Käthe Kollwitz', 27.1.1961.

32. See for example Peter Hübner, *Konsens, Konflikt und Kompromiss–Soziale Arbeiterinteressen und Sozialpolitik in der SBZ/DDR 1945–70* (Berlin: Akademie Verlag, 1995), pp. 85–86. See also Knortz, *Innovationsmanagement*, p. 195.

33. Deich, Kohte, *Betriebliche Sozialeinrichtungen*, p. 166.

34. Karin Zachmann, 'Frauen für die technische Revolution–Studentinnen und Absolventinnen Technischer Hochschulen in der SBZ/DDR', p. 146, in Gunilla-Friederike Budde, ed., *Frauen arbeiten. Weibliche Erwerbstätigkeit in Ost- und Westdeutschland nach 1945* (Göttingen: Vandenhoeck & Ruprecht, 1997), pp. 121–56.

1970s, the position of production workers was strengthened once more, often forcing works directors to concessions that had a negative impact on productivity.[35] However, the tide turned in the 1980s, again favouring technologists.[36] These repeated shifts in social relations caused tensions and influenced individual careers.

The 1960s allowed for social mobility, and in the 1970s and 1980s, there were at least some economic functionaries, even works directors, who had started right at the bottom of the hierarchy and worked their way up. Women in particular appreciated the opportunity for qualification and social advancement, both in comparison to pre-war and post-GDR times.[37] From the middle of the 1970s onwards, one could argue that class differences had been blurred sufficiently to allow for more cordial relations at least in transition areas. Advances in the education system certainly contributed to this, as most young people, including women, were able to acquire a professional qualification by the 1970s. Specifically within the socialist system social relations were shifting over time, blurring the traditional Marxist division of classes in the process.[38]

Nevertheless, there was certainly a recognition of and insistence on distance between various social layers. In spite of the SED's repeated attempts at levelling social differences, these gaps never entirely disappeared; sometimes they widened or narrowed depending on central policy or local conditions at the time. In factories, these gaps were closely linked to difficult working conditions.[39] Blaming the 'other' for inefficient production was common but at least partly based on a lack of information, which was typical for the East German economic and political system.[40] Nevertheless, in retrospect, former employees regularly stress the good relations to both subordinates and superiors, although or possibly because the latter could be and had been openly confronted with criticisms concerning working conditions and work organisation.[41] Animosity mostly affected the most

35. Steiner, *Von Plan zu Plan. Eine Wirtschaftsgeschichte der DDR* (Munich: DVA, 2004), p. 167.

36. Kott, *Le communisme au quotidien*, p. 167.

37. See answers to questionnaires (in possession of the author), especially regarding women already working in the 1960s or before. See also Chapter 13, below.

38. See particularly Heike Solga, *Auf dem Weg in eine klassenlose Gesellschaft? Klassenlagen und Mobilität zwischen Generationen in der DDR* (Berlin: Akademie Verlag, 1995). See also Johannes Huinink and Karl Ulrich Mayer et al., *Kollektiv und Eigensinn–Lebensverläufe in der DDR und danach* (Berlin: Akademie Verlag, 1995).

39. Kott, *Le communisme au quotidien*, p. 172.

40. For a positive exception, see Knortz, *Innovationsmanagement*, p. 214.

41. Martin Kohli, 'Die DDR als Arbeitsgesellschaft? Arbeit, Lebenslauf und soziale Differenzierung', p. 49, in Hartmut Kaelble, Jürgen Kocka, and Hartmut Zwahr, eds., *Sozialgeschichte der DDR* (Stuttgart: Klett-Cotta, 1994), pp. 31–61.

immediate social environment and was only rarely directed at those far above or below.[42]

Furthermore, it needs to be remembered that the impact of central policy was never realised seamlessly. Orders from the centre, for example, aspects of economic reforms, often needed some time to filter through to every factory. Their implementation could be delayed for various reasons, including lack of trust, competence, will or means. Also, the chain of command offered many loopholes. At a broad intermediate level, in between central decision makers and the workforce, there existed many institutions and functionaries. They all had their own agenda and often were intent on finding a balance between the aims of the centre and the interests of the periphery, in order to keep the system functioning. This constellation contained the possibility and the need for dialogue, whereby the building up of structures to accommodate such dialogue was an important part of the normalisation process. The interaction between the various levels had huge implications for stabilisation in the 1960s.

In the 1960s and 1970s, both central authorities and the workforce learned a crucial lesson, in the process of which management and particularly some works directors took on the role of intermediary. It became apparent in relation to both the uprising of 17 June 1953 and the building of the Berlin Wall in August 1961, that central authorities would have to live with a demanding workforce and that the workforce would have to deal with equally severe government and party institutions.[43] This recognition, arguably, was the founding base of normalisation. It enabled stabilisation and, eventually, routinisation within state-owned concerns as workers became more pliable and central authorities more aware and tolerant of the workforce's needs.

This new search for compromises, which was part of a trend to establish, learn, and internalise mutually acceptable rules of the (socialist) game was reflected, for example, in the improvement of working and living conditions that had been an issue since the 1950s, but received much more detailed attention from 1964 onwards. Prior to 1964, the provision of workers with meals and products at their places of work had been the main priority, which provided valuable help to many during times of food rationing. Similarly, medical care was provided to a certain extent, as was childcare

42. Horst Liewald, *Das BGW. Zur Betriebsgeschichte von NARVA–Berliner Glühlampenwerk* (Berlin: Deutsches Technikmuseum, 2004), p. 243. See also Jeannette Madarász, 'Die Realität der Wirtschaftsreform in der DDR. Betriebsalltag in den sechziger Jahren', p. 968, in *DeutschlandArchiv* 6/966 (2003): 966–80.

43. See Hübner, *Konsens, Konflikt und Kompromiss*, p. 208.

and housing. However, from the mid 1960s onwards, social policy contained much more than just those issues that might have been priorities for central institutions but not for employees and management. Specifically, childcare and housing were given a higher priority and, in addition, culture, transportation to and from work, holiday provision, sports facilities, and much more were included in the programme.[44]

In 1964, a programme for the improvement of working and living conditions was being prepared by the SPK. It was discussed in the Politburo in September 1964, where the decision was taken to implement it in selected state-owned concerns.[45] However, following the initiative of some works directors, this programme was expanded to include much more than workers' provision, childcare facilities, and housing. Thereby, with the intention of increasing productivity and counterbalancing deficits of the centrally planned economy, works directors were reacting directly to needs voiced at the grassroots. As part of the NES, but more because of initiatives by middle-level functionaries, central authorities eventually perceived the issue as a complex programme that would not only help to stabilise factories and the economic system, but would also help to ensure social peace.[46]

The remarkable thing about the establishment of programmes for the improvement of working and living conditions as part of the annual contracts between management and workforce was the interaction between central decision makers and the working population. Works directors used the opportunity provided by the economic reforms to stabilise factories in the sense of reducing high turnover and sickness rates. This also meant that works directors reacted to interests, demands, and discontent voiced by the workforce. This independence and flexibility in a constant battle against deficits of the planned economy was crucial, although a factory's specific means depended on its status and the personality and networking abilities of its works director.[47] These changes during the 1960s and 1970s encouraged changes of mentality among the East German population that lasted beyond 1989, at least to some extent. Attitudes to employers, and expectations of the employer or the state regarding social policy, can serve here as examples.

In the following section, the process of routinisation will receive particular attention, to highlight its impact on attitudes and behaviour patterns at all levels of East German society. Routinisation furthered the internalisation

44. See Kott, *Le communisme au quotidien*, pp. 79–83.

45. BAB DE 1 / VA 48523, Report on discussion in Politburo, 30.9.1964.

46. For a more detailed account, see Madarász, 'Normalisation in East German enterprises'.

47. Another example for this attempt to counterbalance the deficiencies of the centrally planned economy was the existence of networks between factories intended to accommodate a semi-legal (if not illegal) exchange of materials. See Steiner, *DDR-Wirtschaftsreform*, p. 35.

of values, but also led to a backlash against standardised lives and the ever more apparent discrepancy between official propaganda and real conditions in the later 1970s. Although, since the 1950s, individual interests had shifted to some extent to suit the conditions of life in a dictatorship and a shortage economy, they were never given up entirely. Routine as a concept seems especially suitable to describe a process of learning and playing the rules of the societal game as it was negotiated after the building of the Berlin Wall in August 1961.[48]

Routinisation and Internalisation

The concept of routine, as employed in this project, differs noticeably from ritualisation,[49] a term that also has been used to describe behaviour in dictatorships. A ritual is stereotyped behaviour in a specific situation; ritualisation takes place when behaviour turns into such a ritual. It implies outward adherence to both political expectations and prescribed procedures for political ceremonies. It also carries connotations of conscious behaviour intended to pretend approval despite both inner retreat and a pronounced lack of interest.[50] In contrast, particularly to this suggestion of outward approval in spite of inward rejection, routinisation intends to highlight long-term socio-political processes within East German society that resulted in internalisation not only of the rules of the game, but also of values and attitudes.

Routine includes both negative and positive aspects; both shall be explored in the following section. It has been argued that the rules of the (socialist) game were both established and learned in the 1960s. From this, predictability ensued, in many cases closely entwined with a progressive lack of real meaning, as for example seen in developments within official language. Functionaries, as demonstrated in the 1980s, often did not know the significance of the slogans they were using routinely.[51]

---

48. See also related concepts, especially 'habitus' (Bourdieu, 1977) and 'structuration' (Giddens, 1984). For a concise discussion of these concepts and their links to 'routine', see George Ritzer, *Contemporary Sociological Theory and Its Classical Roots: The Basics* (University of Maryland) (http://highered.mcgraw-hill.com/sites/007234962x/student_view0/chapter7/chapter_overview.html) (Accessed on 18.08.2005).

49. See Kott, *Le communisme au quotidien*, p. 141.

50. Compare Günther Heydemann and Eckehard Jesse, eds., *Diktaturvergleich als Herausforderung–Theorie und Praxis* (Berlin: Duncker & Humblot, 1998), p. 184. See also Ansorg, 'Ick hab immer von unten Druck gekriegt und von oben', p. 148.

51. See for example SAPMO DY24/14230, 10.1.1989, Eberhard Aurich, 'Probleme und Schwierigkeiten von 1.Kreissekretären', pp. 11–13.

Besides these negative aspects, routine helped to stabilise both political and economic structures. Central authorities, functionaries, and the general population were able to work with established structures that were functioning smoothly even if they were not effective. Routine set in regarding behaviour not just in everyday life, but also in crisis situations. One had learned what to expect and how to achieve a specific goal. By the 1970s, probably reinforced by the experience of the Czech people during the Prague Spring of 1968, the limits of open criticism were known and mostly kept quiet out of fear of MfS involvement.[52] Also, central authorities had acquired a customary way of dealing with crises, namely the avoidance of public awareness and the individualisation of conflict.[53]

Keeping the social peace was an absolute priority following Honecker's rise to power; under Ulbricht, this had been much less the case. Not for nothing, at the beginning of his reign Honecker insisted that 'One can never govern against the workers.'[54] He tried to distance his position from that of Ulbricht, whose rational prioritisation of investment in the economy over the financing of a higher standard of living for the population had been hugely unpopular. In the 1960s, especially just after August 1961 and again following the 11th plenary meeting of the SED's central committee in 1965, socio-political appeasement of the population was deemed desirable, but not at all costs. Ulbricht, for example, had not been reluctant to introduce aggressive policies regarding salaries and the criminalisation of critical voices just after the building of the Berlin Wall. Similarly, both cultural and youth policy underwent radical periods in the 1960s and not just phases of liberation, although, arguably, in these areas the initiator may have been not Ulbricht but Honecker's faction in the Politburo.[55] Honecker, by contrast, always tried to avoid open confrontation.

In the 1970s, routine ensured a comparably smooth functioning of socio-political relations in most sections of East German society. Dialogue had been increasingly institutionalised in the petition system (*Eingaben*) and pressed into an 'official' language that accommodated political expectations. Routine led to internalisation, especially for young people who knew no other socio-political environment, but also, to some extent, for everybody wanting to feel at home under the very difficult political circumstances of life in a socialist dictatorship.

---

52. See also Chapter 1, above.

53. See Renate Hürtgen, *Zwischen Disziplinierung und Partizipation. Vertrauensleute des FDGB im DDR-Betrieb* (Cologne et al.: Böhlau Verlag, 2005), pp. 247ff.

54. BAB, DE 1 / VA 56131, SPK, notes on PB meeting 24.3.1972, p. 8.

55. Monika Kaiser, *Machtwechsel von Ulbricht zu Honecker. Funktionsmechanismen der SED-Diktatur in Konfliktsituationen 1962–1972* (Berlin: Akademie Verlag, 1997), chap. 3.

Within the economic sector, routinisation became apparent in various ways from the late 1960s onwards. Central authorities acquired some routine and became less likely to interfere in the running of factories directly, as long as the plan was fulfilled. In the 1960s, this had been a regular occurrence leading, for example, to a high turnover level of works directors.

In the 1960s, the involvement of central authorities could be either a blessing or a curse. Especially in the early years, at least some works directors still tried to attract the attention of central authorities. They hoped to solve problems by involving those who were felt to have the power to improve a difficult situation. This happened mostly when the factory was still able to fulfil the plan, although with great difficulties. Support from superior institutions such as the VVB or relevant ministries could include lower production plans, credits or simply a better supply of materials. However, when such solutions seemed no longer likely, works directors became more reluctant to call for external support, which often had been provided in the shape of ad hoc measures, including the repeated exchange of works directors. Mostly, there were no real solutions, beyond short-lived rescue missions, within the given circumstances.

Slowly, however, this changed; and in the middle of the second half of the 1960s, the situation became calmer, at least outwardly, although the deficiencies of the centrally planned economy continued to undermine efforts to ensure efficient and profitable production. Between the late 1960s and late 1970s, works directors tended to stay in their positions. Only the new drive to create *Kombinate* initiated a new round of replacements in the late 1970s. Accordingly, TRO had had five different works directors in the 1960s, but only one in the 1970s, and the BGW had to accommodate three works directors during the 1960s, but only one for the 1970s and a large part of the 1980s.

By the 1970s, a reluctance to attract attention from central authorities defined the attitude of most economic functionaries. Possibly it had become clear that no improvements were to be expected from their involvement. Most works directors and their management teams were glad to be able to fulfil the plan, at least officially. Whatever methods seemed necessary were employed, including semi-legal initiatives such as unofficial networks, additional bonuses, and higher wages for the workforce or false bookkeeping.[56] Any detailed attention could have been disastrous in what was, by the late 1970s, an extremely precarious situation in spite of officially fulfilled plans. There were two sides to routinisation: outward calm and inner chaos. Not

---

56. Deich, Kohte, *Betriebliche Sozialeinrichtungen*, 168. See also LAB C Rep. 411, Nr. 1306, Volume 5, *Stellungnahme und Beschluss der Parteileitung in der Leitungssitzung 28.9.1978*. In addition, see interview with K., 30.5.2005 (transcript in possession of author).

either one but the combination of both aspects undermined morale in the long term.

On the one hand, most people adjusted to given circumstances and, on the other hand, many exploited the system. Routinisation had brought with it structures that tended to be ineffective with regard to what they were actually meant to achieve. These structures had acquired some stability and ensured the relatively smooth running of everyday processes, which was a crucial part of the sense of 'normality' that had been growing since the 1960s. Nevertheless, over time the recognition grew that these structures would not be able to help.

By the late 1970s, at the latest, suspicions had arisen that they presented a major aspect of the basic deficiencies of political system. In the 1970s, most structures had become established and were regulated by laws that underwent only minor changes under Honecker. Their behaviour became predictable and, thereby, they could be exploited; exploitation meant in the sense of using given opportunities such as social benefits and educational possibilities to their maximum. The realisation of personal interests without useless confrontation helped many to keep a sense of self-determination in an extremely controlling environment. It allowed the majority of East Germans to create a life for themselves and their families that they felt was worth living.

State-owned concerns were part of these structures and, as has been indicated above, most had been able to stabilise their production processes sufficiently by the 1970s to ensure relatively smooth functioning, at least outwardly. In spite of continuing problems such as unreliable deliveries of material, insufficient investment, and difficult working conditions, officially plans were fulfilled, although the methods used were not always legal and often relied on short-term solutions. By 1971, the intense focus on the improvement of working and living conditions had helped to stabilise the workforce: turnover and sickness rates had declined notably from the high levels of the mid 1960s.[57] However, stabilisation was closely interlinked with routine and the workforce reacted in an ambivalent manner, sensitive to routinisation, a reaction that had a notable impact on company culture. People got used to political and economic circumstances that seemed unalterable and to the fact that fundamental problems would not be solved by central authorities. Neither initiative, nor criticism, nor opposition would make the economic system efficient; at the most, it would enable factories

57. See for example BLHA Rep. 704 HFO 415, 427, 428, 429, 500, 668. See also BLHA Rep. 704 HFO 15; 36 *Erfüllung der geplanten Arbeitsproduktivität*, 21.10.1966, p. 2.

to fulfil the plan without necessarily working profitably. It would at least serve to ensure wages and bonuses.

The brigade movement is one example that highlights this process of recognition and, increasingly, resignation. The first brigade movement was stopped quickly because of its tendency towards independence. In 1958, a second attempt was made to bind together small groups of colleagues into brigades. It was intended that these brigades would ensure higher productivity, greater control, and the social and political education of individuals. In the late 1950s and very early 1960s, the movement was quite effective. Brigade diaries were still kept on a daily basis, noting every success and each problem that arose during the working day.[58] Individual brigades tried to address problems in this way and hoped for support from economic functionaries, whom they confronted with their records. However, already in the early 1960s, it became apparent that the workers' criticisms were not welcome and tended to be ignored.[59] Routine set in, which was manifested in brigade diaries that became more colourful, but had less content; criticism was replaced by politically correct statements and descriptions of social events.[60] The number of brigades increased steadily until 1965, but they experienced decline up to 1967, when central authorities stepped in and ordered new efforts to reinitiate the movement.[61] From then on, ever more brigades were founded although activities of many (but certainly not all) brigades were increasingly limited to those officially expected and necessary for the award of the title '*Brigade der sozialistischen Arbeit*', which included a financial reward. The numbers of brigades were increasing gradually and brigade diaries were kept, but resignation and a new focus on personal interests were growing; routine was taking its toll.

In a similar process towards disillusionment, sickness rates and turnover started to rise again from the mid 1970s onwards.[62] This was partly connected to higher levels of stress at the workplace due to efforts to rationalise production processes, reducing possible gaps in the working day to a

---

58. See Jörg Roesler, 'Das Brigadetagebuch—betriebliches Rapportbuch, Chronik des Brigadelebens oder Erziehungsfibel?', p. 153, in Evemarie Badstübner, *Befremdlich Anders. Leben in der DDR* (Berlin: Dietz Verlag, 2000). See also Kott, *Le communisme au quotidien*, p. 138.

59. See Madarász, 'Die Realität der Wirtschaftsreform in der DDR', p. 970. See also Thomas Reichel, 'Jugoslawische Verhältnisse'?—Die 'Brigaden der sozialistischen Arbeit' und die 'Syndikalismus' Affäre (1959–62), p. 72, in *Herrschaft und Eigen-Sinn in der Diktatur—Studien zur Gesellschaftsgeschichte der DDR* (Cologne et al.: Böhlau Verlag, 1999), pp. 45–73.

60. Roesler, 'Das Brigadetagebuch', pp. 156, 158.

61. Jörg Roesler, 'Probleme des Brigadealltags. Arbeitsverhältnisse und Arbeitsklima in volkseigenen Betrieben 1950–89', pp. 11–12, in *Aus Politik und Zeitgeschichte* B38 (1997): 3–17.

62. BLHA Rep. 704 HFO 1107 Vorlage 6/75, 14.5.1975, 2; 1134 Vorlage 3/78, 26.1.1978, 2; 1143 BGL-Sitzung 5.12.1979, p. 4.

minimum.[63] In addition, the improvement of working and living conditions stagnated because of changes in investment policy, which prioritised Honecker's buildings programme and central social policy. For the economy, this meant first of all, a lack of adequate capacities and materials. Therefore, extensive programmes for the improvement of working and living conditions existed on paper and were agreed upon every year, but their realisation was not ensured. Particularly unsatisfactory sanitary facilities and old building stock such as the cramped and draughty production halls in the BGW could not be dealt with for years. Managers were forced to realise the most urgent tasks as far as possible within their own means. Naturally, the workforce noticed these problems, which reflected growing deficiencies within the production process.[64] Frustration and changes in mentality affected all parts of the workforce, including functionaries, party members, and, especially, young people.

However, long-term processes also influenced the development of different attitudes among workers. The extension of the programme for the improvement of working and living conditions had been a new development in the 1960s. Eventually, it became a significant and obligatory part of the annual contract between workforce and management laying down mutual pledges and promises. The growing breadth of the BKV in the 1960s, at least in this instance, was not a sign of growing routine in all aspects of trade union work, but of a decisive achievement for the workforce. Their expectations and rights were embodied in these contracts, which made it possible to voice demands and criticism. By the 1970s, directors were making vague promises and blaming technical and financial difficulties for substandard working conditions.[65] This was progress: it is crucial to remember here the changes that had taken place in the 1960s. In the early 1960s, it would have been neither acceptable to complain openly about working conditions nor would an economic functionary have stammered an excuse; mostly public complaints either were not made or were ignored. The establishment of programmes for the improvement of working and living conditions enabled the workforce to complain and to be heard, and they did this on a massive scale during the 1970s, when investment shifts under Honecker really did cause additional technical and financial difficulties for individual factories.[66] Increasingly, these benefits were taken for granted and were expected.

63. Gareth Dale, *Between State Capitalism and Globalisation. The Collapse of the East German Economy* (Bern: Peter Lang, 2004), p. 184.

64. See Madarász, 'Normalisation in East German enterprises'.

65. Kott, *Le communisme au quotidien*, p. 169.

66. See for example BLHA Rep. 704 HFO 447.

Furthermore, in the 1970s it became apparent that patterns of behaviour were changing. To take a specific example: the so-called *Neuerer*, workers who suggested technological improvements and innovations, encountered hostility from some of their colleagues in the 1950s and beyond.[67] Management also became afraid of technological improvement very quickly as it disturbed the precarious production process.[68] In addition, potential *Neuerer* seem to have become reluctant to suggest innovative changes to the production process, either because they did not want to upset their colleagues by suggesting innovations that might increase norms or because they cooperated with each other to exploit the system.[69] By the 1970s at the latest, it had become more important (or practical) to uphold cordial relations with colleagues and to avoid confrontations than to work effectively. With routine, the conviction developed that nothing would ever change for the better, causing lethargy, frustration, and a growing concern for one's personal interests rather than those of the factory or society at large.[70]

The strong focus on personal interests affected East German society most severely. It undermined the desired sense of collectivism by concentrating concern on the individual and no longer on the group. Individualisation, however, does not entail autonomy, emancipation, and limitless self-realisation, but rather a combination of self-determination and dependency on existing conditions. Strong tendencies towards individualisation became noticeable in the late 1970s, especially among young people and women, but certainly affected almost all sections of society.[71]

Conclusion

The two faces of routinisation combined stability and outward calm, even social peace, with resignation that was turning into lethargy and, eventually, individualisation. Routine was based on an internalisation of the rules of the game, and on certain norms and expectations, which is a significant part of normalisation. It allowed many to accept 'socialist normality', as it had developed in the 1960s and 1970s, as a given and thereby enjoy its

67. Kott, *Le communisme au quotidien*, p. 123.

68. Steiner, *DDR-Wirtschaftsreform*, p. 38.

69. See Günter Mensching, *Ingenieur M. ppm. Einer unter Millionen. Lebenserinnerungen und Ansichten* (Berlin: Nora, 2005), pp. 189ff. See also Dagmar Semmelmann, *Gespräch mit vier Kollegen aus der Tischlerei des O-Betriebes*, unpublished notes, 6.9.1978, pp. 1–2.

70. See Dagmar Semmelmann, *Gedanken zum sozialistischen Wettbewerb*, unpublished notes, 1978/79, p. 3.

71. See Müller, *Jugend*, p. 13.

advantages, grumble about its disadvantages, and avoid its hazards and pitfalls. This 'socialist normality' included social benefits at the same time as it contained the presence of the MfS. Normal life in the GDR, as experienced by most people, was based not only on shortages increasing the need for personal networks, but also on a surplus of expectations, which the state had unwittingly encouraged in its attempt to uphold social peace, but proved unable to satisfy in the long-term. It was also built on structures and a language specific to the East German dictatorship, and on personal relationships and values that mirrored those in other European societies. Perceptions of 'normality' were shaped by experiences, expectations, hopes, and fears. However, perceptions changed: the early 1960s offered a different 'normality' to that of the late 1970s. Arguably, tendencies towards individualisation from the mid 1970s onwards can be described as a backlash against some aspects of routinisation, especially standardised biographies, inefficient institutions, and rigid structures, but also against the gap between official propaganda and everyday life, between promise and reality.

Normalisation in the 1960s and 1970s had led to relative stability, although fundamental problems were not solved. With time, the majority of the population began not only to adjust to, but also to shape 'socialist normality'. On basic issues at least, common norms and mutual expectations were established. Therefore, it is insufficient to describe the 1970s by pointing at the reliance on mutual arrangements, whereby functionaries were reluctant to insist on a rigid application of central policy and the population adhered only to the required minimum. Such an approach would neither explain the remnants of enthusiasm still existent in the mid 1960s, nor the optimism of the early 1970s, nor the subsequent decline, which certainly had its roots in this first decade under Honecker's rule. Routine upheld outward appearances whilst underneath both ideological tenets and their practical implications, such as the centrally planned economy or the brigade movement, were breaking down. In the late 1970s, however, tendencies towards individualisation not just in the private sphere, but also at places of work contributed strongly to symptoms of disintegration. The long-term consequences of this process did not become apparent until the end of the 1980s.

Chapter 4

Rural Functionaries and the Transmission of Agricultural Policy: The Case of *Bezirk* Erfurt from the 1960s to the 1970s

George Last

With the completion of the campaign for full collectivisation in April 1960, an administrative milestone had been reached. Beyond the paperwork however, the situation was by no means so clear cut. The rural communities of the GDR were fraught with discord and many farmers continued to reject the agricultural collectives, refusing to take part in collective work, and in some cases abandoning their farms and fleeing the GDR altogether. Over subsequent years—particularly with the construction of the Wall in August 1961—the rural population then responded to the end of private farming (on more than a minute scale) by developing ways to safeguard their own interests in resisting, manipulating, but also participating in the new systems of rural organisation. At the same time the SED regime sought to bring its authority more comprehensively and more consistently to bear on the diverse mixture of rural communities, gaining tighter control over agricultural production via its further integration into the planned economy. The difficult task of mediating these two processes at the local level fell to the functionaries of the collective farms. Their developing relationships with one another and with the functionaries of the district state and party bureaucracy, acting and reacting at the crucial overlap of state and society, was a key element of the normalising of rule within the GDR during the 1960s. This essay seeks to highlight some of the characteristics of these relationships and their consequences for the transmission of agricultural policy in the context of one region, *Bezirk* Erfurt.[1]

In the early 1960s, the situation in the rural communities in *Bezirk* Erfurt was very complex. The establishment of agricultural collectives (*Landwirtschaftliche Produktionsgenossenschaften,* or LPGs), organised according to three types of model statutes with varying degrees of collective ownership and collective farming practice, had been underway since the early 1950s—albeit only rapidly since 1958. By the end of the collectivisation campaign, a variety of LPGs of different degrees of longevity, financial solvency, and different structural types[2] thus existed side by side in rural communities. The conditions for farming in the various districts of the *Bezirk* were diverse, varying according to the nature and quality of the land, the quality and quantity of the livestock, draught animals and machinery available. Furthermore, the populations living in rural communities were equally diverse. Religious background,[3] levels of new settlers, and land distribution, as well as local personal and familial ties, defined loyalties and conflicts peculiar to each community. The proximity of urban and industrial centres, the quality of transport, and the patterns of nonagricultural employment all played a role in shaping local conditions. In these diverse circumstances, the SED leadership's project of consolidating collectivisation and bringing effective administrative control to agricultural production was by no means straightforward to implement.

Mass agitation, the use of force, and exemplary terror continued to be used particularly in the early 1960s to encourage participation in the collectivised farms. However, on their own, such approaches could have only limited success in the long term. More consistent and comprehensive means of transmitting agricultural policy were also required at a local level to ensure the ideals and theories of socialist agriculture were reflected to some degree in the actual adoption of new farming practices and the generation of greater productivity as a result. An effective chain of communication was required between farmers and farm workers on the one hand, and the upper echelons of the regime, on the other, which, although top-heavy, worked both ways.

---

1. The GDR was divided from 1952 into 15 administrative regions or *Bezirke.*

2. Of essential importance were the Type I LPGs in which only arable land was necessarily farmed collectively, and the Type III LPGs in which all land, livestock, and machinery were used collectively.

3. Within *Bezirk* Erfurt, there existed Lutheran and Reformed protestant parishes as well as a concentrated community of Catholics in the Eichsfeld region largely within the *Kreise* Heiligenstadt and Worbis.

The regime's agricultural bureaucracy needed to be in a position, given the diversity of conditions on the ground in every sense, to consider and occasionally respond to local peculiarities. It had, of course, also to have the apparatus at its disposal to persuade and educate, as well as threaten and direct, farmers. Of crucial significance to this apparatus was the role played by the leading cadres of the collective farms. The level of LPG leaders' technical ability as farmers and economic functionaries, the degree of their political reliability, and their skills as managers of people defined how farmers' interests and those of the party and state functionaries charged with preparing the implementation of SED agricultural policy within the GDR's regions and districts were aligned at a local level.

Conflict and Consolidation

As far as the SED leadership was concerned, the weaknesses of the structures in place for transmitting agricultural policy in the aftermath of collectivisation were enormous. The problems faced by the leading SED functionaries in the *Bezirk* directing the campaign for full collectivisation had put in relief just how far political unreliability and administrative inefficiency, if not incompetence, pervaded the state and party apparatus responsible for rural communities at a district and local level in the early 1960s.[4] Given the degree of hostility to collectivisation among farmers, it was no surprise that while the new LPGs existed on paper, there were few guarantees for the SED leadership that they existed in reality and functioned in accordance with the model statutes. Moreover, owing to the suddenness of the decision to complete collectivisation in a very short space of time at the end of the 1950s[5] and the rapid expansion in size and numbers of LPGs, there was a glaring absence both in the collective farms

4. Thüringisches Hauptstaatsarchiv Weimar (ThHStAW) Bezirksparteiarchiv der SED Erfurt, Bezirksleitung der SED Erfurt IV/2/2/322 SED Bezirksleitung Abt. Landwirtschaft an das Sekretariat: Bericht über die Vorbereitung der Organisationswahlen der VdgB und ihre Unterstützung durch die Partei. 12.3.1960, pp. 168–76; Bezirksparteiarchiv der SED Erfurt, Bezirksleitung der SED Erfurt IV/2/3/338 Sekretariat der Bezirksleitung, Protokollauszug–Sekretariatssitzung: Brigade in Nordhausen, 18.7.1960, p. 22; Bezirksparteiarchiv der SED Erfurt, Bezirksleitung der SED Erfurt IV/2/3/348 Sekretariat der Bezirksleitung, Brigade Nordhausen der Bezirksleitung Abschlussbericht über den Brigadeeinsatz im Kreis Nordhausen, 28.9.1960, pp. 77–87; Bezirksparteiarchiv der SED Erfurt, Bezirksleitung der SED Erfurt IV/2/3/328 Sekretariat der Bezirksleitung, Vorlage, An das Büro der Bezirksleitung: Bericht über den Einsatz der Brigade der Bezirksleitung im Kreis Apolda, 2.5.1960, pp. 6–16.

5. See J. Schöne, *Frühling auf dem Lande? Die Kollektivierung der DDR Landwirtschaft* (Berlin, 2005) for the latest set of arguments on the subject of the timing and motivation for the completion of the collectivisation campaign.

themselves and the local and district state apparatus of suitably trained agricultural functionaries.

The new scales and patterns of production post-collectivisation required the skills and knowledge not only of new agricultural techniques, but also of man-management and 'socialist' administration. By 1960, insufficient preparation had been made to organise the qualification of sufficient numbers of such agricultural functionaries. A proportion of LPG leaders in the early 1960s were thus seen as deficient, lacking either knowledge of farming or sufficient credibility as leaders. Perhaps more seriously for the regime, very often those with the status in the village to take up leadership of the new collective farms were the least politically reliable or ideologically suitable candidates. The majority of the LPGs in existence in 1961 had adopted the statute of the Type I collective farm, opting for the minimum degree of collective ownership and collective farming practice. These were not only new and barely functional, but also dominated by farmers unenthusiastic about the collectivisation, who in many cases were the only realistic choices as LPG functionaries.

The first years following the completion of the collectivisation campaign were marked in a number of LPGs by fluctuations in the occupation of leading functionary positions. In the first year after collectivisation, LPG chairmen, brigade leaders, and LPG board members resigned in protest as promises of freedom of action or financial support made by agitators during the campaign failed to be met. Beyond this, the willingness of farmers particularly to take on a management role sank when faced with the difficulties of the first years of collective farming. In their role as mediators between the demands of the state and the interests of members of the collective farm, LPG chairmen in particular were under considerable pressure from both sides. On the one hand, with agricultural production dangerously low (thanks in large part to the abandonment of land), failure to meet plan targets could potentially be regarded as a criminal act. On the other, LPG functionaries often found themselves exposed to the resentment of members of the LPG and in some cases even isolated in the community if they too obviously advocated the progress of collective farming.[6]

Collective farmers remained in many cases unconvinced of the positive advantages of implementing the new 'socialist' farming practices that came

6. ThHStAW BDVP 20/065 BDVP Stab/Operativstab, Information 36/60, Einschätzung der Lage in der Landwirtschaft, 20.7.1960; Information über vorkommnisse in der Landwirtschaft 19/60, 4.5.1960; BDVP 20.1/352 BDVP Operativstab, Information 62/61 Landwirtschaft, 5.8.1961, p. 43; BDVP 20/065 BDVP Stab/Operativstab, Auswertung der Vorkommnisse in der Landwirtschaft 20/60; RdB Erfurt L562 Rat des Bezirkes Erfurt, Abt. Landwirtschaft Unterabteilung LPG, Einschätzung der politischen und ökonomischen Entwicklung der LPG des Bezirkes Erfurt, 5.10.1962.

with collectivisation, arguing for 'traditional' methods rather than the 'modern' industrial methods advocated by advisors from the district state bureaucracy.[7] Attempts to fix administratively the size and location of maize plantations as a feed crop and impose the construction of cheap 'open' cow sheds—famously criticised in Erwin Strittmater's *Ole Bienkopp*[8]—remained points of contention in the LPGs well into the early 1960s. Local discussion of when to complete harvesting of different crops and, connected to this, whether outside help should be used to speed the progress of the harvest appeared to be driven all too often by district party and state functionaries' need to assert their authority over LPG chairmen rather than from actual concern for high yields.[9] The justification of the administrative efficiency of an early harvest was not often well received at a local level.[10]

Despite these hindrances to the establishment of a stable body of LPG leaders willing and capable of not only maintaining production levels, but also of carrying out the effective administrative and practical organisation of collective farming, solutions did present themselves. Leaps forward in qualification levels in the agricultural workforce in 1960 and 1961 dramatically increased the number of farmers exposed to basic agricultural training conducted under the auspices of the socialist system, providing the basis for the development of future cadres. At the same time, it increased the number of college and university educated cadres equipped with sufficient technical know-how to lead the development of collective farming in the LPGs.[11] The

7. Nevertheless, relations between farmers and the regime cannot always easily be interpreted in the context of a straightforward dichotomy of tradition and modernisation. Traditional elements of farming and the rural existence survived and in some respects were actively encouraged within the context of socialist agricultural policy. At the same time, farmers themselves were not opposed to certain aspects of modernisation where it was on their terms and could be shown to be of benefit to them, suiting a pragmatic as well as a moral understanding of farming as a profession and as a way of life. By the same token, SED agricultural policy was about more than modernising the methods of farming, but it was also defined by the practical requirements of administration (and repression) as well as radical goals of social transformation.

8. E. Strittmater, *Ole Bienkopp* (East Berlin, 1964).

9. ThHStAW RdB Erfurt L1086 Brief an den Vorsitzenden des RdB Erfurt, 19.9.1962: Beschwerde über die Arbeit mit den Menschen durch den Direktor der MTS Apolda-Heusdorf; Bezirksparteiarchiv der SED Erfurt, Bezirksleitung der SED Erfurt BIV/2/5/44 SED Bezirksleitung Abt. Org./ Kader, Informationsbericht zur Erntesituation in den Kreisen, 5.9.1962, pp. 154–58;

10. ThHStAW Bezirksparteiarchiv der SED Erfurt, Bezirksleitung der SED Erfurt IV/2/3/345 SED Bezirksleitung Abt. Org/Kader, Einschätzung der Bürositzungen vom 2.9.1960 und Ablauf der Halmfruchternte, 13.9.1960, p. 86; Bezirksparteiarchiv der SED Erfurt, Bezirksleitung der SED Erfurt BIV/2/5/44 SED Bezirksleitung Abt. Org./Kader, Informationsbericht Nr. 29/62, undated, pp. 281–91.

11. The proportion of the agricultural workforce with the basic qualification *Facharbeiterprüfung* rose from 4.5 percent to 11.5 percent between 1960 and 1961; while the number of master farmers and those with technical college and university qualifications rose from 2 percent to 3.5 percent within *Bezirk* Erfurt. Statistisches Jahrbuch–Bezirk Erfurt, 1970, Teil I, p. 126.

political suitability of leading functionaries in the collective farms also began to improve. The erection of the Wall in August 1961 was of fundamental importance in reducing incidences of opposition to the collective farms. The end of flight to the west as a last resort for farmers, and subsequent growth in the use of exemplary punitive action against resistant members of collective farms, highlighted not only the futility, but also the dangers associated with even passive opposition to collective farming. It also encouraged acceptance of and adaptation to the new situation in agriculture.[12]

The improved reliability of LPG cadres was in part because of the targeted training of SED members involved in agriculture to enable them to take up management positions and the delegation of a number of functionaries from the district state apparatus, state-owned farms, and other stable LPGs as well as the Farmers' Mutual Support Union (*der Verein der gegenseitigen Bauernhilfe,* or VdgB).[13] A number of functionaries also became free to be delegated from the various branches of the state-run machine pools (*Maschinen-Traktoren-Stationen,* or MTS), which were in the process of being dissolved as machinery was transferred into the ownership of individual collective farms. It is perhaps testimony to the difficulty of the tasks facing LPG functionaries, however, that many eligible cadres sought to avoid delegation into a collective farm.[14]

In early 1963, analyses of the reasons for poor economic performance in a number of LPGs tended to blame the quality of the leading members of the collective farms and their lack of either political or technical credentials. To remedy the situation, functionaries in the SED district administration were directed by their superiors at *Bezirk* level to re-examine the reliability of the various cadres in the villages. Wherever they could be found, expe-

---

12. The clamp down on resistant farmers is described in general terms in: SAPMO BArch DY30/IV 2/7/376 Ministerium für Landwirtschaft, Erfassung und Forstwirtschaft, Einschätzung der Entwicklung der Lage auf dem Lande in Vorbereitung der Wahlen zum 17.9.1961, pp. 65–70; Specific cases of exemplary punishment in Bezirk Erfurt may be found in: ThHStAW Bezirksparteiarchiv der SED Erfurt, Bezirksleitung der SED Erfurt BIV/2/4/59 SED Kreisleitung Sondershausen an die BPKK, Einschätzung über einige Erscheinungen im Kr. Sondershausen, 25.9.1961, p. 344; KPKK Erfurt-Land, Bericht über Feindarbeit im III. Quartal, 25.9.1961, p. 222; KPKK Mühlhausen, Bericht über Feindarbeit im III. Quartal, 26.9.1961, p. 300.; SED Kreisleitung Apolda an die BPKK, Bericht über Feindarbeit im III. Quartal, 29.9.1961, p. 135.

13. ThHStAW Bezirksparteiarchiv der SED Erfurt, Bezirksleitung der SED Erfurt BIV/2/5/043 SED Bezirksleitung Abt. Parteiorgane, Abt. Org./Kader, Informationsbericht Nr. 8/62, pp. 149–157.

14. ThHStAW Bezirksparteiarchiv der SED Erfurt, Bezirksleitung der SED Erfurt BIV/2/7/602 SED Bezirksleitung Abt. Landwirtschaft, Abt. Org./Kader Kaderpolitische Wertung der Qualifikations der Parteisekretäre in den LPG, 23.3.1963, p. 1–4; Abt. Landwirtschaft, Berufsausbildung, 26.7.1965, pp. 26–32; Abt. Landwirtschaft Bericht an Gen. Lüdecke–Stand der Qualifizierung der Werktätigen in der soz. Landwirtschaft, 27.10.1966, pp. 38–39.

rienced political and technical cadres were to be delegated into the LPG.[15] Despite the new economic and political stability given by the Wall to the SED regime in the GDR, the (for the time being) insurmountable shortage of sufficiently reliable cadres seriously limited the extent of regime influence over the practices of agricultural production.[16]

Despite loyalty and obedience to the party and state apparatus tempering the virulence of their response, leading cadres in the collective farms were openly reluctant to implement agricultural policies that seemed ill judged. Given the parlous financial conditions of many LPGs in the early 1960s, policies which threatened to reduce still further the incomes of members of the LPGs were bound to excite anger from collective farmers and opposition on their behalf from LPG functionaries. On this basis, LPG chairmen ignored harvest deadlines and rejected the use of machinery or the deployment of so-called harvest helpers as directed by local and district state authorities—not least in order to ensure their own members would not be deprived of working hours on which to claim their income.[17] Even after the building of the Wall, limits were thus set to the extent to which SED agricultural policy initiatives—as mediated by the managing functionaries of collective farms—were translated into agricultural practice at the local level.

Beginning Economic Integration

The reorganisation of the state administration running agriculture with the creation of the new Agricultural Councils at national, *Bezirk* and *Kreis* level (*Kreislandwirtschaftsräte* or KLRs), marked a number of new departures for the relationship between collective farmers, LPG functionaries, and the

15. As a consequence of the delegation of cadres into LPGs, particularly those Type III LPGs, which were financially unstable, not all LPG functionaries had close personal connections with the other members or with the areas in which they worked. No doubt this was reflected at times in their attitude towards implementing policy and how members responded to them. Functionaries of Type I LPGs were at least initially overwhelmingly selected from among local residents of long standing.

16. ThHStAW Bezirksparteiarchiv der SED Erfurt, Bezirksleitung der SED Erfurt IV/A/2/1/009 Sekretariat der Bezirksleitung, Protokoll der 5. Bezirksleitungssitzung Erfurt am 25.4.1963, p. 116–24; BIV/2/4/299 KPKK Mühlhausen, Bericht über die Untersuchung in der LPG "8.Mai" in Zella, 7.4.1964, p. 170.

17. ThHStAW Bezirksparteiarchiv der SED Erfurt, Bezirksleitung der SED Erfurt BIV/2/5/044 Abt. Parteiorgane, Abt. Org./Kader, 5. Informationsbericht über die Erntesituation in den Kreisen, 7.9.1962, pp. 163–67; Bericht über die Führungstätigkeit des Büros der KL Eisenach und des Staatsapparates im Kreis Eisenach, 10.9.1962, pp. 179–81; Informationsbericht Nr.29/62, p. 281–91; ThHStAW Nationale Front 172, Bezirkssekretariat, Antwort der Gemeinden des Bezirkes auf den Aufruf der Roblinger zu Ehren des 15. Jahrestags der DDR, 4.6.1964, p. 131; ThHStAW RdB L1068 Arbeiter und Bauerninspektion, Bezirksinspektion Erfurt, Ernteinformation, Kreis Gotha, 11.8.1964.

state apparatus. Above all, they promised to result in a better standard of leadership by the state in agricultural matters, with some limitation on direct interference in the production process of the LPGs.[18] The working style of the old agricultural departments of the *Rat des Kreises*, which had overseen the collectivisation process, was criticised for being too administrative and schematic. In contrast, the new Agricultural Councils promised actively to include members of the LPGs in the decisionmaking process at district and regional levels, with the intention of improving the flow of information into the administration from the collective farms themselves.[19] As now true members of the 'Class of the Collective Farmers', the reluctantly collectivised farmers were also now in theory to be seen less in terms of their potential for counterrevolution. Rather, due consideration was to be given to their abilities as productive farmers in addition to their rights (and obligations) as (albeit lesser) partners of the working class.[20] The stage was thus set for a renegotiation of the relationship between the state and farmers.

This renegotiation took place in the context of the completion of the transfer of the machinery from the MTS to LPGs, the announcement of the beginning of the industrialisation of agriculture, and the introduction of the first reforms of the New Economic System of Planning and Management (NES). As such, the rhetoric of reconciliation was certainly balanced by increasing demands on farmers to acquiesce to ever greater leaps forward in the 'socialist' modernisation of agriculture. With the introduction of the NES, it was hoped that LPGs would be encouraged to increase production through more flexible state planning and the construction of a system of economic incentives, which they would then pass on to their members. A new price system was introduced, which made increased revenue available to individual collective farms in order to encourage the development of more intensive mechanised farming of crops and to encourage the creation of collective livestock herds.[21] How this revenue was spent in practice

18. SAPMO BArch DY 30 IV/A 2/2.023/15 Büro Grüneberg, Die besondere Beziehung zwischen genossenschaftlicher und staatlicher Leitung nach dem Produktionsprinzip bei der Verwirklichung des NÖSPL (undated 1964), p. 162.

19. ThHStAW Bezirksparteiarchiv der SED Erfurt, Bezirksleitung der SED Erfurt IV/A/2/3/51 Sekretariat der Bezirksleitung, Protokollauszug von der Bürositzung am 8.2.1963.

20. ThHStAW Bezirksparteiarchiv der SED Erfurt, Bezirksleitung der SED Erfurt IV/A/2/2/38 Protokoll der Bezirksparteiaktivtagung Landwirtschaft am 17.12.1963, Referat Genosse Becker–LPG Söllnitz, p. 68.

21. Where previously production of crops had been encouraged with a dual price system which rewarded excess production, by the end of 1964 a unified price for crops came into effect, graded according to the quality of the produce. On the whole, this unified price was higher than the average of the two purchase and excess prices previously used, allowing the revenues of LPGs to increase. Thereby the means was put at LPGs' disposal to balance the end of the state's subsidisation

remained under careful control. District authorities–within the state administration, the district agricultural banks, and the party apparatus–exerted constant pressure on LPG leaders to ensure that a large proportion of their increased revenue was channelled into a capital fund with which LPGs could invest in the further expansion of industrialised production.[22] More than ever, the functionaries of the KLR pressured LPG managers to implement complex methods of stimulating productivity and to organise the conditions for industrialised agriculture. In these circumstances, the effectiveness of LPG functionaries at persuading their members to adopt new work ordinances came under closer scrutiny. Furthermore, their technical ability as economic managers at organising industrial style farming practice and their grasp of systems of economic levers and material incentives were exposed. As always, political willingness did not presuppose ability nor did ability presuppose willing.

During 1959 and 1960, disregard for the administrative documentation required by the state administration detailing the running of the imposed LPG structure was one means employed by some farmers to resist the actual implications of collectivisation.[23] Although such resistance was not sustained, in subsequent years, additional administrative requirements continued to be opposed to limit outside interference. Particularly, chairmen of Type I LPGs sought in the early 1960s to avoid drawing up the documents of 'socialist competition'. The information contained within these documents provided, of course, the grounds for the state administration to demand increased productivity from LPG members. Chairmen publicly objected on the grounds that such 'competitions' were an extra burden of irrelevant paperwork and provoked unnecessary resentments between members.[24] On the same grounds, members of all types of LPG expressed opposition to

of machinery and pay for the transfer of machinery along with tractor drivers to the LPG. As far as livestock production was concerned, despite the New Economic System, it was still considered necessary to maintain a dual price which favoured the Type III LPGs. Type III LPGs thus continued to receive a lower quota to be bought at purchase price than Type I and II LPGs, which encouraged the latter to merge with or form a Type III LPG, and thus transfer their livestock production from private to collective sheds.

22. For more on NES in agriculture see J. Roesler, *Zwischen Plan und Markt,* pp. 135–43.

23. ThHStAW RdB Erfurt L590 Rat des Bezirkes Erfurt, Abt. Landwirtschaft, Einschätzung der Entwicklung der LPG des Typ I im Bezirk Erfurt 6.7.1960.

24. ThHStAW RdB L599 Bezirkslandwirtschaftsrat, Analyse über die ökonomische Entwicklung der LPG im Jahre 1963, undated; Bezirksparteiarchiv der SED Erfurt, Bezirksleitung der SED Erfurt BIV/2/5/382 Parteiorgane, Abt. Parteiorgane, Informationsbericht, Nr.12/65, 3.5.1965, pp. 116–28; BIV/2/5/044 Abt. Parteiorgane, Abt. Org./Kader, Information, 25.7.1962, pp. 35–48; Abt. Org./Kader, Information 19/62, 30.7.1962, pp. 49–57.

forms of performance related pay.[25] Farmers put forward arguments to the effect that such measures were not only capitalistic and exploitative, but also wholly unnecessary.[26]

An information report on the implementation of the NES in *Bezirk* Erfurt from March 1965 pointed to some progress having been made in winning over LPG cadres. Following a series of lectures and a propaganda campaign to help LPG cadres understand the reforms, twice as many Type III LPGs had reached 'an advanced stage' in the implementation of the NES reforms.[27] Progress had even been made with a proportion of the Type I and Type II LPGs. By May 1965, 40 percent of Type I and II LPGs had implemented a system for sharing livestock fodder, which rewarded farmers who made the most available for sale. Of those, 42 percent farmed pasture land collectively and 72 percent had kept collective livestock.[28] It remained apparent, however, that LPG chairmen were by no means simple conduits of state power and that the process of implementing agricultural policy initiatives would be necessarily drawn out.[29] At the root of the conflict was the wish to resist the extension of administrative regulation–the bureaucratisation–of agricultural production through economic levers. Not only was the paper work considered unnecessary, it represented state interference by stealth in the very internal running of the LPG.

Limitations on the SED's Role

A major factor influencing the attitude of LPG functionaries and the development of the LPG overall was the degree of influence that the SED party organisation had within the agricultural collective. Despite some progress

25. For example, work norms were set determining work units according to measures of quantity and quality of production as well as hours worked.

26. ThHStAW Bezirksparteiarchiv der SED Erfurt, Bezirksleitung der SED Erfurt IV/A/2/2/38 Protokoll der Bezirksparteiaktivtagung Landwirtschaft am 17.12.1963, Referat Genosse Becker–LPG Söllnitz p. 68.

27. ThHStAW Bezirksparteiarchiv der SED Erfurt, Bezirksleitung der SED Erfurt IV/A/2/3/112 Sekretariat der Bezirksleitung, Bezirkslandwirtschaftsrat–Produktionsleitung, Einschätzung der Kreisbauernkonferenzen im Bezirk Erfurt 29.3.1965, pp. 141–51; IV/A/2/3/112 Sekretariat der Bezirksleitung, Einschätzung der Arbeitsgruppe der Bezirksleitung über die Führungstätigkeit des Sekretariats der Kreisleitung Nordhausen, pp. 100–119.

28. ThHStAW Bezirksparteiarchiv der SED Erfurt, Bezirksleitung der SED Erfurt BIV/2/5/382 SED Bezirksleitung Abt. Parteiorgane, Informationsbericht, Nr.16/65, 29.5.1965, pp. 181–191.

29. For example, ThHStAW Bezirksparteiarchiv der SED Erfurt, Bezirksleitung der SED Erfurt BIV/2/7/588 SED Bezirksleitung Abt. Landwirtschaft Bericht über die politische Führungstätigkeit zur Herausbildung von Kooperationsbeziehungen in der soz. Landwirtschaft des Kreis Sondershausen, undated 1965, pp. 476–84.

in recruiting collective farmers into the SED since the completion of collectivisation, and in particular since the building of the Wall, the proportion of SED members in each collective remained low.[30] This was in part because active participation in party life could have considerable social consequences in rural communities. The 'reputation' of SED members in the village was given as a reason by many for not wishing to join the party or to participate regularly in party life. Potential recruits rejected joining the SED with arguments such as: 'we're not joining the party, because the comrades are no model for us'; 'Put your own ranks in order first'; 'teach your comrades to work like we do first.'[31] Speaking to a gathering of leading party members in the *Bezirk* in 1964, the First Secretary of the SED *Bezirksleitung*, Alois Bräutigam, despaired at the number of LPGs without a functioning party organisation. He recommended overcoming the reluctance of potential candidates by persuading them all to sign up in alphabetical order so that: 'no one takes the blame for being the first or for being the last; as that's important in villages.'[32]

One of the central roles of the party organisation, led by the party secretary, was to advise the leading functionaries of the LPGs on how best to implement new elements of agricultural policy. However, even by the mid 1960s, the confluence necessary for the smooth implementation of new agricultural practices of a strong and numerous SED party organisation in the LPG and leading LPG functionaries loyal to the SED existed only in a minority of Type III LPGs. In most Type I LPGs, the SED party organisation (where one even existed) could bring little influence to bear unless the leading cadres of the LPG were also SED members. Even in these cases however, the predominance of non-SED members in other leading positions

30. Between 1962 and 1966, the proportion of SED members in the LPG rose from 6.9 percent to 8.7 percent in Bezirk Erfurt. ThHStAW Bezirksparteiarchiv der SED Erfurt, Bezirksleitung der SED Erfurt IV/A/2/3/186 Abt. Parteiorgane, Analyse der Mitgliederbewegung im Jahre 1966, 9.1.1967, p. 142.

31. ThHStAW Bezirksparteiarchiv der SED Erfurt, Bezirksleitung der SED Erfurt BIV/2/7/500 SED Bezirksleitung Abt. Landwirtschaft, Stand der Mitgliederbewegung, 12.10.1963, p. 115. Some examples, from districts across the Bezirk, of the social conflicts caused in rural communities by SED membership: ThHStAW Bezirksparteiarchiv der SED Erfurt, Bezirksleitung der SED Erfurt BIV/2/4/107 KPKK Sondershausen, Bericht über die Untersuchung in der GO der LPG West-Greussen durch die KPKK, 15.8.1962, p. 22; BIV/2/4/288 KPKK Bad Langensalza, Bericht über die Untersuchungen der KPKK in der PO der LPG Hornsömmern, 20.5.1963, p. 155; BIV/2/4/288 KPKK Mühlhausen, Bericht über die Untersuchung der KPKK in der LPG '4. Parteitag' in Ammern ,24.5.1963, p. 162; BIV/2/4/299 KPKK Erfurt-Land, Bericht über die Untersuchungen in der PO/LPG III "Karl Marx" Grossfahner, 26.10.1964, p. 28.

32. ThHStAW Bezirksparteiarchiv der SED Erfurt, Bezirksleitung der SED Erfurt IV/A/2/2/042 Protokoll der Bezirksparteiaktivtagung, Büro für Landwirtschaft am 18.12.1964, Beitrag Genosse Bräutigam, 1. Bezirkssekretär, p. 171.

and on the board of the LPGs often hindered the implementation of SED proposals.[33]

The running of an LPG depended not only on the LPG chairman but also on the cooperation of the governing board of the collective. Moreover, in theory, if not always in practice, the ratification by an assembly of LPG members was required before major decisions affecting the collective farm could be implemented. Some limits were thus set to what new practices could be introduced in an LPG without the persuasive efforts of a strong party organisation or the repeated persuasive intervention of staff from the KLR. Even where members of block parties and, in particular the DBD, occupied leading positions in the collective farm, their support for the implementation of new agricultural policy was not always forthcoming. Consequently, unless outside pressure was brought to bear on them, LPG farmers were not easily—nor routinely—persuaded to adopt new practices.

Merger, Cooperation, and Forced Transformation

Parallel to the debate over the implementation of the new levels of economic administration in the LPGs was the contentious issue of establishing the conditions for more cost efficient mechanised production. By the mid 1960s, considerable improvements in the numbers and capacity of tractors, harvesters, and other machinery available in the GDR, made large scale mechanised crop production and the beginnings of large scale intensive livestock production possible. However, it was still not clear how individual collective farms ought to be encouraged to combine their resources. Solutions to these problems presented themselves in two forms: the merger of collective farms together to form a so-called '*Gross* LPG', combining crop and livestock production on a larger scale under a single leadership; or the development of cooperative relations between groups of LPGs, who might work together as far as possible to make best use of the economies of scale. The adoption of one solution over another depended enormously in the 1960s on the balance of power between LPG leaders and their relationship with the district party and state apparatus.

33. ThHStAW Bezirksparteiarchiv der SED Erfurt, Bezirksleitung der SED Erfurt BIV/2/7–588 Abt. Landwirtschaft, Abt. Parteiorgane, Sektor Operativ, Erfahrungen und Schlussfolgerungen für die Entwicklung der Parteiarbeit in den Kooperationsbereichen auf der Grundlage der Untersuchungen der KL Erfurt-Land,2.11.1965, pp. 1–11; Bericht über die politische Führungstätigkeit zur Herausbildung von Kooperationsbeziehungen in der soz. Landwirtschaft des Kr. Sondershausen, undated 1965, p. 476.

The tendency by some LPG leaders towards creating a (from one perspective excessively) large single LPG was not easily distinguished from the necessary rationalisation of production through merger. As a rule in the early 1960s, the creation of one LPG per *Gemeinde* or local administrative centre was regarded by the state administration as legitimate rationalisation. The tendency towards a merger of LPGs across a number villages was thought however to smack of excess. Often there was considerable doubt in party circles whether the chairmen of such collective farms should have at their disposal resources far in advance of their proven political reliability or supposed position in the political hierarchy. Nevertheless, the steps that had to be taken on the way either to legitimate merger, excess expansion or the formation of extended cooperative partnerships between farms were outwardly one and the same.[34] Hence, in an analysis by the SED *Kreisleitung* in July and August 1964, discussions between the leaders of the LPGs in Tunzenhausen, Wundersleben, and Schallenburg were regarded with suspicion as indicating covert ('with a wink') intentions to merge.[35]

Some such giant amalgamations of farms nevertheless did indeed go ahead in the course of the 1960s at the insistence of leading LPG functionaries and with the support of the district party and state apparatus. On the whole, however, by the mid to late 1960s most LPGs were stable and independent enough for both their members and the leading cadres to wish to resist a merger with their neighbours. Furthermore, the argument that *Gross* LPGs threatened to limit the long-term possibilities for and the extent of large scale specialised production was increasingly dominant among the SED's agricultural experts. Rationalising production, it was assumed, was best achieved through the extension of cooperative relations between LPGs. As an idea, however, the *Gross* LPG did not disappear, not least because many farmers and agricultural functionaries at all levels struggled to countenance the notion of the administrative separation of crop and livestock production, which cooperation appeared to propose.[36]

---

34. Namely, establishing greater uniformity of pay and organisation and greater exchange of resources and information between LPGs.

35. ThHStAW Bezirksparteiarchiv der SED Erfurt, Kreisleitung der SED Sömmerda IV/A/4.10/077 Sektor Parteiinformation, Einschätzung der MV im Monat Juli und August, 1.9.1964, pp. 120–30.

36. Examples of LPG members opinions to this effect may be found in ThHStAW Bezirksparteiarchiv der SED Erfurt, Bezirksleitung der SED Erfurt IV/B/2/2/022 Protokoll der Bezirksparteiaktivtagung zu den Fragen und Aufgaben der soz. Landwirtschaft am 7.3.1968 Beitrag Genossin Zessin, p. 103; Bezirksparteiarchiv der SED Erfurt, Bezirksleitung der SED Erfurt IV/B/2/13/378 Einschätzung über das Einwohnerforum in der Grenzgemeinde Berka/Werra Kr. Eisenach, 27.1.1969, p. 1.

LPGs had already started in the early 1960s to combine their construction workers in mutual organisations and collaborate on joint land improvement projects. As the decade went on, LPGs were encouraged to expand their participation in local cooperative projects particularly with regard to the use of land and machinery. While few farmers objected in principle to cooperation where there was mutual benefit, there was however growing suspicion of what loss of individual independence cooperation might lead to. By 1965, after a series of (often reluctant) mergers, many collective farmers were anxious not to have control over the finances and land which they had contributed to their LPG diluted still further. Their suspicion was exacerbated too by a desire to consolidate and a growing sense of identification with and possession of the LPG among its members, which rejected the prospect of their LPG losing independent control over its wealth, land, and machinery.

So strong was this sentiment and suspicion that even where it was not shared by LPG chairmen, they found it hard to resist. During the harvest in 1965, the few attempts in *Bezirk* Erfurt at the integrated deployment of machinery by groups of LPGs tended to be halted prematurely. LPG functionaries and their members, it was reported, were too anxious to see to their own concerns before helping their 'partners in cooperation.'[37] Arguments used by district state agricultural functionaries to persuade LPG chairmen of the value of cooperation as a policy inevitably echoed those used to persuade individual farmers during the collectivisation campaign. Cooperation was put forward as the key to rationalising production while maintaining the rights of the individual farmer, just as collectivisation had been. Again, just as they had with collectivisation, many farmers regarded this process, however, as yet another means of restricting their independence.

In contrast to the spring of 1960, however, establishing cooperation by force was not a practicable option. Rather, the transmission of SED agricultural policy relied heavily on the willingness and ability of LPG leaders to explain it and persuade LPG members of its value to them as well as to the society at large. It became clear however that LPG leaders remained themselves more often than not unconvinced of the benefits of further change to the structure of agriculture. The establishment of ever more advanced degrees of cooperation between collective farms was by no means recognised as the panacea for East German agriculture that it was touted to be. Furthermore, the attainment of a reasonable level of profitability in numerous

37. ThHStAW Bezirksparteiarchiv der SED Erfurt, Bezirksleitung der SED Erfurt IV/A/2/2/42 Sekretariat der Bezirksleitung, Protokoll der Bezirksparteiaktivtagung Landwirtschaft am 7.12.1965, p. 160.

collective farms, which enabled LPG members to receive satisfactory incomes, had brought a degree of social harmony and stability to collective farms not seen since the start of the collectivisation campaign. There was thus understandable desire on the part of collective farm leaders, ordinary members, and even members of the state and party administration in some districts not to rock the boat with further change. This attitude was critically dismissed in the rhetoric of party sources as 'the theory of mediocrity', which derided resistance to further change on such grounds as merely signs of incompetence or cowardice among LPG cadres and ideological backwardness among their members.[38]

After the failure of cooperation during the harvest in 1965, the SED *Bezirk* leadership were explicit in their criticism of LPG managers as the weakest links in the chain of policy implementation in agriculture:

> A whole range of leading cadres in the collectives, chairmen as well as crop and livestock brigadiers are not getting to grips with the current problems of society's development. This the result of their level of qualification, even though many of them are themselves state approved farmers or master farmers. . . . In most cases the functionaries appear to be the progressive party in the collective. But already in the boards of the collectives these leading cadres often do not find sufficient support in order to realise the tasks in the collectives individually.

Worse still, many LPG cadres clearly had no desire to continue in a position where they were under constant pressure to push through policies that the majority of their fellow farmers rejected. The report continued:

> In all the districts in which new elections are being held there are problems with filling the posts of chairmen and board members. They refuse to be candidates using in part paper thin arguments. They claim not to understand the integrated deployment of machinery and cite among other things internal difficulties in the collectives, health reasons, age, unreasonable state demands for grain delivery, poor support from the board, differences within the LPG. The real causes lie however not in these arguments but are rather to be found in the fact that these chairmen shy away from confrontations with LPG members over the implementation of the decisions of the party and the government.[39]

---

38. ThHStAW Bezirksparteiarchiv der SED Erfurt, Bezirksleitung der SED Erfurt BIV/2/5/382 Abt. Parteiorgane, Informationsbericht, Nr.16/65, 29.5.1965, pp. 181–91.

39. ThHStAW Bezirksparteiarchiv der SED Erfurt, Bezirksleitung der SED Erfurt BIV/2/7/565 Abt. Landwirtschaft, Einschätzungen über die Vorbereitungen der Neuwahlen bzw. Ergänzungswahlen in den Genossenschaften des Bezirkes Erfurt, 10.12.1965, pp. 206–9.

Even where LPG chairmen did seek to respond to the demands placed upon them by the KLRs and sought to set up cooperative arrangements with their neighbours, mid-level cadres such as work brigade leaders and members of the board continued to put up effective resistance. Without an active party organisation to back them up, LPG chairmen had little choice but to back down, or lose the support and confidence of their subordinates and fellow farmers.[40] In Type I LPGs in particular, LPG chairmen were reluctant even to broach this issue in public discussions.[41] By August 1966, at least on paper, the persuasive efforts largely of agricultural functionaries in the KLR appeared to have paid some dividends. All but 20 of the *Bezirk's* 1062 LPGs were recorded as having joined a so-called cooperative community (*Kooperationsgemeinschaft,* or KOG[42]) with other LPGs. However, the nature and extent of cooperative relations varied considerably in these KOGs. Meanwhile, LPG cadres were still found to be reluctant or unsuccessful at winning their members' support for cooperation.[43]

For cooperation to develop, LPG chairmen and other leading cadres were being asked to do more than just persuade their members; they had also actually to form effective working relations with colleagues in other LPGs. Each KOG formed a cooperative council, in which each LPG was represented, generally by its chairman. In theory, regardless of party membership, LPG chairmen were to be committed to the goals of the SED regime first and foremost. In practice, the content of the discussion of the cooperative councils was still defined to a large extent by LPG functionaries' loyalty to the interests and the wishes of the members of their own LPGs. If, in the reports of the district and *Bezirk* administration, the implementation of the NES was being hindered by a lack of ambition

40. ThHStAW Bezirksparteiarchiv der SED Erfurt, Bezirksleitung der SED Erfurt BIV/2/7/588 Abt. Landwirtschaft, Parteieinfluss im Kooperationsbereich Grossengottern, 5.10.1966, pp. 155–61; BIV/2/7/588 Abt. Landwirtschaft, Abt. Parteiorgane, Sektor Operativ, Erfahrungen und Schlussfolgerungen für die Entwicklung der Parteiarbeit in den Kooperationsbereichen auf der Grundlage der Untersuchungen der KL Erfurt-Land, 2.11.1965, pp. 1–11; BIV/2/5/173 Parteiorgane, Abt. Landwirtschaft, Faktenmaterial für die Parteiaktivtagung der Kooperation Schillingstedt, Kreis Sömmerda am 25.8.1971, 23.8.1971.

41. ThHStAW Bezirksparteiarchiv der SED Erfurt, Bezirksleitung der SED Erfurt IV/A/2/3/150 Sekretariat der Bezirksleitung, Entwurf des Berichtes an das Sekretariat des ZK über 'Die Erfahrungen der Parteiarbeit speziell zur Lösung der ideologischen Fragen bei der Entwicklung von Kooperationsbeziehungen', pp. 37–55.

42. *Kooperationsgemeinschaft* or KOG was the collective term for two or more LPGs contractually bound to cooperate with one another in some aspect of agricultural production.

43. ThHStAW Bezirksparteiarchiv der SED Erfurt, Bezirksleitung der SED Erfurt IV/A/2/3/169 Sekretariat der Bezirksleitung Abt. Parteiorgane, Informationsbericht, Nr 19/66, 24.8.1966, p. 31ff.; IV/A/2/3/169 Sekretariat der Bezirksleitung Abt. Parteiorgane, Einschätzung des Standes des soz. Bewusstseins der Bevölkerung unseres Bezirkes, 8.9.1966, pp. 79–115.

among LPG chairmen, selfishness was often cited as being at the root of the failure of cooperation.[44]

The tendency for LPG cadres to advocate the interests of their collective farm at the expense of implementing the party's agricultural policy was critically dismissed as selfishness and an inability to see the larger picture of overall agricultural (and social) development which cooperation would bring. However, LPG cadres, particularly in Type I LPGs, regarded themselves no less responsible to the membership of the LPGs than they were obliged to follow instructions from the KLR. Not only did no LPG chairman wish to be seen to be the dupe of his neighbour, the day-to-day opprobrium from collective farmers towards LPG functionaries who had failed to safeguard their interests was motive enough to resist cooperation. In several cooperative communities, it became clear in the mid 1960s that relations between chairmen could rapidly deteriorate resulting in the collapse of any real cooperation between LPGs, even where the LPGs involved were supposed to be models of progressive implementation of policy.[45] Within the LPG and the KOG Walschleben, *Kreis* Erfurt-Land, clashes of personalities became a serious problem between 1965 and 1967. At one point, members of the LPG Gebesee were reportedly accusing their chairman of being so subservient that he was little more than the coach driver of the chairman of the LPG Walschleben.[46] As long as there was mutual suspicion between LPG functionaries based on bad experiences in the past, the prospects for developing cooperation were small. Thus it was that a working group from the SED *Bezirksleitung* monitoring the harvest in 1967 in *Kreis* Apolda found a number of LPG chairmen refusing to allow their harvesters to be used in combination with those of other LPGs. One LPG functionary offered the argument: 'last year we were conned by the integrated deployment of machinery. We gave up our harvesters when the weather was good and then all we received was wet grain.'[47]

44. For a dramatic rendering of such conflicts of interest between LPG see: H. Sakowski, *Daniel Druskat*, (E. Berlin, 1976).

45. ThHStAW Bezirksparteiarchiv der SED Erfurt, Bezirksleitung der SED Erfurt BIV/2/7/588 Abt. Landwirtschaft, Protokoll über den Erfahrungsaustausch am 28.3.1967 in Heringen, 11.4.1967, pp. 320–48; BIV/2/7/588 Abt. Landwirtschaft, Information an Genosse Lüdecke, 13.11.1967, pp. 373–75.

46. ThHStAW Bezirksparteiarchiv der SED Erfurt, Bezirksleitung der SED Erfurt BIV/2/7/550 Abt. Parteiorgane Erfahrungen und Schlussfolgerungen, 3.11.1965, p. 100; BIV/2/5/384 Parteiorgane, Information, 27.9.1966, p. 256–58; BIV/2/7/588 Abt. Landwirtschaft, Einschätzung des Kooperationsbereiches Walschleben 6.7.1966, pp. 145–54; Abt. Landwirtschaft, Abt. Parteiorgane, Faktenmaterial zu einigen Problemen der Partei und Massenarbeit der PO der Kooperationsgemeinschaft Walschleben, 23.11.1966, pp. 174–77.

47. ThHStAW Bezirksparteiarchiv der SED Erfurt, Bezirksleitung der SED Erfurt BIV/2/7/557 Abt. Landwirtschaft der Bezirksleitung, Bericht über den Einsatz im Kreis Apolda, 9.8.1967, pp.

While the numbers of SED members in leading positions in LPGs had increased, the KLRs were still reliant on a considerable proportion of mid-level managers in the collective farms who had not joined a party or who were members of one or other of the block parties (primarily the DBD) to implement agricultural policy. Despite the proclaimed loyalty of the DBD to the SED agenda, at the grassroots there was still mutual antagonism between SED members and members of the DBD, who often claimed greater technical expertise. The *grüne Genossen*[48] of the DBD were thus regularly suspected by both the SED and DBD hierarchy of acting primarily in either their own self-interest or the pragmatic interests of their collectives to the detriment of the evolution of socialist agricultural policy. The lack of clarity among such collective farm managers as to what was intended by ever-deeper forms of cooperation was at the core of their inability to persuade their members or, indeed, even agree with one another.

As with the use of the NES reforms in the LPGs, while the positive benefit of cooperation remained unclear, it was dismissed as at best the latest unnecessary fad of policy or suspected of being yet another stealthy method of depriving farmers of control over their own resources.[49] For many LPG members actively involved in the management of the collective farm, the old debate of received farming wisdom and traditional practice versus the SED's progressive agricultural policy was thus recast as pragmatic conservatism in the LPG versus change for change's sake.

Normalisation Tested

By 1968, the gradual implementation of socialist agricultural policy transmitted via the district agricultural councils and the LPG leadership had made some limited progress, as the top-heavy process of communication took its effect. The number of Type I LPGs had been reduced to less than the number of Type III LPGs in most of the districts of the *Bezirk*. Levels of qualification had risen significantly among both leading cadres and

72–76; Bezirksparteiarchiv der SED Erfurt, Kreisleitung der SED Sömmerda IV/A/4.10/077 SED Kreisleitung Sömmerda, Parteiorgane, Einschätzung der MV, 10.9.1967, pp. 50–57; 5.10.1967, pp. 58–63; 27.11.1967, pp. 74–81.

48. 'Green comrades' was a nickname for DBD members among some SED members.

49. ThHStAW Bezirksparteiarchiv der SED Erfurt, Bezirksleitung der SED Erfurt BIV/2/3/278 Sekretariat der Bezirksleitung, Kreisleitung Mühlhausen Monatliche Berichterstattung an den 1. Bezirkssekretär, Monat November 1967, 15.11.1967, pp. 392–96; IV/B/2/5/247 Abt. Parteiorgane, Einschätzung der auf der Grundlage einer Konzeption durchgeführten Untersuchung zu Entwicklungsproblemen in den LPG Typ I des Kreises Eisenach, 12.8.1968, pp. 39–53.

the agricultural workforce as a whole.[50] Much also had been achieved in establishing the conditions for mechanised production on a large scale, with mergers and some forms of cooperation taking effect. While concessions continued to be made to farmers in the form of small private plots and livestock, working conditions had also changed considerably. Many (although not all) residual elements of private farming had been replaced with a collective working culture.[51] Despite resistance to other economic reforms, in most LPGs, performance related pay, bonuses, and detailed accounting of costs and profits had become an accepted part of the production process.

However, impatience was growing in some quarters of the SED leadership with the lack of progress towards the full incorporation of agriculture into the GDR's industrial economy. In particular, the limited adoption of a standardised system of socialist business management (*sozialistische Betriebswirtschaft*[52]) by all LPG chairmen seemed to be holding back progress towards specialisation and industrialisation of production as well as agriculture's integration into the food processing industry, within the New Economic System's flexible planned economy.[53] As with earlier reforms to the economic organisation of the collective farms, LPG functionaries found themselves walking a tightrope between the insistence of the state and party apparatus and the inertia or resistance of their mid-level cadres and members. The failure of chairmen to implement reforms in their collective farms—despite publicly expressing support for them—was noted by the party as a serious obstacle to progress. Without reform, the necessary cooperative relations between farms and the food industry crucial to the further specialisation and industrialisation of agriculture could not be developed.[54]

50. By 1968, the proportion of the agricultural workforce with the basic qualification Facharbeiterprüfung was at 47 percent. The proportion of those qualified as Master farmers, or with a technical college or university qualification, was at 7.8 percent.

51. Private household production (*individuelle Hauswirtschaften*) remained central to life as a collective farmer and was a crucial means of supplementing income for farmers. It came also to be essential to the production of certain items of produce for the GDR as a whole from the late 1970s. See for an example of the meaning of the *individuelle Hauswirtschaft* to members of an LPG, B. Schier, *Alltagsleben im 'Sozialistischen Dorf'* (Munich 2001), pp. 223–37.

52. *Sozialistische Betriebswirtschaft* was a system of accounting and incentive measures designed to improve the efficiency of financial planning under the terms of the New Economic System.

53. BArch, DK 1 VA Neu 2846, Landwirtschaftsrat der DDR, Zu einigen Problemen der Arbeit der betriebswirtschaftlichen Beratungsdienste, Berichte der Bezirksleitungen, 13.3.1968.

54. ThHStAW Bezirksparteiarchiv der SED Erfurt, Kreisleitung der SED Sömmerda IV/B/4.10/197 SED Kreisleitung Sömmerda, Abt. Landwirtschaft, Kreisbauernkonferenz am 3. und 4. Mai 1968, Diskussionsbeitrag H. Reise, LPG Grossbrembach, pp. 104–8, Diskussionbeitrag R. Müller, LPG Bachra, pp. 119–23.

In these circumstances, a fine line had to be trodden by the staff of the district agricultural councils as well. LPG functionaries, responding to the concerns of their farmers, were largely loath to develop what they considered unfair cooperative relations either with other farms or with the major food processing plants. At the same time, if cooperation was administratively imposed and organised, it was likely that there would be negative consequences for production levels as well as personal antagonisms, which would sour relations among LPG chairmen and district functionaries of party and state. Moreover, the disruption that would come with industrialisation and specialisation of agriculture via cooperation would be a bitter enough pill to swallow for rural communities if gradually introduced, let alone if imposed.[55] In some respects, the confusion created by an administrative imposition of cooperation threatened to be more severe than had been the case with collectivisation. As the LPG chairman in Vehra put it in June 1968,

> the step to a common crop production [between LPGs in a KOG] and the development of various cooperative relations is comparable to the step from being a private farmer to being a collective farmer. But back then there was a clear statute which indicated to each person what his rights and obligations were and everyone knew exactly, from their neighbours experience too, how things would proceed and what awaited them. With the common crop production there is still a great deal unclear and we can't give concrete answers to the questions members pose.[56]

At the seventh Party Congress of the SED and the tenth German Farmers Congress in 1968, what appeared to be a new uncompromising agenda for the rapid development of industrialised farming in the GDR was, however, laid out. The apparent advocacy of immediate specialisation in crop production, and greater integration between agriculture and the food processing industry sparked some party zealots–both in LPGs and in the district and *Bezirk* administrations–into action. Pressure was stepped up on collective farms to accept new advances (prematurely) in the extent of their cooperation with one another in crop production. Rumours spread of separate cooperative crop production units being established without due consultation and ratification from LPG members' assemblies. The individual collective

---

55. SAPMO BArch DY 30/IV A/1/7/139 ZK der SED, Abt. Landwirtschaft, Erfahrungen und Probleme der Arbeit der Partei bei der Verwirklichung der Beschlüsse des VII. Parteitages und des X. DBK. 30.8.1968.

56. ThHStAW Bezirksparteiarchiv der SED Erfurt, Bezirksleitung der SED Erfurt IV/B/2/7/268 SED Bezirksleitung Abt. Landwirtschaft, Faktenmaterial zu Aktivtagung der KOG Straussfurt am 26.6.1968, p. 47.

farm appeared as a result increasingly redundant as an autonomous administrative unit, and fears grew among farmers and LPG chairmen that an administrative expropriation of collective farmers was imminent, as collectivised farming was relegated to a branch of the food processing industry.

Having been made aware of the widespread concerns of those in agriculture at this development, Walter Ulbricht himself sought to allay fears, roundly denouncing any such premature moves in this direction in his concluding remarks at the tenth Plenum of the Central Committee of the SED in April 1969. Certain aspects of the party line had, he claimed, been misinterpreted: firstly, too much power had been given to administrators in the food industry and undermined the independent status of LPGs; and secondly, a minority of LPGs in advanced states of cooperation had gone too far too quickly in the development of independent crop production and ought consequently no longer to be considered as models for other LPGs.[57] Central to his comments was the notion of the inviolability of the LPG as an economic unit, in which the principles of collective democracy were to be meticulously implemented. Ulbricht argued that the development of cooperative relations in crop production must and could only occur gradually in consultation with LPG members.

Rather than prompting a return to order and calm, this pronouncement from on high, however, caused considerable disruption. In *Bezirk* Erfurt, in the immediate aftermath of the tenth Plenum of the Central Committee, there was a degree of rebellion in the air as well as considerable confusion among collective farm managers and district agricultural functionaries as to quite what the import of Ulbricht's remarks was.[58] The members of the LPG Lützensömmern in *Kreis* Bad Langensalza took the opportunity to object publicly to their treatment at the hands of the cooperative council and the district agricultural council, suggesting that they were always being forced to accept *faits accomplis*. In *Kreis* Arnstadt as well as Bad Langensalza, some collective farmers suggested that they had been right all along to reject initiatives towards establishing cooperation, going so far as to question the future existence of cooperation between LPGs at all. The chairman of the LPG Kalteneber in Heiligenstadt expressed his confusion and disillusionment:

57. SAPMO BArch DY30/IV 2/1/395 Tagungen des ZK–10. Plenum des ZK, 24.4.1969, Schlusswort des Genossen Ulbricht, pp. 211–21.

58. ThHStAW Bezirksparteiarchiv der SED Erfurt, Bezirksleitung der SED Erfurt IV/B/2/5/183 Abt. Parteiorgane, Kurzinformation 21.5.1969 Abt. Parteiorgane; IV/B/2/7/267 Abt. Landwirtschaft Information über den Stand der Entwicklung der Kooperationsbeziehungen im Bezirk Erfurt und die sich daraus ergebenden Schlussfolgerungen. . ., 19.1.1970, pp. 79–95.

> the question which concerns me is whether agricultural policy has changed since the 10th Plenum? There are currently many discussions, cooperation is going to be broken up, or cooperation is leading to the liquidation of the class of the collective farmer. I'm not against new things, but it's not so easy for us up here as it is in the lowlands. . . We're losing the will to work.[59]

Reports, compiled by the DBD during May 1969 just after the tenth Plenum, on the mood in LPGs in the *Bezirk* highlighted the sense among LPG members that recently they had been rather bullied into things. In Erfurt-Land in particular, DBD members complained about the damage done to the independence of their LPG by the district authorities.[60] In later reports, it was clear that DBD members were still struck by uncertainty about how to proceed, not least because LPGs were reportedly no longer receiving guidance from staff from the SED *Kreisleitung* or the district 'agricultural council', who themselves no doubt were unclear what the correct path ought to be. In Steinrode, *Kreis* Worbis, some DBD members pointed out that representatives of the district authorities used to participate in every meeting of the cooperative council (*Kooperationsrat,* or KOR[61]), but had not turned up since the tenth Plenum.[62] In *Kreis* Heiligenstadt, as in *Kreis* Mühlhausen and *Kreis* Erfurt-Land, SED Bezirksleitung reports complained, the district agricultural councils were now unaware of what was going on in the LPG assemblies.[63]

A meeting of the SED *Kreisleitung* Sömmerda in July 1969 to discuss Ulbricht's concluding remarks heard a report on the reaction of farmers in the district. It was claimed hopefully that the majority of the collective farm members understood correctly that the tenth Plenum did not mean a correction of agricultural policy, but was rather a continuation of the resolutions

59. ThHStAW Bezirksparteiarchiv der SED Erfurt, Bezirksleitung der SED Erfurt IV/B/2/5/183 Abt. Parteiorgane, Kurzinformation, Stimmen von Genossenschaftsbäuerinnen und–bauern. . ., 21.5.1969, p. 326.

60. ThHStAW Bezirksparteiarchiv der SED Erfurt, Bezirksleitung der SED Erfurt IV/B/2/5/410 DBD Bezirksverband, Bericht an den 1. Sekretär der Bezirksleitung der SED ,23.5.1969, p. 174–80.

61. The *Kooperationsrat* or KOR was a body compromised of delegates from each of the LPGs in the cooperative community (KOG), usually the LPG chairmen, but also other leading members of the LPG, including brigade leaders or SED party secretaries. The primary purpose of the council was to arrange and agree upon the terms on which LPGs, and later the so-called LPG *Pflanzenproduktion* and LPG *Tierproduktion* cooperated with one another.

62. ThHStAW Bezirksparteiarchiv der SED Erfurt, Bezirksleitung der SED Erfurt IV/B/2/5/410 DBD Bezirksverband, Auswertung der Berichte der Kreisverbände über Meinungen unserer Mitglieder zum 10. Plenum des ZK der SED und unserer 5. Parteivorstandssitzung, undated, pp. 181–86.

63. ThHStAW Bezirksparteiarchiv der SED Erfurt, Bezirksleitung der SED Erfurt ThHStAW Bezirksparteiarchiv der SED Erfurt, Bezirksleitung der SED Erfurt IV/B/2/5/183 Abt. Parteiorgane, Kurzinformation über den Stand der Durchführung. . ., 17.7.1969, p. 392.

of the seventh SED Party Congress, with the reminder that this process must not be destroyed through impatience. In the first days and weeks after the tenth Plenum, however, mid-level cadres were marked out as being particularly problematic by spreading the opinion that 'thanks to the 10th Plenum that they could all now take their time and that cooperation would be scaled back.' More seriously, it was reported that LPG functionaries were now questioning the connection between collective democracy and democratic centralism. Ulbricht's remarks were thus being interpreted as a license for collective farms to assert their individual independence from outside interference, be it from other LPGs or the state apparatus.

One chairman of an LPG was reported to have collected all of the newspaper articles he could find on the subject of collective democracy, in order, at the given moment, to be able to back up his opposition to cooperation.[64] The wishes of the members of LPGs rather than the directives of the district state authorities were seen now in some quarters as the central consideration in a LPG chairman's decisions. In *Kreis* Sömmerda, it was reported that in a number of LPGs, the attitude of the members was that the cooperation in crop production should be broken up and LPGs should be allowed to be independent again. In a letter sent by the chairman and party secretary of the LPG 'Neuer Weg' Kölleda to the chairman of their cooperative community, they explained the decision of the LPG's board to withdraw from cooperative crop production. The letter concluded with the chairman and party secretary expressing their regret at this decision having been reached. They pointed out however that even they could not get around the words: 'the farmers decide'.[65]

Although by the end of the year, claims were made by the district agricultural council that clarity had been achieved as to the meaning of the tenth Plenum, the issue of how to proceed with cooperation in crop production was not resolved in all LPGs for several years.[66] During 1970, *Kreise* Worbis, Sondershausen, and Erfurt-Land were found to have made no headway in restarting developments in cooperative crop production. Worse still, in a number of existing cooperative crop production partnerships, there was serious disillusionment

64. ThHStAW Bezirksparteiarchiv der SED Erfurt, Kreisleitung der SED Sömmerda IV/B/4.10/190 SED Kreisleitung, Abt. Landwirtschaft, Kreisleitungssitzung, 3.7.1969, pp. 136–55.

65. ThHStAW Bezirksparteiarchiv der SED Erfurt, Kreisleitung der SED Sömmerda IV/B/4.10/200 SED Kreisleitung Sömmerda, Abt. Landwirtschaft, Probleme der Kooperation–Politbüro Beschluss vom 25.7.1969, pp. 150–59; Information über Beratung der Produktionsleitung am 14.8.1969, pp. 160–62; LPG 'Neuer Weg' Kölleda an den Vorsitzenden der KOG Kölleda, 28.8.1969, p. 163.

66. ThHStAW Bezirksparteiarchiv der SED Erfurt, Kreisleitung der SED Sömmerda IV/B/4.10/70 SED Kreisleitung Sömmerda, Abt. Landwirtschaft, Protokoll über die Schrittmacherberatung am 11.9.1969 in der Kreisleitung, 12.9.1969, pp. 3–6.

with the whole project.[67] As late as 1972, the leading cadres of a number of LPGs in *Kreis* Sömmerda expressed their doubt over the value of developing another cooperative crop production partnership, as they were not sure that there would not soon be 'another 10th Plenum', which abandoned the administrative separation of crop and livestock production.[68] The response to the tenth Plenum had clearly highlighted the dangers of any neglect of the chain of communication at the local level. The SED regime's authority in agriculture continued to depend on the mediation of LPG chairmen.

From Ulbricht to Honecker: Regaining the Initiative

The Eighth Party Congress in 1971 marked the final transition of power from Ulbricht to Honecker. There was, however, no u-turn in agricultural policy, with gradual development of greater cooperation in crop production still at the heart of the industrialisation of farming. This was in large part because Gerhard Grüneberg[69] remained the central figure in the formation of agricultural policy in the *Politbüro*. Reports on the situation in *Bezirk* Erfurt in 1971 made clear, however, that there was little chance of a new structure of agricultural production being established without at least some consultation. While in the Sömmerda and Apolda districts more than 70 percent of land was being farmed cooperatively, this was the case for only 20 percent of land in Worbis and Sondershausen districts, where a number of the remaining Type I LPGs continued to resist cooperation.[70]

Over the course of the next five years, the remaining Type I LPGs in the *Bezirk* that had retained their independence, allowing their members to continue to keep their livestock privately, were threatened with severe financial penalties unless they abandoned private livestock holding and transferred to Type III status or agreed to merge with a neighbouring Type III LPG. Objections to mergers by Type I farmers were mitigated by their

67. ThHStAW Bezirksparteiarchiv der SED Erfurt, Bezirksleitung der SED Erfurt IV/B/2/7/267 Abt. Landwirtschaft, Stellungnahme zur Information der Produktionsleitung des RLN (B)…, 11.12.1970, p. 239.

68. ThHStAW Bezirksparteiarchiv der SED Erfurt, Kreisleitung der SED Sömmerda IV/C/4.10/171 SED Kreisleitung Sömmerda, Abt. Landwirtschaft, Zuarbeit zum Informationsbericht über das Thema 'Erfahrungen und Probleme der Kooperation in der Pflanzenproduktion…', 26.09.1972, pp. 50–56.

69. Gerhard Grüneberg (1921–1981), from 1960–1980, was Secretary for Agriculture in the Central Committee of the SED and from 1966, a member of the *Politbüro* of the ZK.

70. BArch Abt. DDR, DK 1 VA neu 2464 Ministerium für LFN, Probleme der Führungstätigkeit im Bereich der Landwirtschaft und Nahrungsgüterwirtschaft im Bezirk Erfurt, 1971; Abt. Wissenschaftliche Führungstätigkeit und Inspektion, Bericht–Erfurt, 1972.

being allowed in some cases to continue to keep the same amount of livestock privately as they had before, despite now being part of the Type III.[71] At the same time, the re-education of the agricultural workforce continued to advance rapidly.[72] Between 1967 and 1971, as the numbers of those working in agriculture dropped, the proportion of farmers in *Bezirk* Erfurt holding a technical qualification rose from 48.6 percent to 76.5 percent,[73] rising again by 1975 to 82.6 percent.[74] In line with this development, the workforce became increasingly specialised and used to an industrial style work pattern, with shift work being widely introduced.[75] As a consequence, the level of resistance to the development of cooperation reduced steadily among the LPG membership who themselves were increasingly specialised.

At the same time, LPG cadres who had not supported the development of industrial style production and the formation of specialised crop production units began to be excluded from leading positions in LPGs, either through merger or through the reorganisation of management of crop production. As far as the SED Bezirksleitung was concerned, the failure of LPGs to advance with establishing cooperative crop production following the tenth Plenum was the continuing lack of sufficient SED presence on the cooperative councils or among LPG leaders in general.[76] Certainly, DBD members in cadre positions were reported in a number of cases to be at the root cause of opposition to the development of independent crop

---

71. D. Gabler *Entwicklungsabschnitte der Landwirtschaft in der ehemaligen DDR* (Berlin, 1995), p. 227; The number of Type I/II LPGs decreased from 121 in 1970 to 49 in 1974. Statistisches Jahrbuch–Bezirk Erfurt, Teil I, p. 173.

72. As part of a poll of farmers by the Institut für Gesellschaftswissenschaften beim ZK in 1970, the following question was asked: 'When you consider the development of your LPG in last years, which are the main changes which have occurred among the people?' The most popular response by some margin was: 'The increase in technical qualification'. SAPMO BArch DY30 IV/A/2.023/83 Institut für Gesellschaftswissenschaften, Lehrstuhl marxistisch-leninistische Soziologie, Die Entwicklung des politischen Verantwortungsbewusstseins der Genossenschaftsbauern. . ., Frage 15, 17.2.1971.

73. ThHStAW Bezirksparteiarchiv der SED Erfurt, Bezirksleitung der SED Erfurt IV/C/2/7/344 Abt. Landwirtschaft, Analyse der Probleme der Entwicklung des gesellschaftlichen Lebens in den Gemeinden des Bezirkes, pp. 14–35.

74. ThHStAW Bezirksparteiarchiv der SED Erfurt, Bezirksleitung der SED Erfurt IV/C/2/7/344 Abt. Landwirtschaft, Rat des Bezirkes, Stellv. Vorsitzende für LFN, Bericht über die Verwirklichung des VIII. Parteitages und der Bezirksdelegiertenkonferenz der SED in der LuN des Bezirkes, Jan. 1976, pp. 192–201.

75. ThHStAW Bezirksparteiarchiv der SED Erfurt, Bezirksleitung der SED Erfurt IV/C/2/3/164 Abt. Landwirtschaft, Material für die Mitarbeiterberatung am 27.8.1973, 23.8.1973, pp. 184–207.

76. ThHStAW Bezirksparteiarchiv der SED Erfurt, Bezirksleitung der SED Erfurt IV/B/2/4/123 BPKK, Analyse über die Parteiverfahren im 2. Halbjahr 1970 und Probleme die sich aus der Tätigkeit der KPKK Weimar ergeben, 2.12.1970, p. 86; Bezirksparteiarchiv der SED Erfurt, Kreisleitung der SED Sömmerda IV/B/4.10/078 SED Kreisleitung Sömmerda, Abt. Landwirtschaft, Bericht über die Arbeit der PO der KOG Straussfurt, 7.6.1971, pp. 44–47.

production partnerships and the resurgence of arguments in favour of the large-scale mixed crop and livestock production of the *Gross* LPG.[77] Those who were not a member of any political party increasingly could not expect to rise beyond the position of work brigade leader, nor would they have access to the highest qualification levels possible without party membership. Although DBD members did occupy some top positions in collective farms, the DBD became the party of mid-level agricultural cadres in the 1970s and 1980s. From the mid 1970s, for those that wished to rise higher, SED membership appeared to be a prerequisite.[78] With these developments, the means for communicating and implementing SED agricultural policy had achieved unprecedented consistency and coherence.

* * *

The nature of SED rule in East Germany is by no means easily characterised. Certainly in the sphere of agriculture, the manner in which the SED leadership communicated its authority was neither static nor monolithic. The transformative effects of industrial and technological development played an integral part in shaping the experience of dictatorship in the East German countryside. Against this background, it is however possible also to trace an, albeit heavily skewed, process of conflict and compromise at the grassroots of agriculture in the GDR. It is in the light of this process that the unprecedented stability and coherence of the Honecker regime in the 1970s must be seen. A normalisation of rule had taken place in agriculture. However, as the economic decline of the 1980s would demonstrate, it could not protect against the decay of the material and epistemic bases of the SED regime's claim to legitimacy.

77. SAPMO BArch, DY60/2973 DBD Parteivorstand, Abt. Parteiorgane, Wertung des Weiteren Verlaufs der Diskussionen zur Vorebreitung des Perspektivplanes; DBD Bezirksverband, Parteiiformation, 11.8.1970; DBD Bezirksverband, Abt. Parteiorgane, Neuwahlbeschlussbericht, 21.1.1970; ThHStAW Bezirksparteiarchiv der SED Erfurt, Bezirksleitung der SED Erfurt IV/B/4.10/198 SED Kreisleitung Sömmerda, Abt. Landwirtschaft, Kreisbauernkonferenz am 4. und 5.3.1970, Diskussionsbeitrag K. Schwarz, LPG Mannstedt, p. 157–65; IV/B/2/5/165 Abt. Parteiorgane Erste Einschätzungen der Kreisleitungssitzungen zur Auswertung der 14. Tagung des ZK, 19.1.1971, pp. 568–74.

78. ThHStAW Bezirksparteiarchiv der SED Erfurt, Bezirksleitung der SED Erfurt IV/C/2/15/517 SED Bezirksleitung, Abt. Befreundete Parteien, Aktennotiz, Dec. 1972, p. 39.

Chapter 5

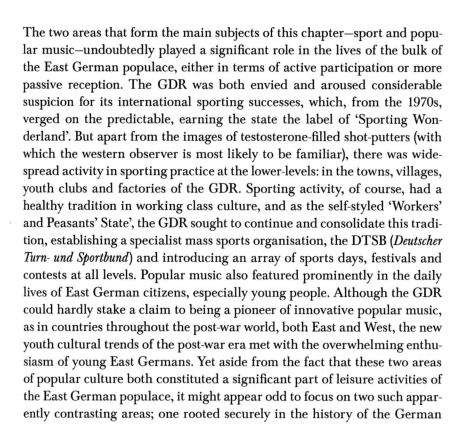

The 'Societalisation' of the State: Sport for the Masses and Popular Music in the GDR

Dan Wilton

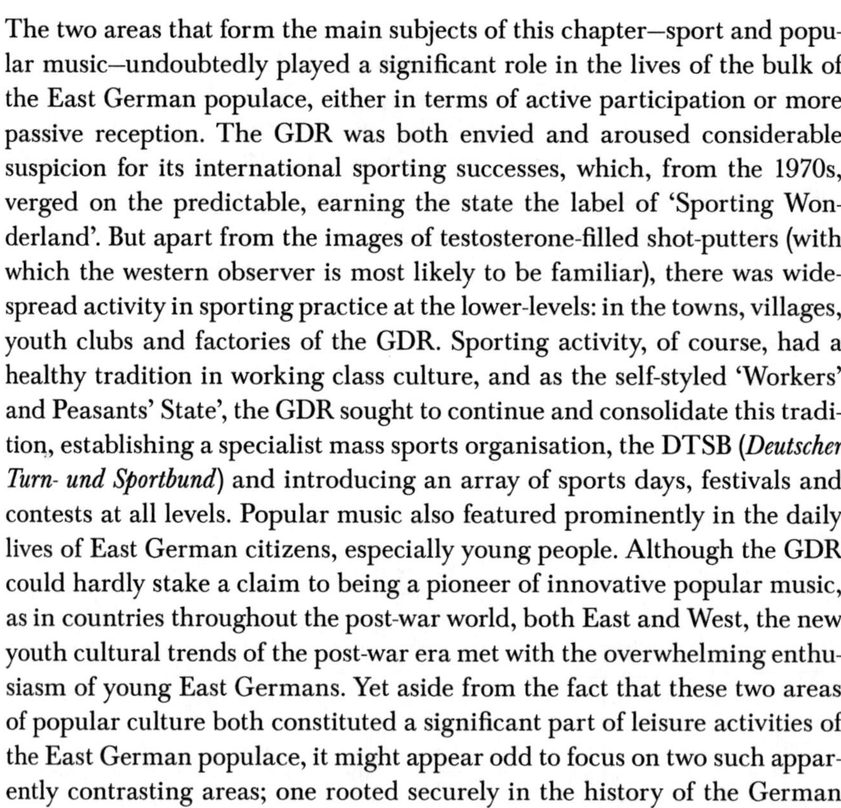

The two areas that form the main subjects of this chapter—sport and popular music—undoubtedly played a significant role in the lives of the bulk of the East German populace, either in terms of active participation or more passive reception. The GDR was both envied and aroused considerable suspicion for its international sporting successes, which, from the 1970s, verged on the predictable, earning the state the label of 'Sporting Wonderland'. But apart from the images of testosterone-filled shot-putters (with which the western observer is most likely to be familiar), there was widespread activity in sporting practice at the lower-levels: in the towns, villages, youth clubs and factories of the GDR. Sporting activity, of course, had a healthy tradition in working class culture, and as the self-styled 'Workers' and Peasants' State', the GDR sought to continue and consolidate this tradition, establishing a specialist mass sports organisation, the DTSB (*Deutscher Turn- und Sportbund*) and introducing an array of sports days, festivals and contests at all levels. Popular music also featured prominently in the daily lives of East German citizens, especially young people. Although the GDR could hardly stake a claim to being a pioneer of innovative popular music, as in countries throughout the post-war world, both East and West, the new youth cultural trends of the post-war era met with the overwhelming enthusiasm of young East Germans. Yet aside from the fact that these two areas of popular culture both constituted a significant part of leisure activities of the East German populace, it might appear odd to focus on two such apparently contrasting areas; one rooted securely in the history of the German working class culture of the twentieth century, and the other regarded (at least officially) as an unwanted intruder from the capitalist West. How, then, can an examination of such different spheres of popular culture fit in with and contribute to the debates about the 'normalisation' of rule in the GDR? In order to address this question, it is important to consider (albeit very briefly) the way in which both (mass) sport and popular music relate to the more general debates about the nature of GDR state and society and their (inter)relationship with one another.

Crudely put, accounts relating to the developments of sport and popular music in the GDR have, in different ways, reflected the dominant trends in the GDR historiography of the last decade or so: on the one hand, those which posit a view of society as being heavily, if not exclusively, determined by politics and according to which the 'people' were in thrall to the whims and will of a small circle of power holders in Berlin; on the other hand, those which put forward a view of a more autonomous society, the developments of which were shaped far more by the people themselves, who were able to evade or resist the prohibitive prescriptions of the central authorities.[1] In short, (the relatively limited number of) works dealing with sport have tended to fall in with the first category, and reflect the preoccupations with control and imposition 'from above'.[2] By contrast, accounts of popular music in the GDR have largely focused on tendencies on the part of the populace to evade the prohibitive prescriptions–in other words, they correspond to and complement the notion of the 'limits' of the dictatorship, referring to deviant, 'resistant' trends 'from below'.[3] Fundamental to the arguments that follow is the contention that, for all their apparent differences, these dominant depictions of popular/mass sport (as imposed from above) and popular music (as an expression of resistance from below) are predicated on

1. There is by now an extensive collection on the main trends in GDR historiography after 1989, all of which cannot be noted here. The most recent comprehensive overview is offered in R. Eppelmann, B. Faulenbach, and U. Mählert, eds., *Bilanz und Perspektiven der DDR Forschung* (Paderborn: F. Schöningh, 2003). See also C. Ross, *The East German Dictatorship. Problems and perspectives in the interpretation of the GDR* (London: Arnold, 2002).

2. See e.g., G. Holzweißig, *Sport und Politik in der DDR* (Berlin: Holzapfel, 1988), esp. chaps. 2 and 4; W. Rossade, *Sport und Kultur in der DDR* (Munich: tuduv-Verlagsgesellschaft, 1987); H-D Krebs, 'Die politische Instrumentalisierung des Sports in der DDR', in *Materialien der Enquete Kommission. 'Aufarbeitung von Geschichte und Folgen der SED Diktatur in Deutschland' des Deutschen Bundestages, Bd. III*, no.1, pp. 1315–69; also Protokoll der 35. Sitzung des Sportausschusses: 'Rolle des Sports in der DDR', in *Materialien der Enquete Kommission*, Bd. III, no.1, pp. 662–75.

3. See e.g., P. Wicke and L. Müller, eds., *Rockmusik und Politik–Analysen, Interviews und Dokumente* (Berlin: Ch. Links, 1996); M. Rauhut, *Beat in der Grauzone. DDR-Rock bis 1972–Politik und Alltag* (Berlin: Basisdruck, 1993); Idem, *Schalmei und Lederjacke. Udo Lindenberg, BAP und Underground: Rock und Politik in den 80er Jahren* (Berlin: Basisdruck, 1996); R. Galenza and H. Havemeister, eds., *Wir wollen immer artig sein. Punk, New Wave, Hip-Hop, Independent Szene in der DDR, 1980–1990* (Berlin: Schwarzkopf & Schwarzkopf, 1999).

a similar and misleading assumption of there being a clear-cut dichotomy between the 'regime' and the 'people'. Sport, in which the agents of change were the political elites, was imposed upon the people against their will. Coming from the opposite direction, the pursuit and practice of popular music, which restores agency to 'ordinary' people, was directed against the explicit will of the authorities. Both, in short, pitch 'state' against 'society'. The essential difference lies in the emphasis on agency, on the matter of who acted against whom. Importantly, then, this suggestion of there being a constant state of conflict between 'regime' and 'people' would seem difficult to reconcile with any notion of a 'normalisation' process in the GDR.

As I shall attempt to argue below, however, developments in the sphere of mass sport cannot be merely explained in terms of 'state' imposed policies from 'above', nor can the developments in popular music be reduced to evasive and deviant practices of subversive elements of the population. Although such factors undoubtedly played a role, particularly during the rather more unstable early years of the GDR's existence, there were far more significant processes of negotiation, compromise, and interaction both within and between 'state' and 'society' which need to be drawn into an examination of both these areas of popular culture.

In considering such processes, it is necessary to focus more closely on the role of the (lower-level or local) functionaries as active carriers of and participants within the system of rule, rather than as merely simple apathetic yes-men, or complicit opportunists, unquestioningly carrying out dictates from 'above'.[4] There is a point of considerable import to be made in connection with this: namely that the predominant tendency in GDR historiography of defining the 'state' as a tightly knit, unitary block of decision-making apparatchiks located in Berlin needs to be modified in favour of a more expansive definition of what and who constituted the 'state'.[5] Quite contrary to the notion of the 'withering away of the state', as envisaged by Marx in the shift towards communism, it is evident that, in the GDR, the number of those involved in the administrative and organisational structures–and hence could be seen to make up the 'state'–was overwhelming and, indeed, increased over time. While this 'growth of the state' could be interpreted simply as a tightening of the administrative bodies' grip over 'society', it would be more useful to see this expansion as a blurring of the boundaries

---

4. For such a view of functionaries employed in the state system, see for example the entries on 'Kader and Kaderpolitik' and 'Massenorganisationen' in Rainer Eppelmann, Horst Möller et al., eds., *Lexikon des DDR-Sozialismus*, Bd. 1 (Paderborn: F. Schöningh, 1997), pp. 438–39, pp. 546–47.

5. In this sense, this study builds on the work of Corey Ross and Jeffrey Kopstein.

between state and society. In other words, through incorporating ever-greater numbers of 'ordinary' citizens into the organisational and administrative system, one could regard this expansion from the opposite perspective: as the 'societalisation' of the state. Adopting this notion, coined in the first instance by Ralph Jessen,[6] allows for greater scope in considering how the system was carried, in an active sense, by participating citizens.

Below, I first consider how this 'expansion of the state' (or, conversely, incorporation of greater numbers of 'ordinary citizens' into the state apparatus) brought about a greater degree of coordination and efficiency in the implementation of policy in mass sport and popular music. In looking at this period of greater stability and efficiency, I also suggest, however, that it was not just a question of there being more effective transmission from 'above' to 'below': with reference to the 'Mach Mit' citizens' programmes of the 1970s, I suggest that there was, during this brief period, a greater sense of common interests between the 'regime' and the 'people'—a consensus of sorts, which was nevertheless based on a condition of mutual cooperation between different groups within 'state' and 'society'. Once there were signs that such cooperation was not being honoured or upheld, then this precarious consensus was replaced by a growing despondency, not only amongst 'ordinary' East Germans without any official responsibility, but also amongst many holding positions, however lowly, within the 'state'. In the latter part of this brief study, then, I suggest that this process of 'societalisation', while allowing for a degree of stability in the 1970s, paradoxically also created conditions for the growing disillusionment of the functionary classes, contributing at once to a diversification in popular cultural practices (both in sport and music) and, ultimately, to the disintegration of authority in the 1980s.

Expanding the 'State', or, Incorporating 'Society'? Cooperation and Coordination in the 1970s

Even if, in contrast to the 1950s, the GDR had become far less unstable in the 1960s, uncertainties and deficiencies in the working habits and practices of lower-level functionaries continued to hamper the consistent implementation of policy during Ulbricht's second decade in power, not least in the spheres of mass sport and popular music.[7] By the turn of the

6. Ralph Jessen, 'Die Gesellschaft im Staatssozialismus. Probleme einer Sozialgeschichte der DDR', in *Geschichte und Gesellschaft*, 21 (1995): 96–110.

7. Put briefly, although there had been concerted efforts at the end of the 1950s to promote sporting practice at the grassroots, such factors as overburdened and inexperienced functionaries, or simple lack of organisation in the localities, as well as rivalries and misunderstandings between

decade, however, it is generally agreed that the GDR, which by now constituted a more permanent fixture on the political landscape of post-war Europe, enjoyed an enhanced period of stability. While the simple passage of time ensured that functionaries became more proficient in pursuing their tasks and so played a role in the smoother functioning of the system, there were other factors that contributed to greater efficiency. First, there were important changes in the state apparatus itself, with new committees being created and educational workshops and programmes established and carried out with greater regularity and thoroughness than at any time previously. Secondly, and just as crucial (and in part related to this 'expansion of the state'), was the fact that policies relating to sport and music (and indeed other areas) themselves became broader based and more 'integrative'. In partial contrast to the 1960s, central policies were not so restrictive, perhaps reflecting a degree of confidence within the state apparatus.

Streamlining Popular Music: Festivals, Committees, and Workshops

Attempts to channel the chaotic and disparate practices of popular music, which had been so evident in the 1960s, into a coordinated policy, found expression at the ground-breaking first national Dance Music Conference of 1972, which took place on 24–25 April in Berlin. In recognition of the previous lack of direction in popular music policy, Werner Rackwitz, the chairman of the department of Music in the Ministry for Culture called for efforts to:

> overcome the discontinuity in the development of dance music, which still relies too often on individual actions, and apply with greater consistency those methods and activities which have been recognised and been proven as correct. . . [This can be attained] by means of a more comradely, creative cooperation with the popular musicians and through a common approach (*Vorangehen*) of all who are active in this area.[8]

In particular, the Free German Youth (FDJ) was to play a greater role in ensuring the implementation of a more streamlined policy through more

functionaries active in differing spheres of responsibility, severely undermined the policies introduced to increase participation. Similarly in popular music, uncertainties and inconsistencies amongst responsible functionaries often stymied the implementation of central directives in this sphere. (This is discussed in greater depth in D. Wilton, *Regime versus People? Public opinion and the development of sport and popular music in the GDR, 1961–1989* [PhD thesis, London University, 2004]).

8. SAPMO-BArch, DY30/IVB2/906/85, fo. 3 (Thesen zum Einleitungsreferat der Tanzmusikkonferenz, Information Abt Kultur, 11.4.72).

focused work with the musicians themselves and through staging central and local workshops, competitions, and festivals.[9] In the 1960s, there had been frequent complaints about FDJ functionaries ignoring or being unaware of directives and hence neglecting their tasks of guiding and encouraging youths in their choice of leisure activities.[10] Whilst it might be expected that such neglect and poor work would have led to a tighter rein being placed on the youth organisation, in the 1970s the FDJ was endowed with greater responsibility in helping to contribute to cultural policy and assisting in staging more significant events. Giving the FDJ more responsibility, for example, in the staging of events, meant that they were more likely to act out their role with a more positive sense of commitment and contribution. One such major programme that was introduced in the 1970s was the FDJ *Werkstattwoche Jugendtanzmusik*, the first of which took place in Frankfurt-an-der-Oder from 21–28 October 1972. Implicitly acknowledging its previous negligence and past failures to stage events of the desired standard, the central council of the FDJ stated its new intent to be more efficient in a report of that summer:

> The basic concern of the FDJ *Werkstattwoche* is to establish and consolidate the influence of the FDJ in this important area of youth policy. It is thus necessary to form a closer and friendlier relationship with the young musicians and, together with them, seek out ways in which the level of youth dance events and concerts... can be steadily improved. The FDJ *Werkstattwoche* should help us to properly incorporate youth dance music into the cultural-political activities of the youth organisation, to determine the tasks needed for the cooperation between the leaders of the FDJ and the young musicians and allow us to embark on an objective discussion about the profile of youth dance music and youth dance bands.[11]

Notwithstanding the possibility of homogenised reports, there are definite indications that such attempts to coordinate and ensure tighter organisation and agreement were successfully realised. The workshop weeks of the FDJ were established as a regular fixture in the cultural calendar of the

9. There were, of course, FDJ events and programmes in the 1960s, not least of which were the (somewhat short-lived) *Gitarrenwettbewerb* as well as the *Singebewegung*. The former was, however, relatively quickly dissolved in the wake of the growing disturbances at events in the mid 1960s. The latter, which was intended to offer an alternative to the more westernised strands of youth music, existed throughout the years of the GDR's existence, but was variable in its level of success. Olaf Schäfer considers the Singebewegung in greater detail in his book, *Zur Musikkultur der FDJ*.

10. This is discussed more thoroughly in my PhD thesis (chapter 2).

11. SAPMO-BArch, DY24/12031, 'Beschluss des Sekretariats des Zentralrates der FDJ, 20.7.72'.

GDR, taking place biennially right up until 1988, whilst youth dance music festivals–including preliminary, qualification rounds for national events–were frequently staged at the local level. Particularly at the local level, where the discrepancies and diffuseness in implementing popular music policy had been so evident in the 1960s, there appears to have been a greater success in organising the events in line with central policy. For example, the third dance music festival in the region of Karl-Marx-Stadt was praised in the most enthusiastic terms. It had attracted a large audience, had been efficiently organised and executed smoothly, and had provided a forum for a 'harmonious balance of artistic performance' all within the 'marvellous surroundings of the recently opened city hall.'[12]

Perhaps the most significant indication of the endeavour to address the hitherto inconsistent implementation of popular cultural policy, and a move which seemed to reflect Rackwitz's call for a more 'comradely approach' to dealing with popular musicians, was the creation of the Committee for Entertainment Arts in 1973. In an attempt to put into practice the intentions stated at the Dance Music Conference a year earlier and following a directive of the *Politburo* in January of 1973, the committee brought together cultural functionaries and entertainment artists (amongst them disc jockeys, actors, musicians, and even circus performers) under the same umbrella organisation. The committee members pledged, amongst other things, to encourage the development of young talent and to monitor and guide these talents by way of *Förderverträge* and the extended use of music schools and higher education institutions. On the whole, the committee was allotted the task of 'making possible the improvement of consensus and coordination amongst the diverse institutions active in the area of entertainment arts.'[13] The committee was responsible to the *Generaldirektion für Unterhaltungskunst*, which, as part of the Ministry for Culture, was assigned with the task of working out new conceptions for work in the area of entertainment arts.

Achieving greater cooperation and efficiency was not just restricted to the central flagship bands of the GDR, who were affiliated to the central Committee for Entertainment Arts. Indeed, perhaps mindful of the fact that it was the local-level amateur bands which, in conjunction with the functionaries prepared to tolerate their programmes, had proved to be most problematic in the 1960s, the regional cultural councils also set about introducing training programmes, to familiarise their musicians and artists with the

---

12. SstAC, RdB,Abt Kultur, 117286; Einschätzung des III Tanzmusikfestes des Bezirkes Karl-Marx-Stadt (23 Nov. 1974).

13. SAPMO-BArch, DY30/IVB2/906/85; 'Information über die bisherige Verwirklichung des Beschlusses des Politbüros vom 30.1.1973 . . .'.

complexities of cultural policy. In *Bezirk* Karl-Marx-Stadt, for instance, and following the directives of the *Ministerrat* of the 30 March 1976 on measures for the influence on youth dance events, the regional council issued its own directive on 12 December of that year, determining that a 'basic education' course be made available to band leaders and members of bands in general. The course, lasting a maximum of 10 months, would familiarise the course participants in 'theories of music, basic cultural political and aesthetic knowledge', equipping them with the necessary training to present 'expert interpretations full of ideas' and thus to 'exert an influence on raising the level of dance events.'[14]

Even disc jockeys were not exempt from attempts to create a more uniform, thoroughly vetted system of entertainment. Largely as a result of the increasing costs and practical requirements of setting up equipment for concert performances, youth club houses and 'culture houses' began to stage dance events without bands with increasing regularity in the 1970s. Rather than paying bands, it proved much more cost-effective and indeed popular amongst young people to employ a single *Schallplattenunterhalter* or *Disco-Sprecher* to play records for the entire evening.[15] The recognition that these disc jockeys could possibly exert an influence on the behaviour of the youngsters both through their choice of music and their own appearance and attitude, meant that it was deemed necessary to establish a means of vetting those wanting to undertake such a role. In order to practise as a disc jockey, it was, as in the case of bands wishing to perform in public, necessary to acquire a permit. The official requirement of gaining a permit evidently did not deter large numbers from wanting to practise as disc jockeys—people were evidently quite prepared to count themselves amongst the many honorary state functionaries. As one report from the district of Zwickau put it:

> *Disco Sprecher*, or those who want to become one, are shooting up everywhere like mushrooms. After word had got around that one has to first register with the district council for cultural work in order to acquire the desired permit, there have been new applications coming in everyday. The number of those showing an interest has already exceeded three hundred. [16]

14. SStAC, RdB, Abt. Kultur, 117278, 'Auswertung des 1. Grundlehrganges für Kollektivleiter und Mitglieder von Amateurtanzorchestern vom September 1976 bis Juni 1977'. (In detail, the course constituted ten hours of instruction on socialist cultural policy, eleven hours of Marxist-Leninist aesthetics, seven hours of 'leadership lessons', five hours of music history and eighty hours of practical music lessons (including harmonisation, melodics, improvisation and dynamics)).

15. See the reports on the development of discos in SStAC, RdB, Abt. Kultur, 117274, 117292.

16. SStAC, RdB, Abt. Kultur, 117302, Report of 7.2.73 ('Neues von den Diskotheken'). I should point out here that the apparent interest in those voluntarily showing up for registration would seem

Common Programmes and Coordination in Sport

In recognition of difficulties in encouraging increased participation in sports pursuits at the grassroots level—difficulties often occasioned by conflicting priorities of functionaries responsible for different spheres of policy—the 'Common Sport Programme' of the DTSB and the Free German League of Trade Unions (FDGB) was introduced. Initially launched in 1970 and then expanded to include the FDJ in 1974, the purpose of the programme was to ensure that sport was not seen in any way as incompatible with economic success or improved working practices of the employees. On the contrary, the official programme determined that the committee members and leading representatives of the FDGB and DTSB included sporting activity in the companies' plans, through, for example, the preparation and staging of company and district sports festivals. Through launching a programme common to both the sports mass organisation and the Trade Union organisation, the aim was clearly to remove or at least alleviate any in-fighting between functionaries and to try and unite efforts in promoting voluntary and non-competitive sports.

> In order to achieve greater progress (*in encouraging FES*[17]), . . . it is a matter for the committees and leaderships of the DTSB to achieve well coordinated and comradely cooperation of the (*sports*) commissions (*in the factories*), and of the functionaries responsible for leisure and recreational sport in the specialist committees, sports communities and sections with the union leaderships, the leaders of the FDJ and the state authorities.[18]

There was, too, an acknowledgement that coaches and referees—particularly those working in a voluntary capacity—required more effective training and education. The DTSB organisation was allotted the task of providing this for all of those who were involved in some capacity in the sphere of sport, regardless of which organisation they were affiliated to.[19]

While there were teething problems in establishing the programmes and some of the problems that had afflicted the promotion of sport in the

---

to speak against the tendency to 'shrink away' from the state and pursue private activities.

17. FES was the acronym in official GDR parlance for 'Freizeit- und Erholungssport'—in other words, sport practised by the broader mass of the population at grassroots level.

18. SAPMO-BArch, DY12/574; report of 6 Apr. 1972, folia 426–427. See also, SAPMO-BArch, DY12/798, 'Vorlage für das Präsidium des DTSB. . .', 31 Oct. 1972, fo. 53.

19. Ibid., fo. s 426, 429; see also SAPMO-BArch, DY34/12111, Report of FDGB Kreisvorstand Borna, 23 Oct. 1972, in which it states that 'a good means of support for the improvement and further development of leisure and recreational sport in our district were and are the regular qualification courses for sports organisers and members of the sports commissions (arranged) through the regional executive of the FDGB' (of Bezirk Leipzig).

1960s continued into the 1970s, it does appear that by the mid to late 1970s, the common programme was beginning to bear fruit. Again, not forgetting the possible tendencies of report writers to skim over problems, there were indications of increased commitment on the part of the functionaries and the efficiency of their work.[20] The most positive developments had been attained where there was effective cooperation between the company union leadership (the BGL), the sports club of the company (the BSG), the FDJ organisation and the state leadership of the company.[21] By the mid 1970s, in spite of the occasional infringement and continuing difficulties in some aspects, reports from all regions attest to predominantly positive developments and to an increased commitment and cooperation on the part of the functionaries.[22] In *Bezirk* Suhl, for example, it was noted that the situation regarding the commitment of the functionaries had improved considerably, particularly in relation to the promotion of leisure and recreational sports:

> Through concrete leadership activities we have made good progress amongst our functionaries and members [which] expresses itself in an open attitude and growing preparedness to cooperate in the realisation of 'higher' tasks.[23]

The relative degree of success of the programme and the improved efficiency and cooperation between the functionaries of the two mass organisations were reflected in the growing number of participants in the district and company sports festivals. In the region of Cottbus, for example, there was a significant increase in the number of company sports festivals in 1975, totalling 599 (up from 475 in 1974), in which 166,428 workers participated (in contrast to the 153,311 of the previous year).[24] The results achieved by the regional organisation of the DTSB in Suhl apparently showed clearly that 'in the breadth, diversity and quality of leisure and recreational sport

---

20. SAPMO-BArch, DY34/12111 contains a whole series of reports from the district executive committees of the FDGB referring to the results of the 'Gemeinsames Sportprogramm', many of which attest to positive improvements.

21. Ibid., Informationsbericht, ('Wie hat das gemeinsame Sportprogramm vom FDGB und DTSB beigetragen, die regelmäßige sportliche Beteiligung der Gewerkschaftsmitglieder zu fördern? 23.10.72. It was noted that large companies in particular were succeeding in organising high-quality and well-attended sports events for their workers. For example, the company sports festival (*Betriebssportfest*) BKK Epsenhain attracted participation from eleven football teams, thirty-nine teams playing in a bowling contest, six handball teams and nine volleyball teams.

22. Cf. for example, SAPMO-Barch, DY34/12081 (Einschätzung der Ergebnisse und Erfahrungen bei der Verwirklichung des Gemeinsamen Sportprogrammes, Cottbus, 16 Feb. 1976).

23. ThStAMgn., IV/D/2/16/603, Bericht zur Arbeit mit dem Beschluss, 'Die Aufgaben des DTSB der DDR zur weiteren Entwicklungen des Freizeit- und Erholungssport', Anlage 1 (no date, ca. 1977).

24. SAPMO-BArch, DY34/12081 (Einschätzung. . .16 Feb. 1976).

visible progress has been made and an increasing number of citizens have been won over to practising regular sport.' The number of sections within the DTSB also increased, with a greater tendency to create 'general sports groups' (*Allgemeine Sportgruppen*) to cater for those sports (such as aerobics) which, as non-Olympic sports, had previously been regarded as a lesser priority.[25]

'Opening up': Popular Music, Sports Policies, and the 'Mach mit' Programmes in the 1970s

Although, at first, one might tend towards the view that the creation of new committees, along with the introduction of workshops and combined programmes, testifies to the desire of the SED to exercise excessive control and impose its will, it should be pointed out here that this 'expansion of the state' at the same time entailed the incorporation of further members of 'society' into the administrative structures. The state was, in other words, becoming increasingly 'societalised' or '*vergesellschaftet*'. This process had important implications for the actual content and formulation of policies, as well as for the way in which such policies were interpreted and then implemented. How did this process more specifically affect the areas of popular music and sport?

Where music was concerned, the incorporation of new and 'expert' voices into committees such as the Committee for Entertainment Arts allowed for a departure from some of the more prohibitive and restrictive measures that had characterised the policies of the 1960s. Then, many complaints of the more hard-line functionaries (as well as members of the public) had been based on their objections to what they perceived as shabby clothing and 'decadent', unkempt appearance, long hair or 'hectic' dancing rather than on the music itself. By the early 1970s, however, once rock/popular music had come to be accepted as an official form of entertainment culture, the revised wisdom was that such objections were only a hindrance to the effective coordination of policy. This shift was reflected in a report of the State Committee for Radio, which stated:

> Clarification of ideological and aesthetic questions should be at the forefront of the discussions (on popular music), not debates about clothing, hairstyles and beards, which still make up a large part of the conflicts.[26]

---

25. ThStAMgn., IV/D/2/16/603, (Bericht zur Arbeit. . ., Anlage 1).

26. SAPMO-BArch, DY30/vorl. SED/11542, 'Konzeption für die Weiterführung der Arbeit auf dem Gebiete der Tanzmusik.'

This was not to say that free licence would be given to musicians to appear in whatever shape and form they desired. Particularly on occasions when they were performing on television programmes or in large-scale official events, they were required to maintain some sense of decorum. But this was to be achieved less by punitive and prohibitive measures than it was through a more measured and apparently conciliatory approach, which was reflected in the language of the apparatchiks themselves.[27]

Such work was to include the introduction of so-called *Förderverträge* according to which promising young musicians were allotted supervisors within the Committee for Entertainment Arts. This practice would not only allow them access to more advanced facilities and equipment (insofar as they were available in the GDR[28]), but also ensure greater publicity in terms of guaranteed media appearances as well as further 'expert' training in a more diverse range of musical styles, including Beat and 'Beat-influenced' pop music.[29]

Perhaps more noticeable–and marking an even more noticeable shift away from any notion of a distinct socialist popular culture–was the sanctioning of rock music. Official encouragement of GDR rock bands brought with it an increase in material ambitions among some of the more high-profile artists, which were evidently tolerated within the administrative apparatus. By the 1970s, many of the artists began to accrue considerable wealth, with monthly 'salaries' of 10,000 Marks and more, and western cars, elaborately decorated flats, and even 'dream villas' being reported.[30] In spite of the fact that the accrual of material possessions evidently undermined the principles of the supposedly 'classless society' to which the GDR elites staked claim, it appears that a blind eye was turned to infringements regarding possession of western currency or importation of western goods, particularly where those who were deemed to be valuable in boosting the profile of GDR popular music were concerned.[31] There were further indications that a less prohibitive line was to be taken in the suggestions of a greater (albeit tentative) embracement or adaptation of those elements of western

27. See for example SAPMO-BArch, DY30/vorl. SED/12944, report from Heldt to Hager (24 Sept. 1973) on the activities and tasks of the Committee for Entertainment Arts.

28. For problems on provision of equipment such as amplifiers and musical instruments, see e.g. SAPMO-BArch, DY30/IVB2/9.06/85, 'Information. . .', 3 Mar. 1973; ibid., 'Information. . .', 28 Feb. 1974.

29. SAPMO-BArch, DY30/vorl. SED/12944, report of 24 Sept. 1973; SAPMO-BArch, DY30/IVB2/9.06/85, 'Information über die bisherige Verwirklichung des Beschlusses vom 30.1.1973. . .'.

30. See SAPMO-BArch, DY30/IVB2/9.06/18, 'Zur materiellen Lage bzw. zu Einkünften von Schriftstellern und Künstlern. . .' and 'Anlage'.

31. See, e.g., the comments about those bands who were to perform at the *Weltfestspiele* in Berlin, in SAPMO-BArch, DY30/IVB2/9.06/85, 'Abschrift. . .', 22 Feb. 1973.

entertainment culture, which could be seen as 'progressive' and even in proposals that mutual 'commercial exchange' between the GDR and western European agents should be encouraged so as to further the international profile of GDR artists.[32]

In short, that which, by and large, had been regarded as a threatening area of foreign hostility in the 1960s had, by the 1970s, been incorporated into the socialist system and a much greater focus placed on more positive, constructive action.

While some of the changes in popular music policy appeared fairly striking, it is perhaps more difficult to pin down such fundamental changes in mass sports policies. With its longer-standing tradition in working class culture, the promotion and embracement of sporting practice had, in contrast to popular music, never been a contentious issue in the GDR. Nevertheless, in line with the attempts to improve the participation of the people through such initiatives as the common sports programme, there were some indications of a shift from the emphasis on the functional advantages of undertaking sports pursuits—the idea that it was fundamental for the 'creation of the all-round development of the socialist personality', and crucial for the improvement of working productivity—to a greater focus on the benefits of sport in terms of relaxation and enjoyment.

Although this shift was perhaps more noticeable in the 1980s, when more commercialised, western-type *Modesports* became increasingly popular and were incorporated into the official sports structures (discussed further below), the basis for the incorporation of such sports was already being laid down in the 1970s. In recognition of the considerable changes that had come to pass in the everyday lives of GDR citizens since the earlier years under the Ulbricht administration, including the increased amount of leisure time, higher living standards, and a more advanced level of education, the DTSB undertook to capture the interests of those who had hitherto declined or been unable to engage in sporting activities. In addition to the pledge to broaden the range of sports on offer within the DTSB organisation,[33] there was a more pronounced emphasis on the health and recuperative benefits of pursuing regular exercise. Perhaps most importantly though, and in acknowledgement of the more diverse requirements of citizens in relation to their family, personal, and work circumstances, the department for leisure sports in the DTSB determined that greater possibilities had to be opened to families in common sports ac-

---

32. SAPMO-BArch, DY30/vorl. SED/12944, 'Analyse..' 16 Jan. 1973.

33. The number of sports groups in disciplines such as gymnastics and fitness, bowling, and table tennis increased considerably in this period. See SAPMO-BArch, DY12/800, 'Bericht an das Präsidium des DTSB Bundesvorstandes. . .', 17 Oct. 1973, folia 203–204.

tivities as well as in more 'fun-oriented' community and local events. Efforts were made to realise these improvements through the introduction of events such as '*Eile mit Meile*', the '*Tischtennisturnier der Tausende*, the family sports programme '*Für Dich*',[34] as well as the development of 'public practice evenings', and events such as '*Turnier für Jedermann*' and '*Tennis im Urlaub*'.[35]

If, in contrast to the rather more inconsistent and unpredictable 1960s, the early to mid 1970s can, broadly speaking, be described as a period of relatively effective coordination and efficiency in terms of the implementation of popular music and sports policies, the notion of coordination–and hence of 'success'–would bear some qualification. Reference to improved coordination might generally convey the sense that the administrative structures were tightened and more stringently regimented and organised. Yet, in the GDR, the means by which coordination was apparently improved were a little more ambivalent. Rather than merely tightening the reins on those active within the state and party apparatus, the introduction of common programmes, the proliferation of workshops and educational programmes, and even the creation of new committees signified a strategy of 'branching out', so as to capture a more diverse palette of interest and incorporate them into the official state structures. Of course, this improved cooperation through means of greater inclusion did, to an extent, result in a more effective transmission of centrally formulated policy to the grassroots, as was reflected on occasions such as the aftermath of the concerts staged at the millennial celebrations of the town of Altenburg.[36]

At the same time, the incorporation of functionaries into positions within the state apparatus who, in many cases, were more eager to fulfil practical tasks in relation to their own specific area of responsibility and contribute to the functioning of day-to-day life in the GDR (and hence who were perhaps more in tune with the people in their respective localities), also created conditions for more effective coordination between 'people' and 'regime'. This was perhaps most noticeable in the large number of citizens' initiatives–which came under the umbrella of the 'Mach Mit' programmes–within the localities. Such initiatives involved the committed contributions of local citizens in

34. See for these and other examples, SAPMO-BArch, DY12/626, 'Vorlage. . .', 23 Nov. 1977, folia 135–136.

35. SAPMO-BArch, DY12/629, 'Vorlage. . .', 29 Mar. 1978, folia 47–48.

36. The incidents involving a large number of Tramper youths following a series of rock concerts at the 1000 year celebrations of the town of Altenburg did occasion a fevered rush of central and local directives relating to youth music concerts and events, which, in stark contrast to the decrees following incidents such as the Leipzig Beat riots in 1965, were by and large implemented with a great degree of success. See in particular the series of reports in file BLHA, Rep. 930 (SED Bezirksleitung Cottbus), 2670.

building sports facilities, youth clubs, and other amenities, sometimes over a period of several years.[37] It is important to emphasise that those initiatives and projects that met with the greatest success were undertaken both with the blessing (and, of course, financial support) of the local authorities, and with the cooperation of local companies and LPGs. The projects, then, were not *just* dependent on a willingness to contribute on the part of the citizens, or even on a resigned attitude of simply 'getting on with things' and making the best out of a 'bad situation'. Nor were the projects' successful realisation reliant solely on the smooth functioning and efficiency of the local state and party authorities and on their ability to gently coerce or persuade the local residents into sacrificing their valuable free time. It was rather a combination or interdependence of both of these factors that made such projects realisable. The local inhabitants' knowledge that there was the possibility of improving their own day-to-day lives with the backing of the local authorities and companies meant that such a sacrifice of time and energy would be worth the effort. And likewise, if the authorities knew that there was the voluntary man- (and woman-) power available to bring such schemes to fruition, then the necessary administrative and organisational tasks could be carried out in good faith. Rather than there being a division between the regime (in this case those at the lower-levels of the apparatus) and the people, there was, it seems, a *common belief* that conditions on the ground could be improved with the required effort on the part of *both* the authorities and the 'people'.

This period of relative success did not come without a considerable price. The greater commitment–if not to any abstract principles of socialism, then at least to improving the situation on the ground–of a more diverse base of functionaries within the state and party apparatus brought with it an increased expectation of recognition on the part of such active contributors. Any signs of fading recognition, or any sense that their efforts were not being reciprocated by those in the higher echelons of power, could soon loosen the precarious bonds that had been formed during the earlier period of the Honecker era.

Disillusionment, Diversification and the Disintegration of Authority

The improved efficiency and coordination of policy in the spheres of popular music and sport was, then, relatively short-lived. Certainly by the latter

37. For some examples of local initiatives, see for example the reports on the programmes in Bezirk Karl-Marx-Stadt in SStAC, RdB, Abt Jugendfragen, Körperkultur und Sport, 5930–5931; 95113.

years of the 1970s and, increasingly, throughout the 1980s, problems with functionaries at the lower-levels of the state and party apparatus were again proving to be a major headache for the central authorities. Through their own contributions to the functioning, and indeed to the successes of the GDR, many functionaries saw themselves as stakeholders in the system, in which they had invested much time and effort. Their expectations that they should receive some recognition for their commitment and contributions were rarely fulfilled, leading to considerable disgruntlement. In the spheres of sport and popular music, the signs of disgruntlement and the growing problems with authority were particularly pronounced. The following section will examine more closely this growing despondency on the part of functionaries. In addition, I will briefly look at the ways in which many functionaries came to deal with such frustrations at the higher-level authorities. Disillusionment amongst functionaries did not, in short, necessarily result in immediate meltdown of the system as a whole: there were instances in which local level functionaries continued to commit themselves, if not to the higher cause of socialism, then at least to the needs and desires of their local communities.

State Musicians and their Misgivings

There were particularly revealing instances of growing frustration at the central administrative authorities on the part of state-sponsored popular musicians—*Staatskünstler*, who were also 'regime carriers' of a sort. These *Staatskünstler*, involved as they were in bodies such as the Committee for Entertainment Arts, and as regular contributors to official festivals and concerts, held the firm belief they had played a positive and crucial role in the development of the GDR as a whole, and more specifically in the relative success of the 1970s GDR music scene. As such important contributors, they, like the functionaries in the sports organisations, also expected some recognition and reciprocal cooperation on the part of the administrative authorities. Certainly from the late 1970s onwards, there were growing indications that such reciprocity on the part of the authorities was not forthcoming and that the lines of communication necessary for the efficient functioning of the state apparatus (and thus for the exercise of authority) began to crumble, setting into motion an accelerating process of disintegration. A series of detailed correspondence from a variety of popular musicians collected in the files of Kurt Hager and the cultural department of the ZK reveals the obvious sense of indignation of many artists regarding the lack of trust and necessary recognition afforded to them by those in the higher administrative bodies.

The tone of the correspondence of course varied from case to case, ranging from clear outrage and disbelief to more measured and sometimes veiled threats and criticisms. For those bold enough, or for those whose exasperation at the lack of support and cooperation on the part of the administrative authorities was beyond redemption, the most extreme tactic was to request a permanent exit visa and expatriation to the West.[38] This was the case with the group *Magdeburg*. Although not averse to light controversy, the group could claim to have become one of the most popular live bands in the GDR. Having performed at a number of official music festivals, including the 1973 *Weltfestspiele* in Berlin and the National Youth Festival of 1977, they asserted that their participation in such high-profile events was testament to their 'very positive attitude'. Yet despite their evident popularity as a live band and their own readiness to make certain compromises—they had toned down their slightly more unconventional performances and changed the name of their band from the *Klosterbrüder* to the rather less controversial name of their hometown—any notable support on the part of the cultural authorities in developing their profile was not forthcoming:

> The support that had been promised by the Committee for Entertainment Arts did not materialise. Only through persistent commitment on our part were we able to maintain our popularity... With such songs as 'Lied einer alten Stadt' and 'In meinem Land' we had proven that our attitude was really positive, yet that didn't seem to interest anybody... Other bands received prizes and were clearly encouraged [but] official recognition of our band was never forthcoming.... GDR television also treated us with condescension. On the very few occasions when we performed on television, there were always discussions about the hair length of our singer... Is this the sort of attitude to expect towards a band which has, for years, shown commitment and has contributed to the development of GDR rock music?[39]

It was on the grounds of this deficiency in state support, and the group's resulting conviction that they requested a visa to settle in the West.[40] Similar sentiments were expressed by Barbara Thalheim, a popular GDR singer-

---

38. Of course, this was also a tactic which, in some respects, helped to stabilise the system as a whole, since it rid the GDR of its most outspoken critics. It was a tactic employed by the cultural authorities with increasing frequency in the late 1970s and early 1980s, after the Biermann affair.

39. SAPMO-BArch, DY 30/vorl. SED, 32816. Correspondence from Magdeburg to the *Konzert und Gastspieldirektion* Magdeburg, 21 Sept. 1981.

40. Ibid. The visa was ultimately granted to the singer of the group on the grounds that if he were not given permission to leave, he would stoke up trouble amongst the ranks of his musician colleagues. (See ibid., 'Hausmitteilung' ZK SED Abt. Kultur to Kurt Hager, 26 Nov. 1981).

songwriter in the 1970s, who renounced her party membership at the beginning of the 1980s:

> When I joined the Party of the Working Class, I had different ideas as to how I could be effective in the party and I think, to the best of my knowledge, that through my artistic work both at home and abroad, I represented the ideology of my party well. Now the Party is taking away from me this opportunity to be artistically and ideologically effective, and with it my faith in the Party. . .[41]

Although much of the current literature on cultural developments in the GDR has tended to focus on the (often retrospective) accounts of 'regime opposition' on the part of the more unconventional and apparently 'non-conformist' bands, such as the Punks, it is the reactions of those such as Thalheim, Magdeburg, and other artists including City, Karat, and Electra, so frequently dismissed as complicit *Staatskünstler*, that provide a more convincing indication of the gradual disintegration of authority in the GDR of the 1980s.

Failing Facilities and Problems of Provision–the Complaints of the Sports Functionaries

There were comparable expressions of growing frustration amongst those involved in the sports organisations (and the various branches of the DTSB). Such complaints largely related to the lack of provision and facilities that would allow for increased participation in popular sports. During the 1970s, as noted above, there had been concerted common efforts between local populations and the authorities and local 'People's Own Factories' (*Volkseigene Betriebe*, VEBs) in improving facilities–particularly sporting facilities–throughout the GDR. These common efforts were based on a mutual interest in improving the situation in the localities, and the relative success of the programmes was dependent on the citizens' and local functionaries' hope and belief that the central authorities would reciprocate their commitments. As it became more evident that the higher-level authorities were unwilling, or unable, to provide the necessary finances and facilities for the implementation of the policies they propagated, despair and weariness amongst their representatives in the localities increased.

That which particularly aggrieved those involved in promoting popular sport at the grassroots was that, while the SED energetically continued to

---

41. SAPMO-BArch, DY 30/vorl.SED 32815 (Declaration printed in document of the *Komitee für Unterhaltungskunst*, Parteileitung), Berlin, 8 Nov. 1980.

promote the practice of popular sport through press campaigns, for example, they showed no signs of being able to provide the practical and financial backing for transforming their propaganda into reality. The leader of a running group of a BSG rather neatly summed up this discrepancy between the ideal of an East German sporting nation and the reality on the ground. Pointing out the willingness on the part of the members of the club to participate actively, but then remarking on the obstacles that prevented them from undertaking their desired pursuits, he noted in a petition:

> It's all very nice in theory, but in practice it seems that we long distance runners don't have the opportunity to purchase suitable running shoes either in sports shops or through our company sports club. . .[42]

Stressing that the matter was an altogether broader problem, not only with implications for his own immediate area of interest of long-distance running, he continued:

> The discrepancy between the extensive propaganda used for encouraging mass sport on the one hand, and the absolute lack of provision in some areas, affecting for example hiking shoes and rucksacks on the other, is incomprehensible to me.[43]

Another sport seriously affected by the problems of facilities was swimming. In spite of the optimistic claims on the part of the central authorities about the creation of new facilities for swimming, there were severe difficulties in transforming the policy of encouraging greater activity amongst the populace into practice.[44] While it appears that the capital, East Berlin, benefited from some investment in new buildings, in other areas, swimming facilities were being closed down, deemed unsafe for public use or had fallen into disrepair.[45] Echoing the sentiments of the functionary of the BSG cited

---

42. SAPMO-BArch, DY30/4987, *Eingabe* of 2 Sep. 1982, p. 30.

43. Ibid. The matter of the lack of running shoes was an extremely widespread problem, demonstrated by the multiplicity of complaints regarding the matter sent to different committees and departments of the administration. For further examples see e.g., BArch, DR5/2025; BArch/2026. Both of these files contain a broad collection of letters of complaint concerning sporting equipment in general.

44. See SAPMO-BArch, DY30/4963, report 'Übersicht der Zu- und Abgänge von Sportplatzanlagen, Sporthellen, Schwimmhallen und sonstigen Sporteinrichtungen in der DDR 1984', 2 May 1985, pp. 126–27.

45. See SAPMO-BArch, DY 12/661, report 'Einschätzung der Arbeit auf dem Gebiet von Körperkultur und Sport im Neubaugebiet Marzahn', 31 Mar. 1983, folia 140–151; see also, e.g. SAPMO-BArch, DY 30/4983, p. 166, letter of 1 Feb. 1986, which refers to the considerable number of new swimming facilities in Berlin in contrast to the poor provisions in the provinces.

above, the leader of the swimming section of BSG Empor in the Dresden community of Löbtau again pointed out the incongruity of the popular propaganda and the real possibilities of pursuing sports activities:

> [I]n books and magazines we are told again and again that swimming benefits peoples' health, enjoyment of life, well-being and capacity to achieve in a diversity of ways. . . The possibilities of practising swimming in pools as a hobby or as a competitive and training pursuit are however completely unsatisfactory in our regional capital.[46]

A colleague of a different BSG in the same region underlined the problem in another letter of complaint to the regional party leadership. In this letter, he drew attention to the dedication of the functionaries in the group. Though eager to improve the situation, it was made clear by the complainant that meetings and good will on the part of the functionaries could only achieve so much:

> Unfortunately, in the last few years we have been unable to fulfil the wishes of the DTSB. . . and of the population for a constant improvement in training possibilities for an ever increasing number of interested children, youths and adults. The problem does not lie in the unwillingness of our trainers, but in the precarious situation of Dresden's swimming facilities. . . . The situation, which, particularly when one considers the growth of Dresden as *Bezirksstadt*, with its extensive new residential estates, is not exactly conducive to the development of mass sport at the BSG level, and has been regularly discussed in the town committee [of the DSSV*] and amongst our section leadership.[47]

Such was the frustration amongst the lower-level mass organisation functionaries at the lack of cooperation from the higher authorities and, consequently, at being faced with public complaints, it is hardly surprising that temptation crept in to throw in the towel, to draw the conclusion that their commitment was no longer worth the effort. As a leader of the rowing section of BSG Einheit in Neuruppin, put it on behalf of his colleagues:

> We have to confirm that in our sport-political activity, we are unfortunately faced with a lack of understanding on the part of the state organs and have [thus] had to abandon previously successful activities. The efforts of our BSG leadership,

---

46. SAPMO-BArch, DY 30/4979; Letter of 13 May 1985 from *Sektionsleiter Schwimmen*, BSG Empor, Dresden Loebtau, pp. 58–59.

47. SAPMO-BArch, DY 30/4983, (*Eingabe*sent to SED Bezirksleitung Dresden and Staatssekretariat für Körperkultur und Sport, 4 Jan. 1985), pp. 168–69. *DSSV was the *Deutscher Schwimmsportverband.*

> both written and oral, have met without response. The sports functionaries have let it be known to me, as chairman, that they will give up their responsibilities if their work continues to be hindered through the heartlessness, bureaucratic talking and lack of understanding of the [administrative] organs.[48]

Carrying on Regardless: Functionaries' Initiatives and the Diversification of Sport and Popular Musical Culture

While this growing despair may then have resulted for some in the decision to give up their positions, this was not the sole response. Indeed, faced with lack of cooperation from above, many functionaries appeared simply to get on with the job regardless, insofar as this was possible. In other words, in spite of the growing problems concerning facilities and the evident inability of the central administration to resolve them, there was not a complete and universal collapse throughout the mass organisations and the local state and party administrations in the GDR. In some cases, the incompetence of the higher authorities merely made the local level functionaries more determined to commit themselves to the task in hand. Life did not come to a stop at any time in the GDR, and in order for everyday (leisure) practices to continue, some semblance of functioning administrative mechanisms had to remain in place. In spite of their increasing doubt about the competence of the higher elites, then, and thus in spite of evidently dwindling loyalty to the political creed of the GDR's ruling power, there were still functionaries at the lower levels who continued to do their job and to take the initiative, seeing it more as their task to satisfy the needs of the citizens in their localities than to simply relay or transfer orders from 'above' to the populace. This continuing commitment, which also appeared to testify to a certain confidence, or at least a more pronounced sense of independence, was evident in cases of both grassroots sports functionaries and those involved with music and youth cultural issues. Rather than there being a wholesale collapse into chaos in leisure and popular culture—which would have more likely come about had functionaries simply 'given up' en masse—the functionaries' continuing commitment, coloured by a greater degree of confidence and independence (at least in their own restricted spheres), instead seemed to lead to a diversification, a kind of 'splintering' of the policies (at the local, micro-level) and practices of popular sport and music.

The tendency on the part of functionaries to continue in their roles and do their utmost to promote their own particular area of responsibility is

48. BArch, DR 5/2180, letter of 10 Jul. 1978 (no pagination).

perhaps best reflected in the growth of what one might term as less strenuous 'leisure' sports: those sports which, by virtue of their non-Olympic status, were categorised as *Sportarten II* in official GDR parlance. Such sports included karate, tennis, aerobics (or *Popgymnastik,* as it became known in the GDR), hiking, and jogging. One could add to the list further leisure pursuits such as fishing, more 'therapeutic' exercise activities such as Yoga, and even fashion sports like skateboarding or break-dancing. These various sporting disciplines had grown in popularity in western capitalist countries and hence, because of their supposed links to commercial interests or the 'reactionary' middle classes, were initially frowned upon within the higher ranks of the DTSB and the sports department of the Central Committee. Insofar as they have at all been considered in existing literature, the growth in the practice of these sports has been thus portrayed as a 'subversive' act of (mild) resistance. It is suggested that such pursuits were undertaken within the context of a 'private sphere' that the 'people' were able to carve out for themselves, where they would be unencumbered by the interventionist auspices of the 'state'. In other words, the fact that such activities grew in popularity is seen as testimony to the existence of the supposed 'niche society'—a politics-free area of society—and to the fact that, for all its attempts, the 'regime' was ultimately unable to control all aspects of leisure.[49] A closer examination of the DTSB documents referring to the development of these 'new' (or bourgeois) branches of sporting pursuits suggest, however, that the categorisation of these disciplines as 'niche' society sports, practised outside of the sphere of the 'state', is misleading. It seems more the case that participants, trainers, and those generally involved in organising events relating to these modern strands of leisure attempted to 'officialise' these activities—that is to say, to incorporate them into, or boost their profile within, the DTSB. As such, they would constitute part of a more diverse spectrum of activities *within*, rather than outside of, an expanded, but increasingly fragile state apparatus.

Some examples indicative of these efforts to incorporate such 'new' sports into the official organisation of the DTSB were karate and skateboarding. A ban had been imposed on karate following an initial flurry of interest at the end of the 1970s, but it had failed to halt the expanding popularity of the sport.[50] In spite of the stubborn intransigence on the part of the central executive of the DTSB, the practice of karate carried on within the framework of the judo sections, in the *Allgemeine Sportgruppen*

49. This is the view put forward by Theo Austermühle, 'Konflikte und Konfliktlösungen im Sport', in Hinsching ed., *Alltagssport in der DDR*, pp. 135–57.

50. SAPMO-BArch, DY12/640, 'Vorlage für das Sekretariat des DTSB, Bundesvorstand des DTSB der DDR, Abteilung Organisation', 15 Oct. 1979, fo. 610.

(the general, or miscellaneous sports associations) and within the BSGs and *Hochschulsportgemeinschaften* (HSSGs), with enthusiasts and trainers continuing to lead and establish new clubs. This persistent pressure from below eventually persuaded the central executive to retract its directive of 1979 and to finally create an official karate association—the *Deutsche Verband für Karate in der DDR*—in 1988.[51]

Viewed from one perspective, on the basis of this statement, it could be argued that this formal recognition of karate and the sport's incorporation into the DTSB merely underlined the ceaseless attempts of the 'state' to control. But at the same time, and from another perspective, one could emphasise the initiative and dogged determination of these lower-level functionaries to push forward the case for their sport, attempting to popularise it in spite of the refusal of the central executive to cede ground on the matter. In other words, this 'about-turn'—the resigned acceptance on the part of the central DTSB executive that a karate association had to be created after all—signified a distinct *lack of ability* to control trends. As such, the continuing commitment of lower-level functionaries contributed to a diversification of popular sports policies.

A further revealing instance in these later years of lower-level functionaries throwing down the gauntlet to the higher authorities involved the Roller-sport association (the *Deutsche Rollsportverein,* or DRV); more specifically, the skateboarding section within the association.[52] Again, instead of viewing this western-style pastime as an example of practices carried out in the 'niche' society, it appears that after its incorporation into the DRV (and hence into the DTSB), those practising and advocating the popularisation of skateboarding were just as eager to use the structures of the state to their advantage as those further up the state and party hierarchy were to control such maverick activities. The incorporation of a skateboarding section into the DRV, in other words, allowed lower-level functionaries some bargaining power, or at least endowed them with a sense of empowerment. Rather than 'giving up' and simply complaining, perhaps sensing that the leading party (at least its centre core) was fading, functionaries involved in this particular sphere were able to use their positions *within* the formal structures of the DTSB to pose challenges and

51. SAPMO-BArch, DY12/716, 'Protokoll der 211. Sitzung des Sekretariates des Bundesvorstandes des DTSB der DDR', 29 Nov. 1988 (Anlage), fo. 217.

52. A skateboarding section had been incorporated into the DRV in the winter of 1986–87 at the behest of the DTSB committee responsible for secondary sports (*Sportarten II*). This was as a result of apparent dissatisfaction on the part of skateboarding aficionados that they had no official 'political and organisational cradle' (*Heimstadt*) for their activity (SAPMO-BArch, DY12/1207, fo. 73).

make demands to improve the profile of the 'Modesport' for which they were responsible.[53]

It was not only the advancement of these so-called fashion sports that attested to the tendency of lower-level functionaries to challenge the authority of the higher authorities, or at least to demonstrate a greater degree of independence. Sports which, on account of their implicit connections with the 'bourgeois' classes, had not been officially encouraged in the GDR, also began to enjoy something of a boom in the 1980s, not only in terms of people's participation, but also regarding the number of officials who were eager to play some role in boosting the profile of the sports in question. This was particularly the case with tennis.[54] Between 1977 and 1984, membership in the *Deutscher Tennisverein* had risen from just under 35,000 to almost 44,000, while the number of qualified coaches grew almost four-fold in the same period, from 841 to 2,852.[55] By the end of 1988, the membership numbers had risen to 47,274, while the number of officially trained coaches increased to 3,185.[56] Such a significant increase, in particular in the number of those holding some position of responsibility, is again indicative of the fact that the disintegration of the GDR's internal structures was not tantamount to 'collapse' or 'breakdown' in any absolute sense.[57] Disintegration here was more a case of diversification, of a splintering in the direction of policy and practices—a disappearance of any semblance of cohesion and consistency that seemed to be evident, for however limited a time, during the 1970s. Willingness to undertake or continue in official roles within the formal structures of the state and party organisations did not entail being ardent political and ideological supporters of the socialist system. Functionaries in the tennis section of the DTSB organisation, for example, while certainly not openly criticising the party and state or calling into question the tenets

---

53. See the reports in SAPMO-BArch, DY12/1207, fo.s 73–78 for some striking examples of lower-level functionaries taking matters into their own hands and throwing down the gauntlet to the apparently flaccid central sports administration.

54. For official views on 'bourgeois' sports such as tennis, see SAPMO-BArch, DY34/14445, manuscript of radio interview of 4 Dec. 1983 (no pagination).

55. SAPMO-BArch, DY12/1202, 'Kurzeinschätzung der Abteilung Sport II, pp. 35–36.

56. Statisches Jahrbuch der DDR, 1989 (Berlin: Staatsverlag der DDR, 1989), p. 330. The growth in membership in this sport was paralleled by a growing popularity in other more modern, leisurely and/or 'bourgeois-tinged' sports in the 1980s.

57. Indeed, even in the last gasps of the SED dictatorship, some functionaries at the grassroots appeared determined to get on with their jobs as they had done before. Thus on 3–4 November 1989, the secretariat for the *DTV* continued their work, in spite of events going on around them, even discussing the broad outline of progress to be made in their branch of the DTSB over the following ten years. This perhaps reflected their belief that while situation was far from ordinary, life had to go on. Certainly, they did not envisage such a rapid process of absolute collapse and integration into the Federal Republic. (SAPMO-BArch, DY12/1196, 'Protokoll der Präsidiumstagung', 3. Nov. 1989; 'Gemeinsame Beratung . . .', 4 Nov. 1989).

of Marxist-Leninist ideology outright, preferred to advocate more neutral values as part of their work. This reduced emphasis on political and ideological concerns was reflected in the end of year report of the *DTV* of 1983, in which it was stated that characteristics such as 'a sense of responsibility, a spirit of community, a readiness to help, fairness, discipline, a readiness to run risks, moral strength, modesty and an openness to criticism' were to be encouraged.[58] Although qualities such as these were not entirely alien to the professed goals of socialism, the combative calls to use sport as a means to engage in class struggle, and to be 'Ready for Work and Defence of the Homeland', so prominent in earlier years, were nevertheless conspicuous by their absence. Indeed, appeals to such qualities were not so different from those that one might have expected to come across in advertisements for participation in sport in western, capitalist countries.[59]

Where music was concerned, there were also indications of functionaries attempting just to 'get on with the job' and accomplishing their tasks to the best of their ability. In many cases, this meant going along with that which was popular amongst youths. While it may be tempting to regard such insouciance as an open defiance of the leading party's dictates–after all, there were continued references to the dangers of western decadence in the official discourse–it appears to be more the case that the functionaries simply turned a blind eye to the rather more pedantic and unsustainable appeals for ideological purity and socialist morality. There was no real subversion intended: rather the actions that they sought to undertake seemed best suited to the circumstances in which they found themselves. Thus, youth club functionaries or even local town authorities made efforts to accommodate their local young populations, seeing this as preferable to letting the young people wander aimlessly around the villages and towns with nothing to do.

In the district of Reichenbach, for example, members of the local town council took it upon themselves to provide a group of young heavy metal fans with facilities where they could meet and pursue their interests.[60] In Annaberg-Buchholz, another FDJ functionary defended his decision to allow youngsters in his charge to found a Depeche Mode fan club under

---

58. SAPMO-BArch, DY12/1202, 'Entschließung des VII. Verbandstag des DTV der DDR', 7. Apr. 1984, p. 37.

59. Karate was another sport that, at least according to the official reasons for the creation of the *Karateverband*, should seek to promote these more 'neutral' qualities such as agility, speed, fairness, self-discipline, even courtesy. There was no mention of the need to use it as a means of increasing work productivity, for example. Cf. SAPMO-BArch, DY12/716, 'Protokoll der 211. Sitzung. . .', folia 216–217.

60. BstU, Ast Chemnitz, RB-178, 'Berichterstattung. . .', 5 Jan. 1989, pp. 10–11.

the umbrella of the local youth organisation. Claiming that the youngsters were all harmless, and had diligently participated in the 'scrap metal' action for the struggling 'young national states', he suggested that accommodating their wishes would prevent the youths from going 'underground' with their interests.[61] Similarly, in the same region of Karl-Marx-Stadt, following difficulties involving a young group of break-dancers who had been pursuing their interests in the vicinity of the gigantic bust of Karl Marx's head in the city centre of Chemnitz (at that time called Karl-Marx-Stadt), the headmaster of the youngsters' school, together with the local district administration, determined to provide more suitable facilities for these youths and their decidedly western interests.[62] There was also a forum set up for heavy metal musicians in Karl-Marx-Stadt by the local *Bezirkskabinett für Kulturarbeit*. Again, in the context of the heavy emphasis in existing literature on oppositional and sub-cultural groups of the 1980s, one might at first interpret such a step as clearly going against the grain of 'official policy'. But the point is that these initiatives and programmes on the ground were indicative of the very diversity of those involved in the state apparatus and that there was, particularly in these last years, no absolute blue-print for regime policy. By introducing such a workshop, the local cultural administration in Karl-Marx-Stadt was undertaking what it saw as a necessary step to try and pacify the situation.[63]

Even in the face of obvious incompetence on the part of higher-level authorities, as in the sphere of popular sport, functionaries involved in youth cultural and popular music events attempted to do their utmost to do their job and undertake what they thought to be the best course of action. Certainly, their enthusiasm and commitment was sometimes combined with criticism and expressions of discontent at the lack of support they received from their superiors, which hinted at the gradual grinding down of the administrative apparatus, or at least demonstrated the growing distance between lower-level functionaries and the apparatchiks at the top of the administrative tree. Such was the case involving an obviously highly committed functionary of the regional branch of the FDJ in Schwerin, who had spent many hours of his own time attempting to arrange a summer festival, which was to include rock music performances, for the young people of the area. While clearly exasperated at the conduct of his superiors, this particular functionary was clearly not willing simply to give up the ghost and energetically attempted to muster up the cooperation that he required from the responsible authorities in order to

61. BstU, Ast Chemnitz, An-126, 'Information..', 24 Aug. 1989, pp. 36–37.
62. BstU files, Ast Chemnitz, AKG 190, Bd. I, pp. 65–66.
63. SStAC, RdB, Abt. Kultur, 117290, 'Einschätzung. . .', 4 May 1988.

provide the youths with a memorable cultural spectacle.[64] His greater sense of responsibility, and impassioned appeals for something to be done, were indicative of an overall shift in the alliances, it would seem, within and between different groups in the state and the lay-population. In short, there was a shift from the role of the functionaries as 'representatives of the state', to a role that could perhaps be better described as 'representatives of the people.' It was this shift–the growing exasperation of committed functionaries towards the lack of cooperation and reciprocity on the part of their superiors and the concomitant increase in sympathy and common grievances with their fellow local residents–which seemed to be so crucial in undermining and weakening the regime.

Conclusion

While the process of *Vergesellschaftung* or 'societalisation' allowed, for a restricted period, for some stability and brought about a more cohesive, yet also more expansive network of allegiances between different elements within the state, it was also instrumental in the process of disintegration in the 1980s. The incorporation of new members into the state did not entail an unconditional act of loyalty being expressed on their part. The lines of allegiance were very much contingent on bargains being upheld on all sides: functionaries, who invested much of their time and energy in their endeavours to improving the situation in their particular areas of responsibility, were reliant on the higher-level authorities delivering on its promises to provide, and expected a degree of reciprocal cooperation for their efforts.

The crucial factor about those who had been incorporated into the state is that they did not see themselves merely as mouthpieces for the wishes and whims of their superiors. The so-called *Staatskünstler*, for example, who had been instrumental in the relative success of the GDR popular music scene of the 1970s, expected something in return for their evident contributions and commitments. Similarly, those who had taken it upon themselves to contribute to the development of sports, training, and acquiring extra qualifications, sacrificing their weekends and evenings to make their contribution to the local sports society, were resentful when their efforts were stymied by poor provisions and broken promises on the part of the higher

64. For details see SAPMO-BArch, DY30/vorl. SED 42272, Bd. II., correspondences of 21 Jul., 4 Aug., 31 Aug., and 3 Sep. 1989. For similar examples of local-level functionaries showing their sympathies with the youths and accompanying exasperation at the higher authorities' unwillingness or incapacity to deliver the goods, see e.g. SStAC, RdB, Abt. Kultur, 150605, letters of 28 Apr. 1986 and 18 Sep. 1986; 150606, letter of 4 Mar. 1987; 150607, letter of 28 Oct. 1988.

authorities. It was they, the functionaries, after all, who were faced with the more direct disgruntlement of the local populace. For some, such problems could only result in taking a step back, rescinding their posts. For others, while any sense of 'political' loyalty that had existed was severely weakened by the inability and prevarication of the higher-level authorities, a sense of commitment to their local 'constituents' and diverse interest groups within the towns and villages remained. In this sense, the system as a whole did continue to 'tick over'–music events continued to be organised, even new fan clubs were created within the official framework of the youth organisations, people still participated in their local sports communities. In some cases there were even increases in levels of participation, particularly in those sports which, as pursuits more distinctly related to commercialism, were deemed as more western 'bourgeois' sports.

Thus, if the more efficient coordination and streamlining of popular sport and music policies had served to alleviate the confusion regarding sports and music policies which had certainly been evident in the localities during the 1960s, this process of *Vergesellschaftung*, of incorporation into the state, did not remove the sense of self-interest of the functionaries. This continued to exist, with new or better trained and (hence more confident) functionaries, hoping to use the broader formal structures within which they now found themselves to their advantage. Hence the boundaries of both the state, and the fundaments of the policies that were devised and formulated, were pushed further out. In short, *Eigen-sinn* and authority, as defined by the localised negotiation and interaction between regime functionaries and the 'ordinary' lay populace, continued to exist within the broader framework of the 'societalised' state.

Chapter 6

Communication and Compromise: The Prerequisites for Cultural Participation

Esther von Richthofen

Throughout the forty-year history of the GDR, the SED aimed to fill people's free time with ideologically sound and intellectually stimulating cultural activities. First, in mass organisations such as the *Kulturbund* and in factories, GDR citizens were encouraged to apply themselves to the pursuit of a particular artistic or cultural endeavour by joining a cultural circle. The party leadership pledged to provide such circles for any officially sanctioned artistic activity or hobby, which meant that, theoretically, no individual had to pursue a cultural interest outside the state-organised cultural network. Secondly, state institutions, like cultural houses, and mass organisations, such as the FDGB, organised events and activities in order to capture those people in their free time who were not members of cultural circles. Through these two strategies, the SED leadership hoped to guide and control people's free time, and hoped to further the process of turning East Germans into 'socialist personalities', who were morally upright, intellectually stimulated, and, above all, instilled with socialist values. The SED leadership wanted to attract people away from the lures of Western 'lowbrow' mass entertainment by providing only 'decent' and 'qualitative' leisure time activities.[1]

The nature of state-organised cultural activity developed quite differently to how the party leadership had imagined it, however. People who became involved in cultural activity usually sought to satisfy personal interests, and they

1. Stiftung Parteien und Massenorganisationen, Bundesarchiv (SAPMO BArch) DY 30/IV 2/1.01/407, *Kulturkonferenz 23–24. Oktober 1957, Referat von Alexander Abusch*, pp. 73–75.

had their own ideas about what shape they wanted their cultural activity to take. Already in the early years of the dictatorship, an independent spirit manifested itself among culturally active people, which remained a prominent aspect of cultural life for the remainder of the GDR. Many cultural functionaries recognised this fact, and rather than stringently enforcing the party-political line, they adapted the organisation of cultural activities to suit the interests and needs of the participants. This state of affairs was not, however, a threat to the SED's claim to power. On the contrary, it served to stabilise the state-organised cultural structures, because it secured the participation of many interested individuals who felt that the organised cultural structures represented their interests, and who consequently identified with state-organised cultural life to a degree.

In analysing these developments in cultural life, the concept of 'normalisation' provides a highly useful tool, particularly for evaluating the GDR's middle period, namely the 1960s and 1970s. During these years, many areas of life and rule in the GDR experienced a high degree of stability, routinisation, and predictability. Moreover, during these years, the majority of the population showed that they had internalised the 'rules of the game': they had learned how to construct their lives according to their own liking without engaging in non-conformist behaviour. They were able to utilise limited forms of agency, for example, the interaction with state organs, in order to control and steer developments in a desired direction. This becomes particularly apparent in the analysis of cultural life. As the following analysis will show, people were not powerless subjects of the SED. Through a mixture of complex behaviour patterns, which included the targeted dialogue with local, intermediate, and central functionaries, they ensured that the state-organised cultural facilities represented their cultural interests and desires.

Straddling the Line between Ideology and Reality: Cultural Functionaries

In historical analyses, the GDR is often divided into 'state' and 'society'—two entities that are described as existing in separation of, or even in juxtaposition to, one another. This dichotomy is evident, for example, in totalitarian theory, which argues that all power emanated from the party-controlled state organs and that the populace could only accept or resist party control.[2]

2. For an overview of the totalitarian theory and its flaws, see Konrad Jarausch, 'Care and Coercion: the GDR as Welfare Dictatorship', in Konrad Jarausch, ed., *Dictatorship as Experience: Towards a Socio-Cultural History of the GDR* (New York, Oxford: Berghahn Books, 1999), pp. 52–54; see also Mary Fulbrook, *The Two Germanies 1945–1990: Problems of Interpretation* (Basingstoke: Macmillan, 1992), pp. 1–10.

This dichotomous characterisation of the GDR is not only apparent in the totalitarian model, however: it is also evident in certain social analyses of the GDR. It is, for example, reflected in the model of the 'durchherrschte Gesellschaft', and in some applications of the *Eigen-Sinn* concept. While both of these concepts are social analyses and argue that people had a degree of control over their own lives, they still describe social developments as being delimited from governing and administrative processes.[3] 'State' and 'society' are, to summarise, frequently described as static, well-defined entities, while intersection, interaction, and interdependence between 'rulers' and the 'ruled' are not sufficiently taken into account in current GDR historiography. The insufficiency of this approach becomes nowhere clearer than in the analysis of functionaries. Historians whose argument follows the totalitarian theory often characterise functionaries as being a part of the SED's power apparatus, and thus see them as part of the 'state' category.[4] But is that characterisation really legitimate? There were many different functionaries, fulfilling a variety of roles. These functionaries cannot merely be regarded as the long arm of the SED. In the cultural field, they interacted and communicated with each other, but they also communicated with those people who were culturally active. They were at the same time guarantors of a limited degree of autonomy of cultural life at the grassroots and of the interference of state organs in cultural life. As a result of their ambiguous role, functionaries need to be regarded as a group within their own right, which means that the 'state' versus 'society' dichotomy has to be abandoned.

The group that is here summarised under the heading of 'cultural functionaries' is a very large one. It comprises, for example, functionaries working in the upper echelons of the state and party organs in *Bezirk* Potsdam, who were in close communication with the central decision making bodies in Berlin. On the other end of the spectrum were those functionaries who led remote cultural circles, and exercised their functions as infrequently as once

---

3. The term 'durchherrschte Gesellschaft' was explored in different contributions to the edited volume Hartmut Kaelble, Jürgen Kocka, and Hartmut Zwahr, eds., *Sozialgeschichte der DDR* (Stuttgart: Klett Cotta, 1994). See Jürgen Kocka's summary of the debate: 'Eine durchherrschte Gesellschaft', pp. 547–54. The term means: a 'ruled' society, but the idea is that this is a society where rule cannot extend everywhere because there are certain boundaries. The term *Eigen-Sinn* was introduced by Alf Lüdtke in *Eigensinn: Fabrikalltag, Arbeitererfahrungen und Politik vom Kaiserreich bis in den Faschismus* (Hamburg: Ergebnisse, 1993). It was adapted to the GDR by historians like Thomas Lindenberger in 'Die Grenzen der Diktatur. Zur Einleitung', in Lindenberger, ed., *Herrschaft und Eigen-Sinn in der Diktatur. Studien zur Gesellschaftsgeschichte der DDR* (Köln: Böhlau Verlag, 1999), pp. 13–44, and it is here that the dichotomy becomes evident: Lindenberger argues that people could only exercise 'Eigen-Sinn' in their immediate surroundings, which had no impact above the administrative level of the *Kreis*. Cf. Corey Ross, *Constructing Socialism at the Grassroots: The Transformation of East Germany, 1945–65* (Basingstoke: Macmillan, 2000), pp. 64–65.

4. See, for example, Klaus Schröder, *Der SED Staat* (München, 1998), pp. 407–12.

a month. These functionaries could not have been much further removed from the SED's ruling elite. In between these two sorts of functionaries were a multitude of individuals who were in charge of running the GDR's cultural network: on a full-time and part-time basis; in administrative, consultative, and organisational roles; some were artistically gifted, some pursued a particular hobby, and others were looking for a way into a political career; some were utterly inept and others highly committed. While appreciating the differences between these various positions, this chapter focuses on the commonality of these functionaries: they all relied on communication with each other and on compromises with the participants in order to make the state-organised cultural system work.

It is best to divide cultural functionaries of *Bezirk* Potsdam into two factions: firstly, there were those functionaries in the administrative units, working in the *Bezirk*, *Kreis*, City, and Community Councils and in the trade union leadership of the factories. They were responsible for disseminating the party's political dictates to the localities, for ensuring that the cultural network was functioning, and for overseeing the bureaucratic demands that arose. These functionaries will be called the 'administrative functionaries'. Secondly, there were those cultural functionaries who were responsible for the actual running and organisation of the cultural facilities, in cultural houses and clubs, in mass organisations and in factories, or as the leaders of individual circles. Individuals in this group tended to take up their roles out of a strong interest in cultural life and artistic endeavours. They were rarely in pursuit of a political career.[5] These functionaries will be called 'executive functionaries'.

Most cultural functionaries tended to complain about their working conditions, as they believed themselves to be over-burdened and poorly paid.[6] Frequently, once an individual had been recruited into a position in the cultural field, he/she quickly became dissatisfied, and left the position after a short while. This was particularly the case with leaders of cultural houses, who had a great deal of responsibility, but who also had to contend with

5. These functionaries had often pursued a particular interest in cultural activity for a long time before taking up their positions: see, for example Brandenburgisches Landeshauptarchiv (BLHA) Rep. 538 Kulturbund (KB) 35, *Schreiben Philatelistenverband P. an das Kreissekretariat P. des Kulturbundes, 16.8.64*: the leader of this stamp collector's circle has been collecting stamps for 50 years. See also BLHA Rep. 426 BfK Nr. 249, *15 Jahre Zirkel Schreibender Arbeiter in W.*, p. 1: the person who founded this circle had engaged in literary activity for over 25 years. These functionaries got a sense of enjoyment out of the cultural element of their work, and resented outside interference if it interrupted their cultural work: Landkreis Oberhavel, Kreis- und Verwaltungsarchiv, Oranienburg LkO III 92 Gransee, *Protokoll der Kulturgruppen Vollversammlung am 13.4.62.*

6. See, for example: BLHA Rep. 538 KB Nr. 31, *Schreiben von der Kreiskommission Brandenburg an den Bezirksvorstand*, 25.9.66: this is an example of a functionary who complains about his workload.

immense material shortages.[7] As a result of the high functionary turnover, the levels of qualification among cultural functionaries could be quite low: in some cases, positions were vacant for so long that the criteria for hiring someone were substantially watered down and people were taken on board who were not fully trained for the position.[8] There were other problems that faced cultural functionaries. In face of the economic problems that dominated the GDR, cultural aspects ranked quite low on the general agenda.[9] As a result, the difficulties of cultural functionaries received little attention from the higher levels of authority, particularly in the factories. Consequently, many cultural functionaries felt they were fending for themselves, and that no one cared about their difficulties.[10]

In the late 1950s and early 1960s, these problems were recognised by the party leadership, and the state administration did try to address them. The SED leadership believed that functionaries could only tackle their growing workload if they underwent excessive qualification and training. Over the course of the 1960s and 1970s, the efforts to train cultural functionaries remained a prevalent factor in the administration of cultural life. This applied to functionaries across the board—the functionaries who were in charge of cultural activity in a single factory brigade, as well as the directors of the Cultural Department in the *Bezirk* Council were told to attend relevant training programmes.[11] These training programmes primarily focussed on giving functionaries a detailed understanding of the political and ideological goals of the party, which was followed up with cultural training,

---

7. BLHA Rep. 401 Rat des Bezirkes (RdB) Nr. 22562, *Information über Kaderprobleme auf dem Gebiet der Kultur*, 13.11.72. The problems with high turnover were also evident among other functionary groups: BLHA Rep. 401 RdB Nr. 22562, *Einschätzung der Arbeit zur weiteren Qualifizierung der Kaderentwicklung der Fachorgane der Kreise* 28.6.77, p. 3; BLHA Rep. 401 RdB Nr. 22561, *VE Lichtspielbetrieb Potsdam, Kaderanalyse der Belegschaft*, 30.9.71.

8. BLHA Rep. 547 FDGB Nr. 1758, *Vorlage des Sekretariats, Bericht über die Verwirklichung des Aufrufes zur Initiative der Bibliotheken der DDR aus Anlass des 100. Geburtstages Lenins*, 5.5.1970.

9. BLHA Rep. 547 FDGB Nr. 1685, *IV. Protokoll der Beratung mit Kulturfunktionären aus den Kreisvorständen FDGB, Klubhäusern und Kommissionen Kultur und Bildung der BGL der Betriebe in Potsdam* 30.9.64 and Neuruppin 28.9.64. See also ibid., *Bezirksvorstand, Abteilung Kultur, Einschätzung der Beratung mit hauptamtlichen Gewerkschaftsbibliotheken*, 21.10.64.

10. Ibid.; see also BLHA Rep. 538 KB Nr. 35, *Schreiben an den Bezirksvorstand Potsdam*, 18.4.70.

11. The increasing focus on the importance of qualifying functionaries began in the late 1950s: BLHA Rep. 547 FDGB Nr. 1075, *Industriegewerkschaft Metall Zentralvorstand*, 18.3.57: here, a functionary is reprimanded for not turning up to the requisite qualification courses; BLHA Rep. 547 FDGB Nr. 2245 *Klubhaus Stahl- und Walzwerk Brandenburg, Klubleitung an den Bezirksvorstand Potsdam*, 17.2.60: this document concludes that *Kulturobmänner*, who were in charge of cultural life in brigades, are to be trained better. The number of available qualification courses and attendances increase over the 1960s and 1970s: see for example BLHA Rep. 401 Rat des Bezirkes (RdB) Nr. 22558: here is a statistical analysis sent from the *Bezirk* Academy to the *Rat des Bezirkes* on 11.2.1983, which shows the steady increase of participants in the annual teaching cycles—in 1973/73 there had been 99 participants, whereas in g82/83 there were 237.

to enable an understanding of the cultural model of the SED.[12] To a limited extent, the efforts to qualify and educate cultural functionaries showed some effects, but only among those functionaries who worked in the upper echelons of the administrative faction. Among this group, tough recruitment principles were applied to ensure that only politically 'sound' individuals and well-trained candidates could rise to positions of responsibility.[13] Among cultural functionaries in intermediate and local administrative and executive positions, however, the overall political and cultural qualification of functionaries did not improve drastically, because it was far too difficult to fill these positions to apply strict recruitment and qualification guidelines. Frequently, those functionaries who were recruited in the 1960s and 1970s lacked either political or cultural training (or both) and in some cases, they had political backgrounds that were dubious to the SED (some even had a Nazi past).[14] As the levels of political and cultural training were quite poor among cultural functionaries, it would be misleading to simply describe them as well-qualified, reliable, and loyal puppets of the SED.

What did this mean for the development of cultural life? One important factor that needs to be considered is that, while the intermediate and local functionaries may not have been reliable and loyal pawns of the party, many of them took up their positions out of an attachment to cultural activity. Their primary interest was to see cultural life flourish. In order to achieve this aim, however, the functionaries relied on the animated participation of interested individuals from the population. People only participated, however, if the state-organised cultural life met their expectations. This meant that functionaries had to engage in continuous dialogue with the participants and had to respond to their interests and needs, even if that meant compromising certain party dictates.[15] The executive functionaries engaged in this kind dialogue with the participants throughout the history of the GDR and they showed a readiness to make compromises in order to fulfil popular in-

---

12. BLHA Rep. 426 Bezirkshabinett für Kulturarbeit (Bfk) Nr. 243, *Laientheater–Mittelstufe (no date, written after the second Bitterfeld conference in 1964, but before the seventh party conference in 1967)*: this is a set of questions for an oral examination of students studying 'lay theatre'. The main focus is on political-ideological content, but technical aspects like the fire regulations are also a part of the course.

13. The pressures of ensuring the political reliability of leading functionaries of the 'administrative group', particularly in the 1970s, are evident in BLHA Rep. 538, KB Nr. 175, *Eingabe aus Kleinmachnow, an das Bezirkssekretariat des Kulturbundes der DDR*, 17.8.78: in this *Eingabe*, a person remarks that he was not considered for a leading administrative position because he was not an SED member.

14. BLHA Rep. 401 RdB Nr. 33652/4, *Konzeption zur Qualifizierung der haupt- und ehrenamtlichen Leitungskader auf dem Gebiet der Kultur und Volkskunst 27.12.71–Anlage II, Analyse über die haupt- und ehrenamtlichen Kulturkader im Kreis Königswusterhausen*: here, the lack of qualification among various administrative and executive functionaries is striking; see also footnote 8.

15. This will be discussed in more detail in the next section.

terests. Of course, these functionaries had to fulfil certain political dictates, but they did so at a minimum, and otherwise implemented their own ideas to ensure that cultural activity represented the desires of the participants. In cultural circles, for example, the leading functionaries ensured that at public events, the cultural groups performed or exhibited 'progressive' socialist material. The daily repertoire of the groups, however, was aligned with the expectations of the majority of the active members, even if this meant that it had a low socialist content.[16]

Because the executive functionaries were so willing to adhere to their own interests, the participants came to regard them as their representatives and not just as the long arm of the SED. Even the executive functionaries saw themselves as the people's representatives, and were increasingly prepared to take on this role vis-à-vis the state organs. Over the course of the 1960s and 1970s, the executive functionaries became more and more confident about making compromises that adapted to the interests and needs of the participants.[17] Furthermore, in the 1970s, they increasingly challenged functionaries in higher levels of authority when they felt that the interests of 'their' participants had been neglected by the state. They addressed the higher-ranking functionaries on behalf of their participants in a very demanding and annoyed tone and insisted that certain problems were rectified.[18]

The readiness to compromise and adapt to the situation at the grassroots did not remain restricted to the executive functionaries. Towards the late 1960s, the intermediate administrative functionaries had also begun to realise the advantages of responding to people's interests and needs. Rather than enforcing strict, educationalist guidelines, the intermediate administrative functionaries now also tried to secure higher levels of popular participation by focussing on popular interests and needs.[19] In the following

16. BLHA Rep. 538 KB Nr. 29, *Protokoll der Kreisdelegiertenkonferenz des Kreisverbandes des Philatelistenverbandes der DDR, Oranienburg, 5.9.70*, p. 2; BLHA Rep. 538 KB Nr. 31, *Protokoll über die Kreiskonferenz, 23.5.70*, pp. 1–2; BLHA Rep. 538 KB Nr. 615, *Bezirkskommission Foto, zwei Jahre nach der letzten Bezirkskonferenz, vier Monate nach der Bezirksfotoschau, 39.3.68*, pp. 1–2.

17. BLHA Rep. 426 BfK Nr. 249, *Letter from E.S. to R. in the Bezirkskabinett für Kulturarbeit Potsdam*, 28.9.1972, p. 2: this is an example of a functionary who was criticised by the higher levels of authority for putting on plays that were not of sufficient artistic quality, but he vehemently defends his decisions, arguing it was more important to draw people away from their televisions than to concentrate on artistic content.

18. See for example BLHA Rep. 538 KB Nr. 30, *Schreiben von dem Kreisvorstand des Philatelistenverbandes an den Bezirksvorstand des Philatelistenverbandes im Kulturbund*, 6.05.79: here, a functionary complains on behalf of the members of his philatelist circle that they had not been sent their stamps.

19. This change could occur because of a changing climate that was developing in cultural policy: the strict application of educationalist principles was abandoned by the party leadership over the course of the 1960s in favour of a greater focus on people's interests and needs. This political change is briefly outlined in the section 'Normalisation of rule' of this chapter.

example from 1972, the minutes from a meeting of the *Kreis* leadership of the *Kulturbund* in Falkensee highlight this newly developed readiness of administrative functionaries to compromise:

> *The chair*: According to the plan, there has to be a monthly Wednesday talk, but that is not realisable. From experience, it can be said that Wednesday talks are not as well frequented as club evenings on weekends. . . Financing the Wednesday evenings is far too costly considering the attendance levels.
>
> *Friend 1*: The *Bezirk* conference was quite resolute about how important it is for the Kulturbund to stage these Wednesday talks.
>
> *Friend 2*: We need to decide on the character of these Wednesday talks. Having a club evening with the brigades is out of the question. Most of the workers have to get up at 5am, and go to bed at 10pm in order to be ready for work in the factory. What would be best would be to have Wednesday talks with relatively few people and find experts from their own ranks. Club evenings with brigades have to take place on weekends.[20]

Though this example may seem quite stilted, it nevertheless emphasises an important point: it was the functionaries' ability to compromise that underpinned the functioning of the organised cultural system. The SED's institutions were carried, and some of the SED's dictates were fulfilled, but at the same time, the participants in the cultural sphere were not driven away by inflexible and unrealisable party guidelines.

The functionaries' growing readiness to compromise and their increasing assertiveness was an important aspect of cultural life: without a close connection between functionaries and participants, the organisation of cultural life would have been seriously hampered. Bad relations between functionaries and participants could result in people's withdrawal from the cultural network.[21] The interaction between functionaries and participants was not the only aspect of functionary work, however. While adjustments were made to people's interests, cultural functionaries were still a part of a wider cultural network and had to interact with other functionaries.

Over the course of the 1960s, cultural functionaries were increasingly required to perform bureaucratic tasks. These demands ranged from organising a certain number of 'political' events to keeping detailed records on all of their participants. If the local functionaries did not fulfil their duties

20. BLHA Rep. 538 KB Nr. 363, *Protokoll in F.; Kreisleitungssitzung,* 15. 11.72, pp. 1–2.

21. BLHA Rep. 471/15.2 Volkspolizei Kreisbehörde Brandenburg Nr 124, *M., Volkspolizeikreisamt Greifswald, 24.1.72.*

adequately, they were reproached by functionaries at higher levels.[22] By the 1970s, it was not uncommon for the administrative functionaries to perform 'checks' on the executive functionaries to see whether the latter were fulfilling their duties. In the worst cases, the outcome of these investigations could be a demand for functionaries to chastise unruly participants, and if necessary, to exclude them from the cultural group or circle.[23] In some cases, the executive functionaries were even prevented from exercising their hobbies if they had not performed their duties properly.[24] This interference of the state organs in the affairs of local cultural groups meant that the autonomous development of cultural life was always restricted, and that compromises with the participants could not be taken too far.

Yet, this does not mean that cultural life can be reduced to repression and state control. It is important to realise that the dialogue with functionaries in higher positions of authority was not merely enforced on the local administrative and executive cultural functionaries. Over the course of the 1960s and 1970s, many of these lower-ranking functionaries actually began to seek interaction with their superiors. This development occurred as a result of the increasing bureaucratic and organisational tasks that the intermediate and local functionaries had to deal with. As these tasks increased in the 1960s and 1970s, local functionaries increasingly turned to the administrative functionaries for help, guidance, and advice in order to deal with their growing workload. They wanted guidance and assistance from the higher levels of authority instead of criticism from afar. This was already becoming evident in the early 1960s. For example, at an FDGB meeting in 1963, the leader of a clubhouse made the following complaint:

> Our room is in a catastrophic state. Here, people meet for gymnastics and do all sorts of things. But we do not receive means for any kinds of repairs. It is looking very bad. There are always some functionaries from the leadership who appear and criticise, but no one helps.[25]

Towards the later 1960s and 1970s, the local functionaries increasingly turned to higher positions of authority with their concerns. By the 1970s, they even asked leading functionaries in the *Bezirk* administration to inter-

---

22. BLHA Rep. 538, KB Nr. 30, see correspondence between W., K., and K.

23. BLHA, Rep. 471/15.2 Bezirksbehörde Deutsche Volkspolizei Potsdam Nr. 940, *Einschätzung des Männerchors 1882 in B, 18.11.68.*

24. BLHA Rep. 538 KB Nr. 25, *Schreiben Kü. an W.* 14.2.72; ibid., *Antwort von W.* 15.2.72; ibid., *Antwort von G.*,16.2.72.

25. BLHA Rep. 547 FDGB Nr. 1682, *Protokoll über den Erfahrungsaustausch mit Klubhausleitern und Sekretären für Kultur der Kreisvorstände der FDGB, 21.5.63*, p. 7, Kulturhaus Neuseddin.

vene at the local level in order to sort out certain problems. A stamp collector's circle in Pritzwalk, for example, ran into a few problems fulfilling the demands for increasing the membership and keeping the circle going in the early 1970s. The circle leader wrote to the head of the *Bezirk* leadership of the *Kulturbund*, expressing:

> Had I known then what kind of work I was taking on, I would certainly not have done it. What is missing is not good will, but the right people, who would then also take on a youth group. I myself don't know what to do anymore in order to activate the work in Pritzwalk. We would really appreciate some help.[26]

When this help did not materialise, the local functionary in Pritzwalk expressed feelings of anger and resentment towards the *Bezirk* leadership of the *Kulturbund*:

> Years ago, we were promised help from the *Bezirk*. Not just once, but several times. Nothing happened. Our members regard that as a failure to appreciate our circle and its work. Our disappointment still lasts today. We are of the opinion that we can't talk about our problems in Potsdam, but only in Pritzwalk.[27]

These appeals for help were also becoming evident among cultural functionaries who worked in the factories. Here, too, levels of discontent were high among executive functionaries if the organisation of cultural life was ignored by the factory leadership or by the trade unions.[28]

Low-level administrative and executive cultural functionaries did not therefore necessarily resent interference from higher-ranking functionaries, but actually sought it when they could not deal with the organisation of cultural life on their own. This shows that functionaries constantly engaged in dialogue in two directions: they responded to the participants' needs *and* they willingly integrated into the state-organised cultural network. Functionaries do not, therefore, slot either into the 'state' or 'society' category. They created cultural structures that were acceptable to the population, and yet ensured that these cultural structures were tied to the state organisation.

---

26. BLHA Rep. 538 KB Nr. 35, *Schreiben an den Bezirksvorstand Potsdam*, 18.4.70.

27. Ibid.

28. BLHA Rep. 547 FDGB Nr. 1685, *IV. Protokoll der Beratung mit Kulturfunktionären aus den Kreisvorständen FDGB, Klubhäuser und Kommissionen Kultur und Bildung der BGL der Betriebe, in Potsdam* 30.9.64 and *Neuruppin* 28.9.64. See also: ibid., *Bezirksvorstand, Abteilung Kultur, Einschätzung der Beratung mit hauptamtlichen Gewerkschaftsbibliotheken*, 21.10.64.

Playing by the Rules and Using the Rules: The Participants

What about those who participated in state-organised cultural activities? Some historians, like Rüdiger Henkel, argue that pursuing cultural activities within the state structures of the GDR meant losing one's freedom of self-expression. Henkel insists that state-organised cultural activity was not a private affair in the GDR, but became an area that facilitated the fulfilment of the SED's totalitarian aims.[29] In contrast to this, other historians highlight the limitations of central control over cultural life that resulted from understaffing and underfunding, which made it impossible to monitor and guide every aspect of organised cultural life. These historians support the notion that cultural life existed in 'niches', which meant that cultural activity had a great deal of autonomy, as long as people did not challenge the supremacy of the SED.[30] Both reflections about the levels of control, and about the autonomous development of cultural life in the GDR are very important aspects for understanding this sphere of people's everyday lives. Nevertheless, the participants' behaviour patterns cannot purely be viewed from either angle. People's engagement with cultural activity cannot simply be boiled down to either repression or withdrawal.

Those who participated in organised cultural activities had to tolerate a degree of interference from the state's or the party's organs throughout the existence of the GDR. As early as 1949, the SED introduced a regulation for the registration of all cultural associations (*Vereine*), which decreed that their independent status was to be abolished. From now on, all cultural groups had to be registered with a state institution, a mass organisation or a factory. In the name of bureaucracy, the details of all members of these circles were to be recorded meticulously, and the functionaries were expected to write regular reports about the circle's progress. If these requirements were not fulfilled, then the administrative units could prohibit the groups from carrying on with their activities.[31] This officially required registration enabled the administrative bodies and the police units to monitor

29. Rüdiger Henkel, *Im Dienste der Staatspartei, über Parteien und Massenorganisationen der DDR* (Baden-Baden: Nomas Verlagsgesellshaft, 1994), pp. 221–37.

30. Simone Hain 'Die Salons der Sozialisten: Geschichte und Gestalt der Kulturhäuser in der DDR', in Simone Hain, Michael Schroedter, and Stephan Stroux, *Die Salons der Sozialisten: Kulturhäuser in der DDR* (Berlin: Ch. Links, 1996), p. 53; Meier, Helmut Meier: 'Der Kulturbund der DDR in den 70er Jahren: Bestandteil des politischen Systems und Ort kultureller Selbstbetätigung', in Evemarie Badstübner, ed., *Befremdlich Anders, Leben in der DDR* (Berlin: Karl Dietz Verlag, 2000), pp. 599–625.

31. BLHA Rep. 538 KB Nr. 25, letter from K. to W. on 14.2.72, letter from G. to K. on 16.2.72, and letter on 15.2.72 from W. to K.

and control cultural development in these circles throughout the 40-year history of the GDR. They analysed whether a cultural circle was progressing in the 'correct' way, whether the leaders of the cultural groups were reliable, law-abiding citizens, and whether the members of the cultural groups were trustworthy individuals.[32] If such analyses found an element that gave cause for concern, then action could be taken by interfering directly in the cultural group. One choir in *Kreis* Pritzwalk, for example, came under investigation in 1965, because it frequently sang at church events, and when doing so, seemed to know the required songs very well, whereas it sang the *Sozialistenmarsch* and the *Gefangenenchor* from the opera Aida 'not with rejection, but showing as little enthusiasm while singing these songs as they do singing other songs . . . the main focus is the melody . . . the text does not attract much interest'.[33] The fact that mere lack of enthusiasm whilst singing a particular song could attract negative attention shows the limits of autonomy of cultural groups.

The members of cultural groups and circles were thus not free from outside intervention. At the same time though, this control was not perpetual and absolute: in many cases, the administrative units were too busy to occupy themselves with the streamlining of every single cultural circle. This becomes evident by looking, for example, at the so-called 'culture and education plans' in factory brigades. From the late 1950s onwards, the SED leadership wished to engage more workers in cultural activities through the brigade movement. Increasingly, brigades that participated in factory award schemes were expected to plan a certain amount of cultural activity that the members would participate in throughout the year. By the 1970s, the brigades were expected to draw up annual 'culture and education plans' as part of their commitments for competitions. These plans were meant to include activities of 'highbrow' culture, as well as intellectually stimulating and educational events. Only very few brigades adhered to these educationalist goals of the party, however. Most brigades organised events of a 'lowbrow' nature that appealed to a majority of brigade members, such as evenings of playing card games, boat outings with families or dances.[34] The factory leadership and the trade unions were

---

32. See BLHA Rep. 471/15.1 Bezirksbehörde der Deutschen Volkspolizei Bezirk Potsdam (DVP) Nr. 308, Nr. 309, and Nr. 310.

33. BLHA Rep. 471/15.1 DVP Nr. 310 *Protokoll über die Ermittlungen zur Überprüfung der Tätigkeit des Männerchors L. in B.*, pp. 1–2, side 73–74. See also all reports in BLHA Rep. 471/15.2 DVP Nr. 940: this file contains several analyses of the amount of 'progressive' material in their repertoire.

34. BLHA Rep. 506 VEB IFA Ludwigsfelde Nr. 1758 *Kultur- und Bildungsplan*, 27.9.72. To see variations between brigades, compare BLHA Rep. 502 Stahl- und Walzwerk Brandenburg Nr. 2072, *Wettbewerbsbeiträge der Brigaden TK1 Meisterbereich 2/S. III, Wettbewerbsverpflichtung 1970*, with BLHA

too busy to ever control this development. In the 1960s, there were still concerns about the inability to guide people's cultural development. One report written by the *Bezirk* Council in 1968 expressed such concern: 'Party decisions are not put into practice. Cultural life and the development of the Socialist personality are more or less left to chance'.[35] Over the course of the 1970s, though, these practices became increasingly accepted by the local and intermediate administrative cultural functionaries in factories. The responsible functionaries did less and less to counter the workers' refusal to engage with 'highbrow' activities, and the workers became bolder about their inclination for 'lowbrow' activities.[36]

This shows that people had some scope for shaping cultural activity according to their own desires. Nevertheless, the limitations that existed due to actual and potential interference from state organs should not be left out of the picture. As a result of the existing demands and constraints that were present alongside some degree of leeway for more autonomous developments, people engaged in a variety of complex behaviour patterns: they subjugated themselves to outside interference, they withdrew, and they interacted with the functionaries who administered and organised the cultural network of the SED. This complex combination of strategies will now be outlined. Over the course of the argument, it will become evident that through this combination of behaviour patterns, people could regain a sense of self-determination over their cultural activity: they gradually learned that they could steer the course of events in their favour, not just by withdrawing from, but also by integrating into the organised cultural structures.

It is important, first of all, to analyse why people engaged with cultural activities that were organised by the organs of the state, thus subjugating themselves to outside interference. To put it simply, people participated in these activities because they felt that they could adequately exercise their interests and needs there. By the 1960s, many people realised that they could exercise their cultural inclination most effectively within the state-organised cultural structures, because these provided materials,

---

Rep. 502 Stahl und Walzwerk Brandenburg Nr. 2072, *Wettbewerbsbeitrag der Brigade 'J.G.'*. The first contains more sociable commitments, whereas the second includes more activities of 'high culture'. See also Sandrine Kott, 'Zur Geschichte des kulturellen Lebens in DDR-Betrieben, Konzepte und Praxis der betrieblichen Kulturarbeit', in *Archiv für Sozialgeschichte*, 39 (1999), p. 189.

35. BLHA Rep. 401 RdB Nr. 6449, *Probleme des Teilsystems Kultur im Industriegebiet Teltow*, 3.5.68, p. 1.

36. BLHA Rep. 503 Chemiefaserwerk Premnitz Nr. 4189, *Erfüllung der kulturpolitischen Aufgaben unter besonderer Berücksichtigung der Durchsetzung der sozialpolitischen Arbeitskultur, 30.10.74*; ibid., *Kultureinschätzung zur Vorlage–Erfüllung der kulturpolitischen Aufgaben, 15.11.74*; ibid., *Vorlage für die Betriebsparteiabteilung, Einschätzung über kulturelle Fragen, 18.11.74.*

equipment, organisation, and the chance to meet other like-minded people with whom to discuss one's interests.[37] The interests that people sought to satisfy within the organised structures varied. Some individuals wanted to pursue a particular hobby, or a specific cultural activity, such as stamp collecting, singing or painting, and joined a cultural circle for that reason. In many cases, people who became active in cultural circles had engaged with its particular activity beforehand, and, once they were members of a cultural circle, they tended to stay in it for a period of time.[38] The fact that people had a personal interest in a particular kind of cultural activity made them quite protective about it. They had a tendency to take themselves quite seriously as representatives of this activity, and because the activity was important to them, they wanted the state administration to take it seriously as well.[39] Nothing other than a strong personal interest would have motivated these individuals to become so active in cultural circles and so protective about their hobby; being culturally active could be a time-consuming exercise that required a lot of dedication and sacrifices. People had to attend rehearsals and meetings, and spend their free time practising or collecting.[40] As a result of the time constraints involved in participating in cultural activities, a high proportion of culturally active people were retired—particularly in the Kulturbund.[41] This was a great thorn in the flesh for the SED leadership, who wanted young people and workers to become involved in state-organised cultural activity. In the 1970s, the state administration frequently called

37. Increasingly, the participants wanted their circles to be registered with an institution that looked after their interests adequately. If the participants of one circle felt let down by the carrying institution or organisation, they ended their contract with it and registered with a different organisation. See, for example: BLHA Rep. 538 KB Nr. 24, *Deutsche Kulturbund AG Philatelie Nauen, Rechenschaftsbericht für das Jahr 1969, 4.4.70*, p. 2, and BLHA, Rep. 426 BfK Nr. 196, *Zirkel Schreibende Arbeiter, VEB EPW Neuruppin, 20.11.78, Kündigung der Trägerschaft über unsere Zirkel.*

38. BLHA Rep. 538 KB Nr. 29, *Mitgliederliste der AG Philatelie Birkenwerder, 30.6.72:* The average membership of this circle is 10 years.

39. BLHA Rep. 505 Schwermaschinenbau Heinrich Rau Wildau Nr. 2031, *Sammeln aus Spaß an der Freude*, pp. 1–2: in this brigade diary, a collector of match boxes described his hobby with loving vocabulary and remarks resentfully that the *Kulturbund* shows little interest in this cultural pastime; BLHA Rep. 538 KB Nr. 306, *Erster Zwischenbericht über die durchgeführten Jahreshauptversammlungen, Bezirksleitung Potsdam an den Zentralvorstand*, 6.5.64, p. 2. Here, *Kulturbund* members complain about paying fees, which are not used for their benefit, but for attracting new members—they demand that they, as fee-paying members, are taken more seriously.

40. BLHA Rep. 401 RdB Nr. 702, *Einschätzung zur Verwirklichung der Direktive des ZK vom 14.3.62 zur Verbesserung der kulturellen Massenarbeit der Klubs und Kulturhäuser*, 26.11.62, p. 4, side 39; This remained a prominent factor in cultural life: BLHA Rep. 538 KB Nr. 234, *letter from Sch. to J on 10.6.80*: here, dedicated members sacrifice their holiday to attend a cultural event.

41. BLHA Rep. 538 KB Nr. 294, see for example *Statistischer Jahresbericht 1974*: out of 9,500 *Kulturbund* members in *Bezirk* Potsdam, 1,332 were 'non-working people' (a figure was mostly made up of retired people).

upon the executive functionaries to combat the so-called 'over-ageing' of cultural circles.[42]

Not everyone became active in state-organised cultural life in pursuit of a particular hobby, however. There were many who largely desired relaxation, fun, sociable pastimes, and interaction with other people. This is particularly evident in cultural life in the factories. The example of the 'culture and education plans' in brigades has already been mentioned, where workers committed themselves to cultural activities that were largely of a 'lowbrow' nature. Particularly favourable were outings with families, or festive evenings with a cultural content that was not too challenging, and that included food, dance, and, of course, drink.[43]

The fact that personal interest was such a strong determinant in joining cultural activities is an important factor in cultural life. It meant that when people participated in organised cultural activities, they did so with a particular expectation: they wanted to see their interests and desires fulfilled. Over the course of the 1960s and 1970s, people increasingly demanded that their needs should be attended to by the state. They had internalised a specific part of the SED's cultural rhetoric: the SED insisted that the organisation of cultural life rested with the state and that there was no 'privately' organised cultural life. This meant, however, that in the eyes of the culturally active population, the state organs had the duty to provide an interesting and stimulating cultural life that lived up to people's expectations. In other words, over the course of the 1960s and 1970s, people were increasingly aware that they could wield the SED's own rhetoric to their advantage: if the provision of cultural life was perceived to be inadequate, people engaged in targeted dialogue with various functionaries in order to ensure that the situation altered. They were devising ways of 'playing the rules' such that organised cultural structures increasingly suited their needs.

Over the course of the 1960s and 1970s, participants frequently communicated their expectations and irritations to higher levels of authority by writing *Eingaben* (letters of complaint). Admittedly, *Eingaben* are a very difficult source, and should be treated with care. They were written by individuals who wanted to have a certain aim fulfilled, and who hence used a certain kind of language with which they hoped to achieve their goal. This means that *Eingaben* are not necessarily an adequate reflection of what people really thought and felt. Nevertheless, in this instance, they are a

---

42. BLHA Rep. 538 KB Nr. 357, *Quartalsbericht I/76;* BLHA Rep. 538 KB Nr. 35. *Schreiben Pritzwalk an Potsdam am 18.4.79.*

43. See footnote 34.

useful source, because they show what people had come to expect from the SED.[44] In many cases, people complained about a functionary who had not done his or her job properly, or about a lamentable state of affairs that they expected to see rectified. A frequent mechanism of articulating a complaint was to write an *Eingabe* as a group in order to give the complaint more weight. This practice was evident throughout the middle period of the GDR. In the following *Eingabe* from 1973, for example, a male choir complained bitterly about not having been given an award that the members felt the choir ought to have received:

> We expect our artistic and social achievements to be acknowledged, and we will simply not be satisfied with being under-valued by not being given the award . . . we expect not only an apology, but also a noticeable improvement in the assistance that is given, particularly to those groups that have for years, despite great difficulty, been active in the area of culture.[45]

There are very many similar examples throughout the 1960s and 1970s of cultural groups who collectively complained to a higher level of authority because they felt that the state institutions and functionaries needed reminding about how to do administer cultural life properly.[46] Just as in the case of local cultural functionaries, participants in the cultural sphere did not simply withdraw from state intervention–when they felt that it benefited them, they actively sought dialogue with higher authorities in order to sort out shortcomings inherent in organised structures. The participants therefore realised that official structures not only imposed control, but that they could also be exploited for their own purposes: they could utilise SED rhetoric and force higher ranking cultural functionaries to do things *for* them.

Collective complaining was not the only form of communication that existed between participants and higher-ranking administrative functionaries: in some cases, people took matters into their own hands and

44. Felix Mühlberg, "Konformismus oder Eigensinn? Eingaben als Quelle zur Forschung der Alltagsgeschichte der DDR", *Mitteilungen aus der kulturwissenschaftlichen Forschung*, February 1996, pp. 331–45; Ina Merkel, Felix Mühlberg, 'Eingaben und Öffentlichkeit', in Ina Merkel, ed., *Wir sind doch nicht die Meckerecke der Nation! Briefe an das Fernsehen der DDR* (Berlin: Schwarzkopf & Schwarzkopf, erweiterte Neuausgabe, 2000), p. 15.

45. BLHA Rep. 401 RdB Nr. 20294, *Eingabe des Männerchors der E.B.K. an das Ministerium für Kultur über die Handhabung des Auszeichnungswesens*, 8.11.73.

46. To see examples from the 1960s: Stadtarchiv Potsdam (StA Potsdam), Nr. 2773, *Eingabe Grenzbahnhof Frankfurt/Oder, 14.8.63*: here, the workers of a brigade complain about functionaries in the city administration in Potsdam; StA Potsdam, Nr. 2773, *Klub H. Potsdam, an die ständige Kommission für kulturelle Massenarbeit beim Rat der Stadt 4.10.63,* pp. 1–2: here, the members of a club complain about the state of pubs in Potsdam.

addressed higher levels of authority as individuals. Frequently, these individuals turned to the state administration in order to settle a personal dispute. This was particularly evident in the *Kulturbund*. People who had been members of the organisation for a long time believed that their membership entitled them to institutional support from the organisation when they had personal problems. In some cases, they involved the *Kulturbund* when they had a dispute with another institution, hoping that the backing of the *Kulturbund* would increase their chances of settling the issue in their favour.[47] Not all cases revolved around battling with institutions, though: some *Kulturbund* members tried to use the organisation to help them settle personal differences with other individuals with whom they had a dispute. This could go as far as asking the *Kulturbund* to track down one of its members to settle a monetary dispute.[48]

The articulation of expectation through *Eingaben* and the targeted exploitation of the state organs for securing a personal advantage shows one crucial factor of cultural life in the GDR: as time progressed, people increasingly tried to realise their interests *through* the state organisation. They realised that interacting with organised cultural structures could bring with it certain advantages, such as institutional support for settling personal disputes. But communication with higher-ranking functionaries was only part of the picture. People did not just integrate into organised cultural structures in order to fulfil their cultural interests. When they saw their interests would be better fulfilled by withdrawing from public cultural life, then they did so. The clearest evidence of this withdrawal can be found in people's interaction with the church: particularly in the villages, the church could provide an alternative to state-organised cultural facilities. In the 1960s, many young people sought church-organised cultural events, because they resented the lack of personal freedom that existed in state-organised cultural activity. Within the realms of the church, these youths were allowed to pursue their interests, such as playing Beat music.[49] But young people were not alone in frequenting cultural events in the church. In the 1970s, when the relations between the church and the SED were beginning to relax, attendance at cultural church events rose considerably. The church organised sociable afternoons with tea and coffee, and

47. BLHA KB Nr. 175, *Eingabe Frau G, 11.5.69*, BLHA Rep. 538 KB Nr. 32, *Eingabe 14.8.70*; BLHA Rep. 538 KB Nr. 30, *Brief an den Deutschen Kulturbund Potsdam am 16.10.68;* BLHA Rep. 538 KB Nr. 19, *Brief von Bundesfreund N., am 17.7.80.*

48. BLHA Rep. 538 KB Nr. 35, *Brief vom 20.11.66*; BLHA Rep. 538 KB Nr. 19, *Eingabe W., Karl Marx Stadt, 31.8.81.*

49. BLHA Rep. 471/15.2 Kreisbehörde Brandenburg Nr 124, *Einschätzung der Kirchenarbeit im Monat Februar in 27.2.68.*

they supported musical groups that preferred to sing religious songs.[50] When people felt that they could not fulfil their interests and needs within the state institutions or mass organisations, either because of political constraints or because of poor organisation, they increasingly attended these kinds of church events instead.[51]

To conclude this section, it can be said that people who participated in cultural activity employed different behaviour patterns and strategies to ensure that their cultural interests were satisfied. As a result of inadequate controls, they were able to steer the cultural repertoire in a direction that appealed to them. Here, they benefited from the cooperation of local and intermediate functionaries, who were willing to engage in compromises because they wanted to keep participation levels high, but could only do so by responding to popular interests. Another strategy that was employed by the participants was interacting with state organs in order to address certain grievances. On many occasions, people were therefore more than happy to realise their interests *though* the organised cultural structures. At other times, nonetheless, the participants preferred to withdraw from the state's cultural network in order to exercise their cultural inclinations elsewhere. By making use of all of these different coping strategies, people could regain a partial sense of self-determination: to a degree, they could control the nature and development of their cultural lives.

Conclusion: The Normalisation of Rule in the Sphere of Organised Culture

The analysis of the previous two sections has shown that over the course of the 1960s and 1970s, cultural life developed in a way that simultaneously satisfied the interests of the participants and upheld the influence of the state over the organisation and development of cultural activities. An important factor that contributed to this situation was the functioning of channels of communication among functionaries at different levels, and between functionaries and participants. Local functionaries did their best to shape cultural activities so that they suited the interests of participants and in order to keep discontent at bay. At the same time, they engaged in dialogue with functionaries in higher positions of authority. Participants also engaged in many kinds of dialogue with cultural functionaries

---

50. BLHA Rep. 401 RdB Nr. 6450, *Rat des Kreises Potsdam an den Rat des Bezirkes, Kurzinfomation–Aktivitäten der Kirche im kulturellen Bereich, 18.20.71.*

51. BLHA Rep. 471/15.2 Kreisbehörde Brandenburg Nr 124, *M., Volkspolizeikreisamt G., 24.1.72.*

in order to maximise the fulfilment of their interests. They had learned how to use the rules of the game to their advantage. In order to attend to their needs, they interacted with the executive functionaries, but they also turned to higher-ranking administrative functionaries with certain grievances. The participants can consequently not be described as passive subjects of the SED having had no power over their own destiny at all. To a degree, they can be seen as actors who knew how to regain a limited degree of control over their own cultural lives.

The high levels of integration and communication that are here shown to have characterised the 1960s and 1970s had not always existed in cultural life. During the late 1940s and early 1950s, the situation had been quite different, and it changed only very gradually over the course of the late 1950s and early-to-mid 1960s. During the first decade of the GDR, participants and executive functionaries had frequently engaged in acts of nonconformity and resistance in order to protect established cultural traditions. In the early 1950s, many cultural groups that had existed before 1945 tried to resist being incorporated into state-organised cultural structures, and it took a lot of effort on the part of the state administration to introduce the 1949 ruling.[52] Moreover, even after these cultural groups finally acceded to the 1949 ruling and gave up their independent status, the members often did not become more acquiescent to the cultural project of the SED. Throughout the 1950s, many culturally active individuals engaged in acts of nonconformity in *Bezirk* Potsdam. These acts could range from having contacts to cultural groups in West Berlin to upholding traditions that had been forbidden in the new dictatorship.[53] Some of these acts of nonconformity still occurred in the mid 1960s.[54] What made the situation worse was that in these cases of resistance and nonconformity, many local executive functionaries supported the participants. This meant that the interaction between administrative and executive functionaries was, in these years, not functioning properly. The state authorities and police forces responded to this situation with a very heavy-handed approach. They intervened directly in the cultural groups to make them

52. See, for example BLHA Rep. 471/15.2 DVP Nr. 930, file section 'Chor B.' VR/ I/21, *Überprüfung der Chorgemeinde B., Volkspolizeikreisamt Potsdam, 11.8.56*; BLHA Rep. 471/152 DVP Nr. 936, file section 'Skat Klub' Sachgebiet E, *Bericht, 2.2.60,* side 2.

53. BLHA Rep. 472/15.1 DVP Nr. 268, *Maßnahmeplan der Abteilung Erlaubniswesen bis zum 15. Jahrestag der Deutschen Volkspolizei, 5.1.60,* p. 4, side 26: here, cultural groups had contacts to groups in West Berlin. BLHA Rep. 471/15.1 DVP Nr. 308, *Beschlussüber die Ermittlungs des Männerchor W. 16.3.61*, side 169: in 1957, it transpired that this choir sang songs like 'Deutsches Vaterland', and 'Deutschland, Deutschland über alles'; see also BLHA Rep. 471/15.2 DVP Kreis Rathenow Nr. 88, *"Spaatz"* (without a date, but probably written in 1957, which was when the event took place).

54. BLHA Rep. 471/15.1 DVP Nr. 310, *Betreff Sängertreffen in der Gemeinde B., 5.7.65,* p. 2, side 92.

more conformist, but achieved only further alienation of and resentment among participants and local executive functionaries.[55]

It was only over the course of the 1960s that dialogue and compromise became part of the established routine, and that people began to fulfil their interests by integrating into the organised cultural structures and using them to their advantage—a development that has been outlined above. Participants and functionaries were not the only ones whose behaviour became more pragmatic over the course of the 1960s and 1970s. It became more and more obvious to the party leadership in the early 1960s that a heavy-handed approach and an educationalist cultural model threatened to alienate the population.[56] Over the course of the 1960s, adjustments were made in cultural policy as a result. By the late 1960s, the party leadership recognised that people's interests and needs were highly diverse, and that this diversity had to be reflected in organised cultural life in order to reach more people in their free time. Consequently, the party leadership now advocated catering for 'lowbrow' as well as 'highbrow' cultural interests in order to appeal to more people.[57] This was officially endorsed in cultural policy after the regime change from Ulbricht to Honecker in 1971.[58] It is important to stress that these policy adjustments were made in reaction to developments at the grassroots. The party leadership recognised that people's interests and needs could not always be steered, moulded, and controlled from above. It was necessary to adjust the party's cultural model to popular developments,

---

55. See, for example, BLHA Rep. 471/15.2 DVP Kreis Jüterborg Nr. 54, *Sachstandsbericht Verein T.*, 24.7.58, *Verfügung, 30.7.58; Aktenvermerk, 6.2.59.*

56. Ideas about making reforms in cultural life and taking people's interests into account began to appear around the introduction of the youth communiqué in 1963: SAPMO BArch DY 30/IV 2/9.06/92, *Für ein kulturvolles Leben der jungen Generation (No date, but the youth communiqué is mentioned, hence it has to be have been written later)*; SAPMO BArch DY 30/IV A 2/9.06/36, *Information über einige neue Probleme im künstlerischen Schaffen der DDR, 21.10.65*, pp. 12–14.

57. In the late 1960s, these ideas were becoming more and more prevalent, which can be particularly seen around the introduction of the 5-day week in 1966: SAPMO BArch DY 30/IV A 2/9.06/90, *Bericht der Abteilung Agitation über die Erfahrungen der massenpolitischen Arbeit unter Berücksichtigung der Einführung der 5-Tage Woche in den Industriegebieten*; SAPMO BArch DY 30/IV A 2/9.06/90, *Kurze Darstellung neuer Probleme in der kulturellen Massenarbeit (no date, but the introduction of the 5-day week is mentioned, so it must have been written in 1966 or after)*; See also SAPMO BArch DY 30/IV A 2/9.06/1, *Hausarbeit: theoretisches Grundsatzmaterial zum siebten Parteitag*, 12.1.67, pp. 8–10. This development was also advocated by cultural theoreticians such as Dieter Heinze and Gerd Rossow, *Der Parteiarbeiter, kulturpolitische Aufgaben nach dem VII. Parteitag* (Ost Berlin, 1968), p. 33.

58. See, for example, SAPMO BArch DY 30/IV 2/1/458, *Protokoll der 6. Tagung des ZK, 'Zu Fragen der Kulturpolitik der SED', Berichterstatter Genosse Kurt Hager, 7.7.72*; for developments in cultural theory, which furthered this process, see Helmut Hanke and Manfred Weißfinger, Christa Ziermann, *Kultur und Freizeit. Zu Tendenzen und Erfordernissen eines kulturvollen Freizeitverhaltens* (Ost Berlin, 1971), p. 11; and SAPMO BArch, DY 30/IV A 2/2.024/7, *H. an Hager, 13.10.70*: H. attached two theoretical essays about the tendencies in recent cultural development. The second essay is: *Helmut Hanke, Die sozialistische Kultur in den siebziger Jahren*, pp. 9–10.

in the same way as the culturally active population was forced to accept outside interference from state organs in cultural activity at the grassroots.[59]

These developments reflect a process of 'normalisation' in cultural life. There is a clearly discernible development over the course of the 1950s, 1960s, and 1970s towards stabilisation, routinised implementation of compromise, and internalisation of the 'rules of the game'. Whereas the 1950s were characterised by resistance, nonconformity, coercion, and alienation, the 1960s were increasingly dominated by high levels of integration and interaction between participants and functionaries. Among all actors in the cultural field–functionaries, participants, and SED party leadership–there was a growing sense of pragmatism in the 1960s and 1970s. This manifested itself in the compromises of the functionaries, in the changing behaviour patterns of the participants, who realised their interests by integrating into the organised structures, and in the greater acceptance of a variety of interests and needs in official cultural policy.

In the analysis of cultural life, it has become evident that the application of the normalisation concept is a very useful tool for analysing the middle period of the GDR. The importance of cultural functionaries as a 'hinge' is particularly evident during these years. Functionaries played a major role in adapting political dictates to the situation at the grassroots, while simultaneously ensuring communication with the administration. They enabled a degree of autonomy in cultural life, but they also upheld the structures of the cultural system. These developments benefited the participants. As a result of the functionaries' willingness to compromise, and because they learned how to take advantage of the cultural system, people could regain a sense of control over their own lives. Their ability to fulfil their interests and needs did not just result from withdrawing into 'niches', but also occurred as a result of willing integration into the organised structures. To conclude, coercion from the central party organs was not the only factor that determined cultural life in the GDR. The satisfaction of people's interests was an equally influential factor. This means that the foundation of cultural life in the East German dictatorship was perhaps more similar to that in free, democratic Western societies than one might assume at a first glance.

---

59. Manfred Jäger, *Kultur und Politik in der DDR: 1945–1990* (Köln: Ed. Deutschland Archiv, 1995), p. 139.

Chapter 7

Learning the Rules: Local Activists and the Heimat

Jan Palmowski

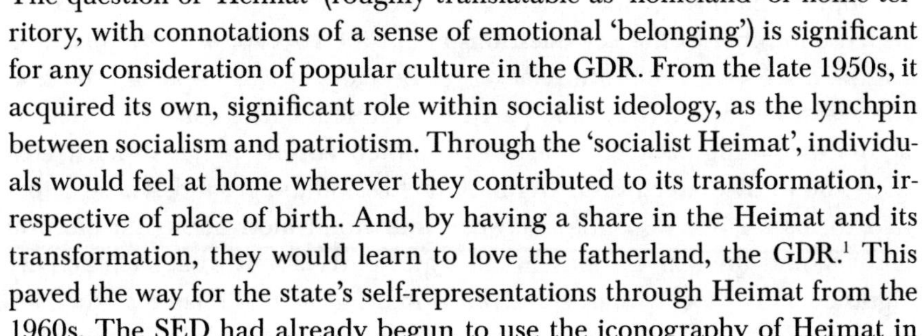

The question of 'Heimat' (roughly translatable as 'homeland' or home territory, with connotations of a sense of emotional 'belonging') is significant for any consideration of popular culture in the GDR. From the late 1950s, it acquired its own, significant role within socialist ideology, as the lynchpin between socialism and patriotism. Through the 'socialist Heimat', individuals would feel at home wherever they contributed to its transformation, irrespective of place of birth. And, by having a share in the Heimat and its transformation, they would learn to love the fatherland, the GDR.[1] This paved the way for the state's self-representations through Heimat from the 1960s. The SED had already begun to use the iconography of Heimat in its propaganda as early as the 1950s,[2] and by the time of its twentieth anniversary in 1968, the idea of the GDR as the socialist Heimat had become an important theme that combined history and transformation, tradition, and industrial change.[3]

Heimat became important not just for the ways in which the state represented itself to its population and to the 'other' Germany. Expressions of individual identification with the locality or a particular region were extremely popular in everyday life, and they had remarkable staying power throughout the GDR's existence. The popular resonance of the Heimat is easily missed if one concentrates on the one official Heimat organization in the GDR,

1. Jan Palmowski, 'Defining the East German Nation: The construction of a Socialist Heimat, 1945–1962', in *Central European History*, 37 (2004), pp. 365–799.

2. Alon Confino, 'Heimat, East German Imagination, and an Excess of Reality', forthcoming.

3. This is discussed further in chapter two of my forthcoming book on 'Potemkin's Nation: Heimat in the GDR'.

the 'Heimat friends' organized within the cultural league (*Kulturbund*). From their creation in 1950, the 'Nature and Heimat friends' were, until they were split up into interdisciplinary societies between 1976 and 1981, the largest individual organization within the cultural league, with about a quarter of its total membership. However, this only translated into around 50,000 members GDR-wide. In terms of membership, Heimat friends were a significant factor for the cultural league, but less so in relation to almost any other mass organization in the GDR. Heimat was much more popular than this figure would indicate. Folklore and Heimat music constituted a staple of cultural life where the majority of the population lived during the 1950s, in villages as well as mid- and small-sized towns. Moreover, the popularity of Heimat and folklore entertainment persisted into the 1980s. One indicator of this is the disproportionately high audience, which Heimat shows such as 'Klock Acht, achtern Strom', or the 'Oberhofer Bauernmarkt' reached on GDR television throughout the 1970s and the 1980s.

The significance of Heimat in the self-representation of the GDR, and in popular culture at the 'grassroots', provides an important context in which a number of the key questions about the concept of 'normalisation' can be discussed. If culture relating to the Heimat was important both at the grassroots and to state and party, local functionaries come into view as actors mediating between officially promoted visions of the socialist Heimat, and individual cultural Heimat practices on the ground. These actors had to manoeuvre every day between individual motivations for cultural activity, and the expectations by state and party about what such activity signified. Any processes, or state, of normalisation as it related to the Heimat would be likely to be reflected–and in turn, reinforced–by these actors, their experiences, and their activities. By looking at actors concerned with the Heimat, we can uncover processes of 'stabilisation', in terms of how culture could be mediated between official encouragement and individual activities in the everyday.

Normalisation as a concept relates not just to a particular state of 'stability', however that may be defined. Any question about the nature of regime stabilisation in the GDR is also inherently one about when that stabilisation set in. In the sphere of popular culture, the longevity of the Heimat ideal offers the great advantage of considering the 'timing' of stabilisation and normalisation from the longue durée. Folk music, choral singing, and local dialect were not equally popular in all parts of the population, but they retained an average popularity between the late 1940s and the late 1980s, which invites comparative questions about what might constitute a 'normalised' experience of the Heimat, and when we might observe this phenomenon.

Finally, the sphere of Heimat and of popular culture invites a consideration of how 'stabilisation' and normalisation, such as it existed, entailed a 'learning the rules' of behaviour in everyday life. The ideal of the socialist Heimat was predicated on individual initiative and activity. In this regard, Heimat friends within the cultural league did acquire significance completely out of proportion to their numbers. They were the ones who could be relied upon to set up Heimat exhibitions, organize the signposting of footpaths, and, most important of all, take a leading part in the organization of Heimat festivals. The socialist Heimat, and socialist cultural activity in general, worked in as much as it was popular, and in as much as it encouraged individual activity. In this regard, one question inherent in the normalisation concept, about individual voluntary activity and initiative, is crucial, and it is a question that leads back to the activists. For their task, in the sphere of Heimat, was to encourage individual activity and initiative within the confines of the political and economic environment. At the same time, the individual initiative they encouraged continued to provide a constant potential challenge to the desire of the party to control and direct individual activity. How did activists, then, learn the rules of changing what could be changed, of accepting what could not be changed, and of distinguishing one from the other? And at what point, if any, did a normalisation of such rules set in?[4]

This chapter considers these issues related to the 'normalisation' paradigm by looking more closely at two individuals who played an important part in their respective local 'Heimat' culture. As the central issue under investigation is under what conditions individuals were able to initiate and encourage Heimat activities, it makes little sense to look at 'functionaries' as a clearly defined category. Individuals could acquire an important role in encouraging the active and passive reception of Heimat in a variety of ways. Both of the individual 'actors' under consideration here lived in small- to mid-sized Thuringian towns: Altenburg in Leipzig district, and Mühlhausen in Erfurt district. Neither individual nor the towns in which they lived were 'typical' in any way; but that does not diminish the potential importance of this chapter's findings, for two reasons.

First, as regards the two individuals under consideration, both were recommended to me as prototypes of successful Heimat activity, albeit from very different perspectives. Heinrich Gemkow, a former vice president of the cultural league in the 1970s and 1980s, recommended Günther Hauthal, the first actor under scrutiny here, as someone I should interview as a

4. On the concepts of normalisation and 'learning the rules' that this article discusses throughout, see Mary Fulbrook's introduction to this volume.

good example of someone enriching the socialist Heimat through research on working-class history.[5] The second actor investigated here, Jürgen Thormann, was pointed out by Kurt Ludwig, the former Erfurt district secretary of the cultural league, as a good example of an active and successful cultural league secretary working at the county level.[6] Both actors under consideration here were naturally unique in their individuality. However, in as much as successful cultural activity rested, in the GDR as elsewhere, on individual initiative and drive,[7] the conditions under which both succeeded, and the arenas in which they were less successful, does suggest a validity beyond these two cases. Second, as regards the local environments Hauthal and Thormann acted in, these, too, were highly specific. Nevertheless, Heimat engagement by definition was about accentuating the distinctiveness of any locality. It is the specificity of each locality, and the attempt by the two Heimat activists to reinforce and help articulate this, which makes them representatives for other Heimat enthusiasts.

A Heimat of Workers and Peasants

The son of a stoker, Günther Hauthal was born near Gera in 1925, and in 1945–46 he was trained as a teacher (*Neulehrer*). He taught in and around Gera, but after taking further courses he moved to nearby Altenburg, where he became a history teacher at the Institute for Teachers' Education (*Institut für Lehrerbildung*). Hauthal became interested in the history of the local working class through his father-in-law, whom he helped to write a local history of the working class in his native Liepschwitz.[8] This publication caught the eye of Heinrich Gemkow, who worked at the Institute of Marxism and Leninism in Berlin and who, as vice secretary of the Nature- and Heimat friends within

---

5. I spoke to Gemkow towards the beginning of my oral history research, and at the time I had collected more interviews with central cultural league functionaries than with activists on the ground. Gemkow's recommendation had come at my request.

6. These recommendations were not just taken at face value. More than two dozen local Heimat activists I interviewed confirm that, within their passions and interests, neither Hauthal or Thormann were particularly out of sync with other enthusiasts—though Hauthal's passion for working class history remained, as this chapter also shows, definitely a minority interest throughout the existence of the GDR. The activities and relative positions of the two within their local communities and their actions were also cross-checked against other types of sources, including interviews with other Heimat activists, printed sources, and archival material.

7. Knut Kreuch, 'Jede Zeit braucht Leitfiguren und Arbeitstiere.... oder, wer sonst kann eine hoch motivierte ehrenamtliche Herde führen und sie immer wieder mit neuen Visionen zur Mitarbeit begeistern?', *Der Heimatpfleger* (Autumn, 2003).

8. Rudolf Behr, *Die Entwicklung der Arbeiterbewegung von Liebschwitz und Taubenpreskeln bis 1946* (Gera: Kulturbund zur demokratischen Erneuerung Deutschlands, 1956).

the cultural league, was responsible for approving all Heimat publications in the GDR that appeared outside the big publishing houses. Gemkow evidently took his duties very seriously, because it entailed educating Heimat friends in socialist values, so that these friends could then act as replicators of these values in their own environments.[9] Gemkow met Hauthal at a local history conference in Jena. Both were of the same age, both were loyal members of the SED, and both were committed to a new, socialist Heimat. To Gemkow, who experienced so much frustration in his efforts to encourage new approaches to the writing of Heimat history amongst especially older Heimat enthusiasts, Hauthal was a welcome ally who could change things from the bottom up, on the ground. Gemokow encouraged Hauthal to pursue local history in his new place of work, Altenburg, and to do so not just within the local history committee of the SED, but to work in and through the cultural league as well. It was an encouragement that Hauthal never forgot.[10]

Gemkow was not concerned about adding a new recruit to the membership lists of the cultural league. What was at issue was the very nature of Heimat activity in Altenburg. The city of almost 50,000 inhabitants is dominated visually by the castle, the former residence of the dukes of Saxony-Altenburg. Following the war, local popular culture mushroomed in Altenburg county as everywhere in the Soviet Occupied Zone. Local choirs proliferated, and if they offered a mixture of folklore and classical singing in the town itself, village choirs in the surrounding countryside sang almost exclusively folkloristic Heimatsongs.[11] Naturally, the cultural authorities tried hard to exert their authority over these activities, but during the late 1940s and the early 1950s, the demand for fare that sang of a Heimat idyll remained the staple of popular entertainment, much to the frustration of cultural officials in Thuringia.[12] Meanwhile, one topic relating to the Heimat exercised Altenburgers more than any other: the return of the 'Skatbrunnen', a statue of four figures representing the Jacks on a deck of cards. Altenburg considered itself as the town

9. Many of Gemkow's exchanges with a number of Heimathistorians 'on the ground' are preserved in BArch-SAPMO DY 27 2615. Gutachten zu Manuskripten über regional- und Heimatgeschichtliche Themen 1954–59.

10. Hauthal continues to acknowledge his debts to Gemkow's encouragement at the time. Interview with Günter Hauthal, 19 May 2003. See also the new introduction to his dissertation manuscript, which he wrote in 2001 (Günter Hauthal, der kampf der arbeiterbenegung gegen militarismus und imperialismus im Land Sachsen-Altenburg 1890-1916 (Diss. Potsdam, 1974). This is subsequently referred to as Hauthal, 'Introduction', here p. 8.

11. ThHStA Altenburg, Deutsche Volksbühne 33. Table: Deutsche Volksbühne: Laienkunst Gruppen. A good insight into some of the programmes offered at choral concerts in Altenburg between 1949 and 1950 is in ThHStA Altenburg, Deutsche Volksbühne 20.

12. ThHStA Altenburg, Deutsche Volksbühne 20. Programm 1.12.1949 Altenburger Akkordeon Orchester. See also: Brief an den Landesvorstand der Deutschen Volksbühne, von der Abteilung Volkskunst Landesregierung Erfurt, 29 October 1949.

where Germany's most popular card game, Skat, was invented. It was a matter of local pride that both the money and the raw materials were collected to restore the bronze figure, which had been melted in 1942. This issue exercised local minds for years, until in November 1955 a new statue was erected.[13] For Altenburg citizens, their ability to restore traditions and artefacts in the face of the financial difficulties and the material shortages that characterized life in the GDR only heightened their sense of accomplishment and local pride.

It is unlikely that Heinrich Gemkow would have been aware of the particularities of the popular culture in Altenburg in the early 1950s. However, Altenburg was by no means peculiar in the pervasiveness of folklore and traditional Heimat tropes in popular entertainment after the war.[14] Nor was it unique in the citizens' desire to reconnect to prewar Heimat traditions. To Gemkow, Hauthal was in a perfect position to make an impact. At a time when the state was evidently too weak to impose socialism in popular culture (in Altenburg as elsewhere),[15] an individual like Hauthal, a young, energetic socialist working at the prestigious institute for teachers' education, was ideally placed to bring socialism to the activities of fellow Heimat enthusiasts.

Following Gemkow's advice, Günther Hauthal became active in the 'subject group' (*Fachgruppe*) for Heimat history in the Kulturbund. With a number of other enthusiasts, he founded a working group on the history of the local workers' movement. Hauthal and his group met regularly to discuss their findings, and from time to time they also presented their work to the subject group for Heimat history in public meetings. He also encouraged many of his students at the Institute of Teachers' Education to engage in research on local working class history. Hauthal also became a prolific writer, and over the next year alone he published thirty-four articles in local publications, most frequently in the local edition of the SED district newspaper, the *Leipziger Volkszeitung*.[16] Hauthal was also invited, by the Altenburg Heimat friends in the cultural league, to publish a booklet on the Altenburg workers' movement from 1900 to World War I.[17]

---

13. Eberhard Heinze, 'Unser Skatbrunnen ist wieder da!', *Altenburger Kulturspiegel* (October, 1955).

14. For a detailed account of the revival of traditional Heimat folklore in Saxony, see Thomas Schaarschmidt, Regionalkultur und Diktatur. Sächsische Heimatbewegung und Heimat-Propaganda im Dritten Reich und in der SBZ/DDR (Cologne/Weimar/Vienna: Böhlau, 2004).

15. I have described the difficulties faced by the state in achiving 'realism' in Heimat culture in Jan Palmowski, *Inventing a Socialist Nation. Heimat and the Politics of Everyday Life in the GDR, 1945–1989* (Cambridge University Press, forthcoming 2009), ch. 2. On the constraints faced by the state in other spheres of popular culture, see Uta Poiger, *Jazz, Rock and Rebels. Cold War Politics and American Culture in a Divided Germany* (Berkeley: University of California Press, 2000).

16. List of Publications, presented by Günter Hauthal.

17. Günter Hauthal, *Die Altenburger Arbeiterbewegung von der Jahrhundertwende bis zum 1. Weltkrieg*, ed. Rat der Stadt Altenburg (Schloßmuseum) in Zusammenarbeit mit der Arbeitsgemeinschaft 'Natur- und Heimatfreunde' der Ortsgruppe Altenburg des Deutschen Kulturbundes (Altenburg, 1959).

To Hauthal, joining the cultural league offered access to older generations, those who had been engaged in local history research since long before 1945. Many of these were, according to Hauthal, also glad to have him in their midst. As Hauthal explained:

> At the foundation of the GDR they no longer knew how to respond. They withdrew completely... and no longer organized public events. Well, when these tensions were over, and they re-entered public life in 1951 with talks made by the group, they also had quite a few listeners. Well, but they had nobody who had done work on the workers' movement, this was the 'in' topic at the time. . . . That is how they welcomed me, a good part welcomed me immediately, five or six people, while I became familiar with, and was accepted by, the others after a while.[18]

Hauthal gave a number of presentations to the Heimat friends during the second half of the 1950s, and remembers lively discussions afterwards. And yet, he stopped going to meetings after a while. The other Heimat historians could not really relate to his interests, while Hauthal found the discussions at the Heimat historians' meetings too far removed from his own concerns.

Hauthal's enthusiasm soon became threatening to the entrenched activities of Altenburg Heimat friends. Like many Heimat groups at the time, the Altenburg cultural league published a cultural magazine, the *Altenburger Kulturspiegel*, which provided readers in the county with news about cultural events, reviews, and articles about the local Heimat. The *Altenburger Kulturspiegel* was run by Eberhard Heinze, a conferencier without party affiliation, and the political direction of the journal attracted frequent criticism in the local pages of the *Leipziger Volkzeitung*, with Hauthal emerging as the central critic. In 1956, Hauthal suggested that his newly founded group on Heimat history should publish its findings in the *Altenburger Kulturspiegel*.[19] This would be one way of politicizing the journal, another being the introduction

18. The full quotation is: Die wußten auf einmal bei der Gründung der Republik nicht mehr was sie machen wollten. Die haben sich dann ganz zurückgezogen, waren aber schon im Kulturbund. Die nannten sich Untergruppe des Kulturbundes, fühlten sich also nicht engstens verbunden. Da haben sie sich also zurückgezogen, keine öffentlichen Veranstaltungen mehr gemacht. . . na ja, und als diese Spannungen vorüber waren, sind sie 1951 wieder an die Öffentlichkeit getreten mit Vorträgen im Kreise ihrer Gruppe, [da]hatten sie auch immer ne ganze Menge Zuhörer. Naja, aber se hatten niemanden der so Arbeiterbewegung [erforscht hat], das war ja sozusagen 'in'. Sie hatten dann einen Lehrer, aus der Weimarer Zeit, der hatte aber nur bis zur '48er Revolution gemacht. . . . Naja, so kam das, das ich da reinkam und die mich wollten, zumindest ein ganzer Teil, fünf bis sechs Mann sofort, [mit] den anderen wurde ich später bekannt, oder warm, sozusagen.

Interview Günter Hauthal, 13 May 2003.

19. Leipziger Volkszeitung (Altenburg), 15 January 1956 ('Jedes Mitglied des Arbeitskreises erhielt einen Forschungsauftrag').

of new rubrics on, for instance, the history of the working class, general Heimat history, educational life, the local economy, and so forth. This should take the place, he argued, of discussions of films shown in the local cinema, and of advertisements. The cultural magazine should connect more to the life of schools, in other words, and to the life of workers.[20] In this way, Hauthal argued, culture could become truly integrative, and relate to the life not of a few elites, but of the whole community.

Hauthal was not alone in its criticisms. In 1957, the local SED leadership criticized the local cultural league and urged it to become more political.[21] The Kulturspiegel responded immediately by printing a number of political discussions,[22] but soon the 'politicisation' of the journal had lost momentum, and the articles reverted to their original choice of style and topic. In its May issue of 1958, it printed a poem by a reader, Herbert Schiffmann, on the 'love of duty'. In its lines, Schiffmann described how 'duty' allowed all to suffer hardships beyond endurance, closing with the line that 'She [duty] is the soul of German history, hence Germany will never go under.'[23] In theme and in diction, this poem had clear resonances to the Third Reich, and this caused another storm in the *Leipziger Volkszeitung*, initiated once again by Hauthal.[24]

Over time, the debate about the meaning of socialism in the Heimat did have consequences for the public activities of the cultural league, as their magazine became more politicised. However, this politicisation took much more than just Hauthal's persuasive attempts, it took the direct intervention of the party. Not until 1963 was Eberhard Heinze relieved of his duties as chief editor of the journal.[25] The *Kulturspiegel* that emerged from 1963 was less erratic in its support for socialism, and no longer offered a home for overly critical articles about the state of the Heimat, for instance, about the

---

20. Günter Hauthal, 'Wie wäre es, wenn der "Altenburger Kulturspiegel" so gestaltet würde?', in Altenburger Kulturspiegel, March 1956, p. 58.

21. 'Der Weg des Kulturbundes', in Altenburger Kulturspiegel, December 1957, pp. 239–40.

22. 'Das sozialistische Altenburg wird schöner sein!' in Altenburger Kulturspiegel, January 1958, pp. 2–3. 'Wie gefällt Ihnen unserer "Kulturspiegel"?' in Altenburger Kulturspiegel, February 1958, p. 39. 'Wo liegt die Heimat?' in Altenburger Kulturspiegel, June 1958, p. 121.

23. 'Sie ist die Seele vom deutschen Geschehn/und deshalb wird Deutschland nie untergehn!' Herbert Schiffmann, 'Die Liebe zur Pflicht', *Altenburger Kulturspiegel*, pp. 90–110.

24. Leipziger Volkszeitung (Altenburg), 15 May 1958 ('"Gartenlaube"-Ideologie'). See also the ensuing discussion between Heinze and Hauthal (who wrote in the name of the *Leipziger Volkszeitung*'s editorial team): *Leipziger Volkszeitung* ('Gartenlaube Ideologie. Antwort der "Kulturspiegel"-Redaktion auf die Kritik vom 15. Mai'). And, registering Heinze's defeat, see the article written by the *Kulturspiegel*'s editorial team: *Leipziger Volkszeitung* (Altenburg), 26 June 1958 ('Gartenlaube Ideologie'). I am grateful to Günter Hauthal for sending me these three articles.

25. 'Das interessiert auch Sie', in *Kulturspiegel Altenburg Schmölln*, April 1963, pp. 116. Heinze was extremely vague about the reasons for his dismissal, and stated that he never found out what had led to it. The only reason he did name was the fact that he had not been a party member. Interview Eberhard Heinze, 19 May 2005.

desperate state of repair of many historic buildings. Henceforth, the *Kulturspiegel* worked hard to propagate the socialist Heimat, for instance, in its promotion of new socialist Heimat festivals. However, the *Kulturspiegel* still did not become the paedagogic instrument along the lines Hauthal had suggested. In this important respect, the party still shied away from the kind of confrontation with traditional Heimat attitudes that Hauthal sought to fight head-on. As far as Hauthal was concerned, representing the new beginning and engaging in the socialist Heimat did not guarantee the support and gratitude of either the Heimat friends or the party.

Hauthal continued to work on the Heimat, but from the late 1950s onwards, he became more detached from the cultural league and the Altenburg cultural elites. There were plenty of other outlets for his energies. During the 1960s, he continued to publish in the local pages of the *Leipziger Volkszeitung*, while also researching as part of a working group attached to the local SED. In his spare time, Hauthal took his university examinations, and from 1970 he wrote his doctoral thesis about the history of the workers in Altenburg County, 1900–1918.[26] However, whereas in 1966, the SED had enthusiastically supported his endeavours to publish a commemorative volume on the history of the local SED,[27] in 1974 the local SED refused to support the publication of his dissertation. Hauthal continued to publish articles in the *Leipziger Volkszeitung* during the 1970s and the 1980s. However, after working so hard to bring the local cultural league into line in the late 1950s, the lack of party support for his dissertation came as a real shock. Hauthal increasingly went into 'internal emigration' from the SED local history group, and in 1985 he formally resigned his position as the chair of the (by now largely inactive) committee for research on the workers' movement.

Günter Hauthal was, like thousands of other activists, passionately engaged with his Heimat. In many respects, Hauthal was also extremely successful: in fifteen years, between late 1955 and late 1970s, he published over one hundred short articles, mostly in local newspapers, on the history of workers in the local Heimat. In this respect, and as a public speaker, he did become well known and influential in his Heimat. However, where Hauthal had failed was in the attempt to transform the Heimat, and change the meaning of Heimat in socialism, or at least to bring socialism to the majority of activists interested in the Heimat.

---

26. Günther Hauthal, 'Der Kampf der Arbeiterbewegung gegen Militarismus und Imperialismus im Land Sachsen-Altenburg 1890–1917', (PhD diss., Pädagogische Hochschule "Karl Liebknecht", Potsdam, 1974).

27. Günther Hauthal, *20 Jahre SED–Zur Entwicklugn im Kreis Altenburg*, ed. Kommission zur Erforschung der Geshcichte der örtlichen Arbeiterbewegung der SED-Kreisleitung (Altenburg, 1966).

Hauthal's biography demonstrates the difficulties of constructing a popular culture that was infused by socialism 'on the ground'. By the time Hauthal began his Heimat activities in Altenburg, the difficulty of infusing the Heimat with socialist connotations had already become apparent in Altenburg, as elsewhere. Nevertheless, if Heimat could acquire a new meaning in socialism, then this could only happen through individuals like Hauthal, those with the education, the conviction, and the commitment to make visible the socialist aspects of the Heimat. Yet, the case of Altenburg shows that commitment was just not enough. 'Learning the rules', in this case, meant appreciating the resistance of traditional local elites. The essence of the socialist Heimat contained the principle that birth no longer mattered for one's belonging to the Heimat. Yet, in places like Altenburg it clearly still mattered. It would have been difficult for anybody to convince the local notables of Altenburg of the merits of working-class history, and of a popular culture for workers' edification. However, the fact that he had just moved there and that he was not a native son, meant that Hauthal started his quest from a position of disadvantage for which no political loyalty to the new order could, over the long run, compensate. For, as the SED's lukewarm commitment to Hauthal's activities, especially from the 1970s, demonstrates, the political rules of engagement proved much more fickle than local ties and local networks.

Hauthal's example brings into focus another important 'rule' of Heimat engagement in the GDR, namely the importance of individuals. Hauthal's commemorative book on the history of the local SED had been encouraged, in 1966, at the behest of Werner Heinecke, the first secretary of the local SED who was from Altenburg itself. He was succeeded by an 'outsider', who had little time for local history, and who refused to take any responsibility for it. Under this new regime, the *Altenburger Kulturspiegel* was discontinued in March 1970. Moreover, as Hauthal's doctoral dissertation on the pre–1918 workers' movement dealt mainly with social democrats rather than the communist party (KPD), the SED leadership never expressed an interest in printing this part of its own history.[28]

Hauthal's Heimat engagement does not end in the 1970s, however. Although he was no longer closely involved with the cultural league, he did give occasional lectures there. He also lectured for the URANIA society for the spread of knowledge, and he continued to write for the *Leipziger Volkszeitung*. Hauthal also wrote the history of the ceramic works Hermsdorf,

---

28. For this reason, it is particularly ironic that a (West-) German post-unification dissertation on the social democrats in Saxony-Altenburg asserted that Hauthal's dissertation, even though it was never printed for political reasons, could be regarded as a 'Paradebeispiel für die marxistisch-leninistische Geschichtsschreibung der DDR'. Hauthal, 'Foreword', p. 5.

and in 1982, he popularized his Heimat's tradition to a wider and national audience by designing a pack of commemorative Skat cards with traditional local folk designs.

Hauthal continued thus to contribute to Heimat history in Altenburg, but he did so very much as his own agent. Yet in 1980, a further context to Hauthal's work emerged. In that year, he received a visit from the head of the agricultural cooperative in Altkirchen. This village was ten kilometres away, but it lay in a different county, Schmölln. They knew each other because during the 1950s, Hauthal had supervised his students at the institute for teachers' education during a year of practical work in agricultural production. When they renewed their acquaintance, the visitor from Altkirchen had an unexpected request: the village wanted to have a small Heimat museum, and the cooperative, which was interested in maintaining its status as one of the model cooperatives in the district, helped with the funding. Hauthal accepted the commission, and even managed to have a new building constructed for the purpose. The museum was opened in 1982, but Hauthal's connection with the village and its people did not end there. The cooperative built him a datcha at the edge of the village. Subsequently, Hauthal spent his weekends and the summer evenings in Altkirchen, he continued to advise the village on the representation of its Heimat in the museum, and he wrote the book for Altkirchen's 850th anniversary celebrations.[29]

In Altkirchen, Hauthal had finally found a context in which he felt appreciated. Altkirchen was situated in a different county, Schmölln. Here, Hauthal felt that, in marked contrast to Altenburg, the SED leadership was more embedded in the locality (not least by origin). The Schmölln SED was much more open to his work, and did not mind hearing about social democrats as part of the county's working class traditions. More importantly, Hauthal experienced in Altkirchen what he had missed in Altenburg, a combination of political and social support and recognition. Altkirchen became what Altenburg had never quite become: Hauthal's Heimat.

The Three Golden Rules

Twenty-five years separate Günter Hauthal and Jürgen Thormann in age. Born in 1940, Thormann was socialized entirely in the GDR. Like Hauthal, Thormann was a member of the SED, and where Hauthal had developed a passion for local history, Thormann had developed a passion for music. He

29. Günter Hauthal, *850 Jahre Altkirchen. Unsere Dörfer, Unsere Landschaft, undsere Geschichte bis 1850, Unsere Chronik bis 1990* (Altenburg, 1989).

loved (and played) jazz, and, by 1969, he had become the leader of the trade union ensemble in his native Mühlhausen. In 1970, Jürgen Thormann, a baker by profession, accepted the position of first secretary to the cultural league in Mühlhausen County.

Before Thormann took up his position, the local organization had declined in numbers and activities, a development that was not untypical for this period in the GDR's history. In Mühlhausen, the demoralization of cultural league members had developed its own particular forms. During the 1960s, the aquarists' energies, for instance, were taken up in a running battle with the director of the Heimat museum. The fish enthusiasts had set up an aquarium in the museum, but from 1963, the group accused the museum of not supplying the aquarium with sufficient electricity so that the fish suffered. In return, the director accused the group of not taking sufficient care of the aquarium. This became so acrimonious that the aquarists split up over the issue, and had to be reconstituted in 1970.[30] The dialect speakers were also under pressure in the 1960s, because the majority of attendees at the meetings refused to join the cultural league. Meanwhile, the forest enthusiasts challenged the local army over its (lack of) respect for environmental laws.[31] More generally, cultural league members voiced repeatedly their frustration at the lack of support and recognition they received from the town council and the SED. Finally, the club of the intelligentsia also concerned the cultural league leadership. Even though discussion evenings on local politics were well attended, meetings on most other issues were not, with outside speakers frequently finding that no audience (apart from paid officials) had turned up.[32]

When Jürgen Thormann took up his office in 1970, therefore, he had his work cut out for him. Yet, under his leadership, the cultural league in Mühlhausen blossomed. Membership levels increased markedly, from 980 members in the county in 1972, to 1180 in 1979, to 1466 in 1988.[33] The increase during the 1980s is roughly equivalent to an increase in membership levels that the cultural league experienced GDR-wide. However, at the national level,

---

30. StA Mühlhausen. Kulturbund Mühlhausen 18. *Protokoll über die am 26.2.1964 durchgeführte Jahreshauptversammlung der Ortsgruppe Mühlhausen*; *Protokoll über die am 3.11.66 stattgefundene Ortsleitungssitzung*; *Protokoll über die am 30.10.70 durchgeführte Ortsleitungssitung des deutschen Kulturbunds, Ortsleitung Mühlhausen*.

31. The question that excited the working group 'Wald und Wandern' was: 'Sind die Naturschutzgesetze nur für die Bevölkerung, oder auch für die NVA, gültig?'. StA Mühlhausen, Kulturbund Mühlhausen 18. *Protokoll über die am 5.5.1964 geführte Leitungssitzung*.

32. StA Mühlhausen, Kulturbund Mühlhausen 18. *Bericht über die gesellscahftliche Wirksamkeit des Klubs der Kulturschaffenden in Mühlhausen* [no date and signature, but evidently written for the central membership meeting of the club on 3 April 1963].

33. StA Mühlhausen. Kulturbund Mühlhausen. *Berichterstattung, Mühlhausen, den 14.10.1988*. (Membership level on 30 September 1988).

membership levels of the cultural league were relatively stagnant during the 1970s, and so the membership increase by 20 percent in Mühlhausen was out of the ordinary.[34] This impression of numerical progress is confirmed by an examination of some of the cultural league's activities. One of the cultural league's innovations of the 1970s, the 'small galleries', which were designed to bring art to smaller communities, found a particularly successful manifestation in Mühlhausen. A small gallery was created inside the town's largest factory, the Mülana clothing factory, and the exhibitions there received generous funding. This link to the Mülana factory gave photography enthusiasts, philatelists, and other collectors added opportunities and encouragement for creating exhibitions, while many hobby groups also participated actively at local Heimat festivals, elections, and anniversary celebrations through displays and exhibitions. As the effective leader of the local cultural league, Thormann did not create these events himself, but he facilitated them. In that sense, he did have an impact on the local cultural league's fortunes from the 1970s. Thormann was clearly successful in his work, and this was recognized not only by his superiors.[35] After the collapse of the GDR, the cultural league was refounded as a voluntary association, and over 400 members 'voted with their feet' and rejoined the cultural league, which Thormann continued to direct.[36]

34. Statistics in the GDR clearly need to be treated with caution. See, for instance, Burghard Ciesla, 'Hinter den Zahlen. Zur Wirtschaftsstatistik und Wirtschaftsberichterstattung in der DDR', in Alf Lüdtke und Peter Becker eds., *Akten. Eingaben. Schaufenster. Die DDR und ihre Texte* (Berlin: Akademie Verlag, 1997), pp. 39–55. However, there are good grounds for assuming that cultural league membership levels were more indicative than membership statistics for the German-Soviet Friendship organization, for instance. Those who wanted to join a mass organization to protest their allegiance to the GDR could do so more effectively through other organizations. Moreover, although there was always the problem of inactive members, any local secretary who artificially inflated membership numbers would have had to justify this to his hobby activists, who were in the cultural league out of enthusiasm for their hobby. This is not to exclude the fact that some joined the cultural league also in order to appear to be loyal to the state. However, the cultural league at the local and GDR-wide levels never appeared to do much to hide the slight decline in membership levels during the 1960s, or the stagnation in the 1970s. Together with qualitative indicators, which are present also in Mühlhausen, there are thus grounds for taking these increased membership levels seriously.

35. In fact, Thormann was recommended by his erstwhile boss, Kurt Ludwig, who was the first district secretary of the cultural league in Erfurt in the 1970s and 1980s. Ludwig may have had a variety of motives for pointing me to Thormann's direction when I asked him for names of county secretaries, but it is unlikely that Thormann would have received Ludwig's recommendation had he not appreciated his work.

36. The cultural league still exists in many areas of the GDR, and a 'rejoining rate' of one third of the former membership is high, but not completely unusual. The bulk of the hobby enthusiasts, such as ornithologists, environmentalists, aquarists, and so on, normally joined (or rather: were 'reunited' with) the relevant West German head organizations. Usually, Heimathistorians and folklore enthusiasts were large enough to create their own local organizations, as they were keen to connect to their pre-GDR roots. As a result, a third of the former membership, consisting mostly of the smaller subgroups and more specific local interests, as well as debating groups, was about the maximum number available for rejoining the cultural league in any local setting.

I conducted two interviews with Jürgen Thormann, one in 2003 and one in 2005. When I asked him whether he thought the Mühlhausen cultural league had been particularly active, Thormann did not answer directly, but explained instead the basics of cultural league engagement in Mühlhausen. In the 1970s, he began, cultural work became easier because the restrictions of the 1960s, caused by the 'Bitterfelder Weg' and other movements, ebbed away. And, in consequence of the Basic Treaty and other external developments, culture was promoted once again by the local party. At the same time, he continued,

> those who wanted to collect stamps properly, had to join the cultural league. Those interested in sundials, or the stars, had to do this within the cultural league. There, the specific hobby was central... these were idealists, [dedicated to] their hobby. They did not come for political motivations as to the German-Soviet Friendship organization, where they [the party] forced them in, they came voluntarily. And now it was the specific skill of the local leadership to guide this.

For his part, Thormann had three principles that determined his work:

> First, no criticism directed at the party, but not in the slightest. In plain language: asslicking for eternity. Even in subject specific matters. One could tell umpteen examples...: they were always right. One had to avoid these disputes, they did not yield anything.[37]

The second principle was that there should be no contacts, in the name of the cultural league, with individuals or organizations abroad. Thormann included contacts to socialist countries in this, and all such requests he directed immediately to the district leadership. Third, there should be no contact with the Church as an institution.

There was a further crucial activity that Thormann estimated cost him up to a third of his working time: attending meetings in the National Front and wherever else the cultural league participated. These were meetings that were almost completely irrelevant for the work of the cultural league, and where the cultural league, in turn, was not taken seriously. But attending, '*That* was important. *There* one had to be present' [Original emphasis in the interview]. Thormann had one piece of good fortune: the head of the local cultural league organization, a voluntary position, was occupied by

37. In Thormann's own words: 'Erstens: keine Kritik an der Partei, aber nicht die geringste. Auf deutsch gesagt: Arschleckerei bis zum geht nicht mehr. Auch in fachlichen Fragen, man könnte zig Beispiele erzählen, wo's nicht um politische Fragen sondern [um] fachliche Fragen ging: die hatten immer Recht. Und diesen Auseinandersetzungen mußte man aus dem Wege gehen. Die brachten gar nischt.'

the director of the Mülana works. This not only enabled Thormann and the cultural league to create the small gallery and have access to occasional practical help. The director, Fries, also was in good standing in the town in general, and in the party in particular, and 'when he took the word for us, then that had an effect, also amongst the powers that be'.[38]

Thormann, in other words, tried to act as a buffer between the political and ideological expectations that state and party had of the cultural league, and the aspirations of his members to be left alone with their passions. 'If I say to the numismatists, let's do a course in ideology or some other nonsense, they would say to me: you must be insane'.[39] Thormann saw his role as one of leaving his members alone as much as he could, and this proved crucial to his own standing among his members. Thormann remembered the reservations with which he, the baker, had been met originally by some of the local elites, which were organized in the cultural league's club of the intelligentsia. Thormann had sought advice from his district secretary on how to deal with this situation, not least because he was intimidated himself. Given the vast array of hobbies and specialisms of cultural league groups, the district cultural league secretary Kurt Ludwig, who was his superior, advised Thormann to 'make a wise face, and pretend to be ignorant.' Thormann kept to his organizational tasks and refrained from interfering in the subgroups themselves. After one and a half years, the club of the intelligentsia thanked him by offering him the address they had reserved when they were amongst themselves: 'colleague' instead of the more formal 'league friend' (*Bundesfreund*).

The modus vivendi which ensued between the cultural league and the local SED meant in practice that the cultural league became much more visible to the party in its activities. Philatelists, for instance, organized a county exhibition every two or three years. They made sure that the exhibition was dedicated to a current political event, such as the party's ninth plenary session. The first exhibits were dedicated to the SED, the history of communism, or another appropriately political topic. This, according to Thormann, ensured that the local party supported and funded the exhibition, while the cultural league could point to its contribution in preparation of the ninth plenary session of the SED. Meanwhile, the philatelists could, for 80 percent of the exhibition space that remained, display their collections on the topics of their choice—all for the ninth plenary session, of course.

---

38. '. . .er war ein hervorragender Leiter, war sehr angesehen, auch hier bei der Partei, und wenn der bei einer Tagung in die Bütt ging, und sagte: unser Kulturbund hat das und das, dann wirkte das auch bei der Obrikgeit.'

39. 'Wenn ich jetzt zu den Numismatikern sage: wir machen einen Parteilehrgang oder irgendwelchen Firlefanz, würde er sagen: Du spinnst wohl!'.

In addition to such tactics, which ensured that the relationship between the local SED and the cultural league improved markedly, Thormann was also concerned to diffuse problematic areas before they came to a head. For instance, the dialect speakers, the 'Müllhisser Schpellstoppn', were, in the early 1970s, renamed into the working group on Heimat poetry (AG Heimatdichtung). In Thormann's subsequent reports and protocols, there were no hints that the problems of control which had existed during the 1960s continued to exist. This was formally a different organization now, and the dialect speakers were subsequently left to themselves.

The kinds of compromises found by the Mühlhausen cultural league can be replicated for everyday life in the GDR with ease, as cultural activists everywhere were concerned with manoeuvring between the ideological demands of the party on the one hand, and their particular passions, on the other. Dedicating particular activities to the political event of the day became a ubiquitous ritual, a code that could be learned by active and passive consumers of culture with relative ease. More importantly, from the point of view of this chapter, is that not all cultural activity could be ritualized in this way. Cultural engagement created individual spaces that created zones of ambiguity which even Thormann's three golden rules could not circumscribe easily.

One such instance was the plan of the National People's Army (NVA), in the early 1970s, to use the residential villa that served as the cultural league's headquarters as the site for selecting, twice per year, its recruits for the army (*Musterung*). This caused great consternation within the cultural league, and Thormann decided to oppose this plan resolutely. The NVA's plans would have made sustained cultural work impossible, and Thormann emphasized how this contravened the pronouncements and decisions of the party both in the locality and at the national level. Thormann succeeded, and the NVA moved elsewhere to conduct its selections.

In 1975, Mühlhausen was officially awarded the title 'Thomas-Müntzer-Stadt', on the 450th anniversary of the peasants' rebellion led by Thomas Müntzer. Although the town had honoured its favourite son before, from 1975 onwards, the pressure in Mühlhausen, but also in the entire region and beyond, to name schools, factories, and anything else after the revolutionary leader increased yet further. Mühlhausen's club of the intelligentsia was also encouraged, by the local SED, to award itself this name and be called 'Thomas-Müntzer-Klub'. Instead, the club's members wanted to name the club after Wilhelm Gottlieb Tilesius von Tilenau. Tilenau was born in 1769, and became a natural scientist, doctor, and drawer at the University of Leipzig. He accepted a position at Moscow University in 1803, and in that year took part in the first Russian circumnavigation of the Earth, a journey from which he published three volumes of drawings and sketches of peoples and animals from different parts of the globe. He died in Mühlhausen in 1857.[40]

The club argued that Tilesius von Tilenau had not just been an important scientist and a native son, but that he also represented the interdisciplinarity that constituted such a fundamental principle of the cultural league with its many subgroups. The local SED continued to insist on the name of Müntzer, but the Club was not impressed: if it could not use the name of Tilesius, it would not have any name. In 1983, the issue was finally resolved: the club was named 'Tilesius-von-Tilenau Klub'. Not only had the Mühlhausen intelligentsia avoided being associated with the ubiquitous beacon of the workers' and peasants' state; but the timing of the naming, which was accompanied by a series of eight talks and other events on Tilenius von Tilenau, also meant that the Mühlhausen intelligentsia largely avoided participating in the GDR-wide commemorations of Martin Luther's heritage in the GDR.[41]

These two incidents are very revealing about the 'rules of engagement' with state and party. This first rule was, of course, that one had to confront the state and the party with its own rules and arguments. In other words, the political language of the SED had to be appropriated and turned against the local authorities (never the party itself). It is, at first sight, surprising that the cultural league prevailed against a mighty agent such as the army; and it is quite possible that this was an exceptional case. But here, the cultural league itself was affected as an organization. It was clearly one of the least of the mass organizations in the GDR, but it was part of the country's political and cultural fabric nevertheless. On that basis, Thormann could rally the cultural league's district leadership, and he could make a number of allies within the town itself. The naming of the club is a striking illustration of 'Eigen-Sinn', of club members demarcating spaces of their own in relation to the local SED.[42] Tilenius von Tilenau represented an impeccable choice, because he was a native son who had performed his major services to human knowledge on a Russian payroll. Moreover, club members were able to link in their demands with the contemporary 'heritage' debate that began in the

40. <http://www.uni-leipzig.de/journal/heft698/S44.htm>. Accessed on 20 May 2005.

41. StA Mühlhausen. Kulturbund Mühlhausen 4. Kulturbund der DDR Kreisleitung Mühlhausen, [Summer 1984], p.5. See also Bericht des Klubs der Kulturschaffenden Mühlhausen des Kulturbundes der DDR zur politisch-ideologischen Arbeit im Karl-Marx-Jahr 1983. gez. Fries (23 Sept. 1983).

42. Alf Lüdtke, 'Lohn, Pausen, Neckereien. *Eigen-Sinn* und Politik bei Fabrikarbeitern in Deutschland um 1900', in Alf Lüdtke, *Eigensinn: Fabrikalltag, Arbeitererfahrungen und Politik vom Kaiserreich bis in den Faschismus. Ergebnisse* (Hamburg: Ergebnisse, 1993), pp. 85–119. Thomas Lindenberger, ed., *Herrschaft und Eigen-Sinn in der Diktatur. Zu einer Gesellschaftsgeschichte der DDR* (Köln: Böhlau Verlag, 1999), pp. 23–26.

mid 1970s. The cultural league put itself in the forefront of the endeavour to explore the rich heritage of the GDR, and this meant, above all, underlining the diversity of influences on the GDR's past and present. Honouring Tilesius von Tilenau in a town identified by the party with Thomas Müntzer could be made to fit this cultural trend perfectly.

For the cultural league, such successes were important. The poor levels of activity in the club of the intelligentsia during the 1960s in part reflected, according to Thormann, a general disgust that the original aims of the cultural league, the promotion of German unity, had been betrayed in 1961. To such a club, the name of Tilesius von Tilenau made an important statement about the Wall, too, because of Tilesius von Tilenau's globetrotting past. Perhaps more importantly, both events created a sense of agency, of self-determination vis-à-vis the party. This promoted not just a feeling of unity among the membership, in pursuit of a common cause, but it also suggested a feeling of 'justice' (promoted by such acts as citing the law to the lawmakers) and achievement.

These moments of affirmation for Thormann and the cultural league were particularly important because they knew also that these small 'victories' were only possible not because of the force of their own pleading, important though that was, but because of the will of the party. 'And yet: the party did whatever it wanted, end of story!'[43] In the early 1980s, rumours emerged that the SED county section (SED Kreisleitung) wanted to build their headquarters on an old, historic cemetary. Preservationists and amateur historians within the cultural league treasured the gravestones there, while dendrologists studied the old bushes and trees on the cemetary. Thormann went repeatedly to the SED county leadership, since the rumour refused to die down. However, Thormann was assured, on each occasion, that the rumours were groundless. One day, Thormann remembers, he was in a meeting with all of the section leaders of all the different groups and sub-groups of the cultural league, when a cultural league member entered the room to say that he had just come from the cemetary where he had witnessed that tanks and the army had moved in to destroy the cemetary and make room for the building.

As with other decisions, the SED contradicted its own pronouncements about the importance of the Heimat, and it contravened the state's laws about the protection of nature and the environment. Nevertheless, such pleas were of little consequence when it came to the desires of the SED leadership—a typical experience of everyday life in the GDR, which reminded cultural league activists just how much their activities on behalf of the

43. Thormann: 'Und trotzdem: die Partei machte, was sie wollte, aus die Maus!'

Heimat depended on the goodwill of the party. This lesson had an important impact on everyday cultural activity. During the 1980s, the delapidation of the old town became an increasingly urgent problem, in Mühlhausen as elsewhere. However, even though he led such an active cultural league organization, Thormann had great difficulties in creating a subgroup devoted to preservationism (*Arbeitskreis Denkmalpflege*), and to find a leader for this group.[44] For it was clear that this would be a thankless task, and that whoever led the group was bound, according to Thormann, to get into trouble.

Cultural activity in Mühlhausen thus relied on rules that were learnt every day, through regular exhibitions or other activities of cultural participation, as well as through confrontational encounters with state, party, or an agency of the state. This was a learning process that had no beginning and no end. And it was a process that was learnt and relearnt not just by 'functionaries', but it was communicated to, and appropriated by, cultural activists more generally. This is best demonstrated through Mühlhausen's biggest cultural event that lay outside the realm of the cultural league, the annual Kirmes (church fair).

The Kirmes was prepared by between forty and fifty communities (*Kirmesgemeinden*), which met throughout the year, and each of which contributed to the main event of the Kirmes, the pageant. Each individual community was presided over by a 'mayor', and the mayors in turn elected their 'lord mayor'.[45] As before 1949 and after 1990, so also during the GDR, the main point of the pageant was to criticize authority. This created, every year, potential for conflict with the authorities, not least because the lord mayor and his committee were not shielded by the cultural league, but were directly answerable to the cultural department of the town council. Four weeks before the Kirmes, a detailed programme of the festival and of the pageant had to be submitted to the council for authorization. This evidently inspired the ingenuity of many communities to give a title to their themed representation at the pageant, which seemed to be innocuous, but whose 'real' meaning revealed itself visually, through the design of costumes or the cart at the procession.

From the second half of the 1960s, the SED leadership of the county tried hard to appropriate the festival and make it ideologically more palatable. In 1967, an article in the local newspaper argued that the pageant should be interpreted as a giant festival of political participation (*Ein*

44. StA Mühlhausen. Kulturbund Mühlhausen 4. *Selbsteinschätzung der Kreisleitung des Kulturbundes zu den Schwerpunkten der weiteren Arbeit 1982*.

45. The following paragraph is based, in addition to the quoted written sources, on an interview with Günter Würfel on 21 April 2005, who has been lord mayor since the 1970s.

großartig gelungenes Einwohnerforum). The pageant highlighted a series of local problems, it held, and this democratic way of raising concerns constituted a perfect act of local democracy.[46] The local council's attempt to appropriate the festival reached its highlight in 1969, when it ordered that the name be changed, from 'Kirmes' to the 'Festival of Socialist Joy'.[47] The Kirmes communities protested against this, but the council refused to allow any material to be printed which did not feature this title. In 1970, a compromise was found, when the festival was named 'Kirmes–a festival of socialist joy'.[48] For Mühlhausen citizens, it became a matter of local pride not to refer to the event as the festival of socialist joy, but to remain true to 'their' Kirmes. Eventually, references to the 'festival of socialist joy' were quietly dropped, but not until the late 1970s.

In Mühlhausen, the process of 'learning the rules' in the sphere of popular 'Heimat' culture, therefore, affected not just members of the cultural league and their families, it also affected dozens of communities besides. These communities learned every year afresh how boundaries and rules shifted. The majority of themes represented at the Kirmes pageant was never rejected by the town council, because individuals adapted to the rules of the possible, and if they did not do so of their own accord, the Kirmes committee headed by the lord mayor was there to oversee the programme and judge what would be permissible and what was not. The example of the Kirmes points to another important fact: the rules of engaging in Heimat activities did not just affect the relationship between individual communities and the party. Perhaps more important for these communities were experiences of organizing materials from the place of work, or from associated factories or agricultural cooperatives. Here, too, rules developed about what was permissible and what was not, a matter quite distinct from the question of what was legal and what was not.

The Mühlhausen example demonstrates a final crucial point. In the cultural sphere, the rules shifted and changed constantly, and they had to be learned not just by cultural activists, but also by the party. This process cannot really be described as one of 'negotiation', because the rules were set by the party. However, the party had conflicting interests, and these shifted over time. In the case of Mühlhausen, for instance, the party had an interest in ensuring that the cultural league managed to rally the intelligentsia in its club, as a form of integration and control. From time to time, the

---

46. Das Volk (Mühlhausen), 5 September 1967 ('Eine knappe Stunde Spaß').

47. Das Volk (Mühlhausen), 4 September 1969 (Anzeigenteil–Mühlhausen).

48. See, for instance, the festival's schedule in: *Das Volk* (Mühlhausen), 26 August 1970 (Anzeigenteil Mühlhausen); *Das Volk* (Mühlhausen), 19 August 1976 (Anzeigenteil–Mühlhausen).

county party secretary and the secretary for agit-prop had to decide which concessions to make in order not to endanger this aim of individual cultural engagement. In fact, as it was with the cultural league, so also was it with the Kirmes communities: every hour of an individual's commitment for the Heimat could be (and was) passed on by the local SED to the district as an example of socialist commitment. The SED, in other words, could and did try to impact upon cultural life, and, 'as a rule', it could forbid anything it wanted. However, if it aimed at fostering individual cultural activity while influencing it at the same time, it, too, had to learn how it could best achieve this in the face of constantly shifting political, personal, and material conditions.

Conclusion: Normalizing the Rules?

Günter Hauthal was in many ways the ideal type of a socialist enthusiast for the Heimat, who was committed to bringing the socialist perspective into the knowledge, reception, and practice of Heimat. Hauthal did not just have commitment; he also had energy and enthusiasm. Hauthal was not afraid to speak his mind, and did not hesitate to point to the shortcomings he witnessed in the transition of his local Heimat to socialism. However, neither these attributes, nor the additional support of the party, were sufficient to turn Altenburg into a socialist Heimat. For Hauthal to have had impact upon the way others related to their Heimat, it would have been necessary, apart from an ideological commitment, to relate to traditional local structures, form relationships, and make compromises. In fact, as Hauthal found out in the 1970s, local ties and structures proved much more enduring and important than party support, for local party hierarchies changed, bringing with them often abrupt changes in the interpretation of party guidelines, while local elites and structures transformed themselves much more gradually.

Jürgen Thormann was also an outsider in important respects. He did not have a university degree, and the fact that he was in the SED had clearly been an important factor in his selection to head a malfunctioning organization. Yet Thormann had grown up in the GDR, he had no reason to believe, as Hauthal had been perfectly entitled to assume, that a belief in socialism and in the party would guarantee success in the 'new Germany'. Thormann was successful because he shielded the cultural league members as much as possible from politics, while doing his utmost to conform to the rules of every-day local politics in style, language, and appearance. When a conflict of interest arose, Thormann sided with 'his' cultural league and not with the SED. He could be successful in encouraging Heimat activity amongst Heimat friends in the cultural league because he was accepted as 'one of them'.[49]

Thormann's success at influencing the cultural league in Mühlhausen and in encouraging a growing number of members to pursue the 'sensible use of free time' which the party proposed as its cultural ideal came at a price. Attempting to shield individuals meant, in effect, a surrender of the party's ultimate goal, to create socialist citizens not least through the ways in which these citizens spent their free time. This had been a price which Hauthal had never been prepared to pay. To Hauthal, exploring the socialist Heimat meant pursuing new themes for a newly dominant class. Hauthal was committed, in effect, to shaping a new memory based on remembering working class activists, and more generally the traditions of the working people, within the particular locality. From the late 1950s, Hauthal had to accept that he would not be able to pursue this commitment with other cultural league activists. Rather than submitting to the personal and ideological continuities among Altenburg Heimatfriends, Hauthal chose instead to go his own way, and stuck with his interests in working class history.

Thormann succeeded because he knew and applied his 'three golden rules' and many other rules besides. Yet the real art lay in knowing which rules to apply when, at what point to yield to political pressures, and when to resist. Learning the rules, and learning how to apply them, was a process that never ended. Hauthal confirms this from a very different perspective. Hauthal had a more difficult start than Thormann, because his 'founding generation' had no precedents that they could follow in their political and cultural engagements. At the same time, it is possible to see Hauthal's path as one of choosing which set of rules to follow. Having failed to make his mark within the Altenburg cultural league, Hauthal worked more closely on behalf of the SED during the 1960s. Following his disappointment by the local SED leadership, Hauthal managed, during the 1970s, to create a remarkably independent role for himself, until 1980, when he chose his new socialist Heimat, Altkirchen. There was, then, not just a set of rules to be learnt, but also a choice of rules that could be followed in the pursuit of Heimat activities.

---

49. The importance of this for successful cultural league activity on the ground was also underlined explicitly by another interview partner of mine, Gertrud Glandt, a successful and long-serving secretary of the cultural league in Rudolstadt County. Glandt was more ideologically committed to the state than Thormann (she was an evacuee from the Rhineland who, after the war, opted to stay in the GDR and joined the SED). Yet she, too, emphasized the importance of shielding 'her' members (*meine Leute*) from political pressure. Interview with Gertrud Glandt, 30 April 2003.

Beyond the comparison and contrast of Günter Hauthal and Jürgen Thormann, there are a number of observations that both activists and their respective environments suggest. The first is a distortion of national cultural politics, which often made it very difficult to discern what the rules in the locality were. To highlight but the two most obvious instances here. First, the concern by the Altenburg SED leadership about the ideological significance of Hauthal's work on the SPD, and its ban on the cultural monthly *Der Kulturspiegel* seems strikingly at odds with the cultural context of the early 1970s. Such ideological rigidity would not have been out of place from 1956, when work on the history of social democrats as part of working class history could be—and often was—attacked as 'revisionism'.[50] Moreover, the difficult decade for Heimat journals was the 1960s, when most of these publications were discontinued for economic and ideological reasons. From the early 1970s, by contrast, cultural Heimat activities became much more diverse, with a relaxation of attitudes that can be traced back to the growing demand for Heimat activites following the introduction of the five-day working week in 1966.[51] The early 1970s, indeed, are notable for the expansion of the concept of 'tradition' (*Erbe*) into the sphere of Heimat and popular culture. From 1974, the party encouraged individuals to explore local traditions in all of their richness and diversity. For the local SED to reject Hauthal's dissertation at precisely this point runs counter to contemporary GDR-wide trends.

Moreover, establishing a new festival culture was a hallmark of SED cultural politics during the 1960s. Mühlhausen was far from the only town in which a 'festival of socialist' joy was invented. However, for the county not to attempt to transform the Kirmes into the festival of socialist joy until 1969, and to hold on to this idea until the end of the following decade, is late to the point of apparent anachronism. Even in democratic centralism, then, local individuals filtered directives and laws from above according to local conditions, their own political and social networks, and their individual personalities.[52]

---

50. This happened, for instance, to Kurt Ludwig in Erfurt. As first secretary to the Erfurt district cultural league, Ludwig was Thormann's boss. In 1958, Ludwig drew the ire, among others, of Heinrich Gemkow.

51. On the fundamental importance of this event as a turning point in the organization of leisure, and the cultural significance of this, see Jan Palmowski, 'Regional Identities and the Limits of Democratic Centralism in the GDR', in Contemporary European History, 41 (2006), pp. 503–26. The significance of the introduction of the five-day working week is also highlighted in Esther von Richthofen's contribution to this volume.

52. An excellent introduction to the significance of the individual for local culture is Lu Seegers, '"Schaufenster zum Westen". Das Elbefest und die Magdeburger Kulturfesttage in den 1950er und 1960er Jahren.', in Adelheid von Saldern, *Inszenierte Einigkeit. Herrschaftsrepräsentationen in DDR-Städten* (Stuttgart: Franz Steiner Verlag, 2003), pp. 107–144.

This meant also, in the spheres of popular culture, that the transition from Ulbricht to Honecker was less marked than has often been asserted. It is true that the demand that the Heimat culture should reflect the diversity of local traditions set in from the 1970s, and by the early 1980s this had led to a genuine diversification of the ways in which the Heimat could be celebrated and discussed. At the same time, Günter Hauthal was frustrated, in the 1950s and the 1960s, precisely by the diversity of research into the history of the Heimat, which left so little room to concentrate on what he considered to be so essential for the socialist heimat, working class history. The ways in which the Heimat was experienced at the grassroots is better seen in terms of persisent evolution, rather than in terms of dramatic change.

A further point to emerge is the problematic nature of the term 'functionary' when it comes to the sphere of popular culture. This is because in this realm, the ideal was for individuals to engage in cultural activity themselves, and this is true for both cultural activity sponsored by the factory, as well as activity within the cultural league. Although Thormann was actually paid by the cultural league, cultural leaders at the village level, for instance, were not, and such activists at micro-level were crucial for the development of popular culture in their particular communities. In places like Altenburg, the development of Heimat activites, of hobby groups, choirs, or Heimat festivals were often the result not of the work of cultural functionaries, but of individual activists who, for a wide variety of motivations, became active on behalf of their communities, and of their Heimat.

It is helpful in many ways to consider this process of cultural activity in the GDR as one of learning the rules and learning how to apply them, particularly so if the rules included are informal and elastic. Basic rules were valid throughout the GDR: cultural activists anywhere would have done well to follow Thormann's three golden rules, and the other rules that existed in everyday life. If philatelists, ornithologists or anybody else conducted an exhibition, they had to acknowledge the politics of the GDR. Any pageant at a Heimat festival had to include references to the achievements of the socialist Heimat. And virtually any attempt to create a vibrant culture of the socialist Heimat in new towns was doomed to failure. Yet, in their application and elasticity, these rules varied according to the economic structure, the history, and the size of a locality. They differed in the way they were interpreted and applied through the individuals in any locality, both those in the local party hierarchy, and those active in popular culture.

If we consider cultural activism on behalf of the Heimat as being in part about learning and applying the rules, then this helps greatly to complicate our understanding of the GDR. It takes further the endeavour to explore the limits of power, of 'Herrschaft'.[53] Culture was, like politics and social policy, designed as an instrument of state power, a tool to help realize socialism in and through every human being. Looking at the putative protagonists of the socialist Heimat in their local environments allows one to observe the strength of social networks, of local pride, and traditions which were reconfigured over time, but which retained many of their pre–1949 features. The perspective of 'learning the rules' allows one to go one step further, and to try and determine more clearly the relationship between traditional norms and new rules, whether written or unwritten. And they allow one to explore the dynamics in this shifting relationship as the rules of cultural activity and cultural success changed constantly, over time and between locations.

At the same time, a focus on 'learning the rules' makes it more difficult to apply the concept of 'normalisation' to cultural activity, at least in the wide cultural realm that related to the socialist Heimat. There are three reasons for this. First, there is a definitional problem. On one level, Heimat activities may represent the ideal type of a desire to return to the way 'things used to be', and to represent how things 'ought to be'. And in many respects, this is a valid characterisation. Ornithologists wanted to watch their birds as they did before the war, free from political interference. The people of Mühlhausen wanted to celebrate their Kirmes just as they had done for over fifty years. However, the problem arises because such Heimat activities rarely existed in isolation. Ornithologists did not just watch birds, they also became upset at local pollution levels, and endeavoured to do something about this. Kirmes enthusiasts not only tried, on occasion, to complain about local issues, they were also greatly affected by local politics–the construction of new towns, for instance, destroyed entire Kirmes communities.[54] Engaging with the Heimat could thus never be simply about wishing to flee into the past, accepting the present, or wishing things were different. Put in these terms, Heimat activities were often linked to a respect for the past, they indicated an acceptance of the present, but they always also entailed a po-

---

53. On the concept of a 'durchherrschte Gesellschaft', see Alf Lüdtke, '"Helden der Arbeit"–Mühen beim Arbeiten. Zur mißmutigen Loyalität von Industriearbeitern in der DDR', in Hartmut Kaelble, Jürgen Kocka and Hartmut Zwahr, *Sozialgeschichte der DDR* (Stuttgart: Klett Cotta, 1994), here p. 188. See also Jürgen Kocka, 'Eine durchherrschte Gesellschaft', *op. cit.*, pp. 547–53.

54. Even such apparently stable forms of activity were subject to constant 'subversions' and challenges up to the end of the GDR's existence. Jürgen Thormann, himself part of a Kirmes community, remembered how in the late 1980s, his community contributed to the pageant a cart on the theme of the polluted air in Mühlhausen. They knew that this cart had no chance of being approved, so they did not submit the suggestion in the first place, but just 'snuck' in the cart as the pageant was on the way–an act that would have been inconceivable in earlier decades, but that reflects again how even in this most constant cultural activity that Mühlhausen had to offer, the rules were constantly learnt and tested for their elasticity.

tential challenge to the way things ought to be. The key analytical task lies in exploring the tension between these assumptions, and this cannot be done through a concept of normalisation that encompasses these dimensions in equal measure.

A second problem, beyond the definitional one, is the usage of the term by contemporaries as has been noted in other contexts. In around forty different interviews with cultural activists from nine different districts whose activities covered almost all of the areas of Heimat activity, I cannot recall a single respondent using the term of 'normality' or any derivative in any context. Other interviewers may have had different experiences, and it is likely that these depend upon the context in which individuals are approached. In my case, my interview partners had all taken some active stance towards the Heimat, and this is what I wanted to ask them about. The question as to whether their experience represented one of 'normality', or whether any particular activity within their range of experiences lent itself to the description of being normal, clearly did not arise to them. Since Heimat activities were about individual passions and the accentuation of local distinctiveness, the term 'normality' or 'normalisation' suggests itself neither from contemporary usage, nor from archival sources, nor from oral history interviews.

Finally, what is at issue is whether the 'normalisation' term passes the major litmus test for its usefulness as an analytical concept and its ability to allow us to see what we otherwise would not see. The problem is that in the sphere of Heimat, the normalisation concept obscures rather than enlightens. This may be different in other spheres of popular culture, such as the small gardeners' association. With regard to Heimat activities, there was never one period one could identify as something of an ideal-type framework for Heimat activity in the GDR. From the 1950s to the 1980s, the rules of engagement shifted constantly at the local, regional, and national levels, and these levels interacted with each other in different ways. The problem with an analysis of Heimat activities, of course, is that this is a category that denotes a very wide variety of interests, from philatelism to ornithology, from local history to environmental engagement. If one narrowed one's focus towards folklore dance groups or dialect speakers, for instance, one might well uncover relatively stable and conducive conditions for the activities of such enthusiasts from the late 1970s to the late 1980s. However, many of those who engaged in local folklore were also concerned about the preservation of their built environment, or the pollution of the natural environment. And in environmental questions, the attitude of the state and the conditions for individual activism changed quite dramatically in the same period. Throughout the existence of the GDR, the conditions under which Heimat activists pursued their hobbies constantly changed depending on

GDR-wide ideological, political, and economic shifts, local personalities and conditions, and the specific dynamic between GDR-wide and local developments. Heimat activists experienced their engagement in everyday life less in terms of a process of normalisation, but rather as activities that were subject to shifts and ruptures forcing them constantly to fine-tune and adapt their own responses.

Part II

Normalisation as Internalisation?

Conformity, 'Normality', and 'Playing The Rules'

Chapter 8

Practices of Survival—Ways of Appropriating 'The Rules': Reconsidering Approaches to the History of the GDR

Alf Lüdtke

How to Recognize Historical Dynamics?

The study of domination revolves around socio-political structures and processes. For decades, this polarity provided a firm basis for research on societal relations and transformations. Yet, efforts to relate both anew and to explore 'structuration' (Anthony Giddens, William H. Sewell) have broken new ground in their emphasis on the processual limits of stability in the realms of the social.[1] Still, even such refined versions of a *systemic view* also claim calculability for their results. The limits of this assumption became only too obvious when 'actually existing socialism' was overthrown and imploded in 1989/90, betraying all assumptions about its coherence and prospects. It is on this basis that a fresh look at the *potential of people to act (or not to act)* is needed. Whatever the take on historical actors is—systemic views frame them as reacting. They appear as

1. Anthony Giddens, New Rules of Sociological Method: a Positive Critique of interpretative Sociologies (London: Hutchinson. 1976), and Giddens, Central Problems in Social Theory: Action, Structure and Contradiction in Social Analysis (London: Macmillan, 1979); see also Mike Sewell, 'Three Temporalities: Toward an Eventful Sociology', in Terrence J. MacDonald, ed., The Historical Turn in the Human Sciences (Ann Arbor, 1996), pp. 245–80.

operating under 'constraints' or because incentives 'stimulate' their perceptions or actions (or both).

In particular, this perspective is blind to the 'inner face' of the practices people employ when coping with what they encounter day by day. Hence, such a view ignores the multi-facetted ways in which individuals or groups nuance, twist, or change what only too often appears as 'given'. Thus, the multiple forms of people's 'distancing' themselves openly or in a concealed manner remain out of sight, including the forms of breaking away or 'letting go'. Even more, systemic approaches do not render the dynamics of people's life-course, especially their ways of '*meandering*' between different if not antagonistic poles.

To turn this question around: how and why did people 'act' in the GDR? What were the settings from which they decided to 'voice' grievances or to 'exit'?[2] Did not most people in the 1960s and 1970s avoid this very choice under the impression of increasing 'normalisation'[3]? In other words, how should one account for both the *relative satisfaction* of the many and the *relative stability* of the GDR as a whole during the four decades prior to its implosion in 1989? How and to what avail did many people develop their own mode of '*Eigen-Sinn*'[4], whether silently or even conspicuously, for that matter? Such questions demarcate the task of restarting research. A fresh look at people's manifold practices would be a good beginning!

The effort to reconstruct 'normalisation' aims at bridging that gap. In particular, it is a question about forms and ranges of 'internalisation' of institutional settings, procedures, and modes of interpretation that people might have 'taken in' or internalised. Still, 'internalisation' operates on the level of society as a whole (as do the accompanying 'stabilisation' and 'routinisation'). And even if this view emphasises 'process', this emphasis remains framed by its bipolar mode. The quest is for mapping societal developments on a scale of 'more' or 'less'—for instance, 'more' routinisation in the treatment of citizen's grievances by state and party functionaries, and how this might affect the 'stabilisation' of rule.

---

2. Albert O. Hirschman, 'Exit, Voice, and the Fate of the German Democratic Republic: An Essay in Conceptual History', in World Politics 45 (1993): 173–202.

3. This was the main focus of several monographic studies on the GDR, which were discussed at the Erfurt conference in July 2005; see for the conceptual frame Mary Fulbrook, Normalisation: a contested concept (MS, 2005), also her book 'Anatomy of a Dictatorship. Inside the GDR 1949–1989 (Oxford: Oxford University Press, 1995).

4. Cf. Alf Lüdtke, Eigen-Sinn. Fabrikalltag, Arbeitererfahrungen und Politik vom Kaiserreich bis in den Faschismus. (Hamburg: Ergebnisse, 1993); Thomas Lindenberger, 'Herrschaft und Eigen-Sinn', in Lindenberger, ed., Herrschaft und Eigen-Sinn in der Diktatur (Köln: Böhlau Verlag, 1999).

Representations

The Impact of the 'Diagonal'

Representations of historical settings and practices relate the particulars of specific cases to notions (and images) that denote what is accepted as a general trend or profile. For instance, researchers take individual workers or, perhaps, workers' families as exemplary for a certain phase or feature of industrialisation, at least for the fate of a social entity such as class. In this effort, numbers seem imbued with a special power to demonstrate the plausibility of a certain point. Visual representations further enhance the truth-claim of these numbers. In other words, tables or graphs suggest the ultimate plausibility, even instantaneously, at one glance. By these tokens, one can convincingly 'show' the advancement of working people in industrialised societies–or, by contrast, the conjunctures of insecurity, if not misery.

Not only written printed texts or, for that matter, oral utterances, but also those tables and graphs revolve around the 'diagonal'. This 'diagonal' stands for and represents what emerges as a principal trend or a 'typical' profile of things or events. Such privileging of the diagonal also shapes the production and acceptance of pictorial representations. Amateur photographers perhaps even more than professionals preferred well-composed and 'nicely' arranged people for their portraits of individuals or groups. Social documentary photographers (to a large extent professionals) veered off from that practice. However, their critical takes on established visual as well as social conventions rarely reached a wider audience. Thus, both, the stills of photography and the moving images of film did not capture those moments that preceded and then followed the moment that is actually preserved in the picture, which preserves the split second when the shutter of the camera was opened. In other words, dynamics and what might be in stock or was a potential in and of that moment kept in the photographic or filmic representation remains strikingly absent, except for rare cases when pictures render a 'punctum'.[5]

Roland Barthes has made the point that some photographs contain elements, which disturb, if they do not actually destroy, the codes and efforts to present a standard or something typical. However, crucial in this argument is that such a 'punctum' is not a result of a determined framing or way of handling the camera by the photographer. On the contrary, this 'punctum' seems to sneak in whether the author of the representation wants it or not.

5. See on this Roland Barthes, *Camera Lucida*, (New York, 1980).

Thus, the question still remains open of how to reorganize and change the conceptual and methodical tools for enhancing the awareness and sensitivity for the potential, for the 'not yet' in a certain setting or activity.

As to the GDR, the 'diagonal' normativity as part of the 'public transcript' (James W. Scott[6]) provided space in a comparable way for certain deviant paths, at least for renderings of other people's ways of coping and self-willed activities. For instance, a company performance report of a department might read: 'Although youth brigade X is lacking in work discipline, the collective as a whole accomplished great success in increasing productivity and in presence on the job during official working hours'. In this very formulation, however, previous noncompliance to norms of discipline and keeping to the officially prescribed working hours is clearly noted; in fact, the continuation of such behaviour in the relevant youth brigade is not denied, but rather explicitly stated. Here, the general 'trend' of such behaviour, even if in the end overcome, provides the very space for alluding to what the official view only viewed as either not or no longer typical.

Acceptance and/or Accepting?

Interpretations of politics in modern societies, in particular in dictatorial regimes, tend to emphasise people's 'acceptance' or 'consent'; the other dimension of possibilities is marked by 'opposition' and 'resistance'. However, even the wording implies a stasis—a rather stable way of acting, particularly of granting loyalty or withholding it. The very terms signal predictable ways of acting. What remains out of sight is the potential of people to move between and even connect, for instance, accepting and distancing.

Therefore, I want to propose a shift not only in perspective, but also in the usage of respective terms and words—a switch to 'accepting' or (if it is a more active way of cooperation) perhaps of 'consenting'. Accordingly, 'distancing' and 'resisting' would operate in similar ways and refer to a multitude of tactics and their forms of behaviour (hidden, semi-hidden but also visible if not demonstrative). Still, it does not suffice to supplant substantives by verbs. The issue might not be exhausted by emphasising practices or their (again, assumed) matter-of-fact-way of doing them. In the 1970s and 1980s in Western societies, the many (the 'masses') tended to accept the given state of things. And in 'socialist' societies, people appeared to be acting in similar ways. Only in hindsight does the profile emerge of the gulf that separated 'Eastern' feelings of resignation or bitterness from those of 'Western'

6. James W. Scott, *Domination and the Arts of Resistance: Hidden Transcripts*, (New Haven/ London, 1990), pp. 4f, 25–28.

satisfied numbness. Can all of this be lumped together under the heading of 'acceptance' or accepting (or even of 'consent' or of 'consenting')? A closer look would undercut such grand but simultaneously flat notions. Only then would observers reckon for the GDR both a wide variety of modes of coping with if not supporting the 'powers that be', *and also* of resigning and 'giving in', and of distancing *and* (occasionally, at least) of withholding or denying support. Whichever way people acted and behaved, they did things 'their way'–they concomitantly entertained highly individualised sets of feelings.

(Re)Capturing Everydayness: 'Inadequate but Indispensable' Notions (Dipesh Chakrabarty)?

Was it wishful thinking (or, for that matter, wishful advertising) when in 1978 the West German Deutsche Verlagsanstalt advertised the West German edition of Erich Loest's *Es geht seinen Gang oder Mühen in unserer Ebene* to its West German readers: 'This novel is surprising precisely in the degree to which so little of it is surprising for us. Certainly we learn lots of new things about everyday life in the GDR. However, this is shown so much 'von Mensch zu Mensch', that everyday life as well as the wishes and also the toil of the common man reflects itself in the everyday life, the longings and the toil of people here [West Germany] and, thus, can be instantly understood'.

This blurb on the book's back cover does resonate, of course, with the gist of Western social science research of that time. Peter Christian Ludz and his team underlined for the GDR the interrelationships of industrialisation, societal modernisation, and–as an aspired final result–the possibilities for democratisation of the GDR. Contemporary political rhetoric could easily be filled in. Still, however, is this claim of increasing similarity if not identity of East and West German settings, practices, and, perhaps, emotions a point in case of 'normalisation' in both respects–more 'normal' rules, but also more 'normal', that is, semi-autonomous handling of the rules by the majority of the people?

In order to investigate this issue, central dimensions of East German society ought to be demarcated. I restrict myself to three aspects I find 'characteristic' of the GDR, chosen more or less at randomly. The necessary comparison to Western or capitalist and also to other socialist / East European societies can only be mentioned here.

1) The growing impact of repression on society as a whole during the history of the state. This is certainly a trait of the GDR appearing in hindsight in a new light, at least to most observers. The strengthening of state violence,

and in particular the ever more present interventions of its various 'organs' as documented in the growth of MfS surveillance, especially from the early 1970s onwards; both were thoroughly underrated by most Westerners in the 1960s and 1970s. This holds for the application of brute force in its various forms, and is evident in the observable boost given to police measures against those who were viewed as 'a-socials' from the late 1960s. One has to include the harsh measures of incarceration of suspects and convicts alike, from long sentences to rude treatment, and also the high presence of military force and violence on many levels from the party rhetoric to its imminent presence at the border to the West, with force not only designed but applied in order to kill. However, the disciplinary furor of and within institutions, and in almost all spheres and arenas of society, did not stop here. The wider emphasis on stressing 'good order' and 'orderliness' in obviously almost all settings, including niches, have to be included too.

2) The emphasis on and multiple meanings of work and working, as has been repeatedly emphasised, and rightly so.
3) Rarely mentioned but almost ever present in people's everyday lives: the aesthetics of public space. Such 'greyness', however, also pervaded many tangible and palpable items that people acquired for their household or leisure time, as particularly visitors from the 'West' lamented over and over again. Still, citizens of the GDR themselves had similar concerns. And a number of them relentlessly tried to stem the tide and to contribute to improvement in these fields, some of them by joining official campaigns as those for public beautification ('*Verschönerung unserer Städte und Dörfer–Mach mit!*')

In such interpretive efforts one issue should, however, not go unnoticed; the significant distance of today's observers from the settings of pre–1989 GDR. To what extent do the notions of current researchers capture the specifics of experiences and practices—the 'inner face', as people who lived inside the GDR saw and tasted it? In other words: how to account for the scale of, for instance, 'order' or 'beauty' that people applied 'then' and 'now'? While difference here seems difficult to discern—what made a term like 'career' sound so starkly different for Westerners and Easterners? This is about 'making' the socio-political 'systems' in both East and West Germany into specific entities, turning them from a mere 'being' into respective trajectories: on both sides, generational dynamics had an enormous impact and contributed towards extending what was 'orderly' or 'beautiful' from the 1950s to the 1980s. Here, one might find a parallel to the puzzle Dipesh Chakrabarty stated in his 'Provincializing Europe': 'Western categories' prove 'inadequate but indispensable'.[7]

7. Dipesh Chakrabarty, *Provincializing Europe* (Princeton, 2000), p. 19.

Against this background: do the notions that we nowadays employ in our research on the GDR capture the experiences and practices people aimed at or aspired for? Do words such as 'order' or 'beauty' denote the same–do they, at least, refer to similar experiences and imaginaries of reality? More generally: do the *'Western' concepts* suffice? At this point I have to resort to Dipesh Chakrabarty's remark that 'western categories' are '*indispensable* and inadequate'.

Practices of Work–and Their Emotional Charges

The 'hero of work' was one, if not *the,* pivotal figure, especially in the first years of the Soviet Occupation Zone (SBZ) and GDR. On the level of propaganda and rhetoric, the Soviet model was certainly a central blueprint. However, engrained in the notion of society and politics that had dominated the socialist and communist workers' movements since the late nineteenth century was the energetic, muscular male figure, aspiring for a better future, who embodied the anti-bourgeois or proletarian hero of history. In the concrete setting of 1945, the shock of violence and the ensuing rubble, turmoil, and forced mass migration, as well as the terrifying pictures and accounts from the extermination and concentration camps, occupied people's mind and hands. Thus, reorganising production in agriculture and industry had absolute priority in order to give people a chance of survival. Campaigns for getting people back to work, if not to steady work, prevailed in all four zones of Allied occupation.[8]

Under the leadership of the SED, local functionaries as well as union activists called for increasing and sustained 'activism' on the part of all of the people working in their respective jobs. Reports about the narrow limits of such actions were abandoned. The complaints emphasise that in contrast to good old working class traditions, the emphasis on doing 'a good job' and being a 'quality worker' obviously had no meaning any more. People strove to get by, whether or not they ransacked the company and took away supplies–in the views of the party activists, nobody seemed to care. Campaigns like the one organised around the miner Adolph Hennecke (in October 1948) failed to stem the tide. This and other campaigns got a cold if not often hostile reception. Still, the official efforts did not stop or slow down: campaigns to honour Hennecke and other 'activists of work' were regular

8. See for a general account of the East German economy André Steiner, *Von Plan zu Plan: eine Wirtschaftsgeschichte der DDR* (Munich: DVA, 2004); for the aftermath of the war, Rainer Gries, *Die Rationen-Gesellschaft: Versorgungskampf und Vergleichsmentalität*, Leipzig, München und Köln nach dem Kriege (Münster, 1991).

features, as were competitions. And it fitted this strategy perfectly that outstanding performers were honoured as 'heroes of work' (those honoured received a bonus as well as a medal and media attention).[9]

Of course, it was a protest against another attempt to push up norms by official decree that triggered first a strike and, then, direct action against state and party authorities. Public protest rapidly spread on 16, 17, and 18 June 1953, not only in cities and towns, but also in the countryside. Although the party stepped back and signalled a new attentiveness to consumers' needs, it did not change its policy of preferring production over consumption, in particular heavy industry and its output. Let us finally consider five individual examples (or individual cases):

Demystifying Heroism

It is against this background that contemporary literary authors took up the issue. Many of them had themselves participated in campaigns to boost production and productivity.[10] The young writer Brigitte Reimann addressed the topic in this context. She, however, chose a different take: in her *Ankunft im Alltag* (published in 1961), she presented a story and portrayed the interactions of the leading figures of this book, set in one of the large construction sites where the 'new cities' materialised in oftentimes hard and strenuous work. Here she presented views of, in particular, young working people who in different ways deviated from the prevailing emphasis on heroising work and workers.

The title of Reimann's book, 'Arrival in the Everyday', demarcated a stance that differed generationally from the experiences of those who had designed and directed the first steps (and years) of what they claimed to be the 'New Germany' in the GDR. In her fictitious treatment of work in a lignite processing plant, Brigitte Reimann directly addresses the need to de-heroise perceptions and accounts of work (of course, at stake is toilsome manual labour). As they watch the sun rise on a cold winter morning after a long 'special shift', the young worker, Nikolaus, blushing somewhat towards the end of his reflections, comments to his friend Recha that what surprised him most was the:

---

9. See on this Alf Lüdtke, 'Helden der Arbeit'–Mühen beim Arbeiten. Zur missmutigen Loyalität von Industriearbeitern in der DDR, in Hartmut Kaelble, J. Kocka, H. Zwar, eds., *Sozialgeschichte der DDR* (Stuttgart: Klett-Cotta, 1994), pp. 188–213; Peter Hübner, 'Die Zukunft war gestern: soziale und mentale Trends in der DDR-Industriearbeiterschaft', in Kaelble, *Sozialgeschichte der DDR*, pp. 171–87; *Parteiauftrag: ein neues Deutschland. Bilder, Rituale und Symbole der frühen DDR* (Munich, 1996).

10. Among them were people who were by no means just propagandists such as, for instance, Franz Fühmann who contributed in the late 1950s *Kabelkran und blauer Peter* (Rostock, 1961).

> sheer ordinariness of the whole affair... No, it was not at all dramatic or romantic or anything, and certainly no-one felt himself to be a hero. They work through the night and make a gift to the state of several thousand tons of good coal, and afterwards they go and drink a beer and talk about dripping taps.... But it is, after all, something special... one feels as if one had done something special; don't you think?... One has to correct one's idea of heroism.[11]

Workers' Honour

In December 1962, some SED-activists in the *VEB Kombinat Werkzeugmaschinenbau '8. Mai'* noted self-critically in an internal report their scepticism about their coworkers in showing very unheroic behaviour. What the activists found particularly lacking was any sense among most colleagues that it would be 'normal' and necessary to work regularly. Instead, they observed widespread failure to understand basic needs of regular and well established 'rules for and of *normal work*' (not the least directly affecting one's wages, as one of the authors sarcastically added!). And those already trained prior to 1945 had 'mostly forgotten' (in the first draft the author had written 'totally forgotten') the 'extent to which they had devoted much of their energy in achieving higher quality work in the capitalist era'. However, in socialist times that kind of enforced self-regulation did not operate any longer. Hence 'some' (the first draft had 'all') disrespected the 'law of quality work'.

What had to be done? The '*proper worker's honour*' could only be re-established if everyone would be careful, for instance, in connecting pipes or handling tools when adjusting screws properly; such were basic characteristics of proper working. In addition, the authors called for everyone to pitch in and to clean up his workplace upon leaving, just as he had to return tools: *good order and reliability* were the main clues they emphasised.

The irony is that it was precisely this situation that had stimulated SED-functionaries to invite literary authors and other people from the arts to get actively involved with workers and to give artistic accounts of their strivings!

'Flyerin': a Female Worker in the Eichsfeld

Biographical accounts allow us to pursue individuals and trace their behaviour over time. It is especially important to explore the range of articulations and forms of behaviour. Only then is it possible to understand

11. Brigitte Reimann, *Ankunft im Alltag*, (Berlin: Verlag Neues Leben, 1961), p. 212 (translation by MF).

the ways of appropriating specific settings or 'the rules', at least by specific individuals.

I am thinking of E. B., who was born in 1921 in a small village between Worbis and Leinefelde in the only overwhelmingly Catholic patch in East Germany, the Eichsfeld. She was married to a small farmer whom she married in 1946, she became mother to eleven children and in 1962 (one year after her tenth child was born) she followed the call for workers at the newly established cotton-spinning factory at Leinefelde. Here, she advanced rapidly and became one of the workers who had to train incoming young women (thus, she was not a brigadier, but did fulfil this specific task of training others). She was officially represented in December 1963 as one of those staunch supporters of the socialist state and its programme of industrialising.

When I interviewed her in 1999, she *proudly* told stories of her work, and how well she and her colleagues had got along, at least most of the time. Still, from the late 1970s her wage was cut back, and she lost that job she liked so much (namely the training of incoming new workers). She obviously left the company for good prior to retirement—but she returned to the small plot in the context of a LPG almost one hour by bus away from the company: she devoted *cheerfully* much of her energies to what she had already done before—writing stories in *Plattdeutsch* and, even more, composing an immense chronicle of her life.

Had she ever participated in a political action? Well, she had seen and liked Hitler, she told me. So, what about politics later on, I asked. She shrugged and did not elaborate.

The Engineer—the Loner: Reputation Paid

D. V. was an engineer who had graduated from a *Fachschule* (Nordhausen) in the mid 1970s.[12] After leaving school at the age of 16, he had started as an apprentice in a motor repair workshop in the city of Erfurt, close to his home village. After having completed this stint, he did his military service and upon his return, in 1963, he started to work for a local repair unit, the machine and tractor lending station (*Maschinentraktorenstation*), which was responsible for maintaining the moving gear and heavy machinery for working the land and especially its engines. This was either a one-person job or, at most, he accompanied a colleague or was accompanied by a colleague.

12. See on this case my piece, 'Meister der Landtechnik oder Grenzen der Feldforschung? Annäherungen an einen "Qualitätsarbeiter" auf dem Lande im Bezirk Erfurt', in Daniela Münkel, Jutta Schwarzkopf, eds., *Geschichte als Experiment. Studien zu Politik, Kultur und Alltag im 19.und 20. Jahrhundert. Festschrift für Adelheid von Saldern* (Frankfurt/New York, 2004), pp. 243–57.

Since D. V. was intensely engaged with his job and was obviously 'good at it', there were no problems with his non-participation in social work or '*gesellschaftliche Arbeit*'; in the union, he remained passive. Repeatedly, he made the point that he had withstood numerous efforts to recruit him for the '*Betriebskampfgruppe*'. In fact, in interviews I did in the late 1990s, he complained furiously about those 'incompetent lazy boys' who sneaked away under the pretence of doing 'socio-political work', but, in fact, simply took a break and enjoyed the company of buddies and, not least, some beer and hard liquor. Still, our man was 'delegated' to *Fernstudium* (a distance learning course) for engineers, which he successfully completed in the early 1970s. He was then promoted to become the leading mechanic of the moving gear in cooperatives in the whole district of Erfurt.

In this new capacity he was, again, working basically on his own. In particular, he was responsible for maintaining and solving guarantee claims for tractors built in the Soviet Union, Czechoslovakia, and Romania. Thus, his job had an international dimension. This was challenging and rewarding at the same time. The challenge came from the different technical standards and, in particular, the lack of proper information to prepare him for his task. But he had learned to cope with inadequate supplies and information, and since he obviously managed well, he got 'reward trips' to visit the respective companies, which he obviously enjoyed and was visibly proud of, both at the time as well as in hindsight.

This was in many ways a rather straight line: the pursuit of engaging oneself with one's work and task. Here, he relied on his own experiences and dexterity, but also on networks of colleagues in the neighbourhood and afar (in most districts of the GDR and even reaching beyond the borders, although still within the Soviet block). Still, whether D. V. 'internalised' any of the specific goals the SED offered or propagated seems rather unlikely.

Working as an IM–the Craze of Writing?

This particular person I got to know through the lenses of *Stasi* files. Upon searching for Stasi surveillance in industry, a two-volume file turned up labelled 'Harry Baumgarten'. As usual, the file included the CV of this man by the name of T. He was born in 1948 in Leipzig in a 'worker's family', as one of the assessments noted.[13] However, in another file someone else had remarked that T. had not known his parents and had grown up with a foster mother. Whether he had trained as a mill hand or an electrician remains unclear (two different reports mention either one). After completion,

13. BStU Außenstelle Leipzig, AIM 227/92, Bl. 159.

in 1965, he had volunteered for the riot police (*Bereitschaftspolizei*), but was dismissed five years later for disciplinary reasons (which were not specified in these reports). However, during his stint with the police, he had become a member of the SED and had also begun to cooperate with the secret police or MfS. This cooperation T. carried on when he got a job as a turner in a machine construction shop in Leipzig. From then on he regularly reported on his superiors and mates. The summary report of 1979 commented on the 'disciplined way' T. had worked for the MfS for (at least) eleven years, and that he 'was fully reliable in his cooperation with the MfS'. The file also testified to the range and intensity of his cooperation: T. had reported continuously. He met his liaison officer every week (or every fortnight). He obviously also regularly wrote reports himself, sometimes half a page in long hand, but often, however, two or three pages.

Is this not a rather straightforward case? Someone who tried 'to make do' and 'get by', thereby making use of possibilities to make some extra money. But the cooperation with the MfS also provided more: constant recognition by the respective liaison officer, and occasionally, by his superiors as well. Of course, the writing testified also to the sense of T. that he had some 'influence'. While reading his reports, I could not help but get the impression that it might not be primarily what he reported that mattered to T. It seems that at least as important for him was—to do this writing. Did he 'internalise' workings of state and party by his doings?

Afternote:

What do these individual cases show? First, I want to underline the fact that these examples are chosen at random. I have not done any systematic scrutiny in a wider array of similar materials. On the contrary, I found them during the vagaries of doing research in archives and among those who were ready to testify on 'their' past. Thus, these vignettes bear every mark of the irregularities that cannot be detached from 'tracing' the past. In other words, this is nothing but a case of ordinary research.

Still, cases like the ones outlined here allude to the room for manoeuvre which, at least, these particular individuals recognised or, to some extent, seized and shaped, if they did not actually create, by the way they went about the tasks they wanted or had to fulfil. By this token, these cases reference the multiple techniques and styles of pursuing 'projects of one's own'. They also reveal the enormous range of viewpoints and temporalities that people pursued, obviously at the 'same time'. Moreover, however, they serve to illustrate encounters and practices in and through which people not only survived, but also gained satisfaction, if not pleasure. In all of these cases, people cooperated with given settings, if not with the powers that be. In one way or another, they cooperated with authorities and policies of the GDR, and not just the informal informant to the Stasi, but also the worker in the spinnery or the mechanical engineer in the countryside. In fact, it was less a matter of direct cooperation, but rather the striving of the many to do a good if not better job. Their energy and, to some extent, their enthusiasm in 'not giving up' at work served to sustain if not propel the existing socio-political order of the GDR.

However, in what ways and to whom such forms of behaviour can be rendered as 'normalisation' is, at least in my view, impossible to ascertain. To turn this around: since these cases can be summed up as examples of 'normalisation' notwithstanding their stark differences, the question returns: what, then, does 'normalisation' actually reveal about historical actors and both their ways of behaving and of making sense of what they did or tried to do?

Chapter 9

The GDR—A Normal Country in the Centre of Europe[1]

Ina Merkel

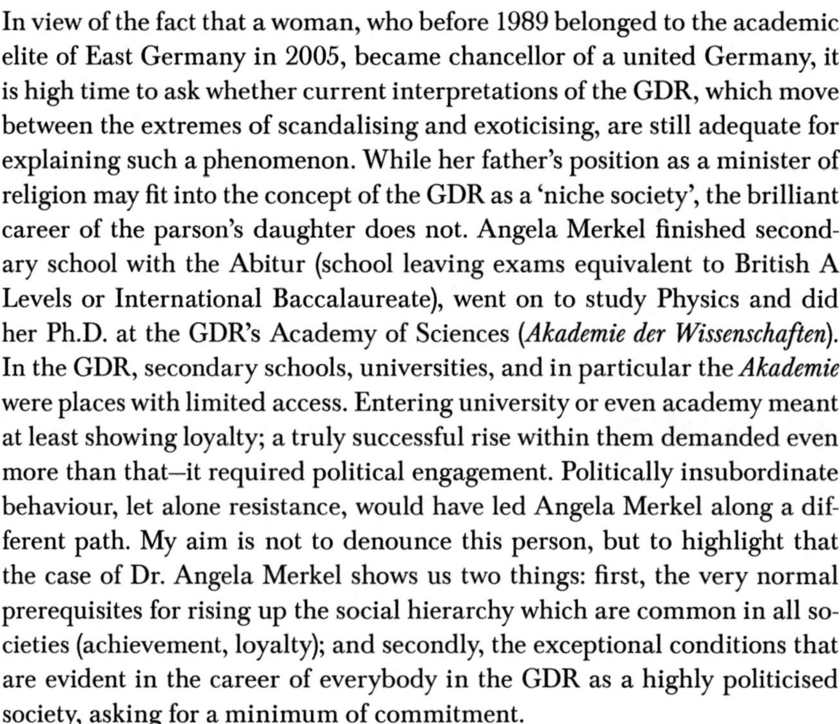

In view of the fact that a woman, who before 1989 belonged to the academic elite of East Germany in 2005, became chancellor of a united Germany, it is high time to ask whether current interpretations of the GDR, which move between the extremes of scandalising and exoticising, are still adequate for explaining such a phenomenon. While her father's position as a minister of religion may fit into the concept of the GDR as a 'niche society', the brilliant career of the parson's daughter does not. Angela Merkel finished secondary school with the Abitur (school leaving exams equivalent to British A Levels or International Baccalaureate), went on to study Physics and did her Ph.D. at the GDR's Academy of Sciences (*Akademie der Wissenschaften*). In the GDR, secondary schools, universities, and in particular the *Akademie* were places with limited access. Entering university or even academy meant at least showing loyalty; a truly successful rise within them demanded even more than that—it required political engagement. Politically insubordinate behaviour, let alone resistance, would have led Angela Merkel along a different path. My aim is not to denounce this person, but to highlight that the case of Dr. Angela Merkel shows us two things: first, the very normal prerequisites for rising up the social hierarchy which are common in all societies (achievement, loyalty); and secondly, the exceptional conditions that are evident in the career of everybody in the GDR as a highly politicised society, asking for a minimum of commitment.

The quest for discovering the connection between the common and the exceptional is also an integral part of the normalisation concept developed

1. Discussion paper. Translated from the German by Esther von Richthofen.

by Mary Fulbrook and her colleagues. Using this as an ideal type, any historical episode or period can be analysed by looking for both general developments and exceptional moments. Similarities and differences between societies or nations can be interpreted as different solutions to one and the same problem. They no longer need to be measured according to a given or a dominant norm. Stabilisation, routinisation, and internalisation are the prerequisites for supporting and upholding every functioning system. Such a set of conceptual categories opens up new possibilities for interpreting the GDR in two directions.

The first point I want to make here is that we should stop looking at the GDR in isolation as a self-contained society, but look at it rather in the context of post-war European modernisation. That requires analysing the GDR in relation to the macro-structures of broader social orders (Europe, industrial societies, etc.), as well as enquiring about the role of 'circulating cultural meanings, objects and identities', cultural transfers, and exchange processes under the conditions set by the Cold War and the Berlin Wall.[2] (Most historical analyses regard the GDR as an autarchic, self-contained structure. There are, for example, analyses of GDR art, DEFA films, GDR rock music, but neither artists nor GDR citizens ever went to the cinema exclusively, or even uniformly, to watch DEFA films.)

Secondly, I understand the everyday actions of individuals as a process of negotiation, which cannot be satisfactorily described in terms of the extremes of conformity and resistance. Society is a lived web of interconnections among individuals, imbued with different meanings. The system of norms and values representing the basic pattern and order of these interconnections does not define the particular meanings, but is, so to speak, a resource for individuals to draw on when attributing potential significance to individual meanings. It is open to interpretation. This ambiguity enables the members of a society to participate in different aspects simultaneously. They situate themselves in this field of forces up to the point where their own cultural interests are concerned. Everyday culture is the ability to make do with what is there–it is a creative process.[3] This is where the question

2. I am referring to the concept of a 'multi-sited ethnography', which was developed in George E. Marcus, 'Ethnography in/of the World System: The Emergence of Multi-Sited Ethnography', in *Annual Review of Anthropology* 24(1995): 95–117. The point of departure here is that the distinction between 'system' and 'life-world' can no longer be sustained, which means that ethnography, which focuses on the local, can also no longer be sustained. Every closed perspective should be abandoned in favour of new approaches that search for connections, relations, links, and could expand that part of traditional ethnography focusing on agency, symbols, and practices of everyday life.

3. Michel de Certeau, *Die Kunst des Handelns* (Berlin, 1988); John Fiske, *Understanding Popular Culture* (London/Sydney/Wellington, 1989); see also the debates about 'doing gender' and performativity.

arises of how (GDR)-society is created and how it is normalised so that a belief in its unchanging nature emerges. Individuals do two things at the same time: they create or reproduce the social structures, and within these structures, they fashion their very own lives.

Historical societies are always analysed and described from the viewpoint of the respective situation of the present. Contemporary conditions (federal German, European) have been in a fundamental state of change since 1989. No matter whether this state of change is described as the dissolution of bipolarity, as the collapse and transformation of socialist society, as the transition into a 'second modernity', or as an erosion of a workers' society, changing contemporary conditions alter the need for historical interpretations. Hitherto dominant West German interpretations—dictatorship and modernisation theories—cannot permanently claim to be valid within united Germany. This is not only because these interpretations exercised hegemonic interpretative dominance over the Eastern part, but also because the old Federal Republic is changing fundamentally. New perspectives on GDR history are emerging, which is also the case with the normalisation concept under discussion here.

The new questions emerging in relation to the history of the GDR—this small, poor country with its short lifespan—reflect issues that are currently being discussed under the heading of a *second*, or *reflexive*, modernity.[4] The essence of this debate is the assumption that today's 'late industrial societies' are experiencing radical changes (individualisation and globalisation). These changes are accompanied by an erosion of old certainties, such as the 'taken for granted nature' of economic growth and technological progress and the dissolution of borders of nation states along with their inherent securities (the end of the society of work, the failure of family models, the new fragility of social conditions, fragmented identities, and so on). Basic principles of action consequently have to be renegotiated or refounded, both in general terms and in specifics. The central question is how social security, identity, and democracy are possible beyond full-time employment.

Beck and collaborators characterise the 'first' modernity, which attempted to offer precisely that degree of security and probably did offer it periodically in certain national societies, as half-modern, mixed-modern societies. Thus, we are dealing with structures made up from modern elements that are combined and merged with elements of counter-modernity. This applies to all industrial societies, including those in the socialist camp, though with a different mélange—and one worth analysing. The concept of

4. Ulrich Beck, Anthony Giddens, and Scott Lash, *Reflexive Modernisierung. Eine Kontroverse* (Frankfurt M., 1996).

a 'second modernity' therefore offers a starting point that transcends the polarities of capitalism and socialism, the two political camps, and could restore the interdependence and correlation between the two, though without becoming universalist.

Ultimately, the concept of a second modernity means questioning the very notion of our own society as a western, modern industrial society. Western development can no longer be seen as normative. The hegemonic notion of interpretative supremacy in contrast to other developments can no longer be sustained. This means that an already pre-interpreted historical field is once again opened up for discussion.

Understanding the GDR as part of the 'first' modernity makes it possible to contextualise it as a moment in world history and as integrated into European and global developments, and to cease to treat it as an autarchic, self-contained construction that can only be comprehended in terms of its own particularities (scandalous, exotic). Conceptualising the GDR as a 'completely normal' European country, a 'half-modern' industrial society, does not overlook its special characteristics (secret police/ *Stasi*, repressive political system, command economy, and so on), but declares these characteristic elements to be particular solutions to general questions that were also evident in other European countries of that time.

The central questions of these years were how to attain the peaceful coexistence of peoples after destructive war and inhuman genocide, how Germans could live with shame and disgrace, and how a renewed upsurge of aggression and violence could be prevented. The GDR's answer was to embark on a route of expropriation, dictatorship of the proletariat, and state socialism. Western nations chose democracy, the public sphere and social free-market economy. However, they shared the idea of creating wealth through work and industrialisation.

Cultural Transfer in the Context of the Wall

Post-war modernity was characterised by the development of an incredible mobility of people, goods, and ideas across given national borders, and special limitations regarding system boundaries. After 1961 GDR citizens were no longer able to enter western countries.

Apart from the fact that the Wall entailed a very real borderline, it had different meanings for different generations, for different social environments, for East and West Germans. It did not simply shut out the world; rather, it gave it a very special meaning. In terms of the normalisation concept under discussion here, the building of the Wall was for some people a political and economic necessity, and for others it was scandalous. While people born until 1961 could decide whether to stay or leave, generations who were young in the 1970s (that is, the birth cohorts of 1955 to 1965) grew up with an insurmountable state border. This age group was used to the Wall as simply being there. The existence of the Wall was an accustomed normality. But what are we to make of that? Even if the Wall could definitely not be crossed, it was nonetheless imagined as surmountable. The Wall was one form of normality. Modernity, which includes the free transgression of borders, was another. How can we relate these two competing normalities to one another, and what did that entail for an individually lived 'normal' life and for images of normality? Did they coexist next to one another, did they accommodate themselves to each other, or were they mutually exclusive? How was the Wall incorporated into everyday behaviour?

On the one hand, the Wall meant shutting out the western world; but on the other hand, it also meant precisely the opposite, namely permanent virtual transgressions of the border. The emigration of people, experiences, goods, and ideas determined life in the GDR in a decisive manner. Because of the Wall, those objects, people, ideas, metaphors, plots, and so on that did manage to cross it attained a very special meaning.[5]

Cultural exchange has so far barely been examined, and if at all, then only in terms of the cultural hegemony of Americanisation in the West and Sovietisation in the East. But how can we grasp cultural transfer, cultural exchange, and so on in the normalisation concept? To begin with, it is necessary to see the GDR as a sovereign state, and to ask in this context what goods, ideas, and people could legally cross the border and were even politically encouraged to do so, and which parts of the outside world could therefore be publicly present in the GDR.

Looking at the example of cinema in the GDR, it is noticeable that—aside from the dominance of Soviet and Eastern European films—modern European films from Scandinavia, Italy, France or Great Britain were very present. They often entered the cinemas in synchrony only a few months after their original release date. Popular American cinema arrived in the GDR in the form of a few selected films that appeared some years after their original release, but were sometimes shown for years on end to a never tiring public. This was certainly not merely the result of the restrictive policy relating to film and cinema, but also of the perpetually precarious foreign currency situation. The GDR's policy of international cultural exchange paid

5. Compare Ina Dietzsch, *Grenzen überschreiben? Deutsch-deutsche Briefwechsel 1948–1989* (Köln/Weimar/Wien, 2004).

most attention to other 'culturally marginalised' societies in Eastern Europe or other new nation states. These were wooed, made visible, and made accessible to the East German public. From an official perspective, it was a matter of a consciously selected section of the world, which, however, was very quickly and irreversibly contradicted by Western television. In the perfectly normal process of globalisation, goods, ways of life, values, and news crossed the borders of the GDR, where they took on a life of their own, since individuals appropriated them according to their own needs, norms, and principles. The world was present even in the GDR, and here it unleashed yearnings, comparisons, and dreams.

Aside from the virtual experiences of the world, there were also real encounters in the form of travel (even for a few–travel overseas, work-related trips), visitors (relatives, artists, sports teams, politicians, business people, and so on) and events (Leipzig trade fair, World Festivals, documentary film festivals, etc.). In the perceptions of foreigners–relatives, Western television, and radio commentaries, etc.–life in the GDR was reflected in a particular way. Encounters with strangers have consequences for one's perception of oneself. The Other functions as a mirror in which one can perceive and understand the Self quite differently. In these encounters, a conception of normality is developed.

In the mentalities of everyday life, normality appears as a relational and evaluating concept. This means that a given situation is seen as different, deviant or uncomfortable–in short, deficient–when opposed to other historical or social situations or desirable conditions. The concept of normality is therefore first of all based on a comparison: a comparison with the past, with other societies, with cultures or ideals. The fact that it is a relational concept means that it inevitably entails notions of comparison and of measurement. These notions are not permanent and unchanging, but are always filled with new, concrete historical contents. There is no universally applicable anthropological scale of measurement against which circumstances can be measured and assessed in terms of their normality. And no measure can be applied to a society from outside. (What is normal from a Western European perspective does not necessarily apply to Eastern European situations.)

Conceptions of normality are formed not only by one's own experiences and through the tales of older generations; rather, real experiences (of things or people) and virtual experiences of other worlds (stories, films, music, etc.) also play a significant role. Standards for one's own life are derived here, and on occasion, articulated. Clothing styles play an important role here as well.

Wearing jeans, for example, was a way of symbolising border transgression. Young people in the GDR wore jeans to show that they belonged to universal youth. The desire to own a pair of genuine jeans and to wear them in public, for example, in school, should not in the first instance be interpreted as a provocative demonstration against the 'socialist way of life', but could rather be seen simply as an expression of young people's conception of normality, namely that they could also wear an article of clothing that was seen as modern 'everywhere'. In the 1960s, this was still regarded as problematic (evidence of Western attitudes and hence hostile); in the 1970s, in the context of attempts at internationalisation (international recognition), jeans were regarded as 'normal'; and in the 1980s, Honecker had them imported into the GDR. Whereas the youth of the 1960s had to endure the contradiction between the Wall as segregation and wearing jeans as virtual transgression of the border, the youth of the 1970s could regard this contradiction as having been negotiated, and the youth of the 1980s interpreted the importing of jeans as an anticipated crossing of the border in the foreseeable future.

Popular culture—the ways in which people use, reject, and subvert cultural-industrial products and thus create their own meanings and messages—always contains marks of power relations, traces of the dominant and subordinate forces that are so central to each social system and to social experiences therein. At the same time, it contains signs of resistance or evasion. The power of popular culture lies in the negative, in the capacity to use jeans in the 1960s to transgress boundaries and thus to express opposing social values. A society's popular culture not only provides insights into competing norms and values, but also material which one can interrogate as to how individuals give significance to this 'text' for their own conceptions of their lives.

It is in the essence of popular culture to transgress boundaries, it includes visions of different ways of life, it provokes comparisons with one's own life, and offers material for desires and dreams. These are not necessarily directed at escaping from one's own world—they can also facilitate a form of arrangement with it, or even make it possible in the first place. The presence of the outside world and of globalisation processes is not something external or foreign, but rather was inherent within life in the GDR. The questions of how the world was incorporated into the GDR, how it was present, and how it was appropriated, are in my opinion highly interesting topics for analysis that could help to rescue the GDR from its special status.

The GDR as a Negotiated Society—Conceptions of Normality

A second dimension of normality can be determined when looking at everyday life: namely, normality as 'unquestioned naturalness' (*Selbstverständlichkeit*), or, to put it differently, normality as habitual actions. Mary Fulbrook uses the terms stabilisation, routinisation, and institutionalisation to discuss this naturalness at a societal-institutional level. These terms primarily evaluate the capacity of individuals to live their lives under particular circumstances. Following the theories of Michel de Certeau, this could also be understood as the 'art of action', in other words, as the ability of individuals to 'make the best' of given conditions and circumstances, or as creativity and innovation in negotiating social relations. It is the question of how society is not just endured by individuals, but rather is negotiated and formed by them, and ultimately, is made by them.

In such a concept, the question of the limits of Ulbricht's and Honecker's power is not just posed at the level of structures and reduced to the dichotomy of authority and resistance, but rather is seen as the outcome of processes of negotiation. It is a question of how far older social patterns, such as bourgeois/ proletarian heritage or tradition/modernity, continue to exist, and how far individuals retained their habits (work ethos, family ties) within them–and thus the extent to which individuals could retain a degree of autonomy. This entails searching for limits, gaps or weaknesses in the system of domination and orientating oneself according to individual strategies within given circumstances.

An exemplary field for studying these issues is pleasure. There are many areas of people's lives that are structured, determined, influenced, and enforced by the state and the system, but pleasure and enjoyment are not among them. They can be regulated, to be sure, but they cannot be forced into existence. If that is the case, then how can it be that, despite such admittedly different experiences and ways of life in the East and West, people laughed at the same films and idolised the same stars? Is this a case of anthropological constants? If people's laughter is subversive, then we need to ask why the state does not intervene to forbid the relevant film–or does everybody interpret a filmic situation in the light of their own individual conditions, thereby rendering it harmless for the system?

In relation to these questions, the normalisation concept makes a lot of sense, because it allows us to ask what assumptions and standards individuals use to evaluate their own lives and the circumstances in which they live. The question is therefore how given social conditions, socially propagated norms and values, and value systems, which are circulated through virtual reality, affect individual constructions of norms. Individuals put together their own systems of norms and values. From the reservoir of norms and meanings, they pick out orientation markers that are relevant for their own individual lives. In this process, there will be moments of agreement with socially standardised perceptions (working hard), or stubborn retention of norms that are 'outdated' (obedience), 'western' (fashion, hedonism), 'bourgeois' (social distinction, entrepreneurial spirit), or norms which are otherwise denounced, dismissed or tolerated. The cultural reservoir on which individuals draw contains all socially circulating norms and values, including those that are seen negatively, and those that are in competition with each other.

The 'art of action' (de Certeau) or 'playing the rules' (Fulbrook) are categories directed at the simultaneity of discipline and doubt, agreement and disagreement, conformity and resistance. One can behave according to established norms without agreeing with them. I can voice opposition towards them and yet simultaneously regard them as necessary in an exceptional situation. That is what is meant by negotiation: in the knowledge that, for example, forbidding bourgeois rights and freedoms (freedom of speech, free elections, freedom to travel) is a politically restrictive act of interference, which is not 'normal', I can temporarily regard this intervention as necessary. There was, for example, no public protest when the Wall was built. Rather, this measure was met with a certain kind of agreement, and a minimum of acceptance and political understanding within society. This acceptance was not, however, secured in the longer term—in other words, after a few years these measures were increasingly questioned: restricted travel, subventions, the electoral system, and so on were criticised ever more strongly.

The 'normal condition' of the GDR was that its citizens did perceive themselves as a 'not quite normal' society, but as one which did absolutely aspire to 'normal' conditions in the near and the more distant future. Many GDR citizens shared with each other the hope that with international recognition, a solution to the question of citizenship, an end to the arms race, and so on, the borders would be opened. The conception of normality had as its goal a society in which all restrictions would be lifted. The GDR or perhaps socialism was seen as a transitional phase of society that was necessarily afflicted by weaknesses—and, to be precise, weaknesses that were different from those experienced by western societies. This means that every period has its own (negotiated) normality, even if it has come off the rails, but that in every period conceptions also circulate about what is not quite right, not correct, not 'normal', that is, what cannot be accepted in this way in the long-term.

The mass exodus and the peaceful revolution of 1989 can be interpreted in many different ways, but they can also be seen as a forcible reclamation of conceptions of normality: these included street demonstrations and demands, public discussion of social questions of general concern, problems and possible solutions, participation in power, getting to know Europe, articulating the right to a private sphere, protection of the environment, and urban preservation. That such a normality was, in the end, only attainable by giving up other normalities (state sovereignty, full-time employment) points to the fact that normality is always the result of negotiation, a historically concrete compromise, in which not all perceptions can be realised at the same time.

The concept of normalisation is well suited to looking at these kinds of compromises and processes of negotiation and asking how individuals in given circumstances make something out of them—namely, their own lives. This concept allows us to do so without evaluating the perceptions of normality that circulate and compete at any given time. It makes it possible to describe normalities as temporarily accepted and simultaneously questioned conditions of social stability, which, for a certain period of time, can give individuals a necessary security of action.

Chapter 10

How Do the 1929ers and the 1949ers Differer?

Dorothee Wierling

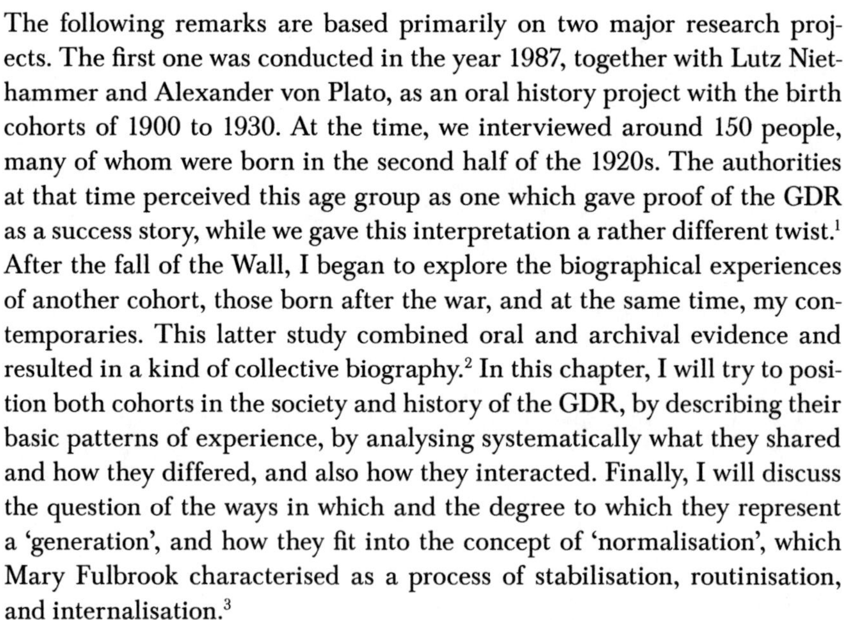

The following remarks are based primarily on two major research projects. The first one was conducted in the year 1987, together with Lutz Niethammer and Alexander von Plato, as an oral history project with the birth cohorts of 1900 to 1930. At the time, we interviewed around 150 people, many of whom were born in the second half of the 1920s. The authorities at that time perceived this age group as one which gave proof of the GDR as a success story, while we gave this interpretation a rather different twist.[1] After the fall of the Wall, I began to explore the biographical experiences of another cohort, those born after the war, and at the same time, my contemporaries. This latter study combined oral and archival evidence and resulted in a kind of collective biography.[2] In this chapter, I will try to position both cohorts in the society and history of the GDR, by describing their basic patterns of experience, by analysing systematically what they shared and how they differed, and also how they interacted. Finally, I will discuss the question of the ways in which and the degree to which they represent a 'generation', and how they fit into the concept of 'normalisation', which Mary Fulbrook characterised as a process of stabilisation, routinisation, and internalisation.[3]

The '1929ers' and the '1949ers' on one level refer to the exact birth cohorts. But they both also represent a broader age group, in the case of the

1. Lutz Niethammer, Alexander von Plato, and Dorothee Wierling, *Die Volkseigene Erfahrung. Eine Archäologie des Lebens in der Industrieprovinz der DDR* (Berlin, 1991).

2. Dorothee Wierling, *Geboren im Jahr Eins. Der Geburtsjahrgang 1949 in der DDR. Versuch einer Kollektivbiographie* (Berlin, 2002).

3. See Chapter 1, above.

1929ers, those who were between 15 and 20 years old in 1945, that is, the so called Hitler Youth generation–born in the second half of the 1920s and living their childhood and early youth in Nazi Germany. In the case of the 1949ers, I can show that those born between 1945 and 1955 share basic experiences (which I will elaborate on later), although I hesitate to label them anything other than 'the first post-war generation'. This brings me to a last preliminary remark in regard to 'generation' as a concept for historical research and analysis.[4] In this article, I use the term in a most general way, that is, as an age group with 'shared patterns of experience' (Mannheim's *Generationszusammenhang*). To what degree these age groups form a conscious unity (Mannheim's *Generationseinheit*), or could even be regarded as a 'political generation', needs to be discussed differently for each age group in question.[5] But even on a more basic level, it should be obvious that not all members of a certain age group or birth cohort share all of the experiences suggested below or were shaped by these experiences in the same way. In this chapter, I focus on what I believe are the most commonly and broadly shared experiences and biographical consequences. Naturally, not each and every member of the cohorts will see my descriptions as mirroring their personal memories. The major differences along such categories as gender, region, class, education, and political affiliation can only be touched upon here.

The 1929ers

Whenever an interviewee or somebody in an audience begins a narrative or statement with the information that he or she was born in 1929, I fear the worst. And very often, I am right. Indeed, it is striking to what degree the anxieties, humiliations, and disorientations of 1945 still dominate the memories and feelings of the Hitler Youth generation and are often expressed as a set of barely hidden resentment and *Ressentiment*. In West Germany, this could easily happen in public, while in the East, official anti-fascism forced the individuals to be silent outside their private circles. And yet, they shared a biographical youth pattern, in which their adolescent megalomania had been fed by an irresponsible and immoral regime. They were terrified by often traumatic experiences at the end of the war, deprived of the hermetic

4. In the last few years, there has been an abundance of generational studies and discussions about the concept of generation among historians and sociologists alike. See most recently, Michael Wildt and Ulrike Jureit, eds., *Generationen. Zur Relevanz eines wissenschaftlichen Grundbegriffs* (Hamburg, 2005).

5. Karl Mannheim, 'Das Problem der Generationen', in Mannheim, *Wissenssoziologie* (Berlin: Luchterhand, 1964; orig. 1928), pp. 509–65.

Nazi worldview, and left without guidance and credible authorities after the breakdown of the regime. Many of them experienced a major personal crisis in the immediate aftermath of World War II, which has left its marks still today.[6]

In the Soviet Zone and later GDR, this age group was targeted early on as mass basis for the recruitment of personnel to fill in the positions of fallen soldiers and former Nazis, and in addition to create a group of functionaries for the new political parties and mass organisations and to be educated as a new intellectual, cultural, and political elite. The older generations, in particular the teaching and law professions, were largely tainted by NSDAP membership or otherwise active support of the Nazi state—the younger ones had not had this opportunity, although they might have been even more attracted by Nazi ideology and its goals of world domination. Their youth, however, and the critical biographical stage they found themselves in at the end of the war, made them an ideal group in the eyes of the new authorities, a group which promised to be needy of support, of a structure to begin with, of a future perspective, and of a new belief system. The socialist ideological and political system in its Stalinist form satisfied many a young person's need for new orientation, a new authority, and a new system of meaning. To put it bluntly, in the minds of many a 1929er, Stalinist socialism turned out to be an ideal substitute for the Nazi ideology: Stalin could take over the position of Hitler and the Soviet Union offered itself for identification with the invincible country that Germany had failed to be. While those members of the 1929ers who came from a middle class, upper class or educated class background tended either to find any potential cooperation rejected by the new authorities or themselves refused any cooperation, the response from the lower middle and working classes to this offer was overwhelming. Without being able to give exact numbers, we can assume that a large minority of the Hitler youth generation enjoyed, or at least experienced, a major upward mobility, and soon dominated certain professional groups, such as teachers, judges, the middle levels of local and district administration as well as political parties and organisations; and last but not least, they entered the industrial management of the state-owned companies. Many were trained on the job, such as teachers or judges who had to function immediately; others went through the 'Workers and Peasants College' (*Arbeiter- und Bauernfakultät, ABF*) before they entered the universities and the new GDR elites.

6. It is interesting that for West Germany, this generation has been referred to more as the 'Flakhelfergeneration', those members of the cohort who as high school students were drafted to man the anti-aircraft guns at the end of the war. See Heinz Bude, *Deutsche Karieren. Lebenskonstruktionen sozialer Aufsteiger aus der Flakhelfergeneration* (Frankfurt M., 1987).

Most of them stayed in these positions until the end of the GDR, while only a few made it to the top of real power—a third of the members of the SED's Central Committee belonged to this generation in 1989.[7]

The social success of the 1929ers referred to more than a specific constellation of options after 1945. Its attractiveness was heightened by a biographical pattern of upward orientation in the lower classes of the Weimar Republic, which had resulted in a low birth rate and growing investments in education, especially with girls. Thus, biographical interviews inform us about a pattern of social mobility that was prepared for in the 1930s through an education meant to help working class youth into white-collar jobs. This was brutally interrupted by the war, although girls in particular at first seemed to profit from the loss of male competition. After 1945, the massive gaps in the workforce and the naïve trust in the young working class led to options that from the perspective of the young seemed like the unexpected and undeserved opportunity they had thought lost.[8]

Yet this upward mobility came with the price of political loyalty and a strict political and social control. Those who had made a commitment to a career as a rule had to make a political commitment as well; and although this might have met their need for a clear framework and order, as indicated above, at the same time it meant discipline and moral pressure beyond the work sphere. In the 1950s in particular, but also way into the 1960s, the SED functioned as a second—and for its members, the primary—disciplinary institution of setting the rules, sanctioning all transgressions, and granting or denying forgiveness and community. Every task could be turned into a party order (*Parteiauftrag*). Oneself, but also one's partner and children, were under constant observation and expected to lead an exemplary life, according to the saying that the party is represented by each of its members at any place at any time (*Wo Du bist, ist die Partei).* But loyalty also came with gratitude: gratitude for the social options that were seen as a gift, especially in comparison to West Germany, where the old elites had not cleared the place for a younger generation; here, the GDR compared favourably. They also felt gratitude for being forgiven and re-educated. And thus, most narratives of the Hitler youth generation in the East focus around 1945 as

7. Alexander von Plato, 'The Hitler Youth generation and its role in the two postwar German states', in Mark Roseman, ed., *Generations in Conflict* (Cambridge: Cambridge University Press, 1995), pp. 210–26. Dorothee Wierling, 'The Hitler Youth generation in the GDR: Insecurites, Ambitions and Dilemmas', in Konrad Jarausch, ed., *Dictatorship as Experience. Towards a Socio-Cultural History of the GDR* (New York, Oxford, 1999), pp. 307–24. Mary Fulbrook, 'Generationen und Kohorten in der DDR' in Annegret Schüle et al. (eds.), *Die DDR aus generationsgeschichtlicher perspektive* (Leipzig, 2006), pp. 113–130.

8. See the portraits of Johanna Maczek ('Die Quittung'), Bertha Uhlig ('Die älteste Schwester'), Lisa Gabert ('Die Brücke'), Rudolf Kamp ('Gewalt und Gesetz') in Niethammer, von Plato, Wierling, *Volkseigene Erfahrung*.

a moment of despair as well as hope, of guilt as well as conversion. Behind this biographical pattern, however, a basic insecurity always prevailed. Politically, it was present in the SED's statement: 'The party forgives, but does not forget'. Personally, it was expressed in a deep feeling of insufficiency vis-à-vis those older anti-fascists, whose sacrifice they could not repeat under the conditions of the GDR. It may be for this reason that, for this part of the Hitler youth generation, the events of the workers' uprising in June 1953 appeared as such a challenge to prove their loyalty under the condition of a threat.[9]

The 1949ers

The 1949ers are in the centre of an age group whose essential experiences are first marked by the end of the war, the effects of which were seen and felt in the East much longer than in the West. Material and mental conditions of the post-war period were harsh, and it took the entire decade of the 1950s to overcome food rationing and secure the satisfaction of basic needs. At the same time, Stalinist politics shaped the atmosphere of fear and opportunism, while many East Germans made for the West. On the other hand, an authoritarian educational system was combined with radical educational reforms that made access to higher education easy for those social groups who had always been excluded from it. In the 1960s, cautious liberalisation was countered by repression of adolescent attempts at claiming greater autonomy. The end of the Prague experiment also put an end to any encouragment for a more democratic socialism in the GDR. In the 1970s, this age group entered the workforce and experienced a more than usual reality shock, especially on the higher level, and in consequence, took a leading stand in a general trend towards private life and family as the most important elements of a good life. Thus, the first post-war cohort was stuck between high expectations built up during childhood and youth on the one hand, and limited options in their adult lives, between a promise of future and its loss, on the other.[10]

Those actually born in 1949 became more specifically the object of politics. The GDR began to celebrate itself as a personalised project, first in 1959, at the occasion of its 10th 'birthday', and much more optimistically

9. Lutz Niethammer, 'Where were you on the 17th of June?' A niche in Memory, in Luisa Passerini, ed., *Memory and Totalitarianism, International Yearbook of Oral History* (Oxford, 1992), pp. 45–69.

10. Dorothee Wierling, 'Wie (er)findet man eine Generation? Das Beispiel des Geburtsjahrgangs 1919 in der DDR', in Jürgen Reulecke, ed., *Generationalität und Lebensgeschichte im 20. Jahrhundert* (München, 2003), pp. 217–28.

and self-assuredly in 1969, at the height of its economic and political success—then as an innocent child of ten, now as a beautiful blonde of twenty. The 1949ers were encouraged on these occasions to identify with the state and think of themselves as a biographical project, as part of building a utopian future combining technological with social progress.[11]

In life history interviews conducted in the first half of the 1990s, respondents born in 1949/1950 shared significant narrative patterns, some of which I would briefly like to characterise. One was the focus on their families' lives before their birth, that is, the hardships their parents had gone through at the end of the war and in the first post-war years. These family stories centre very much on the parents as victims of war and post-war living conditions. Obviously, the scenes that made up the tableau of the parents' biographical and historical experiences were very close to the post-war cohorts, who often narrated them in the interview as if they had personally been present. I therefore understand the 1949ers as virtual war children, not just because they identify so much with the family's war experience, but also because they tend to understand their own lives as an obligation to compensate for their parents' losses and broken biographies. This obligation is particularly strong for those whose parents had the typical Hitler youth biography as indicated above. One crucial instrument for this age group was, however, the past in another sense than that of private losses and new beginnings: as the past of fascism and the sacrifices of anti-fascists, who at the same time represented the state at its very top. The 1949ers were the last age group for which places like Buchenwald represented an obliging and dramatic legacy, linked with the highest respect for those who had risked their lives. This powerful presence of the past coexisted with a powerful promise of a better future, given both by the parents and the new state; and indeed, much was invested in these children, especially in education, so that I speak of a specific 'mission to happiness' that shaped the lives of the post-war born.[12] It was not until the early 1960s, however, that the GDR managed to establish a broad system of institutions, organisations, and personnel to shape the new generation in regard to a consistent set of socialist norms and ideology, especially through school and the children's organisation 'Young Pioneers' (JP) and the youth organisation 'Free German Youth' (FDJ). In

11. Dieter Vorsteher, '"Ich bin zehn Jahre". Die Ausstellung im Museum für Deutsche Geschichte anlässlich des zehnten Jahrestages der DDR', in Monika Gibas et. al, eds., *Wiedergeburten. Zur Geschichte der runden Geburtstage der DDR* (Leipzig, 1999), pp. 135–46; See also Wierling, *Geboren im Jahr Eins*, pp. 316–25.

12. Dorothee Wierling, 'Mission to Happiness. Comparing the Birth Cohort of 1949 in East and West Germany', in Hanna Schissler, ed., *The Miracle Years. West Germany in the 1950s* (Princeton University Press, 2001), pp. 110–25.

1965, an institutional system of 'total' education seemed to be in place; but the state never succeeded in making this system perfect or excluding alternative influences from family and peers.

The 1960s brought to the GDR a 'foreign' phenomenon, the effects of which cannot be overestimated for the 1949ers in particular: a wave of popular culture, especially music, from the West, sucessfully infiltrated the GDR through tape recorder, transistor radio, TV, and the electric guitar. By means of these technical and cultural goods, the GDR youth of the 1960s became part of the West–despite the Wall, and in a very specific way that differed from West Germany.[13] While the idols of this movement–the Beatles, the Rolling Stones–were the same, the restrictions on access to the music and the cultural items and practices which came with it, and–more generally–the disciplinary threats of the authorities gave the music a higher meaning of an existential opposition to the authoritarian traits of the regime. East German youth had to improvise more, had to risk more, and consequently enjoyed more when consuming and reproducing Western popular culture to make it their own. Different factions inside the SED tried to win over youth either through a more liberal or a more strict attitude vis-à-vis young peoples' wishes for autonomy. The support of the Politburo, and especially Ulbricht, for the more liberal faction ended in the late 1960s with a renewed attempt for total control under the emerging authority of Erich Honecker. The 1970s brought a more pragmatic attitude, not just in regard to popular music. The regime had understood that they could not win the culture war against Western popular music and encouraged a home-grown rock music scene.[14] But in more than one realm, the belief in the possible creation of a socialist personality broke down. Disappointment made way for pragmatism, both with the rulers and the ruled, when the 1949ers entered jobs and founded families. We know about their disillusionment through surveys conducted by the Leipzig Institute for Youth Research, the results of which were widely ignored among the authorities, and never became subject of public debate. Certainly, there was no option for changes in politics to address the basic societal problems in the GDR of the 1970s. What was left was the promise of a ever better material life, of growing consumer possibilities, and of continuous technological progress, promises which also turned out to be empty in the 1980s and made the GDR a 'grumbling' society (Fulbrook).[15]

---

13. See also Chapter 9, above.

14. Michael Rauhut, *Beat in der Grauzone: DDR-Rock 1964–1972. Politik und Alltag* (Berlin, 1993).

15. See also Mary Fulbrook's most recent descripton of the GDR 'culture of complaint' in her book *The People's State: East German Society from Hitler to Honecker* (Yale: Yale University Press, 2005), pp. 269–88.

Differences

When I now discuss more systematically the question of how the two age groups in question differ, I want to ask in addition, what might they have in common? First, they were both shaped by the war, albeit in very different ways. The 1929ers represent a group that had often been fascinated by Nazi ideology and the War, and in the end had become active parts of the war effort, be it on the front or on the home front. At the same time, they were needy young adolescents who were overwhelmed by the death and violence that surrounded them—and after the war, the GDR became for many an alternative that provided forgiveness, security, and orientation, along with the—almost uninterrupted—integration into an authoritarian order. In any case, the war presented the most important and often traumatic experience of their lives, an experience that marked the dramatic end of their childhood. For many, it also marked a new dramatic beginning in a system that claimed the future for itself and offered a future to the young—meaning, first of all, re-education.

In contrast, the 1949ers knew about these things only through family narratives—that is, their own parents—and state propaganda, and they found themselves luckily spared from living through these events. At the same time, however, they were also excluded from these bonding experiences, their own lives being lived in the routine of a ready-made system. They were profiting from the new beginning of an anti-fascist state and private reconstruction while the dramatic past their family and society had gone through was present as a collective memory and frightening fantasy. The main feature resulting from this constellation was gratitude—and here the 1949ers were again similar to the 1929ers, for whom gratitude also played a major role.

In 1945, the 1929ers were offered a new ideology, social position, and life out of the ashes, which made them deeply grateful for these undeserved gifts. Given their vague feelings of guilt, however, they remained vulnerable when they were compared, and compared themselves, to those who could claim authentic anti-fascism out of communist roots. That life could change dramatically, that these changes could be violent and dangerous, these were lessons the 1929ers had learned in a very direct way. The result was a deep longing for authority and order, which provided the framework for a life under control—control of others and of a vulnerable self. While the 1929ers had experienced their adolescence in a phase of societal breakdown, the 1949ers entered youth in the early 1960s, when the GDR, safely shut against the West, began its project of modernising socialism. Their childhood appeared as a continuous improvement towards stabilisation and order, the renewed order of state socialism. When they grew out of childhood, however, the discipline to which they had been exposed began to feel like a prison. Together with the experiences provided by the products of popular culture mentioned above, youth for them was a concept linked to a very liberating, exciting, playful acting out of passions and dreams, which were almost impossible to control by the state and party authorities.[16] Even the restrictions which followed in the late 1960s could not totally destroy the spaces of personal freedoms that people had created for themselves. I see the beginning of the so-called niche society here, which developed parallel to the party state's attempts at total institutional control over peoples' lives.[17] In contrast to the 1929ers, the 1949ers did not seek, but rather tried to avoid the control of authorities, thanks to the conditions that had allowed them, but not the 1929ers, to experience autonomous realms in their youth. While the longing for order came out of the disastrous breakdown of society for the young 1929ers, the 1949ers' wish for autonomy came out of the controlling and disciplinary system of their own childhoods. But the 1929ers had been able to reconcile their wishes with those of the state, while the 1949ers necessarily put themselves in contradiction to the state, which had by no means given up its control; on the contrary, the state had sought to perfect it.

Thirdly, the 1929ers were the only GDR generation of upward mobility. They achieved what had never been promised to them, or rather, what they had given up expecting at the end of the war—and they were very aware of this as a favour, as an offer that depended not only on their own ambitions, but on a generous state—especially in contrast to the West. Most of them had been trained on the job, and their peculiar position as a badly prepared new elite made them especially dependent on the authority of the state. Thus, their leading positions on the local or company level were not always comfortable, and their lack of training for each new step up the ladder would sometimes go beyond their strength and capacities.[18] The 1949ers, in comparison, started out with the promise of a near future of technological and social revolution, a society where they would be able to reach anything, if

---

16. This argument needs qualification not only in regard to the immediate end of the war, where youth were practically on their own, but also in regard to the so-called 'Halbstarkenproblem' (rowdyism), that is, the young, male working class, who presented a major problem throughout the history of the GDR, including the 1950s. See Uta Poiger, *Jazz, Rock and Rebels. Cold War Politics and American Culture in a divided Germany* (Berkeley: University of California Press, 2000), esp. pp. 91ff.

17. The concept of the so-called niche society was developed by Günther Gaus, in his book *Wo Deutschland liegt*. It has since turned out to be a favourite term of description—and self description—for GDR society, at least that of its later period.

18. Most of our interviewees, who in 1987 held a management position, mentioned some major psychosomatic illness, had asked to be downgraded or planned to do so.

they only believed in this future and in themselves and did not shy away from the hard work it needed. The education they needed to master this future was provided, at least for those who were either believers in, or willing to give lip service to the achievements of socialism. But the future indeed seemed bright. High expectations were raised in all social strata—a blue-collar worker at times was regarded as superior to his more educated colleague, although in the 1960s the engineer became the essential figure of socialist progress. But the reality of working life seldom fit the expectations, and this was true in particular for those with higher education and the prolonged adolescence it came with, which in the GDR meant being somewhat sheltered from the reality of society and the work sphere. The lack of open positions for those who had been trained for them at university resulted in a rather flat curve of upward mobility, if not stagnation. Compared to their aspirations, this led to frustration and resignation, and a fading away of the early gratitude they had felt vis-à-vis the enormous efforts of family and state to provide a good life and glorious future for them.[19]

Inter-generational Dynamics

The 1929ers and 1949ers interacted in a very specific way and this interaction had a deep effect on the texture of social relations and conflicts in the GDR. Given the demographic situation in Germany after 1945, men between 20 and 40 representing the age group with the largest percentage of war dead, the older segment of the Hitler youth generation made up the bulk of the parents of the 1949ers, both mothers and fathers, while some parents were relatively old.[20] At the same time, the overwhelming majority of teachers and low-level functionaries in the mass organisations and on the local level were members of that same Hitler youth generation. Thus, in most educational constellations, be it at home, in school or in the childrens' or youth organisation, this generation represented *the* generation of reference for the 1949ers—and it is worth looking closer at this generational dynamic.

First, the family bonds between parents and children were very close, and there is little evidence of a generational conflict in the families. Children

19. See the studies of the Leipzig Institute quoted in Wierling, *Geboren im Jahr Eins*, pp. 358ff.; and Johannes Huinink, Karl-Ulrich Mayer, and Heike Trappe, 'Staatliche Lenkung und individuelle Karrierechancen: Bildungs- und Berufsverläufe', in Johannes Huinink et. al, eds., *Kollektiv und Eigensinn–Lebensverläufe in der DDR und danach* (Berlin: Akademie Verlag, 1995), pp. 89–143.

20. *Statistisches Jahrbuch der DDR 1955* (Berlin, 1956), p. 36, gives the age of the mothers. Fathers tended to be of the same age or much older.

and youth tended to bond with their parents vis-à-vis the state, so that families could serve as a community of mutual support in material, emotional, and social ways. Certainly, there is nothing similar to the generational conflicts that dominated many families in 1960s West Germany, where cultural and political protests were acted out in the living rooms, at least in those of the middle classes. In particular, GDR parents in the 1960s were not challenged by questions about their attitude and activities in Nazi Germany, but were regarded as victims of the Nazi regime and spared any critical doubts. Children, as is evident in contemporary sources such as school essays, and certainly in life history interviews with 1949ers, were not only aware of the daily hardships their parents had to endure, but they also identified with the parents and their attempts to build a new life, and this included identification with those who had decided in favour of re-education and re-politicisation. And although many observed the costs of these attempts, such as political pressure and fear of state authorities, the reaction was solidarity and a wish to conform, to make the parents' lives easier. In some cases, the children also followed their parents on their path of political commitment, taking their examples as an obligation for themselves.

There was a generational conflict, however, but it was acted out in schools, in the workplace, and on the streets. Indeed, although the existence of a public sphere—or its special features—can be debated for the GDR,[21] the generational conflict between the 1949ers and their elders was more a public than private one, and the 1929ers and 1949ers confronted each other about various issues.

First, there was the issue of education. The Hitler Youth generation were largely to build the group of new teachers and public educators. By the 1960s, the older generation of teachers from the Weimar Republic had vanished from the schools. The 1929ers very much depended on the idea that education was necessary and possible—beginning with their own re-education after the war, and fed by Marxist-Leninist concepts of the power of education to create a new kind of man (and woman), as soon and as long as all of the circumstances of childrens' upbringing were under control. Since the 1949ers had been born after Nazism, after the war, and even after the chaotic early post-war years, it was expected that they would be the first to realise this dream of a 'socialist personality'. As children they seemed promising—as adolescents, however, they disapppointed and eventually destroyed the pedagogical optimism of the teachers, functionaries, and masters. The fact that the SED and the state would make the educators responsible for

21. See Fulbrook, *The Peoples' State*, p. 250ff.

the failures of the educated was an important reason why disappointment often turned into hatred.

Secondly, there was the more specific issue of discipline and authority. For the 1929ers, discipline was crucial. They had learned it in school and in the Hitler youth, it had been demanded from them during the war, and afterwards discipline and the recognition of a new authority had rescued them from chaos and despair. Discipline and authority meant security, that is, protection from the dangers of outside and inside anarchy. For the 1949ers, this basic security was a given, provided by families, by institutions, and by the promise of a peaceful and structured life. Thus, the restrictive effects of discipline and authority became more obvious, and the children growing into adolescents began to long for autonomy instead of authority, and for pleasure instead of discipline. But their teachers, foremen, and youth leaders were there to keep up work discipline, make sure that hair was cut short, that dance steps were not wild, that dress codes were kept, and gender roles respected–and with a mixture of envy and fear, the elders tried to impose their values and rules on an obstinate youth.

Thirdly, the workplace became a major field of generational competition. In the 1960s, apprentices and young workers threatened many older workers and employees with their hedonism, their lack of discipline and ambition, as well as their better education and the greater ease with which they grasped technological change. In 1963, the SED-Politburo issued the 'Youth Communiqué' praising youth as the social group that naturally tended towards progress, a group which would and should challenge the older ones as the avantgarde towards modernisation; the reaction among the elders, namely the Hitler youth generation, was mixed, sceptical, and sometimes outright defensive: they saw the recognition for their achievements and the recognition of their authority endangered, when young people were encouraged too much to question them.[22] In the 1970s, however, the generational balance of power had changed: those coming from the universities were ready to take over leading positions, but they found that these were largely occupied by the Hitler youth generation, who would stay in their place up to the very end of the GDR. The younger ones were put in positions that were far below the formal level of their education, and the money they earned and the tasks they were in charge of were way below

22. 'Jugend von heute–Hausherren von morgen. Der Jugend Vertrauen und Verantwortung.' This document, created by a reformist group established by Ulbricht and issued as an official Politburo declaration, is published in *Dokumente der Sozialistischen Einheitspartei Deutschlands*, vol. 9 (Berlin, 1965): 679–706.

their promised options and their theoretical and often practical skills. This would not change until the end of the GDR.

Self-understandings

Although people would use the term 'generation' when they referred to an older or a younger birth cohort, using it in the everyday sense they had learned with the German language, 'generation' with capital letters was not a legitimate social or political category in the GDR, nor was generational conflict. Instead, no other concept than that of class could be used to indicate basic differences and conflicts, and in that sense, all antagonistic differences had been eliminated in the GDR.[23] Consequently, the public sphere to develop a sense of generation was missing in the GDR, at least the public sphere as it existed under the control of the SED. However, the former Hitler youth was granted a limited space to identify themselves as a generation, the *Aufbaugeneration*, the 'generation of reconstruction', and they developed a specific biographical pattern—meaning both a pattern for their lived and narrated biographies—which focussed around 1945 as the moment of their personal conversion. This fit well with the public narrative of a weak and broken Germany, activated and elevated by socialist conversion into a new Germany with a bright future. The Hitler youth generation thus stood for the basic possibility of turning national-socialism into socialism, war into peace, Nazis into socialists; but also for the basic tragedy of a murderous and vicious past.

In a way, the 1949ers also provided the stuff generations are made of: the children of this new beginning, the first generation blessed by socialism, the proof of what a good socialist education could do, their lives parallel to the state. As I mentioned above, the GDR celebrated its 'birthdays' by linking the lives of those born in 1949 to its life as a socialist state, and the 1949ers had to perform who they were supposed to be as ten, twenty, thirty, forty year-olds.[24] But the real 1949ers turned against this concept and instead became proof of the limits of education and the limits of authoritarian control. They chose their own heroes from the West, they shared basic orientations with an international post-war youth, and although they were surprisingly loyal and by no means rebellious, they were regarded as a failure and indeed

23. Thus, when the politics of reform were denounced after 1965, the Politburo issued a letter to all First Secretaries at the district and local levels, which bluntly proclaimed that young people did not pursue any 'class goals' (Klassenziele) that differed from those of the older generation. Wierling, *Geboren im Jahr Eins*, p. 211.

24. In 1984, the 'Oktoberklub' came up with a rather melancholic song about the 'Wir über Dreißig' citizens of the GDR: *Oktoberklub, Das Beste* (Berlin, 1995) (CD).

represented the failure of educational dictatorship as such. In the end, they stood for stagnation and resignation, for those who had got lost in the *Mühen der Ebenen* (travails of the plains).[25]

How the 1929ers and the 1949ers experienced the society they grew up in, how they tried to find their place and their happiness, how they interacted—all of these became important aspects of social change in the GDR and had political implications at the same time. To look at generations therefore is to look at one origin of societal dynamics and change. But it would be wrong to try to analyse the history of the GDR through a generational pattern alone or even to structure its history in the rhythm of generations, meaning nothing more than mechanical cohorts.[26] If we go back to Mannheim, we can conclude that, if any, only the 1929ers—that is, the Hitler Youth generation—may be defined as a political generation, given their political commitment and willingness to keep the GDR functioning. In contrast, the 1949ers (or the first post-war generation) had no active political impact, even if we concede that the active body of the small GDR opposition of the 1980s was formed by the post-war cohorts. But by doing so, they did not experience or define themselves as a generation; rather, the phenomenon of a relatively homogeneous age group in the opposition was due to the older ones having left for the West before 1961, leaving the younger ones to grow up in the East almost without older mentors.[27]

Generation and Normalisation

The two cohorts in question differed in the share they had in a 'normal' life. While the 1929ers had lived their childhood and youth through the most dramatic periods of German history, through violence, death, and enormous material and human losses, through often traumatic upheavals with long-term psychological effects, the 1949ers were born, albeit under the shadows of these catastrophes, under a private and public promise of 'normality'.

All of the 1950s can be defined as the tough struggle for normalisation in its crudest meaning of stabilisation. Families were reunited, left for good or were newly founded; people established themselves in apartments, even if

---

25. Bertolt Brecht.

26. Bernd Lindner: '"Bau auf, Freie Jugend!"—und was dann? Kriterien für ein Modell der Jugendgenerationen der DDR', in Reulecke, *Generationalität*, pp. 187–215.

27. Robert Havemann is a rare exception, an 'original' anti-fascist of Honecker's age and an important figure for someone like Wolf Biermann and others. His refusal to leave the GDR was probably—from the perspective of the SED leadership—his most annoying oppositional activity.

their quality was still poor; they also gained new positions in the worksphere, they made decisions in terms of their political commitment or abstinence, they found a more or less permanent social place, at least direction to follow—and be it to the West. All of these acts of stabilisation were hard biographical work for the cohort of the 1929ers—their children, however, found these new stable structures ready made for them to fit in. And, as it turned out, below these new structures, central mental dispositions, sets of rules and beliefs, had survived the upheavals and would now contribute to stabilisation as the normative side of normalisation.[28] The 1949ers, as children, felt quite comfortable and secure in the framework of normative order in a 'normal' life, where war belonged to a past that was shared in family stories. The fear of war, this latent danger of the early Cold War period, fed the longing for this kind of normality long into the 1960s.

It was not until the 1960s that routinisation came about. Then, the educational dictatorship was established in the remotest villages, all of the institutional and organisational structures were in place, and the generational change towards the Hitler Youth generation was finished, keeping the very top in the hands of the political 'activists of the first hour' and leaving only a few technical experts in place. The country was closed off against the West and those who had dreamt of the West German option. The basic precondition for routinisation, the confidence of finding everybody still in place the next day, was thus ensured. For the 1929ers—certainly not all of them—this was the historical period of their breakthrough and of the fulfillment of their hopes: having gained considerable positions in society, they lived in a world with clear rules and a more or less transparent hierarchy. The authorities were there for support, sanctions, and appeal.

Unfortunately, it was in this historical moment of gained security that the 1949ers began to feel the normative pressure of normalisation, the depressing boredom of stabilisation, and the emptiness of routinisation. They wanted autonomy, passion, and adventure—something that the GDR as it was could not provide or grant them. The cultural rebellion that evolved out of these deficiencies and was fed by an international cultural youth revolt became the thorn in the flesh of the 1929ers. The conflict was about much more than political and cultural hegemony; it meant a direct attack on the self-understanding of the 1929ers—that authority was an absolute necessity for society, and for themselves, to function. The 1929ers had rescued this knowledge over the gap of 1945. It was the frame of their innermost existence.

28. Christoph Klessmann, 'Die Beharrungskraft traditioneller Milieus in der DDR', in Manfred Hettling, ed., *Was ist Gesellschaftsgeschichte?* (München, 1991), pp. 254–70.

The degree to which 'playing by the rules' was finally secured by internalisation is a very difficult question to answer. First, following rules is an activity which can be, but is not necessarily, driven by internalised norms; thus, nothing can be concluded from the obedience and conformity we observe or find proof of in the archives. On the other hand, we may ask what following the rules and participation in routines–especially those routines which claim deep personal commitments–do to people, if these activities can be performed without the slightest impact on the performer; at the very least, we may assume a continuous and growing experience of humiliation, a notion which might be avoided or denied by beginning to believe in what you are doing. If we follow standard psychoanalytic interpretation, constant and strict external control is counterproductive for the process of internalisation of the normative set–since internalised rules could and would be followed according to personal beliefs and needs that have become independent of the authority who originally established them. The implosion of the GDR and the mental heritage it left without a controlling state and the rules it had imposed, the so called East German identity, also give a mixed message. It seems most likely that it was not so much the explicit, but the implicit rules developed on the societal level, often against the outspoken rules of the socialist state, which have been internalised to stay, at least into the foreseeable future.[29]

It is possible, however, also to look at these 'official' rules as internalised values, as long and as far as they fulfil basic emotional needs, such as security, order, equality, peace, predictability, and authority.[30] The case of anti-fascism can serve as an example. Certainly, the dramatic and powerful story about those anti-fascists who died as martyrs or survived to create a new Germany of morality and justice had an enormous, deep, and long-lasting effect on the 1929ers and also still on the 1949ers. It was only a younger generation on whom this religious message was lost, worn out by constant repetition and the discrepancy between proclaimed values and everyday life. Thus, we would see a weakening of internalised norms, norms questioned ever more by the normality of daily experiences.

Still, living one's whole or half-life in the GDR left its mental marks, as we all know. These marks, however, are not as deep or as conspicuous for everyone; age, cohort, and generation are important factors here; and they are not the absolute other of what West Germans learned after the war. How the 1929ers and the 1949ers in the East differ from those in the West–this is another question.

---

29. Wolfgang Engler, *Die Ostdeutschen, Kunde von einem verlorenen Land* (Berlin, 1999).
30. See also Chapter 13, below.

Chapter 11

Producing the 'Socialist Personality'? Socialisation, Education, and the Emergence of New Patterns of Behaviour

Angela Brock

This essay focuses on the ways in which two decades of socialisation in the education system of the GDR left their mark on young people growing up there from the late 1950s to the late 1970s.[1] It centres on the enigmatic concept of an 'all-round developed socialist personality', the ubiquitous formula of the SED used to describe its supreme aim and ideal: a new kind of human being endowed with impeccable traits of character on whose ardent socialist convictions rest the fate and future of socialist society.

What makes a personality in the first place? No man is an island, but lives within the framework of society. Children are born into 'the smallest cell of society',[2] the family, and initially tend to adopt their parents' values, views, and behaviour. Growing up, however, other influences come into their lives: playground friends, kindergarten, school, first loves, first job. As the child passes through adolescence into adulthood, these influences are likely at first to rival, then to complement parental influences. This immediate social framework plus other aspects such as traditional morality, politics or culture surrounding them make up a unique cocktail of formative influences

1. Angela Brock, The making of the socialist personality–education and socialisation in the German Democratic Republic 1958–71978 (unpublished PhD thesis, University College London, 2005).

2. This was the view prevalent in the GDR. Cf. *Familiengesetzbuch der DDR vom 20.12.1965* (Berlin, Staatsverlag dev DDR 1970, 4th ed.), preamble, p. 13.

which, in addition to any innate character, give each human being his or her distinctive 'personality'. The flavour of this cocktail depends strongly on the kind of society into which one is born. In the socialist society of the GDR, the SED strove to be the greatest influence and attempted to shape young people's personalities by impressing upon them particular convictions and principles using the comprehensive education system, with the aim that they adopt these as their own.

This essay first introduces the concept of the 'socialist personality' within the GDR education system and then examines the extent to which it had any effect on young people for selected areas, focusing on the 1960s and 1970s, which, compared to the previous and following decade, were the calm and stable middle years of the GDR.

The Evolution of the 'Socialist Personality' Made in GDR

Whilst the idea of a 'socialist' personality originated with Marx and Engels, there were a number of historical precursors in classical antiquity, the Renaissance, and the Enlightenment that were seen as exemplary and progressive by the SED.[3] Yet, despite paying tribute to these earlier ideals, GDR historiography emphasised that these had to remain exceptions in their own time, and concluded that 'only under the societal conditions of socialism can a personality fully and consistently blossom.'[4] This was related to the Marxist 'idea of a human being' (*Menschenbild*), which maintained that the future society of socialism and ultimately communism would yield a new type of human being who would possess the following characteristics: communist awareness, highest all-round education, constructiveness, harmony with society and fellow human beings, moral perfection, material wealth, and stable happiness.[5] The thoughts of Marx and Engels on education are widely scattered over their complete works,[6] but their central ideas may be summarised as follows: all children should benefit from free full-time education; educational privileges should be abolished and education made

3. Cf. Johannes Irmscher, ed., *Das Ideal der allseitig entwickelten Persönlichkeit–seine Entstehung und sozialistische Verwirklichung*, Winkelmann Society Papers, vol. 2 (Berlin, Akademic-Verlag 1976).

4. Friedmar Kühnert, 'Zur Entstehung des Ideals der allseitig entwickelten Persönlichkeit im griechisch-römischen Altertum', in ibid., pp. 9–15, here p. 15.

5. Cf. Michael Beintker, 'Marxistisches Menschenbild', in Rainer Eppelmann et al., eds., *Lexikon des DDR-Sozialismus. Das Staats- und Gesellschaftssystem der DDR* (Paderborn: F. Schöningh, 1997), pp. 537–43, here p. 539f.

6. For an overview, see Siegfried Baske, 'Bildung und Erziehung bei Karl Marx und das Bildungssystem der DDR', in Konrad Löw, ed., *Karl Marx und das politische System der DDR* (Asperg, Meyn 1982), pp. 75–94.

accessible to all members of society; education should guarantee free all-round development and combine academic learning and physical education with productive work (polytechnic education); and finally, education should be free of the influence of religion and the state. When comparing these demands with the GDR education system, it is striking how much the latter stayed faithful to these principles, except in one notable point, the non-intervention of the state. The East German model of the 'socialist personality' was also influenced by Soviet pedagogy, especially that of Nadeshda Krupskaya and Anton S. Makarenko, where more attention was paid to shaping the personality on its path to future completeness and less to proclamations of having achieved this perfect all-round personality already, as was the case in the GDR of the 1970s.

After twelve years of fascist ideology, the watchword in 1945 (in both East and West) was 'New Germany–New People'. Those Germans who happened to live in the Soviet Zone of Occupation were immediately exposed to a radically different ideology. The *homo sovieticus* supposedly existing in the Soviet Union served as the model for the new human being that was needed to build the new society. The main demands for the new personality were inextricably linked to the practical needs of moral and economic reconstruction of the time. These were above all: overcoming the fascist legacy left behind in people's minds; the implementation of anti-fascist thinking; as well as fighting the economic problems of the black market and encouraging the work ethic.[7] During the phase of the anti-fascist and democratic school reform (1945–1949), discussions on the merits of the 'new human being' (not yet the 'socialist personality') outside pedagogical circles were rare. Instead, the educational aim of the 'new democratic school' was 'to prepare our children and young people for a life in which they must be Hennecke activists', and to educate them to become adults 'who build up an anti-fascist-democratic order.'[8]

The actual term 'socialist personality' was coined during the second phase of the GDR school system, the 'establishment of the socialist school' (1949–1961), in connection with the SED's proclamation of the *'Aufbau des Sozialismus'* (establishing socialism). From then onwards, education in school had the objective of forming 'socialist personalities'. At the 5th SED Party Congress in 1958, questions of ideology, morale, and personality finally took centre stage.

---

7. Cf. Irma Hanke, 'Vom neuen Menschen zur sozialistischen Persönlichkeit. Zum Menschenbild der SED' in *Deutschland Archiv*, May 1976 (9): 492–515, here p. 494.

8. Paper by 'Kollege Siebert', 'Zur Konkretisierung des Erziehungsideals', 15 February 1949, in Gert Geißler, Falk Blask, Thomas Scholze, eds., *Schule: Streng vertraulich! Die Volksbildung der DDR in Dokumenten*, vol. 1 (Berlin, Ministcrium für Bildung, Fugend und Sport des Lun les Brandenburg. Basisdruck 1996), pp. 104f. NB: Adolf Hennecke (1905–1975) was a collier and initiated the GDR's activists' movement in 1948.

The party leadership did not own up to the fact that a socialist worldview had not yet gained currency on the desired massive scale. Instead, it was claimed that 'new societal relations between people and a new morale' had already developed.[9] In order to promulgate this new morale, the party leadership attempted for the first time to formulate default standards for the population's behaviour. Walter Ulbricht announced the 'Ten Commandments for the new socialist human being', intended to give shape to the moral countenance of GDR citizens. These moral values were very typical of the 1950s (not only in the GDR, but also in Adenauer's FRG), with their focus on strengthening the young fatherland, encouraging the workforce to greater productivity and continuing to stress 'good' Prussian values such as cleanliness and decency. They further purported that in socialism, personal and societal interests were identical. Those who might not have agreed with these guidelines must consequently have been opposed to socialism. For the rest, abiding by these commandments was meant to create pride in belonging to a morally superior community. From the end of the 1950s, the term 'socialist community' (*sozialistische Gemeinschaft*) began to make frequent appearances in the media and politicians' speeches. Initially it described work teams, but it was more and more employed as a reference to the whole of society, which was supposedly made up of socialist personalities. During the 5th SED congress, the party leadership also explained for the first time in somewhat more detail what the anticipated result of socialist education should be: an all-round developed personality of high theoretical and artistic general education, showing combative activity and being capable of acting in a collective and comradely manner, harbouring a scientific worldview, and a high moral view of life.[10] Two of the busier years of innovations and issuing guidelines concerning the education system were 1958 and 1959, with the introduction of compulsory polytechnic instruction in September 1958 and the 'Law on the socialist development of the school system' (*Schulgesetz*) of 2 December 1959, which cemented the school's Marxist-Leninist orientation and increased compulsory schooling from eight to ten years.

The third phase of the school system (1961–1989) was until the mid 1960s characterised by vacillating education policies and experiments, but stabilised in the wake of the Act on the Integrated Socialist Education System (*Gesetz über das einheitliche sozialistische Bildungssystem*), which was passed on 25 February 1965 and remained in force until 1989. A further stabilising factor was the appointment of Margot Honecker as Education Secretary in 1963, a post she held until November 1989. The Education Act laid

9. Monika Gibas, *Propaganda in der DDR* (Erfurt, Landeszentrale für politische Bildung Thüringen 2000), p. 47.

10. Gibas, Propaganda, p. 47.

down moral and idealistic demands as well as the tasks and functions of all state-run educational institutions. The most famous of all definitions of the 'socialist personality' was stated in the first paragraph: 'The aim of the integrated socialist education system is the high education of the whole people, the education and socialisation of all-round and harmoniously developed socialist personalities, who consciously shape societal life, change nature and lead a fulfilled, happy, humanely dignified life.'[11] In the 1960s, the notion of a 'socialist personality' was conceived more as a tool that helped mould society into the required socialist shape, rather than as the paragon of socialist morality that it had been in the 1950s. In the wake of the leadership change from Walter Ulbricht to Erich Honecker in 1971, the focus moved away from community and social order to the 'socialist way of life' (*sozialistische Lebensweise*) led by 'socialist personalities', whose main attribute was now regarded to be 'socialist awareness' or 'socialist consciousness' (*sozialistisches Bewußtsein*). At the 8th SED Party Congress, Erich Honecker named the formation of the socialist personality as the party's principal task of shaping societal order. He gave a much quoted new point of view of this creature:

> One of the noblest aims
> And one of the greatest achievements
> Of socialist society
> Is the all-round developed socialist personality.[12]

By the mid 1970s, it was proclaimed that East Germans had by now developed socialist attitudes such as collectivity, congruity of interests between society and individual as well as the change from the attitude 'this does not concern me' to the new principle 'I am responsible for everything'.[13] The new Youth Law of 1974 evoked once more young people's connection with socialism and the fatherland.

The focus on ideology within education continued into the fourth and last decade of the GDR. Behind a façade of official détente and international recognition, the atmosphere inside the country was one of increasing stagnation; and the inner stability of the regime began slowly and almost

---

11. Kanzlei des Staatsrates der DDR, ed., *Materialien der 12. Sitzung der Volkskammer der DDR und das Gesetz über das einheitliche sozialistische Bildungswesen*, Heft 5 (Berlin, 1965) [henceforth Bildungsgesetz], pp. 83–133, here part 1, § 1, p. 88.

12. 'Ergebnisse und Probleme bei der weiteren Durchführung der schulpolitischen Beschlüsse des VIII. Parteitages' (March 1975), Stiftung der Parteien und Massenorganisationen der ehemaligen DDR im Bundesarchiv Berlin [henceforth SAPMO-BArch] DY30/IVB2/9.05/60.

13. Maria Elisabeth Müller, *Zwischen Ritual und Alltag: der Traum von einer sozialistischen Persönlichkeit* (Frankfurt/Main & New York, Campus Verlag 1997), p. 35.

imperceptibly to crumble. Party and Pedagogical Congresses had nothing new to suggest on the achievement of the socialist personality and the education system. As the years progressed and the gap between the 'superior socialist camp' and the 'doomed-to-fail capitalist world' widened (in what was for the GDR the wrong direction), notably as far as economic success and living standards were concerned, it became ever harder for the propagandists of the regime to mould young people into the desired socialist shape. In 1974, the GDR's chief pedagogue Gerhart Neuner had declared that 'Wishful thinking of any kind is alien to Marxism-Leninism. The method of dialectical materialism demands a *concrete analysis of the actual societal processes*, which determine today's personality development.'[14] It seems that wishful thinking was exactly what the regime was doing: giving the outward impression that society's development was going to plan, whilst the numerous commissioned 'concrete analyses' in *Stasi* (State Security service) reports told a different story. The rigidity of the old guard and the ossified state apparatus meant that the necessary conclusions were not drawn from the reports and that eventually the old guard had to pay the price.

End Product 'Socialist Personality'?

This essay does not aspire to show all of the possible facets of new patterns of behaviour that emerged as a result of socialist education. Rather, it wishes to examine the social history of the GDR as a history of mentalities (*Mentalitätsgeschichte*).[15] Trying to ascertain the effects of the education system on those growing up within its realms, however, means entering a highly controversial and difficult terrain. It means being faced with two problems: on the one hand, it is ultimately impossible to prove what went on in people's minds, since the majority of the East German population did not keep trustworthy diaries now available to historians. Thus, the suspicion that historiography reserves for studies that draw on surveys commissioned by and reports written for the SED as well as oral history interviews conducted retrospectively is understandable. On the other hand, it is very difficult to say how *the* education affected *the* young generation, given that every single East German experienced *the* GDR differently, lived his or her own life in a unique set of circumstances, and hence now holds different memories of the

14. (emphasis in the original). Wolfgang Eichler in Evemarie Badstübner, ed., *Befremdlich anders. Leben in der DDR*, 3d ed. (Berlin: Dietz Verlag 2004), pp. 552–75, here p. 568.

15. See Peter Schöttler, 'Mentalitäten, Ideologien, Diskurse. Zur sozialgeschichtlichen Thematisierung der dritten Ebene', in Alf Lüdtke, ed., *Alltagsgeschichte. Zur Rekonstruktion historischer Erfahrungen und Lebensweisen* (Frankfurt/Main & New York, Campus Verlag 1989), pp. 85–136.

GDR. It is indisputable that these experiences ranged the full gamut from carefree happiness to outright terror. These different realities of life in the GDR must not be forgotten. One must ask however, how reasonable a goal it is to give a true account that would satisfy everybody? Perhaps a more attainable goal would be to provide a new account that redresses certain imbalances of those preceding accounts by seeking to include alternative sources and thus being able to derive from a combination of facts and figures general conclusions that respect individual experiences.

Historians of the GDR cannot ignore sources such as the studies carried out by the ZIJ (Central Institute for Youth Research in Leipzig), MfV (Ministry for People's Education), and MfS (Ministry for State Security) files reporting on current moods and trends, oral history interviews, and contemporary literature.[16] Focussing exclusively on 'official' sources, for example, party decrees and resolutions, such as the proponents of a totalitarian view of the GDR often do, gives a crooked likeness of what life in the GDR was like for its population. In order to assess the changes in young people's mentality from the late 1950s to the late 1970s, I have drawn extensively on the above sources, and enhanced them by additional sources. Individual experiences were reflected in over forty detailed sets of answers to an in-depth questionnaire by people who experienced the education system during this period, be it as kindergarten children, pupils, parents, teachers or functionaries. Of course, forty partial stories do not prove anything, but the choice of my interviewees was made so as to guarantee a wide variety of regional origins, social, professional and age backgrounds, and political orientation, however, with all of them sharing the experience of the GDR's unified school system, which turned out not to be so unified after all. In the following, the effects of socialist education on young people are presented within five pivotal areas where new patterns of behaviour emerged.

The Foundation Stone of Civic Education: Anti-fascism

Anti-fascism was an essential characteristic of a 'socialist personality'. It was the foundation stone on which the GDR was established, distinguishing it from the FRG and also representing a genuine desire to break with the national socialist past. By reference to the historical legacy of the anti-fascists, the SED leadership was able to stabilise the GDR and to legitimise their monopoly on power, not least because the biographies of the political leadership showed them to have been active anti-fascists and victims

---

16. ZIJ = Zentralinstitut für Jugendforschung; MfV = Ministerium für Volksbildung; MfS = Ministerium für Staatssicherheit.

of Nazi terror. Anti-fascism was particularly prevalent in education in the early decades, but never ceased to be a major cornerstone of the curriculum and inculcation in mass organisations.

Children were susceptible to the stories of unfaltering anti-fascist heroes, led by the air-brushed and very popular Ernst Thälmann, whose life and works were presented without any complexities and whom they affectionately called by his nickname 'Teddy'.[17] Anti-fascists were presented as intelligent, crafty, upright, partisan, altruistic, and fond of children. The powerful narrative of anti-fascism also struck an emotional chord with teenagers. Acquainting themselves with the sufferings and merits of anti-fascists by visiting former concentration camps and meeting real life anti-fascists deepened their attachment. Brigitte F., a primary teacher from Eisenach born in 1954, said, 'During the pioneers' meetings (*Pioniernachmittage*) we heard a lot about Ernst Thälmann and how he fought against fascism. I totally adored him and thought he was ever so brave. Workers veterans were also invited and told us about their struggle against fascism.'[18] This emotional attachment was supported by a wealth of songs, poems, and novels for children and young people about anti-fascists that were part of the school curriculum.[19] Songs in particular did not fail to impress. Dating mostly from the 1920s, 1930s, and early 1940s, they had as subjects the communists' fight against nascent and reigning Nazism in Germany and fascism in Spain, as well as the Soviet people's help in the anti-fascist struggle. The songs had emotional power that came from combining catchy dramatic tunes with simple, and often rather shocking words telling of bloodshed and historical situations, the meaning of which might have eluded some very young children.

Stories of the predecessors who paved the way for the communist anti-fascists in their battle for a better world such as Karl Marx, Friedrich Engels, and Rosa Luxemburg were also represented in the literary canon, with the (highly embellished) story of Marx's exile in Britain, *Mohr und die*

---

17. See Irma Thälmann, *Erinnerungen an meinen Vater* (Berlin, 1977); Fred Rodrian, *Paul und Janni finden Teddy* (Berlin, kinderbuchverlag 1978); Ilsgard Gollus, *Teddy und seine Freunde* (Berlin, Junge Welt 1969). On the Thälmann cult and myth in the GDR, see René Börrnert, *Wie Ernst Thälmann treu und kühn! Das Thälmann-Bild der SED im Erziehungsalltag der DDR* (Bad Heilbrunn, klinkhardt 2004); idem, *Ernst Thälmann als Leitfigur der kommunistischen Erziehung in der DDR* (Braunschweig: Universitätsbibliothak Braunschweig 2003); A. Nothnagle, *Building the East German myth. Historical mythology and youth propaganda in the GDR 1945–1989* (Ann Arbor, The University of Michigan Press 1999), chap. 3.

18. Brigitte F. questionnaire (8.3.2004). NB : The surnames of my interviewees have been abbreviated to protect their privacy and, where indicated by an asterisk, have been changed completely. The dates in brackets show the date when the responses were received by the author.

19. For example Bruno Apitz, *Nackt unter Wölfen* (Halle, Milteldeutscher Verlag 1958); Dieter Noll, *Die Abenteuer des Werner Holt* (Berlin, Aufban Verlag 1960); Anna Seghers, *'Das Duell'* in idem, *Die kraft der Schwachen.* 9 Erzählungen (Berlin, 1994).

Raben von London, being a classic.[20] In later years, children's literature also distinguished itself by going beyond the focus on Communists as the only righteous people during the Nazi era by addressing the Holocaust.[21] These empathetic works did not feature on reading lists at school, but had to be discovered and digested by the young readers themselves.[22]

Anti-fascists were also omnipresent in young people's environment thanks to the practice of naming schools, holiday camps, streets, factories, youth brigades, awards, and competitions in memory of those resting in the pantheon of resistance fighters (e.g. Arthur Becker, Hans Beimler, Rudolf Breitscheid). The oft-quoted legacy (*Vermächtnis*) of Ernst Thälmann in particular was perceptible throughout young people's life. It was an old tradition: during the Spanish Civil War, two batallions of the International Brigades named themselves after Ernst Thälmann, for example. His name was widely bestowed in the GDR: to the pioneers' organisation, to schools, to pioneer houses, and the 'pioneer palace' in Berlin Wulheide, to so-called 'memorial corners' in schools, to badges and banners for the best pupils, to research assignments for pioneers (*'Thälmanns Namen tragen wir–sei seiner würdig, Pionier!'*),[23] and to annual campaigns such as the *Thälmann-Subbotniks* in August, and naturally to the annual commemorations on 18 August 1944 of the eleven years he spent in solitary confinement and his death in the Buchenwald concentration camp. Erich Honecker in particular saw himself as his successor and liked to point out their similarities, such as the long time spent in jail and their personal fight against Nazism.[24] Under Honecker, the Thälmann myth occupied a much more prominent role in educating the young generations than under Ulbricht. An image that many young people had of Erich Honecker was that of a 'real' old anti-fascist fighter who liked to inspect military parades with his fist risen in the manner of the *Rotfrontkämpferbund* greeting (which was, not surprisingly, known as the *Thälmann-Gruß* in the GDR).

The SED's use of anti-fascism to gain people's allegiance, legitimise itself, and claim moral superiority for the GDR over the Federal Republic has

---

20. Ilse Korn, Vilmos Korn, Mohr und die Raben von London (Berlin, kinderbuchverlag 1962).

21. See for example Gisela Karau, *Der gute Stern des Janusz K.* (Berlin, 1972); Bodo Schulenburg, *Markus und der Golem* (Berlin, verl-Junge Welt 1987).

22. For a list of books 'which deal with the anti-fascist resistance fight, create in readers hate against fascism and neofascism and educate to proletarian internationalism', see 'Empfehlung von Literatur zur Unterstützung der patriotischen Erziehung' (5.10.1961), Bundesarchiv Berlin [henceforth BArch] DR2/6765.

23. Loosely translates as: 'We carry Thälmann's name–pioneer, be worthy, bring not shame!'. Thus was the slogan for the Pionierauftrag [research assignment] of the Thälmann pioneers in the academic year 1971/72. Cf. 'Schuljahresarbeitsplan 1971/72' (ca. 1971), BArch DR2/6487.

24. Cf. Thomas Wollschläger, review of René Börrnert, Ernst Thälmann als Leitfigur <http://hsozkult.geschichte.hu-berlin.de/rezensionen/2003-3-110> (accessed 12.8.2005) (page 1).

received a lot of attention by historians.[25] Critics have pointed out the deficiencies of this one-dimensional message glorifying the role of communists and neglecting other opponents of fascism. In the anti-fascist narrative as well as in the context of compensation and acknowledgement as *OdF* (Victims of fascism, *Opfer des Faschismus*), victims of Nazism such as Jews, Roma, and Sinti, disabled people, homosexuals as well as anti-fascist combatants from the ranks of Social Democrats and Christians were all given a subordinate role or completely left out.[26] The role of Stalinism was also written out of history after 1956.[27] The critics also argue that anti-fascism failed to convey its values, having been 'prescribed' from above. This sweeping statement, however, is contradicted by archival evidence. Certainly, there are a number of incidents recorded involving young people who daubed fascist slogans and symbols in their textbooks and on photographs of leading members of the government.[28] What is striking though is that the majority of these actions were not done out of fascist conviction. Instead, the status of anti-fascism as an 'untouchable' or taboo claim was used by young people in various ways: to underline their discontent with the government and political events (e.g., 13 August 1961 and 20 August 1968); to express a more general dissatisfaction with life; to shock their teachers; but often also in an utterly unthinking infantile way with pupils being unaware of the political provocation this daubing represented. The fact that anti-fascism was such a sacred cow for the SED could cause them to overreact to insalubrious but trivial behaviour. A father (and SED member) of a pupil who was relegated from school in 1978 for having shouted anti-Soviet slogans and singing the *Deutschlandlied* whilst drunk and watching a USSR vs. FRG boxing match with friends scoffed: 'Well, chewing chewing gum and wearing jeans are now indicative of fascist attitudes, aren't they?'[29]

---

25. See for example Antonia Grunenberg, *Antifaschismus–ein deutscher Mythos* (Reinbek, 1993); Armin Mitter, Stefan Wolle, Untergang auf Raten: *Unbekannte Kapitel der DDR-Geschichte* (Munich, Bertelsmann Verlag 1993).

26. Cf. Annette Leo, Peter Reif-Spirek, eds., *Vielstimmiges Schweigen. Neue Studien zum DDR-Antifaschismus* (Berlin, Metropol Verlag 2001); Christoph Hölscher, *NS-Verfolgte im 'antifaschistischen Staat'. Vereinnahmung und Ausgrenzung in der ostdeutschen Wiedergutmachung 1945–1989* (Berlin, Christoph Links Verlag 2002). On the treatment of the NS past in the GDR, see also Jurek Becker's novel *Bronsteins Kinder* (Frankfurt/Main, Suhrkamp Verlag 1986).

27. Christoph Dieckmann, *Das wahre Leben im falschen. Geschichten von ostdeutscher Identität* (Berlin, Christoph Links Verlag 1998), p. 60.

28. See for example 'Kriminalstatistik Jugendlicher 1965–1967' (6.9.1967), Bundesbeauftragte für die Unterlagen des Staatssicherheitsdienstes der ehemaligen DDR, Berlin [henceforth BStU] MfS-HA IX 12011 MF; 'Abschlußbericht zur Aktion Jubiläum 30' (10.10.1979), BStU MfS-HA IX 18560, 3.

29. Cf. 'Relegierung von Schülern: Frank B., EOS „Hansa" Stralsund' (June 1978), BArch DR2/A7361/5.

It is true, however, that anti-fascist education did not immunise everyone against genuine fascist ideas. While the GDR existed, some teenagers gathered in cliques, exalting Nazi leaders and ideas, vilifying the NVA (National People's Army, or *Nationale Volksarmee*) and Red Army and maintaining that fascism also had its 'good sides'.[30] These groupings largely kept to themselves and did not express their viewpoint in violent actions. It was only after the GDR's demise with the concomitant loss of authority and surveillance by the police and Stasi that East German neo-Nazi groups went public and resorted to violence. The attacks on foreigners motivated by racial hatred in the 1990s and, more recently, the success of far-right parties in the Eastern German federal states, are evidence that anti-fascist education in the GDR failed to reach everyone. However, it must not be forgotten that the post–1989 East German neo-Nazis were 'helped along' by right-wing extremist organisations hailing from West Germany, who 'proselytised' in the East and blamed existing problems like unemployment, uncertainty, and a sense of futurelessness on the foreigners now sharing their everyday life.[31] The resulting actions cannot be blamed exclusively on an overdose of anti-fascism in the GDR education system.

So did the education system produce dedicated young anti-fascists? In reports from the 1950s and 1960s, young people often told of their happiness about living in a state that proclaimed itself anti-fascist and their respect for the relatively recent exploits of resistance fighters.[32] By the 1970s and in the 1980s, the overblown and ever-same references to anti-fascists at school had resulted in widespread apathy.[33] The difficulty that young people were faced with was that anti-fascism seemed to be no longer relevant and, in any case, they had no means of proving their genuine commitment as anti-fascists: the Nazi era was long gone, travels to Western states infested with fascists, as they learned in civics classes, were impossible, the People's Police and the MfS kept a very close eye on any nascent fascist sounds coming from inside the GDR, so there was neither any need nor possibility for young people to

30. See for example 'Bericht aus Halle' (March 1963), SAPMO-BArch DY30/IVA2/9.05/57; 'Information über die Aufklärung einer Gruppierung negativer Jugendlicher an der KJS Güstrow' (6.1.1966), BStU MfS ZAIG-Z 1164; 'Hinweise über gewonnene Erkenntnisse und Erfahrungen bei der operativen Bearbeitung und vorbeugenden Absicherung Jugendlicher des Bezirkes Erfurt' (11.4.1979), BStU Bezirksverwaltung für Staatssicherheit Erfurt, Kreisdienststelle Worbis 516.

31. On xenophobia in East Germany, see Damian Mac Con Uladh, *Guests of the socialist nation? Foreign students and workers in the GDR 1949–1989* (unpublished PhD thesis, London, 2005); Jan C. Behrens et al., eds., *Fremde und Fremdsein in der DDR. Zu historischen Ursachen der Fremdenfeindlichkeit in Ostdeutschland* (Berlin, Metropol Verlag 2003).

32. 'Abschlußbericht der "Umfrage 69"' (ca. 1970), BArch FDJ B 6249.

33. 'Die Herausbildung der sozialistischen Lebensweise bei Schülern in der Freizeit und ihr Einfluß auf die Persönlichkeitsentwicklung' (December 1977), BArch DC4/366.

express their own anti-fascist convictions other than repeating slogans. Over the years, the anti-fascist founding myth had become as ossified as the real life anti-fascists in the Politburo. However, anti-fascism in East German education had real substance and was not just a name. The conviction that anti-fascism is good and fascism a bad thing stayed on in most people's minds, even after its 'prescription' from above had run out.

'The Peace Dove Must Have Claws': Socialist Military Education

Socialist military education (*Wehrerziehung*) did not begin in 1978 with the introduction of *Wehrkundeunterricht* (WKU); it was only the last and most controversial insertion of military education into the curriculum. Its beginnings go back to the year 1952, with the militarisation of the *Freie Deutsche Jugend* or FDJ (Free German Youth) ordered by Stalin, and the founding of the paramilitary *Gesellschaft für Sport und Technik* or GST (Society for Sports and Technology). The 1960s brought two principal innovations: a clause in the 1965 Education Act which bound all educational institutions to direct education towards the service of national defence[34] and the introduction of the FDJ *'Hans-Beimler-Wettbewerbe'* in 1968, which were annual competitions for pupils of years 8 to 10 involving sporting exercises, first aid, orientation running, and theoretical military knowledge. The 'increasing aggressiveness' of western militarism necessitated the intensification of military education in the 1970s, including the introduction of the *AG Wehrausbildung* for pupils of years 9 and 10 in 1973[35] and a clause in the Youth Law of 1974, obliging young people to gain pre-military knowledge and to serve in the army.[36]

Military education was supposed to instil values such as a sense of responsibility for the defence of socialism, patriotism, vigilance, discipline, courage, resourcefulness, endurance, and determination in young people. The adornment that the SED gave to Picasso's peace dove, 'the peace dove must have claws' (*die Friedenstaube muß auch Krallen haben*), encapsulates the contradiction inherent in the regime's policy of military education: it defined itself as peace-loving and anti-militaristic; but it crammed young people's lives with as many military components as possible. Whether in kindergarten, school or spare time, militaristic forms of organisation, rituals, and education were ubiquitous. The youngest played with 'peace toys', i.e., toy soldiers and tanks. They learned to differentiate between 'good' and 'bad' soldiers; the former

---

34. Bildungsgesetz, § 5, section 2, p. 90.
35. Eng.: After-school club 'Defence Formation'.
36. Verfassung der DDR und Jugendgesetz (Berlin, Staatsverlag der DDR 1988), 14th ed., § 24, p. 33.

were there to protect their kindergartens, mum, and dad whilst the latter planned to invade their socialist homeland. At school, the curriculum was peppered with military references in nearly all subjects, from multiplying x-numbers of tanks in maths to throwing fake handgrenades in PE. Familial solidarity was employed when older brothers of pupils visited their school to tell them about the 'Honourable Service' (*Ehrendienst*) with the army (*Nationale Volksarmee*, NVA). Days out meeting NVA soldiers were 'an adventure', or at least 'a welcome change since there would be no school' for pupils, as Petra R.*, a graphics designer from Berlin born in 1960, remembered,[37] when they wandered around army bases, tried out the scrambling wall and looked at the soldiers' barracks and weapons. Technically minded pupils could subscribe to two magazines dedicated to military topics: *Armeerundschau* (Army Review) and the GST magazine *Sport & Technik* (Sport and Technology). The Pioneer organisation and FDJ organised 'pioneer manoeuvres' that involved orientation with a map and compass, first aid, and sporting exercises. They were very popular with youngsters since they satisfied their sense of adventure and offered campfire romanticism, with Soljanka from the field kitchen (*Gulaschkanone*) fondly remembered by several of my interviewees.

Older pupils, both boys and girls, were encouraged to join the GST, whose principal purpose was to secure long-service recruits for the army and prepare boys for the demands of military life and civil defence. The GST was able to offer a range of adventurous sports such as parachuting, shooting, diving, and radio communications, so it was popular with boys interested in technology and motor mechanics. There is little evidence that the military aspects left any impression: the majority of people most appreciated the opportunity to pass, cheaply or for free, a driving test for various vehicles and even boats. GST camps during the holidays were often simply seen as a pleasant contrast to the daily grind at school, although boys with little sporting ability dreaded the military-style exercises (going through the same emotions when called up for military service in the NVA). It is open to question whether the GST did anything to prepare young people for the defence of the socialist homeland: reports show that ammunition thefts increased following the events of 13 August 1961 and 21 August 1968;[38] whilst in the late 1970s, gliders and aeroplanes were stolen 'in treacherous attempts to leave the GDR'. The three such attempts made in 1979 were successful,[39]

37. Petra R.* questionnaire (23.4.2004).

38. Cf. 'Abschlußbericht über Ergebnisse der Arbeit der GST 1961' (ca. 1962), SAPMO-BArch DY59/91; 'Einschätzung der besonderen Vorkommnisse im Jahre 1968' (18.2.1969), SAPMO-BArch DY59/136.

39. 'Bericht über besondere Vorkommnisse im Ausbildungsjahr 1978/79' (6.11.1979), SAPMO-BArch DY59/244.

which suggests that, if nothing else, GST training did instil initiative and some technical skills.

The introduction of WKU (military education classes) was hotly debated in the Western press[40] and by the churches in the GDR. Christian parents in particular petitioned for their children's exemption from classes,[41] which in year 9 amounted to about 90 lessons and in year 10 to 26, dedicated to theoretical questions of national defence and practical exercises (mainly shooting and military drill for boys and first aid for girls). The protests were unsuccessful and the SED sought to defuse complaints by pointing out that WKU would enable Christians to practice brotherly love (*Nächstenliebe*) in case of disaster and provide effective help to others in civil defence.[42] The repetitive and shallow rhetoric used in these lessons as well as in civics and FDJ and GST meetings rendered the whole issue of military education unattractive to young people. A fairly typical comment on young people's attitudes is this one dating from 1969: 'The aggressiveness of West German imperialism is often underestimated and the willingness for aggression of the *Bundeswehr* soldiers is often trivialised (*verniedlicht*)'.[43] Familial ties to the Federal Republic proved to be stronger than the negative propaganda about West German soldiers. Similarly, the notion of internationalism and brotherly feelings amongst people from the socialist camp still had a long way to go, as this highly symbolic incident recorded in July 1968 shows:

> Students from Potsdam were violently threatened in a restaurant in Senec (USSR) by a group of male Czechs, because they were thought to be Soviet citizens. When the students revealed themselves to be from the GDR, the Czechs did the fascist greeting and sang the *Deutschlandlied*.[44]

Also, the more the SED painted the picture of a smartly shaven young man in uniform as the paragon of virtue, the more uncool this sort of personality was for teenage boys, particularly in the 1960s and 1970s, when youth culture made it cool to have the longest possible hair and the scruffiest of clothes. It took great courage to refuse any aspect of military education and expose oneself to accusations of being hostile to the state and to peace. Surely, this argument was unanswerable. Consequences of such refusal

---

40. Newspaper articles relating to military education in the GDR from 1976 to 1979 are collected in BStU MfS ZAIG 8844 and BStU MfS ZAIG 8845.

41. 'Einschätzung der Eingaben gegen bzw. zur Einführung und Gestaltung des Wehrunterrichts' (1978), BStU MfS-HA XX 4269, 74–101.

42. Ibid.

43. 'Abschlußeinschätzung der wehrpolitischen und wehrsportlichen Aktion "Signal 20"' (19.6.1969), BArch DY30/IVA2/12/167.

44. 'Informationsbericht' (1.8.1968), BArch DY30/IVA2/12/24.

depended on individual circumstances, but ranged from non-admittance to or relegation from the EOS to imprisonment for pacifists who did not take up the concession to serve as 'spade' or 'construction' soldiers (available from 1964), but refused military service outright.[45]

The introduction of compulsory military aspects into young people's lives, notably conscription in 1962 and the WKU, was met without enthusiasm and some hostility by the majority of those whom it affected. In 1962, opinions voiced were, for example, 'Now the national hymn has to be changed since it says there "No mother shall mourn her son ever again"', or the question, 'Why was conscription only introduced after the 13 August; if this had been done earlier, all young men would have bunked off to the West.'[46] The shocked reaction by a considerable number of young people, and to a lesser extent also by teachers, to the intervention of the Warsaw Pact armies in Czechoslovakia in August 1968 also showed their disappointment at the way the dream of a 'socialism without tanks', as the dramatist Heiner Müller called it, had died.[47] In 1978, pupils and parents questioned mostly the regime's credibility with regard to its much-vaunted policy of peace and détente, and the necessity to add yet another form of military education: 'The GDR needs skilled workers, not soldiers.'[48]

By the late 1970s, young people were tired of educators clinging on to the old friend-foe way of thinking that disregarded the rapprochement between the two ideological camps. ZIJ studies undertaken in the late 1970s and 1980s underlined their satiation with small calibre shooting, military sports, and socialist national defence. Whilst in 1978, (only) 39 percent of 15- and 16-year olds had vouched their 'willingness to defend the GDR risking my life', 48 percent would do so 'with reservations', 10 percent 'hardly', and 3 percent 'not at all'; for 1988, the corresponding percentages were 18, 39, 25, and 18 percent.[49] Contrary to the image presented in children's books and songs, obligatory military service was mostly viewed as an unwelcome interruption in one's life rather than 'Honourable Service'. Those wanting to make a career in the NVA

45. Between 1962 and 1989, the total number of conscientious objectors amounted to only ca. 6000. Cf. Bernd Eisenfeld, 'Wehrdienstverweigerung als Opposition', in Klaus-Dietmar Henke et al., eds., *Widerstand und Opposition in der DDR* (Cologne, Böhlan Verlag 1999), pp. 241–50, here p. 242.

46. 'Bericht aus Dresden' (January 1962), Barch DR2/6966.

47. Reports and statistics on young people daubing slogans and producing pamphlets against the 'supporting measures' of the socialist states can be found in BStU MfS-HA IX 2670; BStU MfS-HA XX/AKD 804; BStU Bezirksverwaltung für Staatssicherheit Cottbus, AKG 026.

48. 'Stand der Vorbereitung der Einführung des Wehrunterrichtes ab Schuljahr 1978/79' (28.6.1978), BStU MfS-HA XX 3879.

49. Peter Förster, 'Die Entwicklung des politischen Bewußtseins der DDR-Jugend zwischen 1966 und 1989', in Walter Friedrich et al., eds., *Das Zentralinstitut für Jugendforschung Leipzig 1966–1990* (Berlin, Edition ost 1999), pp. 71–165, here p. 155.

were not highly regarded by their classmates. The jingle referring to school grades and future prospects, *'Ob Eins oder Vier, wir werden Offizier',*[50] implied that high academic achievement was not required. Increasingly, career soldiers came from families where the father was already a member of the forces.

It is proper for any state to inform its young people on national defence policy and to motivate them to serve their country as soldiers. This was not only the case in socialist countries; the United Kingdom has the Cadet Force and the USA the Junior Reserve Officers' Training Corps. It is however morally wrong to use an ideological 'concept of the enemy' (*Feindbild*) as the core of the motivation, as was the case in the GDR. Most young people felt this instinctively. They saw no need for the peace dove to have claws; their *Feindbild* was an abstract one, since they had been lucky enough not to experience war, unlike the anti-fascist elders who had been responsible for setting up the system of military education. Ultimately, the attempts to motivate the youth of the GDR to defend their country were futile.

Educational Aspects of Changes in the Class System

Whilst the primary aim of education in the GDR was to produce all-round developed socialist personalities, it had another role to play in changing society, and that was to ensure that the vestiges of the capitalist class system did not perpetuate themselves. It was not thought desirable that the children of aristocrats should all aspire to be good socialist diplomats and those of the bourgeoisie to aspire to good socialist doctors or planners, whilst the children of working class parents limited themselves to becoming factory workers, even if the pay was the same (which it was not, see below). With the end of inherited legal privilege, political control, and industrial control, there was officially no class system in the GDR, only class enemies, although objective observers using more subtle definitions than Marx's would have had no difficulty discerning one.[51] Whether or not the classes themselves could be said to still exist was a point of argument. For practical purposes, i.e., positive discrimination, they did, in a strictly non-hierarchical way: workers, peasants, intelligentsia, white-collar, or 'miscellaneous' (*Sonstige*)[52] was written

50. 'Whether [we get] an A or a D, we will become officers.' From the questionnaire by Erika P., a teacher from Erfurt born in 1932 (10.5.2004).

51. For a statistical overview, see Siegfried Grundmann, 'Zur Sozialstruktur der DDR', in Badstübner, *Befremdlich anders*, pp. 20–62.

52. The classification of white collar workers [Angestellte] was changeable; sometimes they formed their own category, sometimes they were part of 'Sonstige', but they were never counted as workers as this meant primarily industrial workers. 'Sonstige' included the few remaining 'capitalists' in the GDR, for instance, those who were self-employed, private entrepreneurs, tax advisors,

after each pupil's name in the school register to record the circumstances of the parents. But Ulbricht's '*sozialistische Menschengemeinschaft*' was basically considered a classless society, whilst under Honecker it was decided that, although class antagonisms had become smaller, classes as such still persisted: 'Although it is necessary to stress the similarities between classes and the stage of socialist circumstances reached, it is also important not to underestimate or obliterate the existing social differences.'[53]

It was the task of the educational establishment to work towards diluting these differences, and its aspirations were to a large extent laudable. The first twenty years after 1945 were a period marked by genuine concern and success in opening up education to the formerly disadvantaged social classes of workers and peasants by introducing a free, unitary school system that did not depend on parental wealth. During this period in particular, *Arbeiter-und-Bauernkinder* (children of workers and peasants) enjoyed positive discrimination, regardless of whether they actually wanted to climb the academic ladder or not. In the mid to late 1960s however, the effect diminished because a part of the first generation who had benefited were now the socialist intelligentsia and were not happy that their children should be discriminated against with regard to further education. The SED's simple solution to this problem was to extend the definition of 'workers' to such an extent that it included nearly everyone, from true industrial workers to functionaries and policemen. Whether one sees this as a sign of success (children all had the same opportunities), or failure (a new class asserting itself), it is a fact that, from the 1970s onwards, social origins played less of a role.

The ZIJ conducted several surveys on the influence of social origins on the formation of the socialist personality. Empirical data indicated that socialisation instances outside school, primarily the parental home, still decisively influenced the formation of young people's personalities. For example, children of SED party members, functionaries, and teachers 'judged ideologically much more positively than children of non-party parents'; and female students whose mothers were housewives had more 'conventional' ideas regarding family and the status of women in society.[54] Higher educated men chose higher educated women (and vice versa) who would then reproduce children with above-average academic results due to parental

and those working within the Churches. Cf. 'Über die soziale Einstufung der Schüler' (ca. 1961), BArch DR2/6343.

53. Cf. Kurt Hager, Der IX. Parteitag und die Gesellschaftswissenschaften. Rede auf der Konferenz der Gesellschaftswissenschaftler der DDR am 25. und 26. November 1976 in Berlin (Berlin, Dietz Verlag 1976), p. 42.

54. 'Zur Persönlichkeitsentwicklung sozialistischer Studenten' (13.3.1975), BArch Bibliothek FDJ/1475, p. 28.

enthusiasm for learning. A corresponding pattern was noted for academic low achievers.[55] A study from 1975, which claimed to be representative for the overall age group of between 17 and 25 years, established that social origins still had a considerable influence on the thinking and attitudes of young people.[56] Those with a working class background were less likely to be influenced by their parents in issues relating to politics and ethics than those having intelligentsia origins.[57] Social origins also influenced the way young people chose to spend their spare time. Those with an intelligentsia background were less interested in owning a motorbike; more interested in a hi-fi unit than a tape recorder; more interested in spending their holidays abroad and camping compared to those with a working class background. Young people with a peasant background were not at all interested in owning cine or photographic equipment.[58] Those with an intelligentsia background were more atheistic and strove more towards a leadership position compared to those from workers' and peasants' families. On the subject of their willingness to defend the country, they showed the least disposition and 'a greater discrepancy between vague agreement (word) and concrete (deed) than young workers'.[59]

This supports my contention that those wanting to get ahead in the GDR were more likely to play to the tune of the party than to believe wholeheartedly. Working class children were often more honest with themselves and their environment when it came to ideological guidelines. Asked what he understood by the term 'socialist personality', one of my interviewees, Steffen S., an electrician from Sprötau near Erfurt born in 1966, from a true working class home with an electrician father and a postwoman mother, said: 'On leaving school you were a personality when you had something that others needed in this economy of scarcity. I became an electrician and my moonlighting was sought-after. Flag-carrying on Labour Day was not important in whether or not one was appreciated in society.'[60]

For all of its faults, the GDR was not a society riven by class antagonisms. According to the ZIJ, this was a consequence of the public ownership of the means of production,[61] but even if workers did not feel similar to the

55. 'Forschungsbericht "Schüler in Spezialzirkeln"' (June 1979), BArch DC4/368, p. 13.

56. 'Parlamentsstudie 1975. Zusatzbericht: "Zum Einfluß der sozialen Herkunft"' (June 1977), BArch Bibliothek FDJ/6283.

57. Ibid., p. 21.

58. Ibid.

59. Ibid.

60. Steffen S. questionnaire (18.3.2004).

61. Cf. 'Parlamentsstudie 1975. Zusatzbericht: "Zum Einfluß der sozialen Herkunft"' (June 1977), BArch Bibliothek FDJ/6283, p. 20.

managers of their factory, they did at least feel that inequality was being redressed. This was due to various factors. First, the gap between wages was much reduced; the ratio between the lowest and highest salary within an industry or profession was about 1:3.[62] Second, the consequence of the socialist housing policy was that people of all social backgrounds and with differing financial resources lived as neighbours in the *Plattenbauten* (prefabricated high-rise buildings). Third, the economy of scarcity meant that status symbols were limited; there were only two sorts of car, for example. And lastly, the education system was a major contributor to the great social mobility in the GDR by enabling children from any social background to make their way in society, so long as they 'played by the rules'.

Working for Society: Polytechnic Education

In accordance with the Marxist emphasis on production, the education system had always taken care not only to develop pupils' intellectual abilities, but also their practical ones. In the lower years, this was done through elementary courses in woodwork and metal work, gardening, and needlework. In 1958, following the example of the Soviet Union, polytechnic education lessons in the form of the *'Unterrichtstag in der Produktion'* (UTP, Education Day in Production) were introduced into the curriculum. Every other week, pupils in years 7 to 12 had theoretical instruction lessons (*Einführung in die sozialistische Produktion*, ESP), technical drawing (*Technisches Zeichnen*, TZ) and a course of practical work in production (*Produktive Arbeit*, PA). UTP was intended to strengthen the bond between academic learning and the world of work, to familiarise pupils with the economic basics of socialist production, and to promote work-related virtues of a socialist personality, i.e., 'a socialist attitude towards labour through close contacts between pupils and the teams of working people and through independent, responsible execution of production tasks'.[63] The contents differed according to geographical location, so pupils in industrial areas had their polytechnic lessons in local factories whereas pupils from rural areas went to their local LPG and MTS and learned about animal husbandry and agriculture as well as agricultural machinery.[64]

Daring an experimental phase unique in German educational history between 1962 and 1966, EOS pupils studying for their *Abitur* also

62. Cf. Wolfgang Engler, *Die Ostdeutschen. Kunde von einem verlorenen Land* (Berlin, Aufban Verlag 1999), p. 179.

63. Bildungsgesetz, part 4, § 16, p. 99.

64. LPG = Landwirtschaftliche Produktionsgenossenschaft [agricultural collective]; MTS = Maschinen-Traktoren-Station [tractor deposit].

received full vocational training. The 'class enemy' commented on this development 'These young people will become either bad sixth-formers, bad skilled workers, or probably both.'[65] Maybe the *Bonner Rundschau* was right because the idea was abandoned when it became obvious that the demands were too great intellectually and physically and contradicted the Education Act, which stated that the EOS was there to prepare pupils for university education.[66] 'To expect them to qualify as lorry-drivers or post-office technicians, when none of them is likely to pursue these occupations, is an over-generous interpretation of the principle of "linking the school with life".'[67] After this defeat, a subject called 'scientific-practical work' (*Wissenschaftlich-praktische Arbeit*, WPA) was introduced for EOS pupils in 1969, which continued polytechnic instruction but, as the name suggests, focused on introducing pupils to scientific research methods as a preparation for their further studies.

Meanwhile in the POS, UTP received both criticism and compliments. Comments made by parents at the time of its introduction illustrate that traditional notions with regard to girls' education still existed in the late 1950s and early 1960s: there were demands for a differentiation between polytechnic education for boys and girls ('Where are needlework classes for the girls? This is more important for them than metalwork.'),[68] and calls for the inclusion of home economics and baby care into the curriculum.[69] Polytechnic instruction had a bad press in the Federal Republic initially, as the title of a lurid article in the *Berliner Morgenpost* from 1959 indicates: 'They have to toil in the kolkhoz "Dawn"–Children from East Berlin know no holiday bliss–Pupils must fulfil utopian plans–Dearth of workers in the Zone sees a return to 19th century practices.'[70] The western view of polytechnic education as inhumane child labour had moderated by the mid 1960s and changed to an attentive observation of the theoretical and practical implementation of the Marxist idea.[71] It was internationally recognised that, perhaps, this new ap-

---

65. 'Argumentationen in der Westpresse und NATO-Sendern zur Einführung der Berufsausbildung an den EOS' (5.12.1962), BArch DR2/6630.

66. Bildungsgesetz, part 4, § 21, p. 104.

67. Nigel Grant, *Society, Schools and Progress in Eastern Europe* (Oxford, Pergamon Press 1969), p. 221.

68. 'Stand der Diskussion über die neue Schulordnung' (24.12.1959), Thüringisches Hauptstaatsarchiv Weimar [henceforth ThHStAW], Bezirkstag und Rat des Bezirkes Erfurt, V02.

69. 'Beschwerdeanalyse Abt. Oberschulen 1.1. bis 15.6.1961' (19.6.1961), BArch DR2/6829.

70. 'Zeitungsausschnitte ("Lügenpropaganda") des VEB Zeitungsauschnittdienstes Globus', here: Berliner Morgenpost (6.8.1959), SAPMO-BArch DY25/1946.

71. Subject to revision: Writing in 2002, John Rodden, for example, described the GDR's polytechnic school system as 'a faceless, hulking, centralised bureaucracy mired in inefficiency and incompetence'. John Rodden, *Repainting the little red schoolhouse. A history of Eastern German Education 1945–1995* (Oxford, Oxford University Press 2002), p. 15.

proach was the way forward in a 'technological age',[72] and the GDR was seen to be in the vanguard of polytechnic education in the eastern bloc.[73] So much as far as theory was concerned. For those on the receiving end of UTP, it was experienced primarily as a welcome and mildly exciting break from sitting on the school bench and was inevitably subject to the law of unintended consequences. Regine H., an actress from Weimar born in 1951, said:

> UTP was for us pupils hardly inspiring, but we learned to work with different materials, to make something with our hands, and perhaps also unconsciously to appreciate what dirty and boring jobs those people, especially the women, were doing day-to-day. I am glad that I experienced it though, if only to know that this will never be my life.[74]

Dietrich E., a church musician from Guben born in 1957, mentioned another aspect: 'Partly, we experienced socialist production in all its absurdity and paltriness, also in its slackness—workers playing skat all morning! Overall rather repugnant. But at times also humanely impressive or enthralling for those boys interested in technology.'[75] Steffi K.-P., a copywriter from Orlamünde born in 1959, pointed to another problem of the planned economy, saying that during UTP, she met many 'normal workers' with whom the idea of the 'FDJ as the vanguard of the Party' did not wash. 'They were more interested in knowing why there weren't any power points available once again.'[76] These examples explain why UTP was also known amongst pupils as *'Unterschied zwischen Theorie und Praxis'* (difference between theory and practice). Another criticism was that pupils were often made to do menial jobs, for example, boxing bicycle dynamos or filing the tips of soldering irons, which the factory manager was glad to be able to pass on to the youngsters instead of using his paid workforce to do it, with no regard for educational value. Ottokar Domma, a character from a well-known children's book, satirised it thus: 'At the moment we are making key boards. But there aren't enough keys around for the number of key boards that we're making. . . . Our teacher said that he always has to think of the Soviet cosmonauts and that one can't conquer space with key boards.'[77] Whilst not

72. A.J. Peters, 'The changing idea of technical education', in *British Journal of Educational Studies*, no. 2 (November 1963): 142–66. Quoted in Oskar Anweiler, *Schulpolitik und Schulsystem in der DDR* (Opladen, Verlag Leske und Budrich 1988), p. 59.

73. Ibid., p. 74.

74. Regine H. questionnaire (14.2.2004).

75. Dietrich E. questionnaire (22.5.2004).

76. Steffi K.-P. questionnaire (24.2.2004).

77. Ottokar Domma, Der brave Schüler Ottokar (Berlin, Eulenspiegel Verlag 1982, 4th ed.), p. 31.

quite building space craft, sometimes pupils would be entrusted with 'carrying out repairs for customers' in retail and trade, as was the case for the UTP course in electrotechnology and car mechanics in Gotha.[78] And there are even reports of pupils actually enjoying their productive day out: 'We like working here because we can see that we can actively help to fulfil the *Wohnungsbauprogramm* (housing construction programme) with the results of our work. Apart from that, we enjoy the work because we are respected by the colleagues and can prove what we have to offer.'[79] When a survey was carried out by the *Institut für Schulentwicklungsforschung* of the University of Dortmund in 1991, polytechnic instruction received strong approval, 'with only 13 percent of East German parents who were asked saying that it had *not* proved its worth'.[80]

Another way of introducing pupils to societal life and work was through the partnership of every school class with a '*Patenbrigade*', a team of workers from local factories, cooperatives or an army base. They were supposed to have a positive influence on pupils' career choices, pupils visited their place of work, prepared cultural programmes, and sent congratulatory cards on their partners' official honourable day. This idea initially met with little sympathy and a great deal of incomprehension on the part of workers, who were unsure of their role as 'godparents' to the children. The bosses also had problems accepting their workers' engagement as *Patenbrigaden*, as in this example from 1962: 'The EOS "Heinrich Mann" in Erfurt informed us that the director of their *Patenbetrieb*, the Bau-Union Erfurt, stands against the formation of friendship contracts, giving as a reason that the strain would be too large due to production requirements that need fulfilling'.[81] Nevertheless, over the years the idea of *Patenbrigaden* became an integral part of the socialisation process, but the usefulness of this partnership varied widely. Not only were there workers' brigades whose behaviour made them unsuitable as role models for pupils; the joint activities undertaken also depended on the enthusiasm of individual members. In general, the *Patenbrigaden* were most appreciated in their capacity of presenting book vouchers to the best pupils and financing class excursions or Christmas parties. The effect on pupils' career choices was limited, as Ulla M., a kindergarten teacher from Eisenach born in 1950, summarised: 'We had

---

78. 'Schuljahresanalyse 1960/61 der Abt. Volksbildung, Rat des Kreises Gotha' (ca. 1961), ThHStAW, Bezirkstag und Rat des Bezirkes, V41/1.

79. 'Bezirkstag Erfurt, Ständige Kommission Bildung und Erziehung: Stand und Probleme der Produktiven Arbeit' (1977), BArch DR2/D129, vol. 1.

80. (My emphasis). Rosalind Pritchard, Reconstructing education. East German schools and universities after unification (New York, Berghahn Books 1999), p. 34.

81. 'Einschätzung der Arbeit an den EOS unseres Bezirkes' (15.1.1962), ThHStAW, Bezirkstag und Rat des Bezirkes Erfurt, V139.

a very good relationship with our *Patenbrigade*, but no one in our class became a tram driver.'[82] An official assessment of the *Patenarbeit* in 1976 covered all of the above aspects and noticed something else too. Schools in the Thuringian countryside were having difficulties in finding partners for the higher years, with LPG brigades citing 'formal reasons' (hygiene and contagious disease guidelines) for being unforthcoming.[83] Perhaps this was the truth, or perhaps the peasants were simply too busy or too lazy to engage in societal acitivites. But it seems odd that they only objected to older pupils. Could this be an indication that the peasants had inhibitions about meeting the higher-educated young generation?

With productive work being a cornerstone of GDR society, there was absolutely no question that any pupil would not earn a living after leaving school. The SED claimed: 'A formulation that expresses the capitalist work ethic like *"Arbeit adelt, aber wir bleiben bürgerlich"* undermines the dignity of a socialist worker.'[84] In this light, the SED's policy to send unruly pupils to 'work in production to prove their worth' (*Bewährung in der Produktion*) seems very strange: equating work with punishment?[85] The Party failed to make traditional, 'true working-class' jobs involving hard physical labour, at an open cast mine or blast furnace for instance, seem attractive. Agriculture in particular was extremely unpopular with both pupils and parents. In 1963, the reason for this was seen to be that they let themselves be guided by 'prejudices against professions in animal and plant production and not by the true perspective of socialist agriculture'.[86] Especially in the 1950s and 1960s, pupils were encouraged to see it as 'an honourable task' to take up an agricultural profession.[87]

When it came to choosing a career generally, it was inevitable that economic requirements did not coincide with young people's aspirations. The workforce tended to be recruited where it was needed and this caused much frustration. For those young people who fled to the West before 1961 or tried to do so afterwards, this was a principal factor in their desire to leave the GDR. Although career guidance staff tried their best to interest pupils

82. Ulla M. questionnaire (22.2.2004).

83. 'Information über die Zusammenarbeit zwischen den Betrieben, Kombinaten, LPG und Schulen bei der klassenmäßigen Bildung und Erziehung der Jugend' (15.3.1976), ThHStAW, Bezirkstag und Rat des Bezirkes Erfurt, Nr. 013785.

84. Eng.: 'Work makes you noble. We prefer to remain middle-class.' (Source): Peter-Bernd Schulz, 'Sozialistische Arbeit, Menschenwürde und Persäulichheit' in DDR Arbeits-und Lebensbedingungen, Berliner Ausgabe, Supplement, 30.11.1957 (newspaper article).

85. 'Pupils who show such wrong political attitudes have no right to prepare themselves with the Abitur for responsible tasks in state and economy. They have to prove themselves in the socialist production.' Cf. 'Relegierung von Schülern' (June 1978), BArch DR2/A7361/5.

86. 'Eingaben an das Ministerium für Volksbildung im II. Quartal 1963' (6.9.1963), BArch DR2/7783.

87. See for example 'Argumentation für die Berufswahl der Absolventen der EOS' (19.3.1962), BArch DR2/6978.

in careers as toolmakers or a long-term career in the army, the ZIJ stated in 1973 that 'in lots of areas, personal career aspirations and societal requirements have not coincided for many years now'.[88] Pupils continued to have 'unrealistic' ideas of taking up 'fashionable' or 'dream' careers as doctors, pilots, actresses or were 'wrongly' influenced by parents and friends to make their choices on 'wrong criteria': 'gaining kudos, having an easy life, earning lots of money, having a clean job and learning skills that were "useful" in life outside work in household and family'.[89] A large number were disappointed with the world of work; about one in three young people followed a 'vocation' for which they had no personal interest,[90] resulting in deception, discontent, and later, regular changes of jobs.[91]

'Boys Shouldn't Always Think That We're Incapable': Girls Growing Up

The issue of gender in relation to the concept of the 'socialist personality' is remarkable insofar as it is completely absent. None of the definitions or literature on the subject refers to any difference, or differentiations to be made, between boys and girls. Nevertheless, a section on girls is included here since socialist education and socialisation did contribute to the emergence of a new breed of women and mothers, which one of my interviewees, Jan S.*, a physician from Bad Salzungen born in 1959, described thus:

> In the GDR, the mother was a hybrid of a Red Guards woman, Madame Curie, Annemarie Brodhagen, activist and mother sow, i.e. there *were* endeavours to overcome the classical role understanding. Indeed the demand was for children (plenty), but at the same time the woman was also supposed to be employed, spruce and sensual, with a steadfast class standpoint and able to knock up tasty cabbage dishes'.[92]

Right from the start, the education system was co-educational, thus opening up the same career prospects for both girls and boys. From the school's side, everything was done to enable and encourage girls to pursue academic excellence. It took a little more than a decade before girls were academically on a par with the boys, who were traditionally favoured by education and so,

---

88. 'Probleme der Berufsvorbereitung und Berufswahl bei Jugendlichen' (1973), BArch Bibliothek FDJ/6291, p. 3.

89. Ibid., p. 3.

90. Ibid., p. 4.

91. Ibid. Cf. also 'Zum Problemerleben von 17jährigen Jugendlichen' (1974), BArch Bibliothek FDJ/6293, p. 3.

92. (Emphasis in the original). Jan S.* questionnaire (3.2.2004). NB : Annemarie Brodhagen was a popular GDR television presenter.

initially, better achievers at school. In 1961, the girls of a POS were asked to write an essay on the question: 'What do you expect from the boys in your class as part of the completion of the societal demand for the sexual equality of women?' Most demands were for respect, comradely attitudes, and helpfulness: 'The boys should carry the heavy boxes in UTP'. 'They should stop treating us like little girls, but they should also support us when we can't advance in certain subjects like physics.' 'They shouldn't put things past us. Even if many things are easier for them, they should be proud when we work hard to understand the subject matter. The boys shouldn't always think that we are incapable.'[93] The radical changes in traditional thinking that occurred in the 1960s and 1970s are apparent from these essays. Thanks to the approach of the school system, girls became academically very strong and consequently more self-assured. In fact, girls did so well at school and applied so numerously for the EOS that often boys with lower marks were taken in simply to keep parity in numbers. Long-term studies by the ZIJ found that many girls showed better attitudes to learning than boys, more willingness for self-improvement, and later as women, more energy in order to accommodate and accomplish all demands in the best possible way.[94]

By the early 1950s, it was taken for granted that after graduation from school, girls would either learn a trade or go on to gain higher qualifications. In most cases, their profession was not just seen as an interim solution until marriage. Sonja Walter asked in 1958: 'What would one be without work? Nothing. One would not even exist. . . . Yet the technical revolution cannot be accomplished with the professions preferred by many girls. . . . We cannot leave it solely to the boys to shape the future, can we?'[95] Whilst the problem that girls were influenced by their parents to learn a traditional female vocation and themselves preferred areas such as administration, retail, and education persisted throughout the four decades, by the 1960s girls increasingly also took up atypical jobs as construction engineers or crane operators, although by no means to the extent desired by the SED. The equalisation of gender roles, however, took a back seat to economic requirements, demonstrated by the fact that men were missing from typical female professions and that there continued to exist badly paid female labour in spinning mills

93. Cf. 'Schüleraufsätze POS Glashütte' (March 1961), BArch DR2/6772. NB: There was no indication as to the age of the girls.

94. 'Forschungsbericht: Zu Fragen der sozialistischen Persönlichkeitsentwicklung von Mädchen und jungen Frauen in der DDR' [henceforth Frauenstudie] (June 1975), BArch DC4/234, p. 15. For an overview of ZIJ results on gender issues, see Uta Schlegel, 'Geschlechter-und Frauenforschung', in Friedrich, Das Zentralinstitut, p. 373–91.

95. Sonja Walter, *Zwischen vierzehn und achtzehn: ein Buch für junge Mädchen* (Berlin, Verlag Neues Leben 1958), pp. 16f. and 31.

or the textile industry generally. Also, there were far fewer women in higher positions; Margot Honecker being an exception as the *Volksbildungsminister* (Minister for Education; note that the masculine version was her official form of address, lacking the feminine suffix–*in*). An opinion expressed by a girl in the above-mentioned essays underlines the difficulties that girls had in being accepted in a managerial capacity: 'I think that with sexual equality, a girl could be elected to become FDJ secretary, too. But only if she has the knowledge necessary for that.'[96]

In comparison to the education system, it was socialisation in the family that clung on to patterns handed down from one generation to the next. Parents usually granted sons greater autonomy in their spare time at a younger age than daughters, acting out of an 'awareness of greater responsibility for adolescent girls regarding sexual challenges'. Daughters were more strongly integrated into household chores than sons, in anticipation of their future double role as mothers and working women. Sons not only benefited from an advantageous allocation of household tasks, but also from receiving more presents and pocket money. The father as the role model was regarded as crucial to educating socialist personalities at home, and in this respect the ZIJ spoke of a 'success of a socialist reconfiguration of norms', for in two thirds of families, both parents made joint efforts to bring up their children instead of leaving the bulk of this task solely to the mother.[97]

Images of 'women as competent tractor drivers, far-sighted mayors and skilled engineers which populated East German newspapers, DEFA films and novels', to quote Gunilla-Friederike Budde,[98] were not merely propaganda creations, but reality. Already by the mid 1950s, half of all the women in the GDR had a job; and this proportion increased by about ten percent in each following decade, so that by the late 1980s, 91.2 percent of working-age women were in the equivalent of paid employment.[99] But a closer inspection of the GDR media images might reveal another characteristic of these East German 'super-women'–how tired they looked. Despite the state's provision of industrial laundries, factory, and school

96. 'Schüleraufsätze POS Glashütte' (March 1961), BArch DR2/6772.

97. Cf. Frauenstudie (1975), p. 69. Studies undertaken between 1965 and 1970 showed that on average, women spent 37.1 hours per week on household chores such as cooking, cleaning, washing, and shopping. Whilst 'traditional housewives' worked 51.5 hours per week, full-time employed women worked only (!) 30.8 hours for their families. Ibid., p. 87.

98. Gunilla-Friederike Budde, *Frauen arbeiten. Weibliche Erwerbstätigkeit in Ost- und Westdeutschland nach 1945* (Göttingen Verlag Vandenhoeck und Ruprecht, 1997), p. 11.

99. Cf. ibid., p. 10. NB: This figure is inclusive of female students and apprentices. Less those, the figure stands at 80 percent.

canteens (and very modern ideas such as a shopping service and meal-delivery services existing in the early 1960s)[100] that were supposed to alleviate women's and particularly mothers' workloads, throughout the lifetime of the GDR it was the case that women bore the brunt of everyday organisation of family life. So it should have been no surprise for the ZIJ researchers that whilst young men went in for sports in their spare time, women preferred to sleep and rest.[101] And yet, for women as well as for men, working in the GDR was more than a way of earning money. The community spirit of a *Kollegenkollektiv* (colleagues' collective) played a role here, but also the fact that, as Adelheid K., a teacher from Orlamünde born in 1934, mentioned: 'There was no special "mother role" in most families. After having children, mothers quickly took up their work again, i.e. they *wanted* to work again. Work for women was not only important as an income source, but they worked because it added to their sense of self-worth.'[102] An indication of how far emancipation had progressed is that by the 1970s, two thirds of divorce petitions were filed by women, suggesting that women were financially independent from their husbands and did not need to fear material disadvantages.[103]

Despite the high demands made of them by societal life, women generally responded more positively to political demands and the realities of life than men: a more pronounced pride in the GDR, acceptance of the leading role of the SED, a better relation to the Soviet Union, and a better attitude to the FDJ and societal involvement.[104] In this respect, the state's endeavours to improve women's societal standing by means of legislation and material help, most notably in the form of free pre-school education, bore fruit in ensuring women's loyalty. The first generation of women who had been socialised solely under socialist conditions had internalised new mindsets and attitudes by the late 1960s. Halfway through its lifetime, the GDR had made great societal progress, which, according to Marx, can be 'measured exactly by the societal status of the fairer sex, including the ugly ones'.[105] Nevertheless, from the mid 1970s onwards, fewer children were being born, resulting in a declining population; and this prompted the SED to improve its social policies to take account of a woman's family life and her societal duties, for example, by a rise in child benefits and maternity leave

---

100. Helga Ulbricht et al., Probleme der Frauenarbeit (Berlin, Verlag Die Wirtschaft, Schriftenreihe Arbeitsökonomik, Heft 7 1963), p. 13.

101. Frauenstudie (1975)., pp. 10 and 15.

102. (Emphasis in the original). Adelheid K. questionnaire (24.2.2004).

103. Cf. Frauenstudie (1975), p. 82.

104. Along with those positive positions, the ZIJ also stated that beliefs in 'fate' and 'talismans' still persisted in women. Ibid., 7.

105. Marx in a letter to Dr Kugelmann (1968). Cited in Frauenstudie (1975), p. 94.

for the second child.[106] Despite the success of 'emancipation' with regard to overcoming traditional patterns in both professional and private life, the ZIJ was realistic enough to estimate that in socialism, only an 'extensive approximation to full sexual equality' was possible, full equality only being obtainable in the future classless society of communism.[107]

Conclusion: Emergence of the *Homo Germanicus Orientalis*

Growing up in the socialist education system of the GDR could not fail to leave traces on young people. The experiment of trying to mould young people into utopian socialist personalities did not and could not succeed on all fronts; yet the outcome was indeed a particular type of 'East German human being'. The 'end products' of the GDR education system were much more manifold than the woodcut-like model of the intended socialist personality. The point in time when distinct East German 'new human beings'—albeit not the envisaged one hundred percent socialist ones—began to appear can be placed in the mid 1960s. It is hardly surprising that this coincides with the time when the first generation socialised solely in the GDR reached maturity. They grew up exclusively in a socialist world and acquired their ideological and general attitudes under stabilised political conditions. They took for granted their country's orientation towards and connection with the socialist camp with the Soviet Union at its helm. They were more likely to cheer for the East German than the West German football team. Up until the 1970s, to some extent the international situation with the worldwide liberation movements seemed to follow what they learned at school about the 'natural laws of history' and humanity's development towards socialism. Archival evidence such as this contemporary report by a British observer summarises this change: 'To the young who have never known anything but the present regime, the years of living in a different social system with a different vocabulary, different political principles and a different economic organisation are beginning to create a feeling of separateness.'[108] Those who were teenagers in the early 1960s displayed an

106. Simone Tippach-Schneider, 'Sieben Kinderwagen, drei Berufe und ein Ehemann. DDR-Frauengeschichten im Wandel der Sozialpolitik', in Dokumentationszentrum Alltagskultur der DDR, ed., *Fortschritt, Norm und Eigensinn. Erkundungen im Alltag der DDR* (Berlin, Christoph Links Verlag 1999), p. 129.

107. *Frauenstudie* (1975), p. 5.

108. Major General Peel-Yates, General Officer Commanding, British Sector, Berlin: 'Report on the present mood of East German population' (14.8.1965), PRO FO 371/183002 RG1016/31. Thanks to Merrilyn Thomas for this information.

identity that was utterly different from that of the previous generation, who had still been marked by post-war scarcities and stronger moral constraints. Young East Germans did not necessarily 'ape any rubbish that came out of the West', to paraphrase Ulbricht, nor did they dismiss everything that was homegrown in the GDR as 'rubbish'. The new generation was confident enough to decide for themselves how they wanted to live, albeit within the limits given by the regime.

The appearance of a distinct East German identity, however, did not indicate that young people had been moulded as the SED had hoped; nor did it encompass everyone. With regard to the civic demands made of them, many strongly rejected the day-to-day presentation at school of a black and white world-view on the grounds that both familial connections to West Germany and, increasingly from the mid 1960s onwards, western television put claims about the evil enemy on the other side of the border into question. Parental opinion also prompted pupils to have their doubts as to the validity of these claims. A joke was told behind closed doors: 'A GDR citizen asks for permission to leave the country: he wants to go to the GDR portrayed in the newspaper.'[109] The GDR's own media and textbooks gave an over-rosy portrayal, which denied and suppressed the problems and conflicts existing in socialist society as well. By adding to this the practice of penalising those who dared to speak out, the regime produced generations of Janus-faced young people.

The ZIJ undertook numerous studies of young people's mindsets regarding their 'political-ideological awareness'. They reveal that positive attitudes towards socialism reached their peak in the mid 1970s, but this result might be deceptive. It is often forgotten that the ZIJ first conducted their surveys in 1966, and hence that there is no comparative basis for the early Ulbricht years. Asked when they felt most happy in the GDR and at ease with its political system and everyday life, the answers of my interviewees could not have been more diverse. Numerically, both the 1960s and 1970s came out on top, but there were also some who named the period after Stalin's death and the abolition of food tokens until the building of the Wall as the most liberal and enjoyable period, when post-war hardship had gone, people's expectations were still modest, and the freedom to travel to the West still available. The 1980s were nominated very rarely as an enjoyable period, although some felt that by then the regime had slackened the reins regarding issues such as reception of the western media. A feeling of happiness is of course not only related to societal circumstances, but perhaps

109. Erika P. questionnaire (10.5.2004).

primarily to personal life experiences; so any attempt to pinpoint a 'golden age' for the GDR is futile.

To form young Christians according to the socialist image was a particular challenge for the SED. Officially, the Party took the same line as Frederick the Great who supposedly said, 'In my state everybody may go to Heaven in their own way, but the Church is not to meddle in state affairs.'[110] However, given the clash between Marxist-Leninist principles and Christian teachings, the SED attempted to steer young people away from competing convictions. The 1950s were a confrontational phase that had both the Party and churches engaging in a tug of war. Although church youth work often catered better to young people's interests than that of the FDJ and was more readily adopted, by the early 1960s, to the chagrin of the churches, most young Christians too had internalised the norms that were required of them in order to get ahead in the system. Being societally active and showing proof of one's commitment to the GDR via participation in socialist rituals such as the *Jugendweihe* and membership of the youth organisation had become second nature to them as well. Those who were so committed to their faith that they would not compromise in any way suffered the hard grip of the state authorities and were forced either to live their lives within the confines of the church or to apply for permission to leave the country. The slogan from the Ulbricht days 'Ohne Gott und Sonnenschein fahren wir die Ernte ein' (Without the Lord or rays of sun, we will get the harvest done) sums up the SED's attitude towards religion: derision, arrogance, animosity, and the conviction that their own progressive attitude would triumph over belief. To be a good socialist citizen and a Christian was an equation that for the SED could not be balanced. By holding on to the image of the church as an old foe, the Party often deprived itself of young people who were both Christian and proponents of socialism. The church itself also had problems accepting the state's attempt to attach the character of people's personality to class struggle, ideology, and politics. It disagreed with the goal of the 'socialist personality', because it implied that a human being's personality was valued in terms of its ideological conviction and that an individual's interests must agree with those of society. According to Christian belief, human dignity is inherent and not bestowed by society, hence the church opposed the state's exertion of influence in spheres of human life that were none of its business. Eventually the majority of young Christians were able to cope well with having two worldviews, one for home and one for school. Whilst the SED did not quite destroy Christianity in the GDR, it did succeed in the atheisation

110. Popularly attributed.

of large parts of the population. In 1989, only 11 percent of all pupils still said they were Christian.[111] The notion of an active, powerful Christian community in the GDR had by then become only the wishful thinking of the church leadership and the paranoid thinking of the SED, rather than reality. At that time, the State Secretary for Church Questions, Klaus Gysi, had told West German journalists: 'In the GDR, the true Christians are, with 3 million people, a marginal phenomenon on the one side, but the true Marxists are, with 2.5 million people, a marginal phenomenon on the other. Most people believe neither in Marx nor in God.'[112]

Several determining factors would have been necessary for young people to live up to the idea of the 'socialist personality': parents with a socialist and atheist worldview; no 'contamination' with a different worldview through relations in the FRG or Western media; ideologically sound teachers; peers coming from a similar home; success at school; and plenty of positive distraction in their spare time in order to prevent them from straying from the path. The ingredients of this 'recipe' for a socialist personality are by no means exhaustive, but give an idea about the complexity of factors involved in making the outcome successful. My interviewee replies also showed that school in the GDR was just one of many factors of socialisation, the potency of which is often overestimated. A number of them however said that they had not experienced any ideology in their education, which is perhaps an indication of success in the socialisation process: it went unnoticed because it saturated all areas of life, and its consequences remain unnoticed even till this day, for example, with regard to limited freedom of movement. Doris P., an administrator from Sprötau near Erfurt born in 1955, said: 'We lived a quiet life in our village. I never felt constricted. As far as the freedom to travel is concerned, we never had any money for holidays anyway because we built our house.'[113]

An important point with regard to civic attitudes must not be forgotten: age played a crucial role. Most young children accepted political indoctrination, unless parental opinion prompted them to do otherwise. For the most part, they did not call into question the world-view presented in school, and they also enjoyed the activities offered by the pioneer organisation and thought military education in the form of mock manoeuvres and visits to the local army base exciting. The onset of puberty, which roughly coincided with

---

111. Cf. Ilona Schneider, 'Kinder aus christlichen Familien in der DDR', in Deutsches Jugendinstitut, ed., *Was für Kinder. Aufwachsen in Deutschland* (Munich, kösel Verlag 1993), pp. 317–21, here p. 317.

112. Arnold Freiburg, 'Schüler, Ordnung und Disziplin. Deutsch-deutsche Fakten und Überlegungen zur Erziehung und zum Schulalltag', in Barbara Hille, Walter Jaide, eds., *DDR-Jugend. Politisches Bewusstsein und Lebensalltag* (Opladen, Verlag Leske und Budrich 1990), pp. 276–80, here p. 279, n 1.

113. Doris P. questionnaire (21.3.2004).

admission to the FDJ, meant however that many adolescents began to have other interests–and thus lost their infantile enthusiasm–and regarded their collective organisation as a necessary evil or a waste of valuable spare time.

Although it is extremely difficult to make generalisations, it may be concluded that socialist education was most successful in reaching young people's hearts and minds when it came to sweeping across-the-board values and qualities such as love of peace, anti-fascism, solidarity, helpfulness, and collectivity. A majority of them did internalise the 'good' moral and societal values inherent in socialism as a theory; they honestly participated in societal life as proposed by the state beyond a simple outward conformity, whilst stubbornly refusing to be used by the SED for ends other than those they desired for themselves, especially so in their private lives once they had left the education system with its many constraints. By the early 1960s, young people had learnt to play by the rules imposed on them in order to get ahead or to be left alone. Least successful were the SED's attempts at instilling 'civic' values, namely the politicisation and militarisation of young people. This can be deduced from the fact that at no point in time during the forty years of the GDR's existence did the SED feel that it could release the pressure of civic education on young people. It was never confident that they had sufficiently internalised the values of political-ideological education and militarisation for it to do so.

For most people born after 1945, the GDR became not only their geographical, but also their emotional *Heimat*. To the proponents of the thesis that the GDR never did, and never could, become the 'home' of a people imprisoned by mental and physical borders, I put the counter-argument that the majority of people did not feel as if they were living a daily nightmare in a dictatorship because, increasingly, they knew no other form of government. True, there were young people who came to feel the iron fist of the state, because they openly voiced their opposition to the regime, and they then got to know the ugly side of the GDR, which involved unpleasant confrontations with the Stasi or the police. I do not want to whitewash this aspect of the GDR by any means. For the great majority of the GDR's populace at any time in its four decades of existence, however, the following principle applied: those who do not move do not feel their chains.[114] This explains why so many people have rosy memories of life in the GDR, despite it being undeniably a dictatorship. With hindsight, many former GDR citizens have asked themselves, 'How was it possible that we ever

114. Original: 'Wer sich nicht bewegt spürt auch keine Ketten.' Popularly attributed to Rosa Luxemburg.

lived in these conditions?', but at the time of living in the GDR, this question simply did not arise.

The inherent construction defect of the concept of the socialist personality was that for real human beings, it could only be an unobtainable ideal personality designed to live in the halcyon days of a future communist society. The SED had succeeded in achieving young people's outward compliance to its plans. Beyond this, genuine enthusiasm for the social engineering project of the new human being in a new society remained what the idea had been all along–a utopia.

Chapter 12

1977: The GDR's Most Normal Year?

Mark Allinson

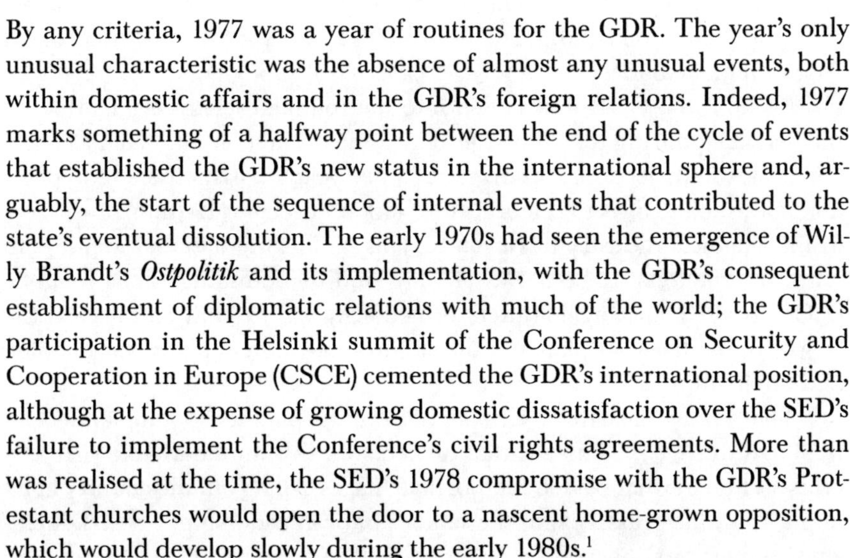

By any criteria, 1977 was a year of routines for the GDR. The year's only unusual characteristic was the absence of almost any unusual events, both within domestic affairs and in the GDR's foreign relations. Indeed, 1977 marks something of a halfway point between the end of the cycle of events that established the GDR's new status in the international sphere and, arguably, the start of the sequence of internal events that contributed to the state's eventual dissolution. The early 1970s had seen the emergence of Willy Brandt's *Ostpolitik* and its implementation, with the GDR's consequent establishment of diplomatic relations with much of the world; the GDR's participation in the Helsinki summit of the Conference on Security and Cooperation in Europe (CSCE) cemented the GDR's international position, although at the expense of growing domestic dissatisfaction over the SED's failure to implement the Conference's civil rights agreements. More than was realised at the time, the SED's 1978 compromise with the GDR's Protestant churches would open the door to a nascent home-grown opposition, which would develop slowly during the early 1980s.[1]

1977 was relatively free of exceptional events. Though the year was marked by the departure of the actor Manfred Krug and the arrest of Rudolf Bahro, author of *Die Alternative* (soon published in English as *The Alternative in Eastern Europe*), 1976 had by contrast witnessed the much higher profile effective expulsion of the singer and songwriter Wolf Biermann, the house arrest of the dissident philosopher Robert Havemann, and the self-immolation

1. Cf. Mary Fulbrook, *Anatomy of a Dictatorship. Inside the GDR 1949–1989* (Oxford: Oxford University Press, 1995), pp. 124–25.

of the Protestant clergyman Oskar Brüsewitz on a public square in Zeitz. The keynote events which marked the passage from one five-year plan to the next–the SED's party congress and the elections to the GDR's parliament, the *Volkskammer*–had already occurred in 1976, along with the FDJ's latest (tenth) *Parlament*. By 1977, the GDR's course had been mapped out as far ahead as 1980, and was essentially in line with the policy initiatives introduced by Erich Honecker in 1971 following his rise to the pinnacle of the SED leadership. In 1977, therefore, it remained only for the bloc parties and mass organisations, including the FDGB trades union, the *Kulturbund* (Cultural League), and the Sorbs' umbrella association, the *Domowina*, to echo the announced course at their own congresses.

Whenever possible, the SED coupled its exhortations to the workforce to increase productivity and its political work to significant events or anniversaries. The SED linked most of its 1977 campaigning to the year's one significant landmark, the sixtieth anniversary of the October 1917 Russian Revolution ('Red October'). This apart, no other anniversary could compete for similar attention in 1977, and even Erich Honecker's 65th birthday on 25 August remained low key.[2]

By 1977, the GDR had settled into the routine cycle of events that remained fixed during the Honecker era. Some of these events, such as party congresses and elections, occurred on a five yearly basis; others took place annually, such as days to celebrate the work of teachers (12 June) or workers in the chemical industry (9 November), as well as the national holidays to mark International Labour Day (1 May) and the founding of the republic (7 October).[3] The struggle (often termed a *Kampf*) to fulfil and exceed the targets of the five-year plan and the subordinate annual plans was ongoing and unrelenting.

The relative dearth of exceptional events–planned or unplanned–in the GDR during 1977 means that we can view this unremarkable year as a cross-section of what passed for 'normal' life, as 'Alltag', in the country at all levels, from the grassroots to the senior political leadership. The GDR citizens' and leaders' view of their country in 1977 is essentially undistorted by

2. Nonetheless, lesser anniversaries were also used to political effect wherever possible. The *Pionierkalender 1977* (Berlin: Kinderbuchverlag, 1977) draws particular attention to the 120th anniversary of Clara Zetkin's birth (p. 59), the 25th anniversary of the first Pionierrepublik "Wilhelm Pieck" (p. 61), the 60th anniversary of the murders of Albin Köbis and Max Reichpietsch, two would-be revolutionaries in the imperial navy (p. 71), and the 20th anniversary of the first Sputnik (p. 77), among others.

3. The list could be considerably extended to include 'Civil Defence Day' (11 February), 'Youth Brigades' Day' (16 May), 'Railway Workers' Day' (8 June), 'Day of the Border Troops of the GDR' (1 December), and many others.

some of the exceptional events that overshadow other years. Here, the term 'normal' is not intended to denote any type of value judgement. It would be hard to counter the oft heard criticism that no state which depended on instruments such as the Berlin Wall and the *Stasi* to ensure its own survival could be described as 'normal' in international or chronological comparison.[4] And yet: within the settled European geopolitical framework of the post-war era, a specific GDR normality emerged, developed, and settled, to which the Berlin Wall and the Stasi were as integral as Spee washing powder and the difficulties of securing regular supplies of bananas and oranges. The aim of this chapter is to sketch the contours of this internal normality in the Honecker era and to evaluate the extent of its stability. However, this brief portrait of 1977 clearly cannot provide a comprehensive overview of life in the GDR in this single year, so the focus is limited principally to the GDR's economic circumstances and to the attitudes of the population to the status and vitality of their state.

Perceptions of the GDR Economy in 1977

In his New Year address, Erich Honecker underlined the ambitious but, in his view, realistic economic plans for the year ahead.[5] The five-year plan, as agreed to the previous year, foresaw a 27.9 percent increase in national earnings, which would finance 'the greatest social programme in our national history'. 'Our aims are realistic,' Honecker declared, while reflecting 'that for the economy of the German Democratic Republic foreign trade difficulties result from the signs of crisis in the imperialist world'.[6] Honecker's public mood was equally positive twelve months later. In an article published on 31 December 1977, he spoke of a year 'of economic upturn'. 'On the threshold of the new year we can say that the hard work of all has paid off. . . . The economic successes have been turned into social policy measures, in accordance with our socialist principles.'[7]

Throughout the year, the campaign to boost economic production was at the core of party work. In January, Günter Ehrensperger, the head of the SED's planning and finances department, emphasised the importance

4. Cf. Mary Fulbrook, *The Concept of 'Normalisation' and the GDR in Comparative Perspective*, elsewhere in this collection.

5. 'Allen Bürgern unserer Republik viel Glück für das Jahr 1977', in Erich Honecker, *Reden und Aufsätze*, Band 5 (Berlin: Dietz, 1978), pp. 102–8.

6. Ibid., pp. 104–5.

7. 'Viel Glück und Erfolg allen Bürgern unserer Republik für das Jahr 1978', in Erich Honecker, *Reden und Aufsätze*, Band 6 (Berlin: Dietz, 1980), pp. 7–14, here p. 7.

of the SED's 'strict management of plan fulfilment from the very first day of the new year'.[8] His article for SED functionaries listed the themes which would recur throughout the year: the plan 'serves the welfare of the working class and of the entire nation', would cement still further the 'unity of economic and social policy', and, with the planned rises in personal income, there would be a greater need 'to offer the population more and better consumer goods to satisfy the quantitatively and qualitatively higher requirements'. A top political priority would be progress within the framework of the plan to construct new residential flats, centred on the 'FDJ-Initiative Berlin'. Though the GDR's increased difficulties in importing fuel and raw materials was not specifically mentioned, the careful reader might also have sensed a period of increasing austerity planning in Ehrensperger's emphasis of 'intensivisation', in other words, 'the acceleration of economic and technical progress with the aim of significant productivity gains'. Technological advancement would be key to achieving 'rationalisation', 'savings of working time', and optimum efficiency in the use of raw materials. Increasingly, firms would move over to shift working so that assets were utilised to the maximum extent.[9]

Despite the positive sounding forecasts at New Year, the real economic difficulties faced by the GDR were apparent in reports compiled for the SED hierarchy throughout 1977. The GDR was attempting to grow its national income by 27.9 percent over the five-year period from 1975 to 1980,[10] but lacked the resources to match the ambitious plans. The shortcomings were exacerbated by the poor quality of goods imported from other socialist countries, and the GDR's inability to fund the necessary imports from hard currency countries. As serious as these problems were, they appeared still greater in the eyes of the population given the obvious mismatch between the failure to achieve results and the oft-repeated aspirations and assertions of success.[11]

A number of distinct themes punctuated public experience and discourse of the GDR's economic performance during 1977. An ongoing theme was the availability of goods. While the retail authorities were generally able

---

8. Günter Ehrensperger, 'Volkswirtschaftsplan 1977—Kurs des IX. Parteitages', in *Neuer Weg*, Nr.1/1977, pp. 1–6, here p. 2.

9. Ibid., passim.

10. *Neuer Weg* (2/1977), endpiece.

11. LDPD members were not alone in commenting that the published figures on the GDR's economic success bore no relationship to the 'inadequate supplies for domestic retail'. 'The many shortages which have persisted over years make the announcement somewhat implausible.' LDPD Sekretariat des Parteivorstandes, 'Information Nr. 26/77', 29 August 1977, p. 3, Stiftung Archiv der Parteien und Massenorganisationen der DDR im Bundesarchiv (SAPMO-BA) DY30/vorl. SED-19406, vol. 2. (Further archival references refer to SAPMO-BArch, except where noted.)

to maintain supplies of food and other goods throughout the country and throughout the year, the precarious nature of the situation was sometimes acutely apparent. During 1977, the GDR experienced huge difficulties in maintaining coffee supplies. The increasing cost of importing high quality beans (world coffee prices peaked in mid 1977[12]) led to the withdrawal of the popular 'Kosta' brand and its replacement with a new 'Kaffee-Mix', apparently containing 51 percent roast coffee beans, but 49 percent rye, although from the smell, many doubted that any real coffee was involved. Only 'Kaffee-Mix' would henceforth be available at all but the most expensive cafés and restaurants, fuelling comments that the GDR was creating a two-class society. The public frequently commented that the new blend effectively wasted real coffee, since it was being mixed to produce a brand which was widely boycotted, and in many cases proved unusable in GDR coffee machines.[13] The poor value for money of 'Kaffee-Mix' also led many to conclude that back door price rises were occurring in the GDR, despite the official denials.[14] With price rises recently announced in neighbouring Czechoslovakia for cocoa products as well as coffee, some panic buying began. Increased sales of cigarettes, alcohol, and chocolate were recorded in Berlin in early September, as (false) rumours spread of imminent price rises in the GDR.[15] As world coffee prices began to sink back, the SED's policy seemed increasingly questionable in the eyes of critical citizens ('We're having problems with coffee, but in the west it's got cheaper. . .').[16] By the end of September, the altered trade conditions and the strength of popular opinion forced a rethink by the state. The price of 'Kaffee-Mix' was reduced, and by November the recipe was changed, while the well known, better quality brands, including 'Mona', 'Rondo', and 'Mokka-Fix-Gold' (the latter of which had remained available in Berlin and Halle during the crisis) were reintroduced throughout the country in time for the state's birthday celebrations on 7 October.[17] The extent of popular discontent prompted Honecker to address the coffee crisis directly in a keynote speech of late September, in which he highlighted the high cost of importing raw beans (some $300

---

12. Cf. David Hallam, 'Falling commodity prices and industry responses: some lessons from the international coffee crisis', in *Commodity Market Review 2003–2004*, viewed at <http://www.fao.org/documents/show_cdr.asp?url_file=/DOCREP/006/Y5117E/y5117e03.htm> (accessed 30.6.2006).

13. CDU Sekretariat des Hauptvorstandes, 'Zur Diskussion der Mitglieder. . .', 13 September 1977, p. 7, DY30/vorl.SED 19680.

14. Nationale Front, 8 September 1977 report, DY30/vorl.SED 18401, vol. 1.

15. SED-Bezirksleitung Berlin, 'Monatsbericht', 12 September 1977, DY30/2200, p. 109.

16. DBD Abt. Parteiorgane, 'Information Nr.20/77', 17 August 1977, p. 3, DY30/vorl.SED 21550.

17. 'Information zu ausgewählten Versorgungspositionen. . .', reports of 27 September and 29 November 1977, DY30/vorl.SED 20223.

million annually).[18] The episode left more than a sour taste: it clearly demonstrated how marginal the GDR's prosperity had become.

Though less remarked upon than the coffee crisis, at year's end oranges proved particularly problematic as supplies were increasingly sourced from Cuba. Unlike Mediterranean oranges, the Cuban variety was frequently greenish in colour as a result of local temperature conditions. With an average of 31 percent of green coloured oranges imported from Cuba in the fourth quarter of 1977,[19] the retail authorities faced a dilemma. While complaints were made to the Cuban authorities about the poor quality of the fruit, and only partial improvements were achieved by attempts to improve the colour by altering storage conditions, there was a choice to be made between withholding the fruit altogether or releasing it for sale and risking negative comments, which would overshadow the otherwise good impression made by the Christmas retail supply situation. Finally a compromise was proposed: to withhold the 'grass green' oranges until they could be coloured or used for other purposes, and to sell the rest before they rotted while issuing public statements about the high juice content and general quality of Cuban oranges–an interpretation not shared internally by the SED's trade department.[20]

More generally, the combination of late deliveries of promised goods and shortages of hard currency to finance imports necessitated a policy of careful balances between goods. For example, the import of additional sweet almonds to meet Christmas baking demands was financed by reducing the planned quantity of imported lemons. Appearances were everything, especially at times of high seasonal demand: the sale of Christmas goods in each district was not to begin too early in case there were not enough goods still on sale immediately before the holiday itself.[21] The SED's trade department was not afraid to note in its report that even where the planned quantities of certain goods had been produced and delivered on time, supplies did not always meet demand. This was true at Christmas 1977 of bags and other leather goods (popular as presents), skis and skates, consumer electrical goods, Christmas decorations, bed linen, and fur-lined coats. For all of the detailed central planning, the SED was not above ordering additional last-minute production of essential or

18. Erich Honecker, 'Die sozialistische Revolution in der DDR und ihre Perspektiven', 26 September 1977, in Honecker, *Reden und Aufsätze*, Band 5, p. 493.

19. 'Information zum Import von Kuba-Orangen. . .', 21 January 1978 [?], p. 3, DY30/vorl. SED-23660, vol. 2.

20. Various memos of early 1978, ibid.

21. Präsidium des Ministerrates, 'Information für das Politbüro. . .', 7 November 1977, pp. 4, 6, DY30/J IV 2/2J/7801.

highly desirable goods,[22] suggesting rather fluid production cycles, a fact not lost on workers at the grassroots whose trust in the political processes surrounding the plan was tested ('. . . what is the point of discussions [about the plan] if the plans are changed anyway?').[23]

The distribution of supplies around the country regularly provoked critical comments, as the SED systematically prioritised the GDR capital with supplies of scarce or luxury goods. The results could be crass and unjust. Residents of Marienberg district (Bezirk Karl-Marx-Stadt), where toys and Christmas decorations were manufactured, could not understand how these goods were available for purchase in Berlin but not at home.[24] The relatively good supply situation in Berlin was, however, deliberate policy, particularly at times when particular festivities placed the image of the capital at the centre of political activism, such as the celebrations of the sixtieth anniversary of the Russian October revolution in 1977. Observers in the provinces believed the party's economic managers had very skewed priorities. 'It's no wonder that there are supply problems in the republic (vegetables, fruit, coffee). There will certainly be an overabundant supply of these goods for the Red October celebrations in Berlin, and meanwhile the population in the provinces will have to suffer the consequences.'[25] Thus in early October, while apples were to be had throughout the country, Berliners could also buy pears and grapes.[26]

These were not consumers' only complaints. Shortages of spare parts were a common complaint, particularly where they rendered expensive goods such as cars and colour televisions useless.[27] This was particularly problematic where spare parts had to be imported.[28] The growing role of the Intershops, where only hard currency could be used for imported and other scarce goods, also caused frustrations and the inequalities they represented in a state apparently striving for socialism represented an own goal in many eyes. SED members in Berlin were concerned that any economic advantages would be outweighed by the potential ideological effects, and activists in the

22. Ibid., pp. 13–16 and passim.

23. FDJ Abteilung Verbandsorgane, 'Schwerpunkte und Probleme. . .', 19 August 1977, p. 6, DY30/vorl.SED 21405.

24. LDPD Sekretariat des Zentralvorstandes, 'Information Nr. 2/77', 25 January 1977, p. 7, DY30/vorl.SED 15733, vol. 1.

25. These comments were reported from around the country. LDPD Sekretariat des Parteivorstandes, 'Information Nr. 29/77', 4 October 1977, p. 4, DY30/vorl. SED-19406, vol. 2.

26. 'Information zu ausgewählten Versorgungspositionen. . .', various reports, DY30/vorl. SED 20223.

27. 'Übersicht über eingegangene Eingaben im 1. Halbjahr 1977', 27 July 1977, p. 7, DY30/J IV 2/2J/7683.

28. For example, of the 122 colour television sets awaiting repair in Berlin in early September, 76 required colour tubes from the USSR: 12 September report (as note 15), p. 113.

Liberal Democratic Party (LDPD) agreed that: 'The Intershop is destroying our ideological work.'[29] Honecker's public defence of the Intershops as an important means of keeping hard currency within the GDR, his promise to extend the chain of 'Exquisit' shops where high quality goods would be available for GDR currency, and his assurance that the goods included in the plan would continue to be available 'in all price ranges and in all shops' cut little ice with the population.[30] Reports compiled by the National Front continued to record 'incorrect or unclear opinions about these measures', with fears that only the highest earners would be able to access the 'Exquisit' stores, and that the Intershops would encourage 'the illegal acquisition of western currency'. Contrary to the state's ideological aspirations to a classless society, citizens believed that these policies would achieve the 'division of GDR citizens into three categories'.[31]

Underpinning the poor experience of the GDR's would-be consumers were chronic logistics and management failures, well illustrated by some of the problems noted in discussions with the workforce of various trade collectives in *Bezirk* Erfurt. Staff at Weimar's wholesale division noted that some goods had to be stored outdoors in all weathers under tarpaulin because the warehouse roof was in such a bad state; at the Erfurt retail dispatch centre, vehicles would wait between two and four hours to be loaded because essential equipment such as forklift trucks was lacking, while the loading ramp at the Weimar branch had been in a poor state of repair since 1968. Even where proposals had been drawn up to improve retail outlets, years could pass before any decision was made; plans to rebuild a shop in Greußen had been on ice since 1960.[32]

Retail problems were exacerbated by the GDR's need to export as many goods as possible in order to secure the required imports. The costs of this policy imperative were apparent to citizens at the grassroots who complained 'that the best products go abroad and we have to make do with lower quality goods which frequently need repairs'.[33] The long waiting lists for cars related to the GDR's export imperative: 77,378 new cars were sold abroad during 1977, some 46 percent of the country's total production.[34] GDR citizens reacted to

29. SED-Bezirksleitung Berlin, 'Zwischenbericht. . .', 21 March 1977, p. 6a, DY30/IV B 2/5/132; 4 October 1977 LDPD report (as note 25), p. 3.

30. Honecker, 'Die sozialistische Revolution. . .', p. 493.

31. Nationalrat der Nationalen Front, reports of 8 November and 13 December 1977, DY30/vorl.SED 18401, vol. 1.

32. SED-Bezirksleitung Erfurt, 'Informationsbericht Nr. 35/77. . .', 18 November 1977, DY30/IV B 2/5/543.

33. 29 August 1977 LDPD report (as note 11), p. 3.

34. *Statistisches Jahrbuch der Deutschen Demokratischen Republik 1978* (Berlin: Staatsverlag der DDR, 1978), pp. 119, 243.

market forces and sold used cars at home for extortionate prices, leading to complaints that these practices were distinctly unsocialist in nature. Why, petitioners to Erich Honecker inquired, was the GDR press printing adverts for these goods and thus fuelling price speculation?[35]

Most worrying of all was the poor availability of medicines. The Erfurt SED reported that supplies of drugs to treat heart and circulation problems had been inadequate for months:

> The shortages and the inadequate provision of medicines for heart and circulation problems are causing great anxiety among patients. Pharmacies are often only able to dispense the necessary drugs in small quantities or not at all. This leads to citizens visiting pharmacies frequently in vain and forming queues.[36]

Besides the everyday difficulties associated with shopping, housing was a problem uppermost in people's minds in the mid 1970s and is a good example of a policy area where the GDR's population had developed unrealistic expectations based on the unrealistic promises made by the SED leadership. Certainly, the starting conditions were poor. As 1977 began, 55 percent of the country's homes had no bath, 50 percent no inside toilet, and 16 percent were not connected to the water mains. It was estimated that in 1975, two thirds of all residential buildings had defects that would need to be repaired to avoid further deterioration.[37]

Although the building programme initiated by Honecker in 1971 was in full swing by 1977,[38] aspirations inevitably grew far faster than the country's ability to construct high quality new homes. However, more than thirty years after the end of the war, those living in unacceptable conditions were increasingly unwilling to wait patiently and, taking the party's promises at face value, measured the GDR's effectiveness against the progress made towards solving the housing crisis. Of the petitions (*Eingaben*) addressed directly to Honecker, by far the largest number (40 percent of the 8,026 received in the first half of 1977, comparable with the proportion of 43 percent in

---

35. 27 July 1977 report (as note 27), p. 7. Honecker's pencil markings indicate he was concerned by these occurrences.

36. SED-Bezirksleitung Erfurt, Bräutigam to Honecker, 21 October 1977, DY30/2221, p. 106.

37. Taken from an analysis accompanying the draft for a 'Beschluß zur besseren Gewährleistung der Erhaltung und Verwaltung des Wohnungsbestandes', 22 March 1977, p. 2, DY30/vorl.SED 30415, vol. 1.

38. In 1977, 106,826 new flats were built, though net growth was 87,811: *Statistisches Jahrbuch 1978*, pp. 142–43.

the first half of 1976) concerned housing issues.[39] Those due to be rehoused from substandard accommodation into anything less than one of the many modern flats being constructed within Honecker's programme were likely to refuse such a transfer, fearing that this would end any prospect of a further move into a new residence.[40] In the meantime, the lack of suitable–or in some cases, any–available accommodation made it practically impossible for key workers to be reassigned to areas where they were needed.[41] The education ministry reported rising numbers of complaints about accommodation issues during the year. In Berlin-Lichtenberg alone, 146 teachers were seeking flats, with 58 citing cases of hardship. However, the borough could only offer 30 communal flats, with a further 25 possible over the following three to four years.[42] When the new school year began, 15 newly qualified teachers complained that they had no accommodation at all, despite having received vague assurances from local mayors. Some of these new teachers felt that their willingness to go where they were needed had been abused.[43]

While investing as heavily as possible in the construction of new flats, the GDR failed to allocate sufficient resources to maintaining the old housing stock or even the newly built flats, where the installation of newer electronic technologies with higher specifications (lifts and ventilation units, for example) placed higher demands on repair services.[44] In 1976, agreed and planned buildings repairs (themselves just a proportion of what was really needed) to a value of more than 380 million Marks had not been carried out. Although numerous citizens undertook repairs in voluntary initiatives (particularly the '*Mach mit!*' (Take part!) scheme) or as paid overtime apart from their normal jobs, the shortage of essential materials (particularly for repairs to roofs, doors and windows), and of spare parts for electrical, heating and sanitary equipment dampened enthusiasm for such efforts, particularly where would-be customers were advised to try securing supplies in the Intershops (for hard currency which they normally lacked). Similarly, the maintenance contractors organised in local state-owned firms (under the

39. 27 July 1977 report (as note 27), p. 2. The next largest proportions concerned applications to emigrate (11.2 percent) and requests to visit the FRG (10 percent).

40. SED-Bezirksleitung Erfurt, Abteilung Parteiorgane, 'Informationsbericht Nr. 27/77', 2 September 1977, p. 3, DY30/IV B 2/5/543. Reports from various departments and regions mention this problem.

41. 27 July 1977 report (as note 27), p. 4. Examples in this report concerned the health service.

42. Ministerium für Volksbildung, 'Analyse der Eingaben für das 1. Halbjahr 1977', p. 22, in: Bundesarchiv DR2/A7493.

43. Ministerium für Volksbildung, 'Analyse der Eingaben für das 2. Halbjahr 1977', p. 6, in ibid.

44. Cf. Instrukteurabteilung beim Vorsitzenden des Ministerrates, 'Information über die Durchführung der Beschlüsse. . .', 13 December 1978, p. 5, DY30/vorl.SED 30415, vol. 2.

title VEB Gebäudewirtschaft) lacked the materials, tools, and equipment to do their work, and were no more able to access spare parts for defective domestic appliances than ordinary citizens. Training in these companies was poor, wages low, and staff turnover high: 33.1 percent of the repair staff in the VEB Gebäudewirtschaft had left between 1974 and 1976.[45] In this respect, the situation was similar to that at local councils' housing departments, where often untrained staff faced the complaints of angry citizens. Typically for the larger cities, 56 of the 130 staff in the Leipzig offices had resigned since 1974, 51 of 175 in Erfurt.[46]

The adoption of a resolution (*Beschluß*) by the Council of Ministers on 21 July 1977 was designed to alleviate these problems of maintenance and repairs to the housing stock. The document called for better resources planning by the local authorities, which held responsibility in this area, and attempted to avoid buck passing between different firms and authorities by allocating specific tasks more carefully. The government prioritised the establishment of around the clock repair services, and placed great emphasis on cooperation between maintenance firms, local councils, individual citizens, and residents' committees. The local VEBs, which ran and maintained public housing, were required to develop centres where residents could hire the necessary equipment to undertake their own repairs. Statistics on completed repairs would henceforth be collected centrally.[47] A draft of this resolution had proposed establishing a 'central body for the management of buildings and flats', but this was energetically opposed by the SED's department for research and development; prime minister Willi Stoph resisted discussing the implementation of aspects of the resolution at the Council of Ministers in September.[48] Instead, central government seemed minded as far as possible to avoid direct involvement in the practicalities of housing policy, and to leave the local authorities to manage the disappointments that seemed certain for many citizens.

By the end of 1978, a government review noted some improvements, but concluded that: 'Overall progress has not yet been sufficient to achieve a

45. Analysis for a 'Beschluß zur besseren Gewährleistung. . .' (as note 37), passim; cf. Sekretariat des Hauptvorstandes der CDU, 'Auszüge aus Informationsberichten. . .', 1 February 1977, p. 1, DY30/vorl.SED 19680.

46. Wettengel to Sorgenicht, 'Information über kaderpolitische Probleme im Bereich Wohnungspolitik. . .', 3 May 1977, pp. 4–5, DY30/vorl.SED 30415, vol. 1. Similar staff turnover problems existed in Berlin. See: 'Material zur Auswertung und Verallgemeinerung der Berliner Erfahrungen. . .', 8 December 1977, in ibid., vol. 2.

47. 'Maßnahmen zur besseren Gewährleistung der Erhaltung und Verwaltung des Wohnbestandes', 21 July 1977, ibid., vol. 1.

48. See the department's 'Stellungnahme', 14 April 1977, and an 'Aktennotiz' of 12 September 1977, ibid.

thorough improvement in the maintenance of residential buildings.' The development of long-term preventative maintenance programmes 'will only be realised over a lengthy period at the current rate of development'. Statistics illustrated the point effectively: on 30 September 1978, there were 35,000 outstanding repair jobs in Magdeburg and some 2,200 in the Mitte district of Berlin alone. Roof repairs were a general concern, and waiting times of up to two years were not unusual. Local authorities were still prioritising new building work over repairs and maintenance, even directing building firms away from working for maintenance departments or residents' associations, and provided little or no money for the purchase of materials and spare parts to support citizens prepared to carry out repair work themselves.[49] The July 1977 resolution had had very limited effects, and as the decade closed, the situation remained untenable in the eyes of the 40,000 Berliners who were still submitting *Eingaben* on housing issues. The catalogue of problems remained much as in the mid 1970s.[50]

Ultimately, the SED was unable to satisfy all of the population's housing demands with the resources available, not least because of the wastage and pilfering of building materials on construction sites.[51] However, although the SED's policies effectively stored up more problems for the future by delaying repairs and maintenance, diverting capacities from the new building programmes would only have exacerbated other grievances, not least from the 57 percent of applicants for new flats who still lacked their own address.[52] In localities with particular difficulties, citizens' comments ('To solve the housing problem by 1990 the whole of old Bitterfeld would have to be erased from the map')[53] indicated that the state's credibility was already stretched to the limits. The apparent preferential treatment of Berlin,[54] where construction workers from around the GDR had been gathered to push forward with new housing projects, prompted complaints comparable to those expressed about retail distribution: 'Unfortunately not every GDR

49. 13 December 1978 report (as note 44), passim.

50. Abt. Staats- und Rechtsfragen, 'Information', 25 October 1979, DY30/vorl.SED 30415, vol. 2.

51. LDPD Sekretariat des Parteivorstandes, 'Information Nr.18/77', 1 July 1977, p. 11, in DY30/vorl.SED 19406, vol. 2.

52. Abteilung Forschung und technische Entwicklung, 'Stellungnahme zu den Beschlußentwürfen. . .', p. 4, 14 April 1977, DY30/vorl.SED 30415, vol. 1.

53. Nationalrat der Nationalen Front, 'Anlage zum Informationsbericht vom 11.5.1977', DY30/vorl.SED 18401, vol. 1.

54. Though Berlin was the focus of FDJ and other construction initiatives, the *Statistisches Jahrbuch 1978* (p. 143) records greater numbers of new flats built in Bezirke Dresden, Halle, and Karl-Marx-Stadt in 1977; however, the total average costs were significantly higher in Berlin than elsewhere.

citizen can be a resident of the capital. But we would like to have nice flats as well.'[55]

The 'Political-Ideological Situation' in 1977

It will be clear from much that has gone before that the GDR population's view of the country's political leadership and prospects was strongly linked to economic factors. Nonetheless, in a state where the leading party placed great emphasis on popular support for and conviction in the benefits of socialism, grassroots reactions to the SED's more purely ideological concerns are also a good indication of the GDR's stability in this 'normal' year.

Since the GDR's very existence depended on the continuing Cold War and the political support of the Soviet Union, the SED had since its inception attempted to nurture close bonds of friendship between the populations of East Germany and the USSR. The sixtieth anniversary of the October Revolution offered the party's propagandists an opportunity both to strengthen ideological support for socialism, and to underline the benefits of good GDR-Soviet relations. The media planned its supporting coverage well in advance; for example, GDR television viewers could look forward to reports, dramas, documentaries, and entertainment throughout the year in support of the Red October theme.[56] With the SED's party congress over, the normal round of pledges for greater productivity was linked in 1977 to honouring the achievements of Red October, as were other initiatives such as the '*Mach mit!*' campaign for voluntary work to improve housing conditions and the appearance of residential areas. The campaign was temporarily relabelled '*Mach mit–auf Oktoberkurs!*' ('Take Part–on course for October!') in Bezirk Dresden, where it was hoped that everyone could be persuaded to join in to work in their communities on Saturday, 24 September. The National Front held numerous 'friendship meetings' in areas close to Soviet garrisons, and the Urania organisation arranged public lectures about the Soviet Union. In Altgliezen, 200 locals and thirty Soviet soldiers attended a ceremony to inaugurate the new shop and post office, built within the 'Mach mit!' project on a square renamed in honour of German-Soviet friendship. Besides the national campaign ('For my best friend') to send presents to the Soviet Union, Bezirk Schwerin excelled in establishing further initiatives

55. Complaints of this nature were reported from all Bezirke in the 1 July 1977 LDPD report (as note 51), p. 10.

56. Cf. Staatliches Komitee für Fernsehen, 'Jahresplan 1977 des Fernsehens der DDR', BArch DR8/157.

such as '*60mal Salut*' (60 salutes), and '*60 rote Nelken zum 60.*' (60 red carnations for the 60th).[57]

Despite the outward expressions of solidarity with the Soviet Union and the other socialist countries on set-piece occasions, such as the Red October festivities or the 'Friendship Meeting' with the People's Republic of Poland held in Frankfurt an der Oder during 1977, relations with the USSR and the other members of the Soviet-led trading bloc, the Council for Mutual Economic Assistance (CMEA), were often viewed by GDR citizens through the lens of trade and the quality of imported goods. There were many concerns that the deepening trade and economic planning links between the CMEA states would limit the GDR's development. Widespread questions included: 'As a highly developed industrialised state, isn't the GDR disadvantaged by socialist economic integration?'; 'Doesn't integration mean economic dependence?'; and 'The socialist countries rightly demand high quality products from the GDR, but why don't we always get the same in return?'. These were questions to which SED propagandists often lacked satisfactory answers.[58] Grassroots comrades were not beyond denouncing Poland and Romania as the 'weakest links' of the socialist community, and expressing their prejudices against these nations.[59] Similar voices could be heard among SED members in Bezirk Suhl:

> We cannot overlook the tendency for the effectiveness of socialist integration often still to be measured against the difficulties, the inadequate quality of goods and the poor availability of spare parts. Too often, the source of the causes is sought in other fraternal countries. Equally certain prejudices still need to be overcome.[60]

For all the efforts put into party education, some comrades persisted in the view that: 'World standards are only to be found in the west.'[61] In the wider population, the year did not pass off without the comment that 'we'd be better off without the Russians'.[62]

---

57. Nationalrat der Nationalen Front, reports of 23 June, 22 August and 21 October 1977 in DY30/vorl.SED 18401, vol. 1.

58. SED-Bezirksleitung Halle, 'Information zum Thema 6 des Parteilehrjahres. . .', 14 April 1977, pp. 3, 4, 6, DY30/vorl.SED 19099, vol. 1.

59. SED-Bezirksleitung Karl-Marx-Stadt, 'Bericht über Hospitationen. . .', 28 March 1977, p. 4, ibid., vol. 2.

60. SED-Bezirksleitung Suhl, 'Information über das Parteilehrjahr. . .', 22 April 1977, DY30/vorl.SED 34937.

61. As at the VEB Maßelektronik works in Berlin: SED-Bezirksleitung Berlin, 'Bericht über das Parteileben. . .', 9 June 1977, p. 8, DY30/IV B 2/5/132.

62. SED-Bezirksleitung Erfurt, 'Informationsbericht Nr. 33/77', 28 October 1977, p. 5, DY30/IV B 2/5/543.

There was greater unity and real concern about the USA's decision during 1977 to develop the neutron bomb. The move was roundly denounced by state and people alike. However, a degree of fatalism and pessimism about the future prospects of the socialist camp also underlay popular reactions to this latest phase of the arms race, with fears that civil defence measures would be ineffective against the new weaponry, and that the Soviet Union's attempts to develop new weapons systems would have negative effects on the standard of living in the socialist countries.[63] The pacifism that would come to the fore in the 1980s was already present in the view that the socialist bloc should demonstrate its moral superiority by taking the first steps towards disarmament.[64] Even amid the general rejection of the USA's plans, critics sought to exploit potential differences between communist countries. Why, LDPD members asked, had the Romanian and Yugoslav communist parties not signed the joint protest of communist and workers' parties against the neutron bomb?[65] Romania's semi-detached relationship with the USSR and the rest of the bloc created frequent opportunities for comment by those who doubted the fraternal unity of the socialist countries.[66] Equally, the SED's seminars offered opportunities for members to pose all types of potentially embarrassing questions, ranging from the position of the GDR and the Soviet Union relative to 'eurocommunism', the political nature of the People's Republic of China, and even why Vietnam had joined the organisations of the non-aligned states rather than those of the socialist bloc.[67]

The travel issue remained a prevalent topic in popular opinion throughout the year. However, as sixteen years had passed since the final closure of the borders, change seemed so unlikely that discussions and complaints about housing, the availability of goods, and the general economic situation were reported more frequently.[68] Nonetheless, travel restrictions remained a live issue, particularly following Honecker's interview with the *Saarbrücker Zeitung* in February. In this text, widely publicised in the GDR's press, he emphasised that there could be no general freedom of travel to the west until

63. 13 September 1977 CDU report (as note 13), p. 2.

64. CDU Sekretariat des Hauptvorstandes, 'Informationsbericht', 22 March 1977, p. 4, DY30/vorl.SED 19680.

65. LDPD Sekretariat des Parteivorstandes, 'Information Nr.25/77', p. 3, DY30/vorl.SED 19406, vol. 2.

66. Cf. also DBD Abt. Parteiorgane, 'Information Nr.17/77', 10 June 1977, pp. 3–4, DY30/vorl.SED 21550.

67. Ministerium für Verkehrswesen, 'Bericht über die Durchführung des Parteilehrjahres. . .', 19 August 1977, Anlage 6, DY30/vorl.SED 19099, vol. 1.

68. In the first half of 1977, 21.2 percent of petitions to Honecker concerned trips to the west or permanent emigration, but 40 percent raised accommodation problems: 27 July 1977 report (as note 27), p. 2.

the Federal Republic recognised GDR citizenship, and in view of his country's shortage of hard currency to finance such trips.[69] These comments did little to alleviate the situation. While Honecker's aspirations for improving relations with the west were widely welcomed, the logic of refusing travel rights on financial grounds found little acceptance,[70] and it was hard to reconcile the general restrictions pending the recognition of GDR citizenship with Honecker's boasts in the same interview about the 1.1 million citizens who had visited the west. To the cynical, it appeared 'that our government is now looking for a new justification to prevent the extension of travel opportunities for the long term. . .'.[71] SED agitators found it hard to persuade citizens that peace would not be furthered by allowing greater travel freedoms.[72] Overall, however, by 1977 extreme discontent on this issue remained principally restricted to those with specific personal grievances about the travel ban, rather than becoming a mass talking point. Nonetheless, there was considerable interest in the Belgrade conference organised to take forward the Helsinki process and which might, many hoped, achieve further progress in east-west relations. No wonder the SED shifted towards a policy of demarcation from the west, mindful of its ongoing failure among most of the population to establish a sense of identity that excluded sympathies for the West German state. The view could still frequently be heard that 'we're all Germans when all's said and done'.[73] Similarly, there was a general 'playing down' of the imperialist tendencies in the FRG and 'illusions' about workers' prospects there.[74]

While the GDR's long-term stability would rest at least in part on the commitment to the socialist ideal which could be inculcated in the general population, the task of sustaining the socialist project from day to day fell to the smaller number of activists gathered in the bloc parties and principally the SED. On the surface at least, the four bloc parties appeared secure. All held their party congresses during 1977, and in this public forum met the aspirations of the SED's political planners.[75] Behind the scenes, however, the

69. 'Interview des stellvertretenden Chefredakteurs der "Saarbrücker Zeitung", Erich Voltmer', 17 February 1977, in Honecker, *Reden und Aufsätze*, Band 5, pp. 137–60 (esp. pp. 141–42).

70. Nationalrat der Nationalen Front, 'Information. . .', 22 February 1977, p. 4, DY30/vorl. SED 18401, vol. 1.

71. Sekretariat des Hauptvorstandes der CDU, 'Erste Information. . .', 24 February 1977, p. 2, DY30/vorl.SED 19680.

72. 28 October 1977 report (as note 62), p. 4.

73. SED-Bezirksleitung Erfurt, Abteilung Parteiorgane, 'Bericht über die Verwirklichung der Direktive. . .', 18 November 1977, pp. 3–4, DY30/IV B 2/5/543.

74. 19 August 1977 FDJ report (as note 23), p. 2.

75. E.g., 'The main message of the LDPD's 12th Party Congress corresponded to the plan laid before the Secretariat of the SED's Central Committee.' Cf. 'Information über den 12. Parteitag der LDPD. . .', 13 May 1977, p. 1, DY30/vorl.SED 21815.

commitment to socialism of bloc party members caused some worries to the SED. In the case of the Democratic Farmers' Party (DBD),

> It must be concluded that some functionaries and local groups still find it difficult to take an offensive and convincing stance on topical political events, always to take basic socialist principles as their starting point and constantly to observe the unity of politics, ideology and economics.[76]

The LDPD inspired similar concerns:

> For all the positive evaluations of the LDPD's activities after their party congress, it must be noted that great differences are still apparent, particularly in political and ideological work. . .[77]

Even among the SED's relatively highly placed allies upon whom the system depended, commitment was lacking. Of the National Front's executive members, 40 percent in the fifteen Bezirke regularly missed meetings, while attendance dropped to just 41 percent in Bezirk Potsdam.[78]

The SED also remained politically heterogeneous in the GDR's apparently established phase. Ordinary SED members were as ready to criticise as non-politically affiliated citizens. They too had difficulties justifying the emergence of the Intershops and Exquisit shops, fearing that the supply of goods to lower earners would be threatened.[79] The '*Parteilehrjahr*' (annual party study programme) was designed to underpin comrades' ideological positions ('This is the forum for communists to obtain their intellectual expertise, . . . and in comradely debate to develop the best arguments for political work with the masses . . .'[80]), and to counter divergence from the central line. However, the results appeared decidedly limited. Though the curriculum for each year was carefully planned in advance around a number of themes,[81] in practice many sessions appear to have concentrated on current international politics (often to circumvent emergent criticisms of the party line) or recent speeches by the leadership. Enthusiasm for the exercise was

---

76. DBD Abt. Parteiorgane, 'Information über einen gemeinsamen Operativeinsatz. . .', 5 January 1977, p. 3, DY30/vorl.SED 21550.

77. Pilz to Honecker, 13 May 1977, DY30/vorl.SED 21805.

78. Nationale Front, 'Information über die im Jahr 1977 durchgeführten Tagungen der Bezirksausschüsse. . .', 20 December 1977, DY30/vorl.SED 18401, vol. 1.

79. 28 October 1977 report (as note 52), p. 6.

80. Kurt Tiedke, 'Revolutionäre Tat erwächst aus unserer Überzeugung', in *Neuer Weg*, Nr.16/1977, pp. 721–26 (p. 24).

81. Cf. 'Themenplan für die Zirkel und Seminare im Parteilehrjahr 1977/78', a supplement to *Neuer Weg*, Nr.5/1977.

clearly lacking. On occasion, participants turned up entirely unprepared, with neither study books nor pencil and paper.[82] Among Dresden groups studying the history of the Communist Party of the Soviet Union, only half the participants possessed the set text.[83]

The sessions revealed some unexpected views among the SED's less ideologically secure members, such as: 'In the GDR the dictatorship of the proletariat is exercised only by the SED, and the party imposes its will on the other parts of the population!'[84], or: 'Is a complete satisfaction of people's needs at all possible in communism?' (apparently a typical question).[85] Even where the correct ideological conclusions were drawn, it proved difficult to extract personal consequences to sharpen the party work of individual comrades, and there was a tendency to view problems experienced in particular factories as systemic to the socialist project.[86] The Neubrandenburg SED was forced to conclude that: 'Many comrades still have problems in reacting convincingly in the dispute with imperialist ideology. It often takes a long time to overcome certain oppositional arguments'.[87] If grassroots members displayed political shortcomings at the seminars, the same was also true of the 'propagandists' entrusted with the implementation of the '*Parteilehrjahr*'. The SED in Bezirk Dresden considered that its seminar leaders generally needed a higher 'theoretical and ideological standard', and some 45 percent of the expected participants failed to attend training sessions in most districts. Only half the districts bothered to send representatives to the Bezirk's training session for the parallel '*FDJ-Studienjahr*'.[88]

The SED leadership found it just as hard to attract new members as to maintain the ideological purity of existing comrades. Recruitment slowed during 1977, and comments from those unwilling to join revealed the party's image in the wider population. Reasons included perceptions that personal freedom would be restricted by party membership (particularly in relation to any prospect of visiting the west), and workers in factories with no SED

82. 'Information. Zirkel im Parteilehrjahr VEB (K) Bau Malcin am 21.2.1977', DY30/vorl.SED 19099, vol. 2.

83. SED-Bezirksleitung Dresden, 'Information über die Durchführung des Parteilehrjahres im Monat November 1977', 9 December 1977, p. 5, ibid., vol. 1.

84. SED-Bezirksleitung Halle, 'Information zum Thema 8 des Parteilehrjahres...', 13 June 1977, p. 4, ibid.

85. SED-Bezirksleitung Karl-Marx-Stadt, 'Bericht über die Durchführung des Parteilehrjahres 1976/77', 11 February 1977, ibid., vol. 2.

86. SED-Bezirksleitung Dresden, 'Information über die Durchführung des Parteilehrjahres im Monat November 1977', p. 5.

87. SED-Bezirksleitung Neubrandenburg, 'Bericht über das Parteilehrjahr...', 18 July 1977, DY30/vorl.SED 19099, vol. 1.

88. SED-Bezirksleitung Dresden, 'Information über den Beginn des Parteilehrjahres 1977/78...', 7 November 1977, p. 5, ibid.

groups feared they would be unable to counter their colleagues' political views: '. . . they shrink from any open discussion.' The requirement to join the workers' militia was also a disincentive.[89]

For all of the difficulties, the year saw just one violent explosion of public dissatisfaction, following an accident on the Alexanderplatz in Berlin during the festivities for the 28th anniversary of the GDR's founding on 7 October.[90] When nine youths climbed on scaffolding that had been erected over a ventilation shaft, it collapsed under their weight and they fell some two metres. All were injured, three seriously. This chance accident sparked spontaneous anti-state protests. Most of the large crowd were unaware of the reason for cordoning off the area of the accident, and the police were subjected to individual insults and chanted slogans. 'A spontaneous polarisation of the two forces occurred in which 100 young people formed a mob on one of the balustrades of the television tower . . .', though the majority of the crowd remained passive or distanced themselves from the brewing trouble. Fans of the Berlin football club 1. FC Union who had been robustly policed at football matches in June and September,[91] saw an opportunity to assert themselves against the authorities, and began mass chants, increasingly anti-socialist in nature. These included 'Down with the police state!', 'Down with the GDR!', 'Down with the Wall!', 'Germany awake!' and, still somewhat topically, 'Honecker out—Biermann in!'. Anti-GDR lyrics were sung to the tune of Germany's traditional national anthem, the '*Deutschlandlied*', and the police were physically attacked (mainly by youths aged between fifteen and seventeen). As many as 66 people were injured, and damage to buildings and property was estimated at 50,000 Marks. Order was fairly quickly restored: 313 arrests were made,[92] although many of these people were quickly released. Later investigations demonstrated that the disturbances had not been premeditated.

The incident very clearly demonstrates a latent potential for broad opposition to the GDR among younger citizens, ready to explode even from very specific causes if once given a vent. The Interior Ministry's analysis of those involved in the violence, though clearly politically coloured in its language, foreshadows a key factor that empowered the individuals involved in the huge

89. 9 June 1977 Berlin SED report (as note 61), p. 15.

90. This paragraph is based principally on: Ministerium des Innern, 'Schwere Vorkommnis. . .', 10 October 1977, DY30/J IV 2/2J/7762.

91. Generalstaatsanwaltschaft der DDR, 'Erfahrungen der Staatsanwaltschaft. . .', 1 November 1977, DY30/vorl.SED 19513.

92. A further 155 arrests were made following later investigations; in all, 95 people were given prison sentences; cf. a report to Honecker from the SED's ZK-Abteilung Staats- und Rechtsfragen, 9.1.1978, p. 1, ibid.

but peaceful demonstrations of September and October 1989: 'Believing themselves anonymous and to be acting in unison with like-minded people, they felt themselves strengthened in their aggression and egged one another on.'[93]

Though this was the most significant act of political protest during the year, there were others. In schools, 1977 saw a total of 350 incidents classed as 'political provocations' by the education ministry, involving 646 participants. This represented a minor increase on 1976, but both years compared badly for the SED, with the much lower levels recorded in 1975 (150 incidents).[94] These incidents included fascist graffiti and greetings, the singing of the '*Deutschlandlied*', anti-semitic comments (sharply up on the previous year), 'discriminatory' remarks against the GDR state and representatives of party and government (also sharply up), anti-Soviet utterances, and desecration of the GDR flag. Officials also included in this category the four cases where a minute's silence was held for the West German industrialist Hanns Martin Schleyer, assassinated by the Red Army Faction in October 1977, and support for West German sport clubs.[95] Though the year saw no cases of 'gang formation', there were 168 cases of 'rowdiness' involving 362 pupils. Such incidents involved violence against teachers, petty theft and intimidation and blackmail of other pupils. There were no signs of coordinated activities or concentrations of individuals working to undermine the state.

Conclusions: How stable was the GDR in 1977?

Outwardly, the GDR appeared stable and peaceful in 1977, and nothing occurred either internally or internationally that seemed capable of prompting a significant change in the state's circumstances. Even the publication in January of the Charter 77 manifesto by dissidents in neighbouring Czechoslovakia was barely remarked upon by the East German population. Yet, in 1977 the very foundations on which the SED relied for the effective continuation of its rule were shaky.

One prerequisite for the GDR's success was a widespread willingness to support both the political aims and the economic activity that would sustain the state in its socialist form. However, the SED's incessant efforts to

93. 10 October 1977 MdI report (as note 90), p. 6.

94. Ministerium für Volksbildung, Hauptschulinspektion, 'Information über die Entwicklung besonderer Vorkommnisse im Jahre 1977', 31 January 1978, Anlage 4, in BArch DR2/A8520. Comparable reports in the same file indicate a near doubling of such incidents in 1978, but a fall back to 1977 levels in 1979. The number of participants remains tiny compared to the total number of pupils, estimated at 2,594,418 in 1977: *Statistisches Jahrbuch 1978*, p. 286.

95. Ministerium für Volksbildung report, 31 January 1978 (as above).

promote passion for the cause had long since ceased to bear fruit. The Red October ceremonies were barely complete when on 18 November, the SED announced a big campaign to mark the GDR's 30th anniversary in 1979.[96] Enthusiasm was lacking. Comments included: 'All these calls to action will create a lot of unrest'; 'For goodness' sake leave us in peace just for a moment'; and 'We rush from one highpoint to the next–it's the citizens who suffer'.[97] DBD members had been similarly unimpressed by the launch of the Red October celebrations in the spring: 'There's always something new we have to get involved with. Who on earth is supposed to read and deal with it all?'[98] Even FDJ members were cautious about the announcement of the '*FDJ-Aufgebot DDR 30*', a new programme for young people to work to improve the GDR in honour of the latest anniversary: 'There's nothing new about it at all, it's just a new name!'[99] Given this rejection of party strategies, it was hardly surprising that some local functionaries simply wrote their group's pledges to support the latest campaign themselves, '. . . without the power, the knowledge and the commitment of the membership',[100] as the central FDJ bureaucracy wearily noted.

Not only was enthusiasm lacking, but criticisms also could be heard. The steady stream of important party and government delegations from socialist and other friendly countries had to be greeted by flag-waving crowds, but this prompted concerns about the associated loss of working hours. Berlin students, who bore the brunt of much of this work, were becoming particularly disenchanted at being used in this way.[101]

Most worrying for the party was the willingness of many in the population to draw general conclusions about the viability of the socialist project from the difficulties faced in their everyday lives. The lack of certain goods and spare parts prompted widespread doubts about the SED's assurances of economic growth and that plan targets were being met. Such views were linked to comments 'in which doubts are expressed about the strength of socialism'.[102] By 1977, it was clear to many that the SED's early hopes of building a strong economy were unravelling: 'When will these productivity increases be over? Will it never

96. Ulrich Dähn et al., eds., *Unser Staat. DDR-Zeittafel 1949–1988* (Berlin: Dietz, 1989), p. 179.

97. Nationale Front, Abteilung Ausschüsse, 'Information über Meinungen und Fragen der Bürger. . .', 8 September 1977, DY30/vorl.SED 18401, vol. 1.

98. DBD Abt. Parteiorgane, 'Information Nr.9/77', 8 March 1977, p. 3, DY30/vorl.SED 21550.

99. FDJ Abteilung Verbandsorgane, 'Information. . .', 1 December 1977, p. 1, DY30/vorl.SED 21404.

100. FDJ Abteilung Verbandsorgane, 'Schwerpunkte und Probleme. . .', 22 December 1977, p. 2, DY30/vorl.SED 21405.

101. 9 June 1977 Berlin SED report (as note 61), p. 13a.

102. FDJ Abteilung Verbandsorgane, 'Schwerpunkte und Probleme. . .', 19 July 1977, p. 4, DY30/vorl.SED 21405.

end? Ever year we're told that next year will be the most decisive year.'[103] Farmers in particular believed that there were natural limits to productivity, and that higher output in each successive year was becoming unrealistic, particularly given shortages of fertiliser and animal feed.[104] The coffee crisis appeared exemplary for the fundamental problems of the socialist bloc, buffeted by fluctuations in world prices, and the misleading nature of the party line: 'We're told over and over that the CMEA countries are the most dynamic economic region in the world. But how stable are we really if we have to make compromises to the capitalist world even to get goods like coffee?'[105] And for all the crises in the west's economy, and the apparent progress in the east, why, citizens asked, did so few people emigrate to the GDR?[106]

Even the much vaunted improved social security measures and reduced working hours, which took force in May 1977, though welcomed in practice, inspired fundamental doubts and some criticisms. In many sectors, workers and managers could not quite see how the new policy could be practically implemented. In the transport sector, as elsewhere, the only answer seemed to be overtime,[107] but what then was the point of reducing working hours while the state also encouraged additional voluntary shifts to fulfil the state plan?[108] There were also serious doubts about the practicality and wisdom of these changes in the health sector, where there were already serious staff shortages and which depended to a great extent on the female workers, particularly mothers of young children who could henceforth refuse night shifts and overtime. 'Some directives still seem to be far ahead of real life.'[109] Against a background of poor planning and widespread local difficulties, many concluded: 'We don't believe that the aims of the social policy programme can be fully realised. The GDR's current economic situation just won't run to it.'[110]

There was an acute sense during 1977 that things were getting worse, not better, and that difficulties on the ground were clearly linked to systemic factors: 'The provision of materials and spare parts is becoming increasingly

103. 19 August 1977 FDJ report (as note 23), p. 6.

104. DBD Abt. Parteiorgane, 'Information Nr.21/77', 15 August 1977, p. 7, DY30/vorl.SED 21550.

105. DBD Abt. Parteiorgane, 'Information Nr.20/77', 17 August 1977, p. 2, ibid.

106. SED ZK Abteilung Gesundheitswesen, 'Information zu politisch-ideologischen Problemen. . .', 27 July 1977, p. 3, DY30/vorl.SED 21898, vol. 1.

107. For example, in transport: cf. 19 August 1977 report (as note 67), p. 5.

108. Nationalrat der Nationalen Front, 'Information über Meinungen und Fragen der Bürger. . .', 8 August 1977, in DY30/vorl.SED 18401, vol. 1.

109. SED ZK Abteilung Gesundheitspolitik, 'Information zu politisch-ideologischen Problemen. . .', 27 July 1977, p. 4, DY30/vorl.SED 21898, vol. 1.

110. LDPD Sekretariat des Parteivorstandes, 'Information Nr. 30/77', 14 October 1977, p. 3, DY30/vorl. SED-19406, vol.2. Cf. also 15 August 1977 DBD report (as note 104), p. 2.

difficult. That just shouldn't happen in socialism.'[111] Optimism about the viability of socialism was obviously lacking. The efforts of the television service and of other propagandists to promote the strength of the Soviet Union seemed in vain when, at year's end, citizens around the country believed that it was impossible to claim that the Soviet Union's progress to communism had achieved 'the highest level of societal development' given that productivity and living standards were far behind the developed capitalist countries.[112] Such observations prompted more personal reflections, as young workers noted that: 'You could be unemployed in West Germany and still earn more than me.'[113] Damningly, health workers believed that the difficulties the GDR was experiencing in implementing the new social measures demonstrated '. . . that socialism is also incapable of creating the unity of economic rationality and humanity'.[114]

In 1977, there were still enough citizens willing to rally to the SED flag and to maintain socialism in the colours of the GDR, albeit with no great enthusiasm. But even among those who bore the system aloft, serious doubts about the long-term prospects and viability of the socialist project were common, and widespread doubts occurred in the general population in the face of shortages of basic goods, appropriate housing, and medical essentials. Integration into the economic systems of the socialist bloc appeared an unnecessary hindrance to their prosperity, and the austerity package appeared to be a product of their isolation from the western world rather than an inherent necessity. Even in this typical year in the GDR's most stable decade, there are striking continuities in popular opinion with both the initial decades of construction and the gradual decline through the 1980s. Equally constant was the willingness to express vocal and damning complaints about specific grievances and the system in general, despite the well understood presence of the *Stasi*.[115] The main change since the 1950s appears to have been a widespread loss of belief and enthusiasm in the project.

In discussing these aspects of popular opinion in 1977, we can challenge the teleological instinct to trace the collapse of popular support for, or tolerance of, the GDR to a process which began in the mid-1980s and which continued inexorably to the *Wende* of late 1989. While the organised oppositional

111. 4 October 1977 LDPD report (as note 25), p. 3.

112. LDPD Sektretariat des Parteivorstandes, 'Information Nr.35/77', p. 2, 8 December 1977, DY30/vorl.SED-19406, vol. 2.

113. 19 August 1977 FDJ report (as note 23), p. 2.

114. 27 July 1977 report (as note 109), p. 4.

115. The contours of popular opinion as recorded in files of 1977 are remarkably similar to those reproduced in this author's *Politics and Popular Opinion in East Germany 1945–68* (Manchester University Press, 2000).

structures had not yet emerged in 1977, the motivations to consider radical political change were already well developed and widespread. Clear ideas about adopting the structures of West German capitalism were no more apparent in 1977 than they were in 1989 until some time after the opening of the Berlin Wall. However, had an international catalyst permitted regime change in the GDR in 1977, it seems certain that this opportunity would have been seized as willingly then as proved to be the case in 1989.

Finally, this contribution has attempted to establish a sense of the GDR's internal normality within a typical year, that is, to present a cross-section of the GDR as it was experienced from a (far from exhaustive) variety of perspectives, rather than to portray the GDR in 1977 as being at a particular stage along a continuum of normalisation (or, for that matter, decline). To consider the events of one single year in this fashion logically precludes any firm conclusions about tendencies in the GDR's historical trajectory, for which a diachronic methodology would be required. Yet this approach perhaps does allow some conclusions to be drawn about the extent to which 'normalisation' and 'routinisation' had occurred by this point in the GDR's history. Mary Fulbrook has proposed elsewhere in this volume that there are three principal facets to normalisation. First, there should be a congruence of norms. The material outlined above would certainly support this contention. Second, routinisation should occur. Here, also, there appears more than adequate evidence that the GDR's routines were well established by 1977: the run of official events and the expected responses were very clear to functionaries at all levels, and to the population at large. However, while this phenomenon produced a considerable level of internal stability (people largely behaved as was expected of them), it also resulted in high levels of boredom and outwardly negative reactions to the system, which in 1977 (and doubtless both beforehand and thereafter) were certainly undermining the SED's claimed ideological legitimacy. Finally, Mary Fulbrook proposes that normalisation would be characterised by stabilisation, in other words that there would be no sense of internal threat.[116] This final facet

116. *Editor's comment:* Actually, this is somewhat too restrictive an interpretation of what is meant by the 'stabilisation' aspect of the normalisation concept; stabilisation has less to do with the absence of a 'sense of internal threat' than with practices geared towards a 'restoration' or 'maintenance' of a political order which is, in face of recent political challenges or following a period of upheaval, now assumed to be capable of reproduction over a foreseeable period of time, whether or not there are continued threats both from within and abroad. Mechanisms may have been devised to deal with both internal and external/international sources of insecurity; yet stability is always inherently fragile, open to further challenge. Cf. the longer discussion in Chapter 1, above, and Merrilyn Thomas's discussion of the international situation in Chapter 2.

These theoretical remarks do not, of course, detract from the validity of the substantive point regarding attitudes which Mark Allinson is making here; and indeed, the year 1977 was on the cusp of the descent into ever more visible economic decline, with renewed international tensions and the growth of domestic political challenges increasingly evident from the late 1970s onwards,

appears from the material presented here to be largely absent from the GDR in 1977, since there were widespread doubts about the wisdom of the socialist economic project and little true ideological commitment below the highest levels of the party and state apparatus. Yet, paradoxically, the failure to achieve this third strand of normalisation and the tensions that stemmed from this deficiency were key characteristics of the GDR's internal normality.

culminating in the ultimate collapse of the GDR and the Soviet system more broadly at the end of the 1980s.

Chapter 13

'Normalisation' in the GDR in Retrospect: East German Perspectives on Their Own Lives

Mary Fulbrook

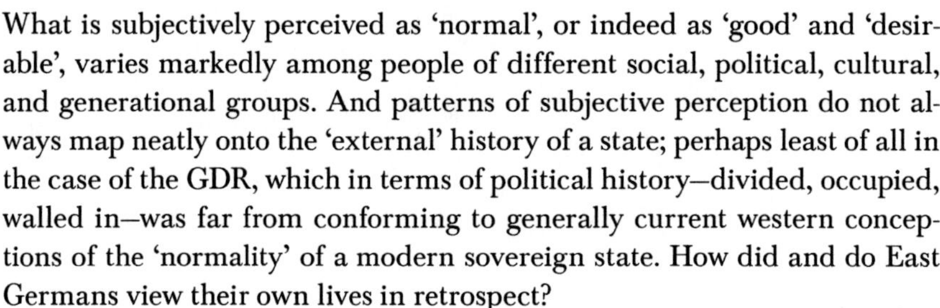

What is subjectively perceived as 'normal', or indeed as 'good' and 'desirable', varies markedly among people of different social, political, cultural, and generational groups. And patterns of subjective perception do not always map neatly onto the 'external' history of a state; perhaps least of all in the case of the GDR, which in terms of political history–divided, occupied, walled in–was far from conforming to generally current western conceptions of the 'normality' of a modern sovereign state. How did and do East Germans view their own lives in retrospect?

The evidence of a survey carried out in 2005, fifteen years after unification, provides insights into retrospective perceptions of 'normality' among East Germans, and highlights what now seems important to them about the GDR in explicit comparison with experiences of life in united Germany.[1] The survey produced some surprising preliminary results, most notably in terms of divergent approaches to the GDR among dif-

1. I would like to thank the Arts and Humanities Research Council (AHRC) for financial support for this research. I am extremely grateful to Silvia Dallinger for her work on this survey during an internship as an Honorary Research Assistant; to Erica Fulbrook for assisting me in inputting data from the questionnaires into an SPSS database; and particularly to all of the anonymous East Germans who were willing to take the time and trouble to assist in the project, to fill in a very lengthy questionnaire and to express their views on the lives they had led and the states they had lived in, both literally and subjectively. I hope I have not done the richness of their views too much of an injustice in the analysis which follows.

ferent generations; these generational patterns will form a major focus of the discussion that follows. This research provides general support for the thesis—widely evidenced in the case of West Germany in the 1950s—that a sense of 'normality' or 'normalisation' is more likely to be pervasive when the experiences of private lives and the intrusions of broader historical-political developments do not seem to run in parallel; when the 'good times' and 'bad times' in one's own life appear, in subjective perceptions, to be unrelated to the wider world in which the individual is living. The material also sustains the view that East Germans lived multi-facetted, many-layered lives, in which 'high politics' was for most people most of the time a matter of relatively subordinate concern; and in which people were capable of simultaneously participating in, sustaining, and criticising state structures, ideas, and institutions, and holding highly differentiated sets of views on different aspects of life in the GDR, rendering suspect any simple distinctions between 'state' and 'society'.[2] The ways in which East Germans reflect on the constraints and parameters of living in and through the specific conditions of the GDR further suggest a very strong awareness of norms and unwritten 'rules' according to which one had to behave; or in the light of which one could predict adverse consequences if one did not; and indeed, surprisingly, some of which many East Germans actively valued in retrospect. The material discussed here, while quite clearly limited in a number of ways outlined below, both tends to support the thesis of normalisation processes as far as internalisation of key norms or 'playing by the rules' is concerned, and suggests key differences in the experience of the GDR across different social groups and generations.

History and Life Stories: Theoretical Considerations

This chapter focuses on how, in 2005, a sample of 'ordinary East Germans' represented their own lives; which is not to suggest that these retrospective self-presentations provide definitive answers to the question of 'what the GDR was actually like', if one may phrase this in rather naïve Rankean terms. The subjective perceptions of individuals, whether captured in some way in records at the time or later, may, if viewed from other perspectives, be entirely mistaken, even reprehensible in their self-centred emphases and related sins of omission (for example, the way in which many 'Aryan' Germans designated the 1930s as the 'good times', ignoring

2. I have developed this argument in Mary Fulbrook, *The People's State: East German Society from Hitler to Honecker* (Yale: Yale University Press, 2005).

the exploitation, exclusion, and repression of those excluded from Hitler's *Volksgemeinschaft*); they are not necessarily any guide to 'how things really were' as far as the broader picture is concerned. On the other hand, people's own perceptions affect how they act and react: whether or not their 'social diagnoses'—over-estimations, underestimations, blind spots, misperceptions—constitute an accurate assessment of the society in which they are living and in which they participate, their subjective perceptions and their retrospective accounts of their life stories are themselves social phenomena with consequences for their behaviour, and hence of considerable interest to historians.

Life stories are not accurate guides to history, nor are they necessarily even truthful versions of an individual biography. The ways in which 'life stories' are later narrated are generally not full and detailed representations even of the individual's own life, but are, rather, ever-developing and frequently changing ways of emplotting or 'making sense' of personal experiences and development in ways with which the narrator can comfortably live; and their construction is generally in some way 'appropriate' to, even actively constructed by, the context in which and the audience to whom the story is narrated, in respect of which certain aspects will be highlighted, others downplayed or even suppressed entirely. This is perhaps clearest with reference to the quite extreme examples of life stories from the Third Reich, and there is by now quite a substantial literature on problems of memory and representation among the survivors and perpetrators of the Nazi system.[3] Some research suggests, for example, that former perpetrators and victims have systematic tendencies to narrate their own stories in rather different ways: those who were (even in a very small way, in the general scale of Third Reich criminality) on the side of the 'perpetrators' tend to play up their own alleged 'victimhood'; yet by contrast, genuine victims of Nazi persecution are more likely to frame their stories in terms of active attempts to deal with an intolerable situation—survivors' tales of escape, of attempted rescue of others—and often find it too painful to talk of failures, separation, or death. While the 'perpetrators' might talk endlessly, recounting stories of heroism in which there are no victims, or in which they appear almost as the only 'victims', genuine survivors

3. See for example: Daniel Bar-On, *Legacy of Silence: Encounters with Children of the Third Reich* (Cambridge, MA: Harvard University Press, 1989); Lawrence Langer, *Holocaust Testimonies* (New Haven: Yale University Press, 1991); Gabriele Rosenthal, ed., *The Holocaust in Three Generations* (London: Cassell, 1998); Harold Welzer, Sabine Moller, and Karoline Tschuggnall, *"Opa war kein Nazi": Nationalsozialismus und Holocaust im Familiengedächtnis* (Frankfurt: Fischer, 2002); and for earlier 'tales', Robert Moeller, *War Stories: The Search for a Usable Past in the Federal Republic of Germany* (Berkeley and Los Angeles: University of California Press, 2001).

often find that the act of talking involves a 'bringing back' or verbal articulation of inchoate emotions and memories that are too painful to live with. These generalisations relate only, of course, to those willing to talk 'honestly' in situations forming part of scholarly research, sometimes with an additional therapeutic dimension.[4] The situation is very different with respect to those recounting aspects of their life stories in the context of investigations into war crimes, where individuals accused of complicity in mass murder will inevitably present merely self-exculpatory tales. Moreover, juxtaposition of the life stories of those accused and the testimonies of people brought as witnesses often reveals that the latter were in no position to have accurate knowledge of who really lay behind the immediate acts of violence and brutality to which they could testify—one of the reasons why the notorious 'desk perpetrators' of Nazi Germany on the whole managed so successfully to evade being brought to juridical account for their involvement in systematic mass murder. In a quite different setting, research suggests that intergenerational transmission of stories will serve to soften and ameliorate the deeds of grandparents by the time the story is the subject of broader familial discussion, with children and grandchildren having a particular interest in reserving an unsullied love for their immediate relatives—an outcome not always possible, depending on how public the misdeeds of the parents or grandparents had been.[5] The problem of intergenerational 'coming to terms with' the Nazi period is often one of a long and slow retelling and reconstructing of both the lives and the life stories which form part of making a new life. The context in which a 'life story' is told, then, will have considerable implications for the ways in which people represent their own past lives.

These general considerations hold true in principle, if in rather different ways in practice, for exploring the ways in which, after the collapse of the GDR and unification with the Federal Republic, East Germans represented their own views and recounted the ways in which they had led their own lives in the GDR. The communist dictatorship in Eastern Germany was an oppressive regime effectively containing its population by the threat or use of force; but those seeking to equate it with the Nazi

---

4. As in the research reported in Rosenthal, ed., *Holocaust in three Generations*, where this argument about the contrasting modes of recounting victim and perpetrator pasts is made.

5. See particularly Welzer et al., *Opa war kein Nazi*. There have been several recent autobiographical accounts by individuals seeking to come to terms with their own families' rather more public Nazi pasts (Frank, Himmler, Scheub), as well as those whose relatives were victims (Monika Maron), or whose relatives, despite Nazi inclinations eventually became part of the resistance (Wibke Bruhns), as well as the highly belated autobiographical revelations of SS-membership as a youngster on the part of Günther Grass.

dictatorship have to be reminded that the GDR was informed by a very different political set of ideals, and that despite the denial of human rights, the GDR was nowhere near either as murderous or as aggressive as the preceding Nazi regime. It was, moreover, unlike the Third Reich, relatively stable—at least during the middle period between the construction of the Berlin Wall in 1961 and the economic decline and renewed Cold War from 1979, with the concomitant growth of political unrest in the Gorbachev era in the later 1980s. Many East Germans, however much they had hated the SED gerontocracy and had criticised the political repression and the mismanagement of the economy to the point of collapse, and however ecstatic they had been about the breaching of the Berlin Wall in November 1989 and unification with the Federal Republic in 1990, were somewhat taken aback and surprised at the character of the discussions following unification. A widespread sense of unease at the simplistic two-dimensional representations of a vilified regime, with an overwhelming focus on repression and fear, was to some extent counteracted by a concomitant rise in '*Ostalgia*', nostalgia for a lost form of society, as well as a belated recuperation of the GDR as comedy in novels and films. Heated public debates on modes of 'overcoming' and representing the East German dictatorship, which exploded in the early 1990s, have continued, if in new forms, in the early twenty-first century. Self-exculpatory autobiographical presentations of former senior politicians or officials of the Ministry for State Security (*Stasi*), for example, or of former unofficial collaborators (*inoffizielle Mitarbeiter*, IMs) continue to be critiqued; individual stories of persecution and political opposition have been highlighted, and members of organisations such as the *Bund der stalinistisch Verfolgten* continue to articulate claims for compensation for injustices suffered at the hands of the communist regime. Controversial commissions have been established to explore ways of interpreting and representing the past, from the Federal Parliamentary Investigative Commissions (*Enquetekommissionen des Bundestages*) of the 1990s through to the 'Sabrow commission' evaluating different memory cultures and modes of representing the past in 2006. People's representations of their own lives in the early twenty-first century were thus taking place in a very different historical context from that of, say, the late 1980s or the early 1990s.[6]

---

6. For an extremely interesting set of oral history interviews carried out by western researchers in the GDR in 1987, see Lutz Niethammer, Dorothee Wierling, and Alexander von Plato, *Die Volkseigene Erfahrung. Eine Archäologie des Lebens in der Industrieprovinz der DDR* (Berlin: Rowohlt, 1991).

The question necessarily arises of whose life stories are being represented, and what implications this selective self-representation has for understanding what the GDR was like for the 'silent majority', given the fact that only the articulate, or those presenting their past in a manner catching the attention of the media or publishing houses, generally find a historical voice in the form of 'ego-documents'. Hence the decision to try to explore the life stories and self-representations of those who were not brought into the limelight by virtue of their political prominence, whether in support of or in opposition to the regime; and those who had no compelling desire–or time, ability, articulacy, funding, publishing outlets–to 'tell their own story', but who often felt that the society through which they had lived was not being appropriately represented through the stories told by others. The findings reported here make no claim to presenting a comprehensive view of life in the GDR; rather, they seek to provide at least some indication of how the GDR was seen, fifteen years after its demise, by arguably the majority of the East German population, who did not have a 'voice' in the published arena with its focus on intellectuals, dissidents, *Stasi* informants, top politicians, church-people, and other prominent individuals.

It has undoubtedly to be borne in mind, when considering in more detail the findings outlined below, that the respondents in this survey were representing their lives in the context of a united Germany in which many felt they were 'losers'. As one put it: 'Since I belong to those who have work, it should be going well for me. Unfortunately not! My husband (a building worker) cannot get work and so I am the sole breadwinner for our family. Money is tight everywhere. We have not been on holiday for ages now. We feel we are the "losers of the nation" (*Verlierer der Nation*).'[7] Others objected to what they saw as the 'victor's viewpoint' (*Siegersicht*) in western portrayals of the GDR–including critiques of this survey as allegedly influenced by such views.[8] Some claimed that 'GDR-people are treated now as 2nd or 3rd class' citizens in the new Germany.[9] A cynic might argue that such views inevitably mean that the GDR is seen in far rosier terms in hindsight–and even some respondents drew attention to this in their own memories, although as one elderly respondent (born in 1919) put it: while people always tend to see 'what has passed as better

7. QN 101, female, born 1961. For details of the surveys, see the methodological discussion below. Comments from the larger study are referenced by QN followed by the relevant number; all statistical analyses are based on this body of material.

8. QN 206, male, born 1948.

9. QN 219, female, born 1948.

than the present . . . who would not like to forget certain [unpleasant] events in the past? But precisely these are the things he can never forget!'[10] A whiff of '*Ostalgie*' or nostalgia for the way things never were in a mythologised lost '*Heimat DDR*' undoubtedly hovers around at least some of the questionnaires. Yet the responses are generally also highly differentiated, with due criticism being targeted at many of the all too evident failings of the GDR system, as well as retrospective praise for aspects of the invisible fabric of social life and relationships which are not so evident to the western observer's eye; the pictures East Germans paint of the past are quite complex. The responses are in any event of interest, given that the very object of analysis is perceived experience. Most interesting, in some respects, is the fact that there are highly distinctive patterns in retrospective perceptions. Once one delves beyond the rough overall view and starts to explore in more detail the variations in patterns of remembered experience between different generational groups, some extremely interesting contrasts emerge, demanding more detailed reflection and further exploration.

Some Methodological Issues: The Survey and the Sample

Before discussing the findings, it is essential to make a few methodological comments about the nature of this particular piece of research. While oral history interviews may be highly suggestive, generalisations based on these can be problematic, particularly when the sample is very small or restricted to one particular social group.[11] The attempt here was rather to combine quantitative and qualitative material across a representative cross-section of the population that might provide a basis for broader conclusions.

Following a smaller survey during 2004/5 using approximately 80 lengthy questionnaires combining quantitative with qualitative and open-ended questions, around 350 revised questionnaires were administered in the summer of 2005 to East German residents born between 1917 and 1977.[12] In total, 271 of

10. QN 253, male, born 1919.

11. For a thorough and insightful example of the use of oral history interviews, see Dorothee Wierling, *Geboren im Jahr Eins. Der Geburtsjahrgang 1949 in der DDR. Versuch einer Kollektivbiographie* (Berlin, 2002).

12. The first set of questionnaires in the smaller-scale survey, which were longer and more qualitative in nature than the version used in the larger study, produced much by way of interesting written material from interviewees, and where the occasional comment is quoted from these it is referenced with the letter L followed by the questionnaire number. They have, however, not been thoroughly analysed or included in the statistical analyses presented below. Discerning readers will be aware that a note of unscientificity has crept in with the use of the words 'approximately' and

this second set of questionnaires were both returned and usable, in the sense that sufficient data was present for them to be coded for most purposes; given my research interest in generational differences, the year of birth was in all cases essential, although it was possible to make use of questionnaires where at least a few other questions were left blank. Since the research project was explicitly based in a UK university and funded by the UK Arts and Humanities Research Council, a fact prominently highlighted alongside the UCL logo on the front cover of the questionnaires, there was no issue of an in-built 'West German / East German' inequality or suspicion as far as the East German respondents were concerned, many of whom expressed some weariness and cynicism about what they saw as typical West German views on the GDR. Nevertheless, and although every effort was made (following a small pilot study of questionnaires for the larger survey) to phrase questions in an open and relatively neutral way, allowing people to give their own views without being unnecessarily 'led' in any particular direction, many respondents commented that they felt the questionnaire had an in-built bias against the GDR; this might partly reflect a wider somewhat defensive stance among many East Germans accompanied by generally rather critical reactions to western representations of the GDR in the media.

This survey, though relatively small by comparison with the activities of professional bodies such as the Allensbach Institut für Demoskopie, made it possible to combine quantitative and qualitative questions, the latter giving respondents scope for presenting in their own language and conceptual framework what they themselves wanted to say about their

---

'around'. Despite rigorous statistical intentions at the stage of research design, there were a number of amendments during the implementation phase. We came to the view, for example, that to achieve a satisfactory response rate among older cohorts, it was preferable to allow administration of the questionnaire by a senior person or carer in a relaxed setting, giving elderly people sufficient time to make their responses; many such questionnaires were photocopied by the institution and then subsequently returned by post. We also adopted a 'snowball technique' in workplaces (such as a copy shop) where staff did not want to take the time to fill in the questionnaire on the spot, but distributed it among colleagues who sent it back later from home. As in any survey, some people who were approached simply refused, both for the kinds of reasons which are the common experience of street survey research everywhere (in haste to get home, to get to work, to meet friends, to catch a train; suspicion of survey research, or people accosting them in the street; not wanting to 'get involved' or have one's privacy invaded) as well as some which seem more GDR-specific, particularly perhaps fear of being potentially exposed to adverse consequences as a result of admitting to particular viewpoints or former political activities. Since we have no means of knowing precisely how many were distributed that did not come back by post, and by definition those who refused to participate are unknown quantities, it is impossible to speculate usefully about the ways in which those who filled in the questionnaire might have systematically differed from those who did not. Nevertheless, the fact that the social profile in terms of patterns of employment and rates of unemployment is fairly representative of the East German population as a whole at the time gives some grounds for belief in the more general validity of these findings.

lives. It was also possible to view individuals 'as a whole', in their different areas of activity at different times in their lives, rather than merely statistical fodder for attitudes on single issues. The corresponding challenge, however, was in analysis; often the material in answers to open-ended questions was both fascinating and extremely hard to code in any sensible way to render it susceptible to meaningful statistical analysis.[13]

There are considerable difficulties with trying to obtain a representative cross-section of the former GDR population in terms of social structure, given the enormous changes in the socio-economic system since 1990. No simple glancing at visible dress codes, as might be possible for a survey of British attitudes in a central London street, will give the interviewer ready clues as to a person's position in the East German class structure pre–and post–1990. In the event, geographical location was taken as a poor proxy for ensuring a degree of social distribution. The questionnaires were distributed in several distinctive locations in eastern Germany: in Eisenhüttenstadt (originally named Stalinstadt), once a flagship 'socialist new town' on the border with Poland at the Oder river; in Königswusterhausen, a small old township (and former royal hunting lodge of the Hohenzollern dynasty) at the end of the S-Bahn line southeast of Berlin; in the Müggelsee/Köpenick area of southeastern Berlin, a relatively pleasant area of old lakeside villas as well as newer housing estates; Marzahn, a northern part of East Berlin characterised by a high proportion of 'Plattenbau' housing estates of high-rise prefabricated apartment blocks built during GDR times, with relatively high rates of unemployment, poverty, and social distress in unified Germany; and in the Lichtenberg area of East Berlin, with a somewhat higher proportion of older housing stock as well as newer estates, and historically perhaps most notable for the presence of the Normannenstrasse complex in which Erich Mielke presided over the headquarters of the Ministry for State Security (*Stasi*), and in which a high proportion of *Stasi* officials lived with their families.

Many of the respondents were interviewed and were prepared to fill out the questionnaire in public spaces: in parks, at playgrounds, while out shopping, at leisure activities or cultural events, on their way home from work, and even in some cases while at work. At the time of the survey, between

---

13. Statistics must, of course, always be treated with the relevant degree of scepticism (to quote the title of one textbook, there are 'lies, damned lies and statistics'; or, in the parlance of one statistics course with reference to highly sophisticated computer packages, there is always the danger of 'rubbish in, rubbish out'). Much depends on how questions are phrased, concepts operationalised, answers coded. If treated carefully, statistics can nevertheless in some respects be highly suggestive for historians, highlighting issues that require more extensive qualitative research and reflection. It is in this spirit that the results of this study are reported here.

Table 13.1. Interview Locations

	Frequency	Percent
Königswusterhausen	**8**	**3.0**
Eisenhüttenstadt	**54**	**19.9**
Lichtenberg	**22**	**8.1**
Marzahn (general)	**44**	**16.2**
Müggelsee / Müggelheim	**36**	**13.3**
Treptow-Köpenick (Arbeitsamt)	**14**	**5.2**
Friedrichshagen, Seniorenfreizeitstätte VITAL	**23**	**8.5**
Marzahn (Arbeitsamt)	**12**	**4.4**
Lichtenberg (Arbeitsamt)	**13**	**4.8**
Other locations	**45**	**16.6**
Total	271	100.0

18.2 percent and 18.9 percent of East Germans of working age were unemployed.[14] Given this high unemployment rate, a total of 14.4 percent of the sample were interviewed while waiting in job centres or unemployment offices (*Arbeitsämter*).[15] Older people were often accessed through day care centres, or residential old people's homes. Some questionnaires were distributed on a 'snowball' basis through personal contacts in a particular workplace, senior citizens' day care centre, church or leisure facility, and subsequently returned by post. While a rough attempt was made to balance the gender ratio, in the event more females responded (169) than males (102).

What follows is an account of some of the key findings of this specific piece of research; to explore these findings further would require embedding in a more extensive analysis of changing experiences and perceptions among different groups across the whole of Germany's turbulent twentieth century, and dense contextualisation in the light of appropriate archival materials.[16]

14. Statistisches Bundesamt Deutschland, at http://www.destatis.de/indicators/d/arb230ad.htm.

15. To be absolutely precise: just under two-thirds (63.8 percent) of the sample were of working age (born 1940–1977); so the total percentage unemployed within the sample was actually 22.54 percent of those of working age, very slightly higher than the average for the area. However, unemployment rates among males aged over twenty ranged from 20 percent to 21.5 percent and among females aged over twenty from 20.3 percent to 22.7 percent during the relevant months, whereas unemployment rates for young people aged under twenty were much lower (from 7.6 percent to 14.5 percent), bringing down the overall averages. Since there were no individuals in the sample aged below twenty (the youngest being 29), the unemployment rate in the sample corresponded very closely to the average for the working population of that age group in the region.

16. This constitutes a far more extensive project, using not merely oral history interviews, but also a wide range of 'ego-documents' and other archival material from across the century. I am extremely grateful to the Leverhulme Trust for a Major Research Fellowship, making this much broader project possible.

Significant Differences: The 'Sore Thumb' Theory of Generations

Striking to any informed observer of the GDR is the large number of prominent people who seemed—like the internationally acclaimed writer Christa Wolf—to have been born in or around 1929. An analysis of those who made a sufficient contribution to the life of the GDR to have been included in the retrospective 'Who was Who in the GDR' *(Wer war wer in der DDR)*–whether by virtue of their activities as functionaries, politicians, senior members of the *Stasi* hierarchy, or as writers, musicians, actors, visual artists, theologians, clowns, sportspeople, oppositionalists—reveals a striking preponderance of functionaries and staunch upholders of the regime among those born in the period 1926–1932.[17] If the 'founding fathers' of the GDR were figures born before the First World War, members of the internally highly divided 'Front generation' and the 'War youth generation' (*Kriegsjugendgeneration*), the GDR was effectively 'carried' by this 'second Hitler Youth generation'. In between was a very different group: the cohort of those born during and shortly after the First World War, the 'first Hitler Youth generation' who, as young people in the 1930s, were the most enthusiastic supporters of the Nazi regime, and who—at least the males among them—were disproportionately decimated by participation in the Second World War.[18] The 'sore thumb' of the group that might loosely be called the '1929ers'—the extraordinary 'sticking out' of a significant cluster of several hundred people born within a few years of each other, between 1926 and 1932—certainly requires further exploration, whether or not they claimed any sense of self-awareness as a generation both 'in and for itself' in Karl Mannheim's sense.[19]

It would at first appear, on a hard-nosed demographic analysis, that a combination of differential birth rates in the early decades of the twentieth century, disproportionate survival rates through the Second World War, and

---

17. See, for further details of this analysis of functional elites and birth cohorts, Mary Fulbrook, 'Generationen und Kohorten in der DDR. Protagonisten und Widersacher des DDR-Systems aus der Perspektive biographischer Daten' in Annegret Schüle, Thomas Ahbe and Rainer Gries, eds., *Die DDR aus generationengeschichtlicher Perspektive. Eine Inventur* (Universitätsverlag Leipzig, 2005).

18. See for a preliminary discussion of this, Mary Fulbrook, 'Changing states, changing selves: Violence and social generations in the transition from Nazism to Communism' in Fulbrook, ed., *Un-Civilising Processes? Excess and Transgression in German Culture and Society: Perspectives Debating with Norbert Elias* (Amsterdam: Rodopi, 2007).

19. Karl Mannheim, 'Das Problem der Generationen', in Mannheim, *Wissenssoziologie* (Berlin: Luchterhand, 1964; orig. 1928), pp. 509–65; and contributions to Mark Roseman, ed., *Generations in Conflict* (Cambridge: Cambridge University Press, 1995). See also Dorothee Wierling's chapter, above, on the differences between the '1929ers' and the '1949ers'.

age at 'entry' into the GDR and associated opportunities for political advancement, together could explain these rather startling findings: those who had survived Hitler's war, and who were in their late teens or early twenties in 1949, were far less likely to be tarnished by the taint of Nazism than those in their thirties who had held positions in the SS, the SA, the Nazi system of government, or who had participated as 'ordinary men' in the racist and ideological war against 'Bolshevism', brutally exterminating communist 'partisans' and Jews on the eastern front.[20] Younger people without such a background–however radical the 'conversion' as a POW might have been in some cases of older men–were, accordingly, far more likely after the war to have been taken on, for example, as 'new teachers' (*Neulehrer*), or vaulted rapidly up the emerging political and functional hierarchies of the communist 'anti-fascist state' after 1949. On this sort of structural explanation, too, one could argue that the relatively low participation in positions of power and authority in the GDR of those born from 1933 onwards could be explained by some form of 'closure', as key positions were already filled by those young enough to retain their status throughout the existence of the GDR as a state, approaching retirement age in their sixties only with the collapse of the GDR itself in 1989.

Thus, as far as the curious preponderance of '1929ers' among the functionary classes of the GDR is concerned, a purely structural argument could be run along the following lines: the differential presence of those born in the later 1920s and early 1930s among the state-sustaining groups in the GDR could be explained by the differential birth rates and survival rates of succeeding birth cohorts in and through the two World Wars, combined with differential post-war opportunity structures with respect to the likelihood of being appointed to and retaining a position of political significance in the new communist regime.

Such a purely structural and statistical analysis works, up to a point, particularly with respect to comparisons between those born during or shortly after the First World War and those born in the later Weimar years; it does not, however (for reasons which cannot be discussed fully here), explain key differences between the '1929ers' and those born in the peacetime years of the 1930s with respect to their later positions in and attitudes towards the GDR. In particular, given the high turnover of functionaries particularly in the first decade or so of the GDR's existence, and the fact that over three million people fled to the West while the border was still permeable, among them many *Neulehrer* and others in promising positions who nevertheless felt

20. The long-term effects on particular cohorts have yet to be fully explored.

they would have better career prospects in the West, the theory of 'closure' in the opportunity structure for those born in the 1930s simply does not hold (although there is undoubtedly some mileage in this when we consider social mobility for younger cohorts of the 'FDJ generation' who reached adulthood in the 1970s and 1980s).[21] It would seem there must have been some attitudinal obstacles to similar forms of active positive participation in the East German functionary system on the part of these slightly younger East Germans.

This raises therefore a number of questions about how people themselves perceived these experiences, and why they were willing–or not, as the case may be–to adopt new roles and play according to the rules of a regime very different from the one in which they had been socialised. And, focussing only on the select group of those whose actions earned them a place in *Wer war wer in der DDR*, it also raises the question of whether those who were willing to take on high-level functionary positions were in any sense representative of their birth cohorts, or were a group apart, distinctively different in key respects from other members of the broader age cohort in the society from which they had emerged. Were they, in effect, a totally atypical 'generational unit' (*Generationseinheit*, to use Mannheim's terminology), rising to prominence by virtue of their differences from others? Or, did those who rose to the top in GDR society and politics in some respects reflect wider attributes of their birth cohort or 'social generation'? And if so, what were these distinctive characteristics, and why were they characteristic of precisely this cohort and not of preceding and succeeding cohorts?

The survey carried out in 2005 of a wider cross-section of 'ordinary' East Germans of different birth cohorts provides some startling preliminary descriptive answers to these questions, and is highly suggestive in a variety of ways, even if the material falls short of suggesting any kind of explanation. To summarise the most important findings: those 'sore thumb' members of the 'second Hitler Youth generation' or '1929ers' who rose to prominent positions in the GDR appear to have been far more similar to 'ordinary' members of their cohort than one might have thought possible. And they seem to be sharply different from those born just a few years later, members of the cohorts born during the Third Reich.

There are many ways of chopping the statistics to represent these differences; but whichever way one chooses to analyse the data and group specific birth cohorts, the peculiarities surrounding the '1929ers' are visible

---

21. See also the discussion in Ralph Jessen, 'Mobility and blockages in the 1970s', in Konrad Jarausch, ed., *Dictatorship as Experience: Towards a Socio-Cultural History of the GDR* (New York and Oxford: Berghahn, 1999).

and striking. In this survey, '1929ers'–i.e., those born between 1926 and 1932–were much more likely to have been a member of the SED than were any other birth cohorts before or afterwards. For all other cohorts, membership of the SED ranged between 11.1 percent and 16.7 percent of the sample in the respective cohort. But among those in the sample who were born between the mid 1920s and Hitler's accession to power, a staggering 41.4 percent professed to have been members of the SED–around three times as many, on average, as for all the other cohorts. The association between birth cohort and SED membership is even stronger if one selects only males: as many as 70 percent of the males in this cohort of the 'second Hitler Youth generation' claimed to have been members of the SED; and this was the only cohort in which those who had been members vastly outweighed those who had not.

The 1929ers were not merely, it seems, far more likely to be committed Communists; they were also far more likely to be 'either-or' people, rejecting Christianity on a massive scale, in stark contrast to those born shortly after them. Those born in the immediately following years–the years of the Third Reich–were, by contrast, far more likely to have been and, more importantly, to have remained Christians: virtually half of the Christians in the entire sample (33 out of 67) were born during these twelve years out of the total of sixty years of birth cohorts. Those born in the Third Reich, unlike those born in the immediately preceding years (who had also been born at a time when belonging to a particular religious confession was well-nigh automatic), retained their church membership throughout the rather anti-religious years of the atheist GDR, when to be a Christian brought with it disadvantages in terms not only of one's own career, but also the school experiences, educational opportunities, and life prospects of one's children.[22] These committed Christians of the Third Reich generation were joined by a small but significant group of young people, born in the 1960s, for whom the church became an important haven for free discussion of political and moral problems during the 1980s.[23] The experience of Christianity of these younger people, following the meeting between Erich Honecker and church leaders culminating in the Church-state agreement of March 1978, was that the church allowed them both metaphorical and physical space to discuss openly the urgent problems of the day–human rights, peace, the environment. While in the earlier twentieth century female religiosity appears to

22. On religion in the GDR, see for example Robert Goeckel, *The Lutheran Church and the East German State* (Ithaca, NY: Cornell University Press, 1990).

23. Cf. my discussion in M. Fulbrook, *Anatomy of a Dictatorship: Inside the GDR, 1949–1989* (Oxford: Oxford University Press, 1995).

have had a strong impact on political position (as demonstrated, for example, in female voting preferences in the Weimar Republic), there was no significant relationship between gender and religion in this sample of former citizens of the GDR. In some respects, this makes the sharp differences with respect to generation even more interesting.

Those old enough to remember clearly a time before the GDR not only had quite distinctive profiles with respect to their perceptions of and participation in the GDR; but particular birth cohorts also differed somewhat from one another with respect to their experiences of and in the Third Reich. Some had been old enough to fight; others had been merely youngsters or children; all had been quite strongly exposed to socialisation within a period dominated by Nazi ideology. It is therefore all the more striking that such children of an 'age of ideology' should have departed from the dominant ideology of the period of their upbringing in such patterned and divergent ways. It is also striking that the 'sore thumb' generational group of loyal GDR supporters appears to run from the birth cohorts of 1925 to 1932, straddling the key year of 1929, which was the cut-off point for the unlucky cohort who experienced compulsory membership of the Hitler Youth organisations at the age of ten in 1939, and participation in military service at the age of sixteen in 1945. There is more that requires explanation here than the notion of the '*Flakhelfer* generation' (the generation of those who as youngsters were just old enough at the end of the war to see military service assisting in anti-aircraft posts) can provide—and indeed far more than can be discussed here.[24]

It is worth considering briefly the ways in which members of these cohorts themselves sought to portray their experiences of the war's end and the subsequent East German regime, in the light of the current (2005) experiences of united Germany. Very large numbers had extremely negative end of war experiences: treks, fleeing their *Heimat*, Russians raping their mothers or other women in their immediate environment, witnessing many dead people; loss of their fathers either in the war or through illness and harsh treatment while subsequently held as a Prisoner of War. Relatively few mention what might be classed as 'political' or anti-Hitler comments (let alone unqualified pro-Nazi comments), although there are passing critical mentions, for example, of youngsters being sent out to 'defend' their village, or seeing dead young boys in the street when emerging from the safety of the cellar.[25]

---

24. To explore adequately the issue of generation formation in relation to diverse war experiences would require far more extensive exploration of contemporary sources than is possible in the context of this essay, where discussion has to be confined merely to the ways in which people sought to represent their experiences decades later.

25. See for example QN 250, female, born 1935.

Quite a few claim to have had experiences as children of kindly treatment by Russians, experiences which are probably not purely imagined figments constructed through the lens of later GDR propaganda; for example, 'The Russians treated us children well and protected us, even though we were all frightened'[26]; 'I was a child and had no bad experiences; [The Russians] were nice to me and friendly'.[27] One remembered 'refugees on the streets—prisoners dead, died of starvation on the road—we children helped to put up notes for [people searching for] relatives, and to distribute warm food—many people shot themselves out of fear of the Russians . . . For me the first meetings with Russians were pleasant, friendly.'[28] These striking experiences and fleeting 'memories' are of course couched in the terms of over half a century later, and are less a record of 'what actually happened' than of the ways in which former East Germans today want selectively and discursively to represent their pasts. What is particularly interesting here, however, is the way in which these 'memories' or 'claimed experiences' of the war's end are then embedded into the narrative of their new lives in the GDR.

A remarkably high number of members of these cohorts see the GDR as having given them good or new life chances (discussed in more detail below); they present themselves as being grateful to the GDR for the degree of security and happiness it eventually provided for them, following the immediate post-war years of misery and hunger. Many were initially relieved that the violence of war had ended, but devastated and uncertain about how to pick up the pieces after the collapse of Hitler's Reich. Yet by the early 1950s, the shapes of new lives—in terms of both work and family—began to emerge; a degree of political commitment often followed, in a fashion. The official East German term, 'Aufbau' (not so much 'reconstruction' as 'building up anew'), often appears quite unselfconsciously and frequently in these vignettes. Again, even though this is only a matter of linguistic socialisation, reflecting nearly half a century of living within a language community in which this term was regularly used, it is significant that respondents did in fact use it so readily.

Innumerable examples could be given: a few stories must suffice here. One woman, born in 1922, comments on 'shattering' experiences at the end of the war, such as witnessing a column of concentration camp prisoners

---

26. QN 60, female, born 1934. These kinds of comments are also very much in line with the findings of Norman Naimark, *The Russians in Germany: A History of the Soviet Zone of Occupation, 1945–1949* (Cambridge: Harvard University Press, 1995), who emphasises that while the Russians raped German women wildly and robbed adults indiscriminately for their watches, wallets, bicycles, and much else, they remained kindly towards children.

27. QN 163, female, born 1934.

28. QN 161, female, born 1938.

on the way through her village on one of the 'death marches'; but after that, 'life in the little village was very quickly normalised' (*normalisierte sich ... sehr schnell*).[29] At first, her mother was suicidal, 'since we stood before the abyss'; but her father prevented this. 'And then, two years later when I started having success in the theatre, and got married, ... [I realised] that one should never give up hope, there is always a silver lining on the horizon.' This woman, who worked for many years in the DEFA film studio as well as with children's theatre, developed a particularly lengthy, complex yet generally positive evaluation of the strengths and weakness of the GDR. Another woman, born in 1923, remembered that:

> I experienced the end of the war in Saxony, when the 'eastern workers' [*Ostarbeiter*] were liberated and ran around the streets, happy. At that time I was 'unhappy' about having lost the war. But then a process of re-thinking began. There must never again be war. I very much hope that my future descendents will experience true Socialism.[30]

A male born in 1924 was active as a soldier in Italy during the war, and was taken into British and American custody in 1943; the 'best years' of his life were 'before 1943', and the 'worst years' during his three-year imprisonment from 1943 to 1946. But he rapidly picked up the pieces in East Germany after his return, claiming that it gave him 'new chances' in the following terms: 'further professional qualifications, no existential fears. Order and security reigned.'[31] He married in 1948, and had at the time of the survey enjoyed 'nearly 57 years of happy marriage and well brought-up children'; his family had been the principal source of happiness in his life. He joined the SED in 1959, and was also a member of the FDGB and the DSF (German-Soviet Friendship Society), as well as being a volunteer in the fire service. A woman born in 1925 provided a lengthy and graphic account of her flight from East Prussia, as one of 3,000 refugees on a boat to Rostock, on a three-day journey remembered principally in terms of constant hunger and fear of death through aircraft bombing or mines.[32] Settled in appalling conditions in a Mecklenburg village, this woman, then aged twenty, experienced the end of the war as a massive 'blow of fate' (*Schicksalsschlag*): 'The "Final Victory" (*Endsieg*) which we had been promised was now history'. The immediate post-war period was recounted in terms of a very high death rate exacerbated by hunger, typhus,

29. QN 254, female, born 1922.
30. QN 44, female, born 1923.
31. QN 165, male, born 1924. ('Berufliche Weiterqualifizierung, keine Exiztenzängste. Es herrschte Ordnung und Sicherheit.')
32. QN 159, female, born 1925.

and other diseases, rapes by Russian soldiers being 'a daily occurrence' (*an der Tagesordnung*); she too was affected by disease and 'battled with death'. In November 1945, the family resettled in the southern part of the Soviet zone, and in 1952, on marriage, she herself moved with her new husband to Berlin. Then began the story of her 'happy' life: recounted in terms of enjoyment of work in the GDR, which gave her new opportunities as an employee in housing administration in the 1950s, with interesting and many-facetted work, as well as work colleagues with whom she still kept up contacts, and later, in the 1970s, retraining as a Kindergarten worker and a salesperson; as well as fifty years of an extremely happy marriage, a son who 'brought us much happiness, is upright (*gradlinig*) and successful in his profession [and] whose well-functioning marriage has now also lasted nearly 25 years . . . [M]y dear grandson has successfully passed his *Abitur*'. This woman became a member of one of the GDR's bloc parties, the LDPD (Liberal Democratic Party), in 1949, a membership she retained throughout the GDR's existence, as well as joining the DFD (Democratic Women's League) in 1958. On somewhat similar lines, a woman born in 1931 reported that:

> I experienced the end of the war as a thirteen-year-old in the former East Prussia with all the horrors of the Second World War. Expulsion in 1947 out of homeland [*Heimat*]. Resettling [*Übersiedlung*] with very ill mother into the former GDR. Father died after being transported in April 1945 to Siberia. Then as a seventeen-year-old, all alone and without any means of support, survived a very difficult time.
>
> After marriage in 1951 and the birth of a son a new life began. We were happy and also contented with our life.[33]

The very language of this particular account—with the use of the first person pronoun omitted in the note form used for the most difficult years, then reappearing suddenly with the 'new life'—seems to reflect the way in which life opened up to agency again with the 'normalisation' of the new family in the 1950s.

These sorts of life stories could be multiplied by many other examples: there was a 'normal' pattern to the lives of those who felt in 1945 that their world had been devastated, but then managed as young adults in the 1950s to pick up the pieces and enter into fulfilling relationships with marriage partners, benefit from new training opportunities, and embark on employment in a society in which work and basic security of existence, if not the risky and unevenly distributed affluence of the West, were guaranteed to all who made the minimum

33. QN 43, female, born 1931.

commitments required of them. A significant number of young adults who were not prepared to make such commitments left for the West in the 1950s. Aspects of life and work in the GDR were, then, subsequently experienced in rather different ways by members of the older cohorts who had remained, and those who had little choice, having been 'born into' the GDR. Yet there were, too, common overriding experiences of life for those who remained in the GDR after 1961 and experienced 'actually existing socialism' as it developed over time, as becomes evident if we consider selected aspects in a little more detail.

The Primacy of the Personal? Best Times, Worst Times

The 'private' is definitely 'political', especially in 'abnormal times'. In times of war, millions of personal relationships are ruptured, damaged, destroyed forever—through death, disfigurement, and disability, physical dislocation, psychological damage from which individuals never 'return' to their former 'selves'. In post-war periods, people may interpret the reformation of personal bonds, the reunion or reconstitution of families, as 'normalisation'. Especially if all else appears to be 'returning to normal'—food supplies improve, communication networks are repaired, physical war damage is dealt with, and new buildings rise on the site of ruins—then a process of 'normalisation' appears to be clearly identifiable. This certainly seems to have been the case in West Germany in the 1950s, where a determination to 'kick over the traces' was also associated with a wilful putting of the Nazi past behind them.[34]

In the GDR, there was initially a period of very radical social upheaval associated at least in part with claims about denazification: expropriation of large estates and of significant sectors of finance and industry was to some degree 'legitimated' by theories of 'fascism' as being rooted in 'monopoly capitalism' and 'imperialism' carried by capitalists, militarists, and the landowning Junker class; the radical turnover of personnel in the teaching and legal professions and in local administration (unlike in the West) was further legitimised by theories of denazification, even if the ultimate goal was to strengthen communist control over the Soviet occupation zone and subsequent GDR. Many of those adversely affected by this radical social upheaval—whose estates and property had been confiscated, whose professional careers were terminated or blighted, or whose children faced bleak prospects—fled West, as did many of those who had only briefly settled on the soil of the Soviet Zone as 'refugees and expellees' from lost German territories further east. Before the building of the Berlin Wall, around one-sixth of the East German population left in this way. For

34. See the discussion in Chapter 1, above.

those who remained, the issue of the Nazi past was by and large disposed of, through the convenient myth of the 'anti-fascist state' which pronounced the ordinary 'workers and peasants' effectively innocent. To this extent, at least, Germans in the East had perhaps even less need to worry about their Nazi past than their fellow former comrades of the Nazi *Volksgemeinschaft*, who had so recently been converted to democracy in the West. Yet, at first glance, there were other things they would need to worry about more, which might, one would think, militate against any early sense of 'normalisation'.

With the lack of any injection of Marshall Aid along the lines experienced in the West, and the difficulties of a war-torn economy further disrupted by reparations to the Soviet Union and radical socio-economic upheaval, in East Germany the outward signs of a post-war society stubbornly resisted removal. Buildings remained ruined, the pock-marks of war damage disfigured older houses and offices right through the next forty years; the post-war economy, while relatively successful in Soviet bloc terms, never quite took off in a manner comparable to the West German 'economic miracle'; and, after a faltering moment of new hopes in the early 1970s, an inexorable slide began into economic decline and eventual near bankruptcy by the end of the 1980s, evident to any casual observer in the high levels of air pollution, rusting industrial landscapes, ill-stocked ordinary shops (in contrast to Intershops offering luxury goods for western currency), dilapidated older housing stock, and un-repaired roads. Despite the high value accorded to work, the system simply was not working; difficulties of supply of materials and spare parts led to constant frustration, while a second 'under the counter' economy was the only way of fulfilling many needs. Politics remained a matter of repression and effective incarceration, infamously symbolised by the Wall. Post-war division and the GDR's status as a separate sovereign state remained contentious, even after the international recognition of the GDR consequent on *Ostpolitik*; and most East Germans remained highly aware of the existence of another, more affluent Germany–an awareness and interest which was not reciprocated by their West German brethren, who generally showed little interest in the GDR. In short, for most East Germans, the outer parameters of life might be regarded as sufficiently uncomfortable that, from a western perspective, they could or should never have been ignored. This is in part what makes it so difficult for western observers to accept that the notion of normalisation could ever be applied to the GDR, except, perhaps, in the politically highly contentious sense adopted by other Soviet bloc states to refer to periods of enforced stabilisation following suppression of challenges to Soviet hegemony.[35]

35. See Chapter 1, above. See also Mark Allinson's discussion, in Chapter 12, of the intrinsic instabilities of the GDR's 'most normal year', prior to its terminal decline.

Table 13.2. The extent to which respondents agreed with the statement that it was possible to lead a 'perfectly normal life in the GDR[1]

	Strongly disagree	Partly disagree	Neither agree nor disagree	Partly agree	Strongly agree
1917–24	11	0	16.7	22.2	50
1925–32	7.1	3.6	10.7	35.7	39.3
1933–45	8.5	6.1	20.7	34.1	24.4
1946–57	2.1	6.3	29.7	29.2	29.2
1958–69	4.2	1.4	28.2	46.5	19.7
1970–79	5.3	0	26.3	31.6	36.8

[1] By percentage of each cohort, omitting non-responses.

And yet: when we look at the evidence of this survey, we have to recognise that there are distinctions to be made. When questioned in 2005, remarkably few respondents—only around 10 percent in total—'strongly' or 'partly' disagreed with the statement that it was possible to lead 'a perfectly normal life' in the GDR; but again, there are some interesting generational variations (see Table 13.2), which give pause for thought.

Both strength of agreement and strength of disagreement are significantly stronger, relative to the cohort, among the older respondents in the survey than among those 'born into' the GDR. The 'first Hitler youth generation'—those who as adults either resisted or sustained the Third Reich—are by far the most polarised in their views about the Communist regime that succeeded Nazi Germany. The children of the Third Reich, born between 1933 and 1945, were most likely to disagree with the view that it was possible to live a perfectly normal life in the GDR, with a total of 14.6 percent disagreeing strongly or somewhat, compared to 8.4 percent of those born in the years after the end of the war when the border to the West was still porous, and a mere 5.6 percent or 5.3 percent of the two younger cohorts born from the later 1950s through to the 1970s, who had grown up entirely within the GDR and had known nothing else with which to compare it during the period of their socialisation. Those born just before and after the building of the Berlin Wall are distinctive, however, in that they seem to have hedged their bets most with respect to both ends of the spectrum of answers; as many as three quarters of this cohort (74.7 percent) gave the rather cautious responses of 'neither agree nor disagree', or 'partly agree', with again the lowest percentage of all, 19.7 percent, prepared to agree strongly with the statement concerning the possibility of 'normal lives'. If the 'first Hitler youth generation' was strongly polarised, with nearly two thirds agreeing or disagreeing strongly, then this 'Wall generation' appears to have preferred, perhaps appropriately, to sit on the fence, clustering in a somewhat non-committal middle, with less than a quarter prepared to give 'extreme' answers.

How can these subjective viewpoints be explained; and in what relevant sets of associations, connections, values, or general evaluations of the kinds of lives they led in the GDR are such assertions of relative 'normality' rooted? Of crucial importance is the question of what really mattered to people. And, on this point, there is no doubt whatsoever: of whatever generation, gender or class background, what mattered most to most people most of the time was their 'personal' life. And although the 'personal' is not a matter to be abstracted from 'politics', and is indeed deeply and intensely affected by the historical events and social and political structures through which people make their lives and by which their lives are shaped, it is not necessarily always interpreted or experienced in this way. It is often only in hindsight that people recognise just how much their lives were shaped by a particular set of historical circumstances, and social and economic parameters. It is this recognition that becomes very evident in reading through the evidence of retrospective perceptions.

Here, a very interesting finding emerges from the survey: there is a marked asymmetry between what actively makes people happy, and what makes them unhappy. Lack of that which makes one unhappy is not necessarily sufficient to make one happy; whereas disruption in what makes one happy is sufficient to make one unhappy. Economic insecurity is a deep cause of unhappiness, but lack of it does not necessarily actively make one happy; it is merely a precondition for other possibilities in life. Personal fulfilment in love, family, and work are what tend to make people actively happy.

These questions were approached in a number of ways, none of them methodologically very satisfactory as far as producing easily quantifiable data was concerned, but extremely suggestive and interesting in relation to the qualitative questions of subjective experience. Open-ended questions on the following lines were posed: 'When were the "best times" in your life? And why?'; 'When were the "worst times" in your life? And why?'; and 'What was your greatest pleasure in life? What made you happy?' (In the light of these questions, it seems hard to uphold the complaint on the part of some respondents that the questionnaire was entirely phrased in gloomy, anti-GDR terms designed to elicit critiques.) The questions were phrased in this open-ended way precisely to elicit free responses from people, to see what they would come up with spontaneously, and in what kind of terminology they would use to describe their experiences.

The asymmetry referred to above lies in the following combination of findings. The overwhelmingly most important factor in 'happiness' for the majority of respondents consisted in personal relationships, family, partner, children, friends; and, for a significant percentage of these–particularly women who came to maturity in the GDR–in the further fulfilment that arises from being able to combine enjoyment of family and friends with personal satisfaction in work or profession (the notion of 'career' appears, by contrast, quite alien to the majority of East Germans and was not used at all by these respondents). Very small numbers indeed gave other responses to the 'what makes you happy' question. A couple of responses to the question of 'What made you happy?' may be taken to stand for many more on similar lines: 'My marriage, my children, my work, travelling abroad in socialist countries, my house, my garden, my family'.[36] 'My husband, regulated work times, no fears about losing my job, many friends, affordable leisure–which is not the case today, for example I was a member of a sailing club (costing 1.30 Marks a month) and after the *Wende* the cost went up to 125.00 Marks and the club eventually had to be disbanded. From today's perspective, I would probably have liked to go to Austria, for example, but at that time I didn't miss it; what you don't know about you don't miss.'[37] 'Best times' also correspond in a very large numbers of cases–again somewhat more so among women than men–with purely 'personal' factors, such as periods of childhood and youth that in retrospect appear carefree and happy, falling in love and marriage, the birth of a child, family holidays, as well as with periods of fulfilment in work and professional life.

'Worst times' inevitably also include a significant number of purely 'personal' moments: the illness or death of a loved one, difficulty in relationships, separation or divorce. But 'worst times', across generational and gender divides, are far more likely to correlate with periods of political and economic insecurity and the acute existential anxiety caused by major historical upheavals, which have the potential to translate major historical events into personally experienced tragedies. The two great 'winners', as far as the 'worst times' were concerned, were, paradoxically: first, the immediate post-war years of the later 1940s and very early 1950s (among those old enough to remember this period–and note that it was generally not the war years, but rather the post-war years, which were the 'worst times'); and secondly, the period since unification in 1990 up to the time of the survey in 2005, which was the 'worst time' in their life for by far the largest group of respondents. Both of these periods were times of widespread extreme anxiety about sheer physical survival. Hunger and the memory of hunger, as well as the experience of being physically uprooted, moving, losing close relatives, worrying about how to survive, how to start a new life, loomed very large in the reports of the post-war period; loss

36. QN 216, female, born 1939.
37. QN 246, female, born 1943.

of employment, continued unemployment, worries about being able to pay the rent, lack of medical care, prospects for one's own future, or that of children and grandchildren, depending on age, loomed very large in the reports of those identifying the 'worst times' as being in the period since 1990. Thus, economic insecurity and '*Existenzängste*' are major causes of unhappiness; but, in itself, lack of economic insecurity is not, apparently, a major cause of positive happiness in the same way as are personal relationships or the combination of fulfilment in family and work.

What people most valued about the GDR in retrospect, therefore, was the possibility of combining personal happiness in their family life with security of employment and an income sufficient to meet basic needs. (Freud appears to have been posthumously vindicated in his emphasis on the importance to individual well-being of love and work.) Many respondents claimed in retrospect that economic and consumer shortages in the GDR were relatively unimportant, or had relatively low salience for them, as compared with the good life chances they enjoyed, the possibility of studying for free, or having a fulfilling professional life; this sort of comment was particularly noticeable among those who could be classed as members of the East German intelligentsia who had come from working class backgrounds, giving some support to the widespread thesis that those who had enjoyed rapid upward social mobility in the 1950s and 1960s 'had a stake in the system' and were appropriately grateful to it for the life chances it had offered them.

The Active Self: Life Chances, Work, and Community

A distinctive value system appears to have become well established, which included not only the high value accorded to and satisfaction derived from work (continuing in some respects with pre-Nazi traditions, but extended in a variety of ways, particularly with respect to women), but also the importance of notions of 'togetherness' (or a sense of *Gemeinschaft,* in contrast to the individualistic *Gesellschaft* of the capitalist 'elbow society'), despite marked tendencies towards 'individualisation' in the growing consumer society of the later decades.

In contrast to western notions of competitive individualism, in which the fruits of inherited capital—whether material or cultural—are often interpreted as the results of individual effort and merit, the GDR was based on a strong official sense of community responsibility. On the one hand, this meant, in official terms, that the 'collective' should be placed above the 'individual'; and that working for a better collective future was to be prioritised over 'bourgeois' notions of individual happiness and personal fulfilment. It also meant that the previously privileged classes were demoted, and displaced, while the previously under-privileged workers and peasants–so long as they were of an acceptable political persuasion–were supported and promoted, at least in the first two decades of 'social revolution' after the war. While this process was extremely uncomfortable (to say the least) for those who were in the process expropriated and discriminated against, for others it meant that they perceived the GDR as having genuinely offered them new, or good, chances in life, of a quality that they would not have expected given their own relatively modest social backgrounds. It was then possible, in the eyes of a surprising and significant majority of those questioned, not merely to lead a 'perfectly normal life', but even to lead a 'good' life in the GDR. A remarkable number felt that the GDR had given them 'good' or 'new' life chances (depending on their age at 'entry' into the GDR–whether as a young person with memories of what had gone before, or whether effectively born into the GDR)–or, to phrase it more accurately, remarkably few disagreed either partly or strongly with this statement.

Significant generational differences in response, however, again suggest the importance of different life experiences and points of comparison in evaluating what was 'objectively' the 'same' situation as far as the outward appearance conveyed by an 'objective' historical representation is concerned. The cohorts most likely to feel that the GDR had given them good chances in life were, proportionately, the older ones: those born before 1945, and, particularly striking, those born before 1925. Those 'born into' the GDR, by contrast, were less enthusiastic about what the GDR had offered them; perhaps because their experience was compared to the West, rather than to expectations rooted in a pre–1945 past; or perhaps because they had had little or no choice about being in the system. Among the older cohorts, in addition to having 'objectively' benefited from the opportunities for upward mobility created by post-war demographic imbalances and the westward flight of others, there might also be the effects of 'cognitive dissonance' (to adopt Festinger's concept), in that they had a subjective interest in having positive views about their own lives in the GDR. Generational differences among women are particularly striking, given the GDR's record on furthering women's education and training, and providing an extensive workplace-based system of childcare and relatively generous infrastructural support for families, to ensure the compatibility of production and reproduction (see Table 13.3). The oldest cohorts were very much more likely to appreciate the chances offered to them by the GDR than were younger women, who perhaps took the new system more for granted; and those born in the Honecker period, who were still teenagers when the Wall fell, were most acutely aware of the disadvantages attached to having grown up in the GDR, perhaps in comparison with the opportunities that had been available to their peers in the West.

Table 13.3. Extent to which females of different birth cohorts agreed with the statement that the GDR had given them 'good' or 'new' 'life chances'. Figures in percentages.

Females only	1917–24	1925–32	1933–45	1946–57	1958–69	1970–79
Strongly disagree	0	0	5.4	3.3	9.1	22.2
Partly disagree	0	5.3	7.1	6.7	2.3	22.2
Neither agree nor disagree	18.2	26.3	17.9	30	31.8	11.1
Partly agree	0	21.1	17.9	16.7	40.9	33.3
Strongly agree	72.7	31.6	44.6	40	15.9	11.1

There are a number of further respects in which both gender and generation were significant. Older GDR citizens were more likely than younger ones to have experienced high levels of work satisfaction in the GDR, and to have been more satisfied with modes of conflict resolution. Satisfaction at work was highest among cohorts who had experienced the rapid upward mobility characteristic of the GDR in the 1950s and 1960s, while those born later tended to be slightly less enthusiastic about their workplace experiences. (The very youngest in the survey had, of course, not been old enough to have started employment during the existence of the GDR.) It is also notable that women, who had historically 'benefited' most from upward social mobility, at least as far as the slightly contentious measure of this in terms of increased participation in paid employment outside the household is concerned, were proportionately significantly more likely than men to claim to have experienced very high levels of work satisfaction. Whatever the debates about the 'double burden' of responsibility for both household and work, women appear in retrospect to have highly valued their high rates of participation in the East German paid labour force.

Interestingly, too, respondents generally claimed relatively high levels of satisfaction with modes of conflict resolution at work, despite the fact that it is conventionally thought that the state-run trade union organisation, the FDGB, barely played a serious role in terms of representation of people's genuine interests (except in so far as it was concerned with distribution of holiday home places and similar). The brigade seems in retrospect to have been particularly important as a locus for conflict resolution: over one-third (36.6 percent) mentioned this as most important, among which one-quarter mentioned it as the sole vehicle, whereas just over 11 percent mentioned a combination of brigade and FDGB; a further 10.7 percent mentioned the

FDGB and/or BGL (the works union leadership) as crucial without mentioning the brigade. Virtually one-quarter of respondents (24.4 percent) thought that conflicts had been successfully resolved through their own individual efforts and initiative; and 8.1 percent claimed that *Eingaben* had been the key to success. Many respondents pointed to the importance in conflict resolution of processes of informal discussions (or *Gespräche*) within the work-based collective. A surprisingly high proportion alleged that there had been no work conflicts. What matters here is less whether these statistics accurately reflect what went on in the workplace, and rather more the emotional tone they convey about satisfaction in and with the lost world of GDR work—undoubtedly remembered in somewhat rosier tones than it was experienced at the time, but arguably conveying an emotional truth rooted in the unemployment of contemporary Germany.

Rather surprisingly, with respect to what most people would immediately see as the worst aspects of life in the GDR, the results of questionnaires highlight the tremendous importance in East Germans' own perceptions of their successful development of coping strategies in the GDR, alongside a sense of control and the exertion of an active self capable of dealing competently with the world. Under the East German system, many felt they knew the parameters and knew how to deal with even the worst aspects of the system.

As far as the ubiquitous economic and material shortages were concerned, East Germans were obviously the first to recognise that their system was, literally as well as metaphorically, not delivering the goods. Relative lack of availability of food and consumer goods is, however, retrospectively seen as less problematic than restrictions on freedom of expression and movement. In relative terms, the results across five separate questions, each asking respondents to rate the extent to which they found the particular aspect in question to be a significant problem in everyday life, were as follows: 16.3 percent agreed either 'somewhat' or 'strongly' that food was a significant problem in everyday life; 30.3 percent agreed 'somewhat' or 'strongly' that lack of available consumer goods was a problem; 37.3 percent thought 'somewhat' or 'strongly' that housing was a problem; 50.2 percent thought 'somewhat' or 'strongly' that lack of freedom of opinion was a problem; and 56.5 percent agreed 'somewhat' or 'strongly' that lack of freedom to travel was a problem. Yet in each case, there were comments qualifying these observations, and demonstrating ways in which they had developed coping strategies, mechanisms for getting around problems or fulfilling needs and aspirations in some other way—or adjusting their aspirations according to availability. In retrospect, for the vast majority of those questioned, economic constraints and material shortages appear to have been experienced as manageable and predictable, and not generally sufficient to make life intolerable. They frequently referred to such problems as non-availability of recordings of western music, the long waiting lists for cars, the lack of exotic fruits (*Südfrüchte*); but many also explicitly queried the notion of 'needs'. Some respondents mentioned that it was necessary to lower one's expectations and aspirations (*Ansprüche*), and to learn to make do with what one had. As one respondent put it: 'Through acquired modesty of aspirations I had fewer problems in this respect'.[38] Others made comments such as 'Well, we lived here after all, and had to survive and adapt'.[39] Expressions reflecting the view that, if one could not change reality, one could only change one's own perceptions to make reality acceptable—or the recognition of what was possible, and the need to adjust oneself accordingly—were common ('*sich arrangieren*', '*sich anpassen*', '*wir mußten aber entsprechend anspruchslos sein*'). Clearly the reflection that 'freedom is the recognition of necessity' found widespread resonance in the GDR.

Thus, alternatives were sought and found; and significant numbers of people professed themselves to have been largely contented with what they did and could do. Many suggested that while it might have been nice to be able to travel in the West, they also had great fun on the holidays they did go on, in the GDR or elsewhere in the Soviet bloc. As one respondent put it, he managed to deal with the problems of everyday life 'without complications, one just had to deal with things as they were'; and his greatest pleasure in life, that which made him most happy, was 'holidays at the Baltic'.[40] At the same time, many mentioned that the economic constraints of today—particularly the difficulties in raising the money required for travel—ultimately have the same effects as the political constraints obtaining in the GDR. Large numbers pointed to the new form of denial of consumer choice in the capitalist united Germany, in that they now had a wide range of goods readily available in the shops, but inadequate money with which to buy the things they desired; some felt in effect worse off than in the GDR. In short, East Germans were highly aware of the relative constraints and opportunities provided by both kinds of system, and the fact that there are different winners and losers in each. Very few agreed with the strident views of a small minority, that the Wall should be rebuilt.

On the other hand, certain aspects of GDR society were in retrospect valued very highly indeed. There were extraordinarily high levels of strong agreement with statements such as, 'The sense of togetherness among

38. QN170, born 1952: 'Durch anerzogener Bescheidenheit hatte ich damit weniger Probleme'.

39. QN 154, female, 1928.

40. QN 214, male, born 1942.

citizens (*Zusammenhalt der Bürger*) was stronger in the GDR than it is today', and spontaneous comments in open-ended questions very often brought up the strong sense of community (such as in the frequent use of the word '*Miteinander*', conveying a sense of togetherness). One or two saw this, perhaps realistically given the high degree of informal inter-reliance for obtaining scarce goods and services through 'connections' (*Beziehungen*), as a 'community of need' or '*Notgemeinschaft*'; and many emphasised the central importance of cultivating 'connections'. Yet the sense of community which this fostered–the need to remain on friendly terms with others, in a network of mutually supportive groups–was one which, particularly perhaps in retrospect, many people claim to have valued highly, in contrast to the loneliness produced by the competitive individualism of the capitalist market society of united Germany. In the words of one respondent, in answer to one of the final open questions asking if there was anything they wished to add: 'There were no specific experiences, apart from the often very good relationships between people [*außer den oft sehr guten zwischenmenschlichen Beziehungen*] and a certain sticking together, both of which disappeared very quickly after the "Wende".'[41] The notion of good relationships between people was brought up again and again in the survey.

Many respondents valued and explicitly mentioned the fact that in the GDR, they suffered lower levels of stress and enjoyed more time for family and friends, than they did in united Germany, particularly with family and friends now scattered over a far wider geographical area (a somewhat ironic by-product of the capitalist labour market, given that one of the most painful features of the GDR was the way in which families were separated by the 'Iron Curtain', and people in the East were physically cut off from any possibility of maintaining routine ties with friends and relatives in the West). Education and training came out rather well: what was seen as good about the GDR was, for example, 'a sensible school education, with guaranteed professional training, and then straight away afterwards a job'.[42] Another commented that 'the school system was without question better. What goes on in schools today is totally unacceptable in the view of people of my age.'[43] One respondent summarised her 'good times' in the following terms: '1961–1989: Life was much more peaceful (*Man lebte viel ruhiger*), everyone had work. No one had to worry about losing their job. Existence was secure. People understood each other better, there was no "elbow society". Children were looked after in child day care centres (*Kitas*) and the school system was

41. QN 214, male, born 1942.
42. QN 211, male, 1976.
43. QN 168, female, born 1961.

much better than nowadays. In free time one was well looked after in the sports association or in the school choir and so on.'[44] Many claimed that, during GDR times, they were able to engage in cultural, sporting, and other leisure activities, to enjoy subsidised holidays and travel, and to spend unpressured time with friends: they thought in retrospect that they used to have the time, the facilities, and the resources to have what was both a satisfying and affordable leisure time. But as one respondent put it, summarising the reasons why she had ticked the box for 'partly agree' in relation to the GDR giving her good life chances: 'a solid education; social security; but also eternal uniformity/stagnation/not being able to have an independent voice (*Bevormundung*) / constriction of the individual personality'.[45] Those—a minority in this survey—who wanted the space to 'think differently', to use the famous Rosa Luxemburg phrase, were well aware of the limits.

As far as political involvement is concerned, the results of the survey demonstrate that the picture is slightly more complex than often portrayed: there was what might be called a widespread 'simultaneity of participation, commitment and dissent'. A small minority were very clearly in the oppositional category, and were discriminated against to greater or lesser degrees for a number of reasons: because they were Christian, political dissidents, and in a few cases, allegedly because they refused to conform or join a political party, although many mentioned that such refusals had never caused them any problems at work or in any other way. Some reported that they felt their careers had been held back, that they had been unable to study the subject of their choice or had been forced to go into an area of work that they did not really want. Ways of coping, subjectively, included the fairly frequent comment that one had to 'adapt oneself' and 'conform to the system' (*sich anpassen*)—but this was often accompanied by the qualification that this was true in any system and it was merely expressed in different ways in the current system of united Germany. There was, then, a very high level of awareness of the unwritten 'rules' of the GDR to which one had to conform in order to achieve one's own ends, and explicit knowledge of the likely consequences of breaking these rules. The majority, on the evidence of this questionnaire, certainly played by the rules; very few were prepared to stick out and take the consequences in terms of personal disadvantages (even, in a couple of cases, imprisonment).

High rates of participation in the East German system, in one way or another, are far from neat: no easy separations can be drawn between 'state' and 'society', those 'supporting' and those 'opposing' the system. East Germans

44. QN 101, female, born 1961.
45. QN 119, female, born 1956.

often simultaneously occupied multiple positions and held highly differentiated sets of opinions on different aspects of life in the GDR. There are quite a few cases where what one might think to be mutually incompatible positions are held simultaneously, such as the Christian who was also a functionary for over twenty years in one of the mass organisations, the German League for Sport and Gymnastics (DTSB).[46] Ordinary membership levels in mass organisations (as we know anyway from statistics kept at the time) were very high: in this survey, 78 percent claimed to have been a member of the Trade Union organisation (FDGB); 68 percent had been a member of a youth organisation (JP, FDJ), and nearly 15 percent had held functionary positions of one sort or another in these organisations; around 60 percent had been a member of one or more of the other mass organisations, with 25 percent claiming to have been a member of two or more. As far as length of membership of one organisation or another was concerned, as many as 60 percent claimed to have remained a member for more than ten years. This was for obvious reasons in case of the FDGB, membership of which was more or less automatic for those in employment; but membership of other mass organisations also seemed to be fairly lengthy, as appropriate, and respondents claimed there were few or no problems if they chose to leave. Length of service as a functionary divided quite sharply: just under a quarter of those who recalled taking on a role as a functionary served for less than three years, while two-thirds claim to have acted in this role for over ten years, with remarkably few managing to escape service at an intermediate length of time; those who were not found wanting, or who did not fall foul of superiors fairly early on, presumably had the commitment and character attributes required to stick it out for a more extensive term of office. Only 6 percent claimed to have been 'very active' in the organisations with which they were involved; a further 39 percent thought that they were 'fairly active' or somewhat active', but a bare majority clearly managed to remain rather inactive in the organisations of which they were nominal members.

Reasons for belonging tended to group around a combination of what was seen as 'just normal' and social or idealistic motives. More than half claimed that they simply joined 'because everyone belonged at the time'; around one-quarter gave as a reason for membership 'because it was fun'; around one-fifth thought that they could help to improve conditions; and one in ten felt that a particular membership 'was expected in my position'.[47] Membership and

---

46. QN 224, male, born 1933; nicely falling at the generational cusp of the cohorts who were disproportionately active in and committed to the GDR and those who remained committed Christians.

47. Statistics are here given in only rough terms, because this turned out to be a somewhat poorly designed question, which was open to a degree of ambiguity in interpretation, with some respondents apparently unsure whether to give one or more reasons for each membership. I have

participation in the structures of the GDR 'societal state' was, then, widely seen as 'perfectly normal': 'everyone belonged' and for significant numbers the activities were enjoyable as well as giving them a feeling they could contribute to improving the world around them. Membership of youth organisations was associated with particularly fond memories for some participants: one young woman, born in 1970, in answer to the question of what was her greatest pleasure in life, what made her happy, identified 'collective outings and arts and crafts afternoons with the class, Pioneer afternoons'.[48] Another, the youngest in the survey, born in 1977, also replied to this question 'life in the Pioneer organisation, togetherness in school!'[49] The 'two lives theory', retreating in to the 'niche society' (Günter Gaus's notion of a 'niche society' or *Nischensgesellschaft*), living on two tracks, speaking with two tongues (*Doppelgleisigkeit, Doppelzüngigkeit*), used to be very popular in secondary literature on GDR, but only a couple of respondents mention anything coming at all close to this notion; the majority seem to have been entirely at one with themselves, if one may put it this way, in their participatory activities.

Only a minority stood out as having not participated in any way at all in the GDR's organisational framework, and this minority was divided between two very different groups: some older individuals who had been too old to join the FDJ, and had evaded joining the FDGB; and a minority of very committed political activists, largely Christians. A very small number claimed they had suffered as a result of their refusal to join in with, for example, the *Jugendweihe* (the state atheist coming of age ceremony, in opposition to confirmation in church); while six said that there were no problems arising from their refusal, three claimed that their refusal to conform or to join an organisation had brought with it 'bad consequences' for them.

Those living through an 'age of ideologies' were, as we have repeatedly seen, in some ways themselves more 'ideological'—more likely to be a member of the SED if they were born between 1926 and 1933, more likely to be and remain a Christian if born during the Third Reich. The '1929ers' were generally more likely to be functionaries, highly active, participatory citizens of the GDR. They were more extreme in terms not merely of their prior experiences, but also their subsequent reactions: their comparisons of standards of living in the GDR tended to be with their own war-time and post-war deprivations. But, very interestingly, they also tended to be far more consciously aware of the 'costs' of the GDR in terms of *Stasi* surveillance:

therefore tried to avoid unduly weighting the answers of the more enthusiastic respondents, but want here merely to convey the general gist that emerges from looking at the overall pattern of answers.

48. QN 240, female, born 1970.

49. QN 237, female, born 1977.

they claimed to have known more about the *Stasi*, and to have had more contact with the unofficial collaborators or IMs (*Inoffizielle Mitarbeiter*) than did younger cohorts of former citizens of the GDR. Those born into the GDR were, by contrast, much less likely to be as satisfied with their work, and less satisfied with modes of conflict resolution at work. They were also less likely to think there were high levels of 'togetherness' or *Zusammenhalt* among East Germans. But they were, at the same time, less likely to have experienced the *Stasi* as important, and less likely to claim to have had any direct experience of the *Stasi* through knowledge of an IM. All of this in part reflects their younger age group and related statuses while in the GDR—occupying relatively low levels in any hierarchy, and hence to some extent having lower relevance for the *Stasi* unless they were a member of one of the tiny minority of dissident groups, which the vast majority were not. This raises, then, very directly the question of perceptions of repression and restrictions on freedom in the GDR; topics about which East Germans held highly differentiated views.

The 'Normality of Evil'? Perceptions of the *Stasi* and the Sense of 'Freedom'

The *Stasi* has loomed very large in writing on the GDR, from the popularisation of the 'repression thesis' view of the GDR in works such as *Stasiland,* or the perhaps more problematic 'rendering harmless' (*Verharmlosung*) of the *Stasi* in works of fiction such as Thomas Brussig's *Helden wie Wir* (Brussig was born in 1965), to an extensive body of highly critical academic and journalistic literature.[50] There is little doubt that, along with the very visible restrictions on freedom of movement posed by the highly fortified inner-German border and Berlin Wall, the *Stasi* has dominated general perceptions of what life in the GDR must have been like for its citizens.

And yet, at least on the evidence of this research, it did not loom so large in most people's perceptions and sense of being able to live 'perfectly normal lives' in the GDR. The fact that the questionnaire even posed a question about the *Stasi* annoyed a surprising number of people. The first survey, which included rather more by way of questions on the *Stasi*, provoked comments such as '*Generally with respect to the Stasi-questions:* My experiences in life

50. Anna Funder, *Stasiland* (London: Granta, 2003); Thomas Brussig, *Helden wie Wir* (Berlin: Verlag Volk & Welt, 1995); for an overview of the academic literature which burgeoned in the first decade after unification, see for example Jens Gieseke, 'Die Geschichte der Staatssicherheit', in Rainer Eppelmann, Bernd Faulenbach, and Ulrich Maehlert, eds,, *Bilanz und Perspektiven der DDR-Forschung* (Paderborn: Ferdinand Schöningh, 2003).

and my own life story in the GDR have in absolutely no way been influenced by the *Stasi*! Why should this play *any role at all* in this questionnaire!?'[51] One of the principal revisions between the pilot study and the questionnaire, which was finally used in the larger survey, was to tone down and reduce the section devoted to questions on the *Stasi*, since so many people were irritated and suspicious about these questions and refused to answer these questions (or indeed to answer the questionnaire at all) on the pilot version. The final version of the questionnaire, then, included only two very simple sets of questions on the *Stasi*: first, 'Was knowledge of the existence of the *Stasi* important to you in your daily life?' (answerable by tick-boxes for 'yes', 'no', and 'somewhat') and, 'If so, in what respects?' (where an open-ended qualitative response was required); and secondly, 'Did you know anyone personally who was active as a *Stasi* informer (IM)?' again answerable in terms of tick-boxes ('yes', 'no', 'not as far as I am aware'), with the correlate question, 'If yes: how did this knowledge influence your relationship with that person?' Even here, there were difficulties with getting responses.[52]

This survey of a significant number of 'ordinary East Germans' produced a rather more multi-facetted view than the pictures conveyed in analyses of selected cases of individual *Stasi* victims or 'perpetrators'. For the vast majority of those surveyed, the *Stasi* was simply unimportant. Three-fifths (60 percent) claimed not to have experienced the *Stasi* as important at all; a further 20 percent found the *Stasi* 'somewhat' important, but even among these there were comments such as '[but] I barely bothered myself about it'.[53] Only one in five (20 percent) experienced the *Stasi* as sufficiently important to tick the box for 'yes'—and among these, a surprising number were actually supporters of *Stasi*, and thought it did a good and necessary job in maintaining 'security'. Methodologically, this may actually be something of an underestimate, since a number of people refused to answer this question, and those refusing are probably disproportionately drawn from those who might well have feared personal disadvantages if such views were brought into the daylight of united Germany.

There were, of course, a number of people in the survey, across all age groups, who had suffered very bad experiences as a result of *Stasi* surveillance, persecution, and incarceration. A former architect was in 1963

51. L18 (1949), emphasis in the original.

52. One colleague working at a senior citizens' home, who kindly agreed to assist with distributing questionnaires and posting back responses from elderly residents, wrote explicitly in his covering letter that unfortunately only two people had been willing to respond precisely because of this question. 'We reassured them about the anonymity of the survey. . . . Nevertheless most of them had difficulties and fears about the questions concerning the *Stasi*.' Letter of 7 July 2005.

53. QN 167, male, born 1966.

subjected to four years imprisonment as a result of seeking to help someone escape the GDR (*Republikflucht*) and spent the 23 years following his release unable to practise his profession, but forced instead to 'work in production' in a VEB ('people's own factory') at the lowest wage level.[54] (This particular individual had a fairly awful combination of historical experiences, having been called up for military service in 1944 at the age of 16, and was in 2005 still suffering from nightmares both about scenes he had witnessed towards the end of the war, such as seeing deserters being hung or having to step over corpses in the street, as well as nightmares about his sleep deprivation, ill-treatment, and interrogations during *Stasi* imprisonment in the 1960s.) One Christian member of an oppositional group for peace and the environment from 1985, and member of New Forum in 1989, lists among her 'worst times' a very specific experience: participation in the demonstration on 6–7 October 1989 at the Gethsemane Church in East Berlin, being surrounded by the *Stasi* and being 'terrified for her life' (*große Existenzangst*).[55] Interestingly, however, in terms of the coexistence of quite different experiences of and a differentiated attitude towards the GDR, this very same person had listed among the 'best times' in her life the period 1985/86, when she had 'intensively pursued her hobbies', including folk dancing, rowing and making music, as well as being young, financially independent, and in love. A number of respondents, without giving any specifics, claimed to have lived with a significant sense of 'permanent surveillance' (*ständige Überwachung*) or a diffuse feeling of being constantly 'under threat' (*Bedrohung*). Others suggested that it made it difficult to talk to friends at the time, and revelations about *Stasi* informers after 1990 had been personally devastating: 'Once I knew it (the IM confessed to me) I immediately broke off all contact–it was a massive loss of trust.'[56]

Many developed coping strategies of one sort or another, such that–almost like swatting unwanted insects at a summer picnic–the *Stasi* became for them a predictable and manageable evil in an otherwise tolerable or enjoyable life. One Christian who was, for example, very critical of the political discrimination in the GDR and the pressure on her children in school, commented about an IM in her acquaintance that she simply 'kept her distance'.[57] (She too had a difficult background: her father had died in captivity as a Soviet Prisoner of War when she was only eleven; the family business had been expropriated; and the 'basis for existence for my mother

54. QN 151, male, born 1928.
55. QN 64, female, born 1966.
56. QN 119, female, born 1956.
57. QN 153, female, born 1934.

and we three children was utterly destroyed (*vernichtet*)'.) Some treated the *Stasi* as a somewhat humourous element in life: 'We made a bit of a joke out of it. We observed the *Stasi* observing us.'[58] Many others simply treated the *Stasi* as quite routine, a 'perfectly normal' part of life, particularly in certain occupations: 'As a teacher, checks were frequently being carried out and questions posed concerning parents of particular children'[59]; 'In the factory–professionally–I saw it as legitimate';[60] 'Anyone who worked in sport and was able to travel abroad (to the USA, Italy, Yugoslavia, Spain) with sports delegations had personal contacts [with the *Stasi*] without being an unofficial collaborator!!!'[61] Some even had something of a friendly relationship with people they knew to be informers; in one case, the neighbour, who was an IM, even directly told the respondent on whom she was reporting whenever she had been questioned about this person by the *Stasi*.[62]

Among those who said the *Stasi* was important to them in their everyday life, there were also a surprisingly large number of positive answers with respect to the role of the *Stasi*: for example, the *Stasi* was important in everyday life by virtue of its 'Protection of our achievement in building up from the ruins' (hard to render the ideological flavour of the original in English: *Schutz des von uns geleisteten Aufbaus*).[63] Another commented in some detail that: 'I have only got to know the expression "*Stasi*" since 1989. Until then, for me it was the MfS, whose rules had to be observed in professional life (*Berufsleben*) in just the same way as the regulations of the police, the education system, the transport system, the health system and so on. As far as I was concerned, the MfS was not the "worst" institution.'[64] A number suggest that being an IM was not important in choosing one's friends: 'But [I knew the IM] only as someone working for the Ministry for State Security. This did not influence my relationship with this friend at all, since every state has an organisation for state security. I chose my friends according to their character traits.'[65] Others, on revealing that they knew someone was an IM, simply said that this did not influence their relationship with the person at all–'garnicht!'[66] Some go on to compare the current situation in united Germany unfavourably with the GDR, as in the comment from a younger

58. QN 263, female, born 1949.
59. QN 166, male, born 1921.
60. QN 206, male, born 1948.
61. L18, born 1949.
62. QN 154, female, born 1928, member of the SED.
63. QN 52, male, born 1935.
64. QN 134, male, born 1936.
65. QN 136, female, born 1934.
66. QN 142, female, born 1959.

East German who claimed that, while knowing a *Stasi* informer had not influenced her relationship to this person at all, in stark contrast 'today we are subjected to surveillance by the BND [secret service of the Federal Republic] and there is no doubt a great deal more going on there that we don't know about. Just think about America–total surveillance (*totale Überwachung*).'[67]

Most East Germans, at least on the evidence of their retrospective claims in 2005, appear to have known how to cope with the *Stasi*: one might want to talk about a process of 'routinisation of evil', in that people knew what to say to whom in what context, and with whom they should maintain a purely formal and distanced relationship. They had expectations about when and where they might have to engage in confrontation–or professional cooperation–with either a paid functionary of the MfS, in the course of their work, or with an unofficial informer. There were significant, indeed massive, differences in the 'density' of exposure to the *Stasi*. Christians and people with oppositional political views obviously experienced the *Stasi* as far more threatening and oppressive, denying them the possibility of leading their lives as they wanted; yet a majority of the East Germans surveyed did not fall into these categories.

Proportionately, those born between 1925 and 1957, who experienced life in the GDR as adults for well over a decade, were far more likely to be affected by knowledge of the *Stasi* than were younger generations. Those most affected by knowledge of the *Stasi* were the cohorts born during the Third Reich, for 27.1 percent of whom knowledge of the *Stasi* had significance in their everyday lives, contrasted with a mere 12.5 percent of those born between 1958 and 1969. This 'Wall generation', however, again hedged its bets slightly: over a quarter (26.4 percent) gave the answer 'somewhat', compared to an overall average of 16.2 percent, with a low of 5.3 percent for 'somewhat' among the more decisive immediately following birth cohorts of 1970–79, and 6.9 percent among the '1929ers'. The least concerned were, perhaps oddly, the oldest and youngest cohorts: over two-thirds (66.7 percent) of those born from 1917 to 1924 thought the *Stasi* was not at all important, and nearly four out of five (78.9 percent) of those born in the 1970s saw the *Stasi* as not at all important in their lives, whereas only a little over a half (54.1 percent) of those born during the Third Reich gave this answer. Certain (28.2 percent) or suspected (25.9 percent) knowledge of someone who was a *Stasi* informer (IM) also clustered disproportionately among those born during the Third Reich, although there is an odd feature here: by far the highest proportions of those who, cumulatively, either thought (41.7 percent) or were certain (22.2 percent) that they knew a *Stasi* informer were to be found among the 'Wall generation' born

67. QN 127, female, born 1976.

from 1958 to 1969. It is curious that nearly two-thirds (63.9 percent) of this cohort thought they knew a *Stasi* informer personally, yet virtually the same percentage (61.6 percent) did not consider the *Stasi* to be important in their lives: there is clearly some degree of routinisation at work here, among cohorts who had learnt through socialisation to negotiate the conditions in which they lived. The fact that significantly fewer people born after 1969—i.e., those aged below 20 when the Wall fell—had either any personal exposure to the *Stasi*, or any sense that it was important in their lives, may help to explain the trend towards a 'rendering harmless' (*Verharmlosung*) and ironic presentation of the 'GDR as comedy' evident among many younger post-*Wende* literary authors.

If women shared with older cohorts a greater probability of seeing the GDR as having offered them good life chances, they now appeared to have a double bonus in their experiences of the GDR. Women are proportionately less likely to claim to have been bothered by knowledge of the existence of the *Stasi*, and less likely to have known an informer or IM, than men. Overall, nearly a quarter of men (24.5 percent) and just under one-fifth of women (18.9 percent) saw the *Stasi* as important; just over a half (53.9 percent) of men and nearly two-thirds (62.7 percent) of women felt it was entirely unimportant (and the rest, of course, were respectively in the 'somewhat' or the 3.3 percent of 'no answer' categories). Around one-quarter of both males (24.5 percent) and females (24.9 percent) were certain they knew an informer, while over one-third (34.3 percent) of males, but again only a quarter (24.3 percent) of females, replied that they 'maybe' knew an IM, leaving considerably more males than females living with a shade of suspicion. Apart from the handful of 'no answers', the remaining 37.3 percent of males and 46.2 percent of females were certain they did not personally know a *Stasi* informer. Thus, while women somewhat disproportionately felt that they were the beneficiaries of GDR social policies allowing the combination of family life and fulfilment in work, at the same time they were less likely to register the shadow sides of the East German dictatorship in terms of repression and surveillance.[68]

Although on the basis of this evidence there is no need at all to revise any moral and political views of the self-confessed practices of the *Stasi* in surveillance, intimidation, and destruction (*Zersetzung*) of the lives, relationships, and careers of individuals, there does appear to be some need for qualification of views concerning the extent to which knowledge of these practices played a role in the lives of individuals who did not come into the net of the *Stasi*, or who indeed themselves approved of the activities of

68. It also has, however, to be borne in mind that women were greater 'losers' in the unification process and economic restructuring than were men; it is possible therefore that their memories and representations of life in the GDR are likely to be marginally more positively tinged.

the MfS in maintaining a measure of 'security'. The GDR was essentially a society which certainly had polar extremes, but where there was a great deal of grey area, of compromise, adaptation, and complexity in between. And for those—probably a majority of the population—occupying an ambiguous position in the cross-currents of the complex middle ground, the *Stasi* was, as one respondent put it, 'not nearly as important as it is portrayed today'.[69]

The 'Normalisation of Rule'? East German Perspectives and the History of the GDR

We know a lot about the dark sides of the GDR: we know a lot about the outward signs of visible repression in a state which prevented freedom of association, freedom of expression, and freedom of movement. We know a lot, too, about the less visible pressures under which many people felt they lived in such a society. These were well summarised by a woman born in 1956, who did not find it easy to come to terms with the state into which she had been born and within which she was socialised:

> You could lead a 'normal' life if your life conformed to the expectations of the state. That meant: not stepping out of line, not attracting attention to yourself politically, no activities on your own initiative or opinions that were not handed down to you; if you were punctual and reliable in your work, if there was nothing out of the ordinary in the personal arena, then a 'normal' life was possible. Difficulties arose if you became active or expressed opinions that were not along the prescribed lines—it was a dictatorship with not a whiff of democracy![70]

A 'normal' life was on this view a life lived within the narrow parameters of the officially prescribed 'norms', which, for those who wanting to think outside these limits, were experienced as highly restricting. All this is well documented and well known.

What is more difficult to get at, however, is a sense of the way in which a significant number of East Germans seem to have valued this notion of a 'normal life', and valued what they saw as the orderliness and security of GDR society—and this too is a real aspect of GDR history, although one which has to date been far less well researched. The sense of knowing the rules, playing by the rules, even valuing the regularities of a predictable life, come across in many ways in people's responses, some in part critical or resigned, others far more

69. QN 206, male, born 1948.
70. QN 119, female, born 1956.

positive about their experiences and the patterns of their lives in the GDR. An eighty-year old woman, who had lived all of her life in Fürstenberg / Eisenhüttenstadt, summed up her life in the GDR very simply: 'We had a normal life with my four children. As far as exotic fruits [*Südfruchte*] were concerned, it was bad. Otherwise it was not bad.'[71] A Christian, born in 1940, commented that 'I came to terms with it and saw it as God's path for me'.[72] A male, 'born into' the GDR in 1966, summarised his view thus: 'One could lead a perfectly normal life in the GDR, if one kept to certain rules (but that is just the same today). One didn't starve, there was always food, maybe not the choice we have today (but is that necessary) . . . As long as one has work [today] things are okay, but if not it's bad. . . . Competition may enliven business, but at what price?'[73] A male, who was still in his teens when the Wall came down, commented that in the GDR one had 'the prospect of an orderly life [*ein geregeltes Leben*], with a sensible job.' A woman born in 1939 said that in the GDR, 'It was peaceful, there was contentment and harmony in family and profession–security on the streets–the health system was in order'.[74] Another woman, born in 1957, simply summarised the GDR thus: 'The GDR was in order (*in Ordnung*), only freedom of travel was limited, that was not in order (*nicht in Ordnung*)'.[75]

The GDR, for all its recognised shortcomings, was for many of its former citizens '*in Ordnung*': it appeared to be an 'orderly' form of society; for those who liked the form of order, and were prepared to live within the rules, it was experienced as 'normal'; and indeed for many East Germans a predictable life with assured employment, a sense of community, and social security, was far less stressful than the uncertainties and the new restrictions on freedom caused by lack of money, as widely experienced in the period since unification. As one respondent put it, 'One had the opportunity of learning a profession, there was no unemployment, everyone had housing they could afford, it was possible to take holidays in other socialist countries. . . . Today one hits one's head against a brick wall because one can't afford things. All in all, [in the GDR] I lived more peacefully and in greater security. . . I had a sense of well-being.'[76] In the words of another: 'Good times: Up to 1990: Life ran in regular tracks with normal ups and downs. Without anxiety.'[77] 'Normal' here means 'what one would expect'–in the sphere of family, friends, leisure, work–where

71. QN 116, female, born 1925.
72. QN 187, male, born 1940.
73. QN 167, male, born 1966.
74. QN 173, female, born 1939.
75. QN 203, female, born 1957.
76. QN 175, female, born 1954.
77. QN 56, female, born 1961. (*Bis 1990: Das Leben war in geregelten Bahnen mit normalen Höhen und Tiefen. Ohne Ängste.*)

all is not necessarily always wonderful, where one expects 'ups and downs', sadness, and discord as well as happiness and success. 'Abnormal' is when the rules change, and when one is constantly anxious about the future and how to survive. One respondent, born in 1941, designated the years up to 1990 as the best years of her life, 'but only in the light of my experience now'; she knew that she had lacked freedom to travel and to express her opinions, but now what she most valued about the GDR was that she 'had lived in a *secure* and ordered' society (*habe sicher und geordnet gelebt*, underlining in original).[78] A slightly older respondent, born in 1938, summarised the contrasts between the GDR and the present in the following list: In the GDR, there was 'social security, security of pensions, a sense of collective responsibility, work, being there for one another, being together . . . a preparedness to help, honesty. All gone now.'[79]

For others in the GDR, this sense of orderliness and regulation was of course by contrast experienced as living in a 'cage' (*Käfig*).[80] That this was a highly apposite description for life in a literally walled-in state should not blind us to the fact that, experientially, the same can be said about the capitalist system for those constrained to operate by its rules or go under—as Max Weber famously reminded us in his use of the term '*ein stahlhartes Gehäuse*', conventionally translated as the 'iron cage' of the 'spirit of capitalism'. As one woman, born in 1960, very appositely put it, in the context of a longer and highly differentiated picture of her life in the GDR:

> Of course I found aspects of everyday life in the GDR very negative, but in many ways I have not been able to shake off these feelings today. . . In the normal working day in the GDR one was constantly subject to political agitation, one was always supposed to be politically engaged and 'do things collectively' in the Brigade, in the FDGB, in the Party etc. etc. etc.—but if you didn't go along with it nothing happened to you either. Of course that meant that you also could not get into 'leading positions', but I never wanted that anyway. Today you still have to spring to attention and do what is ordered 'from above'—and if you do not go along with it, your job is perhaps at risk and your means of livelihood endangered. There are lots of other examples I could give to develop this point.
>
> In general, I do not really feel any more free now than I did in the GDR—pressure is pressure (*Zwang ist Zwang*)—from whatever direction it might come, and everyone has to decide for themselves how far they are prepared to go along with it or to 'jump off the bandwagon' and remove themselves from such influences.[81]

78. QN 213, female, born 1941.
79. QN 161, female, born 1938.
80. QN 168, female, born 1961.
81. QN 152, female, born 1960.

It is these antinomies that lie at the heart of the difficulties in interpreting patterns of 'normalisation' in the GDR. One could go on multiplying examples from the very rich and extensive comments that East Germans made on these questionnaires in the summer of 2005. The differentiated comments, and the detailed evaluations of different aspects of life, reveal just how deeply many of them have registered the contrasting 'rules' of life under 'actually existing socialism' and under the system of capitalism as experienced on the ground among ordinary people in the eastern part of the expanded Federal Republic of Germany. To seek to dismiss these perceptions as a bad case of *Ostalgie* or the long-term consequences of ideological indoctrination would be both historically inaccurate and utterly unfair to the people who have personally lived through, and thought most deeply about, the consequences of living in these two systems; and whose views have directly relevant implications for their own sense of self, security, and future perspectives. The 'people's own voices' perhaps deserve more respect in a democracy than to deny their validity as essentially misguided misperceptions, or (ironically) the effects of suffering from a form of 'false consciousness'. They deserve, at least, to be given a hearing as an authentic expression of subjective experiences, even if the sophisticated observer will pick up on certain patterns of discourse in a given historical context.[82]

It would be too simple to come to more general conclusions about broader normalisation processes in the GDR on the basis of this selection of retrospective reflections. But perhaps the material presented here will serve both to reinsert into a wider comparative context the experiences of people living through the second half of the twentieth century in Eastern Germany; and to problematise any unthinking use of notions of 'normal' and 'normality' from any one hegemonic perspective. The regularity and predictability of even unpleasant aspects of life seem to have been for some East Germans more comfortable than living with new uncertainties, despite greater freedom–a form of Durkheimian anomie. If the concept of 'normalisation' can be constructed as an ideal type, focussing on both changing historical periods of stabilisation and routinisation, and on changing subjective experiences and cultural constructions of 'normality', it will allow us to explore with more open minds the ways in which people sought to make sense of their lives and to pursue what they held to be most important to them under conditions, which were, very definitely, not of everybody's choosing.

82. It is precisely to give them an explicit hearing that I have chosen in this already rather long essay to present extensive quotations.

Contributors

Mark Allinson holds a PhD from UCL and is Head of the School of Modern Languages at Bristol University. His publications include: *Politics and Popular Opinion in East Germany 1945–1968* (Manchester University Press); *Contemporary Germany* (Longman); and *Germany and Austria 1814–2000* (Edward Arnold).

Angela Brock holds a PhD from UCL, and is currently an independent researcher based in Berlin and Weimar.

Mary Fulbrook, FBA, was educated at Cambridge and Harvard, and is currently Professor of German History and Director of the Centre for European Studies at UCL. She was founding Joint Editor of *German History* and served as Chair of the German History Society. Her books include: *The People's State: East German Society from Hitler to Honecker* (Yale University Press); *Anatomy of a Dictatorship: Inside the GDR* (Oxford University Press); *A Concise History of Germany* (Cambridge University Press); *A History of Germany, 1918–2008: The Divided Nation* (Blackwell); *German National Identity after the Holocaust* (Polity); and *Historical Theory* (Routledge), as well as a number of shorter books and edited volumes.

George Last was educated at Oxford and UCL, and was part of the AHRC-funded project on 'The "normalisation" of rule'. He has taught at UCL, and is currently working as a civil servant in London. His publications include *After the 'Socialist Spring': Collectivisation and Economic Transformation in the GDR* (Berghahn).

Alf Lüdtke studied in Tübingen. He has held leading positions at the Max-Planck Institute for History in Göttingen and the Centre for Historical Anthropology in Erfurt, as well as regular Visiting Professorships abroad, including the Universities of Michigan and Chicago. His publications include: *Police and State in Prussia, 1815–1850* (CUP); *Eigen-Sinn. Fabrikalltag, Arbeitererfahrungen und Politik vom Kaiserreich bis in den Faschismus* (Hamburg); and many edited volumes including *The History of Everyday Life* (Princeton); *Herrschaft als soziale Praxis* (Göttingen); *Akten, Eingaben, Schaufenster: Die DDR und ihre Texte* (Berlin); and *The No Man's Land of Violence. Extreme Wars in the 20th Century* (Göttingen).

Jeannette Madarász, educated at Cambridge and UCL, is currently a Research Fellow at the Wissenschaftszentrum Berlin; she formerly held a Research Fellowship at UCL to work on the AHRC-funded project on 'The "normalisation" of rule'. Her publications include: *Working in East Germany. Normality in a socialist dictatorship, 1961 to 1979* (Palgrave) and *Conflict and Compromise in East Germany, 1971 to 1989. A Precarious Stability* (Palgrave).

Ina Merkel studied at the Humboldt University, and is currently Professor of European Ethnology and Cultural Studies at the University of Marburg. She has held positions at Humboldt University and visiting fellowships at Rutgers and at Michigan State University. Her publications include: . . . *und Du, Frau an der Werkbank. Die DDR in den 50er Jahren* (Elefanten Press); *Utopie und Bedürfnis. Die Geschichte der Konsumkultur in der DDR* (Böhlau); as well as co-authored or edited volumes on *Wunderwirtschaft. DDR- Konsumkultur in den 60er Jahren* (Böhlau); *Wir sind doch nicht die Mecker-Ecke der Nation. Briefe an das DDR- Fernsehen* (Böhlau); and *das kollektiv bin ich* (Böhlau).

Jan Palmowski was educated at the universities of York and Oxford, and is currently Head of the School of Arts and Humanities at Kings College London. His publications include a book on *Urban Liberalism in Imperial Germany* (Oxford University Press) and a co-edited volume on *Citizenship and National Identity in Twentieth-Century Germany* (Stanford University Press), as well as *Inventing a Socialist Nation: Heimat and the Politics of Everyday Life in the GDR, 1945-1990* (Cambridge University Press).

Esther von Richthofen was educated at Oxford (BA) and UCL (PhD), and was part of the AHRC-funded project on 'The "normalisation" of rule'. She is currently Personal Advisor to the President of the Humboldt University, Berlin. Her publications include *Bringing Culture to the Masses: Control, Compromise and Participation in the GDR* (Berghahn).

Merrilyn Thomas holds a PhD from UCL, and is a writer, journalist, and researcher focussing on Cold War history. Her publications include: *Life on Death Row* (Piatkus); and *Communing with the Enemy: Covert Operations, Christianity and Cold War Politics in Britain and the GDR* (Peter Lang).

Dorothee Wierling is Deputy Director of the Research Centre for Contemporary History in Hamburg. Educated at the universities of Bochum, Essen and Potsdam, she has also held positions at the University of Erfurt and visiting fellowships at the universities of Tel Aviv, Washington and Michigan. Her publications include: *Geboren im Jahr Eins Der Jahrgang 1949 in der DDR. Versuch einer Kollektivbiographie* (Chr. Links Verlag); *Mädchen für Alles. Arbeitsalltag und Lebensgeschichte städtischer Dienstmädchen um die Jahrhundertwende*; and, with Lutz Niethammer und Alexander von Plato, *Die volkseigene Erfahrung. Eine Archäologie des Lebens in der Industrieprovinz der DDR.*

Dan Wilton holds a PhD from UCL. He is now a teacher of German and French at the 'Grammar School at Leeds'.

Select Bibliography

Ansorg, Leonore. '"Ick hab immer von unten Druck gekriegt und von oben". Weibliche Leitungskader und Arbeiterinnen in einem DDR-Textilbetrieb. Eine Studie zum Innenleben der DDR-Industrie'. In *Archiv für Sozialgeschichte* 39. Pp. 123–65. Berlin: Dietz Verlag, 1999.

Austermühle, Theo. 'Konflikte und Konfliktlösungen im Sport.' In *Alltagssport in der DDR*, edited by Jochen Hinsching. Aachen: Meyer. and Meyer, 1998. Pp. 135–57.

Badstübner, Evemarie. *Befremdlich Anders. Leben in der DDR*. Berlin: Dietz Verlag, 2000.

Bahr, Egon. 'American Détente and German *Ostpolitik*'. *Bulletin of the German Historical Institute*, 1969–1972, Supplement 1, 2004.

Bar-On, Daniel. *Legacy of Silence: Encounters with Children of the Third Reich.* Cambridge, MA: Harvard University Press, 1989.

Barthes, Roland. *Camera Lucida.* New York: Hill and Wang, 1981.

Bask, Siegfried. 'Bildung und Erziehung bei Karl Marx und das Bildungssytem der DDR'. *Karl Marx und das politische System der DDR*, edited by Konrad Löw. Asperg, 1982.

Beck, Ulrich, Anthony Giddens, and Scott Lash. *Reflexive Modernisierung. Eine Kontroverse.* Frankfurt M., 1996.

Behr, Rudolf. *Die Entwicklung der Arbeiterbewegung von Liebschwitz and Taubenpreskeln bis 1946.* Gera: Kulturbund zur demokratischen Erneuerung Deutschlands, 1956.

Behrens, Jan C. et al., eds. *Fremde und Fremdsein in der DDR. Zu historischen Ursachen der Fremdenfeindlichkeit in Ostdeutschland.* Berlin, 2003.

Beintker, Michael. 'Marxistisches Menschenbild'. In *Lexikon des DDR-Sozialismus. Das Staats- und Gesellschaftssystem der DDR*, edited by Rainer Eppelmann et al. Pp. 537–43. Paderborn, 1997.

Bessel, R. and D. Schumann, eds. *Life after Death: Approaches to a Cultural and Social History of Europe during the 1940s and 1950s.* Cambridge: Cambridge University Press, 2003.

Biermann, Wolfgang. *Demokratisierung in der DDR? Ökonomische Notwendigkeiten, Herrschaftsstrukturen, Rolle der Gewerkschaften 1961–1977.* Cologne: Verlag Wissenschaft und Politik, 1978.

Börrnert, René. *Ernst Thälmann als Leitfigur der kommunistischen Erziehung in der DDR.* Brunswick, 2003.

———. *Wie Ernst Thälmann treu und kühn! Das Thälmann-Bild der SED im Erziehungsalltag der DDR*. Bad Heilbrunn, 2004.

Brock, Angela. *The making of the socialist personality–education and socialisation in the German Democratic Republic 1958–1978*. PhD thesis, University College London, 2005.

Brus, W., P. Kende, and Z. Mlynar. *'Normalization' Processes in Soviet-dominated Central Europe: Hungary Czechoslovakia Poland*. Research Project: Crises in Soviet-type Systems, Study No. 1. © Z. Mlynar, 1982.

Brussig, Thomas. *Helden wie Wir*. Berlin: Verlag Volk & Welt, 1995.

Buckow, Anjana. *Zwischen Propaganda und Realpolitik: die USA und der sowjetisch besetzte Teil Deutschland 1945–1955*. Stuttgart: Franz Steiner, 2003.

Budde, Gunilla-Friederike, ed. *Frauen arbeiten. Weibliche Erwerbstätigkeit in Ost- und Westdeutschland nach 1945*. Göttingen: Vandenhoeck & Ruprecht, 1997.

Bude, Heinz. *Deutsche Karieren. Lebenskonstruktionen sozialer Aufsteiger aus der Flakhelfergeneration*. Frankfurt M., 1987.

Caldwell, Peter C. *Dictatorship, State Planning, and Social Theory in the GDR*. Cambridge, New York: Cambridge University Press, 2003.

de Certeau, Michel. *Die Kunst des Handelns*. Berlin, 1988.

Chakrabarty, Dipesh. *Provincialising Europe*. Princeton, 2000.

Ciesla, Burghard. 'Hinter den Zahlen. Zur Wirtschaftsstatistik und Wirtschaftsberichterstattung in der DDR'. In *Akten. Eingaben. Schaufenster. Die DDR und ihre Texte*, edited by Alf Lüdtke und Peter Becker. Berlin: Akademie Verlag, 1997.

Clemens, Petra. *Die aus der Tuchbude–Alltag und Lebensgeschichten Forster Textilarbeiterinnen*. Münster: Waxmann Verlag, 1998.

Dähn, Ulrich et al., eds. *Unser Staat. DDR-Zeittafel 1949–1988*. Berlin: Dietz, 1989.

Dale, Gareth. *Between State Capitalism and Globalisation. The Collapse of the East German Economy*. Bern: Peter Lang, 2004.

Deich, Ingrid and Wolfhard Kohte. *Betriebliche Sozialeinrichtungen*. Opladen: Leske+Budrich, 1997.

Dieckmann, Christoph. *Das wahre Leben im falschen. Geschichten von ostdeutscher Identität*. Berlin, 1998.

Dietzsch, Ina. *Grenzen überschreiben? Deutsch-deutsche Briefwechsel 1948–1989*. Köln/Weimar/Wien, 2004.

Doerry, Martin. *'Mein verwundetes Herz'. Das Leben der Lilli Jahn 1900–1944*. Stuttgart and Munich: Deutsche Verlags-Anstalt, and Bundeszentrale für politische Bildung, 2004.

Eidlin, Fred. *The Logic of 'Normalization': The Soviet Intervention in Czechoslovakia of 21 August 1968 and the Czechoslovak Response*. New York: Columbia University Press and Boulder, 1980.

Eisenfeld, Bernd. 'Wehrdienstverweigerung als Opposition'. In *Widerstand und Opposition in der DDR*, edited by Klaus-Dietmar Henke et al. Pp. 241–50. Cologne, 1999.

Engler, Wolfgang. *Die Ostdeutschen, Kunde von einem verlorenen Land*. Berlin, 1999.

Eppelmann, Rainer, Horst Möller et al., eds. *Lexikon des DDR-Sozialismus. Das Staats- und Gesellschaftssystem der DDR,* Bd. 1. Paderborn: F. Schöningh, 1997.

———, B. Faulenbach, and U. Mählert, eds. *Bilanz und Perspektiven der DDR Forschung.* Paderborn: F. Schöningh, 2003.

Fiske, John. *Understanding Popular Culture.* London/Sydney/Wellington, 1989.

Förster, Peter. 'Die Entwicklung des politischen Bewußtseins der DDR-Jugend zwischen 1966 und 1989'. In *Das Zentralinstitut für Jugendforschung Leipzig 1966–1990,* edited by Walter Friedrich et al. Pp. 71–165. Berlin, 1999.

Frei, Norbert. *Vergangenheitspolitik.* Munich: C. H. Beck, 1996.

Freiburg, Arnold. 'Schüler, Ordnung und Disziplin. Deutsch-deutsche Fakten und Überlegungen zur Erziehung und zum Schulalltag'. In *DDR-Jugend. Politisches Bewusstsein und Lebensalltag,* edited by Barbara Hille and Walter Jaide. Pp. 276–80. Opladen, 1990.

Fulbrook, Mary. *Anatomy of a Dictatorship. Inside the GDR 1949–1989.* Oxford: Oxford University Press, 1995.

———. 'Changing states, changing selves: Violence and social generations in the transition from Nazism to Communism'. In M. Fulbrook, ed., *Un-Civilising Processes? Excess and Transgression in German Culture and Society: Perspectives Debating with Norbert Elias.* Amsterdam: Rodopi, 2007.

———. 'Generationen und Kohorten in der DDR. Protagonisten und Widersacher des DDR-Systems aus der Perspektive biographischer Daten'. In *Die DDR aus generationengeschichtlicher Perspektive. Eine Inventur,* edited by Annegret Schüle, Thomas Ahbe, and Rainer Gries. Universitätsverlag Leipzig, 2005.

———. *German National Identity after the Holocaust.* Cambridge: Polity, 1999.

———. *Historical Theory.* London: Routledge, 2002.

———. *The People's State: East German Society from Hitler to Honecker.* Yale: Yale University Press, 2005.

———. *The Two Germanies 1945–1990: Problems of Interpretation.* Basingstoke: Macmillan, 1992.

Funder, Anna. *Stasiland.* London: Granta, 2003.

Gabler, D. *Entwicklungsabschnitte der Landwirtschaft in der ehemaligen DDR.* Berlin, 1995.

Galenza, R. and H. Havemeister, eds. *Wir wollen immer artig sein. Punk, New Wave, Hip-Hop, Independent Szene in der DDR, 1980–1990.* Berlin: Schwarzkopf & Schwarzkopf, 1999.

Gaus, Günther. *Wo Deutschland liegt.* [Location: Publisher, Year.]

Geißler, Gert, Falk Blask, and Thomas Scholze, eds. *Schule: Streng vertraulich! Die Volksbildung der DDR in Dokumenten.* Vol. 1. Berlin, 1996.

Gerstenberger, Heide and Dorothea Schmidt, eds. *Normalität oder Normalisierung?* Münster: Westfälisches Dampfboot Verlag, 1987.

Geulen, Dieter. *Politische Sozialisation in der DDR. Autobiographische Gruppengespräche mit Angehörigen der Intelligenz.* Opladen: Leske+Budrich, 1998.

Gibas, Monika. *Propaganda in der DDR.* Erfurt, 2000.

Giordano, Ralph. *Die zeite Schuld, oder Von der Last Deutscher zu sein.* Hamburg: Rasch and Röhrig, 1987.

Goeckel, Robert. *The Lutheran Church and the East German State.* Ithaca, NY: Cornell University Press, 1990.

Görtemaker, Manfred. 'The Collapse of the German Democratic Republic and the Role of the Federal Republic'. In the *Bulletin of the German Historical Institute London.* Vol. XXV, no. 2 (November 2003): 49–70.

Grant, Nigel. *Society, Schools and Progress in Eastern Europe.* Oxford, 1969.

Gries, Rainer. *Die Rationen-Gesellschaft: Versorgungskampf und Vergleichsmentalität, Leipzig, München und Köln nach dem Kriege.* Münster, 1991.

Grose, Peter. *Operation Rollback: America's Secret War Behind the Iron Curtain.* Boston, New York: Houghton Mifflin, 2000.

Grunenberg, Antonia. *Antifaschismus–ein deutscher Mythos.* Reinbek, 1993.

Hain, Simone. 'Die Salons der Sozialisten: Geschichte und Gestalt der Kulturhäuser in der DDR'. In Simone Hain, Michael Schroedter, and Stephan Stroux, *Die Salons der Sozialisten: Kulturhäuser in der DDR.* Berlin: Ch. Links, 1996.

Hanke, Irma. 'Vom neuen Menschen zur sozialistischen Persönlichkeit. Zum Menschenbild der SED'. *Deutschland Archiv,* May 1976 (9): 492–515.

Hanke, Helmut, Manfred Weißfinger, and Christa Ziermann, *Kultur und Freizeit. Zu Tendenzen und Erfordernissen eines kulturvollen Freizeitverhaltens.* Ost Berlin, 1971.

Heinze, Dieter and Gerd Rossow. *Der Parteiarbeiter, kulturpolitische Aufgaben nach dem VII Parteitag.* Ost Berlin, 1968.

Heinze, Eberhard. 'Unser Skatbrunnen ist wieder da!' *Altenburger Kulturspiegel* (October, 1955).

Heldmann, Philipp. *Herrschaft, Wirtschaft, Anoraks. Konsumpolitik in der DDR der Sechzigerjahre.* Göttingen: Vandenhoeck & Ruprecht, 2004.

Henkel, Rüdiger. *Im Dienste der Staatspartei, über Parteien und Massenorganisationen der DDR.* Baden-Baden, 1994.

Heydemann, Günther and Eckehard Jesse, eds. *Diktaturvergleich als Herausforderung–Theorie und Praxis.* Berlin: Duncker & Humblot, 1998.

Hirschman, Albert O. 'Exit, Voice, and the Fate of the German Democratic Republic: An Essay in Conceptual History'. In *World Politics* 45 (1993): 173–202.

'The *Historikerstreit* Twenty Years On'. *German History,* Vol. 24 (October 2006): 587–607.

Hölscher, Christoph. *NS-Verfolgte im 'antifaschistischen Staat'. Vereinnahmung und Ausgrenzung in der ostdeutschen Wiedergutmachung 1945–1989.* Berlin, 2002.

Holzweißig, G. *Sport und Politik in der DDR.* Berlin: Holzapfel, 1988.

Howe, Ellic. *The Black Game: British subversive operations against the Germans during the Second World War.* London: Michael Joseph, 1982.

Hübner, Peter. *Konsens, Konflikt und Kompromiss–Soziale Arbeiterinteressen und Sozialpolitik in der SBZ/DDR 1945–70.* Berlin: Akademie Verlag, 1995.

———. 'Norm, Normalität, Normalisierung: Quellen und Ziele eines gesellschaftlichen Paradigmenweschsels im sowjetischen Block um 1970'. *Potsdamer Bulletin* No. 28/29, Jan. 2003: 24–40.

Huinink, Johannes and Karl Ulrich Mayer et al. *Kollektiv und Eigensinn–Lebensverläufe in der DDR und danach.* Berlin: Akademie Verlag, 1995.

Hürtgen, Renate. *Zwischen Disziplinierung und Partizipation. Vertrauensleute des FDGB im DDR-Betrieb.* Cologne et al.: Böhlau Verlag, 2005.

——— and Thomas Reichel, eds. *Der Schein der Stabilität–DDR-Betriebsalltag in der Ära Honecker.* Berlin: Metropol Verlag, 2001.

Jäger, Manfred. *Kultur und Politik in der DDR: 1945–1990.* Köln: Ed. Deutschland Archiv, 1995.

Jarausch, Konrad, ed. *Dictatorship as Experience: Towards a Socio-Cultural History of the GDR.* New York, Oxford: Berghahn Books, 1999.

Jessen, Ralph. 'Die Gesellschaft im Staatssozialismus. Probleme einer Sozialgeschichte der DDR'. In *Geschichte und Gesellschaft*, 21 (1995): 96–110.

Kaelble, Hartmut, Jürgen Kocka, and Hartmut Zwahr, eds. *Sozialgeschichte der DDR.* Stuttgart: Klett Cotta, 1994.

Kaiser, Monika. *Machtwechsel von Ulbricht zu Honecker. Funktionsmechanismen der SED-Diktatur in Konfliktsituationen 1962–1972.* Berlin: Akademie Verlag, 1997.

Kirby, Dianne, ed. *Religion and the Cold War.* Basingstoke: Palgrave, 2003.

Klessman, Christoph. 'Die Beharrungskraft traditioneller Milieus in der DDR'. In *Was ist Gesellschaftsgeschichte?*, edited by Manfred Hettling. Pp. 254–70. München, 1991.

Knortz, Heike. *Innovationsmanagement in der DDR 1973/79–1989. Der sozialistische Manager zwischen ökonomischen Herausforderungen und Systemblockaden.* Berlin: Duncker & Humblot, 2004.

Kopstein, Jeffrey. *The Politics of Economic Decline in East Germany, 1945–1989.* Chapel Hill, London: University of North Carolina Press, 1997.

Kott, Sandrine. *Le communisme au quotidien. Les Enterprises d'Etat dans la société est-allemande. Edition Belin.* Paris, 2001.

———. 'Pour une histoire sociale du pouvoir en Europe communiste'. In *Pour une histoire sociale du pouvoir en Europe communiste, Revue d'histoire moderne et contemporaire 49*, edited by S. Kott. Pp. 5–23. 2002.

———. 'Zur Geschichte des kulturellen Lebens in DDR-Betrieben, Konzepte und Praxis der betrieblichen Kulturarbeit'. In *Archiv für Sozialgeschichte*, 39 (1999).

Krebs, H-D. 'Die politische Instrumentalisierung des Sports in der DDR'. In *Materialien der Enquete Kommission. 'Aufarbeitung von Geschichte und Folgen der SED Diktatur in Deutschland' des Deutschen Bundestages, Bd. III*, no. 1: 1315–69.

Kreuch, Knut. 'Jede Zeit Braucht Leitfiguren and Arbeitstiere. . . . oder, wer sonst kann eine hoch motivierte ehrenamtliche Herde führen und sie immer wieder mit neuen Visionen zur Mitarbeit begeistern? *Der Heimatpfleger* (August, 2003).

Kusin, Vladimir. *From Dubček to Charter 77: A study of 'normalisation' in Czechoslovakia 1968–1978.* Edinburgh: Q Press, 1978.

Kvitzinsky, Juli. *Vor dem Sturm: Erinnerungen eines Diplomaten.* Berlin: Siedler, 1993.

Langer, Lawrence. *Holocaust Testimonies.* New Haven: Yale University Press, 1991.

Lashmar, Paul and James Oliver. *Britain's Secret Propaganda War.* Stroud: Sutton, 1998.

Leo, Annette and Peter Reif-Spirek, eds. *Vielstimmiges Schweigen. Neue Studien zum DDR-Antifaschismus.* Berlin, 2001.

Liewald, Horst. *Das BGW. Zur Betriebsgeschichte von NARVA–Berliner Glühlampenwerk.* Berlin: Deutsches Technikmuseum, 2004.

Lindenberger, Thomas, ed. *Herrschaft und Eigen-Sinn in der Diktatur. Studien zur Gesellschaftsgeschichte der DDR.* Köln: Böhlau Verlag, 1999.

Lüdtke, Alf. *Eigensinn: Fabrikalltag, Arbeitererfahrungen und Politik vom Kaiserreich bis in den Faschismus.* Hamburg: Ergebnisse, 1993.

———. 'Meister der Landtechnik oder Grenzen der Feldforschung? Annäherungen an einen "Qualitätsarbeiter" auf dem Lande im Bezirk Erfurt'. In *Geschichte als Experiment. Studien zu Politik, Kultur und Alltag im 19.und 20. Jahrhundert. Festschrift für Adelheid von Saldern*, edited by Daniela Münkel and Jutta Schwarzkopf. Pp. 243–57. Frankfurt/New York, 2004.

——— and Peter Becker, eds. *Akten. Eingaben. Schaufenster. Die DDR und ihre Texte.* Berlin: Akademie Verlag, 1997.

Mac Con Uladh, Damian. *Guests of the socialist nation? Foreign students and workers in the GDR 1949–1989.* PhD thesis, UCL, London, 2005.

Madarász, Jeannette. 'Die Realität der Wirtschaftsreform in der DDR. Betriebsalltag in den sechziger Jahren', p. 968. In *Deutschland Archiv* 6/966 (2003): 966–80.

———. 'Normalisation in East German enterprises, 1961–79'. In *Debatte* 1/2005: 45–63.

———. *Working life in East Germany, 1961 to 1979. Arriving in the Everyday.* Basingstoke: Palgrave, 2006.

Marcus, George E. Ethnography in/of the World System: The Emergence of Multi-Sited Ethnography. In *Annual Review of Anthropology* 24 (1995): 95–117.

Mannheim, Karl. 'Das Problem der Generationen'. In *Wissenssoziologie*, edited by K. Mannheim. Pp. 509–65. Berlin: Luchterhand, 1964; orig. 1928.

Meier, Helmut. 'Der Kulturbund der DDR in den 70er Jahren: Bestandteil des politischen Systems und Ort kultureller Selbstbetätigung'. In *Befremdlich Anders, Leben in der DDR*, edited by Evemarie Badstübner. Pp. 599–625. Berlin: Karl Dietz Verlag, 2000.

Mensching, Günter. *Ingenieur M. ppm. Einer unter Millionen. Lebenserinnerungen und Ansichten.* Berlin: Nora, 2005.

Merkel, Ina. *Utopie und Bedürfnis. Die Geschichte der Konsumkultur in der DDR.* Cologne et al.: Böhlau, 1999.

——— and Felix Mühlberg. 'Eingaben und Öffentlichkeit'. In *Wir sind doch nicht die Meckerecke der Nation! Briefe an das Fernsehen der DDR*, edited by Ina Merkel. Berlin: Schwarzkopf & Schwarzkopf, erweiterte Neuausgabe, 2000.

Mitter, Armin and Stefan Wolle. *Untergang auf Raten: Unbekannte Kapitel der DDR-Geschichte.* Munich, 1993.

Moeller, Robert. *War Stories: The Search for a Usable Past in the Federal Republic of Germany.* Berkeley and Los Angeles: University of California Press, 2001.

Mühlberg, Felix. *Bürger, Bitten und Eingaben. Geschichte der Eingabe in der DDR.* Berlin: Dietz Verlag, 2004.

———. 'Konformismus oder Eigensinn? Eingaben als Quelle zur Forschung der Alltagsgeschichte der DDR'. *Mitteilungen aus der kulturwissenschaftlichen Forschung.* Pp. 331–45. February 1996.

Müller, Harry. *Jugend im Wandel ihrer Werte.* Leipzig: ZIJ, 1985.

Müller, Maria Elisabeth. *Zwischen Ritual und Alltag: der Traum von einer sozialistischen Persönlichkeit.* Frankfurt/Main & New York, 1997.

Niethammer, Lutz. 'Where were you on the 17th of June?' A niche in Memory. In *Memory and Totalitarianism, International Yearbook of Oral History*, edited by Luisa Passerini. Pp. 45–69. Oxford, 1992.

———, Alexander von Plato, and Dorothee Wierling. *Die Volkseigene Erfahrung. Eine Archäologie des Lebens in der Industrieprovinz der DDR.* Berlin: Rowohlt, 1991.

Nothnagle, A. *Building the East German myth. Historical mythology and youth propaganda in the GDR 1945–1989.* Ann Arbor, 1999.

Palmowski, Jan. 'Defining the East German Nation: The construction of a Socialist Heimat, 1945–1962'. In *Central European History*, 37 (2004): 365–99.

———. 'Regional Identities and the Limits of Democratic Centralism in the GDR'. In *Contemporary European History*, 2006 (forthcoming).

Plato, Alexander. 'The Hitler Youth generation and its role in the two postwar German states'. In *Generations in Conflict*, edited by Mark Roseman. Pp. 210–26. Cambridge, 1995.

Poiger, Uta. *Jazz, Rock and Rebels. Cold War Politics and American Culture in a Divided Germany.* Berkeley: University of California Press, 2000.

Pritchard, Rosalind. *Reconstructing education. East German schools and universities after unification.* New York, 1999.

Protokoll der 35. Sitzung des Sportausschusses: 'Rolle des Sports in der DDR'. In *Materialien der Enquete Kommission*, Bd. III, no. 1: 662–75.

Rauhut, M. *Beat in der Grauzone. DDR-Rock 1964 bis 1972–Politik und Alltag.* Berlin: Basisdruck, 1993.

———. *Schalmei und Lederjacke. Udo Lindenberg, BAP und Underground: Rock und Politik in den 80er Jahren.* Berlin: Basisdruck, 1996.

Reichel, Thomas. 'Jugoslawische Verhältnisse'?–Die 'Brigaden der sozialistischen Arbeit' und die 'Syndikalismus' Affäre (1959–62). In *Herrschaft und Eigen-Sinn in der Diktatur–Studien zur Gesellschaftsgeschichte der DDR.* Pp. 45–73. Cologne et al.: Böhlau Verlag, 1999.

Rodden, John. *Repainting the little red schoolhouse. A history of Eastern German Education 1945–1995.* Oxford, 2002.

Roesler, Jörg. 'Probleme des Brigadealltags. Arbeitsverhältnisse und Arbeitsklima in volkseigenen Betrieben 1950–89', pp. 11–12. In *Aus Politik und Zeitgeschichte* B38 (1997): 3–17.

Roesler, J. *Zwischen Plan und Markt.* Berlin: Haufe Verlag, 1990.

Roseman, Mark, ed. *Generations in Conflict.* Cambridge: Cambridge University Press, 1995.

Rosenthal, Gabriele, ed. *The Holocaust in Three Generations.* London: Cassell, 1998.

Ross, Corey. *Constructing Socialism at the Grassroots: The Transformation of East Germany, 1945–65.* Basingstoke: Macmillan, 2000.

———. *The East German Dictatorship. Problems and perspectives in the interpretation of the GDR.* London: Arnold, 2002.

Rossade, W. *Sport und Kultur in der DDR.* Munich: tuduv-Verlagsgesellschaft, 1987.

Sakowski, H. *Daniel Druskat.* E. Berlin, 1976.

Sarotte, ME. *Dealing with the Devil: East Germany, Détente and Ostpolitik.* Chapel Hill and London: University of North Carolina Press, 2001.

Schaarschmidt, Thomas. *Regionalkultur und Diktatur. Sächsische Heimatbewegung und Heimat-Propaganda im Dritten Reich und in der SBZ/DDR.* Cologne/Weimar/Vienna: Böhlau, 2004.

Schäfer, Olaf. *Pädagogische Untersuchungen zur Musikkultur der FDJ. Ein erziehungswissenschaftlicher Beitrag zur Totalitarismusforschung.* Berlin: Wissenschaftlicher Verlag, 1998

Schier, B. *Alltagsleben im 'Sozialistischen Dorf'.* Munich, 2001.

Schissler, Hanna, ed. *The Miracle Years. A Cultural History of West Germany, 1949–1968.* Princeton: Princeton U. P., 2001.

Schlegel, Uta. 'Geschlechter- und Frauenforschung'. In *Das Zentralinstitut für Jugendforschung Leipzig 1966–1990,* edited by Walter Friedrich et al. Pp. 373–91. Berlin, 1999.

Schneider, Ilona. 'Kinder aus christlichen Familien in der DDR'. In *Was für Kinder. Aufwachsen in Deutschland*, edited by Deutsches Jugendinstitut. Pp. 317–21. Munich, 1993.

Schöne, J. *Frühling auf dem Lande? Die Kollektivierung der DDR Landwirtschaft.* Berlin, 2005.

Schöttler, Peter. 'Mentalitäten, Ideologien, Diskurse. Zur sozialgeschichtlichen Thematisierung der dritten Ebene'. In *Alltagsgeschichte. Zur Rekonstruktion historischer Erfahrungen und Lebensweisen*, edited by Alf Lüdtke. Pp. 85–136. Frankfurt/Main & New York, 1989.

Schröder, Klaus. *Der SED Staat.* München, 1998.

Scott, James W. *Domination and the Arts of Resistance: Hidden Transcripts.* New Haven/London, 1990.

Seegers, Lu. '"Schaufenster zum Westen". Das Elbefest und die Magdeburger Kulturfesttage in den 1950er und 1960er Jahren.' In Adelheid von Saldern, *Inszenierte Einigkeit. Herrschaftsrepräsentationen in DDR-Städten.* Pp. 107–44. Stuttgart: Franz Steiner Verlag, 2003.

Sewell, Mike. *The Cold War.* Cambridge: Cambridge University Press, 2002.

———. 'Three Temporalities: Toward an Eventful Sociology'. In *The Historical Turn in the Human Sciences*, edited by Terrence J. MacDonald. Pp. 245–80. Ann Arbor, 1996.

Simecka, Milan. *The Restoration of Order: The Normalization of Czechoslovakia.* Translated by A.G. Brain. London: Verso, 1984.

Skilling, H. Gordon. *Czechoslovakia's Interrupted Revolution.* Princeton: Princeton University Press, 1976.

Solga, Heike. *Auf dem Weg in eine klassenlose Gesellschaft? Klassenlagen und Mobilität zwischen Generationen in der DDR*. Berlin: Akademie Verlag, 1995.

Steiner, André. *Die DDR-Wirtschaftsreform der sechziger Jahre–Konflikt zwischen Effizienz- und Machtkalkül.* Berlin: Akademie Verlag, 1999.

———. *Von Plan zu Plan. Eine Wirtschaftsgeschichte der DDR*. Munich: DVA, 2004.

Stenton, Michael. *Radio London and Resistance in Occupied Europe: British Political Warfare 1939–1943.* Oxford: Oxford University Press, 2000.

Strittmater, E. *Ole Bienkopp.* East Berlin, 1964.

Thomas, Merrilyn. *Communing with the Enemy: Covert Operations, Christianity and Cold War Politics in Britain and the GDR*. Oxford and Bern: Peter Lang, 2005.

Tippach-Schneider, Simone, 'Sieben Kinderwagen, drei Berufe und ein Ehemann. DDR-Frauengeschichten im Wandel der Sozialpolitik'. In *Fortschritt, Norm und Eigensinn. Erkundungen im Alltag der DDR*, edited by Dokumentationszentrum Alltagskultur der DDR. Berlin, 1999.

Vorsteher, Dieter. '"Ich bin zehn Jahre". Die Ausstellung im Museum für Deutsche Geschichte anlässlich des zehnten Jahrestages der DDR'. In *Wiedergeburten. Zur Geschichte der runden Geburtstage der DDR*, edited by Monika Gibas et al. Leipzig, 1999.

Weigel, George. *Witness to Hope: the Biography of Pope John Paul II.* New York: HarperCollins, 1999.

Weil, Francesca. *Herrschaftsanspruch und Wirklichkeit. Zwei Sächsiche Betriebe in der DDR während der Honecker-Ära*. Cologne et al.: Böhlau Verlag, 2000.

Welzer, Harold, Sabine Moller, and Karoline Tschuggnall. *"Opa war kein Nazi": Nationalsozialismus und Holocaust im Familiengedächtnis.* Frankfurt: Fischer, 2002.

Wicke, P. and L. Müller, eds. *Rockmusik und Politik–Analysen, Interviews und Dokumente.* Berlin: Ch. Links, 1996.

Wierling, Dorothee. *Geboren im Jahr Eins. Der Geburtsjahrgang 1949 in der DDR. Versuch einer Kollektivbiographie.* Berlin, 2002.

———. 'The Hitler Youth generation in the GDR: Insecurities, Ambitions and Dilemmas'. In *Dictatorship as Experience. Towards a Socio-Cultural History of the GDR*, edited by Konrad Jarausch. Pp. 307–24. New York, Oxford, 1999.

———. 'Mission to Happiness. Comparing the Birth Cohort of 1949 in East and West Germany'. In *The Miracle Years. West Germany in the 1950s*, edited by Hanna Schissler. Pp. 110–25. Princeton: Princeton University Press, 2001.

———. 'Wie (er)findet man eine Generation? Das Beispiel des Geburtsjahrgangs 1919 in der DDR'. In *Generationalität und Lebensgeschichte im 20. Jahrhundert*, edited by Jürgen Reulecke. Pp. 217–28. München, 2003.

Wildt, Michael and Ulrike Jureit, eds. *Generationen. Zur Relevanz eines wissenschaftlichen Grundbegriffs.* Hamburg, 2005.

Williams, Kieran. *The Prague Spring and its Aftermath: Czechoslovak Politics, 1968–1970.* Cambridge: Cambridge University Press, 1997.

Wilton, D. *Regime versus People? Public opinion and the development of sport and popular music in the GDR, 1961–1989.* PhD thesis, London University, 2004.

Index